Click Start 9

Computer Science fo

N Meera

CAMBRIDGE
UNIVERSITY PRESS

CAMBRIDGE
UNIVERSITY PRESS

University Printing House, Cambridge CB2 8BS, United Kingdom

One Liberty Plaza, 20th Floor, New York, NY 10006, USA

477 Williamstown Road, Port Melbourne, VIC 3207, Australia

314–321, 3rd Floor, Plot 3, Splendor Forum, Jasola District Centre, New Delhi – 110025, India

79 Anson Road, #06–04/06, Singapore 079906

Cambridge University Press is part of the University of Cambridge.

It furthers the University's mission by disseminating knowledge in the pursuit of education, learning and research at the highest international levels of excellence.

www.cambridge.org
Information on this title: www.cambridge.org/9781107667440

First published 2015

20 19 18 17 16 15 14 13 12 11 10 9 8 7 6 5

Printed in India by Rajkamal Electric Press

ISBN 978-1-107-66744-0 Paperback with CD-ROM

Contents

Overview *vi*

Preface *viii*

1. Computer System 1–33
   - Characteristics of a computer 1
   - Functional components of a computer 3
   - Input unit 3
   - Central Processing Unit 11
   - Memory unit 12
   - Storage devices 14
   - Output unit 18
   - Types of computer 21
   - Applications of computer 23

2. Computer Software 34–54
   - Types of software 35
   - System software 35
   - Operating system 35
   - Language translators 40
   - Utilities 41
   - Application software 45

3. Operating System and Windows 55–89
   - Basic concepts of OS 56
   - Functions of OS 56
   - Popular operating systems 57
   - Desktop 59
   - Windows Explorer 66
   - Files and Folders 67
   - Windows Accessories 70
   - Paint 71
   - Notepad 73
   - WordPad 75
   - Mobile operating system 79

Worksheet 1 *90*

4. Word Processing Tools – I 91–119
   - Microsoft Office Word 2007 92
   - Components of Microsoft Office Word 2007 92
   - Creating and saving a Word document 95
   - Some features of MS Word 2007 100
   - Editing a document 102
   - Formatting a document 105
   - Printing a document 111

5. Word Processing Tools – II 120–148
- Insert tab 120
- Table Tools tab 122
- Page Layout tab 132
- References tab 134
- Mailings tab 136
- Review tab 138

6. Presentation Tools – I 149–172
- MS PowerPoint 150
- PowerPoint 2007 150
- Creating a presentation 152
- Slide group 156
- Formatting slide 157
- Formatting paragraph 158
- Presentation Views 160
- Inserting text in slides 162
- Slide Show 165

7. Presentation Tools – II 173–192
- Inserting tables 174
- Insert pictures 174
- Inserting clip art 175
- Inserting shapes 176
- Inserting SmartArt 176
- Inserting charts 178
- Inserting media clips 180
- Animation effects 182
- Record Narration 184
- Rehearse Timings 185
- Printing presentation slides 185

Worksheet 2 .... *193*
Comprehensive Worksheet 1 .... *194*

8. Spreadsheet Tools – I 196–234
- MS Excel 197
- MS Excel 2007 199
- Working with a workbook 203
- Modifying a worksheet 207

9. Spreadsheet Tools – II 235–262
- Adding pictures and shapes 236
- Inserting charts 238
- Formulae 248
- Cell reference 249
- Formulas tab 252
- Text to Columns 254
- Print titles 254
- Print a selected range 255
- Freeze rows and columns 255

10. Communication Technology 263–282
- Advantages of a network 264
- Topology 265
- Linear Bus topology 265
- Star topology 265
- Ring topology 266
- Tree topology 267
- Types of network 268
- Networking technology 271
- Wired technology 271
- Wireless technology 272
- Internet 274
- World Wide Web 275

11. Content Technology 283–294
- Data 284
- Information 284
- Multimedia 285
- Animation 287
- File types 287
- Conclusion 288

Worksheet 3 .... *295*

12. Programming in C 296–341
- Algorithm 297
- Flowchart 297
- Introduction to C 299
- Structure of a C program 300
- C variable 302
- C constant 302
- C keyword 302
- Data types 303
- Declaring a variable 304
- Input and output functions 305
- Operators 307
- Control structures 312
- Loop structures 319
- Arrays 324
- Functions 327

13. Societal Impacts of IT – I 342–353
- Plagiarism 343
- Intellectual Property Rights 344
- Privacy 346
- Computer Security and Integrity of Information 346
- Careers in IT 347

Worksheet 4 .... *354*
Comprehensive Worksheet 2 .... *355*
IT Applications – I *357*
Sample Test Paper 1 – Solved *371*
Sample Test Paper 2 – Unsolved *378*
Answer Key *382*
Cheat Sheet *385*

Overview

Lesson Number	Lesson Name	Contents	Objectives	ICD Components
1.	Computer System	• Functional components of a computer system • Input, Output and Storage devices • Memory unit • Types of computer • Applications of computer	To make the students understand the functions of a computer and its peripherals devices	Input Output and storage devices: Slideshow + Exercises
2.	Computer Software	• Software • Types of software: System software and Application software • System software • Application software	To make the students learn about software and its types	Application Software – General Purpose, Specific Purpose: Animation + Exercises
3.	Operating System and Windows	• Concepts and functions of an operating system • Components of an operating system • Using Windows 7 Accessories • Mobile OS	To make the students learn about the functions of an operating system	Exercises + Application Based Questions
4.	Word Processing Tools – I	• Word processor • MS Office Word 2007 • Components of Word 2007 • Editing, formatting and printing a document	To introduce the students to Word 2007	Exercises + Application Based Questions
5.	Word Processing Tools – II	• Insert tab • Table Tools tab • Page Layout tab • Drawing Tools tab • References tab • Mailing tab • Review tab	To make the students learn about various advanced features of Word 2007	Exercises + Application Based Questions
6.	Presentation Tools – I	• Presentation software • PowerPoint 2007 • Components of PowerPoint 2007 • Editing and formatting slides • Slide show	To introduce the students to PowerPoint 2007	Exercises + Application Based Questions
7.	Presentation Tools – II	• Inserting tables • Inserting illustrations • Inserting media • Custom animation, Slide transition and Rehearse timing	To make the students learn about various advanced features of PowerPoint 2007	Exercises + Application Based Questions

Overview

Lesson Number	Lesson Name	Contents	Objectives	ICD Components
8.	Spreadsheet Tools – I	• Spreadsheet software • MS Office Excel 2007 • Components of Excel 2007 • Create, save, edit and format a worksheet in Excel 2007	To introduce the students to Excel 2007	Exercises + Application Based Questions
9.	Spreadsheet Tools – II	• Inserting illustrations • Inserting charts • Inserting formulae • Cell reference	To make the students learn about various advanced features of Excel 2007	Exercises + Application Based Questions
10.	Communication Technology	• Network • Advantages of a network • Network topologies • Types of network • Wired and wireless technology • Internet and World Wide Web	To make the students learn about the computer networking and communication technologies	Networking Technology; Internet and its applications: Animation + Exercises
11.	Content Technology	• Data and Information • Multimedia • Animation • Convergence of technology	To make the students learn about information and communication technology	Convergence of technology: Animation + Exercises
12.	Programming in C	• Programming concepts • Algorithm and Flowchart • Introduction to C • Variables and constants • I/O functions • Operators and Arrays	To introduce the students to the basic concepts of programming using C programming language	Exercises + Application Based Questions
13.	Societal Impacts of IT – I	• Plagiarism • Intellectual Property Rights • Copyright • Software piracy • Internet hacking • Privacy • Securing your system • Careers in IT	To make the students learn about the societal impacts of IT	Societal impacts of IT: Animation + Exercises

Preface

In today's modern world, existing and emerging technologies are rapidly becoming an integral part of our work, home and social lives. Therefore, it is important to prepare the students for ever evolving technologies and increasing global communications. In schools, Information Technology (IT) plays an important role as it promotes innovation, increases productivity, enhances quality of education.

Click Start: Computer Science for Schools for classes *9* and *10* have been prepared keeping in mind the rising demand for Computer Science education in schools. The new levels cover the important set of computer skills required by the students to explore and learn things across various disciplines. Each level of the series has been designed as a means for honing problem solving skills associated with the study of IT. These books are primarily based on Windows 7, MS Office 2007, HTML, XML and programming languages, such as C, C++ and Java.

The key features of the books are:

- ***Snap Recap*** to reiterate the concepts learnt earlier
- ***Learning Objectives*** to outline the objectives of the chapter
- ***Fact Files*** to enhance the knowledge of the students
- ***Quick Key*** and ***Try This*** to introduce shortcuts and alternative methodologies
- ***Activities*** interspersed within each chapter to promote application-based learning
- ***Check Your Progress*** to quickly revise and practice the topics learnt
- ***Exercises*** to make tasks interactive and promote guided discussions
- ***Glossary*** and ***Now You Know*** to aid quick revision of the concepts learnt in the chapter
- ***Application Based Questions*** to enhance real-life problem solving skills of the students
- ***Lab Work*** to encourage learning by doing
- ***Updates*** on Windows 8 and MS Office 2010 to keep the students abreast with advancements in the field of technology
- ***Teacher's Notes*** to provide creative suggestions to the teachers
- ***Worksheets*** and ***Sample Test Papers*** to assess the students' understanding of the concept
- ***Answer Key*** to provide answers to the objective-type questions given in the book
- ***Cheat Sheets*** to quickly revise the concepts learnt in the book

Additionally, in-text notes, shortcut methods, troubleshooting tips, concise screenshots and clear illustrations have been used to support and strengthen the process of learning.

The books come with an Interactive CD-ROM which allows the students to make easy connections with the book. It enables effective construction of knowledge and its application in an interactive medium. The CD-ROM offers:

- Concept-based animations to reinforce key concepts
- Interactive activities suitable for self-assessment with automated feedback
- Application-based animations to apply knowledge in real-life situations
- Glossary to introduce vocabulary with clear definitions
- Gaming zone to revise concepts in an engaging manner

All these components will help the students gain more information about IT in an easy and interactive way leading into **Edutainment** (***Edu***cation + Enter***tainment***). Thus, the books will not only make learning fun but also help the students achieve a certain level of theoretical and practical expertise.

N Meera

1 Computer System

LEARNING OBJECTIVES

You will learn about:

1. Characteristics of a Computer
2. Functional Components of a Computer
3. Input Devices
4. Output Devices
5. Storage Devices
6. Types of Computers
7. Applications of Computers

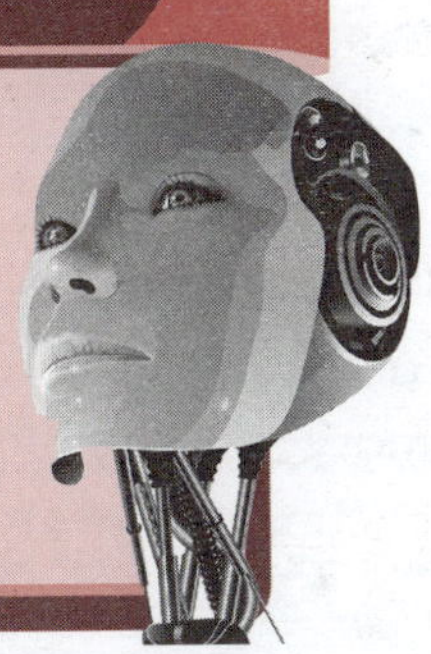

INTRODUCTION

Computers have become an indispensable part of our daily lives, from entertainment to studies, from business to communication, computers have permeated every aspect of our lives. They have become as essential as television, radio and telephone. They have become a necessity that relieves us from exhausting tasks like copying, checking and comparing. *A computer, in simple terms, is an electronic machine that is used to store, process data, and produce the desired output according to the instructions given to it.* Knowledge of computers is essential in modern times as they are used everywhere, in homes and schools, in offices and factories.

CHARACTERISTICS OF A COMPUTER

Computers have revolutionized the world. They are capable of performing highly complex tasks, which a human cannot perform efficiently and in a short time. Some important characteristics of a computer are discussed below.

Speed

A computer works at enormous speed, without making any mistake, according to the given instruction. A computer can simultaneously execute millions of instructions within fraction of seconds. The speed of a computer is measured in terms of MHz or GHz.

Accuracy

A computer performs its task with great accuracy. The accuracy of the computers is almost perfect and non erroneous; and if there is any error, it is due to wrong input or wrong instructions. Only if the computer is given correct data and instructions, it will return an accurate result. This concept is called **GIGO (Garbage In Garbage Out)**.

Diligence

A computer does not suffer from tiredness and boredom. Even if it has to perform a calculation million times, it do so accurately without getting tired or bored.

Versatility

A computer is flexible and capable of doing variety of jobs efficiently. It can carry out all tasks from drawing and painting to calculations and logical operations. It can also transfer the data, surf the Internet, exchange information with the outside world and analyse data. Hence, it is used in science and technology, designing and engineering, hospitals, schools and universities.

Reliability

A computer is more reliable than human beings. It can produce accurate results by performing complicated calculations repeated number of times without getting it wrong or getting bored.

Storage

A computer can store a large amount of data in its memory. This data can be retrieved in no time when needed. The memory capacity of a computer is measured in terms of **bytes**. To store data, devices like CD, DVD, pen drive and magnetic tape are also used.

Softcopy

A computer can store and maintain records in multiple formats. *An unprinted digital copy of any document is known as a **softcopy***. Softcopy makes it easy to retrieve information quickly. In addition, a large amount of paper is also saved.

Quick Key

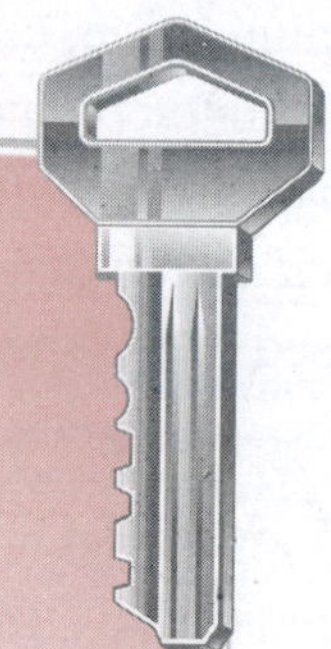

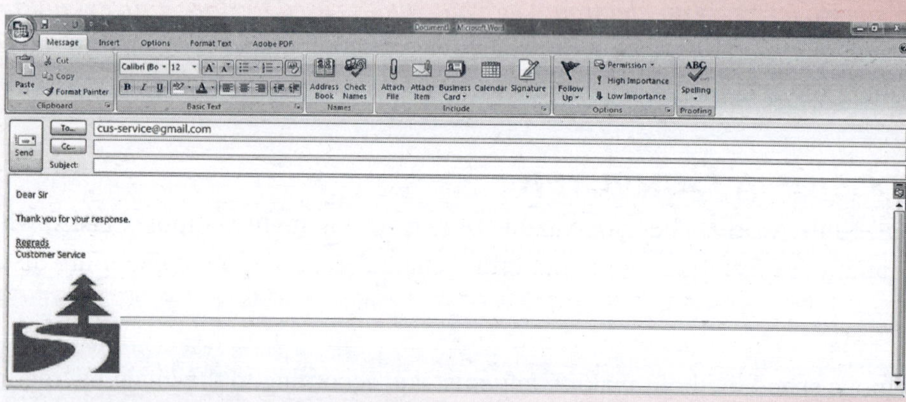

You must have seen this type of digital signature attached in many emails. This **green signature** is added to the emails to save trees. Usually, this symbol along with a green tip is added to the signature line. And thereby, by default appears in every email.

Some popular green tips are:

- Think of the trees... Please do not print off this email unless you really have to.
- 'Save a Tree' – Please consider the environment before printing this email!

CHECK YOUR PROGRESS

A. List five characteristics of a computer.

B. With the help of the Internet, find out more about the following.

1. Bytes
2. Softcopy
3. GIGO
4. Magnetic Tape
5. Digital signatures
6. Storage devices

Functional Components of a Computer

A computer system consists of both hardware and software components that perform tasks based on four components (Fig.1.1). They are:

- Input unit
- Processing unit
- Memory unit
- Output unit

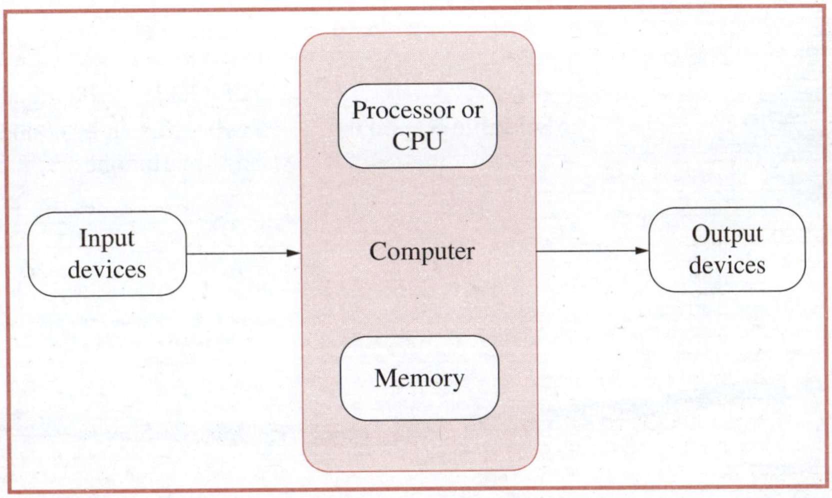

Fig. 1.1 *Functional components of a computer*

Input Unit

Input is the data or set of instructions given to a computer. The input unit receives the data or instruction through input devices and sends it to the main memory of the computer for processing. Some common input devices are keyboard, mouse, light pen, OCR, BCR, MICR, trackball, scanner, microphone, digital camera, webcam and joystick. Some of the input devices and their types are discussed in Table 1.1 (*refer to pages 4–10*).

Table 1.1 *Input devices*

Device	Name of the Device	Purpose
	**KEYBOARD**	A keyboard is used to feed data into the computer. It is used to type letters and numbers. It is the main input device for most of the computers. A keyboard usually has characters printed or engraved on the keys. Each press of a key corresponds to a single written symbol. Though, to produce some symbols you need to press and hold several keys simultaneously. Different types of keyboards are available. Some of these are discussed below.
	**Wired Keyboard**	A wired keyboard is wired to a host computer and sends data through a physical cord.
	**Wireless Keyboard**	A wireless keyboard sends data to a host computer without relying on a physical cord. These keyboards transfer the data to a computer via infrared beams.
	**Foldable Keyboard**	A foldable keyboard, also known as a flexible keyboard, can be connected to portable devices and smartphones.

FACT FILE

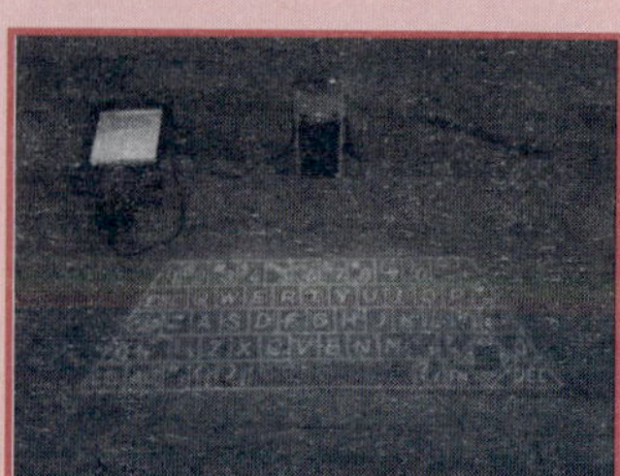

The **Virtual Laser Keyboard** is a computer input device, which when connected to a computer, projects the image of a virtual keyboard onto a smooth surface. When you touch the surface covered by the image of keys, the device records the corresponding keystroke.

FACT FILE

The **Apple Wireless Keyboard** is a wireless keyboard built for Macintosh computers and compatible with iOS devices. It connects to a computer via Bluetooth and has no USB connectors or ports. It runs on AA batteries. Apple Inc. first released it in September, 2003.

Table 1.1 continued...

Device	Name of the Device	Purpose
	**POINTING DEVICE**	A pointing device is an input device that allows you to control the pointer on the computer screen. It is used to move and select objects around the screen and as well as selecting menu commands.
	**Mouse**	A mouse is the most popular pointing device. It has one or more buttons on top and a scroll wheel in the middle. The scroll wheel allows you to scroll up and down the page.

FACT FILE

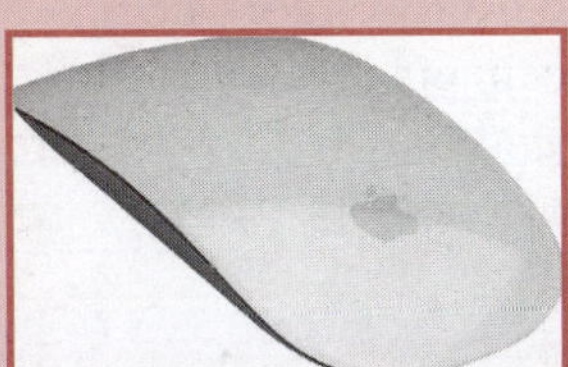

The **Apple Magic Mouse** is a multi-touch mouse that allows the use of gestures like swiping and scrolling. It connects to a computer via Bluetooth and runs on AA batteries. Apple Inc. first released it in October, 2009.

Table 1.1 continued...

Device	Name of the Device	Purpose
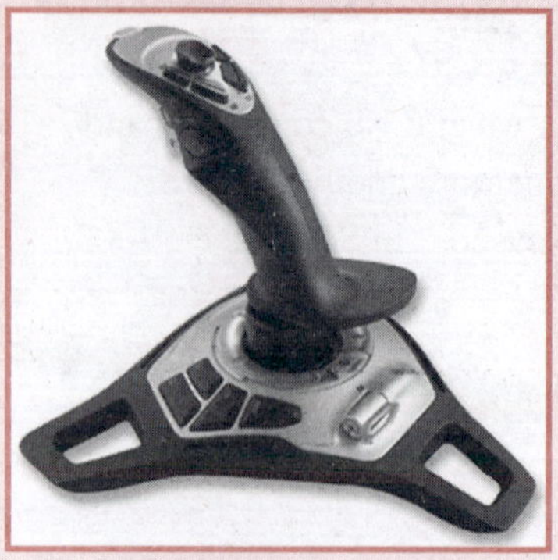	**Joystick**	A joystick is the most widely used input device used for playing games on a computer. It has a rod and a ball attached to its lower end. It is operated by holding the rod and moving it in any direction.
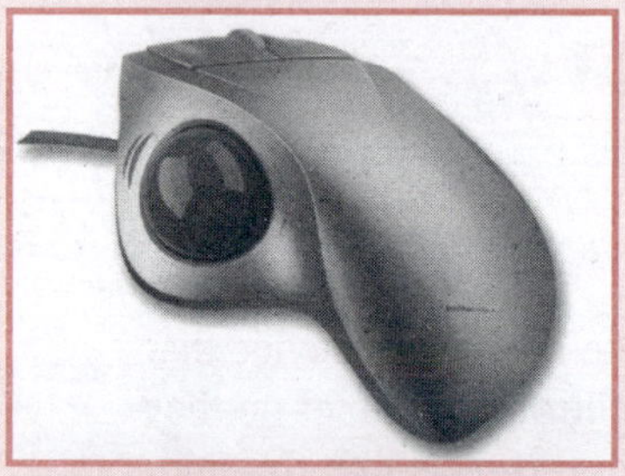	**Trackball**	A trackball is an upturned mouse in which the ball is present on top or on side. Instead of moving the whole device, you need to just move the ball with fingers. It does not require as much space as a mouse does. It is often built-in on portable computers.
	**Light Pen**	A light pen is a light-sensitive wand that is connected to a Visual Display Unit. It is used to point to objects onscreen and draw on the screen. It is very similar to a touchscreen but has greater positional accuracy.
	**Graphic Tablet**	A graphic tablet allows you to hand-draw images, animations and graphics, just like when you do it with a pencil and paper. It consists of a flat surface and a pen-like drawing tool called **stylus**.
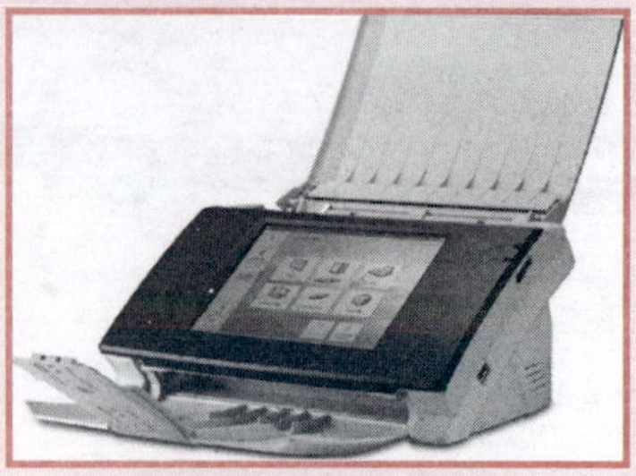	**Scanner**	A scanner is used to scan or copy written documents and photographs into a computer. It converts the file to digitised format. Different types of scanners are available. **Hand-held** models and **flat-bed** models are two available form of scanners.

ACTIVITY

To scan a document using Windows Fax and Scan.

1. Click on the **Start** button.
2. Click **All Programs** and select **Windows Fax and Scan**.
3. **Windows Fax and Scan** dialog box appears.

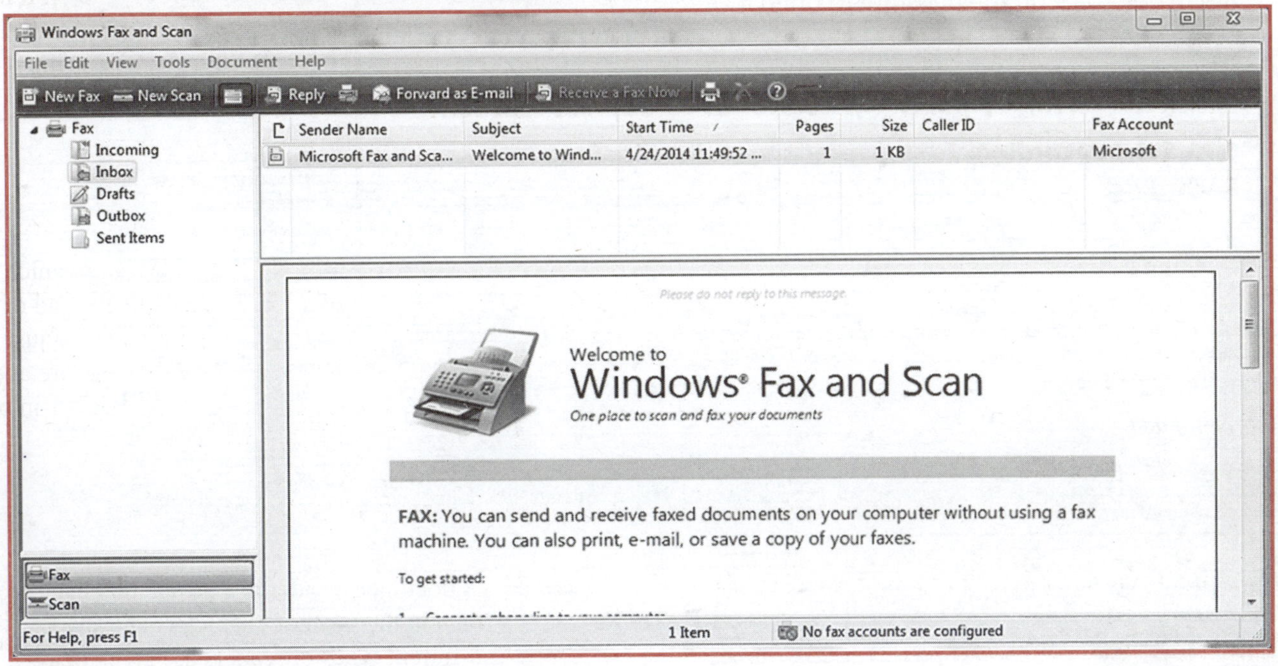

4. Select the **New Scan** option from the toolbar.
5. **New Scan** dialog box appears. In the **Profile list** section, choose **Documents**.
6. To see how your document will be scanned, click on **Preview**.
7. Click **Scan**.

NOTE: Ensure that the scanner is connected and switched on before starting scan.

Table 1.1 continued...

Device	Name of the Device	Purpose
	**MICROPHONE**	A microphone is used to input sound into a computer. It detects the sound and transmit electrical signals to a computer.

ACTIVITY

To record audio using a microphone.

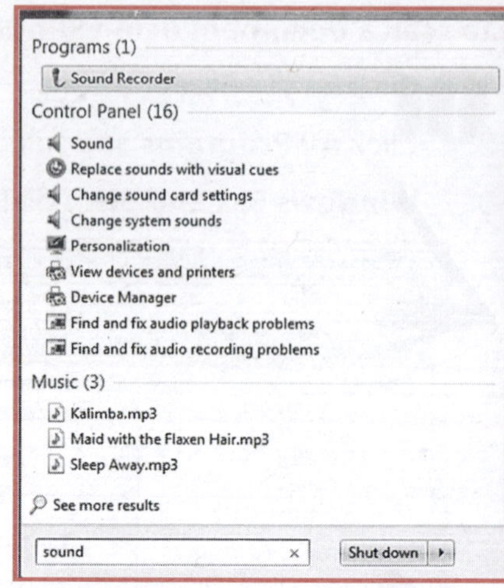

1. Plug a microphone to your computer.
2. Click on the **Start** button.
3. In the **Search programs and files** box, search for the **Sound Recorder**. Click on the program to open it.

   OR

   Click **Start** ⟹ **All Programs** ⟹ **Accessories** ⟹ **Sound Recorder**.
4. Click **Start Recording**. To stop recording audio, click **Stop Recording**.

Table 1.1 continued...

Device	Name of the Device	Purpose
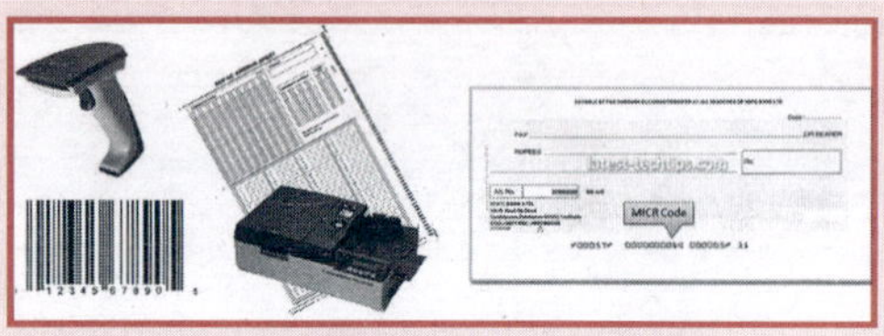	**READER**	A document reader is a device that can read data in the form of characters and marks. Some different types of readers are given below.
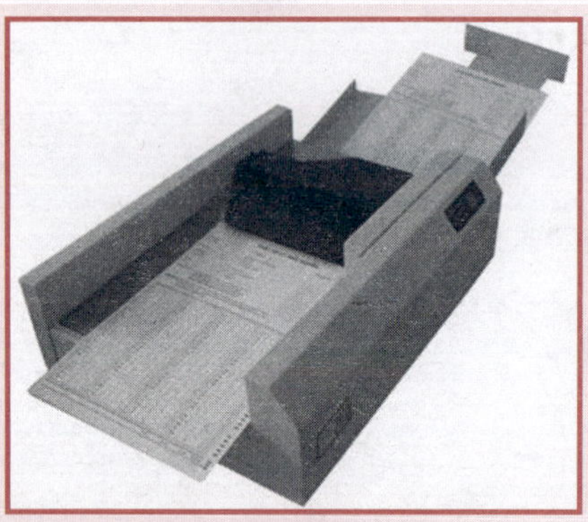	**Optical Mark Reader**	An OMR, also known as sense reader, senses the data directly from the document and into a computer. It reads the marks made by a pencil or a pen on a printed form. It is mostly used in the evaluation of MCQ papers.

FACT FILE

The word **electrographic** is used for punched card and page scanning technology that allow cards or pages marked with a pencil to be processed or converted into punched cards. This technology was developed and sold by IBM, under the term **mark sense**.

Table 1.1 continued...

Device	Name of the Device	Purpose
	**Optical Character Recognition**	An OCR allows direct reading of any printed character written in a specific font. The printed matter is scanned with a photoelectric device.
	**Magnetic Ink Character Recognition**	An MICR is used to read the magnetic code written on cheques or on credit cards. It provides a secure and high-speed method of scanning and processing information.
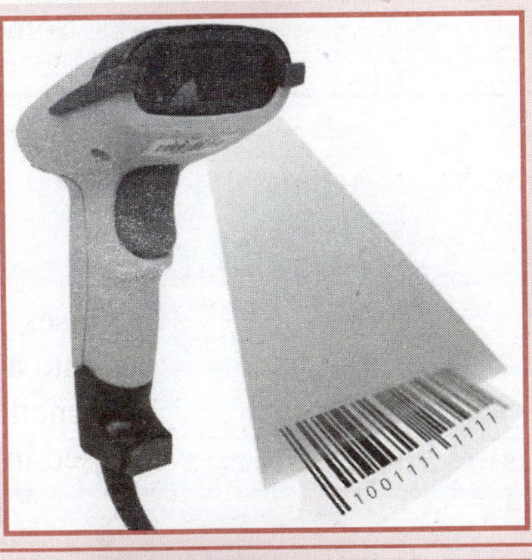	**Bar Code Reader**	A BCR is used to read the pattern of bars on items you buy from the market. The stripes of the bar code are sensed and read by BCR. Bar codes can be read by hand-held optical readers or by fixed readers.
	**WEBCAM**	A webcam is a camera usually placed on the top of a computer monitor. It is used to take pictures and record movies. It is majorly used for video conferencing over the Internet.

ACTIVITY

To install and use a webcam on a Windows 7 computer.

1. Attach the webcam into the USB port of your computer.

   NOTE: Before connecting the webcam, install the webcam software from the CD that comes with it.

2. Download free chat software, such as **Windows Live Messenger** or **Skype**, from the Internet.
3. Follow the steps to install the program and create your account.
4. Your webcam will be automatically activated when you start a video chat.

Table 1.1 continued...

Device	Name of the Device	Purpose
	DIGITAL CAMERA	A digital camera, also called digicam, is a camera that encodes images digitally. Immediately after recording an image, it can display the image on its screen. You can also delete, crop or modify your images using a digital camera.

ACTIVITY

To import pictures and videos from a digital camera to a Windows 7 computer.

1. Connect the camera to a computer with a USB cable.
2. Turn on the camera.
3. In **AutoPlay** dialog box that appears, click on **Import pictures and videos using Windows**.
4. Click on the **Import** button. The file transfer will begin.
5. A new window, containing the folder that has the imported pictures and videos, opens.

Table 1.1 continued...

Device	Name of the Device	Purpose
	TOUCH SCREEN	Touch screen is a special monitor that allows the user to input information by touching the screen that can detect touch. The touch screen monitors are mostly found in airports and ATMs. Nowadays, many mobile phones also have touch screens.

CHECK YOUR PROGRESS

A. List five functions of a computer that you use in real life.

B. How are scanners different from an optical mark reader? HOTS

C. What are different types of mouse available in the market today?

D. Can you input signatures with the help of a graphics tablet? HOTS

E. With the help of the Internet and school library, answer the following questions.

   1. Enumerate different types of scanners. Also, differentiate between flatbed and hand-held scanners.

   2. Give one feature and one photo of each: Microsoft Arc, Optimus Keyboard and Maltron 3-D Ergonomic Keyboard.

F. Name five smartphones that use touch screen technology.

Central Processing Unit

The Central Processing Unit (CPU) is the most important component of a computer. It is used for carrying out calculations and processing data. As it is responsible for execution of instructions, arithmetic and logical calculations, storing and controlling the input and output devices, it is rightly called the brain of the computer.

The CPU consists of three units (Fig. 1.2). They are:

- Arithmetic and Logic unit
- Control unit
- Memory unit

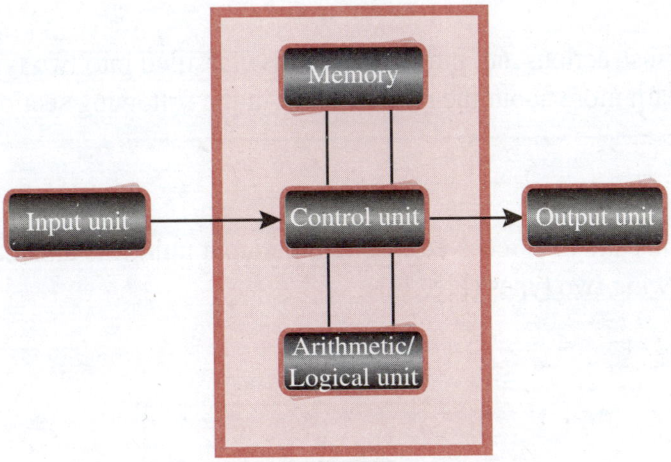

Fig. 1.2 *CPU*

Arithmetic and Logic Unit (ALU)

The ALU is used to perform arithmetic and logical operations on data received from memory and transfer the same to main memory. The ALU can perform four kinds of arithmetic operations: addition, subtraction, multiplication and division. The ALU also executes logical operations. < , > , = , <=. >=, < > are the basic operations that are performed by the ALU.

FACT FILE

The number of instructions executed per second by the CPU determines its speed. This purely depends on the motherboard and the processor of a computer. The speed of processor is measured in **megahertz (MHz)**.

Control Unit (CU)

The CU controls and directs the functions of all components of a computer system. It does not execute instructions; rather, it instructs different parts of the computer system to carry out various tasks. Importantly, it also determines the sequence in which the tasks will be carried out.

The CU must communicate with both the arithmetic/logic unit and memory unit. The CU also controls communication and co-ordination between different devices. It communicates with different devices through **control signals**. In simple terms, it controls how the entire computer system operates.

Some of the main functions of a Control Unit are listed below.

- CU interprets instructions and governs the sequence of execution of instructions.
- It monitors data flow through different areas of a computer system.
- It also controls processor timing.
- It sends and receives control signals from different input and output devices.
- It can handle multiple tasks, such as decoding, execution handling and storing results.

Memory Unit

The memory unit stores all the instructions and information. It is classified into two types: Primary Memory and Secondary Memory. We will learn more about the memory unit in the following section.

▶ MEMORY UNIT

The memory unit stores programs and data received through the input unit. It is an area where all the instructions are stored. It is classified into following two types (Fig. 1.3).

- Primary Memory
- Secondary Memory

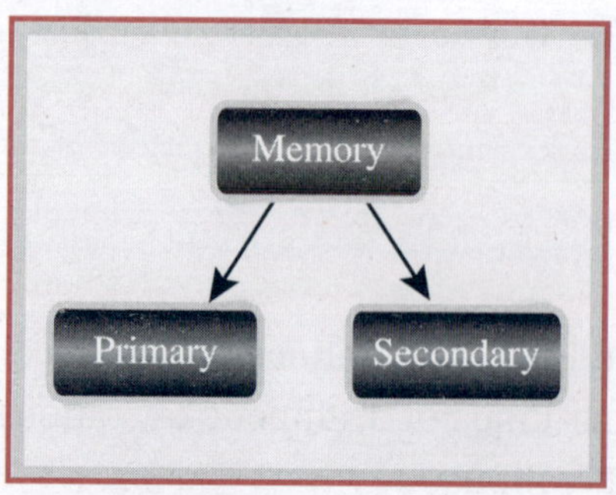

Fig. 1.3 *Memory unit*

Primary memory

Primary memory is the main memory of a computer. It is the area in a computer system wherein the data is stored for quick and direct access by computer's CPU. It is of two types (Fig. 1.4):

- Random Access Memory (RAM)
- Read Only Memory (ROM).

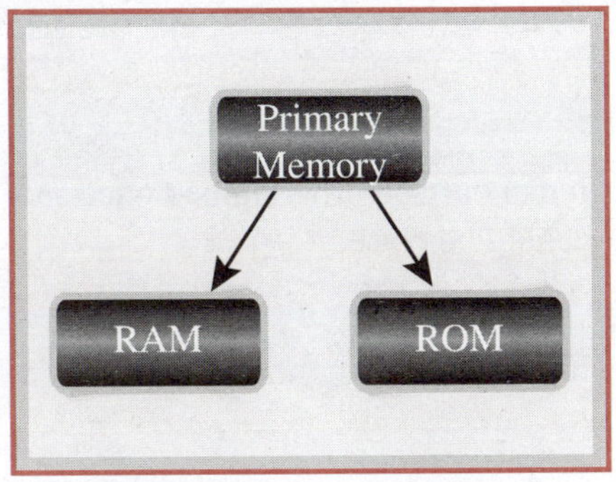

Fig. 1.4 *Primary Memory*

Random Access Memory (RAM)

As it is readily accessible for read and write operations, it is referred as Random Access Memory (Fig. 1.5). It is temporary memory. As soon as you switch off the computer, contents of RAM are erased or lost. Hence, it is known as **volatile memory**. There are two types of RAM: **Static RAM** and **Dynamic RAM**. The difference between both is given in Table 1.2.

Fig. 1.5 *RAM*

Table 1.2 *Different types of RAM*

Static RAM	Dynamic RAM
It retains the data as long as the power is on.	It deletes the data when the power is on; hence it requires refresh command to restore.
It gives fast access to data.	It is very slow.
It is expensive.	It is a cheap memory. Most of the computers contain DRAM chips.

Read Only Memory (ROM)

ROM is a non-volatile memory. The data is neither lost nor erased even when you switch off the computer. Its contents cannot be modified. Hence, it is known as **read only** memory (Fig. 1.6).

There are three different types of ROM. They are:

- ***PROM:*** Programmable Read Only Memory
- ***EPROM:*** Erasable Programmable Read Only Memory
- ***EEPROM:*** Electrically Erasable Programmable Read Only Memory.

Fig. 1.6 *ROM*

The difference between PROM, EPROM and EEPROM is given in Table 1.3.

Table 1.3 *Different types of ROM*

PROM	EPROM	EEPROM
It can only be programmed once and cannot be erased.	It can be erased by exposing it to ultraviolet light.	It can be erased using electric signals.
Its contents cannot be altered.	Its content can be written again but the entire content has to be rewritten, even if there is a small change.	There is no need to delete the whole content for a small change. The part that needs modification can be altered in isolation but the process is expensive.

Secondary memory

Secondary memory is the cheapest form of computer memory. In comparison to the main memory, it is very slow.It is stored in secondary storage devices like hard disk, CD-ROM, DVD and floppy disk. It is permanent in nature.

Storage Devices

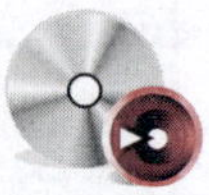

In a computer, data is stored in terms of bits and bytes. A bit refers to the **binary digit**, that is, 1 or 0, where 1 refers to logical value true and 0 refers to logical value false. A bit is the smallest unit of storage.

The memory capacity can be defined in terms of the following units.

4 bits = 1 nibble

8 bits = 2 nibbles, 1 byte

1024 bytes = 1 Kilobyte (KB)

1024 KB = 1 Megabyte (MB)

1024 MB = 1 Gigabyte (GB)

1024 GB = 1 Terabyte (TB)

Storage devices are the secondary devices that are used to store data and programs depending on the capacity of memory they can hold. They are non-volatile, that is, information stored on them is not erased or lost when the computer is switched off. They consist of peripheral devices such as floppy disk and hard disk, which are much cheaper than the computer's internal memory. However, they are also slower. These devices can be categorised into two categories: magnetic and optical. Some of the commonly used storage devices are discussed in Table 1.4 (*refer to pages 14–17*).

Table 1.4 *Storage devices*

Device	Name of the Device	Purpose
	HARD DISK	A hard disk is one of the most popular storage device. It is used for storing large amounts of data. It is made up of **platters**, that is, a collection of disks. A computer comes with a hard disk that has the capacity of several GBs. This is the internally mounted hard disk. You can also attach external hard disk for additional storage space. It is a magnetic storage device.

Table 1.4 continued...

Device	Name of the Device	Purpose
	**CD-ROM**	CD-ROM stands for Compact Disc Read Only Memory. It is used to store data up to 700 MB. This data is stored permanently on the disc. It is an optical storage device. Rewritable CDs, such as, Compact Disc Recordable (CD-R) and Compact Disc Rewritable (CD-W), are also available.
	**FLOPPY DISK**	A floppy disk is used to store data up to 1.44 MB. It is small, portable and rewritable. It is a magnetic storage device.
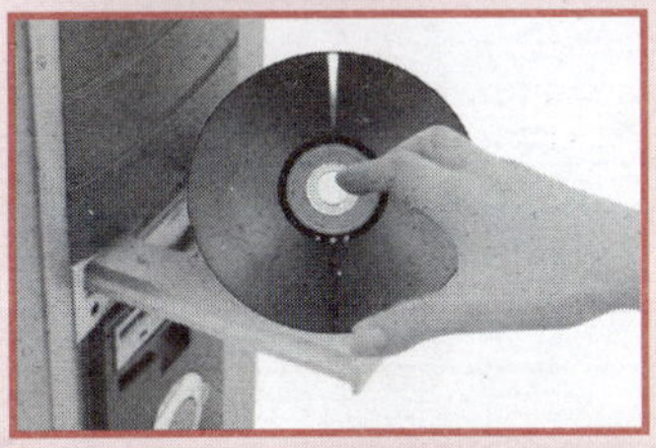	**DVD**	DVD stands for Digital Versatile Disc. It is like CD-ROM but it has more storage capacity. Its capacity varies from 4 GB to 47 GB. It is an optical storage device.
	**PEN DRIVE**	A pen drive is a flash memory storage device. It is easy to carry and copy. It is portable and writable (as many times as you require). The capacity of a pen drive ranges from 256 MB to 32 GB.

ACTIVITY

To safely remove a pen drive from a computer.

1. Click on the **Start** button.
2. In the **Search programs and files** box, search for the **Device Manager**. Click on it to open.
3. In the **Device Manager** dialog box, expand the **Disk Drives** option.
4. You will find that your removable drive is listed there.

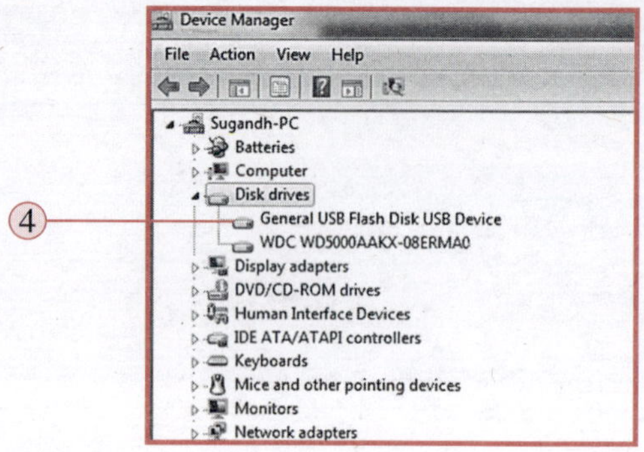

5. Right-click on the name of the drive and click on **Properties**.

6. Go to the **Policies** tab and select **Quick removal (default)** option to safely remove your pen drive.

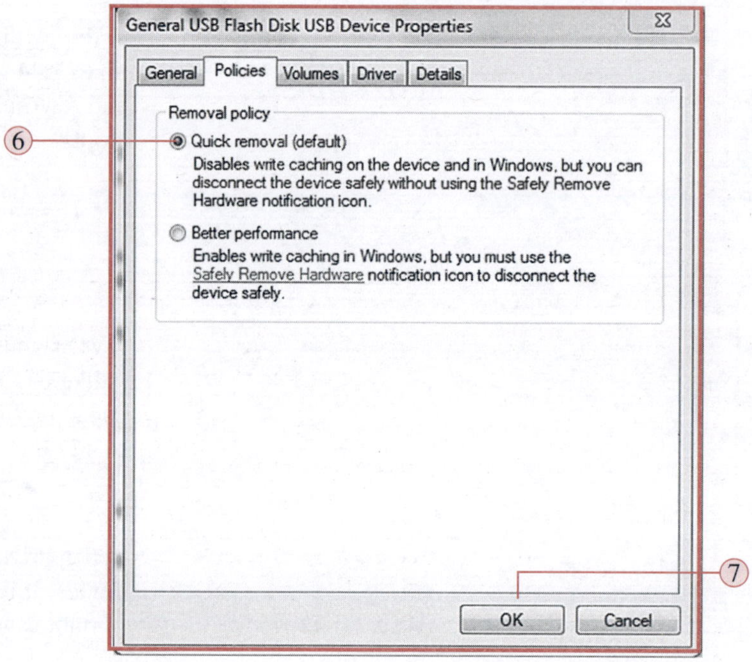

7. Click on **OK**.

NOTE: You can also remove your pen drive safely using the **Safely Remove Hardware** notification icon in the taskbar.

Table 1.4 continued...

Device	Name of the Device	Purpose
	**BLUE RAY DISC**	A blue ray disc can store a large amount of data compared to a DVD. It has a storage capacity of upto 25 GB. It gives a HD (high density) data video experience to the viewer. Hence, apart from DVDs, new movies are being released on Blue Ray.
	**MEMORY CARD**	A memory card is a small, re-writable storage device used for storing digital information. It is used in electronic devices such as cameras, mobile phones and laptops. It does not need power to retain data.

ACTIVITY

To transfer data from a memory card to a computer.

1. Connect a multi-card reader to your computer.
2. Insert the memory card into a designated card slot.
3. Click on the **Start button** ⟶ **All Programs** ⟶ **Computer** ⟶ **Card Reader's Drive**.
4. Select the data you want to transfer and right-click on the selection.
5. From the shortcut menu, select the **Copy** option to copy the data and **Cut** option to move the data.
6. Open the desired destination folder and click on the **Paste** option from the shortcut menu.

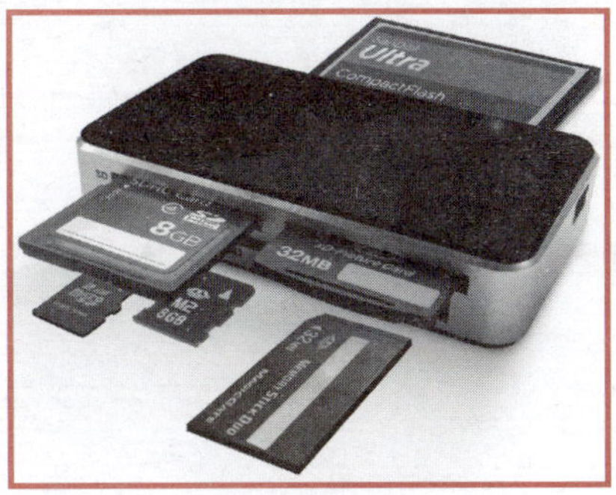

CHECK YOUR PROGRESS

A. Make a flowchart on computer memory. Give examples at each level.

B. The data transfer rate of externally and internally mounted hard disk is different. Find out why. **HOTS**

C. With the help of Internet, find out more about the two types of external hard disk: USB and, Play and Plug. What is the key difference between them? **HOTS**

D. List the commonly used processors.

▶ OUTPUT UNIT

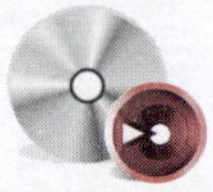

The output unit of a computer system consists of different output devices attached to the computer. It yields the information that the computer processes based on your input. Some of the common output devices are discussed in Table 1.5 (*refer to pages 18–20*).

Table 1.5 *Output devices*

Device	Name of the Device	Purpose
	**VISUAL DISPLAY UNIT (VDU)/ MONITOR**	VDU is the most common output device. It is used to display the output generated by the processing unit, CPU. The output generated is called the **soft copy**.

FACT FILE

The two most popular varieties of monitors being used today are the cathode ray tube (CRT) monitors and thin film transistor liquid crystal display (TFT-LCD) monitors.

Table 1.5 continued...

Device	Name of the Device	Purpose
	**PRINTER**	A printer is used to print the output generated by the CPU on a paper. This is known as a **hard copy**. Printers can be classified into: Impact printers and Non-Impact printers. Different types of printers are:

Table 1.5 continued...

Device	Name of the Device	Purpose
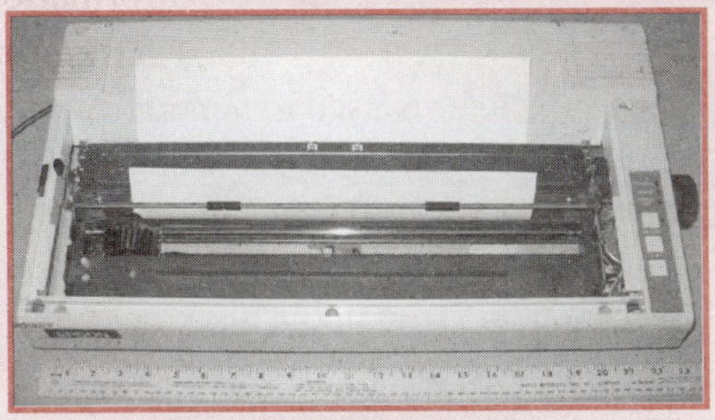	**Impact Printer**	An impact printer is a printer in which the paper comes in direct contact with the printer head during printing. **Daisywheel printers** and **Dot Matrix printers** are examples of impact printers.
	*Daisywheel Printer*	A daisywheel printer print continuous characters with a good letter formation. The speed of this printer ranges from 20 characters per second to 100 characters per second (CPS).
	*Dot Matrix Printer*	A dot matrix printer is the most commonly used printer. It leaves the impression of the characters in the form of dots. The printing speed of this printer can vary up to 100 CPS at 12 CPI (characters per inch). They are less expensive.
	**Non-Impact Printer**	A non-impact printer is a printer in which the paper does not come in direct contact with the printer head during printing. Examples of such printers are **Laser Printers** and **Inkjet Printers**.

Device	Name of the Device	Purpose
	*Laser Printer*	A laser printer is used to generate high quality text as well as images. It can print about 100 pages in a minute without making any noise. Laser printer is used in desktop publishing.
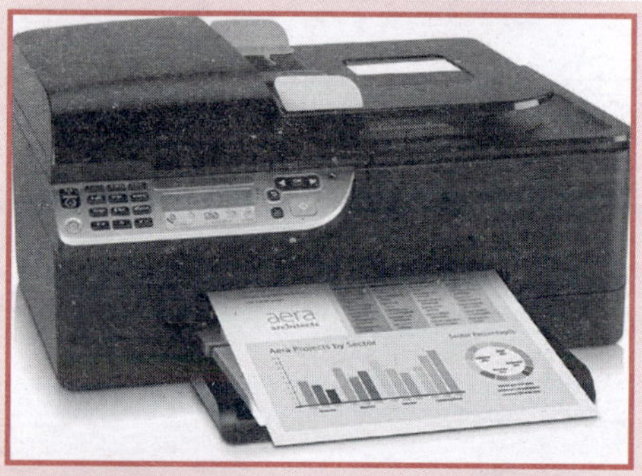	*Inkjet Printer*	An inkjet printer is fast and far less expensive than laser printer. Also, its speed is less than that of a laser printer. These are commonly used in small offices, schools and at home.
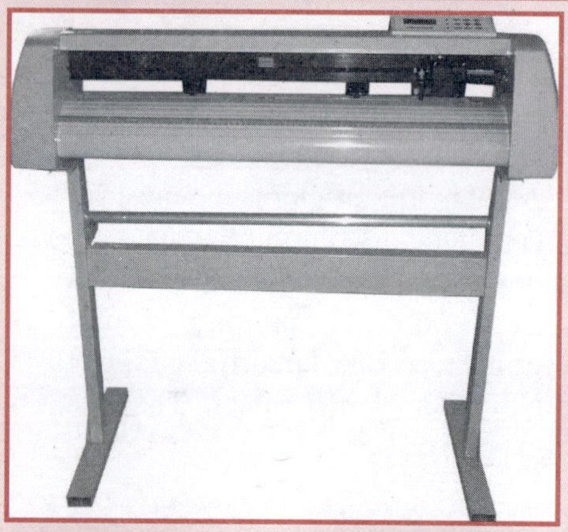	**PLOTTER**	A plotter is an output device used to print graphics, diagrams and maps. A plotter gives a hard copy of the output. There are different types of plotters used for various purposes such as, drum plotters and flatbed plotters.
	**SPEAKER**	A speaker is used to produce audio output. It typically comes in pairs and is connected to the CPU via USB port.

CHECK YOUR PROGRESS

A. Make a presentation on different types of printers available in the market these days. List one place where each type is used.

B. Make a list of different types of plotters.

C. I am an output device. I print continuous characters. My head is like the daisy flower. There is a hub in the center and the characters are in the spokes. Who am I?

D. Computers have inbuilt speakers. Then why do we need additional external speakers? Discuss. HOTS

TYPES OF COMPUTER

Computers are available in many types and sizes. The difference between them is based on their purpose and processing abilities. They can generally be divided into four major categories. They are:

- Micro computer
- Mini computer
- Mainframe computer
- Super computer

Micro computer

A micro computer is a small low cost computer with a single silicon chip processor (Fig. 1.7). Its processing unit (CPU) is called **microprocessor**. All the components of a microprocessor are on a single integrated circuit chip. Personal computers that you see in your school, home and office are all micro computers. The personal computers are small in size compared to other computers like mainframe computers and super computers. Desktop, laptop and palmtop are micro computers. An example of a micro computer is **IBM PC**.

Fig. 1.7 *Micro computer*

Mini computer

A mini computer is a digital computer, whose process and storage capacity is less than that of a mainframe computer and greater than that of a micro computer (Fig. 1.8). It is a multi-user system, where many users work on the same system. It was developed to replace mainframe computers, as mainframe computers occupy too much space. Due to their efficient processor, speed and memory size, mini computers are used in business applications and scientific applications. Examples of mini computers are **VAX 7500** and **PDP 11**.

NOTE: Mini computers are also known as Mid-Range computers.

Fig. 1.8 *Mini computer*

Fig. 1.9 *Mainframe computer*

Mainframe computer

A mainframe computer is an ultra-high performance computer (Fig. 1.9). It is large, expensive and occupy more space. Its memory capacity is measured in megabytes, and storage capacity is calculated in terabytes. It can store huge amount of data and can perform very complex calculations. It is used in research organisations, large industries, airline reservations, and any place where a large database has to be maintained. Examples of mainframe computers are **IBM 4300** and **HP9000** and **VAX 8000**.

Fig. 1.10 *Super computer*

Super computer

A super computer is the fastest computer (Fig. 1.10). The parallel processing of super computer is very fast because it comprises of a number of CPU that operate parallelly. The memory capacity of a super computer is in gigabytes or in terabytes. The storage capacity is in pixabytes. Its processing speed lies in the range of 400-10000 millions of floating point operations per second (**MFLOPS**). Super computers are used in weapon research, weather forecast, nuclear research, rocket research, atomic research and aerodynamics. Examples of supercomputers are **PARAM**, **CRAY-3** and **CYBER 20**.

FACT FILE

PARAM Padma is a super computer designed and assembled by **Center for Development of Advanced Computer (CDAC)** in Pune, India. It has a processing speed of up to 1 teraflop per second (1 TFLOP).

CHECK YOUR PROGRESS

A. Write a short note on different types of computers. Which all computers have you seen?

B. Using the Internet, find out a list of places where super computers are used in India. **HOTS**

C. Visit the meteorological department office, a railway station, or an airport. Collect the details of server they use (its capacity and the temperature it requires).

D. Differentiate between mainframe computers and super computers.

Applications of Computer

In our day-to-day life, computers have become essential and integral. They help in performing various tasks in various fields. Let us discuss some of the common applications of computers in different fields.

Education

Some of the applications of a computer in the field of education are given below.

- They help the students in gathering information, writing reports and developing projects; thereby enhancing their learning process.
- Online teaching helps the students learn through the Internet, without the physical presence of a tutor.
- Students can register and take online exams. This is helpful if the university/test center is at a far of place.
- CAD (Computer-Aided Design) software helps draw or manipulate technical drawings.
- They help the teachers prepare assignments and presentations.
- They provide the teachers different methods to teach a concept.

Fig. 1.11 *Students using computers in classroom*

Bank

Some of the applications of computer in banks are given below.

- Online banking allows the user to create online bank account and manage transactions and other bank related activities from the safety and comfort of their home.
- With the help of the Internet, the customers have the facility to transact with any branch of any bank from anywhere.
- Automated Teller Machine (ATM) allows you to withdraw money from your account from anyplace.

Fig. 1.12 *Computers are used in ATMs*

Business

Some of the applications of a computer in the field of business are given below.

- E-Commerce (electronic commerce), is used for onling buying and selling of products and services. Business today make extensive use of e-commerce, like online shopping through websites like Flipkart and Amazon.
- They are also used for maintaining inventory records, staff records and other transactions.
- They are used for various business functions like billing, accounting and creating reports.

Fig. 1.13 *E-commerce*

Hospital

Some of the applications of a computer in hospitals are given below.

- Computers are used to diagnose diseases.
- They help in maintaining the medical history of the patients.
- They help to monitor the condition of patients.
- Computerised equipment's are helpful in observing and maintaining patient's condition.

Fig. 1.14 *Computers used at hospital*

Press

Some of the applications of computer in press are given below.

- Computers are used for designing and typing.
- Editing and typesetting is also done on computers.
- They are used for inserting pictures, graphs and creating and presenting pages in different styles.

Fig. 1.15 *Computers are used in desktop publishing*

Government organisation

Some of the applications of computer in government organisation are given below.

- Computers helps in maintaining and updating records of employees.
- They help in maintenance of official correspondence with security.
- Uploading general forms and information is done through the Internet.
- They help in the electoral process. They help in casting votes, counting and declaring results during election.

Fig. 1.16 *Computers are used in various organisations*

Communication

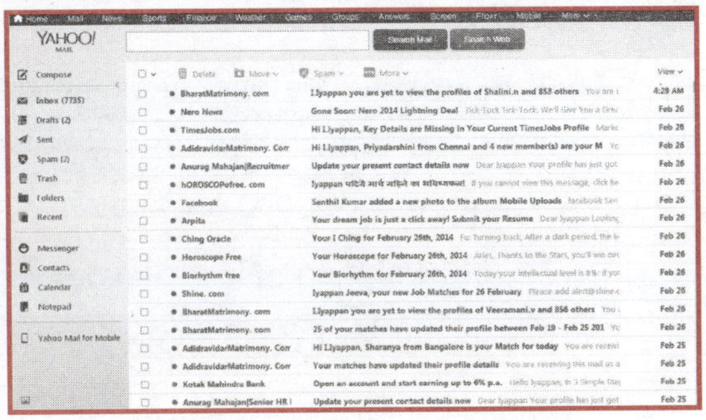

Fig. 1.17 *Inbox view of Yahoo mail*

Some of the applications of a computer in the field of communication are given below.

- Computers are used for sending and receiving emails from any part of the world.
- They allow you to communicate with people across the globe through video conference.
- They allow you to chat with different people over the Internet.
- Events occurring at one place can be viewed and discussed all over the world with the help of computers.

Transportation

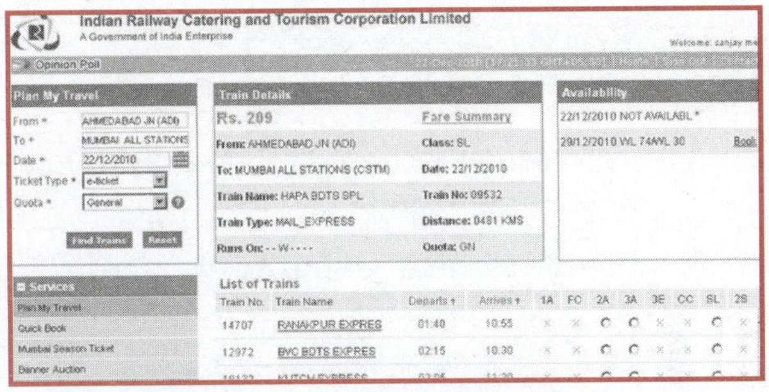

Fig. 1.18 *IRCTC website*

Some of the applications of a computer in transportation are given below.

- Railway and air ticket booking and cancellation can be done online.
- Instant update and information about the availability of seats is available over the Internet.
- They are used to track and control the air traffic.
- They are used to monitor electrical systems in aeroplanes.

Movie and media

Fig. 1.19 *An animation movie*

Some of the applications of a computer in movies and medias are given below.

- They are used in making cartoon and animated films.
- They are used for giving special effects.
- They are used for mixing effects in audio-visual media.

Weather forecasting

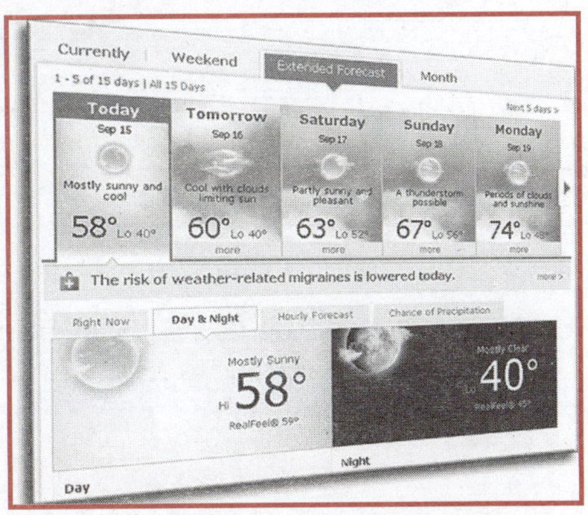

Fig. 1.20 *Weather update*

Some of the applications of a computer in weather forecasting are given below.

- They are used to predict the changes in the weather condition.
- They help forecast weather conditions and wind speed.
- They are used for drawing weather maps.

Entertainment

Computers are used for various entertainment purposes. Some are listed below.

- They allow access to play games.
- They allow you to upload and download music.
- They allow you to watch movies.
- They help you stay in constant touch with friends and relatives through social network.

CHECK YOUR PROGRESS

A. Information technology is heavily used today. Give five uses of information technology in the world of entertainment.

B. Complete the word puzzle given below:

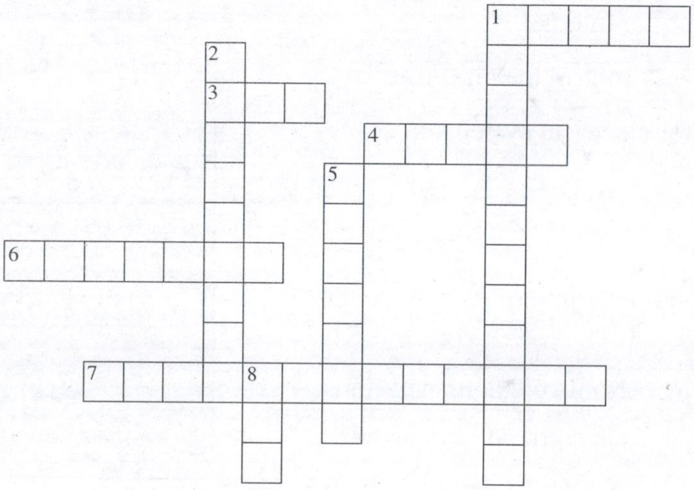

Across:

1. Pointing device used as a common input device
3. Brain of the Computer
4. Sending and receiving messages instantly
6. Input device that converts file into a digitised format
7. Fastest computer

Down:

1. Type of computer used in business and scientific applications
2. Online buying and selling of products and services
5. Output device used to see the softcopy of documents
8. Temporary Memory

GLOSSARY

- **Arithmetic and Logic Unit (ALU):** It is is used to perform arithmetic and logical operations on data received from memory and transfer the same to main memory.
- **Automated Teller Machine (ATM):** It is used to withdraw money from your bank account from anywhere.
- **Bar Code Reader:** It is used to read the pattern of bars on the items you buy from the market.
- **Bit:** It refers to the binary digits (0 and 1).
- **Magnetic Ink Character Reader:** It is used to read the magnetic code written on the cheques or on credit cards.
- **MFLOPS:** It stands for millions of floating point operations per second.
- **ROM:** It is the non-volatile memory.

NOW YOU KNOW

1. A computer is an electronic machine that can be used to store and process data and produce the desired output according to the instructions given.
2. The speed of a computer is measured in terms of MHz or GHz.
3. The input unit receives the data or instruction through input devices and sends it to the main memory of the computer.
4. There are two types of RAM: Static RAM and Dynamic RAM.
5. Dynamic RAM is a cheap memory. Most of the computers contain DRAM chips.
6. There are three types of ROM: PROM, EPROM and EEPROM.
7. Mainframe Computers are ultra-high performance computers, large, expensive and occupy more space.
8. India developed the PARAM Padma Super Computer by Center for Development of Advanced Computer (CDAC) with processing speed up to one teraflop per second (1 trillion process per second).
9. A bit is the smallest unit of storage.
10. Storage devices are the secondary devices used to store data and programs depending on the capacity of memory it can hold.
11. Hard Disk is one of the most popular storage device for storing a large amount of data.
12. Digital Versatile Disc (DVD) is like a CD but its storage capacity is more than the CDs (from 4 GB to 47 GB).
13. Computers can generally be divided into four major categories: micro computer, mini computer, mainframe computer, super computer.
14. Computers are used in education. They help in gathering information, online teaching, online registrations, and many more.
15. Computers are also used in banks, businesses, hospitals, press, government organisations, communication, transportation, movie and media, weather forecasting and entertainment.

EXERCISE

FA

A Fill in the blanks.

1. A .... keyboard sends data through a physical cord.
2. A .... is an input device that allows you to control the pointer on the computer screen.
3. An upturned mouse where the ball is present on top or on side is called ....
4. A graphic tablet consists of a .... surface and a pen-like drawing tool called ....
5. .... is used to read the magnetic code written on the cheques or on credit cards.
6. CPU consists of .... unit, ... unit and .... unit.
7. In .... printers paper comes in direct contact with the printer head.
8. .... are used to print graphics, diagrams and maps.
9. Minicomputers are also known as .... computers.
10. Online buying and selling of products and services is known as ....

B Multiple choice questions.

1. Which computer can be used to type the details of personal expenses while travelling?
   a. Desktop
   b. Laptop
   c. Super computer
   d. Palmtop
2. Which of the following is not an input device?
   a. Speaker
   b. Scanner
   c. Mouse
   d. Joystick
3. RAM stands for ....
   a. Read Access Memory
   b. Random Access Memory
   c. Random Auxiliary memory
   d. Read Allocate Memory
4. A .... looks like a CD-ROM but stores more data than the CD.
   a. CD-RW
   b. Magnetic disk
   c. Floppy
   d. DVD

5. One nibble is equal to ....

a. 4 bits b. 8 bits c. 1 bit d. 1024 bits

6. In super markets, a .... is used to identify the product code for billing.

a. BCR b. OMR c. OCR d. MICR

7. VDU is used as a/an ....

a. input unit b. storage unit c. memory unit d. output unit

8. Primary memory is .... compared to secondary memory.

a. slow b. fast c. cheap d. small

9. The capacity of a floppy disk is approximately ....

a. 1.24 MB b. 1.44 MB c. 1.44 GB d. 134 KB

10. A Blue Ray Disc can store up to .... of data.

a. 4.7 GB b. 10 GB c. 2 GB d. 25 GB

11. The capacity of computer's memory is measured in terms of ....

a. kilograms b. kilometers

c. weight of computer d. kilobytes

12. A laser printer is a ....

a. impact printer b. non-impact printer c. large printer d. slow printer

13. .... is easy to carry, copy, portable, writable and non-scratchable.

a. Pen Drive b. Hard Disk c. External Disk d. None of these

14. .... is used to read the magnetic code written on the cheques or on credit cards.

a. Magnetic Ink Character Reader b. Optical Character Recognition

c. Optical Mark Reader d. Bar Code Reader

15. The speed of a computer is measured in terms of ....

a. capacity b. cost c. size d. MHz

16. Only if the computer is given correct data and instructions, it will return an accurate result. This concept is called ....

a. BIOS b. IPO c. GIGO d. None of these

17. The documents stored and maintained in system to retrieve any information at any time is called as ....

a. copy b. hard copy c. softcopy d. duplicate

18. .... monitor can be easily damaged even with a sharp pencil. HOTS

a. LCD b. CRT c. Color d. TFT

19. .... is a digital computer, whose process and storage capacity is lesser than that of mainframe and greater than that of micro computers.

a. Mini computer b. Micro computer c. Super computer d. All of these

20. .... computer is also called as mid-range computer.

a. Micro b. Palmtop c. Mini d. Mainframe

C State whether the following statements are True or False.

1. Dot matrix printer is an impact printer. ....
2. A bit is the highest unit of storage. ....
3. DVD's can store only up to 2 GB. ....
4. ROM is a volatile memory. ....
5. Super computers are used in weapons research and weather forecasting. ....
6. CD-ROM is an optical storage device. ....
7. You cannot download movies from a computer. ....
8. Dot matrix printers leaves the impression of the characters in the form of dots. ....
9. IBM 4300 is a mainframe computer. ....
10. A large amount of paper wastage is prevented with the help of hard copy. ....
11. Random Access Memory is temporary. ....
12. Computer does not suffer from tiredness or boredom. This character is called as versatility. ....
13. Light pen is an input device. ....
14. Both inkjet printer and laser printer are one and the same. ....
15. Plotters are the output devices used to print graphs and maps. ....

D Write a short note on each of the following topic.

1. RAM
2. ROM
3. Secondary Memory
4. ALU
5. Super Computer

SA

E Differentiate between the following.

1. RAM and ROM
2. CD and DVD
3. DVD and Blue Ray
4. CD-ROM and CD-RW HOTS
5. Primary Memory and Secondary Memory
6. Printers and Plotters
7. Inkjet and Laser jet
8. Impact and Non-Impact Printers
9. DRAM and SRAM
10. LCD and TFT HOTS

F Answer the following questions.

1. Define computers.
2. Mention the characteristics of a computer.
3. Write any two applications of a computer.
4. What are the three main units of a computer?
5. What is the use of control unit?
6. What are the two types of memory?
7. Name any four input devices.
8. Name any four output devices.
9. Name any four storage devices.
10. How DVD is different from CD?
11. Write one advantage of dot matrix printer.
12. What is the use of e-commerce?
13. What is the memory capacity and storage capacity of a super computer?
14. How are computers used in desktop publishing?
15. Identify this: It has a rod and a ball attached to its lower end. It is operated by holding the rod and moving it in any direction.

G Answer the following questions in detail.

1. Write a note on applications of computers in our day-to-day life.
2. Explain any four input devices.
3. What is the use of a storage device? Explain.
4. Draw and explain the functioning of computer.
5. Explain the units of storage.

Application Based Questions

A. Suhail joined a local IT company for a three month internship. As the part his orientation he was shown around the office and then asked to finish a small test. Help him fill the following table, which is the part of the test.

Device	Name and Type	Purpose
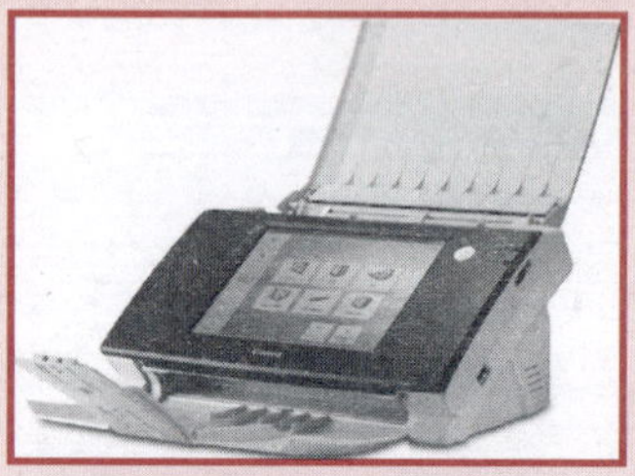		
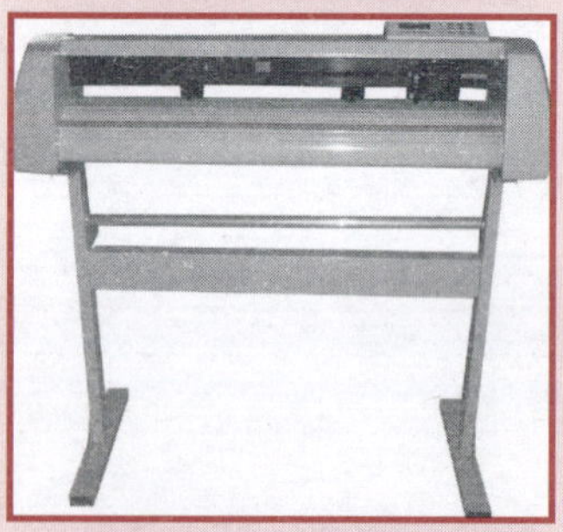		

B. Megha wants to store data of her monthly expenditure for a period of one year and wants to perform some calculations and analysis. She decided to use MS Excel. What input devices will she be needing for this?

C. Farhan is a computer programmer. He developed a software for his friend's retail shop. As he cannot upload the entire software through email, he has to carry the software and a sample data back for testing. Which storage device will you suggest for him to use for this purpose? The device should have high storage capacity and should be rewriteable.

D. Sugandh has bought a new inkjet printer. She has connected it to her computer with the help of a USB cable and has switched the printer on. When she is giving the print command, the printer is not printing. What else is she required to do?

E. Surbhi is going to London for a student exchange program. Her parents do not want her to travel with a lot of money. Is there a way she can withdraw money from her bank in London?

LAB WORK

A. Create a presentation on the topic 'Applications of Computer'.

B. Find out the name of processor used in your home and school computer. If they both are different, then which one is better and why?

C. Investigate and list the input, output and storage devices attached to your computer in school. List the name, model and main functionality of the device.

EXTENSION

Some common acronyms associated with computers are listed in the table below.

GIGO	Garbage In Garbage Out
MHz	Megahertz
GHz	Gigahertz
OMR	Optical Mark Reader
OCR	Optical Character Recognition
MICR	Magnetic Ink Character Recognition
BCR	Bar Code Reader
ALU	Arithmetic Logic Unit
CU	Control Unit
MU	Memory Unit
CPU	Central Processing Unit
ROM	Read Only Memory
PROM	Programmable Read Only Memory
EPROM	Erasable Programmable Read Only Memory
EEPROM	Electrical Erasable Programmable Read Only Memory
RAM	Random Access Memory
SRAM	Static Random Access Memory
DRAM	Dynamic Random Access Memory

CPS	Character Per Second
CPI	Character Per Inch
CRT	Cathode Ray Tube
LCD	Liquid Crystal Display
TFT	Thin Film Transistor
ATM	Automated Teller Machine
CAD	Computer Aided Design
CDAC	Center for Development of Advanced Computer
CD-ROM	Compact Disc Read Only Memory
CD-RW	Compact Disc Rewritable
DVD	Digital Versatile Disc
DTP	DeskTop Publishing
ECOM	Electronic Commerce
MFLOPS	Millions of Floating Point Operations Per Second
BIT	Binary Digit
KB	Kilobyte
MB	Megabyte
GB	Gigabyte
TB	Terabyte

TEACHER'S NOTES

1. Show the students different input, output and storage devices and their real life usage.
2. Talk to the students about the usage of super computers.

2 Computer Software

SNAP RECAP

1. The functional components of a computer are input unit, processing unit and output unit.
2. Computers are classified based on their size and speed. The four major categories of a computer are: micro computer, mini computer, mainframe computer and super computer.
3. A computer has two types of memory: Primary memory and Secondary memory.
4. The Central Processing Unit is responsible for execution of instructions, arithmetic and logical calculations, storing and controlling the input and output devices.

LEARNING OBJECTIVES

You will learn about:

1. Software
2. Types of Software
3. System Software – Operating System, Language Translators and Utilities
4. Application Software – General Purpose and Specific Purpose

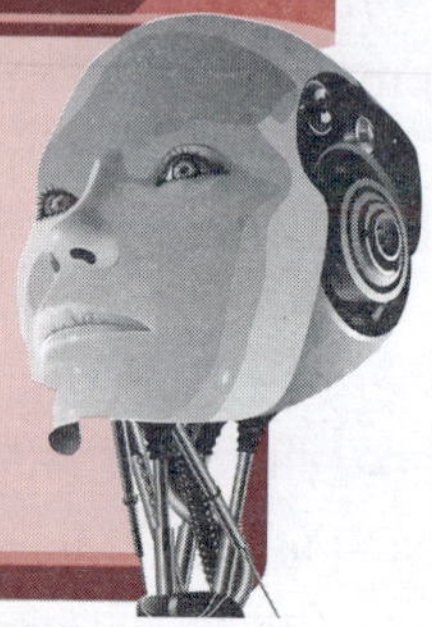

▶ INTRODUCTION

A computer is an electronic device that performs specific tasks based on the instructions given to it. This set of instructions, written using a computer language, is called a **program**. *A set of programs and procedures which helps in performing various operations on a computer is called* ***software*** (Fig. 2.1). Software is the non-tangible component of a computer system.

Fig. 2.1 *Software*

When the computer is switched on, it loads the **System Software–Operating System (OS)**. Then, the OS makes the computer ready for work through different **Application Software** like word processors for documents, spreadsheets for calculations and gaming software for playing games. The software gives instructions to hardware, using input devices, to complete the desired task. Hardware alone is incapable of performing any task. Computer hardware and software have a symbiotic relationship, that is, neither can be used without the other. They need each other to fulfil their potential.

Software can broadly be categorised into two main types: system software and application software. In this chapter, you will learn more about software and its different types.

Types of Software

There are two types of software (Fig. 2.2). They are:

- System software
- Application software.

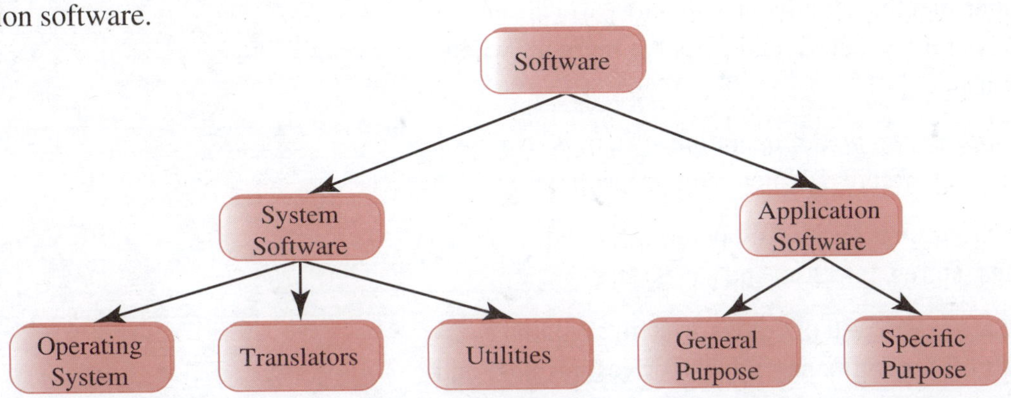

Fig. 2.2 *Types of software*

System Software

The software that controls the internal operations, like input and processing, is known as system software. System software manages, controls and coordinates the hardware component of a computer. It also performs the task of storage management. System software executes automatically when the computer system is switched on. System software includes:

- Operating system
- Language translators
- Utility software.

Operating System

The software program that acts as a means of communication between the user and the computer system is known as the operating system (Fig. 2.3). It acts as an interface and is responsible for smooth functioning of the computer. It controls and coordinates all the operations between the hardware and the software components of the computer.

Fig. 2.3 *Operating system*

Operating system acts as a supervisor for all applications and other types of software. When the user inputs a task that he/she desires to do, then the operating system allocates the task to an appropriate application and allows the hardware and software components of the computer system to interact with each other.

An operating system consists of low-level programs, which interact with the computer at a basic level.

Functions of an operating system

Some of the important functions of an operating system are listed below (Fig. 2.4).

- ***Input and output management:*** An operating system controls the functioning of all the input and output devices.
- ***Process management:*** An operating system manages the working of a processor. It allocates the resources to a process; allows a process to share and exchange information and facilitates synchronisation among different processes.
- ***Memory management:*** An operating system manages the computer memory. It allocates memory to various applications at their request and frees the memory when it is not in use.
- ***Resource management:*** An operating system is responsible for efficient and effective deployment of resources.
- ***Information management:*** An operating system manipulates, stores, retrieves and saves data.
- ***Utility management:*** An operating system contains a number of utilities for managing disk drives, printers and other devices. Utilities analyse, configure, optimise and maintain a computer system.

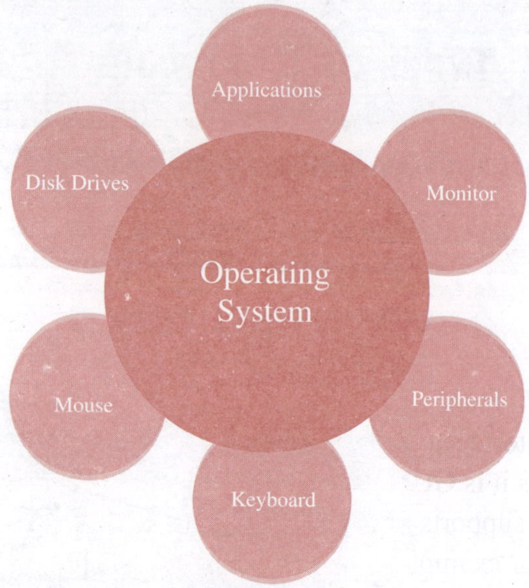

Fig. 2.4 *Functions of an operating system*

Based on the user interface, operating systems are classified into **CUI** and **GUI**. CUI stands for **Character User Interface**, while GUI stands for **Graphical User Interface**.

Character User Interface: A CUI operating system requires you to type commands (using a keyboard) to interact with a computer. It is sequence oriented in nature, that is, each command is executed in an order. A programmer controls the flow of actions in a CUI system. For example, MS-DOS operating system.

Graphical User Interface: A GUI operating system requires you to make use of graphics and images to interact with a computer. GUI makes interactions with computers really easy; a user just has to click the mouse. Microsoft Windows is an example of GUI operating system. A GUI operating system provides windows, menus, buttons, scrollbars, iconic images and icons.

Some of the popular operating systems are listed and discussed below.

- MS-DOS
- Windows
- Unix
- Linux
- Mac OS

MS-DOS: DOS stands for Disk Operating System (Fig. 2.5). It was developed in early 1980s. Before Microsoft Windows was launched, MS-DOS was the most commonly used operating system.

MS-DOS is a single user operating system. It can support only one program at a time. It uses Character User Interface (CUI) or Command/Character Line Interface (CLI).

Fig. 2.5 *MS-DOS*

Microsoft Windows: Windows operating system was developed by Microsoft in late 1980s. It uses Graphical User Interface (GUI). Windows operating system (Fig. 2.6) can support multiple programs at a time, that is, **multitasking**. As it is GUI based, it is easy to use. It can be used in a stand-alone computer system as well as on network systems. It supports multiple user accounts. A GUI interface usually offer more than one option to initiate a particular option. For example, to print a word document you can use the **Print** option in the Office Button menu, or click on the Printer icon, or use the keyboard shortcut **(Ctrl + P)**.

Fig. 2.6 *Windows 7*

FACT FILE

The recent OS of Microsoft Windows for personal computers, mobile devices and server computers are Windows 8.1, Windows Phone 8 and Windows Server 2012 R2, respectively.

Unix: Unix operating system (Fig. 2.7) is a multiuser, multitasking operating system. It is widely used as the master control program in high-end workstations and servers.

Fig. 2.7 *Unix*

FACT FILE

The first operation system coded by Microsoft was **Xenix**. It was a version of unix under a different name. However, it was MS-DOS, that was made for IBM PCs, that gave Microsoft a foothold in the software market.

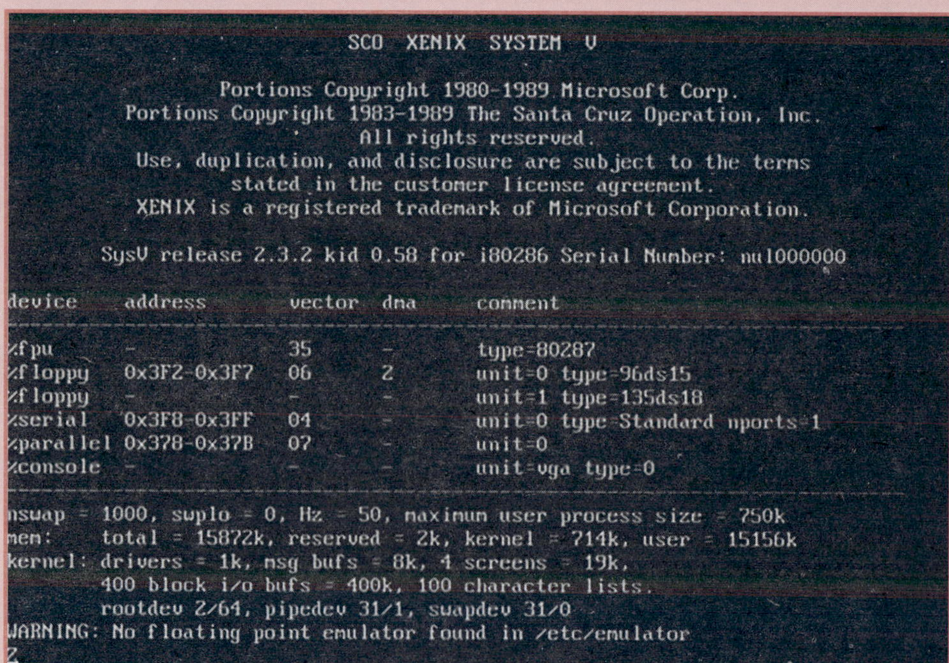

Linux: Linux operating system (Fig. 2.8) is an open source operating system. It was initially developed as a free operating system for Intel x86 - based computers. It is a low cost operating system for computers that helps in maintaining the standard and efficiency. It is also used in servers as it provides security. It is an open source program available free of cost. Its source code is available and may be used, modified and distributed by anyone under licenses, such as, the GNU General Public License.

Fig. 2.8 *Linux*

Mac OS: It is a series of GUI based operating systems developed by Apple Inc. for their Macintosh line of computer systems (Fig. 2.9).

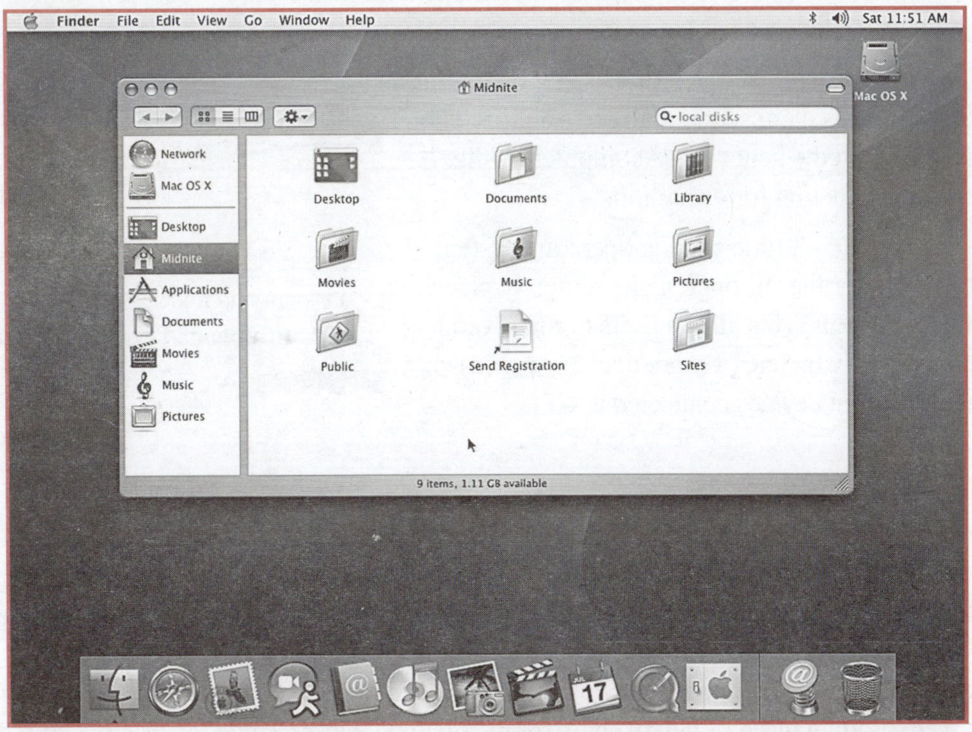

Fig. 2.9 *Mac OS*

Types of operating system

There are different types of operating systems. They are categorised based on their functions. They are:

- Single user operating system
- Multi-user operating system
- Multitasking operating system
- Real-time operating system
- Batch processing operating system
- Time sharing operating system.

> **FACT FILE**
>
> **Network operating system** refers to an operating system that has functions for connecting computers and devices in a network, usually a Local Area Network (LAN). Some popular network operating systems are: Novell Netware, Artisoft's LANtastic and Microsoft Windows Server.
>
> There are some operating systems that have built-in networking features. For example, Unix and Mac OS.

Single user operating system: The most popular single user operating system is MS-DOS. As the processor has to execute only one program at a time, the memory management is not difficult for this type of operating system.

Multi-user operating system: A multi-user operating system allows more than one user to access the operating system at the same time. Network techniques are adapted to establish this. Multi-terminals are attached to the host computer. Unix is a powerful multi-user operating system.

Multitasking operating system: A multitasking operating system allows you to execute more than one program at a given time. It allows different devices to perform their own processing independently, without the involvement of CPU. This technique reduces the idle time of CPU. Microsoft Windows operating system is a popular and powerful multitasking operating system.

Real-time operating system: Real-time operating systems are the most sophisticated systems. They provide random enquiries from remote locations. These are dedicated systems and their tasks are processed immediately. Hence, the response time for any task in these operating systems is very little.

Batch processing operating system: A batch processing operating system accepts tasks and places them sequentially to execute. The tasks can be stored and executed whenever the computer is idle. It does not require the user interaction for execution.

Time sharing operating system: A time sharing operating system allows access to CPU and other files through many remotely placed systems called **remote terminals**. This allows users to run several different programs concurrently on one or more than one processor that consists of input and output devices connected to CPU.

> **FACT FILE**
>
> The process of waiting for the execution of tasks in batch processing OS is called **Spooling (Simultaneous Peripheral Operation On Line)**.

LANGUAGE TRANSLATORS

In **machine language**, all the data and programs exist as long series of 0 and 1. A computer easily understands these machine language programs. The program execution is very quick as the instructions are processed very fast. Programs written in machine language are processor specific. Hence, these languages are called **machine dependent languages** or **machine code**.

However, it is very difficult to read and understand this machine code. Hence, second level languages were developed in which abbreviations were used, in place of binary code, for instructions. For example, *A* for *add* and *CPY* for *copy*. These languages are known as **assembly languages**. As you know, a computer only understands machine language and therefore, a translator called **assembler** is required to translate the instructions to machine code and vice versa. After this, **high-level languages** were developed in which the programs were written in English language, like sentences. High-level languages are not machine dependent. With the help of translators, the instructions were translated to machine code and vice versa. Some of the common translators are discussed below.

Assembler

An assembler converts assembly language programs, that is, low-level language to machine level language programs and vice versa.

Compiler

A compiler converts the high-level language programs like C and COBOL into machine level language programs and vice versa. It converts the entire program in one go and displays all the errors in the program with line numbers.

Interpreter

An interpreter converts high-level language programs like BASIC and Visual Basic, into machine level language programs and vice versa. It converts and executes the program line by line. It cannot proceed to the next line unless the error is rectified.

CHECK YOUR PROGRESS

A. Name any four popular operating systems. Also, categorise them based on their functions.

B. Differentiate between application software and system software using examples.

C. Initially, Apple Inc. logo had Isaac Newton sitting under an apple tree. It was later replaced by the present day logo. Also, to differentiate the shape of the apple from a cherry, the bite was put in. With the help of the Internet, find out 10 more interesting facts about Apple computers and Mac OS. HOTS

D. Why do we need high level language? HOTS

E. Make a list of five commonly used assemblers and five commonly used compilers.

Utilities

Utility software are programs that help in managing the hardware and software of a computer system by performing a range of tasks. The availability of these utilities depends on the operating system of a computer. Utilities protect the computer from virus attacks, loss of data, perform security and storage check by scanning, cleaning, repairing, compressing and by creating a backup of data.

Some of the utility software are supplied as a part of an operating system while others are purchased and updated regularly online.

Some common utility programs are explained below.

Antivirus utility

An antivirus program scans the computer system, recognises a virus, alert the user and cleans the computer system. These are designed to protect the computer against malicious software, such as, Trojan horse and Happy Birthday and from other code that steals the computer data. However, it is not enough to install an antivirus software to protect your computer system. It is also necessary to update the software to the latest versions through the Internet. Some of the commonly used antivirus programs are: Symantec, McAfee, Kaspersky and Avasti.

ACTIVITY

How to scan your entire computer system using an antivirus software?

1. Start the antivirus program installed on your computer system. To do so, double-click on the desktop icon of the antivirus program.

   NOTE: You can also launch the program using the **Start button**.

2. The main antivirus program window opens.
3. Select the **Full Scan** option. This alerts the antivirus program to begin scanning your hard drive(s). If any malicious programs or files are found, they are automatically quarantined and deleted.

NOTE: While browsing the Internet, allow your antivirus program to run. It will scan your emails and downloaded files. The program ensures that they are virus free and protect you from attack sites.

Backup utility

Backing up of a file refers to saving a copy of the file on a backup storage from which it can be retrieved in case the data gets lost. The latest operating systems provide the backup utility to make copies of your data on a regular schedule.

ACTIVITY

How to back up your programs, system settings and files on a Windows 7 computer?

1. Go to the **Start** button ⟹ **Control Panel** ⟹ **Backup and Restore** option.
2. On the left pane, click on the **Create a system image**.
3. **Create a system image** wizard opens. Follow the steps in the wizard to start the backup.

   NOTE: If you are asked for an administrator password, key in the password.

4. System images are saved in the format of **drive\WindowsImageBackup\computer name**.

File compression utility

Maintaining and transferring huge amount of data is time consuming. So, the data needs to be compressed using file compression utilities. These utilities compresses the data so that it occupies less space. It also makes file transfer over the Internet easy and less time consuming. To use these compressed files, the files first have to be decompressed. Winzip is a commonly used file compression utility.

ACTIVITY

How to compress files on a Windows 7 computer?

1. Click on the desired file(s). To select multiple files, hold down the **Ctrl** key while clicking.
2. Right-click on the selected files to open the **shortcut** menu.
3. In the **shortcut** menu, go to **Send to** option ⟹ **Compressed (zipped) folder**. The file will begin to compress automatically.
4. The compressed file will be saved at the same location. It will also have the same name as the original; although, if desired, you can rename it.

Disk defragmenter utility

Allocation of areas for files is done by the operating system. Allocation by the OS is scattered all over the disk as per the different task allotted to it. The term defragment means arranging the files on the disk in a sequential order. The disk defragmenter utility defragments files and thereby reduces the time to access the same.

ACTIVITY

How to defragment a disk on a Windows 7 computer?

1. Click on the **Start** button ⟹ **All Programs** ⟹ **Accessories** ⟹ **System Tools** ⟹ **Disk Defragmenter**.
2. The **Disk Defragmenter** dialog box opens. In the **Current status:** section, select the drive you want to defragment.
3. Once the drive is selected, click on the **Defragment Disk** button to start the process.
4. Click on **Close**.

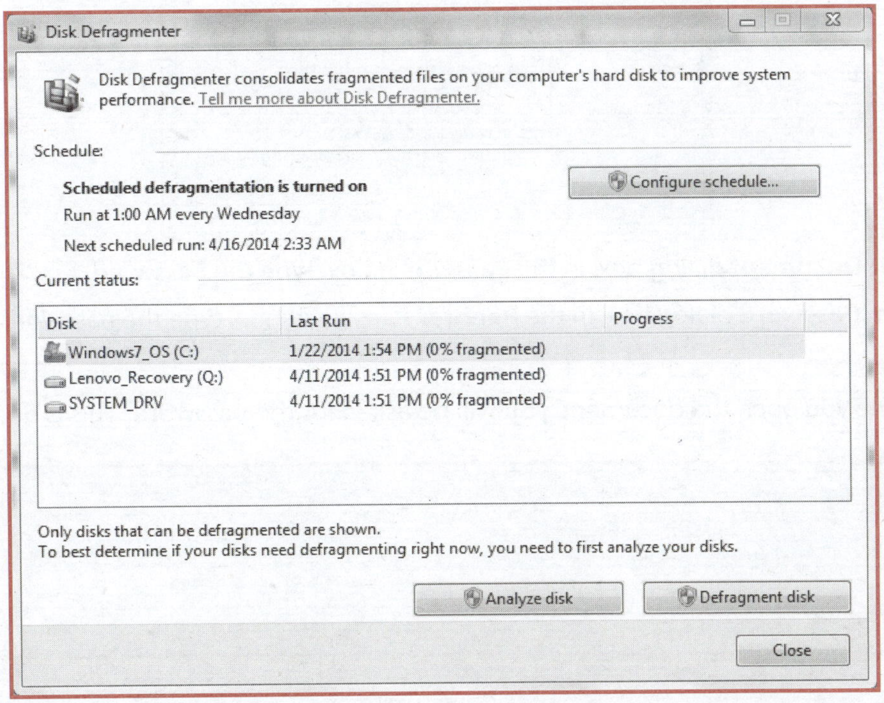

NOTE: You can also schedule defragmentation by using the **Configure schedule...** option.

Data encryption and decryption

Today computers are being used for all kinds of purpose, including creating and storing sensitive information. Therefore, it is essential to ensure security and safety of the information. To protect the data, it can be converted into an unknown form which can only be decoded by the user. *This process of converting data into unknown form is called* ***encryption***. The encrypted data needs to be decoded by the intended user so that the receiver of information is able to read the information. *The process of converting the encrypted code back to its original form is called* ***decryption***.

ACTIVITY

How to encrypt a MS Word 2007 document?

1. Click on the **Microsoft Office Button.**
2. Go to **Prepare** ⟹ **Encrypt Document.**

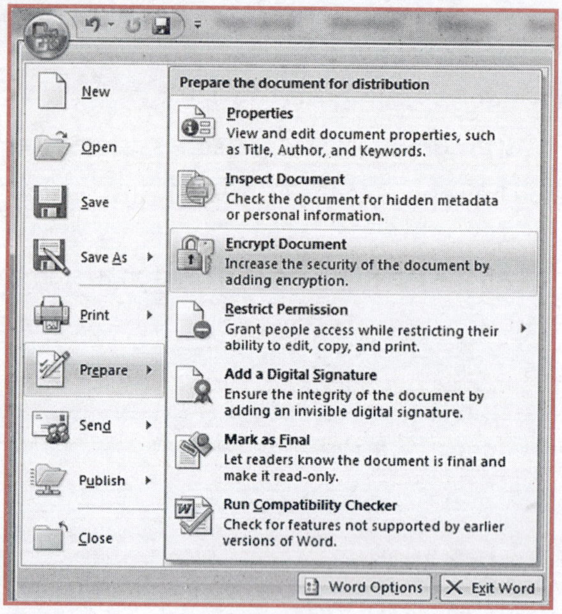

3. In the **Encrypt Document** dialog box, in the **Password:** box, type the password.
4. In the **Confirm Password** dialog box, in the **Reenter Password** box, type the password again to confirm.
5. Click **OK**.
6. Now every time you open the document, you will be asked for the password. This is decryption.

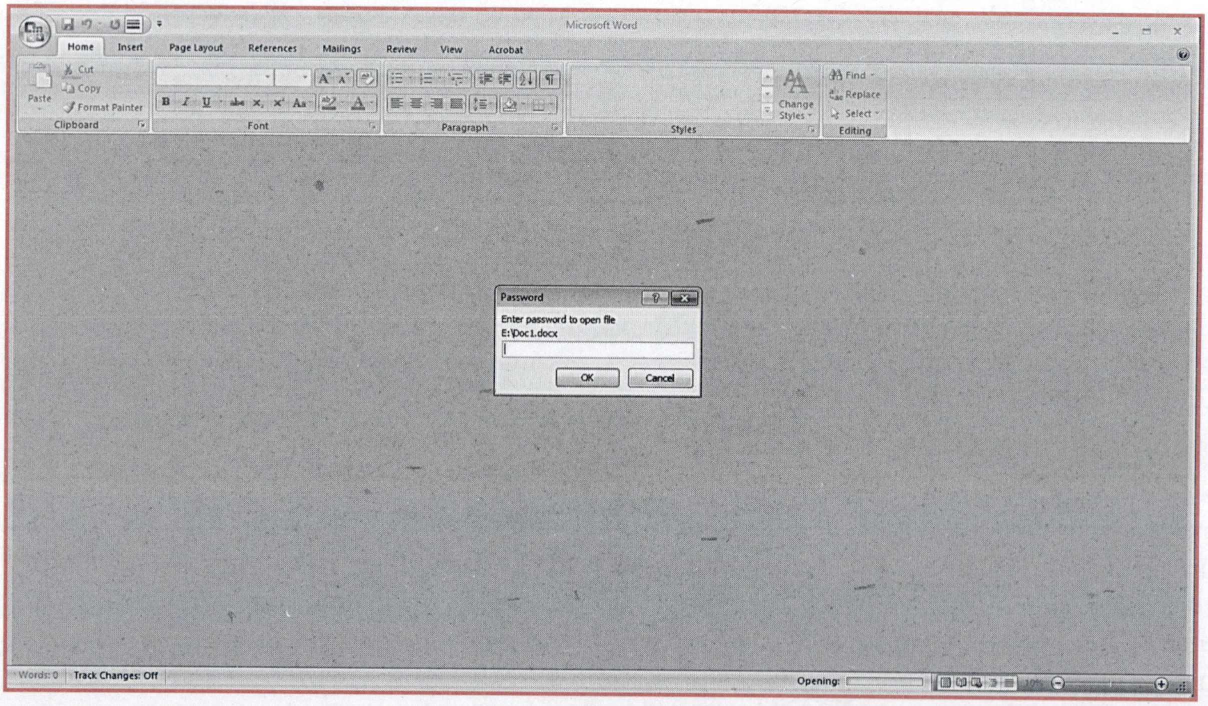

▶ Application Software

Application software are used for a specific purpose of work that benefits the user. These are designed to handle specialised tasks like documentation, creating spreadsheets, drawing, creating graphics, employee payroll and school results. These are also known as **end user programs**. Application software cannot run without the help of the system software.

The application software can be categorised into two. They are:

- General purpose application software
- Specific purpose application software.

General purpose application software

General purpose application software are commonly used in organisations or by people who have to perform similar activities to achieve simple and regular tasks. They are standard software developed, packed and sold. They are relatively cheap and easily available. As general purpose application software are widely used, they are thoroughly tested before they are made available for use and hence, the chances of errors in these software are relatively less. Word processing software, spreadsheet software, database software, graphics software, desktop publishing software, presentation software and multimedia software are some of the general purpose application software.

Word processing software: Word processing software is used to create, edit and format a document quickly and efficiently. It also helps to store and modify the text by entering commands. One can easily rearrange, edit, modify, insert pictures, add tables and shapes to a document using a word processor. It is generally used to create letters, documents and reports. Some popular word processing software are MS Word (Fig. 2.10), WordPad, Notepad, WordStar and WordPerfect.

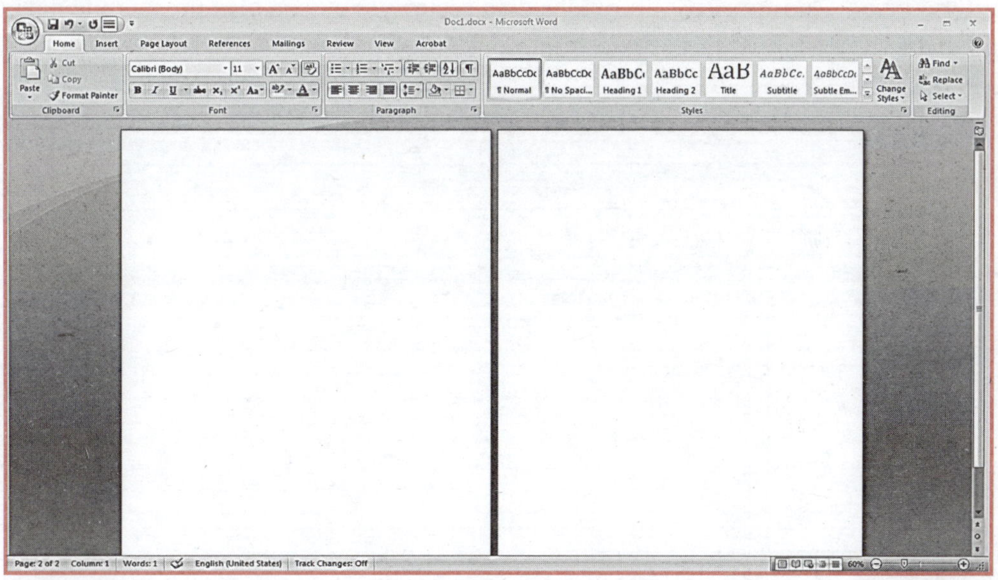

Fig. 2.10 *MS Word 2007*

Spreadsheet software: A spreadsheet is used to enter data in a tabular format, where values are arranged in rows and columns. It is useful for doing calculations, handling data, inserting charts, analysing data and displaying the data in an organised manner. Built-in functions like SUM, AVERAGE, COUNT, MAX and MIN help manipulate the data easily. It also allows the user to insert formulas to work with the data easily. You can also create charts using spreadsheet software. The charts give a better understanding and analysis of data. Some commonly used spreadsheet software are Lotus 123, Star Calc and Microsoft Excel (Fig. 2.11).

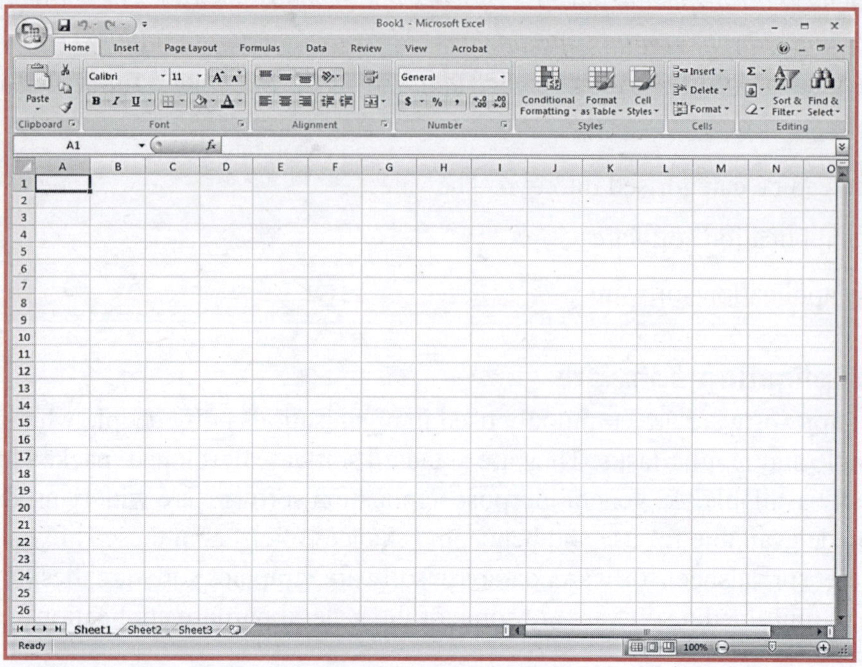

Fig. 2.11 *MS Excel 2007*

Database software: A database is an organised collection of related data. Database software is used for creating databases and managing the information stored in them. Also referred to as database management systems (DBMS), it is used to create, edit, organise, modify and maintain data. It also allows the users to sort, retrieve and filter data according to the criteria given. Additionally, it provides data security. You can also present the data in the form of professional reports using database software. Some commonly used database software are Oracle, SQL Server, MS Access (Fig. 2.12) and Sybase.

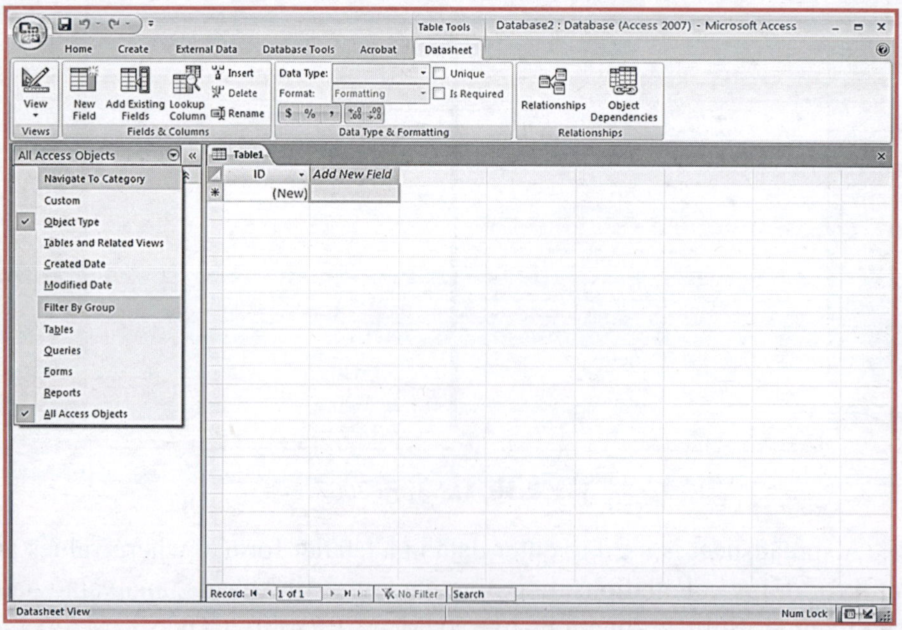

Fig. 2.12 *MS Access 2007*

Graphics software: Graphics software is used to create, edit and manage graphics like images and logos. It is used in architecture and engineering where machines are designed using computers and then implemented. Adobe Photoshop (Fig. 2.13), CorelDRAW, MS Paint and CAD (Computer aided design) are some of the commonly used graphics software.

Fig. 2.13 *Adobe Photoshop*

Desktop publishing software: The page layout, designing and printing documents with text and graphics in a professional manner can be easily done with the help of desktop publishing software (DTP). It is mainly used for designing and printing advertisements, brochures, posters, magazines, newsletters and books. Adobe PageMaker, QuarkXpress, CorelDRAW and Adobe Indesign (Fig. 2.14) are some of the commonly used DTP software.

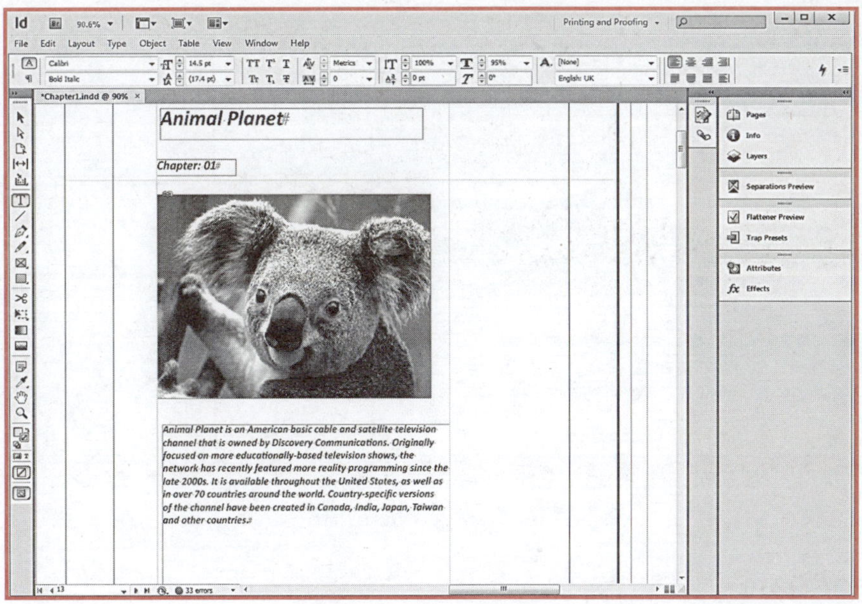

Fig. 2.14 *Adobe Indesign 7.0*

Presentation software: Presentation software is used to display information in the form of slide show on screen by developing slides. The slide includes text, pictures, animation effects, audio and video. It also allows you to record narration in your own voice. Some commonly used presentation software are MS PowerPoint (Fig. 2.15) and Star Impress.

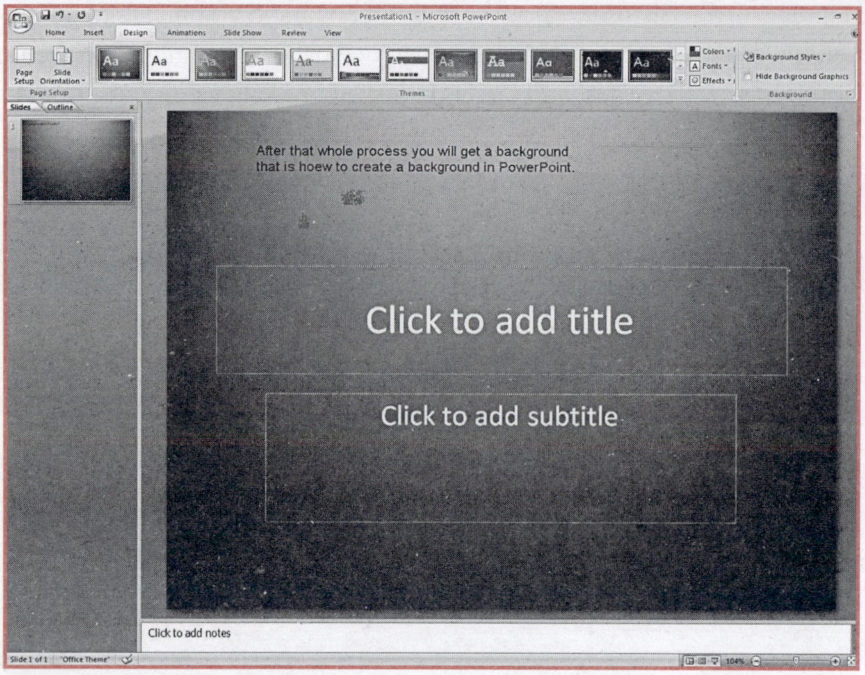

Fig. 2.15 *PowerPoint 2007*

Multimedia software: Multimedia software is used to integrate text, video, sound, animation and graphics and package it to present it as a movie. This provides interactive learning program in the field of education. Adobe Flash is an example of multimedia software (Fig. 2.16).

Fig. 2.16 *Adobe Flash*

Specific purpose software

Specific purpose software is a program designed to perform a specific function. Some of the specific purpose software programs are:

- Billing and accounting software
- Payroll software

- Reservation software
- Attendance system software
- HR management software.

Billing and accounting software: A billing system handles the billing of a product used or purchased. It is used to calculate the total payment to be received from the customer. It gives a simple, efficient and cost effective way to gain full control over accounting processes. Most of the supermarkets use this software to calculate and generate bills.

Payroll software: A payroll software is used by organisations to prepare salary of their employees along with their increments and deductions. It designs the payslip as per a company requirements. It maintains history of payments and deductions of each employee. It also helps to maintain records and to create reports.

Reservation system software: A reservation system is used to manage all kinds of bookings for flight, train, theaters and hotels. Indian Railways is one of the largest services which provide the facility of reservation through online system. Another example is hotel reservation software which helps in managing and booking cottages, hotels and cabins according to your convenience and budget.

Attendance system software: An attendance system software is used to monitor the attendance of the employee of a company. This system records the details of arrival and departure of employees. Finger print recognition and face recognition devices have made this system very sophisticated and useful. The data can be processed quickly and easily. The software also provides the reports generation and security feature for the data.

HR management software: An HR management software is used to recruit, train and educate the employees according to their job position. It is also used to test and measure employees' skills by maintaining performance records.

CHECK YOUR PROGRESS

A. Divide the class into four groups. Each group will be named after a specific purpose software used by the school for different purpose (like Payroll, Student's database and E-Learning). Each group have to collect information about the software, such as, features of the software assigned to the group. Also, find out where (Department – Exam, Office and Library) it is used. Each group will then present the information they have collected and the other groups should identify the software and the department it is used.

B. Categorise the following software and write them in the appropriate table column.

Linux, Payroll System, Word Perfect, Unix, Windows NT, Business Management System, Disk Clean Up, Compiler, Oracle, Lotus 123, Tally, Assembler, K7

Operating system	Language translators	Utility software	General purpose software	Specific purpose software

C. Name two utility software available in Windows 7 for protecting your data.

D. Differentiate between general purpose application software and specific purpose application software.

GLOSSARY

- **Attendance System Software:** It is used to monitor the attendance of the employee of a company.
- **Application Software:** They are designed to handle specialised tasks, such as, documentation, creating spreadsheets, drawing, creating graphics, employee payroll and school results.
- **Billing System:** It handles the billing of a product used or purchased.
- **Decryption:** It is the process of converting the encrypted code back to its original form.
- **Defragmentation:** It is the process of arranging the files on the disk in a sequential order.
- **Encryption:** It is the process of converting data into unknown form for security reasons.
- **General Purpose Application Software:** They are used in organisations or by people who have to perform similar activities to achieve simple and regular tasks.
- **HR Management Software:** It is used to recruit, train and educate the employees according to their job position.
- **Operating System:** It is a set of programs that controls the execution of all other programs.
- **Payroll Software:** It is used by organisations to prepare salary of their employees along with their increments and deductions.
- **Program:** It is a set of instructions written using a computer language to achieve a particular task.
- **Reservation System:** It is used to manage all kinds of bookings for flight, train, theaters and hotels.
- **Software:** It is the set of programs and procedures which helps in performing various operations on a computer.
- **Specific Purpose Software:** It is a program designed to perform a specific function.
- **Spooling:** It is the process of waiting for the execution of tasks in batch processing operating system.
- **System Software:** It controls the internal operations, like input and processing.

NOW YOU KNOW

1. There are two types of software: system software and application software.
2. An operating system acts as a means of communication between the user and the computer system.
3. A word processing software is used to create, edit and format a document quickly and efficiently.
4. A spreadsheet is used to enter data in a tabular form where values are arranged in rows and columns.
5. A database is an organised collection of related data.
6. The page layout, designing and printing documents with text and graphics in a professional manner can be easily done with the help of desktop publishing software.
7. A presentation software is used to display information in the form of slide show on screen by developing slides.
8. A multimedia software is used to integrate text, video, sound, animation and graphics and present it as a movie.
9. A utility software is a program that manages the computer hardware and software by performing a small range of tasks.
10. The process of converting data into unknown form, to provide security, is called encryption. The process of converting the encrypted code back to its original form is called decryption.

EXERCISE

FA

A Fill in the blanks.

1. A set of programs that help in performing various operations on a computer is called ....
2. .... controls and coordinates all the operations between the hardware and the software components of a computer.
3. A .... operating system lets you accomplish more than one task at a given time.
4. The programs that perform specific task, such as database management or payroll management, are known as ....
5. An operating system can be classified into .... and .... based on the user interface.
6. The first operating system coded by Microsoft was ....
7. An assembler is required to convert .... language into .... language.
8. An .... utility protects the system from virus attack.
9. DTP stands for ....
10. The process of arranging the files in sequential order on the disk is known as ....

B Multiple choice questions.

1. DOS stands for ....
   a. Disk Operating System
   b. Data Operating System
   c. Disk Oriented System
   d. Disk Operation System
2. Disk defragmenter is a ....
   a. database program
   b. presentation program
   c. operating system
   d. utility software
3. Which of the following is not an operating system?
   a. MS-DOS
   b. MS Word
   c. Windows
   d. Unix

4. Which of the following is not a specific purpose software program?

   a. Billing software
   b. Payroll software
   c. MS Access 2007
   d. Reservation software

5. Winzip is a .... program.

   a. backup
   b. file compression
   c. billing
   d. antivirus

6. GUI stands for ....

   a. Graphical User Interface
   b. Graphic User Interface
   c. Graphics Use Inference
   d. Graphic User Inference

7. Norton is an example of which utility?

   a. Disk Defragmenter
   b. Antivirus
   c. Decryption
   d. File compression

8. Which operating system has in-built networking functions?

   a. Windows XP
   b. Windows Server
   c. Unix
   d. Linux

9. It is a high level programming language.

   a. Cobol
   b. Visual Basic
   c. Neither a nor b
   d. Both a and b

10. Which of the following is specific purpose software?

   a. MS Word 2007
   b. Office Calc
   c. Tally
   d. Lotus 123

C Answer the following questions briefly.

1. Name one single user operating system.
2. Can you work with an application software without an operating system?
3. A garment factory maintains the details of arrival and departure of its employees through a software system. Which type of software is it?
4. Which software is used to calculate and generate bills in supermarkets?

5. Identify the software.

SA

D **Answer the following questions.**

1. What is encryption?
2. Define software. Briefly explain the two main types of software.
3. What is the use of a presentation software?
4. What is decryption?
5. Enumerate top five features of any two popular operating systems. HOTS
6. What is the use of backup utility?
7. Name any two antivirus software. List what all features they have. HOTS
8. What are the two types of application software?
9. What is CLI? Explain.
10. Give an example for file compression utility software.

E **Answer the following questions in detail.**

1. Define specific purpose software. Write any two advantages of any two of such software.
2. What are the functions of an operating system? Write short notes on different types of operating systems.
3. Give any one advantage and one disadvantage of the following software:
   a. MS Excel
   b. MS Word
   c. MS Access
   d. Paint
   e. PageMaker.
4. What is the use of utility software? Explain any two utilities present in Windows 7. HOTS
5. What do you understand by language translators?

Application Based Questions

A. Mrs. Menon is the head of a preschool. She wants to maintain a database of her students in the school computer system. However, she is not good with computers. Suggest an application she can use to maintain the student database with ease.

B. Whenever Rahul tries to open or save a file, he gets an error message that says 'Disk Full'. Suggest a utility that he can use to rectify this error.

C. Prateek wants to create budget for his firm's upcoming summer retreat. Which software can he use for this? Give a reasoned answer.

D. Shalini wants to create a banner for her schools sports days. She has different images of school logo, emblem and motto. She wants to aesthetically merge the three and use it in the banner. Can she manipulate the images? If yes, then which software can she use?

E. Sanjay is participating in his school's debate competetion. The topic of debate is general purpose application software like MS Excel are different from specific purpose application software like TurboTax. Help him prepare his speech in support of this statement.

LAB WORK

A. Complete the following activity.

1. Observe the computer system provided to you and list out the software installed in that system. Categorise them according to their type. Give minimum 10 software.
2. Using any word processor, create a document to list down the software present in your system.
3. Write any five applications of each in the word document itself.
4. Based on the data you collected, make a PowerPoint presentation on 'Application Software'.

B. Pacific Rim Ltd. has a spreadsheet that contains the contact information of all their top clients. Before sharing this pivotal information with anyone, the company wants to encrypt the spreadsheet and make it password protected. Explore MS Excel 2007 and examine whether it provides any feature that may help them?

C. Schedule disk defragmentation of your C Drive for 1'O clock on Wednesday. Give steps and supporting images (wherever possible) of all the steps involved.

D. Attach an external memory device, such as a pen drive or external hard disk, to your computer system. With the help of the antivirus program installed on your system, run a virus scan and enumerate the result listed.

E. Inspect which operating system you use at home and at school. Examine which utilities come along with the operating system. Make a list of the most commonly used utilities and how they help your computer system?

TEACHER'S NOTES

1. Demonstrate the symbiotic relationship of hardware and software components of a computer to the students.
2. If possible, show a MS-DOS operating system to the students. Help them understand how even the simplest of task in a CUI operating system required detailed instructions.
3. Download and exhibit Bharat Operating System Solutions (BOSS) to students.
4. Explain the process of spooling.

3 Operating System and Windows

SNAP RECAP

1. A computer is an electronic device that can be used to store and process data and produce output.
2. An operating system is an interface between the user and the components of the computer.
3. A mouse is the most popular pointing device used to input data.
4. A word processing software is used to create, edit and format a document quickly and efficiently.

LEARNING OBJECTIVES

You will learn about:

1. Basic concepts of OS
2. Functions of OS
3. Popular Operating Systems
4. Desktop
5. Windows Explorer
6. Files and Folders
7. Windows Accessories
8. Mobile OS

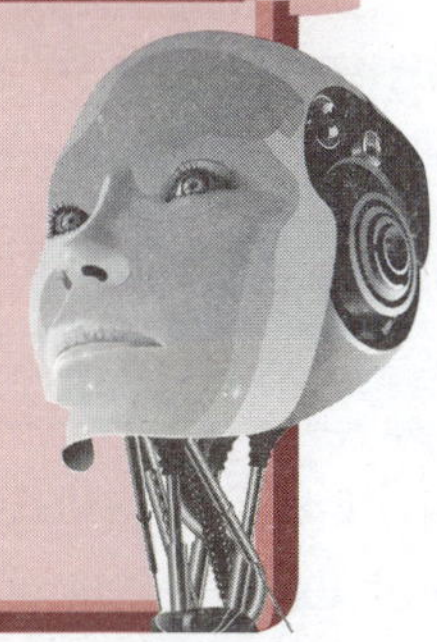

Introduction

The basic components of a computer system, computer hardware and software technologies, have given us reliable tools of processing information. These tools help us in providing and presenting structured and organised work. An operating system (OS) is one such important tool that manages the functions of a computer and provides the information efficiently after processing. An operating system is a means of communication between the user, system hardware and software. In this chapter, you will learn more about operating system and Microsoft Windows operating system (Fig. 3.1).

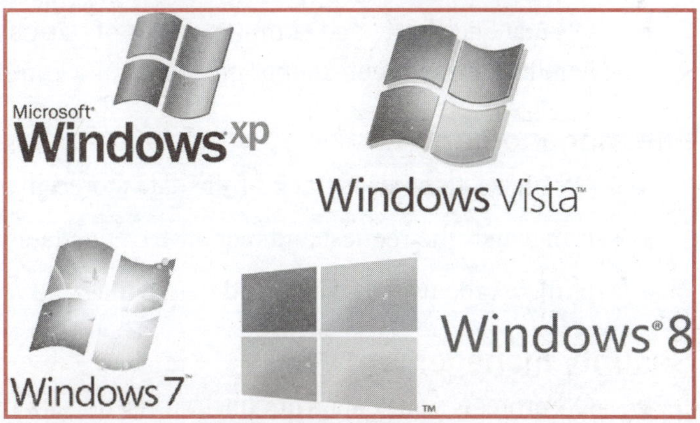

Fig. 3.1 *Different versions of Windows operating system*

Basic concepts of OS

An operating system is a system software that acts as an interface between the end user and the computer hardware and software. It controls, coordinates and manages all the units of a computer. It also controls the allocation of resources to ensure efficient operation.

Operating systems vary with their features and characteristics. Some of the most popular operating systems are MS-DOS, MS Windows, UNIX, Linux and Mac OS.

FACT FILE

Both PlayStation 4 and Xbox have their own operating system, namely **Orbis OS** and **Xbox 360 Dashboard**, respectively.

Functions of OS

The main functions of an operating system are discussed below.

Process management

- OS manages the allocation of the system resources according to priority.
- It controls creation and deletion of the processes.
- It also handles process synchronisation and communication.

Main memory management

- OS allocates and deallocates the memory space for storing data.
- It keeps track of the usage of memory.
- It can create a virtual memory on the hard drive, if the RAM memory is insufficient to store.

Input output system management

- OS takes care of the proper usage of hardware devices (both input and output), such as, disk drive and mouse, based on their speed of retrieving data.
- OS manages basic and complex issues of various computer devices. It communicates with these devices and handles all the input–output processes of a computer system.

File management

- OS file system keeps track of the data stored in a computer system.
- It manages the request and response of the data used in application programs.
- It allows the user to create and delete files and folders for the manipulation of documents on a computer.

Security management

- OS protects your data from unauthorised users by providing password protection.
- It also provides backup and recovery of data in case of system failure.

FACT FILE

The world's first operating system, **GM-NAA I/O**, was built by General Motors in 1956. It was created by Robert L. Patrick for the IBM 704 computer. It only managed basic functions and its main task was to automatically run a series of programs, as soon as the previous program was completed.

▶ Popular Operating Systems

MS-DOS

MS-DOS (**Microsoft Disk Operating System**) is a **CLI** based operating system; where CLI stands for **Command Line Interface**. CLI allows the user to interact with the computer by typing commands in the prompt using a keyboard (Fig. 3.2).

For example, `C:>DIR/P` This command is used to list the files in the C drive pagewise.

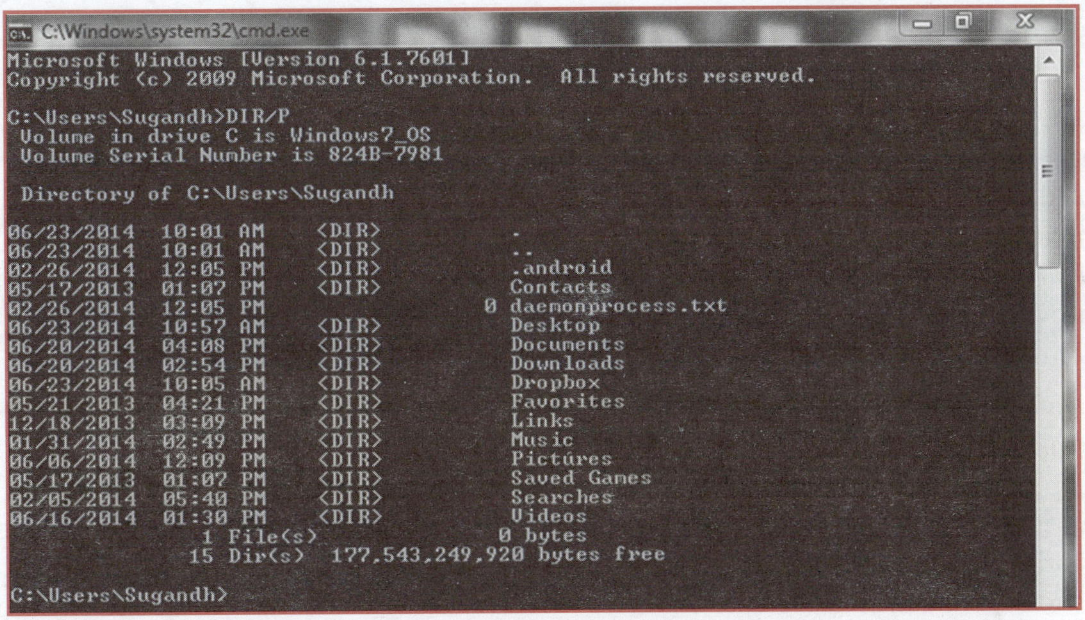

Fig. 3.2 *Viewing C directory*

FACT FILE

MS-DOS can be accessed from any Windows operating system by following these steps. Go to **Start** ⟹ **Run**. In the **Run** dialog box that appears, type **cmd**. The command prompt will open.

Unix

Unix is a powerful and reliable operating system. It is used for big servers as it provides security and complexity and cannot be easily accessed. Due to its complexity, it is not used in personal computers.

GNU / Linux

GNU means that 'GNU is Not Unix'. It was developed to liberate Unix. It is a non-proprietary software and could be freely shared. Linux is an **open source** system software, that is, it allows the individuals and companies to sell, distribute and copy or download its code. Over the years it has gained popularity because of its flexibility and reliability.

FACT FILE

Open Source Software is the software that is available in source code form. It gives users the rights and permissions to study and modify the software.

Microsoft Windows

Graphical User Interface (GUI) is a user-friendly graphical interface that allows the user to interact with a computer by just clicking on the mouse. There is no need for the user to remember all the commands. It contains a collection of tools, programs and resources. It also provides a multitasking environment. It allows the user to view and control multiple windows at once and hence it is much faster than CUI. It also provides connectivity through the Internet.

FACT FILE

Microsoft Corporation was founded by Bill Gates and Paul Allen on April 4, 1975.

Microsoft Windows is a graphical user interface (GUI) based operating system. Microsoft introduced Windows, a graphical user interface for its own operating system (MS-DOS), on November 20, 1985. Over the years Microsoft has developed, marketed and sold several generations of Microsoft operating system. Today, Microsoft Windows dominate the world's personal computer market with over 90% market share. In this chapter, you will be learning more about Microsoft Windows 7. Developed under the codename 'Blackcomb', it was released on October 22, 2009.

Some of the features of Windows 7 are:

- Faster and more responsive performance
- Easy device management
- Improved Taskbar and full screen preview
- Jump list feature
- Peek feature
- Device stage (that is, it helps you to manage cell phones, cameras and printers when they are connected to your computer)

- Math Input Panel (to write math expressions)
- Handwriting Recognition.

Mouse

A mouse is an input device (Fig. 3.3). It is one of the most important device of a GUI based operating system as the user gives instructions to the computer by clicking on the mouse. It is about the size of our palm. It moves on a flat surface called the **mouse pad** and translates the movement into digital information.

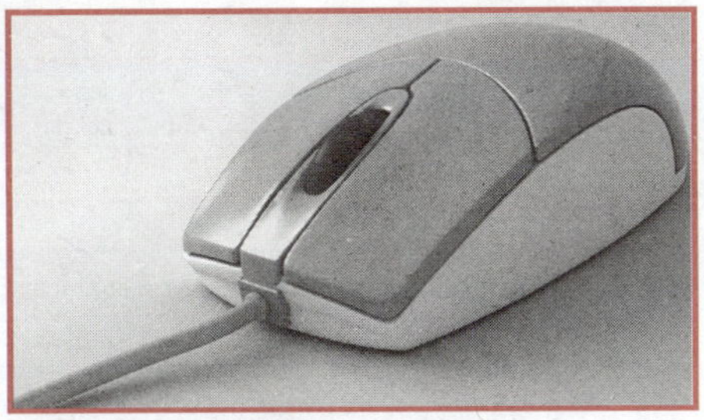

Fig. 3.3 *Mouse*

Some of the common tasks of mouse are listed below.

- ***Click:*** It is used to select a file or an object on the screen (by pressing mostly the left button of the mouse).
- ***Double-click:*** It is used to execute an application, by pressing the mouse buttons twice quickly.
- ***Drag:*** It is used to move any object from one place to another, by pressing the left button and moving the mouse simultaneously.
- ***Scroll:*** It is used to scroll the current screen or a document up and down.

CHECK YOUR PROGRESS

A. Mr. Smith has bought all hardware components required for assembling a computer. After assembling the computer system, which is the very first software he will have to install? Why?

1. Antivirus software
2. Office software
3. Operating system
4. Printer software

B. Aditya is new to computers. Which OS would you suggest for him to start his work? Why?

C. Search the Internet for Ubuntu operating system. Evaluate its pros and cons. HOTS

D. Some of the features/advantages of Windows 7 are given above. Make a list of 10 new features of Windows 7. Also, write a short note on how it is different from previous versions of Windows.

E. Browse the Internet and write short notes on Math Input Panel and Handwriting Recognition. HOTS

Desktop

Desktop is the first screen of the Windows. The main components of a desktop are (Fig. 3.4):

- Icons
- Start button
- Quick Launch bar
- Taskbar
- Notification Area
- Show Desktop

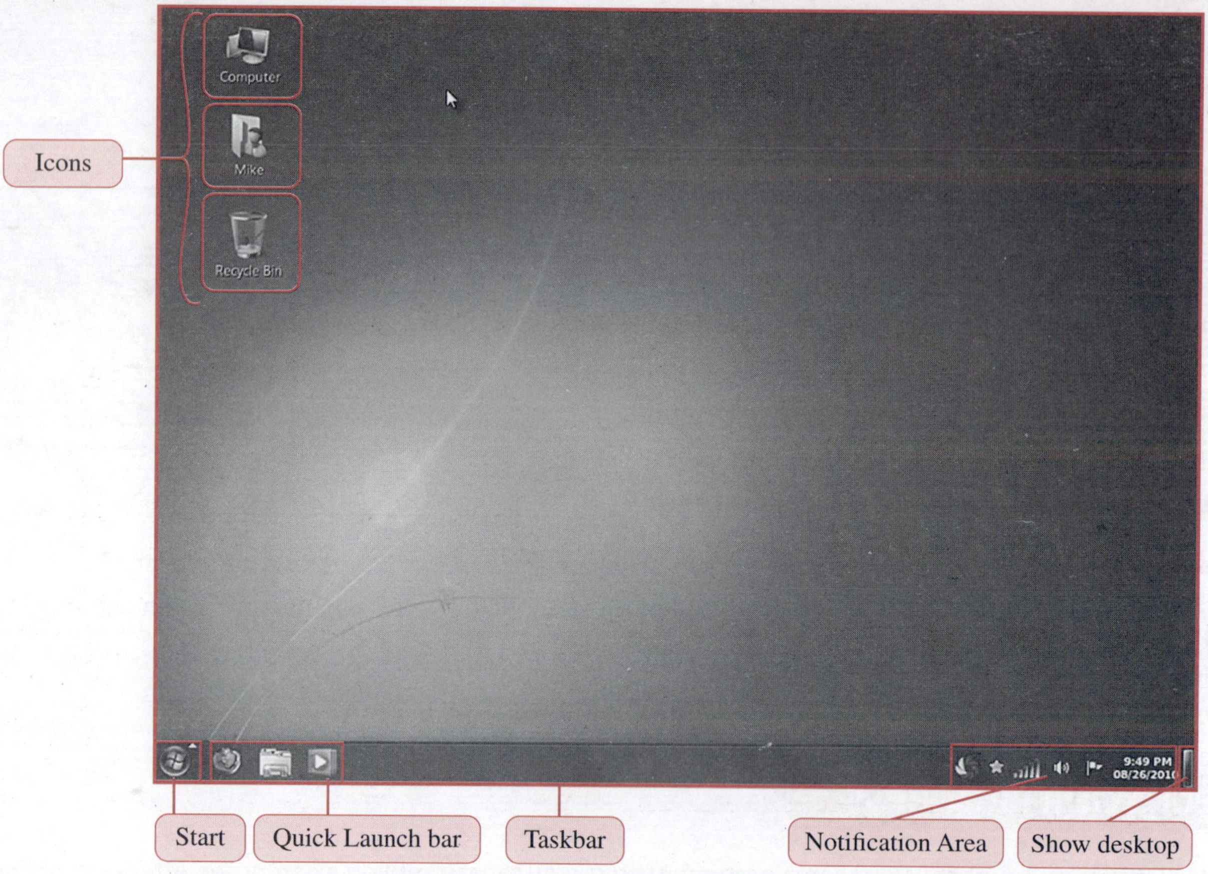

Fig. 3.4 *Main components of a desktop*

Basic Components of a Desktop

After you start your computer, the first screen you see is the desktop. It is your work area. Some of the important components of Windows 7 desktop are explained below.

Desktop icons

The small pictures that represent files, folders, applications and other items on the desktop are called **desktop icons**. Some of the common desktop icons are discussed below.

Computer icon: When you double-click on this icon, it displays all the files and folders available in the system drives. It also allows you to search for a file or folder from any location in the system.

Recycle Bin icon: This holds the deleted files and folders until they are completely deleted from the hard disk. The files or folders in the recycle bin can be restored to their original location or they can be deleted permanently. This tool is opened on double-click.

Network icon: It allows to make connection with the Internet.

TRY THIS!

Does My Documents folder exists in Windows 7?

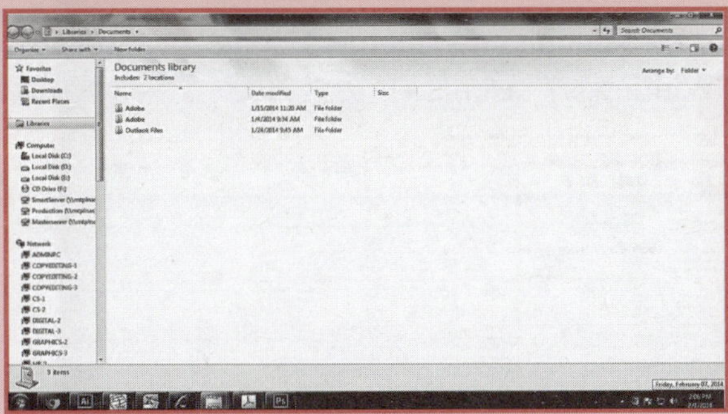

My Documents folder is not available directly on desktop in Windows 7. To open it, click **Start** ⟹ **Documents**.

This will open **Libraries Window** in which four major folders viz. **Documents**, **Pictures**, **Music** and **Videos** are available.

Taskbar

The taskbar is the long horizontal bar at the bottom of your desktop. It shows the applications or programs that are currently opened. You can also place your favourite or most commonly used programs anywhere on the taskbar for easy access. Windows 7 provide thumbnail previews. When you point to a program's icon on the taskbar, you will see miniature views of your documents, images, and even live videos (Fig. 3.5).

Fig. 3.5 *Taskbar*

FACT FILE

The taskbar can be moved to any of the four edges of the desktop just by dragging it.

Start button

The Start button is located on the left of the taskbar. It contains all the programs and tools installed in the system. It is used to explore Windows. Some of the items on the Start button menu are:

- Programs
- Accessories
- Documents
- Help and Support.
- Control Panel
- Devices and Printers
- Submenu

Quick Launch toolbar

The Quick Launch toolbar is used to open programs quickly with a single-click. It is just to the right of Start button (Fig. 3.6).

Fig. 3.6 *Quick Launch Toolbar*

Jump List

The Jump List is a new feature in Windows 7. It takes you to the recent documents, pictures, songs or websites. To open a Jump List, just right-click on a program button on the Windows 7 taskbar (Fig. 3.7).

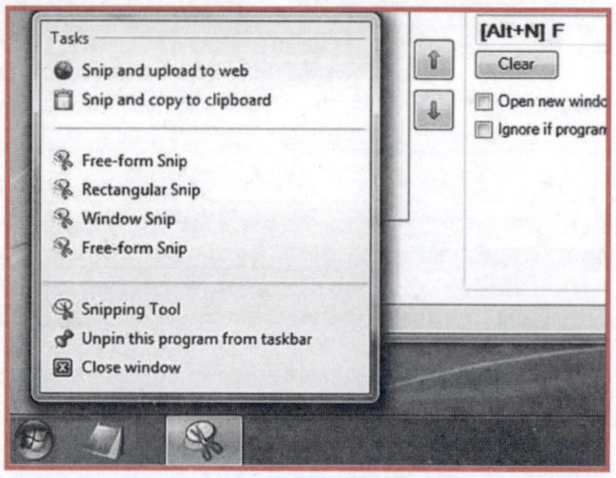

Fig. 3.7 *Jump List*

TRY THIS!

Flip and **Flip 3-D** are two interesting ways to preview your open windows. Press and hold the **Alt** key and then press **Tab** key to open the Flip view of your open windows. Press and hold the **Windows** key and then press **Tab** key for a 3-D version of Flip.

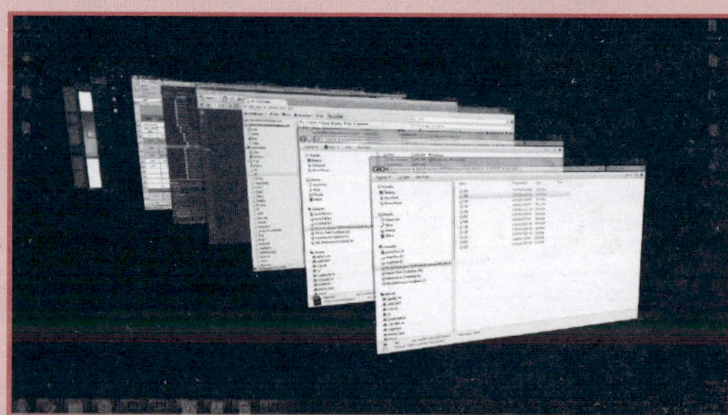

Show desktop

This new **peek** feature allows you to peer past all your open windows and show you the desktop. You can do this by clicking the right edge of the Taskbar. It minimizes all the windows and show the desktop.

Notification Area

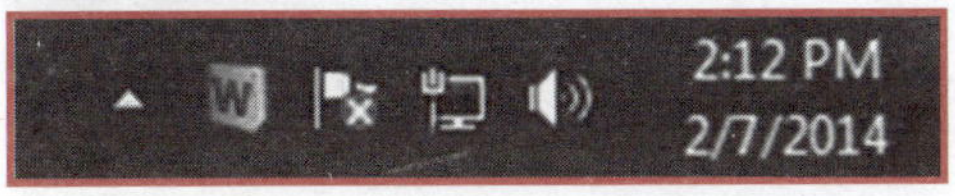

Fig. 3.8 *Notification Area*

The Notification Area is at the right end of the taskbar. It has volume control, system clock and other associated program. It is just to the left of show desktop button (Fig. 3.8).

ACTIVITY

To set system date and time.

1. Right-click on the time in the system tray.
2. Select the option **Adjust date/time**.
3. Click on the **Change date and time. . .** button.
4. **Date and Time** dialog box appears.
5. Set the date and time.
6. Click on **OK**.

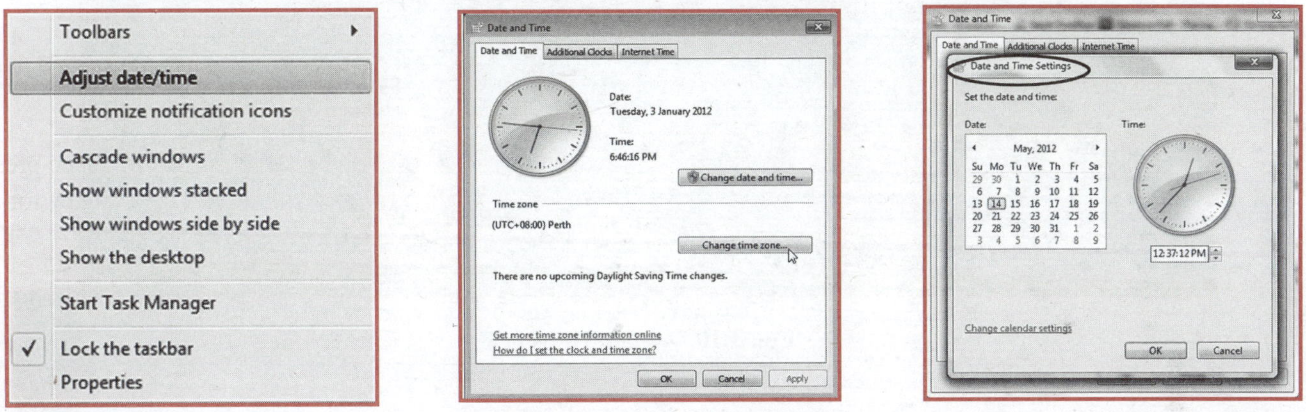

Setting system date and time

Search

It is easy to search files and folders in your computer by typing the search text in the **Search programs and files** box in the **Start** menu (Fig. 3.9).

Fig. 3.9 *Search programs and files box*

Desktop Gadgets

Gadgets are the mini programs that offer information and easy access to the tools that are frequently used. To add gadgets on the desktop follow the steps given below.

1. Right-click on your desktop.
2. Go to **Gadgets** option.

3. Double-click on the gadget you want and it will appear on your desktop (Fig. 3.10).

The gadgets available in Windows 7 are Calendar, Clock, Weather, CPU Meter, Feed Headlines, Slide Show, Windows Media Centre and Picture Puzzle.

Fig. 3.10 *Desktop gadgets*

Shortcuts

A shortcut is an icon that refers to a link to a file, a folder or a program. You can recognise a shortcut by a cross arrow mark on its icon. To create a shortcut on the desktop, follow the steps given below.

1. Right-click on the file.
2. Go to **Send to** option.
3. From the drop-down list that appears, select **Desktop (create shortcut)** option.

FACT FILE

If you copy the shortcut, only the link of shortcut will be copied and not the original file.

ACTIVITY

A. Changing the desktop background

To change the desktop background, follow the steps given below.

1. Right-click on the desktop and select **Personalization** option. **Change the visuals and sounds on your computer** dialog box appears.
2. Click on the **Desktop** option and select the picture of your choice.
3. Click on **Save changes**.

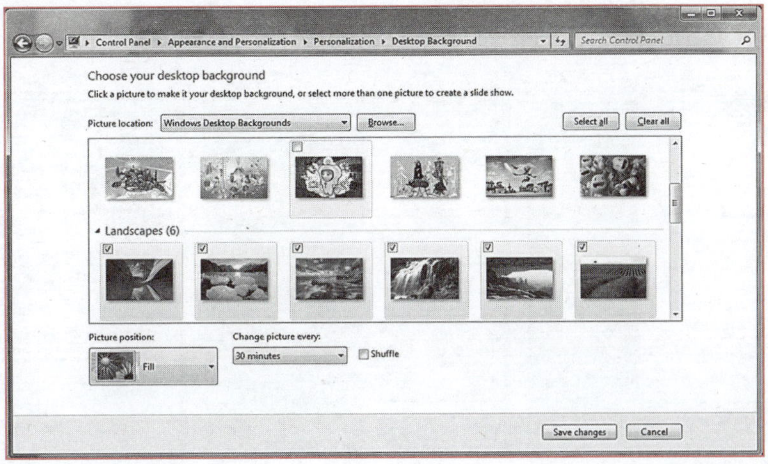

B. Setting the screen saver

Screen Saver is a feature of Windows that automatically appears on the desktop if the computer is idle for a certain period of time. To set the screen saver, follow the steps given below.

1. Right-click on the desktop and select **Personalization** option. **Change the visuals and sounds on your computer** dialog box appears.
2. Click on the **Screen Saver** option. **Screen Saver Settings** dialog box appears.
3. Set the screensaver of your choice and click on **Apply**.
4. Click on **OK**.

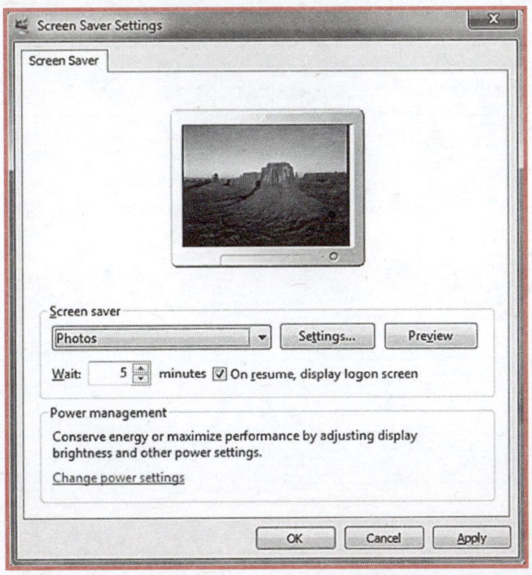

▶ Windows Explorer

Explorer is an application used to list files and folders available on the computer. There are two ways to open Windows Explorer. They are:

- Using Start menu
- Using Computer icon on the desktop.

FACT FILE

The menu that appears when you right-click on any icon is called **Context Menu** or **Shortcut Menu**.

To open Windows Explorer using Start

1. Click on **Start** ⟹ **All programs**.
2. Go to **Accessories**.
3. Select **Windows Explorer** (Fig. 3.11).

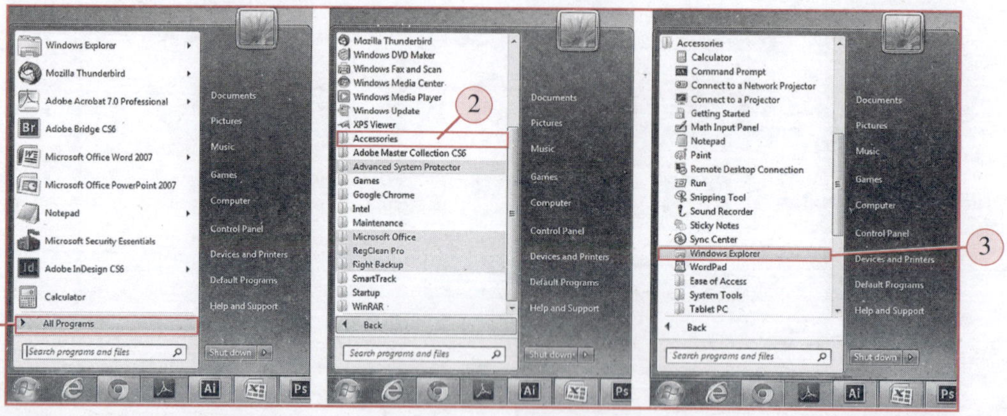

Fig. 3.11 *Opening Windows Explorer using Start*

To open Windows Explorer using Computer icon

Double-click the **Computer** icon on the desktop or select the **Computer** option from the **Start** button. Windows Explorer will open and display all the storage devices of the system such as, hard disk drives, CD drives, floppy drive, pen drive and memory card (Fig. 3.12).

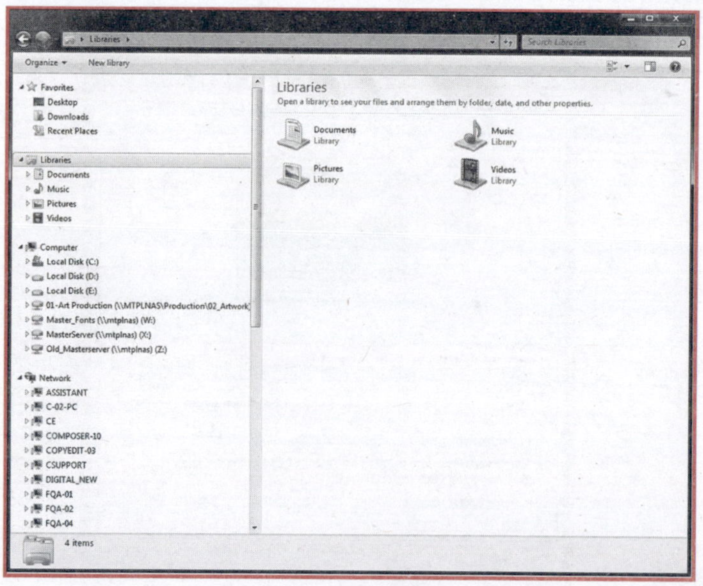

Fig. 3.12 *Opening Windows Explorer using computer icon*

FILES AND FOLDERS

All the tasks in windows involve working with files and folders. Folders are used to store and organise files and other folders on your computer.

> **FACT FILE**
>
> Folders inside other folders are called **sub folders.**

Create a new folder

To create a new folder, follow the steps given below (Fig. 3.13).

1. Go to the location (drive) where you want to create a new folder.
2. Click on the **New Folder** button on the Windows Explorer tool bar.
3. Type a name for the new folder that is created and press **Enter**.

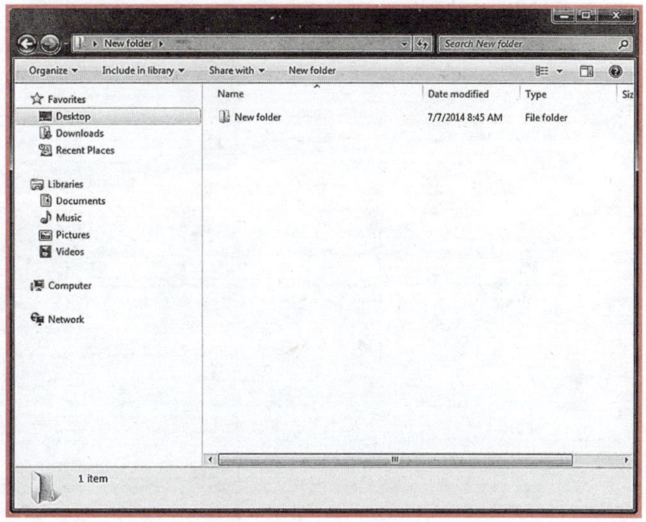

Fig. 3.13 *Creating a new folder*

Rename a folder

To rename a folder, follow the steps given below.

1. Right-click on the folder.
2. Click the **Rename** option in the **shortcut** menu that appears.
3. Type a new name for the folder.
4. Press **Enter**.

Files and folders view

There are many ways to view the files and folders that are stored on your computer system. Click on the drop-down arrow next to **Change your view** button. A submenu containing more options will open. Choose your desired view by clicking on it. The options available are shown in Figure 3.14.

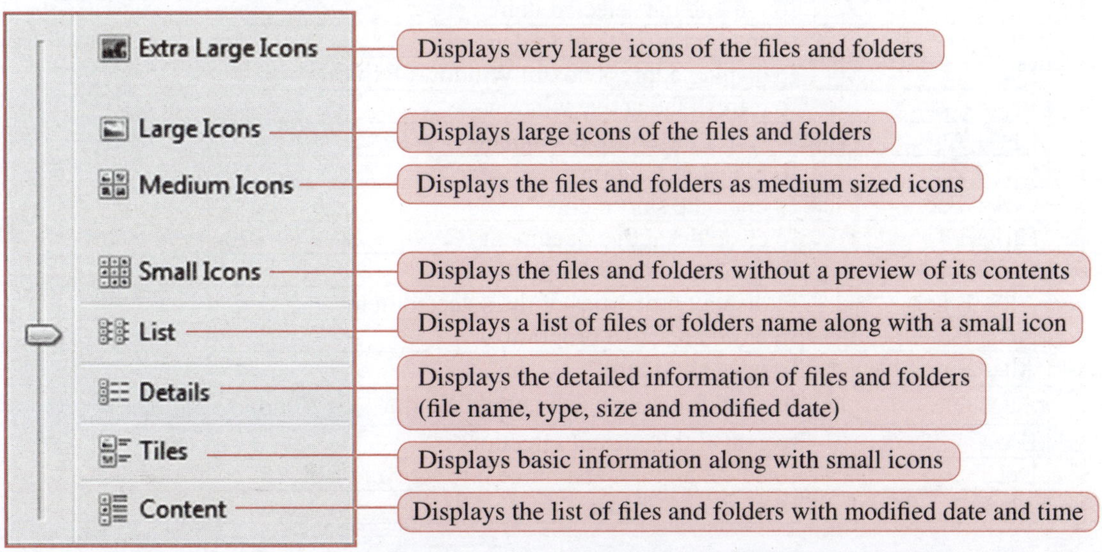

Fig. 3.14 *Different files and folders view*

Displaying two windows

In Windows 7, you can display two application windows side by side. For example,

1. Open MS Word 2007 and MS Excel 2007.
2. Right-click anywhere on the blank portion of the taskbar.
3. Click on the **Show Windows side by side** option (Fig. 3.15).

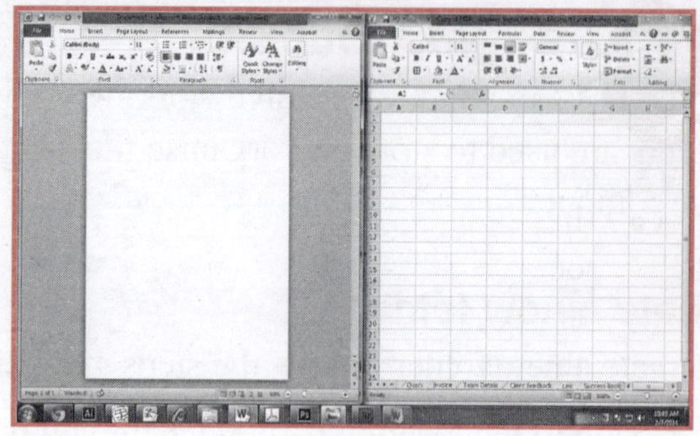

Fig. 3.15 *Displaying two windows simultaneously*

FACT FILE

On-Screen Keyboard is a special feature of Windows that can be operated with a mouse when the keyboard is not working.

To activate On-Screen Keyboard, click on **Start** → **All Programs** → **Accessories** → **Ease of Access** → **On Screen keyboard**. On-Screen Keyboard appears. Use mouse to click on the desired keys.

Quick Key

F1	To display help window
F2	To rename the selected item
F3	To search for a file or folder
F4	To display address box in Windows Explorer
F5	To refresh the active window
Ctrl + A	To select the entire document
Ctrl + Z	To repeat last action
Ctrl + Esc	To open the start menu
Ctrl + F4	To close the active document
Ctrl + F10	To maximize or restore the window
Alt + Enter	To display properties of the selected item
Alt + F4	To close an active program
Alt + Space bar	To open shortcut
Alt + ⇧	To view folder one level up in Windows Explorer
Esc	To cancel the current selection
Del	To delete an item and move it to Recycle Bin
Alt + ⇨	To view next folder

TRY THIS!

- In Windows 7, there are many hidden wallpapers and themes from other English speaking countries like Australia, Canada, Great Britain and South Africa. Usually, you cannot access these backgrounds and themes, but there is a simple method to install and use them. Type **C:\Windows\Globalization\MCT** in the **Search programs and files** box in the **Start** menu and press **Enter** to see and use themes from multiple countries.

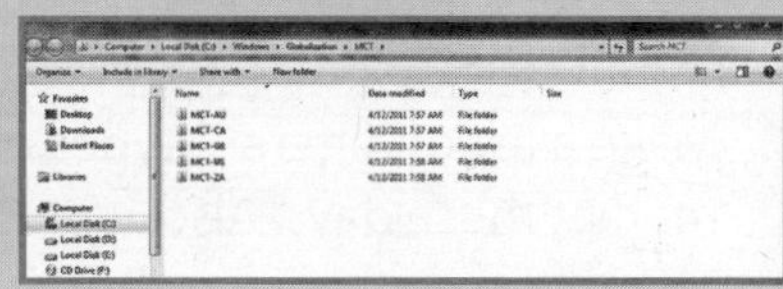

- In Windows 7, in a single step you can minimize all the windows except the one you are currently using. This can be done using the **Shake** feature. Just click and hold the **Title** bar of the window you do not want to minimize and shake it back and forth quickly until all of the other windows minimize to the taskbar.

- Press [Windows key] + **P** or in **Run** dialog box type **Display Switch.exe** to choose your preferred mode of display.

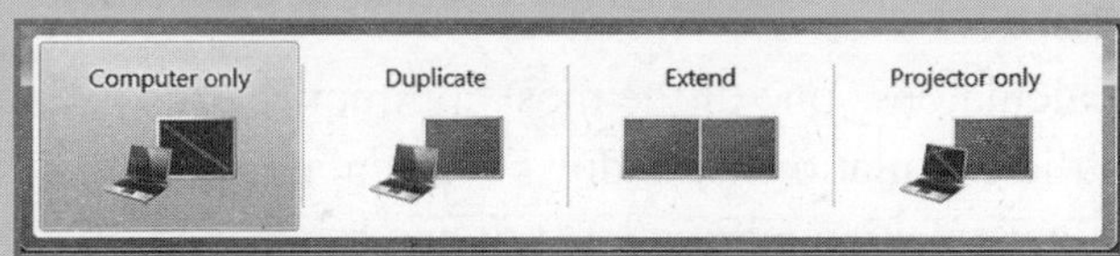

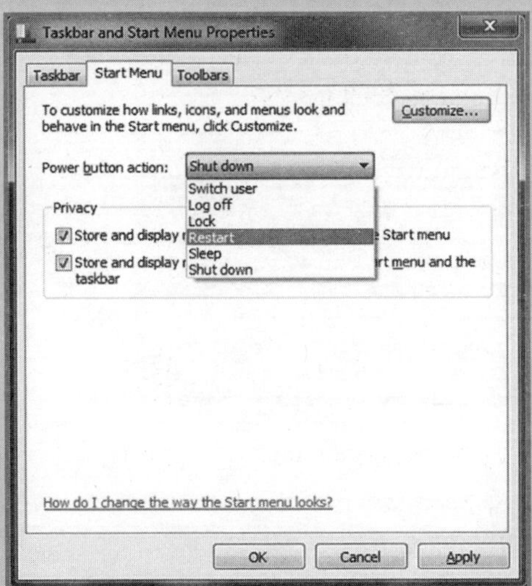

- In Windows 7, you can customise the **Shut down** button. Just right-click on the arrow next to the **Shut down** button and select **Properties. Taskbar and Start Menu Properties** dialog box appears. In the **Start Menu** tab, click the **Power button action:** drop-down menu and select which action you want to set as default. Click on **Apply**.

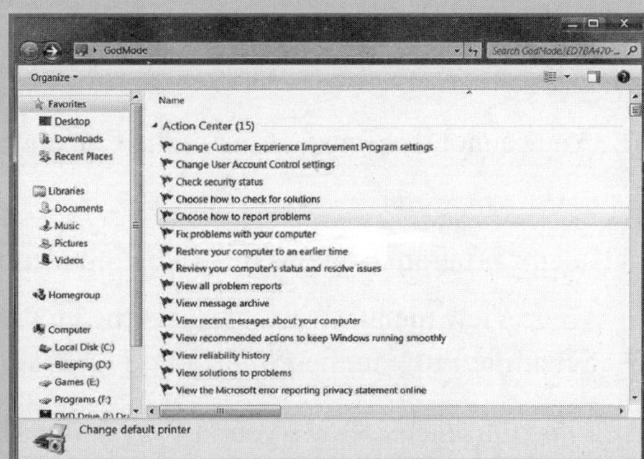

- In Windows 7, you can access all the applets and options of Control Panel in one single folder. Just create a new folder and rename it:

  NewFolder. {ED7BA470-8E54-465E-825C-99712043E01C}.

  Double-click on it and you will find shortcut to all 270 configurable options in Windows 7.

CHECK YOUR PROGRESS

A. Identify the rounded portion of the taskbar.
(**Hint**: This is used to open the program quickly as you see the desktop)

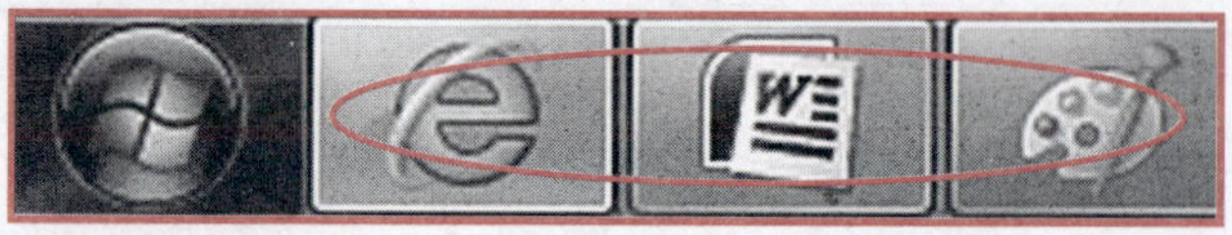

B. Make a list of different types of mice available in the market these days. Also, write a short note on Magic Mouse. **HOTS**

C. There are some keywords that cannot be used for naming a folder. Find out 10 such names. **HOTS**

▶ WINDOWS ACCESSORIES

Windows 7 has many accessories for day-to-day use. Windows accessories are built-in programs that perform basic tasks. Some accessories available in Windows 7 are discussed below.

- Calculator
- Paint
- Notepad
- WordPad

Calculator

The calculator is one of the most commonly used accessory of Windows 7. It helps you to perform arithmetic and scientific calculations. Windows 7 calculator provides the advanced capabilities of a programming, scientific and statistical calculator (Fig. 3.16). It can be opened by clicking **Start button ⟹ All Programs ⟹ Accessories ⟹ Calculator**.

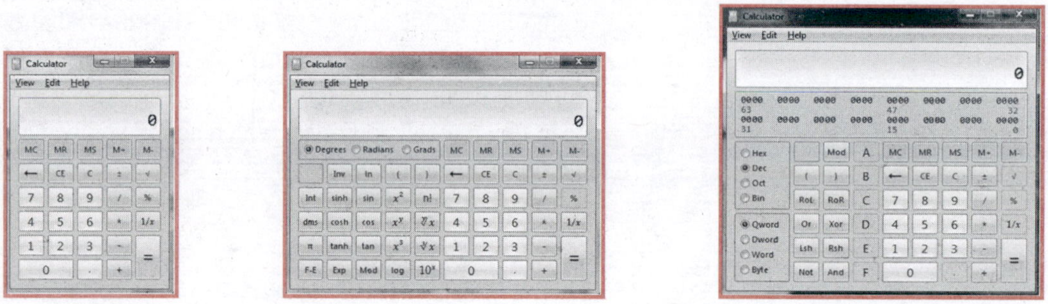

Standard Scientific Programmer

Fig. 3.16 *Different calculators in Windows 7*

NOTE: You cannot maximize or resize the Calculator Window.

Menus in the calculator

The calculator program contains the following menus:

- ***View:*** View menu is used to select the mode you want (Standard/Scientific/Programmer/Statistics) (Fig. 3.17).
- ***Edit:*** Edit menu allows you to copy and paste the results elsewhere.
- ***Help:*** Help menu provides help options to the user.

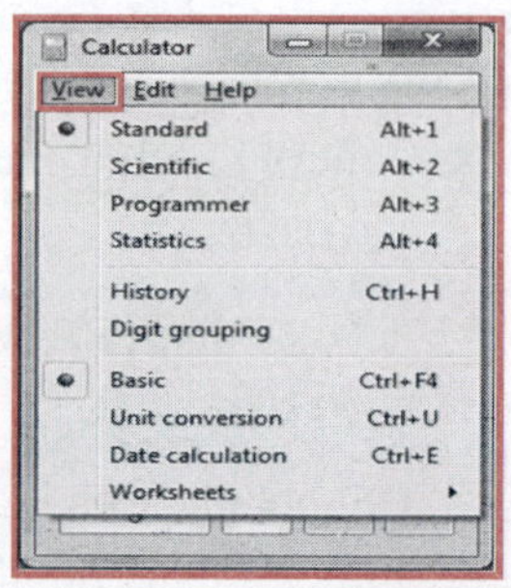

Fig. 3.17 *View menu of calculator*

Quick Key

Calculator shortcut keys

Alt + 1	To switch to standard mode
Alt + 2	To switch to scientific mode
Alt + 3	To switch to programmer mode
Alt + 4	To switch to statistics mode
Ctrl + E	To open date calculation
Ctrl + H	To turn calculation history on/off
Ctrl + N	To open unit conversion
Ctrl + Q	Quit

FACT FILE

Programmer mode is an integer only mode. Decimal portions are discarded in this mode.

PAINT

The Paint program of Windows 7 is used to create drawings on a blank drawing area or in existing pictures. Many of the tools you use in Paint are found in the Ribbon, which is near the top of the Paint window (Fig. 3.18). Paint files are saved with the extension ***.png** (Portable Network Graphics) by default. Using **Save As** option, the file can be saved in BMP, JPG, TIF and GIF formats too.

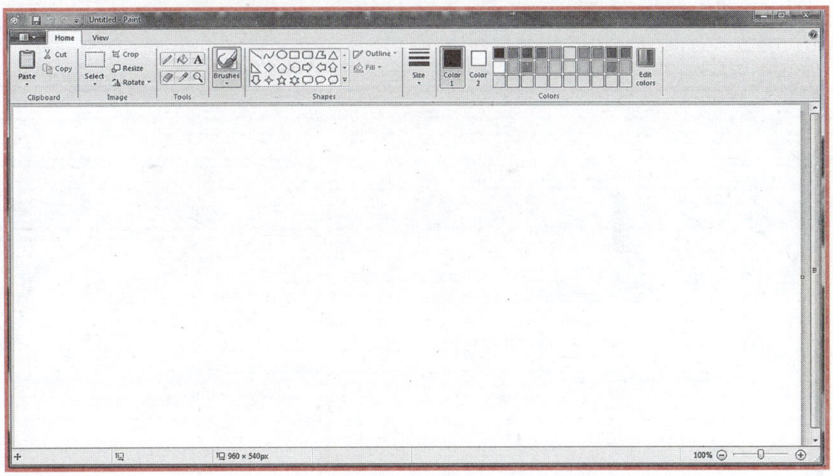

Fig. 3.18 *Paint*

Tools

Some of the tools available in Paint are discussed in Table 3.1.

Table 3.1 *Paint tools*

Tools	Description
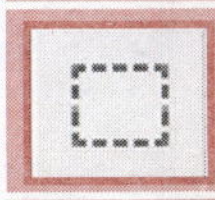 *Rectangular Selection*	To select a rectangular area
 *Free form Select*	To select an area of any shape

	*Pencil*	To draw freehand line
	*Fill with color*	Click to fill the foreground color and right-click to fill the background color
	*Text*	To insert text into the picture
	*Eraser*	To erase a portion of a picture by replacing it with the background color
	*Pick color*	To pick a color
	*Magnifier*	To change the magnification for a part of a picture
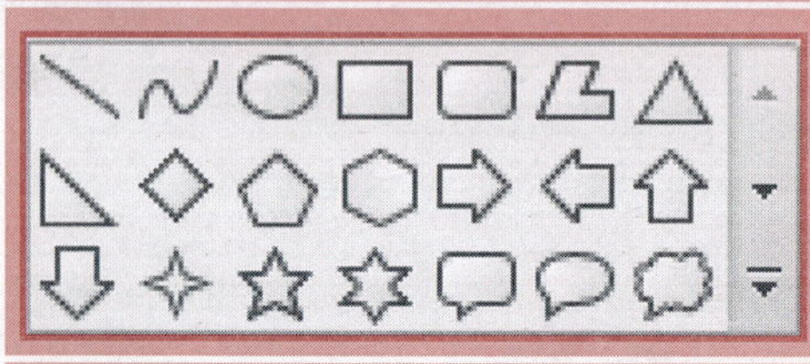	*Shapes*	To insert shapes. Some available shapes are: Line, Curve, Oval, Rectangle, Rounded Rectangle, Polygon, Triangle, Right Triangle, Diamond, Pentagon, Hexagon, Right Arrow, Left Arrow, Up Arrow, Down Arrow, Four Point Star, Five Point Star, Six Point Star, Callouts, Heart and Lightning Shape tools
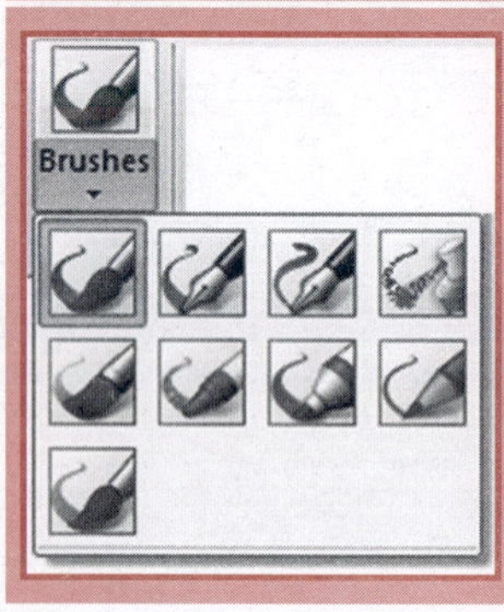	*Brushes*	There are nine types of brushes available in Paint. They are: • Brush • Calligraphy Brush 1 • Calligraphy Brush 2 • Air Brush • Oil Brush • Crayon • Marker • Natural Pencil • Water Color Brush

Quick Key

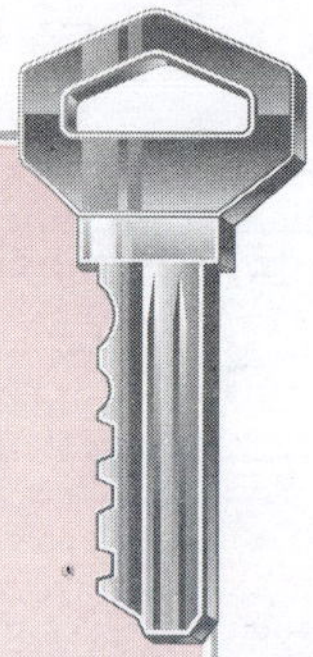

Paint shortcut keys

Ctrl + N	To create a new picture file
Ctrl + O	To open an existing file
Ctrl + S	To save the file
F12	To save as new file
Ctrl + P	To print the picture file
Alt + F4	To close the current paint window
Ctrl + Z	To cancel the last three actions

Ctrl + Y	To repeat the last three actions
Ctrl + A	To select the entire picture file
Ctrl + X	To cut an item
Ctrl + C	To copy an item
Ctrl + V	To paste the last item stored in clipboard
Esc	To cancel the selection
Del	To delete the selected image
Ctrl + B	To make the selected text bold
Ctrl + +	To increase the size of tool
Ctrl + –	To decrease the size of tool
Ctrl + page up	To zoom in
Ctrl + page down	To zoom out

NOTEPAD

Notepad is a simple text editor (Fig. 3.19). It is used for creating simple text files which do not require much formatting. It saves the files with extension **.txt** by default. To open Notepad, click on **Start** ⟹ **All Programs** ⟹ **Accessories** ⟹ **Notepad.** The components of the Notepad window are: Title bar, Menu bar, Working Area and Scroll bar.

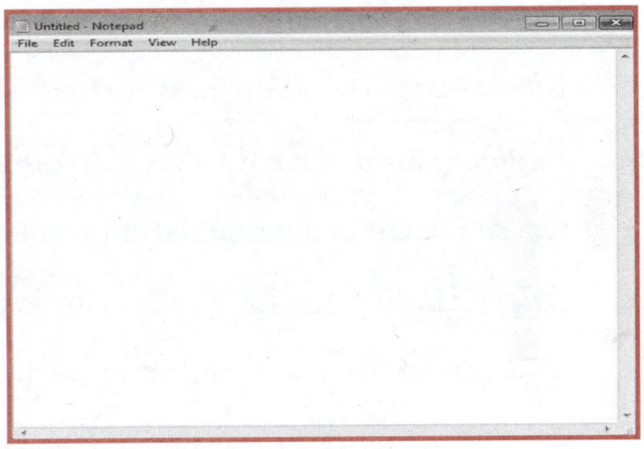

Fig. 3.19 *Notepad*

The menus available in Notepad window are:

- File
- Edit
- Format
- View
- Help

TRY THIS!

Open Notepad and type **.LOG** in capital letters. Press **Enter**. Save the file. Now, every time you open this file, Notepad will automatically insert the current time and date.

File menu

The options available in File menu are listed below (Fig. 3.20).

- ***New:*** To open a new text file.
- ***Open:*** To open an existing file.
- ***Save:*** To save a text file.
- ***Save As:*** To save the file with another name or in different location.

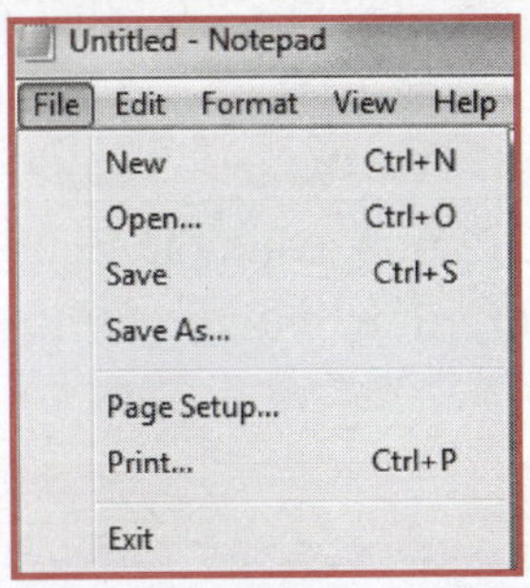

Fig. 3.20 *File menu of Notepad*

- ***Page Setup:*** To set the page orientation and margins.
- ***Print:*** To print the content of the file on printer.
- ***Exit:*** To quit the Notepad window.

FACT FILE

You cannot insert a picture in Notepad files.

Edit menu

The options available in Edit menu are listed below (Fig. 3.21).

- ***Undo:*** To cancel the previous action.
- ***Cut:*** To cut the selected text and store it temporarily on clipboard.
- ***Copy:*** To copy the selected text and store it temporarily on clipboard.
- ***Paste:*** To paste the content stored on clipboard (that you copied or removed recently).
- ***Delete:*** To delete the selected text.
- ***Find:*** To find a text.
- ***Find Next:*** To find the next text.
- ***Replace:*** To replace the text by typing the replacement text on it.
- ***Go To:*** To go to a particular line number.
- ***Select All:*** To select the entire content of the file.
- ***Time/Date:*** To insert date and time in the text file.

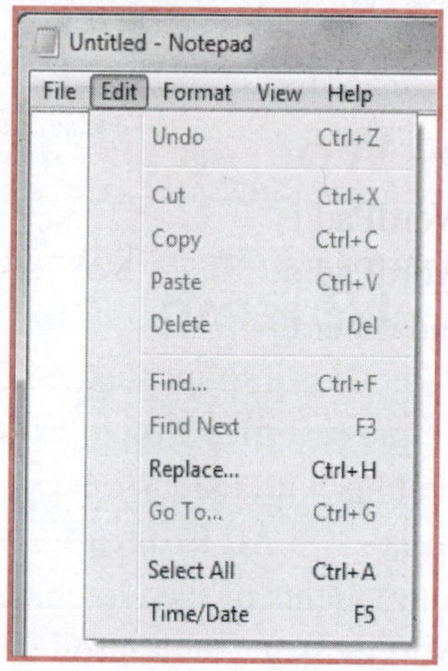

Fig. 3.21 *Edit menu of Notepad*

Format menu

The options available in Format menu are listed below (Fig. 3.22).

- ***Word Wrap:*** If the width of the line exceeds the screen, you need to scroll the window to see the text. Word Wrap automatically adjusts the width of each line of text according to the width of the screen.
- ***Font:*** It displays the font window which enables you to select your font, style and size for the text typed in the text file.

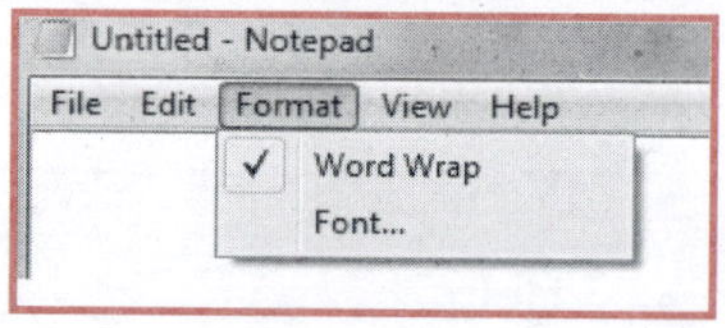

Fig. 3.22 *Format menu of Notepad*

View menu

The option available in View menu are listed below (Fig. 3.23).

- ***Status Bar:*** This option helps you to choose whether the status bar is to be displayed on the screen or not.

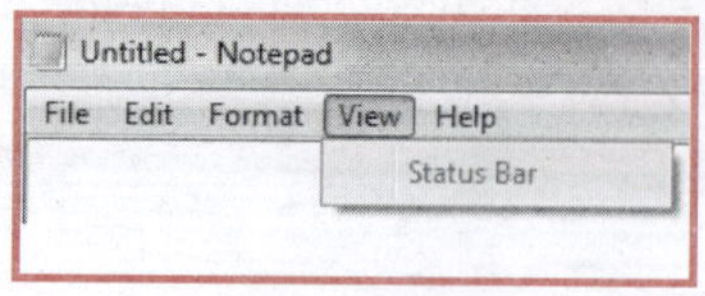

Fig. 3.23 *View menu of Notepad*

Help menu

The option available in this menu is View Help (Fig. 3.24). This option provides the required help to the user. It has information related to Notepad menus and options.

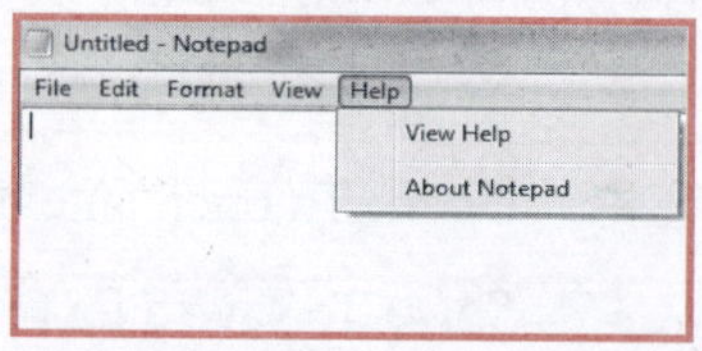

Fig. 3.24 *Help menu of Notepad*

Quick Key

Notepad shortcut keys

Ctrl + N	To create a new file
Ctrl + O	To open an existing file
Ctrl + S	To save a file
Ctrl + P	To print a file
Ctrl + F	To find text

F3	To find next text
F5	To insert time and date
Ctrl + H	To replace
Ctrl + G	To go to a particular line

WordPad

WordPad is a text-editing program that can be used to create and edit documents (Fig. 3.25). Unlike Notepad, WordPad documents can include rich formatting and graphics, and you can link to or embed objects, such as pictures and other documents. It saves the file with the extension ***.rtf** (rich text format).

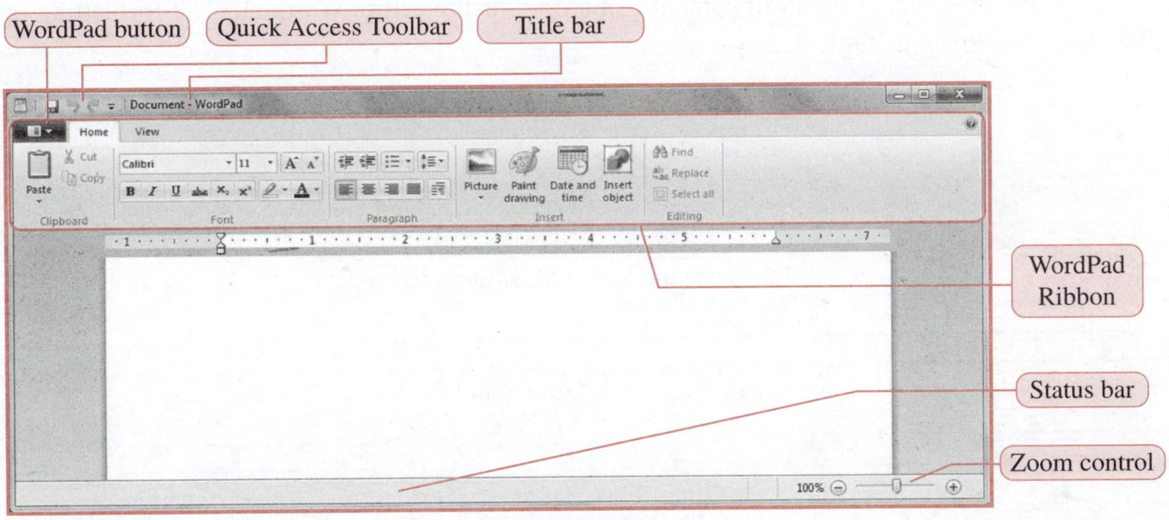

Fig. 3.25 *WordPad*

FACT FILE

WordPad can be used to open and save Notepad files, WordPad files, MS Word files and Open Office files.

When you click on the WordPad **Home** button, the following options appear.

- ***New:*** To create a new document.
- ***Open:*** To open an existing document.
- ***Save:*** To save a document.
- ***Save As:*** To save a document with new name and/or in new location.

- ***Page Setup:*** To set the page orientation and margins.
- ***Print Preview:*** To preview your document before printing.
- ***Print:*** To print the document.

FACT FILE

The Ribbon is placed at the top area of the document. It has several **tabs** like **Home** and **Insert**. Each tab performs specific functions and contains commands arranged in **groups**.

Formatting in WordPad

Formatting refers to the appearance of the text in your document. You can use the Ribbon, located just underneath the Title bar, to easily change the formatting in your document by choosing fonts, font sizes and font color you want. You can also change the alignment of your document using options present in WordPad. The formatting options available in Wordpad are given in Table 3.2.

Table 3.2 *Formatting options in WordPad*

Tools	Description
Calibri ▾	To change the font style of the selected text
11 ▾	To change the size of the font
A▲	To increase the font size
A▼	To decrease the font size
B *I* <u>U</u>	To apply styles to the text (Bold, Italics and Underline)
X_2	To show the text smaller and lower than regular text (Subscript)
X^2	To show the text smaller and higher than regular text (Superscript)

	To highlight a text with marking color
	To change the text color
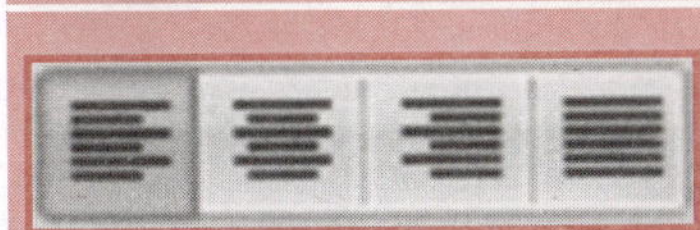	To align the paragraph (Left, Centre, Right and Justified)
	To increase and decrease the indent level of the paragraph
	To choose different list styles (Bullets and Numbering)
	To change the spacing between lines of text
	To adjust the indentation and alignment of the paragraph
	To insert, change and resize the picture
	To insert a drawing
	To insert current date and time
	To insert an object
	To find and replace a text with another text. Select all, is to select the entire document
	Zoom in and Zoom out on the document to magnify or shrink it

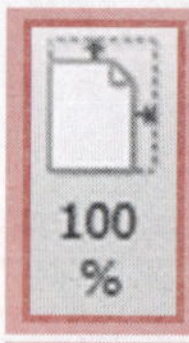	To view the document in 100% of normal size
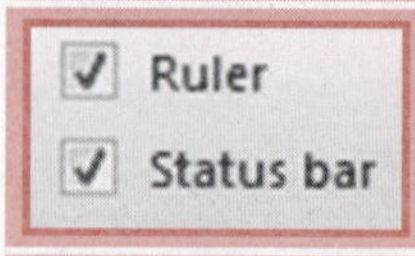	To show or to hide the Ruler and Status bar
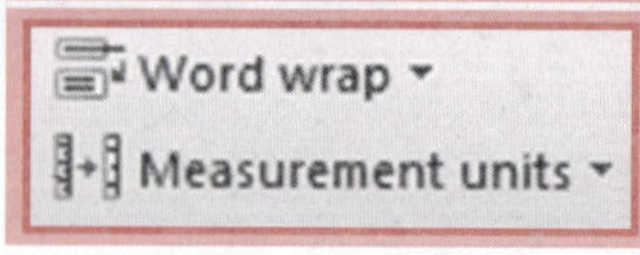	To set the Word wrap and Measurement units to a WordPad window

Quick Key

WordPad shortcut keys

Ctrl + N	To create a new document
Ctrl + O	To open existing document
Ctrl + S	To save the document
F12	To save as a new document
Ctrl + P	To print the document
Alt + F4	To close the document
Ctrl + Z	To cancel last action
Ctrl + Y	To repeat last action
Ctrl + A	To select entire document
Ctrl + =	To make text appear small and below the text base line
Ctrl + Shift + =	To make text appear small and above the text base line
Ctrl + L	To align the text to left
Ctrl + E	To align the text to centre
Ctrl + R	To align the text to right
Ctrl + J	To justify the text
Ctrl + 1	To set single line spacing
Ctrl + 2	To set double line spacing
Ctrl + Shift + >	To increase font size
Ctrl + Shift + <	To decrease font size
Ctrl + Shift + A	To change all the selected text to uppercase
Ctrl + D	To insert drawing created in Paint
Ctrl + H	To find and replace text
Ctrl + Shift + L	To change the bullet style
Ctrl + Home	To go to the beginning of the document
Ctrl + End	To go to the end of the document
Ctrl + F1	To hide or show the Ribbon

MOBILE OPERATING SYSTEM

Fig. 3.26 *A smartphone*

A smartphone is probably best described as a hybrid of a cell phone and a personal computer. A **mobile operating system** operates mobile devices such as smartphone, tablet and PDA. These mobile OS combines the features of a personal computer operating system with touch-screen, cellular, Bluetooth, Wi-Fi, camera and music player. The mobile operating system is responsible for determining the functions and features available on your device, such as thumbwheel, keyboards, WAP, synchronisation with applications, email, text messaging and more. The mobile operating system also determines the third-party applications that can be used on your device such as Facebook and Skype. Different mobile OS are used in different smartphones (Fig. 3.26). Among them, Android and Symbian are the two most popular OS used in smartphones.

Android OS

Android is a Linux-derived OS backed by Google, along with major hardware and software developers (such as Intel, HTC, ARM, Samsung, Motorola and eBay), that forms the Open Handset Alliance. The current Android version is 4.2.2. Android's releases are nicknamed after sweets or dessert items like Cupcake (1.5), Frozen Yogurt (2.2), Honeycomb (3.0), Ice Cream Sandwich (4.0) and Jelly Bean (4.1). Android (Fig. 3.27) has reached, approximately, 52.5% of the global smartphone market share.

Fig. 3.27 *Android OS icon*

Symbian OS

Symbian has the largest smartphone share in most markets worldwide, but lags behind other companies. It has been used by many major handset manufacturers, including BenQ, Fujistu, LG, Mitsubishi, Motorola and Nokia. Though shipments of Symbian devices (Fig. 3.28) have increased, the operating system's worldwide market share has declined from over 50% to just over 40% from 2009 to 2010.

Fig. 3.28 *Symbian OS*

FACT FILE

Apple IPhone uses an operating system called **iOS**, which is derived from **Mac OS X**.

CHECK YOUR PROGRESS

A. Varsha is studying in Class 2. She wants to draw a computer and its peripherals. Suggest a software which does not require an external file installation other than Windows operating system. Also, give a suitable file name with its extension.

B. Kavita is a science teacher. She wants to find the value of tan 45°. Suggest an application available in Windows operating system to calculate the tan value.

C.

These symbols given above corresponds to different alphabets, numbers or characters. Explore Notepad to discover what they match up to.

(**Hint:** Font styles)

D. See the picture below and answer the questions.

a. Which is the active folder?

b. Which is the parent folder of 2011-12 photos?

c. Name two child directories of 2011-12 photos folder?

d. How to create a new folder?

e. How to expand the active folder?

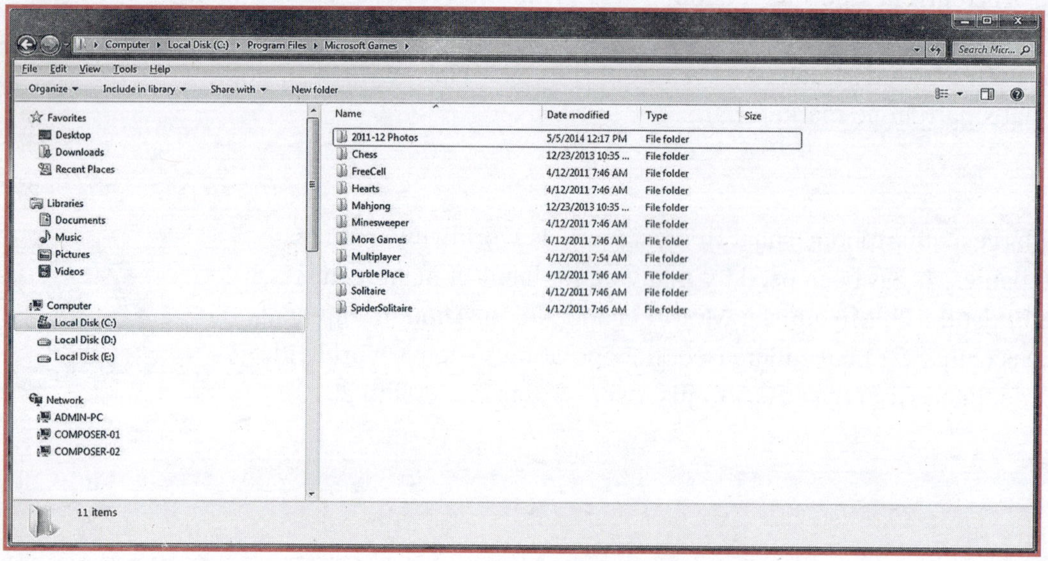

E. Recreate the image given below in Paint and then embed it in WordPad. Also, write a short note on all the tools you used while recreating it.

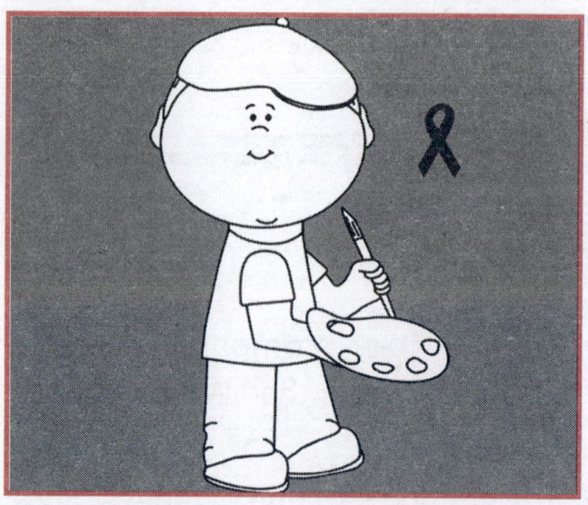

GLOSSARY

- **CLI:** It stands for Command Line Interface that allows the user to interact with computer by typing commands in the prompt using keyboard.
- **Desktop:** It is the first screen of the Windows.
- **Explorer:** It is an application used to list files and folders available in the computer.
- **Formatting:** It refers to the appearance of the text in your document.
- **Folders:** They are used to store and organise files and also folders on your computer.
- **Gadgets:** They are the mini programs that offer information and easy access to the tools that are frequently used.
- **GUI:** Graphical User Interface is user-friendly environment that allows the user to interact with the computer by clicking the buttons of a mouse.
- **Icons:** The small pictures that represent files, folders, applications and other items on the desktop.
- **Operating System:** It is a system software that acts as an interface between the user and the computer hardware.
- **Screen Saver:** It is a feature of Windows that automatically appears on the desktop if the computer is idle for a certain period of time.
- **Smartphone:** It is a mobile phone that is hybrid of a cell phone and a personal computer.
- **Shortcut:** It is an icon that refers a link to a file, folder or a program.
- **Taskbar:** It is the long horizontal bar at the bottom of a desktop.

NOW YOU KNOW

1. Operating System is an important tool that manages the functions of computer and provides the information efficiently after processing.
2. MS-DOS can be accessed from Windows Operating System by clicking Start ⟹ Run and type command or cmd.
3. Recycle Bin holds the deleted files and folders until they are completely deleted from the hard disk.
4. Quick Launch bar is used to open programs quickly with a single-click.
5. The peek feature of Windows allows you to peer past all your open windows and show the desktop.
6. The Notification Area is at the right end of the taskbar. It has volume control, system clock and other associated program.
7. If you copy the shortcut, only the link of shortcut will be copied and not the original file.
8. Folders inside other folders are called sub folders.
9. You cannot maximize or resize the calculator window.
10. In calculator program, programmer mode is an integer mode.
11. Paint program of Windows 7 is used to create drawings on a blank drawing area or in existing pictures.

12. Word wrap automatically adjusts the width of each line of text in a document according to the width of the screen.
13. Notepad is used for creating simple text files which do not require much formatting.
14. WordPad can be used to open and save Notepad files, WordPad files, MS Word files and Open office files.
15. Android and Symbian are the most popular OS used in smartphones.

EXERCISE

FA

A Fill in the blanks.

1. The .... holds the deleted files and folders.
2. A calculator window cannot be .... or ....
3. Decimal portions are discarded in .... mode of a calculator program.
4. .... is the concept of adjusting the width of each line according to the width of the screen.
5. The .... feature of Windows allows you to peer past all your open windows and show the desktop.
6. A .... is an icon that refers a link to a file, a folder or a program.
7. Folders inside other folders are called ....
8. .... are the mini programs that offer information and easy access to the tools that are frequently used.
9. The .... is used to open programs quickly with a single-click.
10. A picture cannot be inserted in a .... file.

B Multiple choice questions.

1. Which of the following is not an accessory in Windows?

   a. Notepad b. WordPad c. Paint d. Excel

2. The following is the default extension of a document saved in Notepad ....

   a. .txt b. . ntp c. . htm d. . rtf

3. Which one of the following is an open source operating system?

a. Windows b. Linux c. Unix d. MS-DOS

4. Recycle Bin is a folder that stores ....

a. saved files b. deleted files c. recent files d. modified files

5. The taskbar appears at the .... of the desktop.

a. top b. side c. bottom d. middle

6. WordPad is a ....

a. word processor b. game software

c. drawing program d. All of these

7. Some specialised programs that come with Windows are grouped under the .... heading.

a. shareware b. desktop c. accessories d. control panel

8. The first software that is loaded into the memory of a computer when a computer starts is ....

a. MS Word b. antivirus c. operating system d. None of these

9. .... key is used to close the active window.

a. Alt + F3 b. Alt + F4 c. Alt + F6 d. Ctrl + F4

10.  This tool is available in .... window.

a. WordPad b. Notepad c. Paint d. None of these

11. Brushes are of .... types in paint.

a. 5 b. 9 c. 6 d. 12

12. The latest android version is ....

a. 3.2 b. 4.2 c. 4.5 d. 1.3

13. Sandwich and JellyBean are the nickname of .... HOTS

a. Android b. Symbian c. Linux d. Mac OS

14. To highlight a text with marking color .... tool is used.

a.  b.  c.  d. 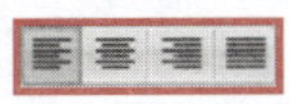

15. WordPad program saves its files with the extension ....

a. .wpd b. .doc c. .rtf d. .txt

16. Which of the following is not a function of an operating system?

a. File Management b. Process Management

c. Memory Management d. Database Management

17. Which symbol in Windows Explorer indicates that there are subfolders in the folder?

a. + b. Δ c. ▷ d. None of these

18. Cut, Copy and Paste options are available in .... tab.

a. Home b. View c. Help d. None of these

19. Which interface allows the user to interact with the computer by typing instructions?

a. GUI b. CLI c. Both GUI and CUI d. None of these

20. To align the text to centre .... shortcut key is used.

a. Ctrl + E b. Ctrl + C c. Ctrl + L d. Ctrl + R

C Identify the tools and write the name of the accessories in which they are available.

1. 

2. 

3. 

4. 

5. 

6. 

7. 

8. 

9. 

10. 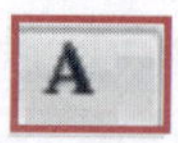

D Answer the following questions briefly.

1. Define operating system.
2. Write the shortcut key to create a new file in Notepad.
3. Mention the different file formats that can be created or saved using WordPad application.
4. What is CLI?
5. Give an example for GUI based operating system.
6. What is the difference between click and double-click?
7. What are the three calculator modes available in Windows 7?
8. 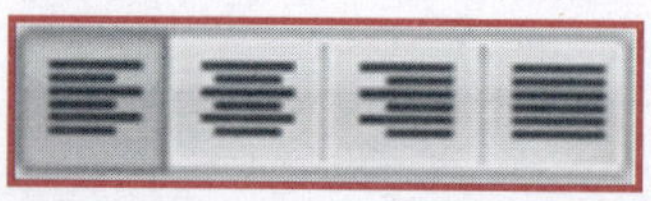 Identify this tool and label it.

9. What does the Recycle bin hold?
10. How do you create a shortcut icon for an application program?
11. What is the purpose of Ctrl and + key in Paint?
12. What are sub folders?
13. Is it possible to list the text with bullets using WordPad application?
14. List out the items seen in Notification Area.
15. How do you open MS-DOS from Windows?
16. What are smartphones?
17. Name any four formatting tools available in WordPad.
18. How do you insert current date and time in the Notepad window?
19. What is the difference between X_2 and x^2 ?
20. What is the purpose of F3 and F5 key in Notepad?

SA

E Answer the following questions.

1. Name some of the items available in Start menu.
2. Explain any two functions of an operating system.
3. What are the main components of a desktop?
4. Name and write a short note on common operating systems used in personal computers.
5. What are the common tasks of a mouse? Write a line about each.
6. Write down the features of android OS.
7. Write down the steps to activate on-screen keyboard. Which device is used to select keys from that?
8. What is the use of Word wrap feature? Name the menu in which it is available.
9. Write any four common features of WordPad and Notepad.
10. What is the default file extension of a Notepad file, a WordPad file and a Paint file?
11. What are the options available in Format menu in Notepad window?
12. Write short notes on any four options available under WordPad button.
13. Name any four types of brushes used in Paint software. Use each of the brush to highlight the difference.
14. How do you display two windows at a time on the desktop?
15. What is the use of print preview option? HOTS

F Answer the following questions in detail.

1. Explain different operating systems used in personal computers.
2. Compare features of symbian and android operating system. HOTS
3. Explain the features of calculator in Windows 7.
4. Explain any five formatting tools used in WordPad.
5. Differentiate between Notepad and WordPad.
6. Give a brief note about functions of the tabs available in WordPad Ribbon.
7. How will you set date and time of your computer?
8. Explain the different view modes available in Windows Explorer.
9. What is the use of on-screen keyboard?
10. Enumerate and explain different components present on Windows 7 taskbar.

Application Based Questions

A. Sabina just visited Holland with her family. She captured over five hundred photographs. She transferred all the photos to her desktop and now wants to set some images as her desktop background. How can she achieve this?

B. Few months back Isha created a resume for an internship. However, before she could apply, the application date closed. The internship is inviting applications again; however, Isha does not remember where she saved her resume. She looked in Documents folder and on her desktop, but without any result. Help her locate the resume.

C. Samir and his brother are learning how to use Windows Accessories like Notepad, WordPad, Paint and Calculator. After three lessons their father asked them to identify, label and explain the use of the following components.

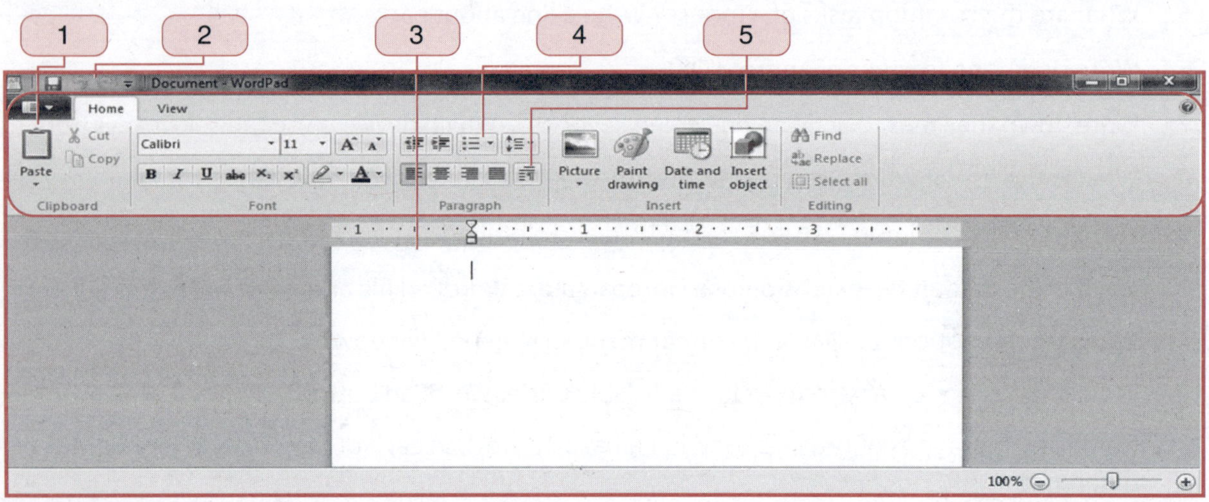

D. Rashmi listed the pros and cons of different mobile operating system in Notepad. However, her teacher asked her to rework her content. To avoid confusion of having multiple files, she wants to permanently delete the files from her hard disk. What should she do?

E. Rajat is a salesman who spends half his working days on tour. He wants to maintain a log of all the days he goes to office. His colleagues suggested he can maintain a log in Notepad. Help him do this.

F. Ratika bought two mobile handsets, one for her grandfather and the other for her younger brother. One phone has symbian operating system and the other phone is android based. Which phone is appropriate for her grandfather, who will just be using the calling and messaging facility of the phone; and which phone is appropriate for her brother who will be playing games and downloading applications.

LAB WORK

A. Complete the following activity using Paint.

1. Draw the Windows logo.
2. Write few lines about Windows using text tool.
3. Save it as a .jpg file.
4. Open another Paint program.
5. Open the first Paint file, press PrintScreen key and paste it in the new Paint document.
6. Using selection tool, cut each tool of paint and place it one below the other.
7. Label the tool using text tool.

B. Using Notepad, write a letter to your friend to share your experience of visiting the recently concluded Computer Expo. Insert date and time at the top of the letter.

C. Complete the following activity using WordPad.

1. Type the following paragraph:

> There are places you must visit before sitting for an exam. Besides the classroom, learn to love the library, the bookshops, the staff room (the place where you go to consult with teachers) and all places where people in the profession of your dreams practice. How can you aspire to be a doctor and do not acquaint yourself with hospitals, clinics, medical shops and other health related places?
>
> There are numerous pitfalls associated with exams that have little to do with the subject material, but much to do with the style of your answers. With a little attention to detail, you can significantly increase your effectiveness, your marks and most importantly your understanding of the subject.
>
> **Muralidharan**

2. Follow the instructions given below to complete the activity.
   a. Align the whole document to both left and right (Justify).
   b. Apply Cambria font for the first paragraph and Algerian font for the second paragraph.

c. Apply font size 16 to the whole document.

d. Align the last line text to right.

e. Insert a suitable picture or draw using Paint drawing button.

f. Change the spacing between lines to 1.5 for the whole document.

g. Save it as 'Exams' in your folder (Create a folder in your name in Documents folder).

D. Complete the following activity using a calculator.

1. Perform the following calculations and write the results in Notepad: 115/22 * 2/4 + 22 – 8
2. Solve the following and write the result in WordPad.

   a. Sin 90 + cos 45 = _________

   b. Sin 45 + cos 30 = _________

   c. Tan 30 + sin 90 = _________

Windows 8 Updates

In Windows 8:

- You have an innovative and dynamic tile-based **Start screen**. The Windows 8 Start screen consists of a grid of tiles which can be arranged into columnar groups. Tiles can display dynamic content provided by their corresponding applications, such as notifications and slide shows. They can also show updates from your friends, new emails, application notifications, the next appointment on your calendar, etc.

- Multiple users can use one single PC. Every user has a personalised experience, with their own start screen, files and applications.
- You can lock and unlock your screen with pictures. You can choose a picture to lock screen. Then, instead of typing a password to unlock, you draw shapes on the picture to unlock.
- You can create a copy of the entire OS along with all the settings, wallpapers, files and even apps, into a USB thumb drive. When plugged into another computer with Windows 8, you can boot up the PC and make it look exactly like the OS you use, with all the same settings. This can be done using **Windows To Go** feature.
- Windows Explorer screen has the Ribbon similar to that of MS Word 2007 or Paint.
  You can manage files and folders with the help of the Ribbon. You can easily add folders to a library. Many options such as Copy, Move, Rename, Create New Folder and Delete are available in the Home tab of the Ribbon.

EXTENSION

Bharat Operating System Solutions (BOSS) is a free and open source computer operating system developed by the National Resource Centre for Free/Open Source Software (NRCFOSS) of India. **BOSS GNU/Linux** is also known by the acronym **BOSS**. The latest version of this operating system is Version 5.0, which was released in August 2013.

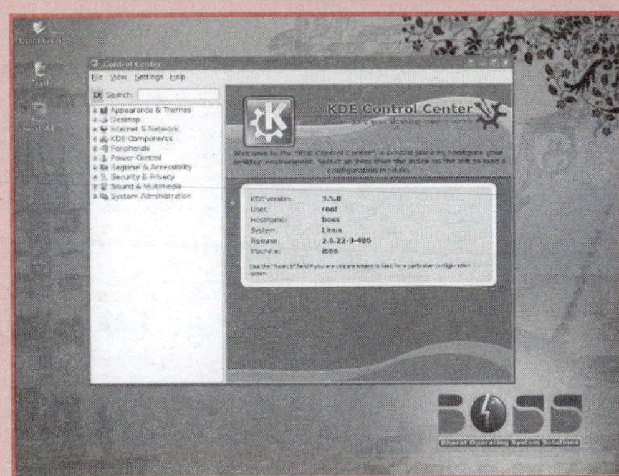

TEACHER'S NOTES

1. Along with the students explore Notepad, WordPad and Paint interface. Demonstrate functionalities of different features available and then give them activities to complete.
2. Explain to the students how advanced mobile operating systems have become and how mobile phones are used today.
3. Download and show the Bharat Operating System Solutions (BOSS) to the students.

Worksheet 1

SECTION A

Fill in the blanks.

1. A ____________________ is a printed copy of information from a computer.
2. A ____________________ computer is also known as mid-range computer.
3. A set of programs that help perform various tasks in a computer is called ____________________.
4. The programs that control the computer hardware are called ____________________.
5. ____________________ operating system lets you accomplish only one task at a given time.
6. A compiler coverts ____________________ language into ____________________ language.
7. The Recycle Bin holds the ____________________ files and folders.
8. ____________________ and ____________________ are two different modes of a calculator program in Windows 7.
9. ____________________ is an application used to list files and folders available in the computer.
10. ____________________ is used to open programs quickly with a single-click.

SECTION B

Answer the questions briefly.

1. What are the three main units of a computer?
2. How DVD is different from Blue Ray?
3. What is desktop publishing?
4. What is the relationship between operating system and application software? Can they exist without each other?
5. Define decryption?
6. What are jump lists?
7. Name the operating system used in Apple products.
8. Why are utilities, like antivirus software and backup software, important?
9. What do you understand by the term desktop gadgets?
10. Give any five features of an android smartphone.

4 Word Processing Tools – I

SNAP RECAP

1. The document that you view on your computer monitor is known as the softcopy.
2. The printed version of the document is known as the hardcopy.
3. A word processing tool is used to create, edit and print documents.
4. MS Word is an effective and powerful word processing tool by Microsoft.

LEARNING OBJECTIVES

You will learn about:

1. Word Processing Tool
2. Components of MS Word 2007
3. Creating and Saving a Document
4. Editing a Document
5. Formatting a Document
6. Printing a Document

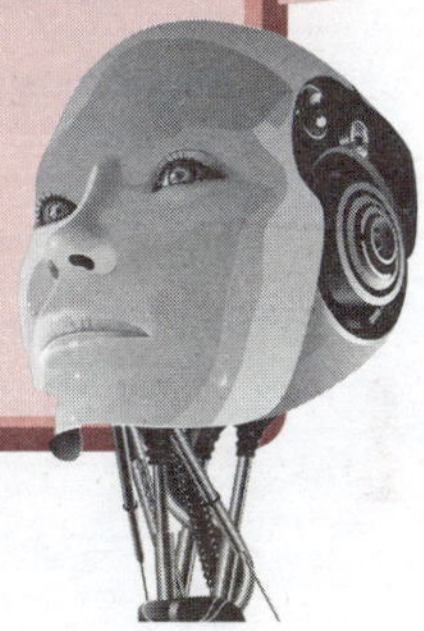

INTRODUCTION

***Word processing tools** are the set of programs used to create, edit, view, search, replace, save and print documents.* Word processing tools are used for text manipulation. They also allow you to insert pictures, charts and tables in a text file. The advantage of any word processor is that you can make changes anywhere in the document without retyping the entire document. It is easy to correct your mistakes, to insert a sentence or a paragraph and to move a section of text from one place to another in a document.

Features of a word processor

A word processor is used to create, review, revise and save documents for future and further use. Some of the common features of a word processing tool are listed below.

- You can save your document.
- The text once written can be modified and there is no need to rewrite the entire text again.
- You can insert text anywhere in the document.

- You can apply different fonts, styles and color to the text.
- Pictures, charts, graphs and tables can be inserted into a document.
- Spell check feature allows you to check your document for incorrect spellings and correct the errors automatically.
- It allows you to define various page sizes and margins.
- It allows you to search and replace a word.
- It helps you produce letters, reports, newsletters and books in a professional manner.

▶ Microsoft Office Word 2007

Microsoft Office Word 2007 is a word processing tool which has a range of editing, formatting and layout options. It was released to businesses on November 30, 2006 and to consumers worldwide on January 30, 2007. It is available both as a stand-alone product and as part of the Microsoft Office 2007 suite. It was preceded by Office Word 2003 and succeeded by Word 2010.

To open Microsoft Office Word 2007, follow the steps given below (Fig. 4.1).

1. Click on the **Start** button.
2. Go to **All Programs** option.
3. Click on **Microsoft Office** option.
4. Select **Microsoft Office Word 2007**.

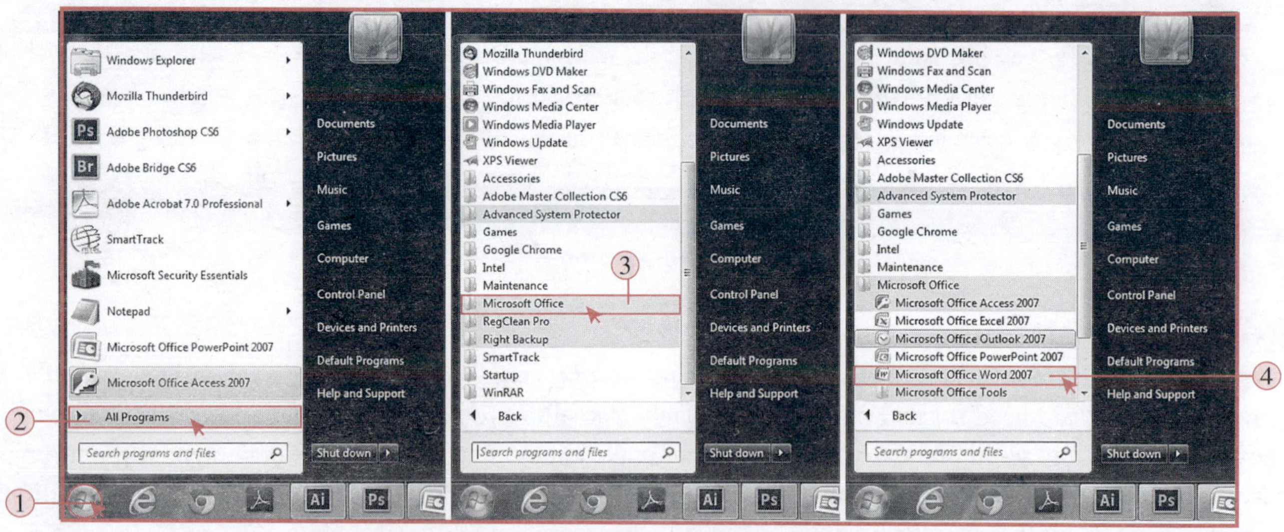

Fig. 4.1 *Starting Microsoft Office Word 2007*

▶ Components of Microsoft Office Word 2007

Microsoft Office Word 2007 has number of components, such as the **Microsoft Office** button, **Quick Access Toolbar**, **Ribbon**, **Scroll Bar**, among others. Some of the most important and frequently used components are (Fig. 4.2) discussed here.

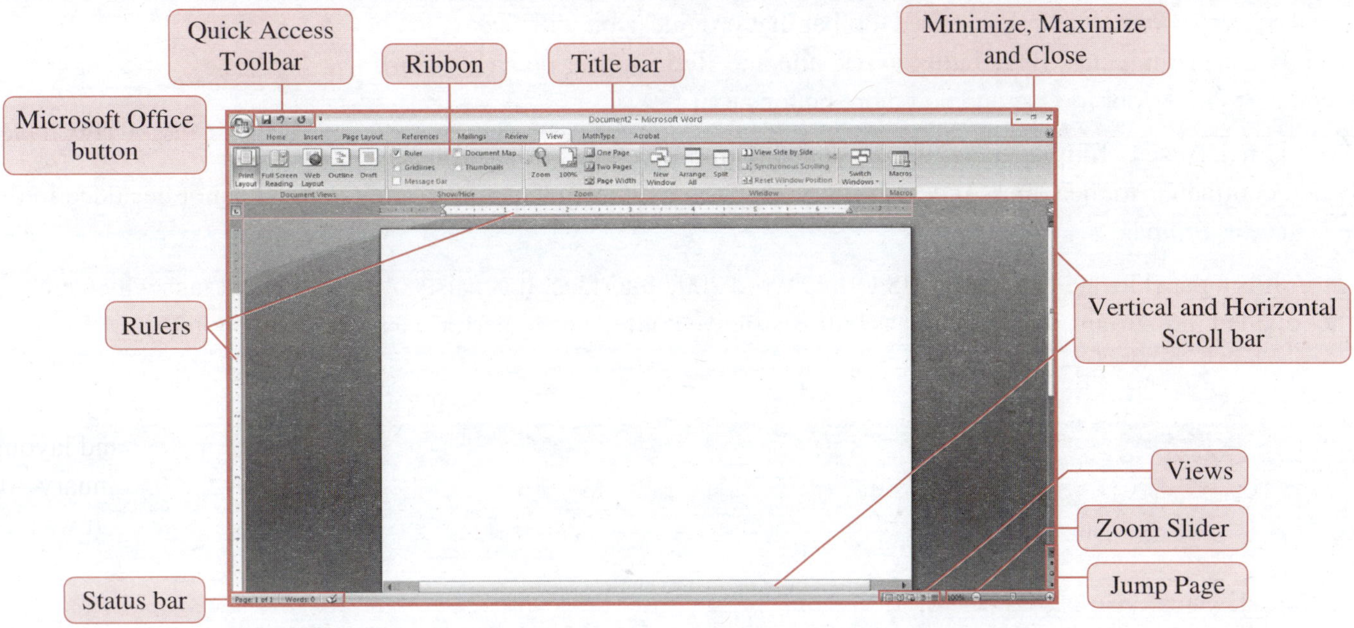

Fig. 4.2 *Components of MS Office Word 2007*

Microsoft Office Button: It is located at the top-left corner and displays a set of options, such as, to create a new file, to open an existing document, to save a document and to print a document. The menu that opens is called **Office Menu** (Fig. 4.3).

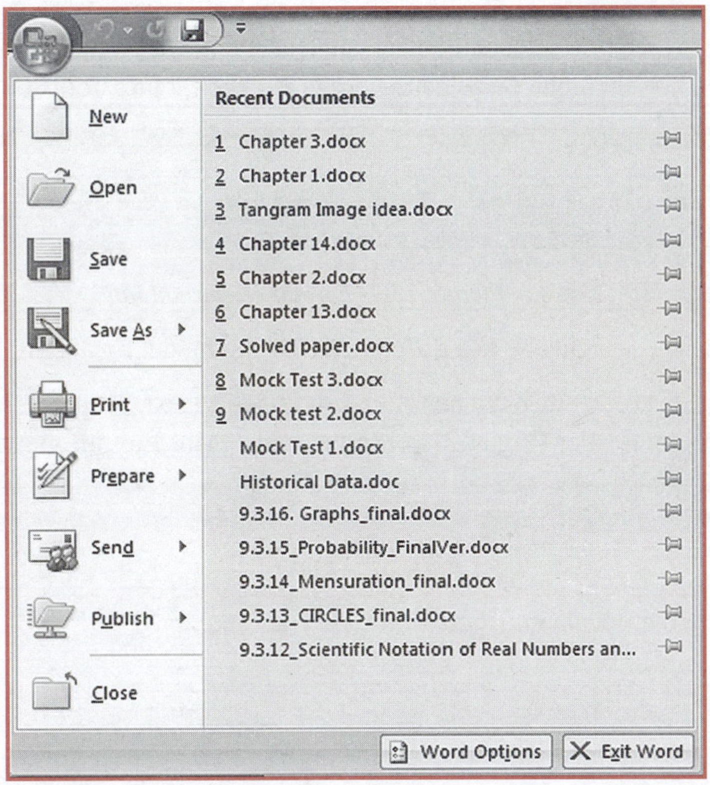

Fig. 4.3 *Office menu*

Quick Access Toolbar: It is a customised toolbar that provides you with access to frequently used commands. By default **Save**, **Undo** and **Redo** appear on it (Fig. 4.4). You can customise your toolbar and add more buttons to it.

Fig. 4.4 *Quick Access Toolbar*

NOTE: Quick Access Toolbar cannot be displayed on multiple lines. Also, you can only add commands to the Quick Access Toolbar. Options such as indent and spacing values cannot be added to the Quick Access Toolbar.

Ribbon: It is a panel located on top of MS Office Word 2007 interface. It consists of seven default tabs which are further divided into groups. Each group has buttons to give commands to perform a specific function (Fig. 4.5).

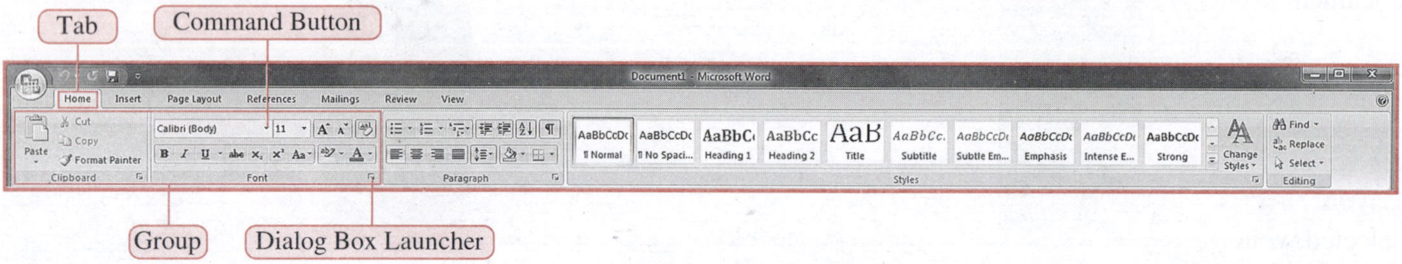

Fig. 4.5 *MS Office Word 2007 Ribbon*

1. *Tabs* are task-oriented.
2. *Groups* within each tab break up a task into sub-tasks.
3. *Command buttons* in each group execute a command or display options of commands.

There are two other kinds of tabs that appear when you need them. They are **contextual tabs** and **program tabs**.

- *Contextual tabs* appear when you select an object, such as a table, a picture or a chart and a corresponding contextual tab appears. For example, on selecting a picture, the Picture Tools Format tab appears (Fig. 4.6).

Fig. 4.6 *Picture Tools Format contextual tab*

- *Program tabs* appear when you change to a different authoring mode. For example, Print Preview tab.

Rulers: The horizontal and vertical rulers in Word are often used to align text, graphics, tables and other elements in a document. To view the horizontal ruler (Fig. 4.7) you must be in Print Layout view.

Fig. 4.7 *Ruler*

Working Area: It is the place in the document where you type your text and work on it (Fig. 4.8).

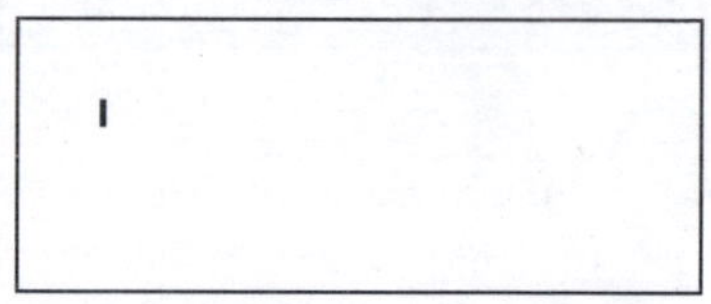

Fig. 4.8 *Working Area*

Status Bar: It displays the page number you are currently working on and the total number of pages in the document. It also displays the number of words used in the document (Fig. 4.9).

Fig. 4.9 *Status Bar*

Title Bar: It contains the name of the document.
By default, a new word document is named Document1. It is the topmost bar of Word 2007 interface and is present just above the Ribbon (Fig. 4.10).

Fig. 4.10 *Title Bar*

Minimize, Maximize, Close: These three buttons are on the right side of the title bar. They allow you to minimize, maximize or close the Word 2007 window (Fig. 4.11).

Fig. 4.11 *Minimize, Maximize, Close*

Vertical and Horizontal Scroll Bar: Vertical scroll bar allows you to move the document up and down. Horizontal scroll bar allows you to move the document left and right (Fig. 4.12).

Fig. 4.12 *Scroll Bars*

Document Views: A document can be displayed in five different views. They are **Print Layout, Full Screen Reading, Web Layout, Outline** and **Draft**. Depending on the view selected, your document will appear as when printed or in web format or just as an outline (Fig. 4.13).

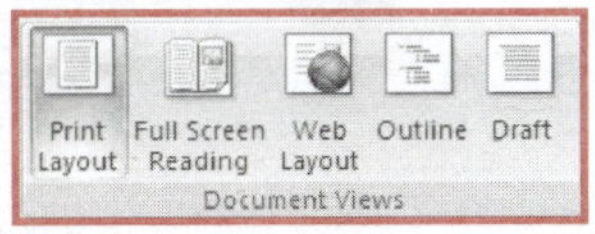

Fig. 4.13 *Document Views*

Zoom Slider: It is available at the bottom right of your screen. You can use this to increase or decrease the size of your page to view (Fig. 4.14).

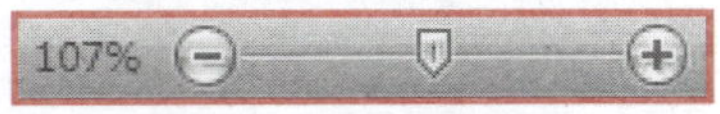

Fig. 4.14 *Zoom Slider*

Jump Page: To jump to the next page or go to the previous page these buttons are used (Fig. 4.15).

Fig. 4.15 *Jump Page*

CHECK YOUR PROGRESS

A. Make a list of all the options available in the Office menu. Also, mention their functionality.

B. Explore and identify these Document View.

1.

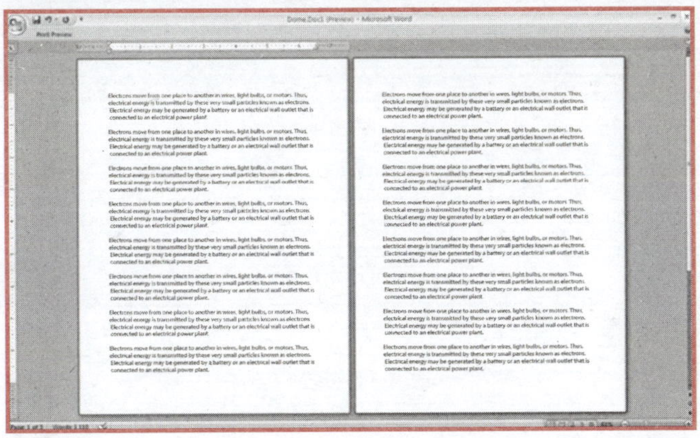

2.

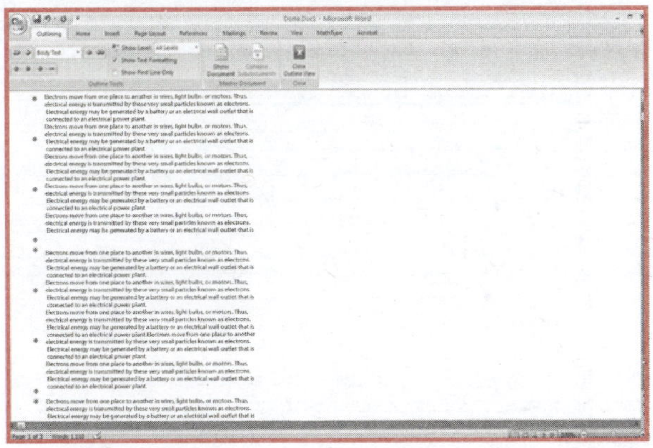

▶ Creating and Saving a Word Document

To write a document in MS Office Word 2007, it is necessary to create a **New Document**. Once you have entered the text and worked on it, it is important to save it for future use. In this section you will learn how to create a new document and save it. You will also learn how to open an existing document and how to close a document.

To create a document in Word 2007

To create a **blank document** in Word 2007, follow the steps given below.

1. Click on the **Office** button and go to **New** option (Fig. 4.16).
2. Select **Blank Document**.
3. Click on the **Create** button (Fig. 4.17).

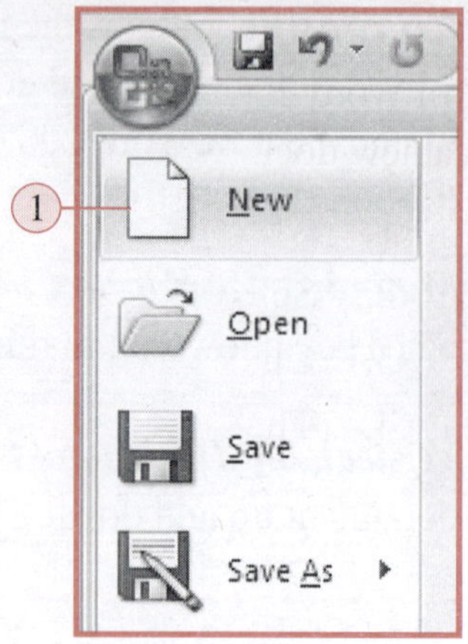

Fig. 4.16 *Office menu*

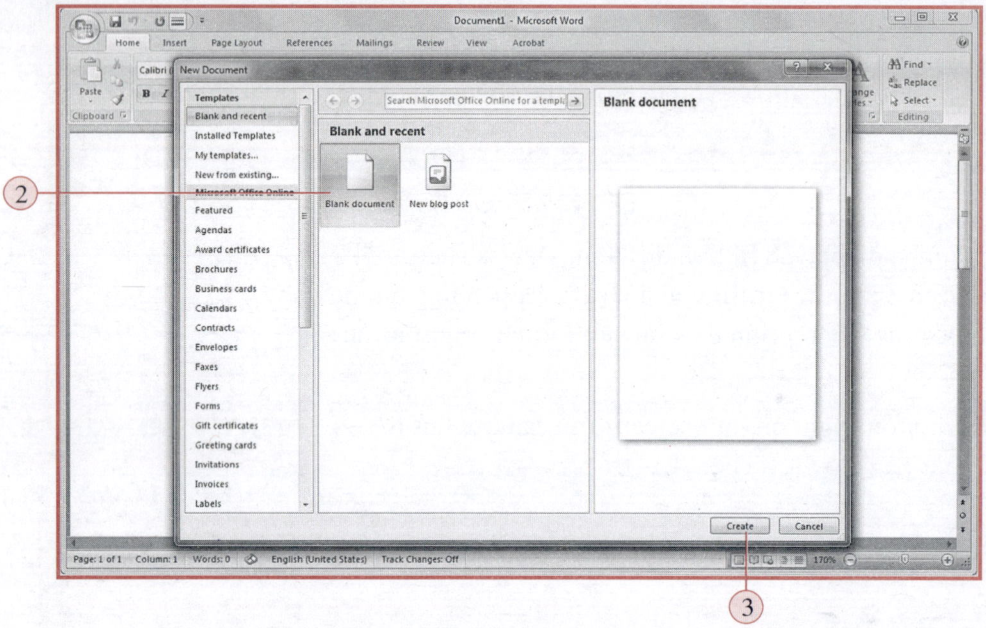

Fig. 4.17 *Creating a blank document*

4. As shown below, a new blank document appears (Fig. 4.18).

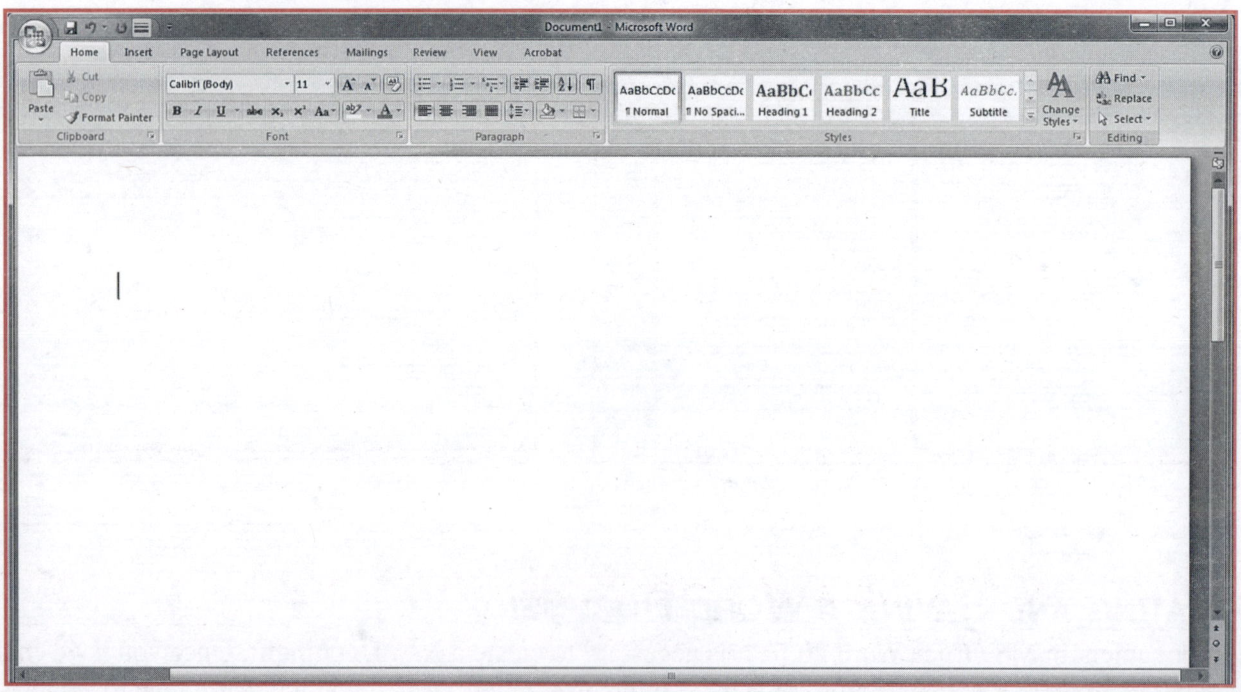

Fig. 4.18 *A new word document*

To create a new document using an installed template

In Word 2007, you can also create a new word document using templates (pre-selected styles and settings). To create a new document using a template, follow the steps given below.

1. Click on the **Office** button and go to **New** option.
2. Select **Installed Templates** and select the type of template you want to create from the list given.
3. Click on the **Create** button (Fig. 4.19).
4. The new template document is displayed.

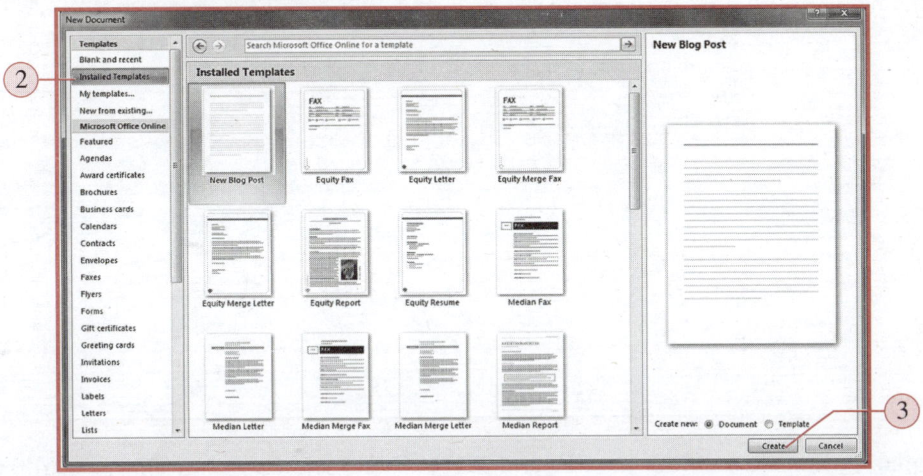

Fig. 4.19 *Creating a new document using installed templates*

To open an existing document

To open an existing file, follow the steps given below.

1. Click on the **Office** button.
2. Click on **Open**. The **Open** dialog box appears (Fig. 4.20).
3. Select the file you want to open.
4. Click on the **Open** button.

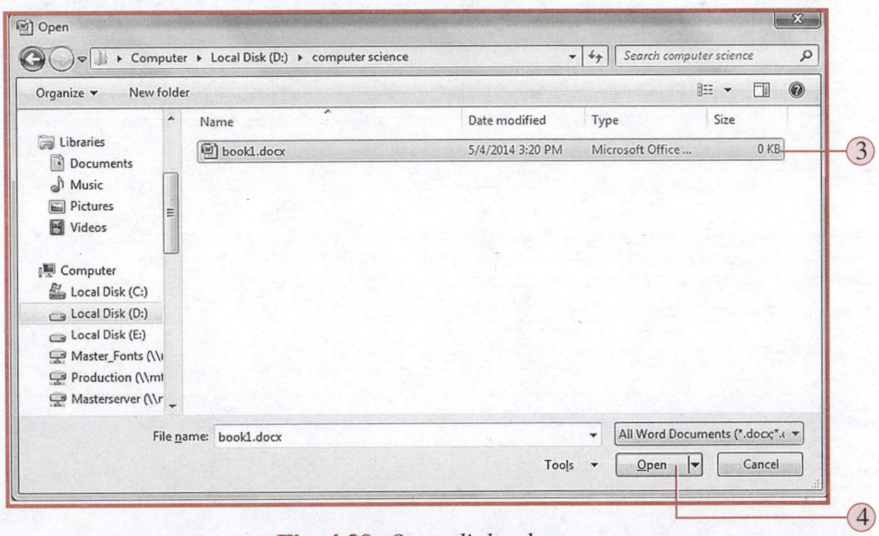

Fig. 4.20 *Open dialog box*

TRY THIS!

You can create games using templates given in Word 2007. In the **Installed Templates** section, go to **Projects** and click on the **Games** category. All the available game templates will appear.

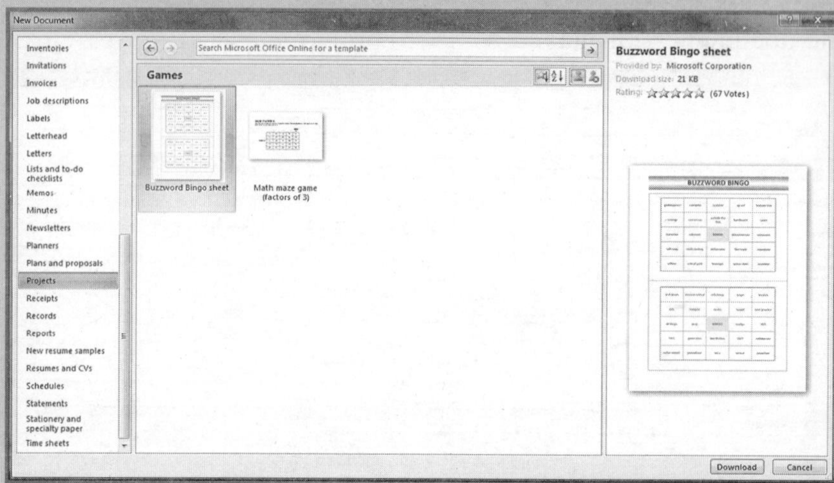

Some game templates available are Buzzword Bingo, Maze! Factor and Crossword puzzles. You can also modify the template according to your needs.

MAZE! FACTOR 3

Find your way through the maze by circling the numbers that are divisible by 3. But watch out for dead ends, which you can mark with an X.

FINISH ↑ (above the right-hand column)

Start ➔ (beside the third row)

7	53	15	53	63
21	37	42	86	54
3	43	16	18	31
13	27	9	14	72
29	67	35	23	55

To save a document

To save your document for reuse, follow the steps given below.

1. Click on the **Office** button.
2. Click on **Save**. The **Save As** dialog box appears (Fig. 4.21).
3. Enter the file name in **File name:** box.
4. Select the file type in **Save as type:** box.
5. Click on the **Save** button.

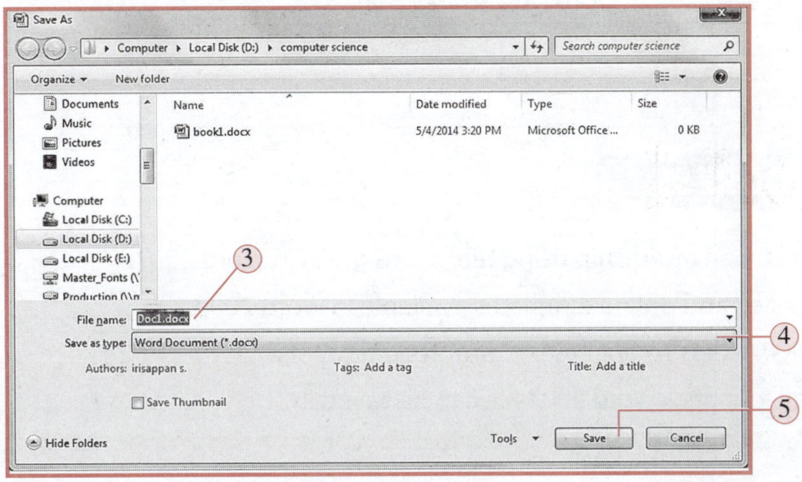

Fig. 4.21 *Save As dialog box*

FACT FILE

The **Save As** option is used to save an existing file with a different name. By default, the Word 2007 files are stored with extension ***.docx** while the earlier versions of Word had ***.doc** extension.

To close a document

Follow the steps given below to close a document in Word 2007.

1. Click on the **Office** button.
2. Select the **Close** option (Fig. 4.22).

OR

Click on the close button on the right side of the title bar.

NOTE: Before closing a document, ensure that you saved it.

Fig. 4.22 *Closing a document*

Quick Key

Ctrl + N	To create a new document
Ctrl + O	To open an existing document
Ctrl + S	To save a document
F12	To save a document with a new name
Ctrl + P	To print a document
Ctrl + W	To close a document

CHECK YOUR PROGRESS

A. Create your résumé for an internship using templates given in Word 2007.

B. Explore all the installed and online templates available in Word 2007.

C. Customise the Quick Access Toolbar as per your requirements.

D. Investigate what all formats a Word 2007 file can be saved in.

▶ Some Features of MS Word 2007

With Word 2007, you can perform many tasks. Some frequently used tasks are given below.

- ***Scroll bars:*** You can move your document in any direction–up, down, left or right–using Scroll bars.
- ***Word Wrap:*** While typing continuously, if the last word stretches beyond the right margin, Word automatically shifts it to the beginning of the next line without pressing the Enter key on the keyboard.
- ***Tabs:*** They are designed to be task-oriented. The groups within each tab break a task into sub-tasks. Command buttons in each group carry out a command or display a menu of commands.
- ***Save Time:*** You get more out of the powerful Word capabilities by selecting from galleries of predefined styles, table formats, list formats and graphical effects.

  NOTE: Explore all the Word 2007 tabs for more options.
- ***Quick Styles:*** You can quickly change the appearance of text, tables and graphics throughout your document by selecting quick styles and document themes (Fig. 4.23).

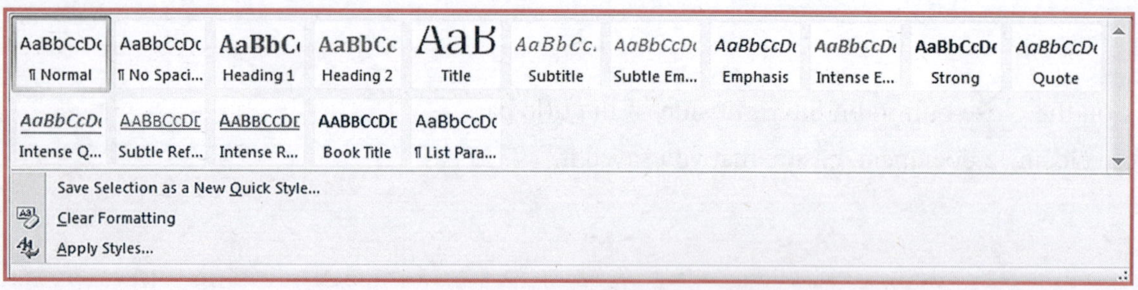

Fig. 4.23 *Quick Styles gallery*

- ***Digital Signature:*** You can add an invisible digital signature to a document or you can insert a **Microsoft Office Signature Line** to capture a visible representation of a signature along with the digital signature (Fig. 4.24).

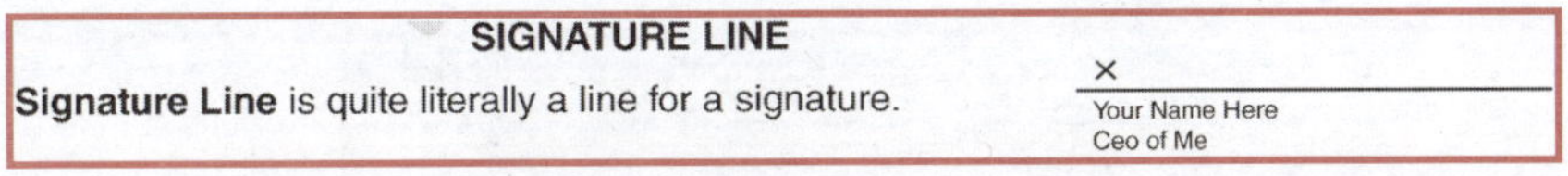

Fig. 4.24 *Digital signature*

- ***Export:*** Word 2007 supports exporting your file to PDF and XPS.
- ***Cover Pages:*** Using Word 2007, you can insert pre-formatted elements like cover pages and pull quotes with just a few clicks (Fig. 4.25).

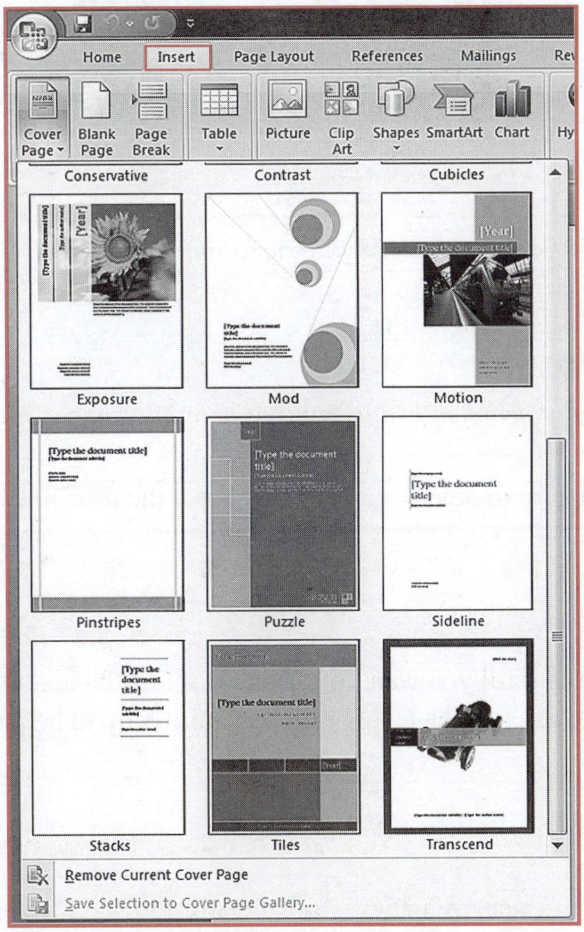

Fig. 4.25 *Cover page gallery*

ACTIVITY

To insert a cover page to your Word 2007 document.

1. Click on the **Insert** tab.
2. In the **Pages** group, click on **Cover Page** option.
3. From the Cover Page gallery, click on the design you like.

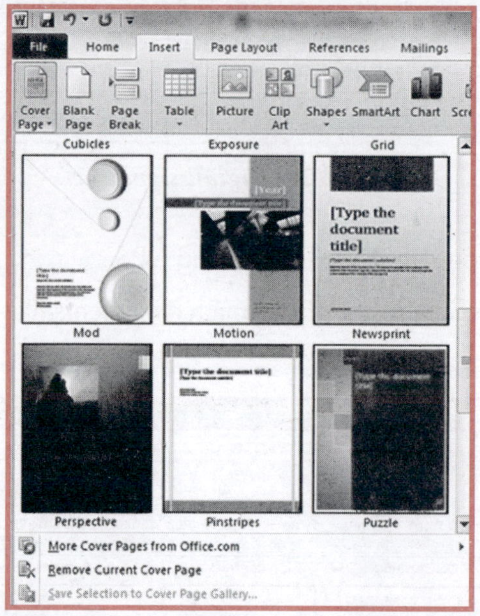

4. The cover page will be inserted at the start of your document.

▶ Editing a Document

The process of modifying an existing document by inserting or deleting some content, or embedding pictures, charts and tables is called ***editing****.*

To edit a document, to move, to copy or to delete, you need to select the text, line or a paragraph. Selection of text can be done in two ways. They are:

- ***By using mouse***
- ***By using keyboard***

To select the text using a mouse, drag it till you want to select. To select the text using a keyboard, use the **Shift** key along with the **Arrow** key till the end. Once the text is selected, it is ready to be moved, copied, deleted or for any other action in the document.

Quick Key

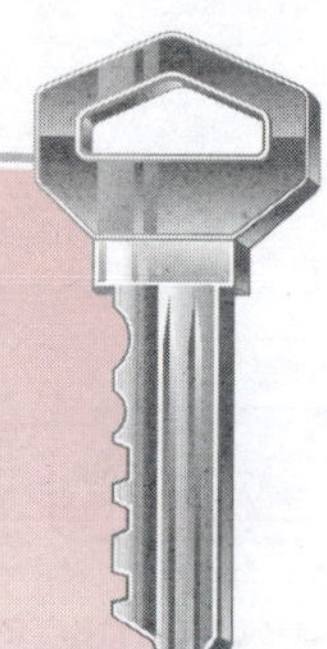

To edit a document you need to move from one word to another word or another line of a document. The following keyboard commands are used to move the cursor anywhere in the document.

Ctrl + Home	To move to the top of the document
Ctrl + End	To move to the bottom of the document
Home	To move to the beginning of the line
End	To move to the end of the line
Ctrl + Left Arrow	To move one word to the left
Ctrl + Left Arrow	To move one word to the right
Ctrl + Left Arrow	To move one line above
Ctrl + Left Arrow	To move one line below

Moving text

You can move text from one place to another in a document. To do so, follow the steps given below.

1. Select the text that has to be moved.
2. Go to the **Clipboard** group of **Home** tab on the Ribbon.
3. Click on **Cut** option to move the selected text to clipboard (Fig. 4.26).
4. Place the cursor where the text has to be moved.
5. Click on **Paste** option from the Clipboard.

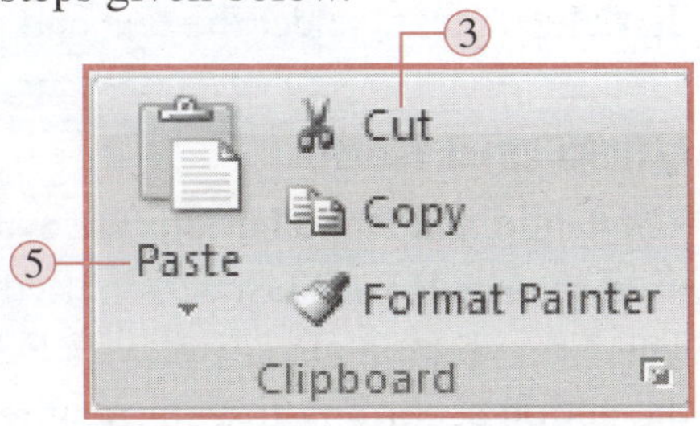

Fig. 4.26 *Cut and Paste options*

FACT FILE

Clipboard is a temporary storage area in Windows. It can hold or store information temporarily.

Copying text

You can copy a portion of text from one place to another in a document or from one document to another. To do so, follow the steps given below.

1. Select the text that has to be copied.
2. Go to the **Clipboard** group of **Home** tab.
3. Click on **Copy** option to copy the selected text to clipboard (Fig. 4.27).
4. Place the cursor where the text has to be copied.
5. Click on **Paste** option from the clipboard.

Fig. 4.27 *Copy and Paste options*

NOTE: The difference between Cut and Copy is that when Cut is applied, the selected text is removed from its original position and copied to the clipboard. However, when Copy option is applied, the text retains its position and at the same time it is copied to the clipboard. Once the text is cut or copied it can be pasted anywhere on the document by clicking Paste button from the **Clipboard** group.

TRY THIS!

You can use the **Spike** feature to gather text from various places in the document, combine it and paste the whole selection together multiple times anywhere in the document. The text that is added to the Spike is cut from its original position. Once created, it can be pasted unlimited times anywhere in the document.

To add text to a Spike, select the text and press **Ctrl+F3**. You can cut different parts of your document and Word will add them to spike.

To paste this text back into the document, press **Ctrl+Shift+F3** or write the word **spike** and **press F3**.

Deleting a text

To delete a text, select the text and press the 

key.

Undo and Redo

Fig. 4.28 *Undo and Redo*

The Undo and Redo buttons are available in Quick Access Toolbar (Fig. 4.28). Undo button is used to cancel your last action. Redo option is used to cancel your last undo action.
The Undo button also displays a list of your last actions so that you can select and cancel the action according to your requirement.

Find and Replace

Find option is used to find a particular text in a document. It is available on the right side of the Ribbon in **Editing** group of the **Home** tab (Fig. 4.29). There are two available options. One is to find a text and the other **Go to...** is used to go to a particular page, section, line or bookmark. **Replace** option is used to find a text and replace it with another text in a document.

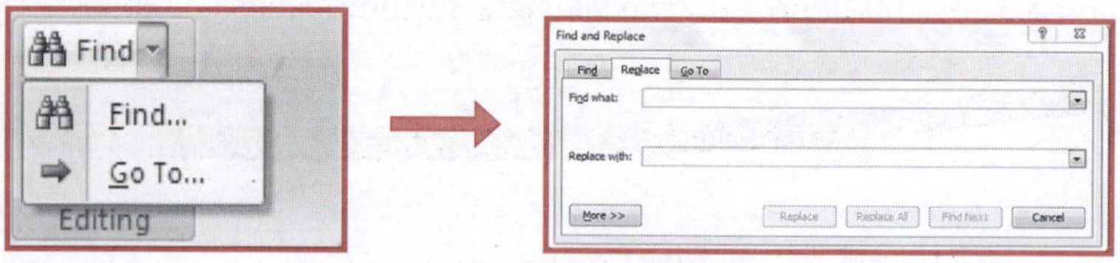

Fig. 4.29 *Find and Replace*

ACTIVITY

To find and replace a text in Word 2007.

1. Go to the **Replace** option in the **Editing** group of the **Home** tab.
2. **Find and Replace** dialog box appears.
3. Click on the **Replace** tab. In the **Find what:** box, type the text that you want to search and in the **Replace with:** box, type the replacement text.
4. Click on the **Replace** button to replace an occurrence of the text. Click on the **Find Next** button to find the next occurrence of the text. Click on the **Replace All** button to replace all the occurrences of the text.

Quick Key

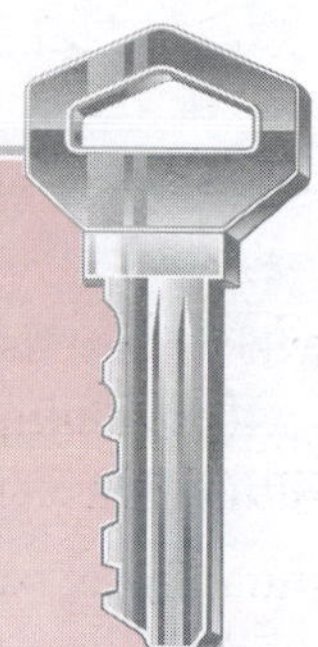

Ctrl + X	To cut a portion of text from a document
Ctrl + C	To copy a portion of text from a document
Ctrl + V	To paste the selection of text stored in clipboard
Ctrl + Z	To undo the last action
Ctrl +Y	To redo the last undo
Ctrl + F	To find a text in a document
Ctrl + H	To replace a text
Ctrl + A	To select all

CHECK YOUR PROGRESS

Complete the following activity.

A. Create a new document in Word 2007.

B. Save it as Success.docx.

C. Type the following in the Success document.

> **Success**
>
> Believe while others are doubting
>
> Plan while others are playing
>
> Study while others are sleeping
>
> Decide while others are delaying
>
> Prepare while others are daydreaming
>
> Take actions while others are still thinking
>
> Save while others are wasting
>
> Listen while others are talking
>
> Persist while others are quitting

D. On the typed text, complete the following task.

1. Cut the first two lines and paste them after the last line.
2. Copy the heading and place it after the last line.
3. Find the word 'Success' and replace it with 'Sure Success'.
4. Delete the third line.
5. Using Undo option, bring back the deleted third line.

▶ FORMATTING A DOCUMENT

*The process of changing the appearance of the text in a document, or to present a document in a very attractive manner is called **formatting***. The text formatting tools in Word 2007 include **Font Type**, **Font Size**, **Font Color** and so on. On the **Ribbon** under **Home** tab there are three areas that control the style of your document. They are **Font** group, **Paragraph** group and **Styles** group (Fig. 4.30).

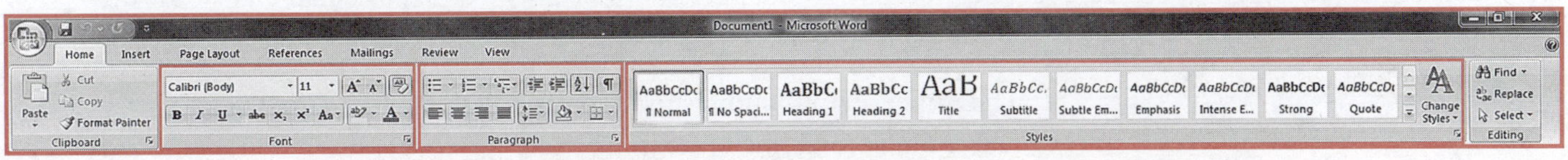

Fig. 4.30 *Formatting text using Font group, Paragraph group and Styles group*

Font group

The font type, size, color and style can be changed using the **Font** group (Fig. 4.31). The tools present in the Font group and their purpose are discussed in Table 4.1.

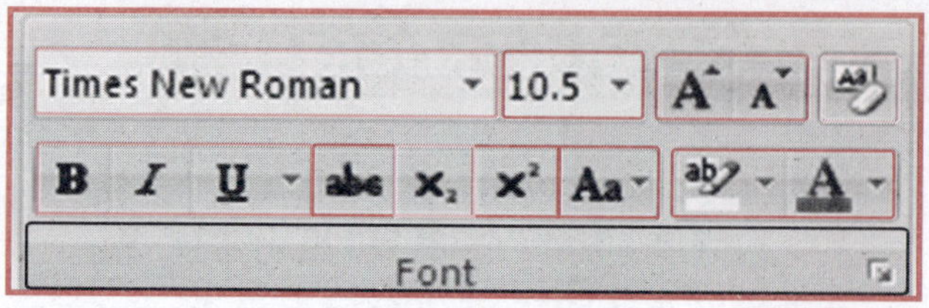

Fig. 4.31 *Font group*

Table 4.1 *Tools present in Font group*

Tools	Purpose
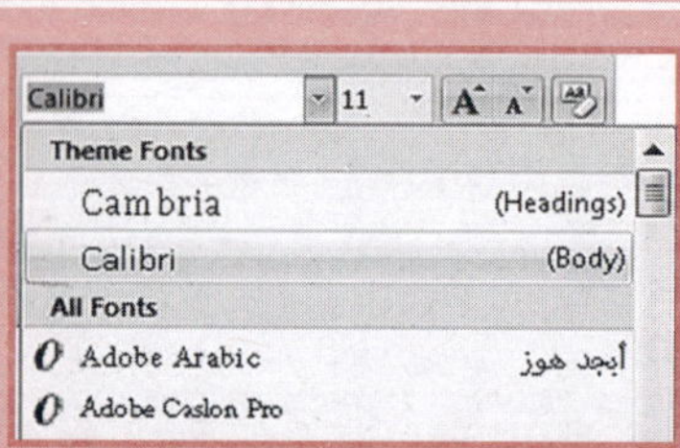	This button is used to change the font type. Click the arrow next to the **Font** option and a list of built-in fonts will be displayed. Choose the font of your choice. The default font in Word 2007 is **Calibri**.
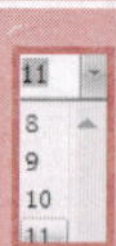	This button is used to change the font size. Click on the arrow next to the **Font Size** option and choose the appropriate size. You can also use **Grow Font** and **Shrink Font** buttons to change the font size.
	The **Grow Font** button is used to increase the size of the font for the selected text.
	The **Shrink Font** button is used to decrease the size of the font for the selected text.
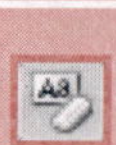	The **Clear Formatting** button is used to clear all the formatting from the selected portion of the text.
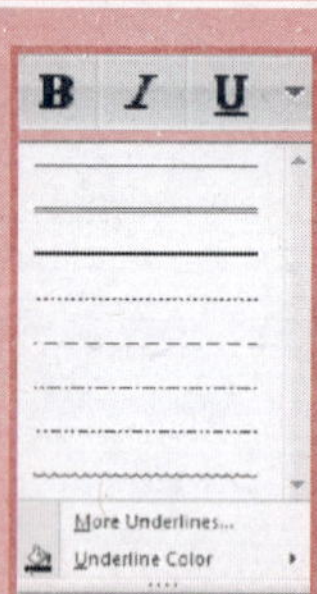	The **Font Styles** are the predefined formatting options which include **B**, **I** and **U** buttons. To make the selected text appear Bold, Italics or to underline it, click on **B**, **I** and **U** buttons. For more underline styles, click on arrow next to **U** button and select different styles of line. Use **More Underline...** option to view more line styles and use **Underline Color** option for colored underlines.
	The **Strikethrough** button is used to draw a line through the middle of the selected text.
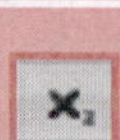	The **Subscript** button is used to display the text as small and below the normal line of text.
	The **Superscript** button is used to display the text as small and above the normal line of text.

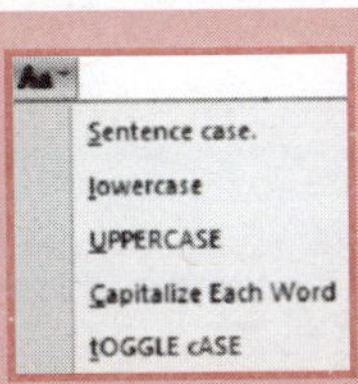	The **Change Case** button is used to change the selected text to UPPERCASE, lowercase, Sentence Case, etc. Click on the arrow next to **Aa** button and select the required style from the drop-down list that appears.
	To highlight the selected text with a color, use the **Text Highlight Color** button. To select a color, click on the arrow next to the button and a drop-down menu appears. Select the color of your choice.
	The **Font Color** button is used to change the color of the text. Click on the arrow next to **A** to select more colors.

You can also change the font styles using the **Font** dialog box (Fig. 4.32). To do so, click on the small arrow on bottom right corner of the **Font group** or press **Ctrl+D** or press **Ctrl+Shift+D**.

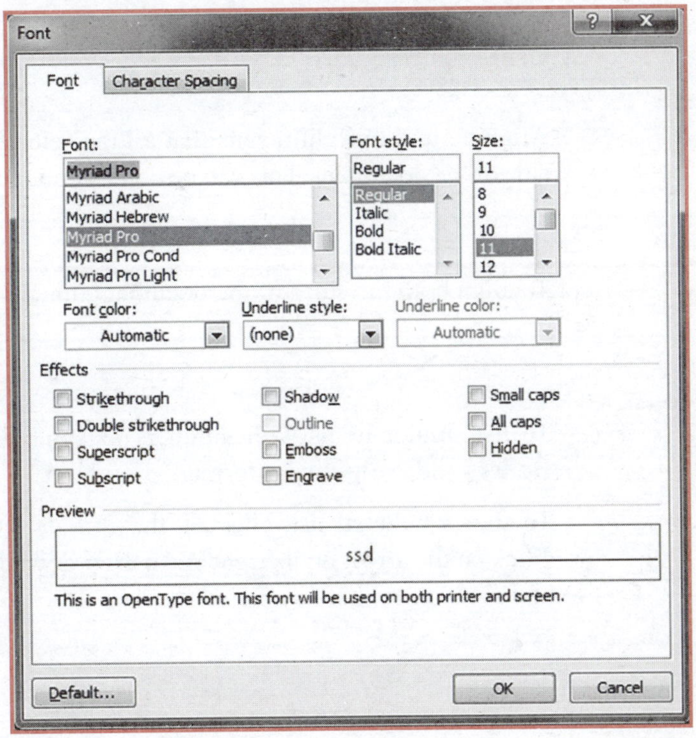

Fig. 4.32 *Font dialog box*

Paragraph group

In a document, it is necessary to align a paragraph to left, right or centre according to the requirements. To list items you need some symbols or numbers to make the paragraph more understandable. The paragraph level formatting includes alignment settings, paragraph indentation, increasing and decreasing line spacing, bullets and numbering, among other things. Tools to carry out these tasks are present in the **Paragraph group** (Fig. 4.33). These tools and their purpose are discussed in Table 4.2.

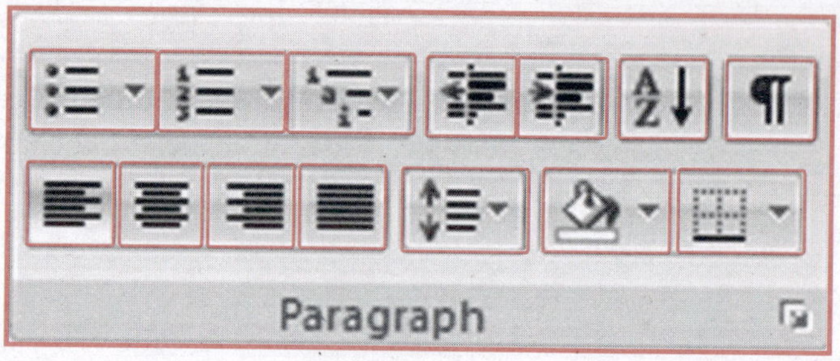

Fig. 4.33 *Paragraph group*

Table 4.2 *Tools present in Paragraph group*

Tools	Purpose
	Aligning text to left means that all the selected lines in a paragraph get aligned to the left side of the document page. But, the right side of the document remains unaligned. To align the selected text to left, select the paragraph and click the **Align Text Left** button.
	Aligning text to centre means that all the selected lines in a paragraph get aligned to the centre of the document. To do this, select the text and click the **Centre** button.
	Aligning text to right means that all the selected lines get aligned to the right side of the document. This can be done by clicking the **Align Text Right** button.
	To align both the sides of the document, the **Justify** button is used.
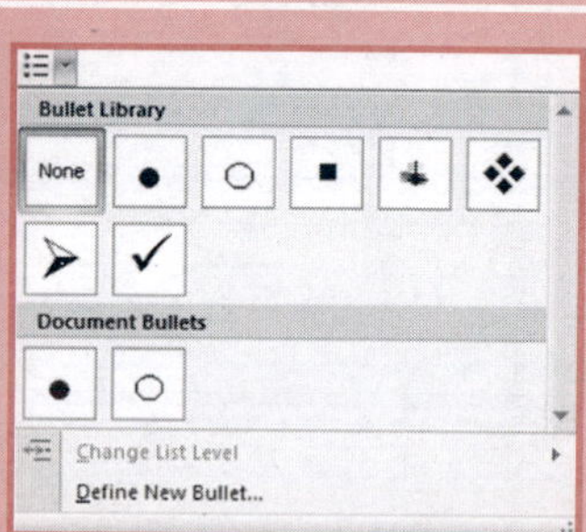	To list similar items with numbers or symbols in a document, you can use **Bullets and Numbering** format. To start a bulleted list, click on the **Bullets** button in the **Paragraph** group. Click on the arrow on its right and a drop-down list appears. Choose bullet style and click on it.
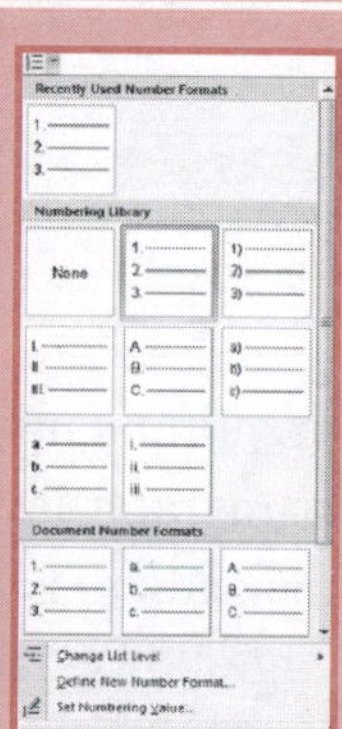	To start a numbered list, click on the **Numbering** button in the **Paragraph** group. Click on the arrow to its right and a drop-down list appears. Choose numbering formats and click on it.

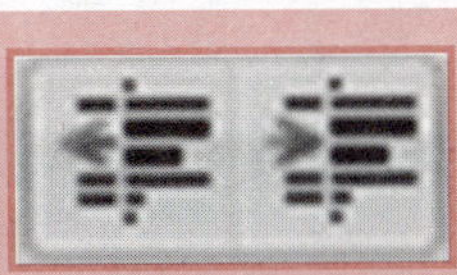

To decrease or increase the indent level of a paragraph, **Decrease Indent** and **Increase Indent** buttons are used. They are available in the **Paragraph** group next to multilevel list button.

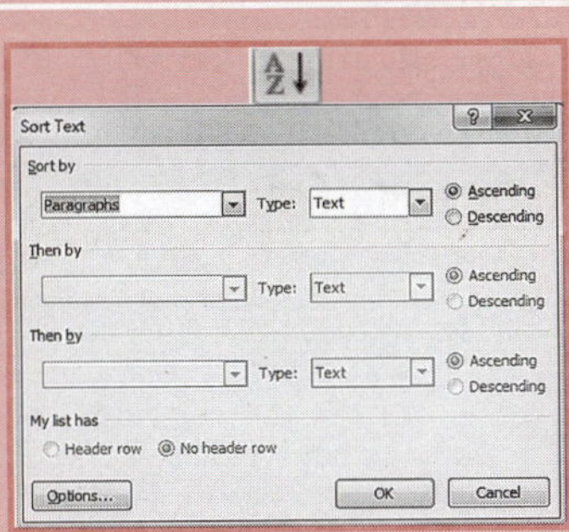

The **Sort** button is used to sort alphabetic data or numeric data in an ascending or descending order.

To sort, select the text and click on the **Sort** button. The **Sort** dialog box appears on the screen. Select the required options in **Sort by:**, **Type:** and **Using:** sections. Select the order: **Ascending** or **Descending** and click on the **OK** button. The sorted text will be shown on the screen.

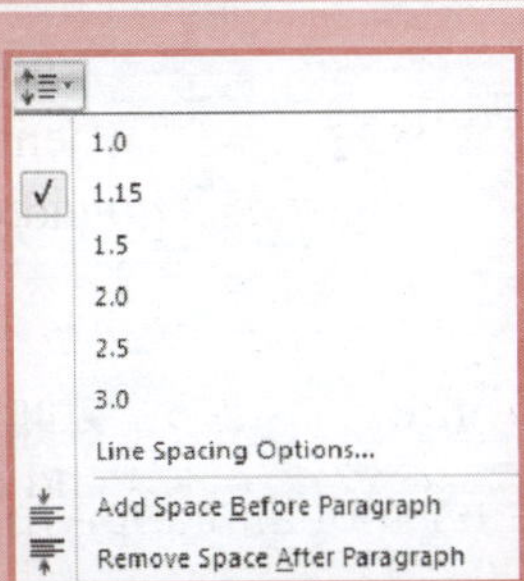

The **Line Spacing** button is used to change the spacing between lines of the text. You can also customise the spaces before and after the paragraph. To do so, click on the **Line spacing** button which is available next to the Justify button and select the spacing option according to your requirement.

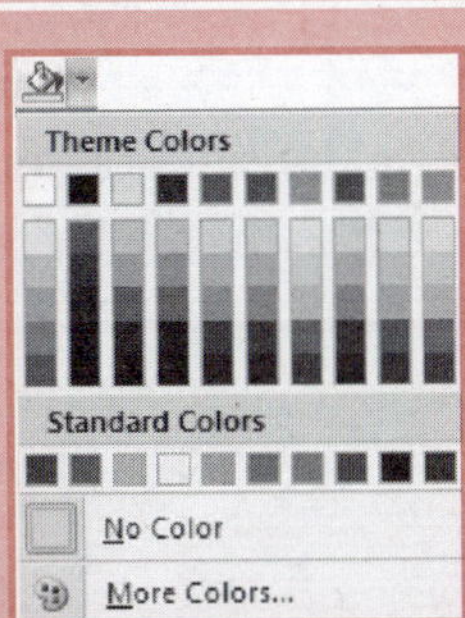

The **Shading** button is used to color the background behind the selected text or paragraph. To do so, click on the arrow next to the Shading button and select any colors for shading.

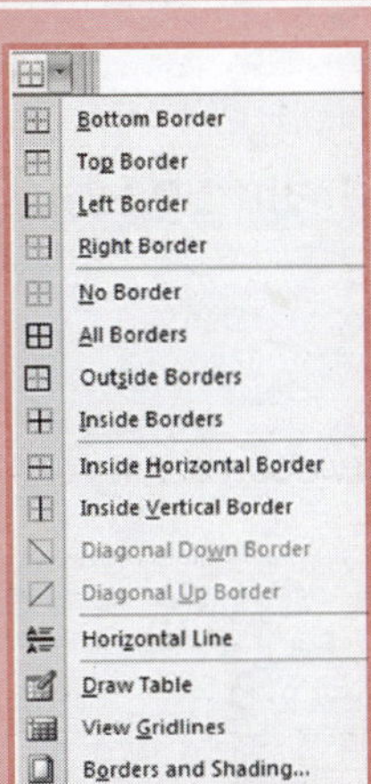

The **Border** button is used to apply and customise borders around selected text or paragraph. To do so, click on the arrow next to the Border button and select the required border.

You can also make these changes using the **Paragraph** dialog box (Fig. 4.34). To open the **Paragraph** dialog box, click on the small arrow on bottom right corner of the **Paragraph** group.

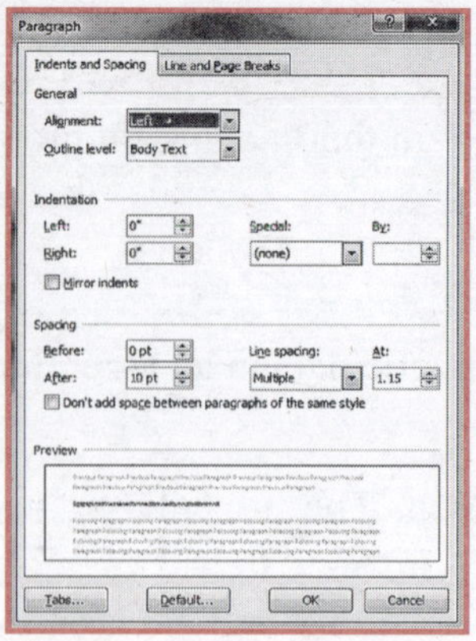

Fig. 4.34 *Paragraph dialog box*

Quick Key

Centre text	Ctrl+E	Two line spacing	Ctrl+2
Left-align	Ctrl+L	Justify	Ctrl+J
Right-align	Ctrl+R	Indent paragraph	Ctrl+M
One line spacing	Ctrl+1	Unindent	Ctrl+Shift+M

Format Painter: This tool is used to copy the format from one place and apply it to another selection (Fig. 4.35). To use Format Painter, follow the steps given below.

Fig. 4.35 *Format painter*

1. Select the text whose formatting effects you want to copy.
2. Click the **Format Painter** tool from **Clipboard** group of the **Home** tab. Note that the mouse pointer changes to a brush.
3. Select the text where you want to apply the same formatting effect and click on it.

NOTE: To copy a formatting effect to multiple texts, double-click on the Format Painter tool and apply it wherever needed.

Styles group

In Word 2007, there are many in-built styles available for your use. They are available in the **Quick Styles** option in **Styles** group of the **Home** tab (Fig. 4.36). You can use a pre-existing style or create a new one and add it to the **Styles** gallery.

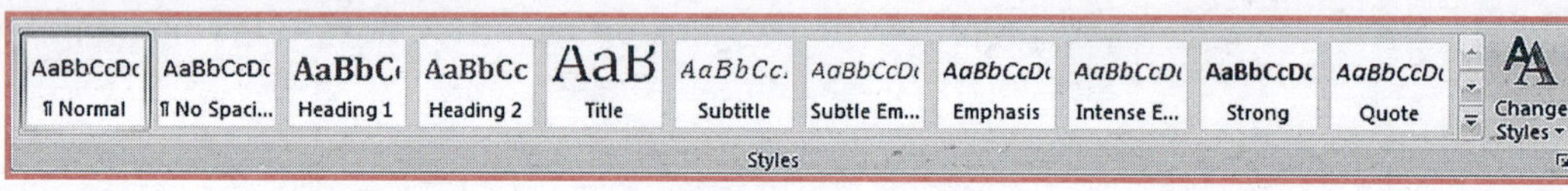

Fig. 4.36 *Styles group*

To apply a style to your text, follow the steps given below.

1. Select the text.
2. On the **Home** tab, in the **Styles** group, click on the dialog box launcher button. In the **Styles** task pane that appears, select the desired style.

   OR

   On the **Home** tab, in the **Styles** group, click on the **More** button and select the desired style from **Styles** gallery (Fig. 4.37) that appears as a drop-down list.

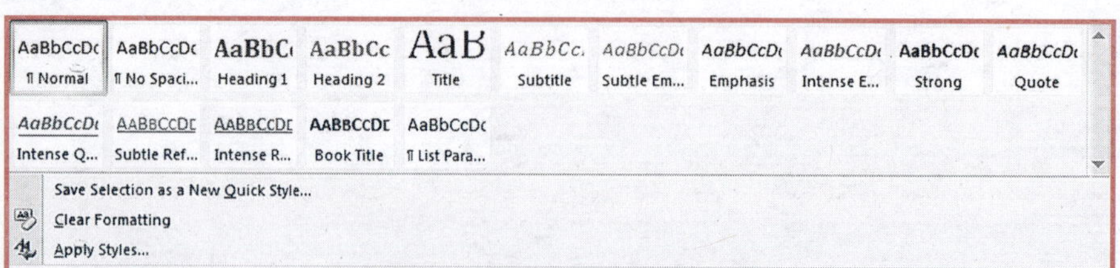

Fig. 4.37 *Styles gallery*

▶ PRINTING A DOCUMENT

The document that you see on your monitor is called a softcopy. If the same document is printed on a paper then it is called a **hard copy**. To take a hard copy of your document, you need to connect your computer to a printer and follow the steps given below.

1. Click on the **Office button**.
2. Select the **Print** option.
3. The **Print** dialog box appears (Fig. 4.38).

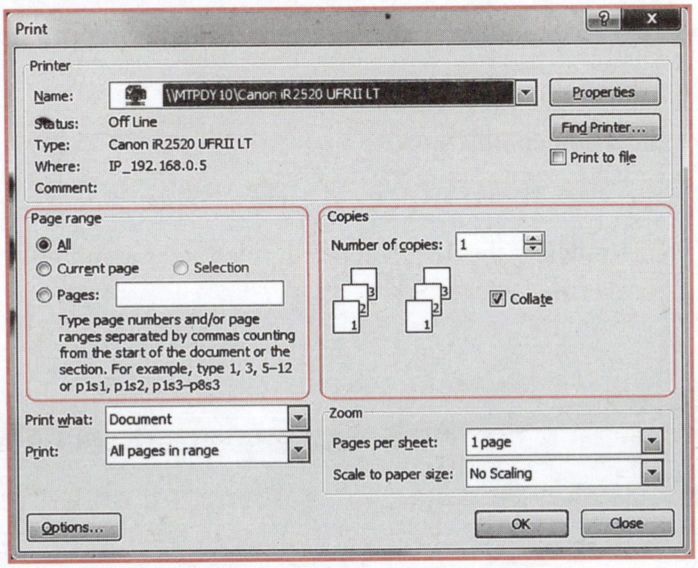

Fig. 4.38 *Print dialog box*

4. Select the printer you are using in the **Name:** box.
5. Under **Page range** frame, select **All** to print all pages; select **Current page** to print only the active page; or select **Pages:** to specify the page number(s) that you want to print.
6. To print more than one copy of your document, under **Copies** frame, type the number of copies in the **Number of copies:** box.
7. Click on the **Properties** button to select the paper size or saved print settings.
8. Click on **OK** to print the document.

Print Preview

Print Preview shows you exactly how your document will look when you print it. It is used to check the correct page layout, adjust margins, reduce document to one page, edit and format text, and check document appearance so that if necessary, you can make changes before printing. All these options are available in the **Print Preview** tab (Fig. 4.39). This tab appears only after you select the **Print Preview** option from the **Office** menu.

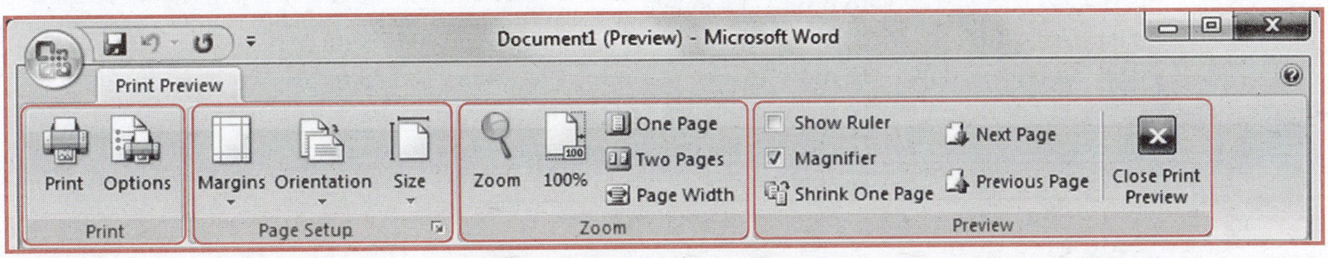

Fig. 4.39 *Print Preview tab*

The **Print Preview** tab has the following groups:

- **Print** group is used to print the document.
- **Page Setup** group has **Margins**, **Page Orientation**, **Size** option.
  - ***Margins:*** To select the margin sizes of the document.
  - ***Page orientation:*** To set the page layout as Portrait or Landscape.
  - ***Size:*** To choose a paper size for printing the document.
- **Zoom** group has **Zoom, 100%, One Page, Two Page** and **Page Width option**.
  - ***Zoom:*** To specify the zoom level.
  - ***100%:*** To zoom the document to 100%.
  - ***One Page, Two page, Page Width:*** To fit the document to one page, two pages or to set the page width.
- **Preview** group allows you to preview the document with ruler and magnifier (to zoom).

FACT FILE

The **Quick Print** option is used to send the document directly to the default printer without making any changes.

Quick Key

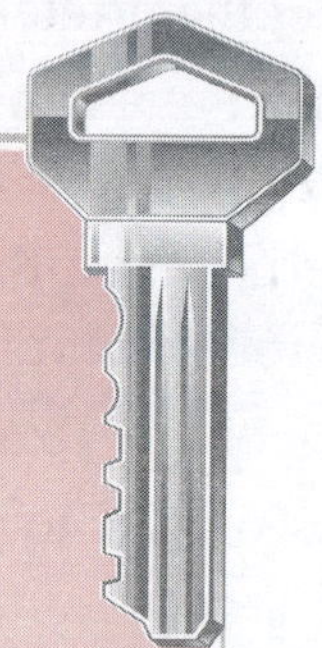

Ctrl + Shift + A	To change all text to capital letters
Ctrl + Shift + K	To change all text to small capital letters
Ctrl + >	To increase the font size
Ctrl + <	To decrease the font size
Ctrl + B	To make the text appear bold
Ctrl + I	To make the text appear italics
Ctrl + U	To underline the selected text
Ctrl + Shift + D	To double underline the text
Ctrl + D	To display the font window
Ctrl + =	To make the text appear as subscript
Ctrl + Shift + =	To make the text appear as superscript
Ctrl + 5	To set 1.5 line spacing
Ctrl + P	To print a document
Alt + Ctrl + I	To switch in or out of print preview
Page up or Page down	To move by one preview page when zoomed out
Ctrl + Home	To move to the first preview page when zoomed out
Ctrl + End	To move to the last preview page when zoomed out
Ctrl + Shift + S	To apply styles
Ctrl + Shift + C	To copy formatting from text

CHECK YOUR PROGRESS

A. Identify the following figure. Explain which tab and group it appears on. Also, give its purpose.

1. 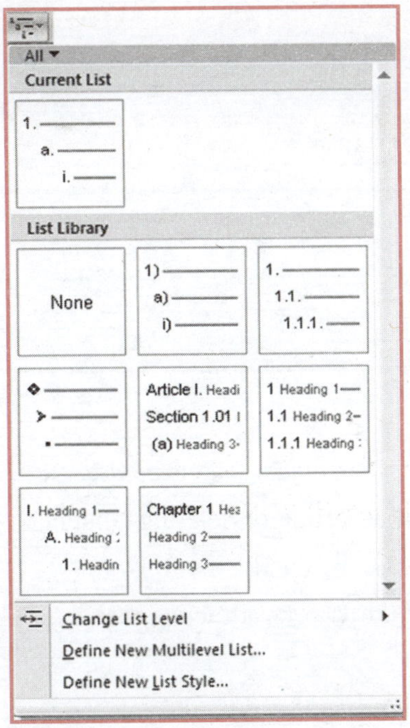

2. 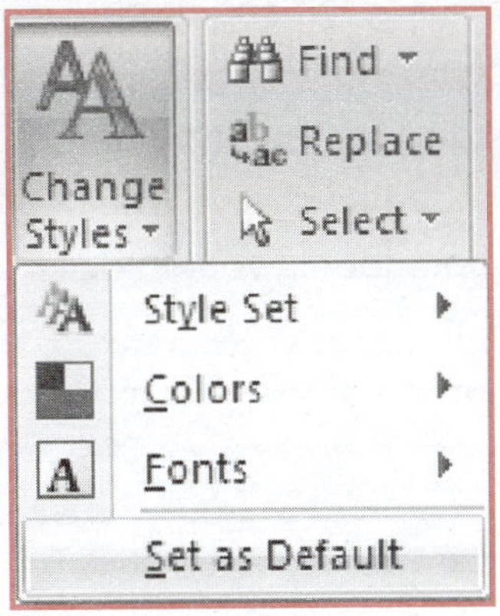

B. Complete the activity given below by following all the instructions.

MOTIVATION

Motivation is enhanced by becoming more realistic and aware of the task ahead and your ability to face the challenge of examination and its anxieties.

Deliberately switch your focus on to the process of studying, rather than the ultimate result (the desired pass or high grade). Study for yourself and not for anyone else.

If there are certain topics that you dread and therefore have a tendency to avoid, break them down into smaller bits; incorporate morale boosters – an enjoyable reward after each small task is completed.

Find out what works for you and what doesn't – avoid the latter. This may sound obvious, but it is surprising how many students persevere with unhelpful and unconstructive methods of studying simply because they always have and it feels strange or worrying to abandon something familiar. Maybe you would find it easier to work with a friend or in a group.

Muralidharan

1. Type the paragraphs given.
2. Set font size to 14 for the heading.
3. Align the heading to centre.
4. Apply bullets for each paragraph.
5. Set font size to 12 for the paragraphs.

6. Set font face as Algerian for the heading and Cambria for the paragraph.
7. Set line spacing as 1.5.
8. Increase the indent at the beginning of each paragraph.
9. Align the paragraphs to left and right.
10. Align the author name to right.
11. Highlight the heading with cyan color.
12. Apply bold and underline style for the heading and author name.
13. Save it as Motivation.docx in your folder.
14. Print the document.

GLOSSARY

- **Change Case:** It is used to change the selected text to uppercase, lowercase, sentence case, etc.
- **Editing:** It is the process of modifying the existing documents by inserting or deleting content.
- **Font Styles:** They are the predefined formatting options and include B, I and U buttons.
- **Formatting:** It is the process of changing the appearance of text into a very attractive manner.
- **Hardcopy:** It is the printed document on a paper.
- **Quick Access Toolbar:** It is a customised toolbar that provides access to commands you use frequently.
- **Quick Styles:** It is used to quickly change the appearance of text, tables and graphics throughout your document by selecting in-built styles and document themes.
- **Softcopy:** It is the document that you see on your monitor.
- **Word Processing Tools:** They are the set of programs used to create, edit, view, search, replace, save and print documents.

NOW YOU KNOW

1. Microsoft Word 2007 is a word processing tool with a range of editing, formatting and layout options.
2. Sort button is used to sort an alphabetic data or a numeric data in an ascending or descending order.
3. Format Painter tool is used to copy the formatting from one place and apply it to another selection.
4. Quick Print is used to send the document directly to the default printer without making any changes.
5. Word 2007 supports exporting your file to PDF and XPS.
6. Microsoft Office Button is located at the top-left corner and displays options, such as, to create a new file, to open an existing document, to save a document and to print a document.
7. A document can be displayed in five different views, namely, Print Layout, Full Screen Reading, Web Layout, Outline and Draft.
8. The default font in Word 2007 is Calibri.
9. Paragraph group contains tools to change the alignment settings, paragraph indentation, line spacing and bullets and numbering.
10. Bullets and Numbering options are used to list a similar item with numbers or symbols in a document.

EXERCISE

FA

A Fill in the blanks.

1. The .... tools are used for text manipulation.
2. The .... cannot be displayed on multiple lines.
3. To jump from one page to another .... button is used.
4. The document views available in Word 2007 are ...., ..., ..., ... and ....
5. Word 2007 allows you to save the word file as .... and ....
6. ...., ... and .... options are present in the Editing group of the Home tab.
7. The .... option is used to strike a line through the middle of the text.
8. To open the Font dialog box, press Ctrl+ .... or Ctrl+ ....+...................................
9. The Quick Styles option is available in .... group of the Home tab.
10. ...., ..., ..., ... and .... are the options available in the Zoom group of the Print Preview tab.

B Multiple Choice Questions.

1. Which of the following is not a Word Processor?
   a. MS Word b. MS Access c. WordStar d. WordPad
2. To set the line spacing as 1.5, ... shortcut key combination is used.
   a. Ctrl + 1 b. Ctrl + 2 c. Ctrl + 5 d. Ctrl + shift + 1
3. The default document name while opening a blank document in Word 2007 is ....
   a. Doc1 b. docx1 c. document1 d. untitled
4. The Replace option is available in .... tab.
   a. Home b. Review c. Mailings d. Insert
5. In a^2, the 2 appears small just above the text. Which effect has been applied?
   a. Decrease font b. Superscript c. Subscript d. Indent
6. The .... tool is used to find out the number of words in a document. HOTS
   a. Count b. Word Count c. Total d. None of these
7. To copy the formatting from one text to another .... tool is used.
   a. Copy b. Copy Format c. Format Painter d. All of these

8. In Word 2007, the .... consists of several tabs in groups with buttons to give commands.

a. toolbar b. menu c. group tool d. Ribbon

9. Word 2007 supports exporting your file to ....

a. PDF and XPS b. PDF and PNG c. DOC and PPT d. None of these

10. To print a document, ... is the shortcut key used.

a. Ctrl + P b. Shift + P c. Alt + P d. Ctrl + Alt + P

C Answer the following questions briefly.

1. What is the Ribbon?
2. Name any four tabs available in Word 2007 Ribbon?
3. You have deleted a portion of your document by mistake. Is it possible to retrieve it? How?
4. What do you mean by formatting?
5. What is the difference between Save and Save As?
6. What is the use of Print Preview tool?
7. What are the tools available in Quick Access Toolbar?
8.  Identify this tool and the tab under which it is available.
9. Is it possible to display you document in different views? It yes, then how?
10. What is a multilevel list?

SA

D Answer the following questions.

1. What is the difference between hard copy and softcopy?
2. Name any two groups and their tools (any two) that are available in Home tab.
3. Name any four themes that can be applied for a document. Which is the default theme? HOTS
4. What are the options available under document views of View tab?
5. What are the tools available in Page Setup group available under Page Layout tab. Write a line about each. HOTS

E Answer the following questions in detail.

1. What are the buttons available under Office button? Write a line about each.
2. Write a note on Format Painter.
3. How are bullets different from numbers? Give steps to apply both. Also, give a real life example where only numbered list can be used.
4. Write steps to customise your Quick Access Toolbar.
5. What are templates? Enlist all the templates available in Word 2007. Write a line on atleast five of them.

Application Based Questions

A. Sameer invited his friends to his house for Bingo game night. Just half an hour before their arrival, Sameer spilled water over all the Bingo cards. Since all the shops near his house are closed, he can't go and buy new cards. He called his sister who suggested that he use Word 2007 to create new cards. Help him achieve this.

B. Meena is a mathematics teacher. She typed the following problem.

$$\text{Prove: } (a+b)^2 = a^2 + 2ab + b^2;$$

$$a^2 + b^2 = (a+b)^2 - 2ab$$

While typing, the text appeared as (a+b)2 = a2 + 2ab + b2; a2 + b2 = (a+b)2 – 2ab. Which formatting feature should she use to make the text appear in the desired format?

C. Piyush created his Curriculum Vitae using MS Word 2007. He wants to preview it before sending it to the printer. Which feature of Word 2007 can he use?

D. Karishma is writing letters to different companies on behalf of her boss. She was given a sample letter by one of her colleagues and was asked to forward it. But on checking she found that the line spacing and listing is not done properly. What options can she use to format the document?

E. Rama is a customer service executive at Cambridge University Press India. She sent an invoice to the librarian of Hill Crest School, Guwahati. The librarian used the invoice as a sample during IT Training. The students were asked to identify atleast five Word 2007 tools used to create the invoice. Look at the invoice and help the students identify, label and explain the tools used.

CAMBRIDGE UNIVERSITY PRESS

INVOICE

Attention: Divya Sharma
Librarian
235-Hill Crest Road
Gauhati, India
Date: 14/04/14

123-456-7890
no_reply@example.com

123 High Street
Anytown County
Postcode

Project Title: Click Start
Project Description: Ty
P.O. Number: 54678
Invoice Number: 55907
Terms: 30 Days

Description	Quantity	Unit Price	Cost
Item 1	55	₹ 10	₹5,500
Item 2	13	₹ 90	₹ 1,170
Item 3	25	₹ 50	₹ 1,250
		Subtotal	₹ 7,920
	Tax	8.25%	₹ 653
		Total	₹ 8,573

Thank you for your business. It is a pleasure to work with you on this project.

Your order will be shipped in 30 days.

Yours sincerely,
Rama Sharma

LAB WORK

A. Create a multi-lingual greeting card. Select your language font and type a greeting message as given below. Apply text effect for the text typed.

B. Follow the instructions given to complete the activity below.

COOL AS A CUCUMBER

Meaning: Very cool, relaxed and in control

Example: Even though Arjun was aware that he was losing, he remained cool as a cucumber.

Origin: 'Cool as a Cucumber' is just alliteration. But alternatively, a cut cucumber can actually feel cool to the touch. This is because they are very moist and evaporation of the moisture provides a cooling effect.

- Type the above content as it is given.
- Align the heading COOL AS A CUCUMBER to centre.
- Apply green color to the heading.
- Apply Tahoma font for the heading, Calibri for the meaning, Comic Sans for example and Arial for origin.
- Insert a suitable picture.
- Apply a suitable page border.
- Add two more pages and apply same format for any two idioms.

C. Type the text given and apply bullets and numbering, as shown below, to complete the activity.

Paulo Coelho – The Brazilian Lyricist and Novelist said:

1. *There is only one thing that makes a dream impossible to achieve: the fear of failure*
2. *A child can teach an adult three things:*
   a. *To be happy for no reason,*
   b. *To always be busy with something, and*
   c. *To know how to demand with all his might that which he desires*
3. *I can choose either to be a victim of the World or an adventure in search of treasure. It is all the question of how I view my life.*
4. *None of us know what might happen even the next minute, yet still we go forward. Because we have faith.*
5. *The simple things are also the most extraordinary things and only the wise can see them.*

MS Office 2010

Updates

In MS Word 2010:

- You have enhanced themes. The **Themes** command is present in the **Themes** group in the **Page Layout** group. Click on the theme buttons and a drop-down list appears which has thumbnail images of built-in themes.
- You have the **paste preview** option that allows to preview the content before it is pasted. It also allows the users to paste only the values or the formatting.
- You have the **Navigation Pane** that appears on the left side of the document. It helps you find text, tables, graphics, comments, footnotes or endnotes, and equations. You can also get a quick look at the structure of your document, or change its structure using the Navigation Pane. You can access the Navigation Pane by clicking **Ctrl + F**.
- You can capture a screenshot using built-in **Screenshot** tool. It is used to grab screen clipping of any program that is not minimized to the taskbar. It is available in the **Illustrations** group in the **Insert** tab.

TEACHER'S NOTES

1. Explain the key difference between editing and formatting to the students.
2. In this chapter students were taught how to print a document. Teach them how to connect a printer to a computer.

5 Word Processing Tools – II

SNAP RECAP

1. Microsoft Word 2007 is a word processing tool that has a range of editing, formatting and layout options.
2. Ribbon is the panel located on top of MS Word 2007 interface. It consists of seven tabs: Home, Insert, Page Layout, References, Mailings, Review and View.
3. Editing is the process of modifying an existing document by inserting or deleting some content, or embedding content in it.
4. Formatting is the process of changing the appearance of the text in a document and presenting it in an attractive layout.

LEARNING OBJECTIVES

You will learn about:

1. Insert Tab
2. Table Tools Tab
3. Page Layout Tab
4. Drawing Tools Tab
5. Reference Tab
6. Mailing Tab
7. Review Tab
8. View Tab

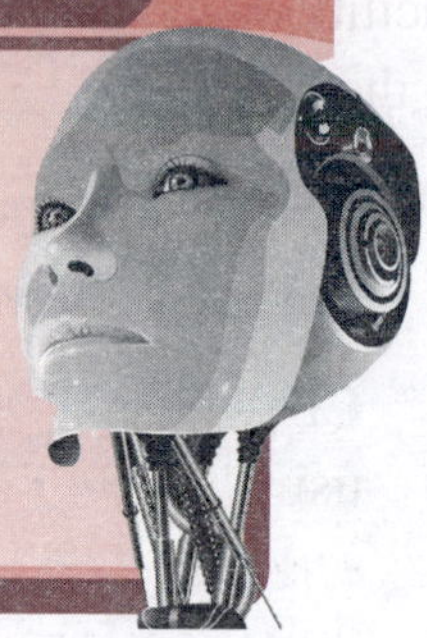

▶ INTRODUCTION

In the previous chapter you learned how to edit and format a document. In this chapter, you will learn more advanced features of MS Word, such as, inserting pictures, charts, shapes, formulae, symbols; reviewing and proofreading your document; mailing your document, adding headers, footers and footnotes. All these options are available in the following tabs: **Insert**, **Page Layout**, **Reference**, **Mailing**, **Review** and **View**. You will learn about these tabs in the following pages. You will also learn about two contextual tabs: **Table Tools** and **Drawing Tools**.

▶ INSERT TAB

Word 2007 allows you to insert pictures, charts, shapes, header, footer, number, text, formulae and more. The **Insert** tab on the Ribbon is used to insert these objects (Fig. 5.1). The **Insert** tab has 7 groups, namely, **Pages**, **Tables**, **Illustrations**, **Links**, **Header & Footer**, **Text** and **Symbols**. Each group is task-oriented and divided into sub-tasks that fulfill a specific purpose. For example, the **Illustrations** group is used to add graphics to a document. Each command/option on the group – **Picture**, **Clip Art**, **Shapes**, **SmartArt** and **Chart** – is there to accomplish this task.

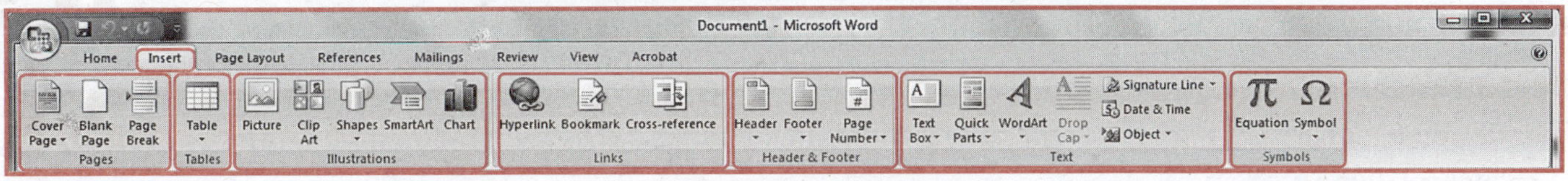

Fig. 5.1 *Insert tab*

Pages group

Pages group helps you to add or delete pages, insert blank pages anywhere in the document or add a cover page at the beginning of a document (Fig. 5.2). There are three options in this group. They are:

Fig. 5.2 *Pages group*

- ***Cover Page tool:*** It is used to insert a fully formatted cover page. The page is fully designed and formatted. All you have to do is to fill in the content. To add a cover page, click on the **Cover Page** button. A drop-down list consisting of different predefined styles of cover pages will appear. Select the cover page you desire to use.
- ***Blank Page tool:*** It is used to insert a new blank page at the current position in the document.
- ***Page Break tool:*** It is used to give a page break.

Tables group

Data can be presented in the form of table, that is, in rows and columns. Word 2007 provides the facility of creating tables in a document. You can insert or draw a table in a document using the options available in **Tables** group (Fig. 5.3) of the **Insert tab**.

Fig. 5.3 *Tables group*

To create a table, follow the steps given below.

1. Place the cursor on the page where you want to add a new table.
2. Click on **Insert** tab and click on **Table** option (Fig. 5.4). You can create a table by using one of the four ways given below:
   - Highlight the number of rows and columns in the grid that appear in the drop-down list.

     OR
   - Click on the **Insert Table...** option and enter the number of rows and columns.

     OR
   - Click on the **Draw Table** option and create your table by clicking and entering the rows and columns.

     OR
   - Click on **Quick Tables** option and choose a table.
3. Place your cursor in the cell and type the content. To move to the next column, press the **Tab** key.

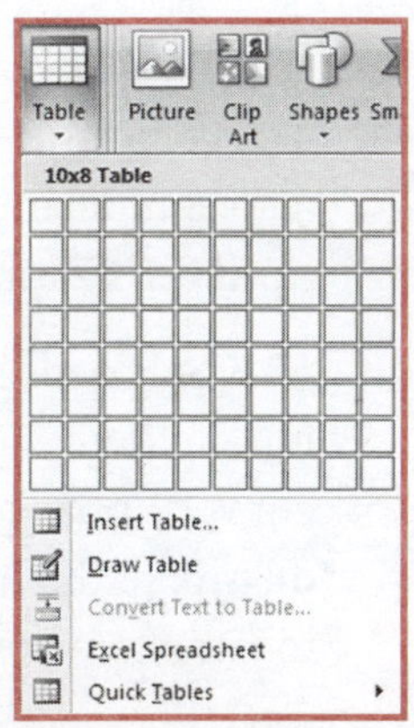

Fig. 5.4 *Inserting a table*

▶ TABLE TOOLS TAB

In Word 2007, you can modify the structure of a table. To do so, click on the table and two new tabs, namely, **Design** and **Layout** appears on the Ribbon. These tabs have options to change the design and layout of the table.

Design tab

Under design tab, there are three different groups pertaining to tables. They are: **Table Style Options**, **Table Styles** and **Draw Borders** (Fig. 5.5).

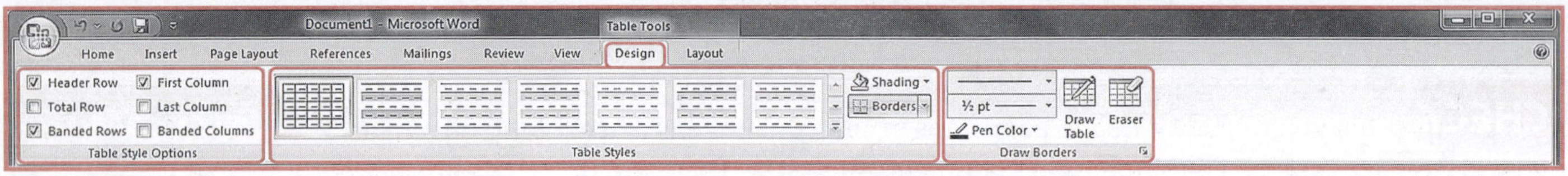

Fig. 5.5 *Design tab*

- ***Table Styles group:*** It provides you a list of pre-formatted tables. To insert a table, select any one design from the **Table Style** group and click on it. To apply a border to a table, click on **Border tool** from the **Table Styles group**. You can apply border for the bottom, top, left and right side or for all sides by selecting the appropriate option. The **Shading tool** is used to apply the background color behind the selected text or paragraph.

- ***Draw Border group:*** It has options like **Line Style**, **Line Weight**, **Pen Color**, **Draw Table** and **Eraser**. The **Line Style** is to change the style of the line. The **Line Weight** is to change the width of the line. The **Pen color** is to change the color of the line. The **Draw Table** is for drawing the border of a table. The **Eraser** is used to erase the border of a table.

Layout tab

To format a table, click on the table and then click on the **Layout** tab on the Ribbon. Layout tab has six groups: **Table**, **Rows & Columns**, **Merge**, **Cell size**, **Alignment** and **Data** (Fig. 5.6).

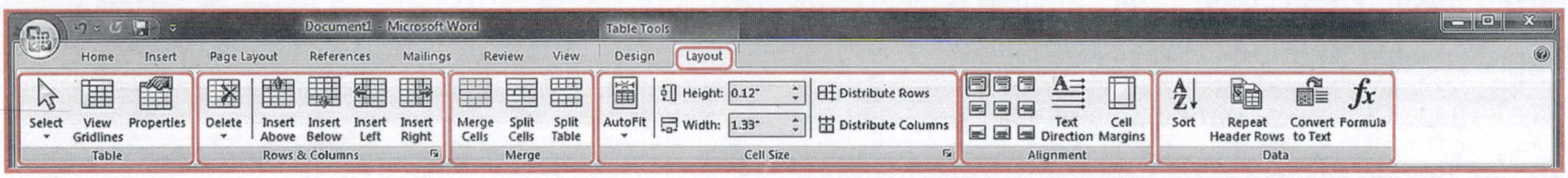

Fig. 5.6 *Layout tab*

- ***Table group:*** You can view and modify tables using **View Gridlines** and **Properties** tool from the **Table** group.

- ***Rows & Columns group:*** To delete or to insert a row or a column from a selected position, click the respective button from **Rows & Columns** group.

- ***Merge group:*** To merge two or more selected cells into one cell, the **Merge Cells** tool is used. You can also split a single cell to multiple cells using the **Split Cells** tool. To split a table into two tables, use the **Split Table** tool.

- ***Cell Size group:*** The **AutoFit** tool is used to resize the column width automatically based on the size of the text in them. You can set the table column width and row height, based on the window size. You can also convert it back to use fixed column width. The **Distribute Rows** and the **Distribute Columns** tool is used to distribute the height and width of the selected rows and columns equally between them. The **Cell Margins** tool customises the cell margin and the spacing between the cells.

- ***Alignment group:*** This tool is used to align the text to left, right, top, bottom and centre of a table. You can change the text direction of a cell by clicking the **Text Direction** tool. Click the button multiple times to cycle through the available direction. The **Cell Margin** tool is used to customise cell margins and the spacing between cells.

- ***Data group:*** In data group, you have **Sort**, **Repeat Header Rows**, **Convert to Text** and **Formula** tools. The data in a table can be sorted in an ascending or descending order. Sorting can be done on both numeric and alphabetic data using the **Sort** tool. The **Repeat Header Rows** tool is used to repeat the header row on every page (that is if the table extends beyond a single page). You can also convert text columns separated by tab characters and commas into a table or a table can also be converted into text by selecting the **Convert Text** tool. To add a formula to a cell and perform simple calculation, the **Formula** tool is used.

CHECK YOUR PROGRESS

A. Identify on which tab and group does the following exist. Describe their function in one line.

1. 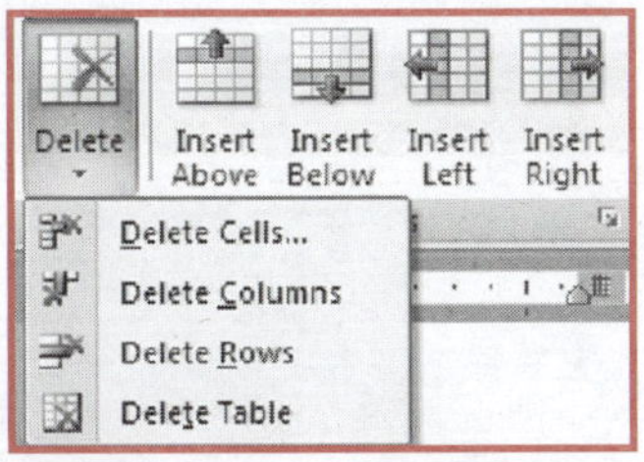

2. 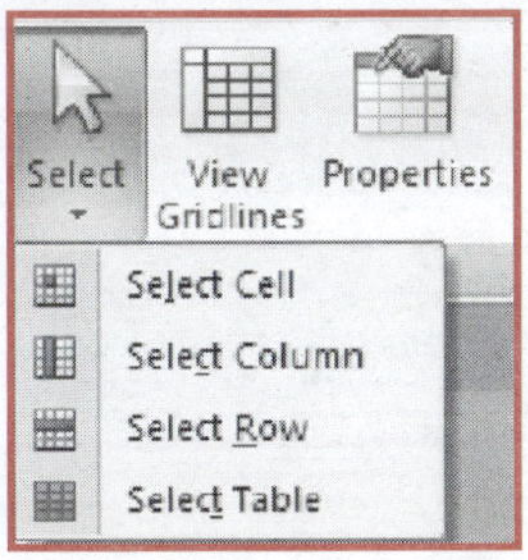

3. 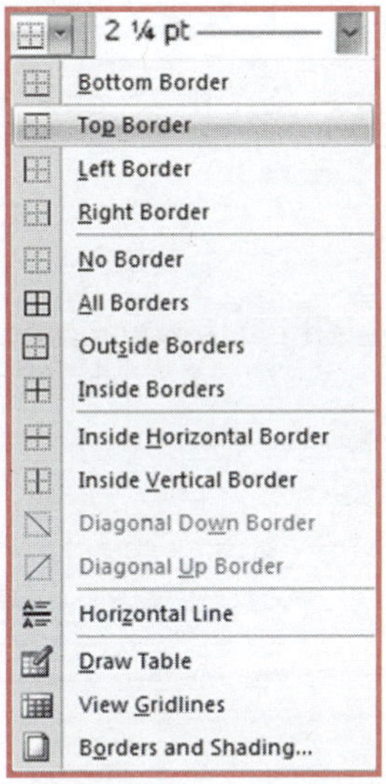

B. Follow the instructions given below to complete the activity.

1. Start MS Word 2007.
2. Create a new document.
3. Insert a table consisting of four columns.
4. Set the height of the row as 1.
5. Create a header with following tab headings: Roll No, Student Name, Class and Section, ICT Marks.
6. Split the column ICT Marks into two cells and name it as Skills and Aptitude.
7. Enter 20 records.
8. Sort the Student name column in alphabetical order.
9. Click Repeat Header Row from Data group of Layout tab to repeat the header for all pages.
10. Using Formula tool, sum up all the marks and find out the average of the same.
11. Apply centre alignment to the whole table.
12. Give a suitable border for the table.

C. Insert a table in Word 2007 to create the following bill.

S.NO	ITEM NAME	PRICE (INR)
1	Boost 500G	175.00
2	Sugar 2KG	90.00
3	Tea 500G	150.00
4	Chocos 500G	120.00
5	Olive Oil 500G	180.00
	TOTAL	715.00

Illustrations group

This group helps you insert pictures, clip art, shapes, SmartArt and charts into a document (Fig. 5.7).

Fig. 5.7 *Illustrations group*

Picture tool

The Picture tool is used to insert a picture file which is already stored on your computer.

To insert a picture file, follow the steps given below.

1. Place the cursor where you want the picture to be inserted in your document.
2. Click on the **Insert** tab on the Ribbon.
3. Go to the **Picture** tool in the **Illustrations** group.
4. The **Insert Picture** dialog box opens. Select the picture you wish to include (Fig. 5.8).
5. Click on **Insert** button at the bottom.
6. The picture is added to your document.

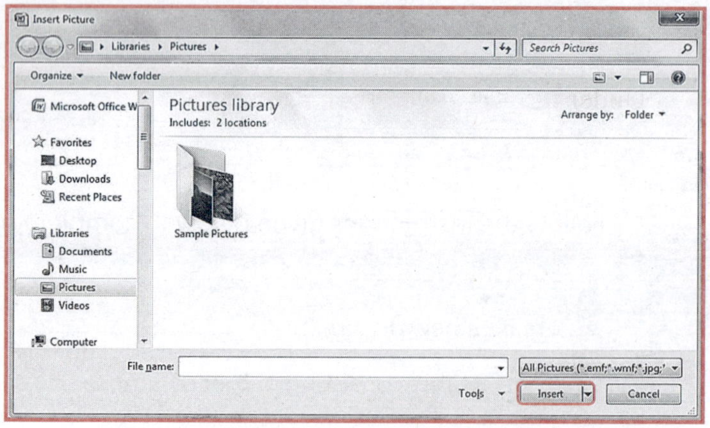

Fig. 5.8 *Insert picture dialog box*

Format tab

When you insert a picture in a document, a new tab named **Picture Tools Format** appears on the Ribbon (Fig. 5.9). This tab is to change the alignment, size, color, frame, style and outline of the picture. You can also remove unwanted portions of the picture using options in this tab.

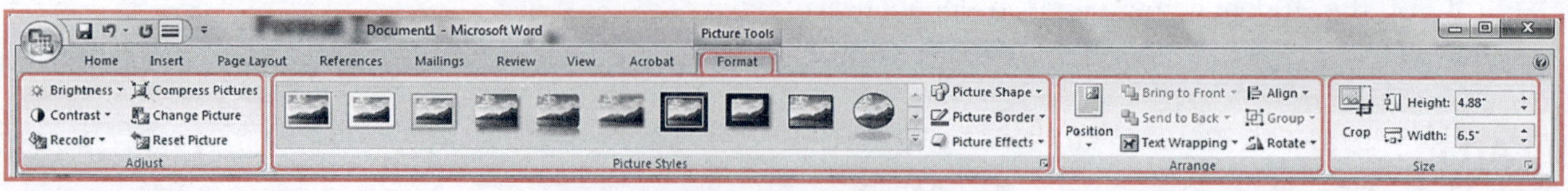

Fig. 5.9 *Picture Tools Format tab*

Picture Tools Format tab has four groups. They are: **Adjust**, **Picture Styles**, **Arrange** and **Size**.

- Under the **Adjust** group you have six tools to adjust various factors of the picture. They are:
  - ***Brightness:*** This tool is used to increase or decrease the brightness of the picture.
  - ***Contrast:*** This tool is used to increase or decrease the contrast of the picture.
  - ***Recolor:*** This tool is used to recolor the picture and to give a stylised effect such as, grayscale and sepia tone to the pictures.
  - ***Compress Pictures:*** This tool is used to reduce the size of the picture.
  - ***Change Picture:*** This tool is used to change the picture while preserving the formatting and size of the current picture.
  - ***Reset Picture:*** This tool is used to discard all of the formatting changes made to the picture.
- Under the **Picture Styles** group you have four tools to format the picture. They are:
  - ***Picture Styles:*** This tool is used to apply a frame to the picture. There are about 28 ready-made frames available in this tool.
  - ***Picture Shape:*** This tool is used to change the shape of the picture all the while preserving all the formatting.
  - ***Picture Border:*** This tool is used to apply the color, width and line style for the outline of the selected picture.
  - ***Picture Effects:*** This tool is used to apply a visual effect such as, shadow, glow, reflection and 3-D rotation to the picture.
- Under the **Arrange** group of **Picture Tools Format** tab you have seven tools. They are:
  - ***Position:*** This tool is used to position the selected picture on the page. The text is automatically set to wrap around the picture.
  - ***Text wrapping:*** This tool is used to change the way text wrap around the selected picture.
  - ***Align:*** This tool is used to align the edges of multiple selected objects.
  - ***Rotate:*** This tool is used to rotate or flip the selected object.
  - ***Group:*** This tool is used to group several objects together so that they can be treated as a single object.
  - ***Bring to Front** and **Send to Back:*** These tools are used to bring the selected picture infront of all objects or send the selected picture to back.
- Under the **Size** group of **Picture Tools Format** tab you have three tools. They are:
  - ***Crop:*** This tool is used to crop the picture as per your requirement.
  - ***Height:*** and ***Width:*** These tools are used to increase or decrease the height and width of the picture.

Clip Art tool

The Clip Art gallery is a collection of predefined pictures based on various categories. The **Clip Art** option is available in the **Illustrations** group of the **Insert** tab (Fig. 5.10).

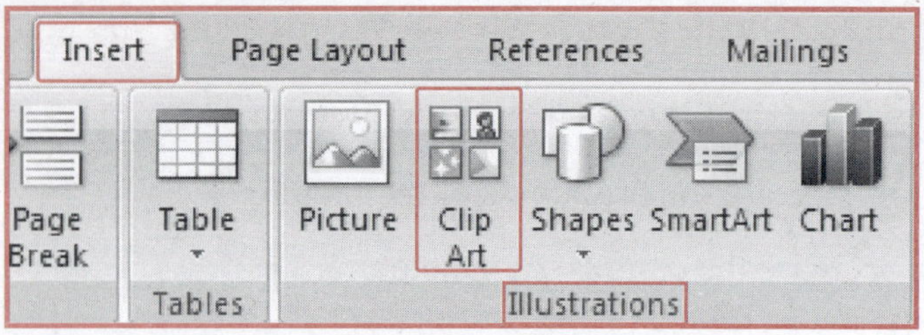

Fig. 5.10 *Clip Art*

Fig. 5.11 *Clip Art task pane*

To insert a picture from Clip Art gallery, follow the steps given below.

1. Place your cursor where you want the picture to be inserted.
2. Click on the **Insert** tab on the Ribbon.
3. Click on the **Clip Art** button.
4. The **Clip Art task pane dialog box** (Fig. 5.11) appears on the right side of the document.
5. Type the desired keyword in the **Search for:** column and click on **Go** to search.
6. Choose the picture you want and click on **Insert button** or just double-click on the image.
7. The image will be added to your document.

NOTE: You can adjust, align and resize this picture using **Picture Tools Format** tab.

Shapes tool

The **Shapes** tool under the **Insert** tab provides various drawing tools such as Lines, Block Arrows, Geometric Shapes, Flowcharts, Callouts, Stars and Banners. You can select, insert and modify these graphics objects using tools given in the **Drawing Tools Format** tab that appears after you insert a shape.

To insert a shape using **Shapes** tool in a document, follow the steps given below.

1. Place your cursor where you want the shape to be inserted.
2. Click the **Insert** tab on the Ribbon.
3. Click on the **Shapes** tool in the **Illustrations** group.
4. Select the ready-made shape from the drop-down list (Fig. 5.12).
5. Note that your mouse pointer changes to the **+** symbol.
6. Drag your mouse to draw the shape on your page.

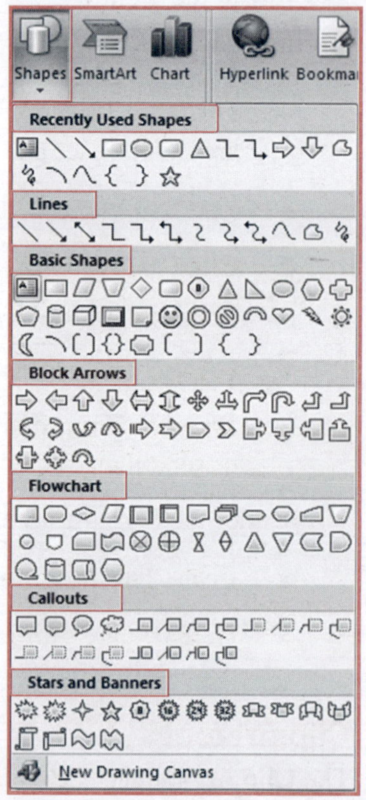

Fig. 5.12 *Inserting shapes*

When you click on the inserted shape, a new tab **Drawing Tools Format** tab appears on the Ribbon (Fig. 5.13). It has six groups.

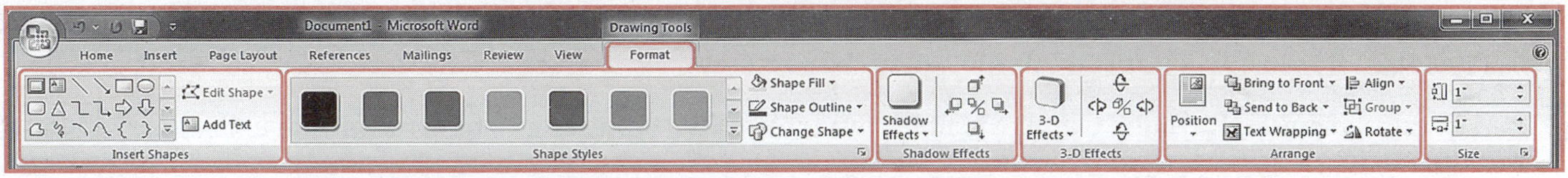

Fig. 5.13 *Drawing Tools Format tab*

- ***Insert Shapes:*** This group is used to insert various shapes into the picture document, edit the added shape and add text to the shapes. It has **Insert Shapes**, **Edit Shape** and **Edit Text** tools.
- ***Shape Styles:*** This group is used to change the overall style of the shape. The **Shape Fill** option is used to fill the inserted shape with a solid color, a gradient, a texture or a picture. The **Shape Outline** option is used to specify the line style, color and width for the outline of the shape.
- ***Shadow Effects:*** This group is used to apply the shadow effects to the inserted shape.
- ***3-D Effects:*** This group is used to apply 3-D effects to the inserted shape.
- ***Arrange:*** This group is used to position the shape along with text.
- ***Size:*** This group is used to adjust the height and width of the shape.

FACT FILE

In Word 2003, you could draw lines and shapes using **Drawing** toolbar.

SmartArt tool

SmartArt is a collection of graphics you can use to organise and visually communicate information within a document. It includes processes, list, workflow, relationship and matrix.

To insert a SmartArt into a document, follow the steps given below.

1. Place your cursor where you want the SmartArt to be included.
2. Click on the **Insert** tab in the **Illustrations** group of the Ribbon.
3. Click on the a **SmartArt** button.
4. **Choose a SmartArt Graphic** dailog box appears (Fig. 5.14). Select the SmartArt you wish to include into your document.

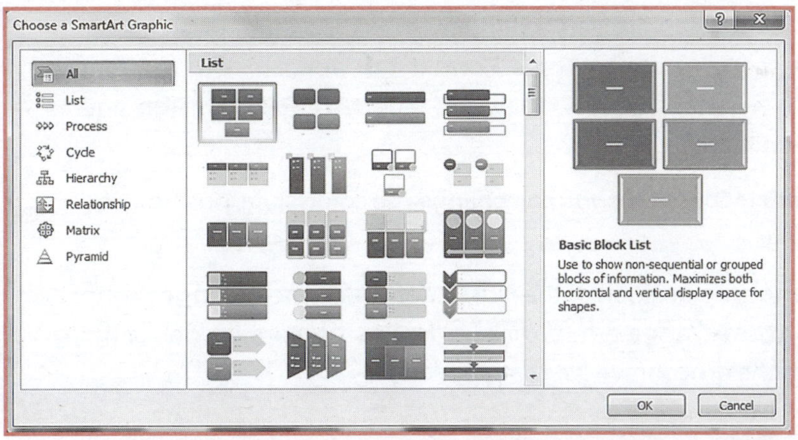

Fig. 5.14 *Choose a SmartArt Graphic dialog box*

5. Click on **OK**.

When you click on the inserted graphic, two new tabs **Design** and **Format** appear on the Ribbon. These tabs are used to change the design and format of the SmartArt graphic.

- **Create Graphic**, **Layouts**, **Change Colors**, **SmartArt Styles**, **Reset** groups are available under the **Design** tab.
- **Shapes**, **Shape Styles**, **Word Art** and **Arrange** groups are available under the **Format** tab.

ACTIVITY

To insert an illustration in a Word document and format it.

1. Click on the **Insert** tab.
2. In the **Illustrations** group, click on the **Picture** option to insert a photograph; on the **Clip Art** option to insert a clip art; the **Shapes** option to insert a shape or the **SmartArt** option to insert a SmartArt.

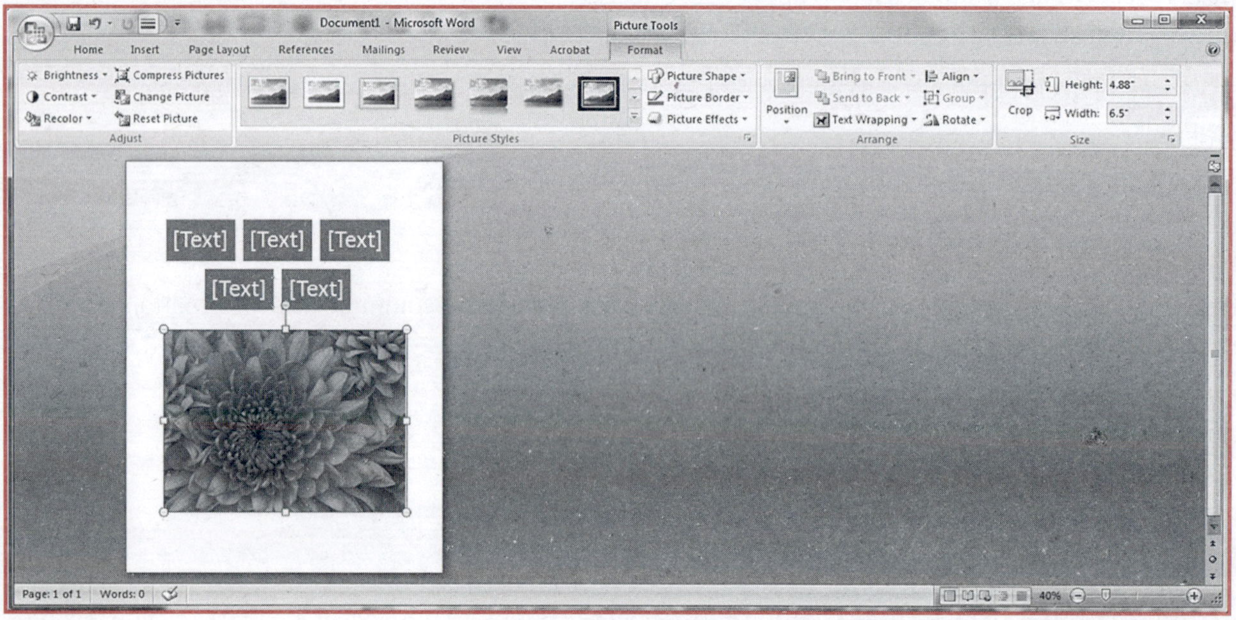

3. The moment you enter an illustration, the corresponding contextual tabs appear. The **Picture Tools Format** tab appears when you insert a picture or a clip art. When you insert a shape, **Drawing Tools Format tab** appears. On inserting a SmartArt, the two new tabs appear. They are: **SmartArt Tools Design** and **SmartArt Tools Format** tabs.
4. Using options present in these tabs you can change the color, style, position and size of the illustrations.

   For example, to change the position of the illustration, go to the **Arrange** group in the **Format** tab. In the **Arrange** group, click on the **Position** option. Select the desired option from the drop-down list that appears.

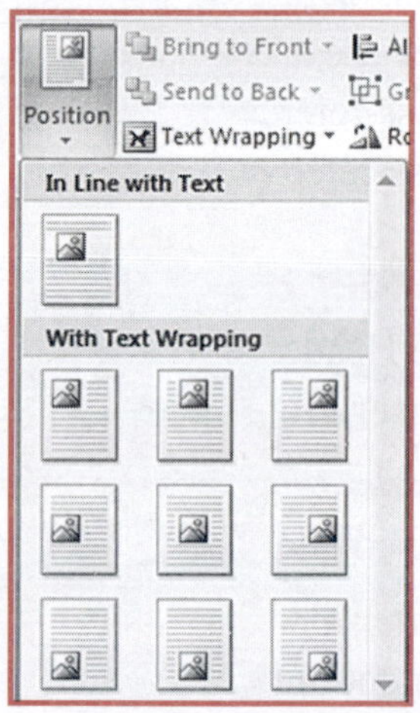

Chart tool

This tool is used to insert a chart into a document. A chart is the pictorial representation of data. It is used to compare data. After inserting a chart, click on it and note that three new tabs **Design**, **Layout** and **Format** appears on the Ribbon. These tabs are used to modify the design, layout and format of the chart (Fig. 5.15).

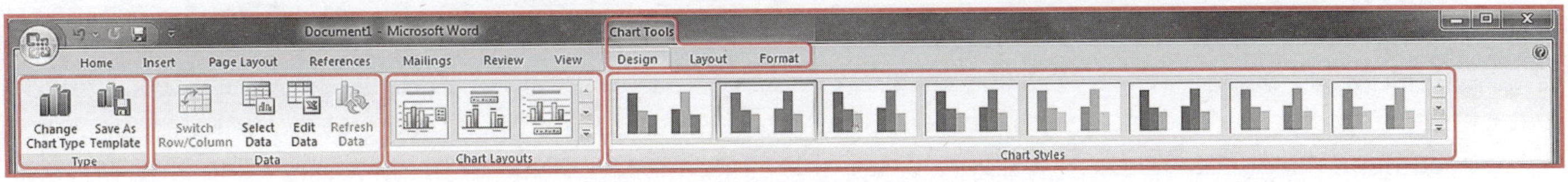

Fig. 5.15 *Chart Tools tab*

NOTE: You will learn more about Charts later.

Links group

Under Insert tab, another important group is **Links**. This group has three tools. They are: **Hyperlink**, **Bookmark** and **Cross-reference** (Fig. 5.16).

Fig. 5.16 *Links group*

Hyperlink: The Hyperlink tool is used to create a link to a web page, a picture, a program or an email address. Select the text or picture that you want to display as the hyperlink. Click on the **Hyperlink** button. The **Insert Hyperlink** dialog box appears. You can create hyperlinks within an **Existing File** or **Web Page**, **Place in The Document**, **Create New Document** and **Email Address**. Select the required hyperlink and click on **OK**.

FACT FILE

Bookmark names must begin with a letter. It can contain letters, numbers or underscore.

Bookmark: The Bookmark tool is used to assign a name to a specific point in a document. You can make a hyperlink to jump directly to a bookmark location. Select the text or picture you want as bookmark. Click on the **Bookmark** button. **Bookmark** dialog box opens. Name the bookmark, select its type and click on **Add**.

Cross-reference: The Cross-reference tool is used to include references from one part of the document to another. They are automatically updated. So, if the content is moved, the cross-reference is automatically updated. Cross-references are inserted as hyperlinks by default. Click on the **Cross-reference** button in the **Insert tab** to add cross-reference. The **Cross-reference** dialog box appears. Select the desired cross-reference and click on **Insert**.

Header & Footer group

The Header, Footer and Page number tools are available under **Header & Footer** group (Fig. 5.17).

Fig. 5.17 *Header & Footer group*

Header tool: It is used to create or edit the header content of the document. The content of the header will appear on top of each page in a document.

Footer tool: It is used to create or edit the footer content of the document. The content of the footer will appear at the bottom of each page in a document.

Page Number tool: It is used to insert page numbers to all the pages of a document.

To insert header and footer information such as page numbers, date or title, you first need to decide if you want the information in the header or in the footer. Then follow the steps given below to insert them into your document.

1. Click on the **Insert** tab on the Ribbon.
2. Go to the **Header & Footer** group.
3. Click on the **Header** button to insert a header, the **Footer** button to insert a footer or the **Page Number** button to add page number. A drop-down list containing all the built-in style will appear. Choose one as per your requirement. The Header/Footer/Page Number section along with the preview will appear on your document. Also, note that a new **Header & Footer tab** appears. Type in the necessary data.
4. Go to the **Header & Footer** tab and click on **Close Header and Footer** option to exit.

Text group

Text Box, **Quick Parts**, **WordArt**, **Drop Cap**, **Signature Line**, **Date & Time** and **Object** tools are available in the **Text group** under the **Insert** tab (Fig. 5.18).

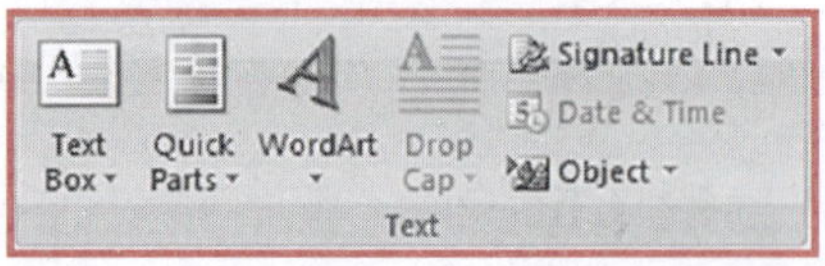

Fig. 5.18 *Text group*

Text Box: This tool is used to insert preformatted text boxes into a document.

Quick Parts: This tool is used to insert reused parts of the content including fields and document properties, such as, title, author name or any other preformatted snippets you create.

WordArt: WordArt is a collection of preformatted text. This tool is used to insert decorative text into a document.

FACT FILE

There are 30 predefined text styles available in WordArt gallery.

ACTIVITY

To insert WordArt in a document.

1. Click on the **Insert** tab.
2. Select the **WordArt** tool from the **Text** group.
3. From the drop-down list select a style.
4. Type the text to be formatted and displayed in the **Edit WordArt Text** dialog box that appears on the screen.
5. Set the font type, size and style.
6. Click on the **OK** button.

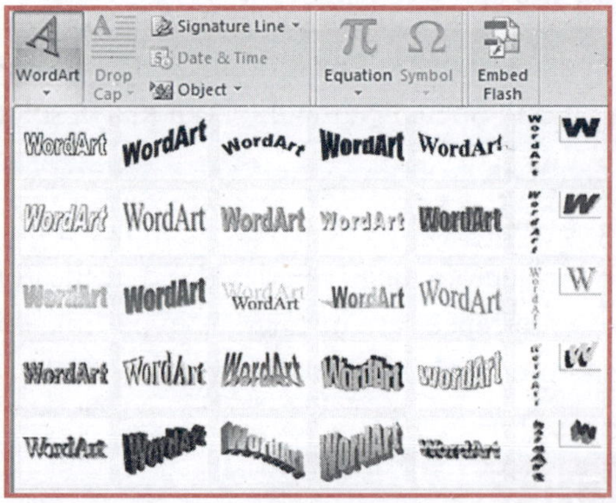

Drop Cap: Drop Cap is a special effect that can be applied to the first letter of the paragraph. It creates a large capital letter at the beginning of the paragraph. This tool is used to apply drop cap effect.

Signature Line: This tool is used to insert a signature line that specifies the individual who must sign. A digital signature requires a digital ID from a certified Microsoft partner.

Date & Time: This tool is used to insert the System Date and Time into a document.

Object: This tool is used to embed an object into a document.

Symbols group

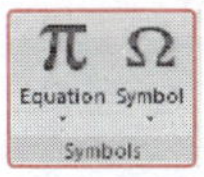

Word 2007 also allows you to insert mathematical equations. **Equation** and **Symbol** tools available under **Symbols** group in the **Insert** tab are used for this purpose.

To access the mathematical equations tool, follow the steps given below.

1. Place your cursor in the document where you want the equation to be added.
2. Click on the **Insert** tab on the **Ribbon**.
3. Click the **Equation** button on the **Symbols** group (Fig. 5.19).
4. Choose the appropriate equation and structure from the drop-down list.

   OR

   Click on **Insert New Equation** tool to write your own equation. To edit the equation, click on the equation to open **Equation Tools Design** tab in the Ribbon (Fig. 5.20).

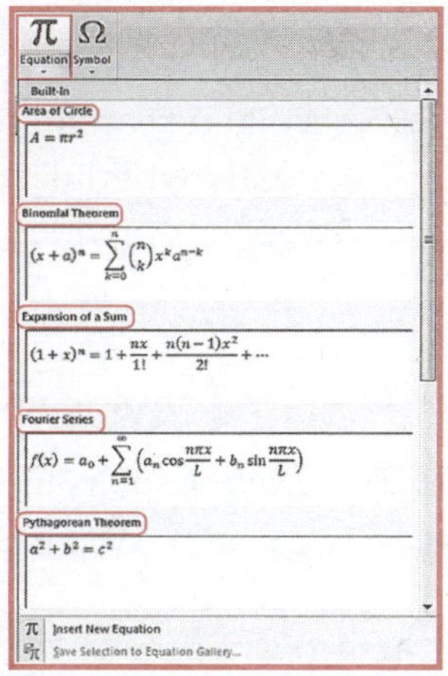

Fig. 5.19 *Inserting equations*

Fig. 5.20 *Equation Tools Design tab*

In Word 2007 you can insert special characters and symbols using **Symbol** tool under **Symbols** group of the **Insert** tab. To insert special characters and symbols, follow the steps given below.

1. Place the cursor in the document where you want the symbol or the special character to be inserted.
2. Click on the **Insert** tab on the Ribbon.
3. Click on the **Symbol** button from the **Symbols** group.
4. From the drop-down list, choose the appropriate symbol (Fig. 5.21).

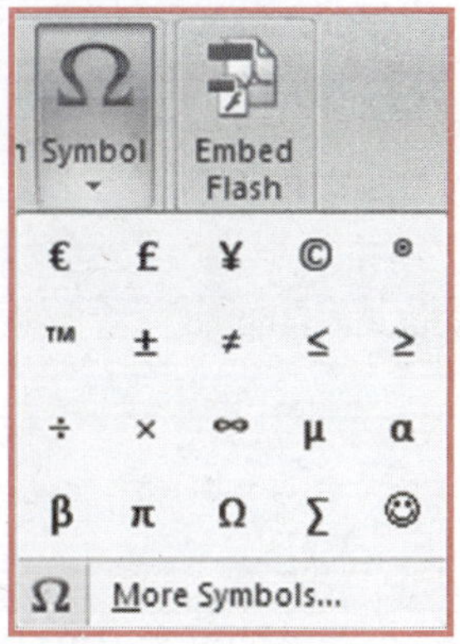

Fig. 5.21 *Inserting symbols*

CHECK YOUR PROGRESS

A. Make two cover pages for your projects. One will be for an English project and another for a Mathematics project.

B. Explore the Design and Format tab of SmartArt. What all groups are present in each tab and what tasks do they perform?

C. Create a new year greeting card using English fonts. Set an attractive page border. Use Auto Shapes tools to draw the pictures. Use Comic Sans font to display the New Year Wishes.

D. Using the Word Art tool, write two lines about the following.

- Positive thinking
- Prayer
- Selfless life

E. While researching on any project you must have visited many websites. Use any one project and create hyperlinks in the project document. Hyperlinking can be done to other projects, documents, websites or videos.

▶ Page Layout Tab

The Page Layout tab is used to work with page settings, themes and apply background options. It has **Themes** group, **Page Setup** group, **Page Background** group, **Paragraph** group and **Arrange** group in it (Fig. 5.22).

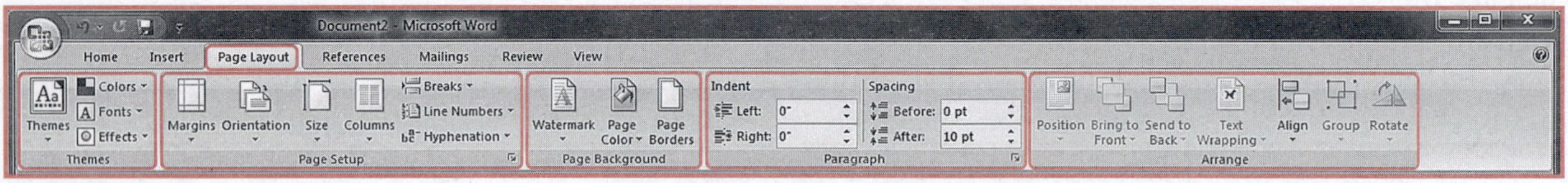

Fig. 5.22 *Page Layout tab*

Themes group

The Themes group is used to change the overall design of the entire document including colors, fonts and effects. The Themes group has the following options: **Themes**, **Theme Effects**, **Theme Fonts** and **Theme Colors** (Fig. 5.23).

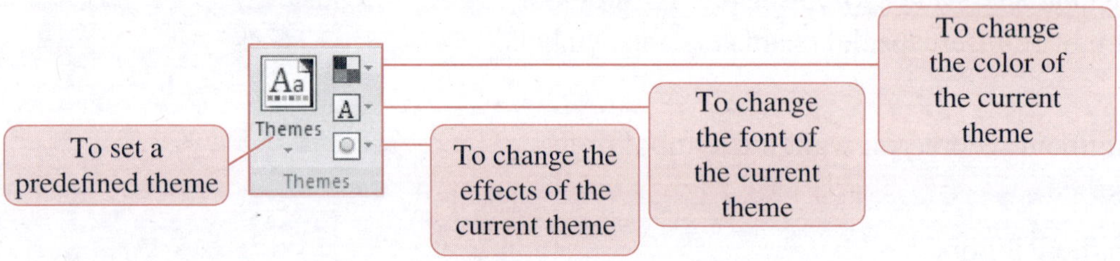

Fig. 5.23 *Themes group*

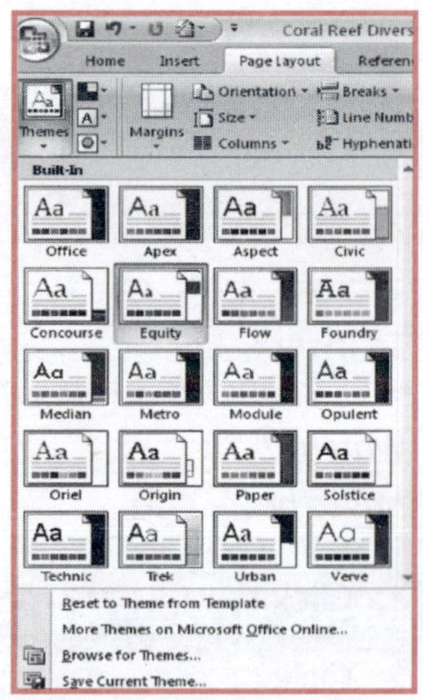

Fig. 5.24 *Built-In theme window*

To select a theme for your document, follow the steps given below.

1. Click the down arrow below the **Themes** button.
2. The **Built-In** drop-down list appears (Fig. 5.24).
3. Select a theme to change the design of your current document.

NOTE: The **Office** theme is the default theme of Word 2007 document.

Page Setup group

The Page Setup group is used to change the formatting options of a page, a section, or an entire document.
It includes adjusting document margins, numbering pages, inserting page breaks, applying columns and hyphenation. The options available in the Page Setup group are given in Figure 5.25.

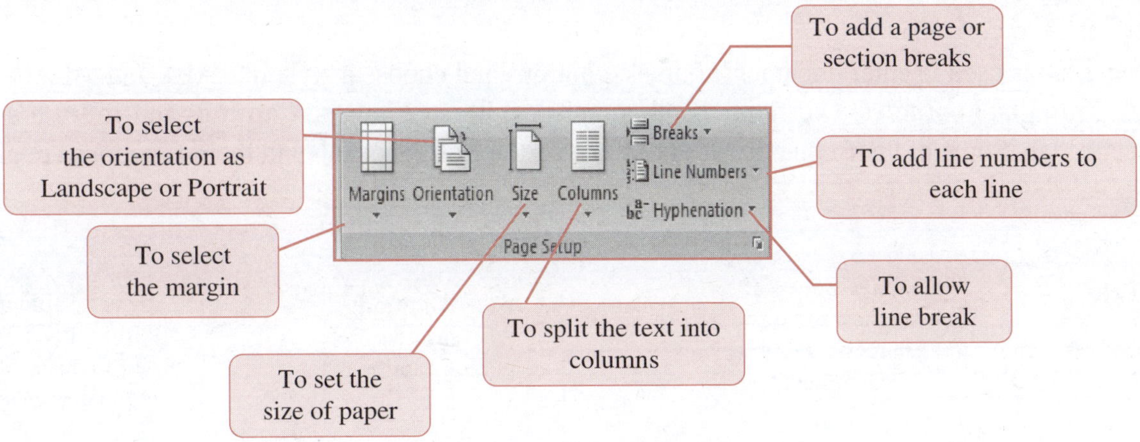

Fig. 5.25 *Page Setup group*

Page Background group

The Page Background group is used for formatting an entire page. The options avilable in the Page Background group are **Watermark**, **Page Color** and **Page Borders** (Fig. 5.26).

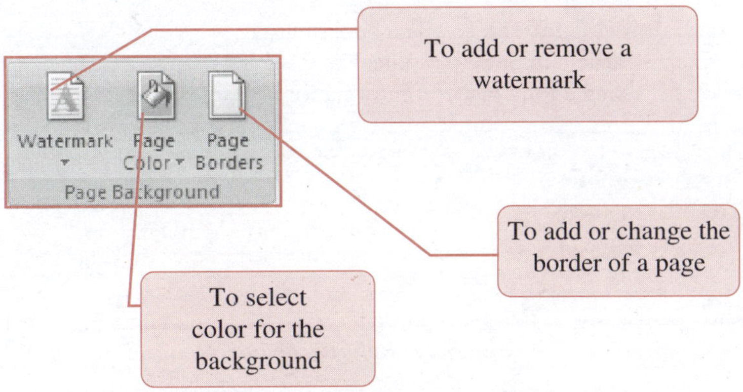

Fig. 5.26 *Page Background group*

ACTIVITY

To insert a watermark.

Watermark is a translucent image that appears behind the text in a document. It is used to indicate that a document has to be treated specially as confidential or urgent. It establishes ownership and status.

1. Click on the **Page Layout** tab in the Ribbon.
2. Click on the **Watermark** button in the Page **Background** group.
3. Select the watermark you want to insert.

   OR

   Click **Custom Watermark...** option to create your own watermark.
4. To remove a watermark, click on **Remove Watermark** option from the same group of **Page Layout** tab.

▶ REFERENCES TAB

The **References** tab is used to enter document sources, citations and choose a style like APA and MLA. Options like **Table of Contents**, **Footnotes**, **Citations**, **Bibliography**, **Table of Figures**, **Captions** and **Index** are available on the **Reference** tab. Some of the frequently used options on the Reference tab and there functions are given here (Fig. 5.27).

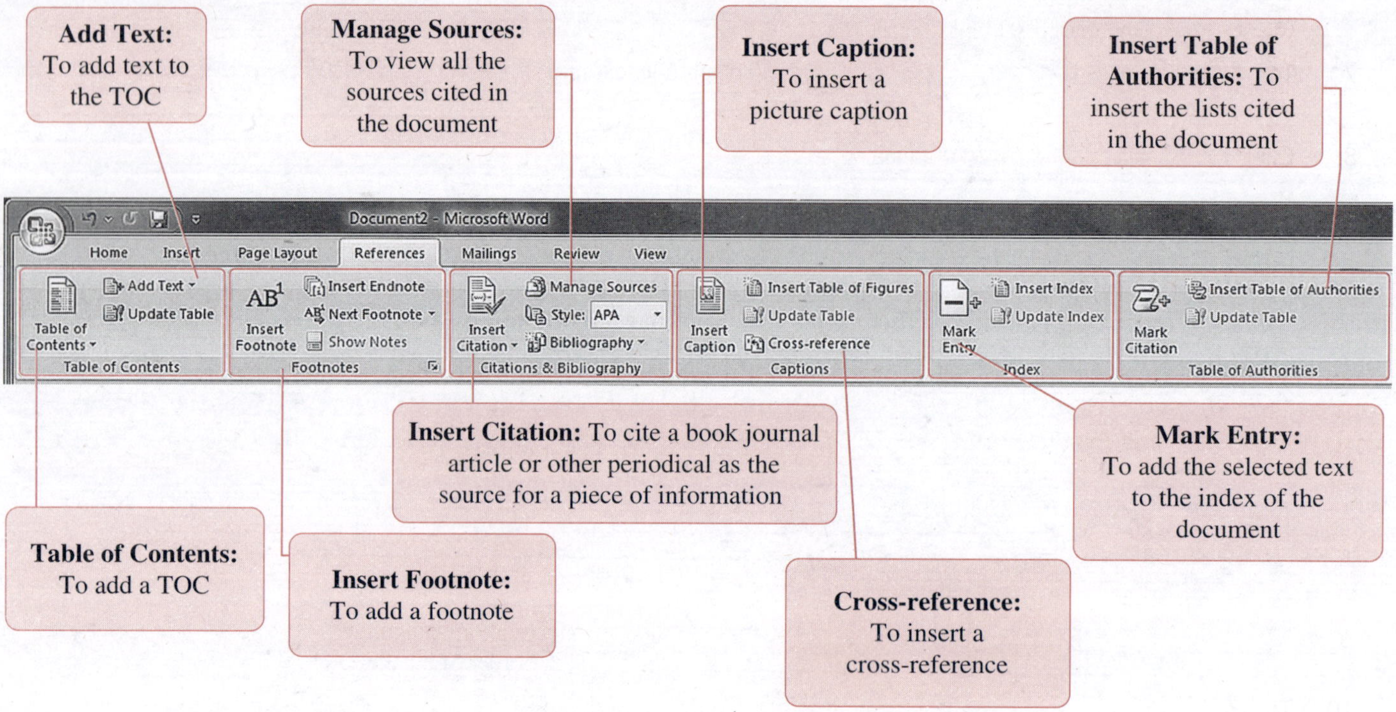

Fig. 5.27 *References tab*

ACTIVITY

To explore and use the References tab.

1. To choose a publishing style, click on the **References** tab on the **Ribbon**.
2. Click on **Style:** option in the **Citations & Bibliography** group.
3. From the drop-down list that appears, choose the appropriate style.

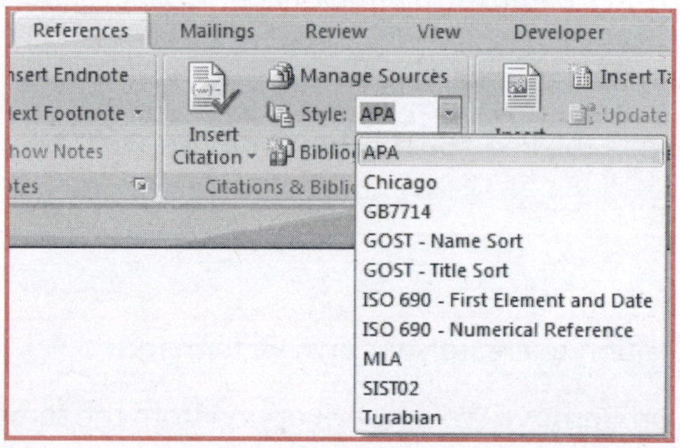

4. To insert a citation, click on the **References** tab on the **Ribbon**.
5. In the **Citations & Bibliography** group, click on the **Insert Citation** option.
6. In the drop-down list, select the **Add New Source...** option to insert a new source. **Create Source** dialog box appears. Complete the form to insert a new source. If you have already created the source, it will appear in the drop-down list (as shown). Just click on it to insert it.

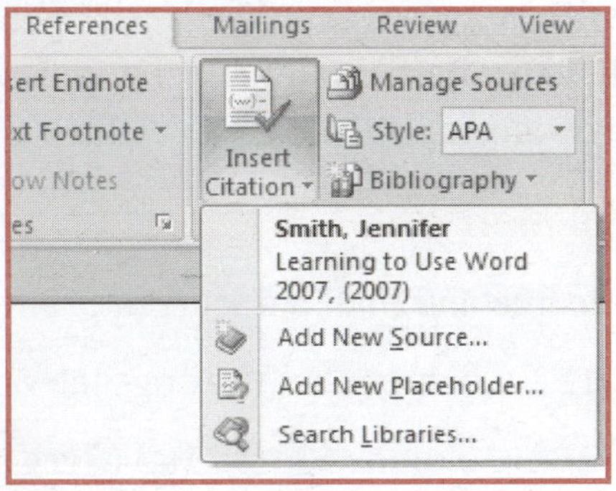

7. To add a bibliography to your document, go to the page where you want to add the bibliography.
8. Click on the **Bibliography** option in the **Citations & Bibliography** group of the **References** tab.
9. Choose an option from the **Built-in Bibliography** gallery to insert a predesigned bibliography format; or choose the **Insert Bibliography** option to add a bibliography which lists all the sources cited in the document.

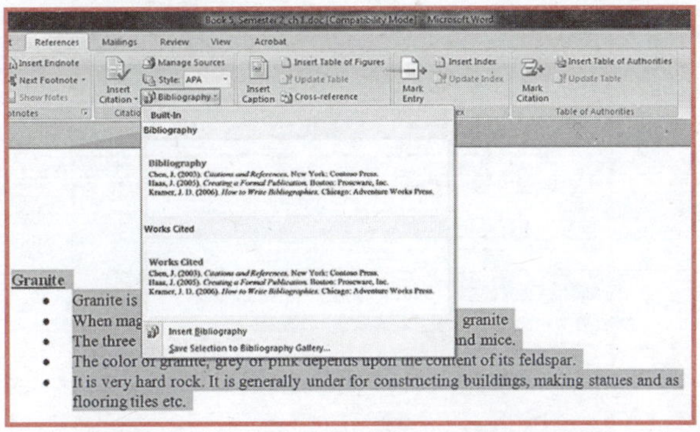

10. To add a table of content to your document, go to the page where you want to add the table of content.
11. Click on the **Table of Contents** option in the **Table of Contents** group of the **References** tab.
12. Select a predefined table of content from the **Built-In** gallery or to insert your own table of content, select the **Insert Table of Contents. . .** option.

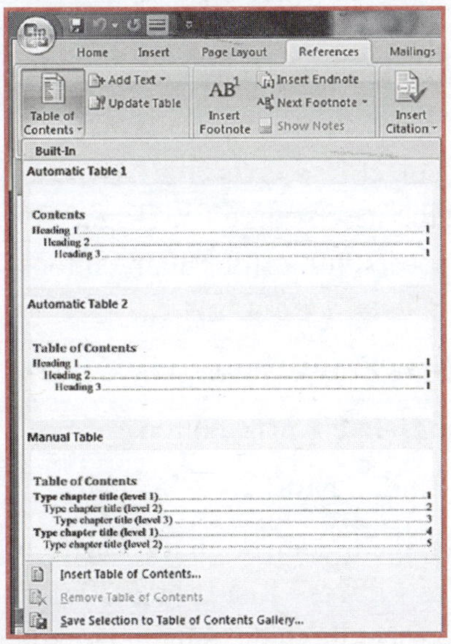

13. Similarly, to add a footnote or a caption, go to the **Insert Footnote** option in the **Footnotes** group and the **Insert Caption** option in the **Captions** group of the **References** tab.

▶ Mailings Tab

Mail Merge (Mailings) provides a way to create custom documents for bulk mailings. Mail Merge combines the main document with a data source file. This is mainly used to send a single letter to multiple addresses by storing the details in data source. The letter, invitation, circular or any other document that has to be sent to many addresses is called the **main document**. The field information like Name, Address, and Phone number, that has to be inserted into the document is the stored in a file called **data source file**.

Mail Merge

To merge and mail a document, follow the steps given below.

1. Click on the **Mailings** tab on the Ribbon.
2. Go to the **Start Mail Merge** button and click on the tool (Fig. 5.28).

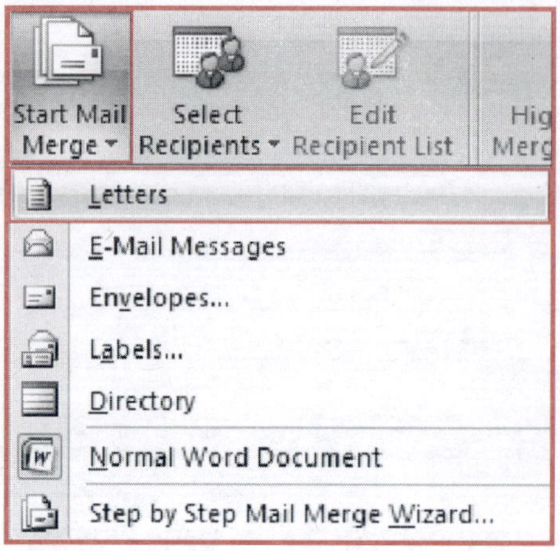

Fig. 5.28 *Starting Mail Merge*

3. From the drop-down list select the **Letters** option.
4. Type the letter or information that has to be send to all the recipients.
5. Now click on the **Select Recipients** tool.
6. If the data source already exists, select **Use Existing List...** and browse for the file. Otherwise, select **Type New List...** option to start the new source file (Fig. 5.29).
7. The **New Address List** window appears. It has four main buttons: **New Entry**, **Delete Entry**, **Find...** and **Custom Columns...**.
   a. To add a record, click on the **New Entry** button (Fig. 5.30a).
   b. To delete a record, click on the **Delete Entry** button.
   c. To find a record, click on the **Find...** button.
   d. To add or delete a column from the file, click on the **Customize Columns...** option. **Customize Address List** (Fig. 5.30b) dialog box appears. From the dialog box, select the field and click on the **Delete** button to delete the selected field or click the **Add** button to add a new field.

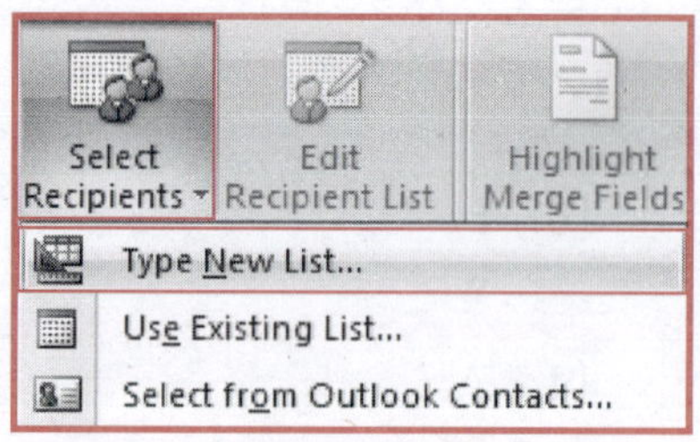

Fig. 5.29 *Selecting recipients*

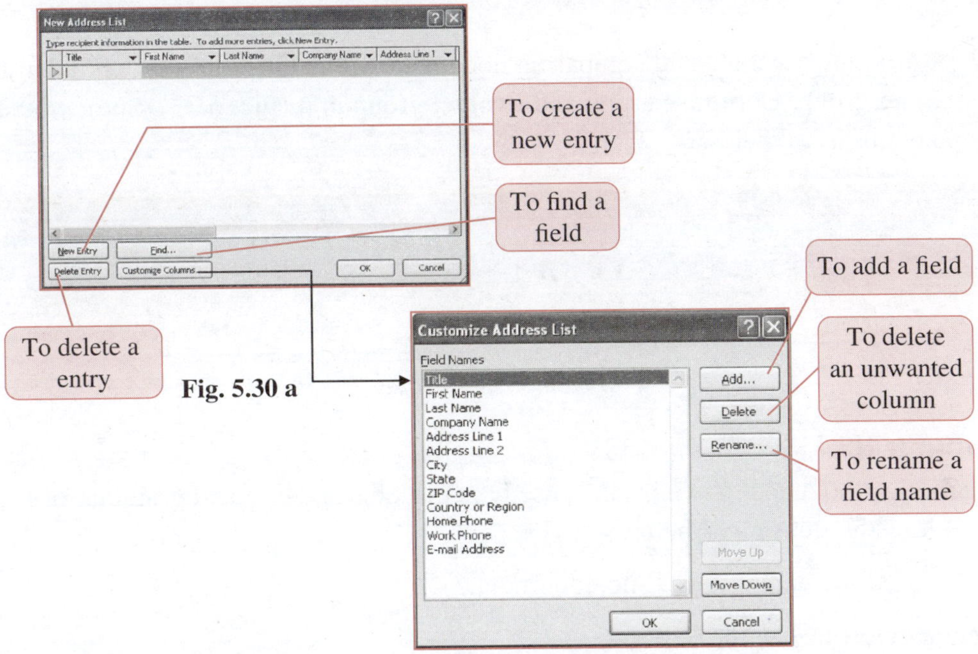

Fig. 5.30 a

Fig. 5.30 b

Fig. 5.30 *Adding and deleting new recipients*

8. After the data entry, click on the **OK** button to save the data source file. The **Same Address List** dialog box appears. Type the name is the box next to the **File name:** and save the file.

   NOTE: The file is saved as Microsoft Office Address Lists.

9. From the Mailings tab, select the **Insert Merge Field** option present in the **Write & Insert Fields** group (Fig. 5.31).

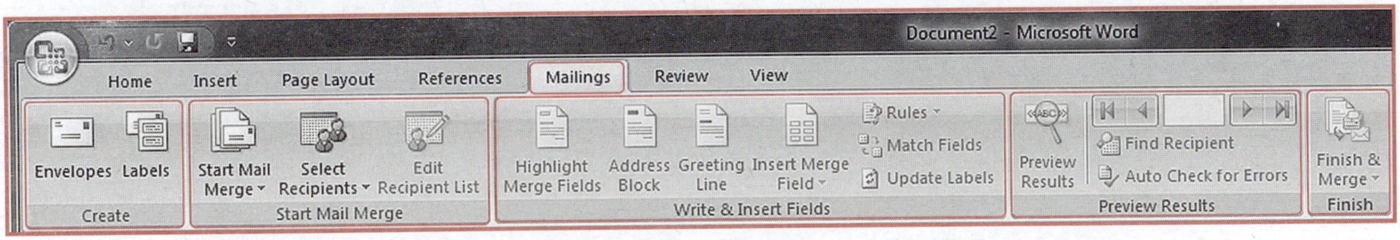

Fig. 5.31 *Mailings tab*

10. From the list of fields available, select and drag the fields one by one and place it on the document where you want to insert.

11. After inserting all the fields on the document, click on the **Finish & Merge** button in the **Finish** group. **Edit Individual Documents...**, **Print Documents...**, and **Send E-mail Messages**... options appear (Fig. 5.32). As per your requirements, choose any out of the three.

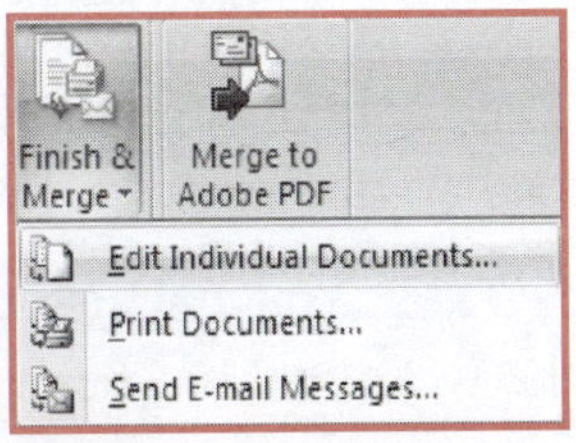

Fig. 5.32 *Finish & Merge*

▶ Review Tab

Review tab is used for proofing, tracking and comparing documents. It has **Proofing** group, **Comments** group, **Tracking** group, **Changes** group, **Compare** group and **Protect** group in it (Fig. 5.33). Some of the commonly used options of this group are discussed below.

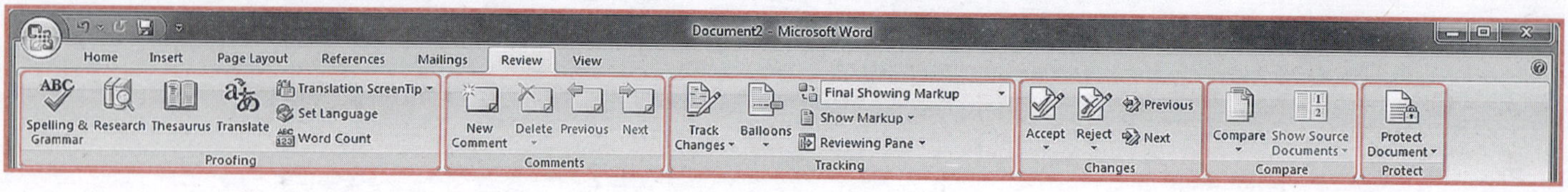

Fig. 5.33 *Review tab*

Spelling & Grammar tool

The **Spelling & Grammar** tool under **Review** tab is used to check the spelling and grammar of text in the document. To check the same, follow the steps given below.

1. Place the cursor at the beginning of the document.
2. Click on the **Review** tab on the Ribbon.
3. Click on the **Spelling & Grammar** on the **Proofing** group. **Spelling and Grammar: English (United Kingdom)** dialog box appears (Fig. 5.34).

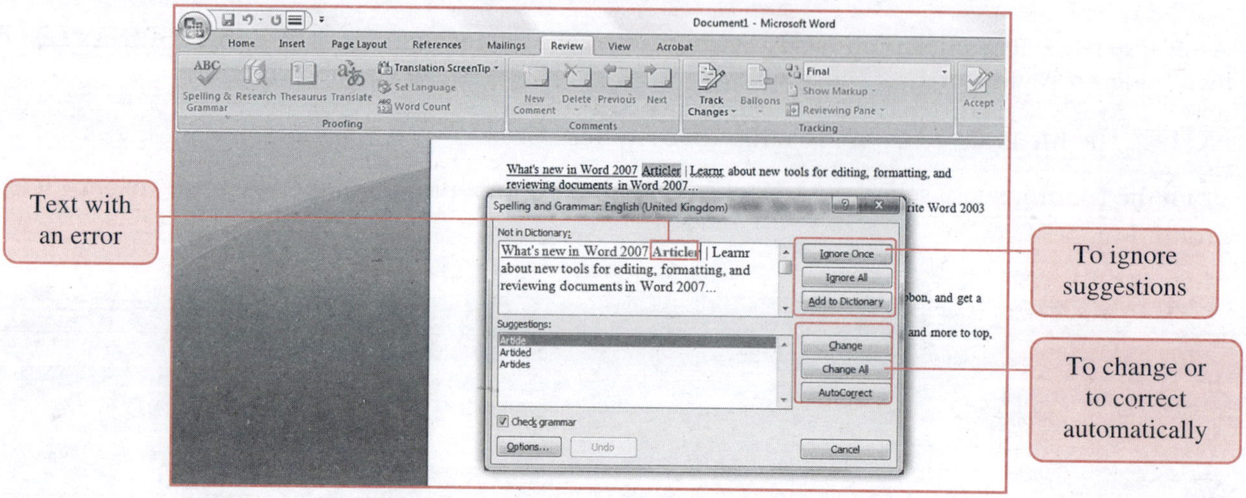

Fig. 5.34 *Spelling and Grammar: English (United Kingdom) dialog box*

4. In the **Not in Dictionary:** frame, the mistakes are highlighted. In the **Suggestions:** frame, word suggestions are given. Click on the **Ignore Once** button to ignore the rule once; click on the **Ignore All** button to ignore the rule throughout the document; click on the **Change** button to change the word as per suggestions given; click on the **Change All** button to make the change throughout the document.

NOTE: You can also check the spelling of an individual word by right-clicking the word that has been underlined and choose a suitable alternative from the suggestions that appear in the **shortcut menu** (Fig. 5.35).

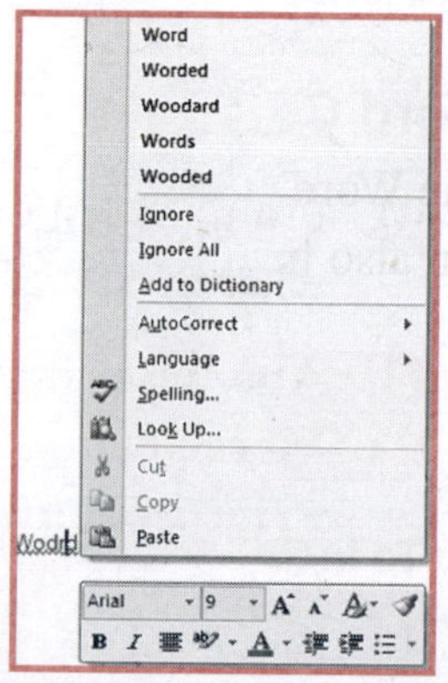

Fig. 5.35 *Spell Check through shortcut menu*

Thesaurus tool

The **Thesaurus** tool enables you to look for synonyms and antonyms of the selected word.

To use a thesaurus, follow the steps given below (Fig. 5.36).

1. Select the text for which you want to find the meaning.
2. Click on the **Review** tab from the Ribbon.
3. Click on the **Thesaurus** tool in the **Proofing** group.
4. The **Research task pane** appears on the right side of the screen.

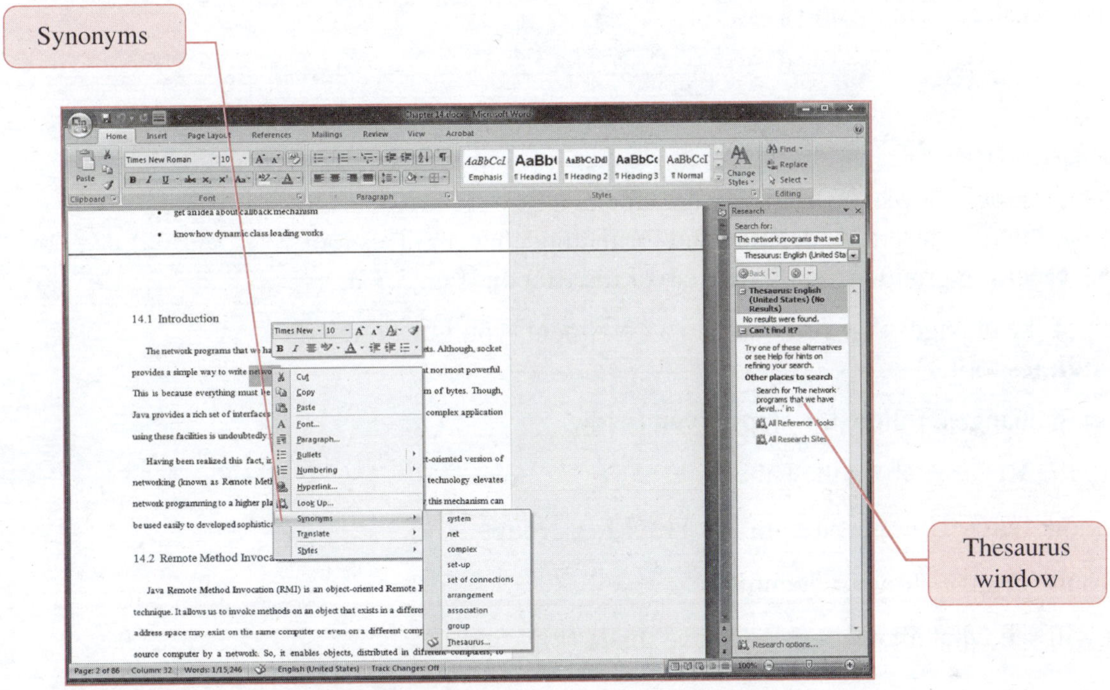

Fig. 5.36 *Research task pane*

5. In the **Search for:** box type the word or phrase and click on the green arrow next to it.
6. Synonyms (and antonyms) will appear as a list below.

NOTE: You can also access the thesaurus by right-clicking the selected word and choosing **Synonyms** on the **shortcut** menu.

Word Count tool

The Word Count tool is used to find out the number of words, characters, paragraphs and lines in a document. You can also find the total word count of a document in the status bar of Word 2007 window.

ACTIVITY

To include text in footnotes, endnotes and text boxes in the word count.

1. Click on the **Word Count** option in the **Proofing** group of the **Review** tab.
2. In the **Word Count** dialog box, select the **Include textboxes, footnotes and endnotes** check box.

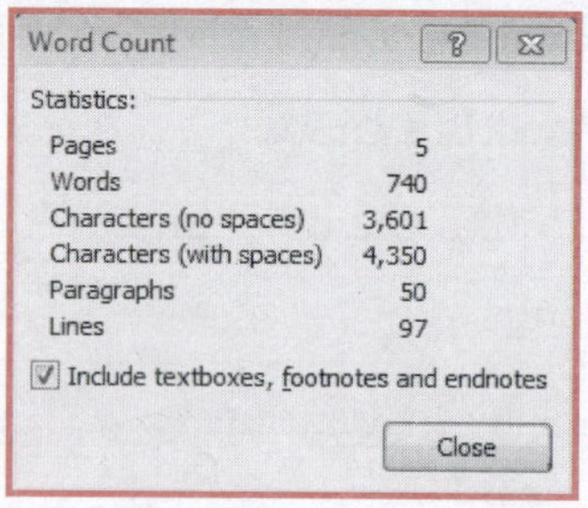

3. The **Word Count** dialog box shows the total number of pages, words, characters (no spaces), characters (with spaces), paragraphs and lines.

Track Changes tool

The Track Changes tool allows you to track what all changes you have made to your document, including insertion, deletion and formatting changes. This tool is found in the **Tracking** group in the **Review** tab of the Ribbon (Fig. 5.37).

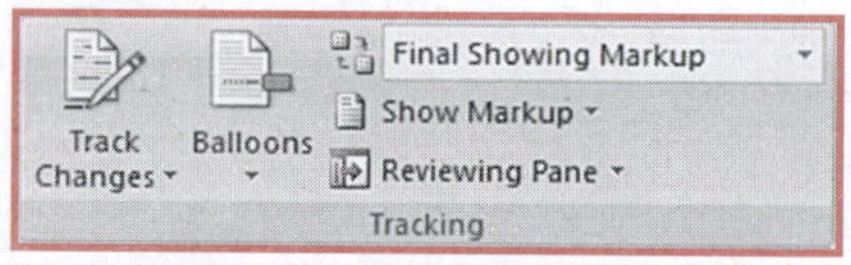

Fig. 5.37 *Tracking group*

To keep track of the changes that you make to a document, you must click on the **Track Changes** tool.

To start tracking changes, follow the steps given below.

1. Go to the **Review** tab on the Ribbon.
2. Click on **Track Changes** tool in the **Tracking** group.
3. Make the changes to your document.
4. You will see what all changes you have made (Fig. 5.38).

Fig. 5.38 *Tracking changes*

Some tools used during tracking are:

- ***Balloon tool:*** It is used to choose how to show revisions to the document. You can show revisions as balloons in the document.
- ***Compare tool:*** It is used to compare or combine multiple versions of a document.
- ***Protect document:*** It is used to restrict access to the document.
- ***Show Markup:*** It enables you to view different mark up items (like comments and formatting) and choose which authors' comments to view.

Quick Key

Ctrl + K	To insert hyperlink
F7	To check spelling and grammar
Shift + F7	To open Thesaurus
Alt + N + W	To insert WordArt
Alt + N + M	To insert SmartArt
Alt + Shift + E	To edit a mail merge data source file
Alt + Shift + F	To insert a merge field
Alt + Shift + K	To preview a mail merge
Alt + Shift + N	To merge a document
Alt + Shift + M	To print the merged document

CHECK YOUR PROGRESS

A. Complete the crossword given below.

Across:

2. The word processing tool of MS Office.
6. A collection of related commands under a tab.
8. A list of frequently used commands that appears when you right-click on an object.

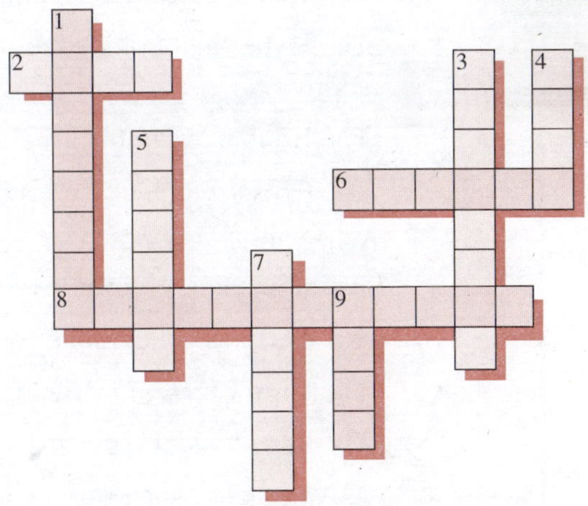

Down:

1. Buttons to do a specific task in Word 2007 document.
3. This refers to the content of the Word page.
4. Click on this for related group of commands that you use in Word 2007 document.
5. This consists of several tabs in groups with buttons to give commands.
7. To move left, right, up or down on the screen.
9. Font effects like font face, style, color and size can be applied to this.

B. Enlist different themes available in Word 2007.

C. Add a Table of Content, Bibliography and Citation, using the References tab in Word 2007, on any school project that you are currently working on.

GLOSSARY

- **Blank Page Tool:** It is used to insert a new blank page at the current position of the document.
- **Clip Art Gallery:** It is a collection of predefined pictures based on various categories.
- **Cover Page Tool:** It is used to insert a fully formatted cover page.
- **Page Break Tool:** It is used to give a break in the current page and start a new page at the current position of the document.
- **Picture Tool:** It is used to insert a picture file which is already stored in your computer.
- **Theme Tool:** It is used to change the overall design of the entire document including colors, fonts and effects.
- **Track Changes:** It allows you to see what all changes have been made to a document including insertion, deletion and formatting changes.
- **Word Count Tool:** It is used to find out the number of words, characters, paragraphs and lines in the document.

NOW YOU KNOW

1. Word 2007 allows you to insert pictures, charts, shapes, header, footer, number, text, formulae and more.
2. The Shapes tool under Insert tab in Word 2007 provides various drawing tools such as lines, arrows, geometric shapes, flow charts, callouts, stars and banners.
3. The Clip Art gallery is a collection of predefined pictures based on various categories.
4. Smart Art is a collection of graphics you can use to organise and visually communicate information within a document.
5. The Hyperlink tool is used to create a link to a web page, a picture, a program or an email address.
6. The Bookmark tool is used to assign a name to a specific point in a document.
7. The Cross-reference tool is used to include references from one part of the document to another.
8. Word 2007 also allows you to insert mathematical equations. **Equation** and **Symbol** tools available under **Symbols** group in the **Insert** tab are used for this purpose.
9. WordArt is a collection of preformatted text. It is used to insert decorative text into a document.
10. The Drop Cap tool is used to apply a special effect to the first letter of the paragraph.
11. The Page Layout tab is used to work with page settings, themes and apply background options.
12. A Watermark is a translucent image that appears behind the text in a document.
13. The **References** tab is used to enter document sources, citations and choose a style like APA and MLA.
14. Mail Merge (Mailings) provides a way to create custom documents for bulk mailings.
15. The Spelling & Grammar tool is used to check the spelling and grammar of text in a document.
16. The Thesaurus suggests other words with a similar meaning to the word you have selected.
17. The Track Changes tool allows you to track what all changes you have made to your document, including insertion, deletion and formatting changes.

EXERCISE

FA

A Fill in the blanks.

1. ...., ..., ..., ..., ...,
   .... and .... are the groups present on the Insert tab.
2. The .... tool is used to insert blank pages into a document.
3. Table Style options is present in .... tab.
4. .... is a collection of graphics used to organise and visually communicate information within a document.
5. The Hyperlink, Bookmark and Cross-reference option are present in the .... group.
6. The .... tool is used to insert a signature line that specifies the individual who must sign.
7. The default theme of Word 2007 document is ....
8. To remove a watermark, ... option is used.
9. Mail Merge combines the .... with a ....
10. The .... tab is used for proofing, tracking and comparing.

B Multiple choice questions

1. In Mail Merge, the main document is linked to the .... of data source.

   a. field names b. data name c. header name d. data file

2. The field names in Mail Merge document are enclosed within ....

   a. << << b. >> >> c. << >> d. >> <<

3. The .... key is the shortcut for spelling check.

   a. F1 b. F7 c. F5 d. F2

4. 

   Identify this tool.

   a. Spelling and Grammar tool b. Change case tool

   c. Style tool d. Text tool

5. The Equations tool is available under .... tab.

   a. Symbol b. Equation c. Insert d. References

6. To work with page settings, themes and apply background options, ... tab is used.

   a. Developer b. Insert c. Page Layout d. View

7.  This tool is available under Insert tab. Identify this.

   a. Web page b. Web Layout c. Hyperlink d. Cross-reference

8. 

This tool is available under .... tab of Tables Tools.

   a. Design b. Format c. Layout d. Table

9. 

This buttons allows you to .... column in Data Source document.

   a. add b. delete c. rename d. add, delete and rename

10. By default, the page orientation in Word 2007 is ....

   a. Portrait b. Landscape c. A4 d. Letter

C Match the following options with the appropriate tabs.

1. Review	a. Citation
2. Page Layout	b. Select Recipients
3. Insert	c. Change Styles
4. View	d. Track Changes
5. Home	e. Page Number
6. References	f. Columns
7. Mailings	g. Zoom

D Answer the following questions briefly.

1. How to insert a row in an existing table?
2. Name the tab in which Header & Footer tool is available.
3. Why are headers and footers used in a document? HOTS
4. What is Mail Merge?
5. What is the use of Track Changes tool?
6. Under which tab are the Proofing group, Comments group, Tracking group, Changes group, Compare group and Protect group available?
7. 

Identify this tool and the tab under which it is available.
8. Name any two options that are available under Select Recipients tool under Mailings tab? Write a line about each option.

9. What are the options available under Document Views of View tab?
10. What is SmartArt?

SA

E **Answer the following questions.**

1. What are the different categories of shapes available under Shapes tool of Insert tab?
2. Define bookmark.
3. What is the use of Equation tool available under Insert tab?
4. What is the purpose of Watermark tool?
5. Define citation. HOTS
6. What is the use of Thesaurus tool?
7. What is the use of Word Count tool? Name the tab under which it is available.
8. What is the purpose of SmartArt graphics tool? Name any two designs.
9. What are the tools available in Page Setup group available under Page Layout tab? Write a line about each.
10. Discuss different themes available in Word 2007.

F **Answer the following questions in detail.**

1. Write down the steps to create Mail Merge using Mailings tab in Word 2007.
2. Explain the Tables group and its sub-tasks.
3. What is the difference between hyperlink and bookmark?
4. Write short notes on all the options in the Text group of the Insert tab.
5. What is the default page orientation and page size of Word 2007 document? How can you change it? HOTS

Application Based Questions

A. Aditi created a document of 10 pages using Word 2007. She wants to number all the pages in the document. Name a feature which will help her achieve the same without opening and typing the number on each and every page. Give steps.

B. Camila is working as an HR Manager in a finance company. She stores her data of monthly expenditures in an organised manner for a period of one year in a word document. Can she use Word 2007 to calculate her total expenditure?

C. Ajith is a student of Delhi Public School. He wrote an article on board examinations for his school magazine. The document is neatly formatted. He now wants to add attractive borders on each page. Name and explain a feature of Word 2007 which will help him to achieve the same.

D. Anant is a spiritual speaker. He is writing a book on his own experience on prayers. He does not have a good command on English language and he cannot afford to hire an editor for the book. Which two features of Word 2007 should he use for basic language corrections?

E. Shivani is writing a chapter and she wants the name of the chapter as header. Which tool can she use to put heading on each page of her document?

F. Kaushik is a clerk in a company. He was asked to create a proposal to be sent to other companies for contract of a building. He wants to merge his main invitation document with the address database. Help him achieve this without wasting much of his time.

G. Bharat is a student of National School. He is composing an article for an essay competition. He wants the title of the essay at the bottom of every page. Which feature of Word 2007 will allow Bharat do the this?

LAB WORK

A. Create a document and type the following paragraph. Insert a picture related to the topic using Picture tool. Use different Word options to format and edit the document.

Walking is one of the best forms of exercise. It confers physical, mental and spiritual benefits. The correct way to walk is to carry the chest high, chin level and throw the legs energetically out from the thigh. Right walking put a tingle in the blood, promotes digestion, clarifies the mind and elevates the spirit. Energetic walking stimulates unsuspected thoughts into action. Walk enough every day, with energetic strides, deep breathing and definite purpose. It will contribute to your health and longevity.

B. Create a document and type the following paragraph. Insert a picture from Clip Art. Use different formatting and editing options to improve your document.

To practice the art of reading, develop a hungry, curious and questing mind. You open doors when you open books, doors that swing wide to unlimited horizons of knowledge, wisdom and inspiration that will enlarge the dimensions of your life.

In studying books we are sometimes deluded into thinking that thereby we are being spiritually helped; but if we analyse the effect of the study of books on ourselves, we shall find that, at the utmost, it is only our intellect that derives profit from such studies, and not the inner spirit.

C. Create a document and type the following paragraph. Insert a picture and a callout to label it. Write some text based on the document.

A person's memory can be divided into 3 stages. Each has a different time span.

- Sensory Memory
- Short-term Memory
- Long term memory

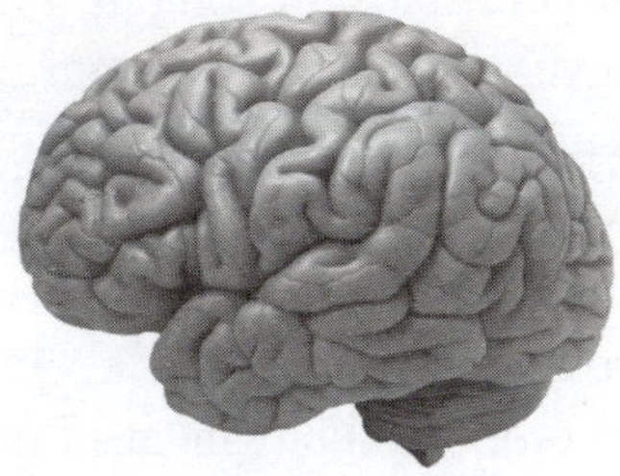

The sensory memory holds information only for an instant. The information passes through your eyes and gets stored in your sensory memory. It quickly fades and disappears.

Short term memory holds a fact for as long as you actively think about. This memory fades after 20 seconds unless you continually repeat the information to yourself.

Long term memory includes a large amount of information which may be retained for a life time. Two factors are responsible for entry of information into long term memory. They are:

- Repetition – by repeating everyday
- Intense emotion – first experience and strong emotions

D. Type the following document and split into two columns using Page Layout tab. Set the first character of the document as a large capital letter of the paragraph.

Soft words in a lullaby will put a baby to sleep. Excited words will stir a mob to violence. Eloquent words will send armies marching into the face of death. Encouraging words will fan to flame the genius. Powerful words will mold the public mind as the sculptor molds his clay. Words are dynamic force.

Words are the swords we use in our battle for success and happiness. How others react toward us depends, in a large measure, upon the words we speak to them. Life is a great whispering gallery that sends back echoes of the words we send out! Our words are immortal too. They go marching through the years in the lives of all those with whom we come in contact.

When you speak, when you write, remember the creative power of words.

-Wilfred A. Peterson

E. Imagine that your school is organizing a COMPUTER EXPO in the school premise. Create an invitation letter to invite various schools in and around your area to participate in that event.

- Format your main document (invitation letter) with borders, colors and pictures.
- Add minimum five records in data source to merge with main document.

F. Type the following paragraphs and find the synonyms for the underlined text.

The Art of Writing

Writing is a private activity but a public service. You may write a protest letter in the solitude of your study, or compile a report in the office or scribble a few paragraphs of your favorite novel but in each case your intention is the same – that eventually your writing will become the reading matter of someone else.

Writing in other words, is above all for communication – for conveying ideas and feelings from your mind to another mind. Apart from a few oddities – filling out a puzzle or writing your name in the sand at low tide is true of all writing tasks. Even taking lecture notes or recording a funny incident in your diary book is to communicate with your future self. The hall marks of good writing are the hall mark of good communication. The ABCs of both are:

- accuracy, appropriateness, attentiveness to your audience and avoidance of ambiguity;
- breebity or conciseness, brightness or buoyancy;
- correctness, clarity, consistency and concreteness.

MS Office 2010
Updates

In MS Word 2010:

- You can apply a number of artistic effects to the pictures. Insert the desired picture and click on the picture. The **Picture Tools Format** contextual tab appears. In the **Adjust** group, click on the **Artistic Effects** tool. A drop-down list appears. Select an effect to make the picture look more like a painting or a sketch.
- You can remove the background of any image using the **Remove Background** tool. Insert the desired picture and click on the picture. The **Picture Tools Format** contextual tab appears. In the **Adjust** group, click on the **Background Removal** tool. The Background removal tab appears. Using the options available in this tab you can remove the background.
- You can co-author a document. Word 2010 allows more than one authors to edit a document at the same time. Word 2010 tells you how many authors are editing the document and their changes can be viewed too.

TEACHER'S NOTES

1. Discuss the Developer tab and the tools available in it. Explain to them that it is not a default tab and has to be added. Show them how to add it and use its features.
2. Talk to the students about the usage of Translate and Language tools.

6 Presentation Tools – I

SNAP RECAP

1. A presentation tool is used to display information in the form of a slide show.
2. PowerPoint is developed by Microsoft and is part of Microsoft Office package.
3. PowerPoint is one of the most powerful software program used for creating presentations.
4. A PowerPoint presentation consists of slides that include text, pictures, animation effects, audio and video.

LEARNING OBJECTIVES

You will learn about:

1. Components of PowerPoint 2007
2. Editing Slides
3. Formatting Slides
4. Presentation Views
5. Insert Tab
6. Slide Show

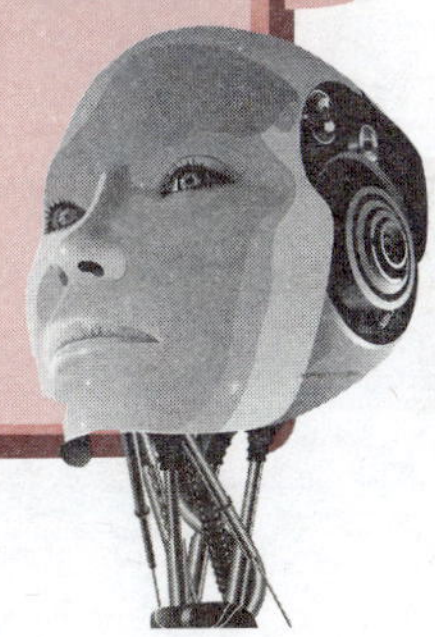

INTRODUCTION

A presentation is an effective and powerful way to communicate ideas and information in this information driven world. Although it is a collection of data and information, directed towards a specific audience, the presentation of data is striking. Presentations are used to inform, advertise, educate and promote.

Presentations are easy and quick to prepare and the end result is polished. Several software packages are available for creating presentations, such as, MS PowerPoint, Office Impress, Apple Keynote and K Presenter.

Advantages of presentation software

Some of the advantages of presentation software are given below.

- Presentation software are easy to learn and use.
- They are excellent for summarising facts.
- Graphs, charts, diagrams can be easily inserted into a presentation through a presentation software.
- They provide many in-built layout and design options.

- It is easy to add multimedia components, such as audio and video files using presentation software.
- They make the presentation interactive and entertaining.

MS PowerPoint

MS PowerPoint is one of the most powerful and simple tool used to design presentations. It is available as a part of the MS Office package. It is a collection of electronic slides that can have text, pictures, graphics, tables, sound and video. Presentations can be created easily by making slides in PowerPoint. It has number of in-built designs, pictures, clip art, graphics and templates, which help the user to design high-impact, dynamic presentation in a professional manner.

FACT FILE

A **slide** is a collection of text, images, pictures, graphs, charts, sound and animation. **Presentation**, on the other hand, is a collection of multiple slides arranged in a systematic order with several components that combine together to present a **slide show**.

PowerPoint 2007

The features of PowerPoint 2007 are very similar to that of previous versions of PowerPoint. However, the functions that were located in the **File menu** of the older versions are now available under **Microsoft Office button**. Also, instead of menus and options that formed the user interface in the previous versions, here you have **Ribbon**, **tabs** and **groups**.

Starting MS PowerPoint 2007

To start PowerPoint 2007, follow the steps given below (Fig. 6.1).

1. Click on the **Start** button.
2. Click on **All Programs**.

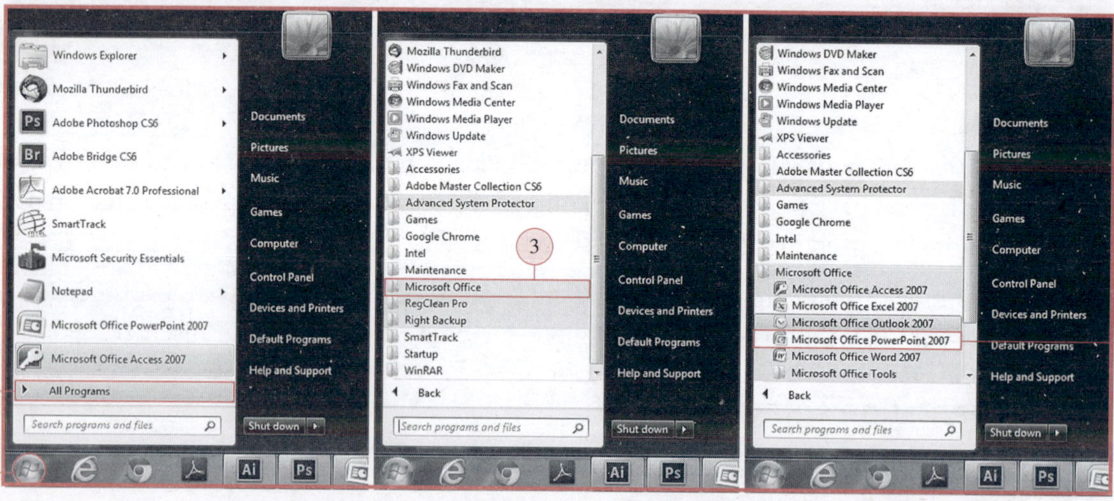

Fig. 6.1 *Starting PowerPoint 2007*

3. Go to **Microsoft Office**.
4. Click on **Microsoft Office PowerPoint 2007**.
5. A new presentation window appears with a blank slide in normal (layout) view (Fig. 6.2).

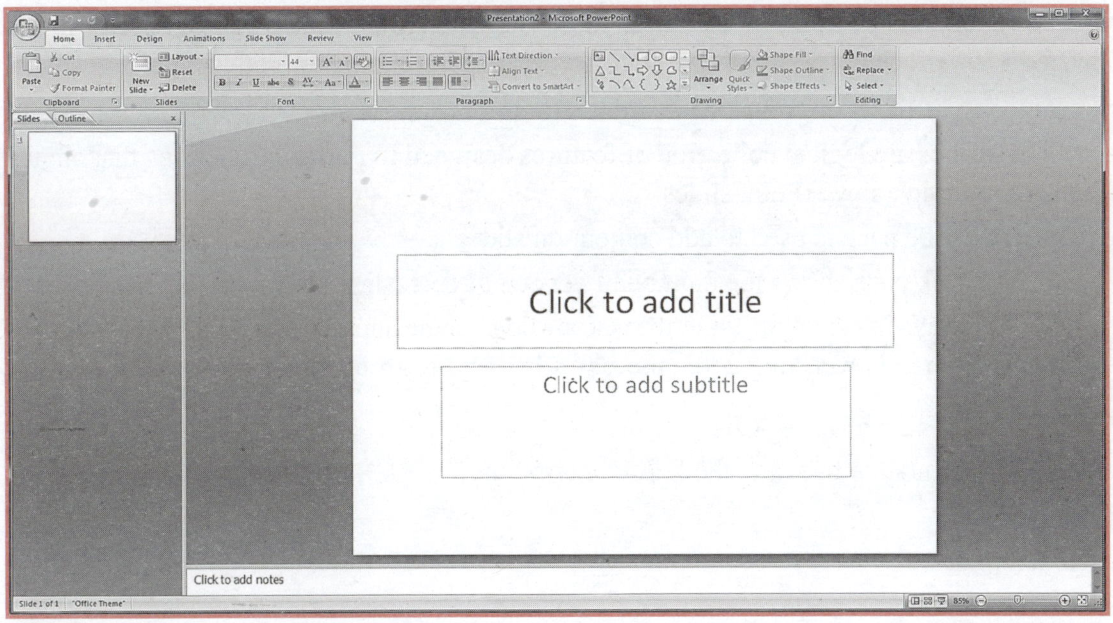

Fig. 6.2 *A new blank presentation*

Components of PowerPoint 2007

PowerPoint 2007 allows you to create visually stimulating and dynamic presentations quickly and efficiently. Its user-friendly interface contributes a lot towards this end. **Microsoft Office button**, **Quick Access Toolbar** and **Ribbon** are the main components of PowerPoint 2007 window (Fig. 6.3).

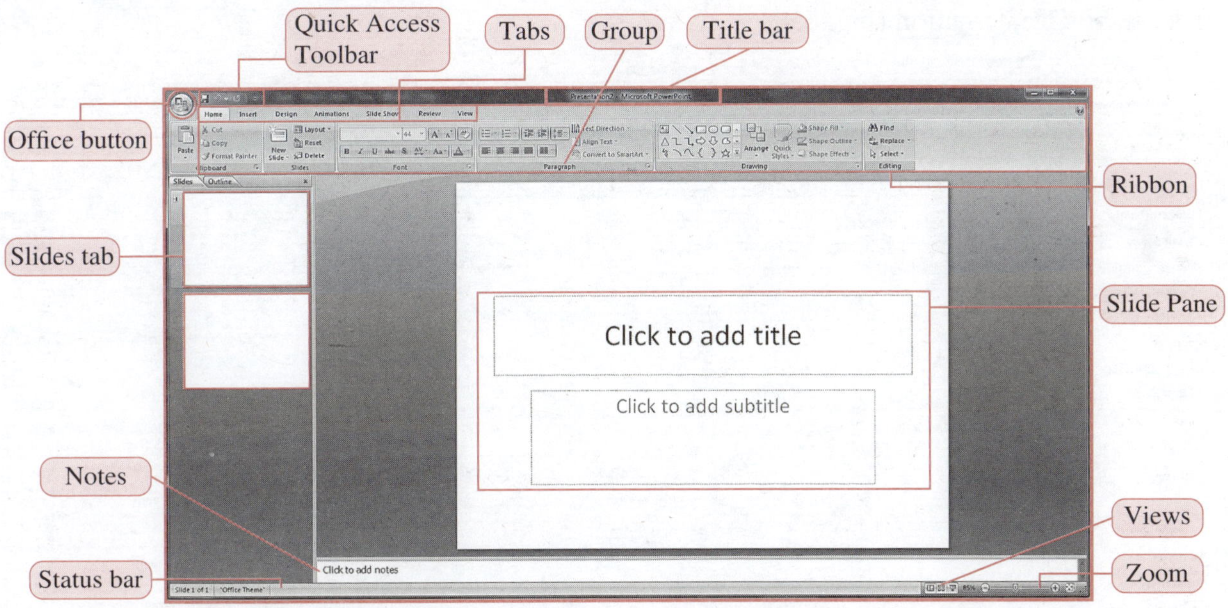

Fig. 6.3 *Components of PowerPoint 2007 window*

The main components of PowerPoint 2007 window are discussed below.

- ***Office button:*** This button contains the functions of File menu options of previous versions of PowerPoint. It allows you to create, open, save and print your presentation.
- ***Title bar:*** Title bar displays the title of the presentation.
- ***Quick Access Toolbar:*** Quick Access Toolbar contains tools that you use very often. You can also add items to the Quick Access Toolbar by right-clicking on any item on the Ribbon and selecting **Add to Quick Access Toolbar**.

- ***Ribbon:*** The Ribbon in PowerPoint has seven tabs. They are **Home**, **Insert**, **Design**, **Animations**, **Slideshow**, **Review** and **View**. Each tab is sub-divided into groups that have tools for both simple and advanced functions.
- ***Tabs:*** A tab consists of set of groups with various tools.
- ***Groups:*** The groups are logical collection of features designed to perform functions that are utilised in developing or editing a PowerPoint slides.
- ***Slide pane:*** The slide pane is used to add content on slides.
- ***Slides tab:*** This task pane shows the thumbnail version of each slide shown on the Slide pane.
- ***Status bar:*** It displays information about the action slide, theme applied, view and zoom options. If no presentation is open in PowerPoint 2007, the status bar area is grouped out.

Creating a Presentation

You can create a new presentation by using the following options:

- Blank and recent
- Installed Templates
- Installed Themes

Creating a new presentation from a blank slide

To create a new presentation from a blank slide, follow the steps given below.

1. Click on the **Office** button.
2. Click on the **New** option. The **New Presentation** dialog box appears.
3. Click on the **Blank Presentation** in the **Blank and recent** section.
4. Click on the **Create** button (Fig. 6.4).

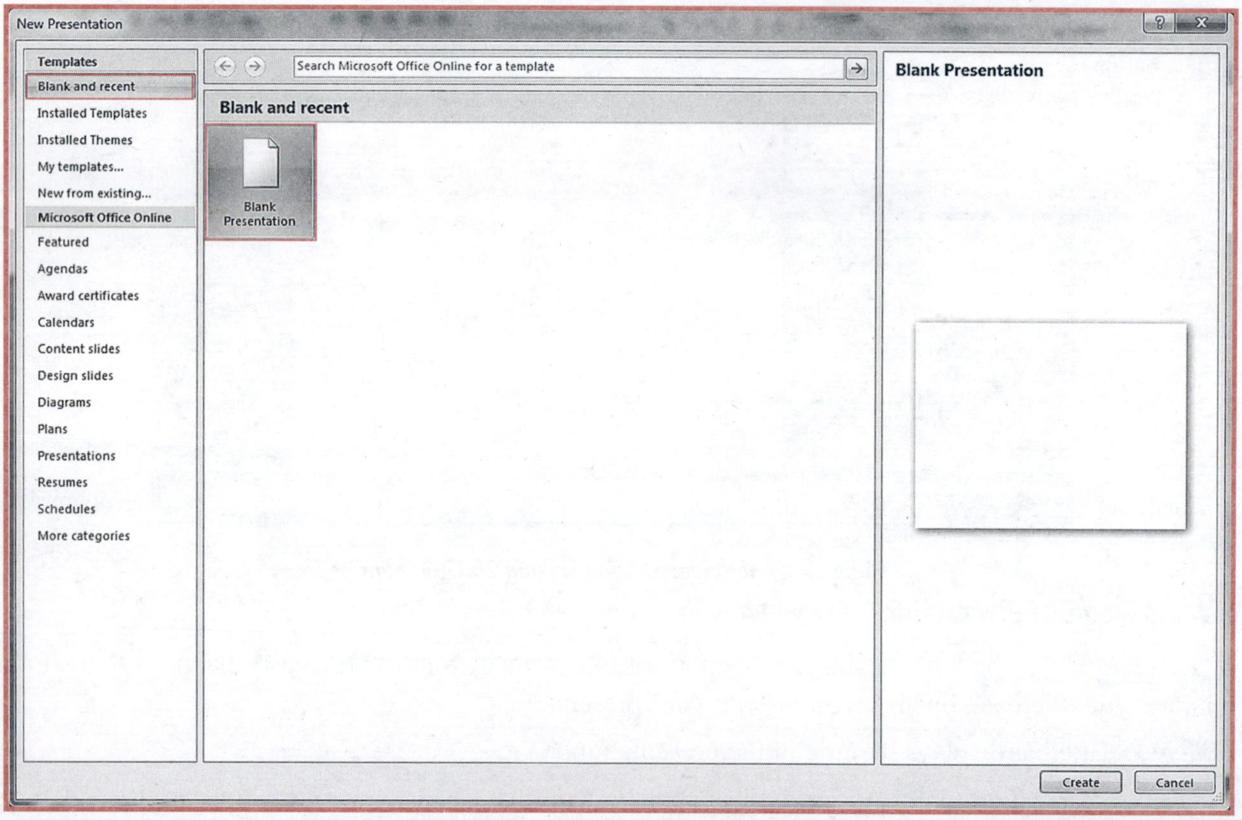

Fig. 6.4 *Creating a new presentation from a blank presentation*

Creating a new presentation from an installed template

PowerPoint 2007 provides a quick and easy way to create a presentation using built-in templates called **installed templates**. It is similar to the **AutoContent Wizard** of the previous versions of MS PowerPoint. It gives you the basic sketch of a presentation. You can further modify it with the text, pictures and sounds according to your requirement.

To create a new presentation from installed templates, follow the steps given below.

1. Click on the **Office** button.
2. Click on the **New** option. The **New Presentation** dialog box appears.
3. In the **Templates** task pane on the left, click on the **Installed Templates**.
4. Select a template and click on the **Create** button (Fig. 6.5).

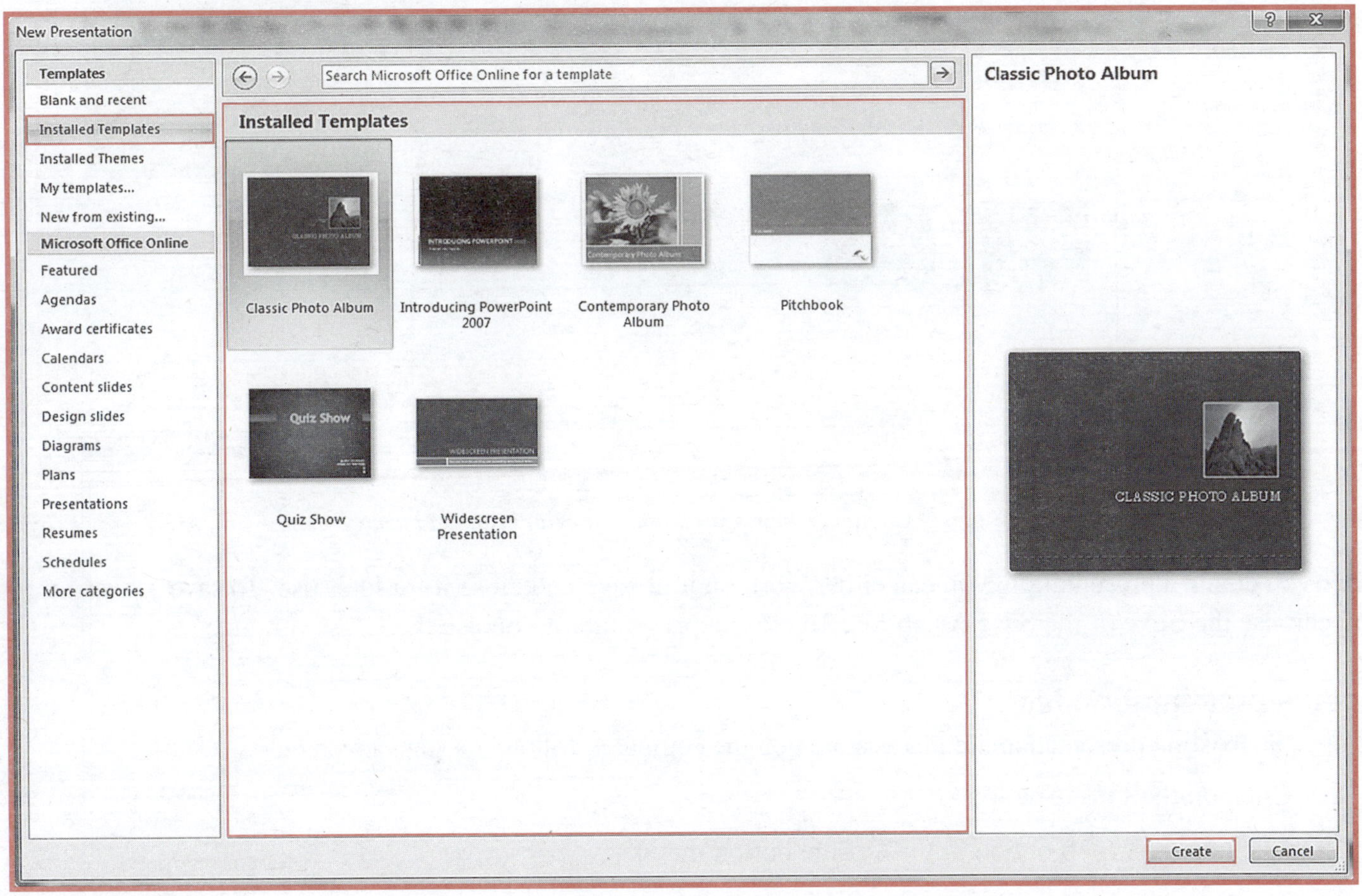

Fig. 6.5 *Creating a new presentation from an installed template*

Creating a new presentation from an installed theme

Installed themes are the set of predesigned formats that include text, layouts, background and color schemes which can be applied to any presentation.

To create a new presentation from installed themes, follow the steps given below.

1. Click on the **Office** button.
2. Click on the **New** option. The **New Presentation** dialog box appears.

3. In the **Templates** task pane on the left, click on **Installed Themes**.
4. Select a theme and click on the **Create** button (Fig. 6.6).

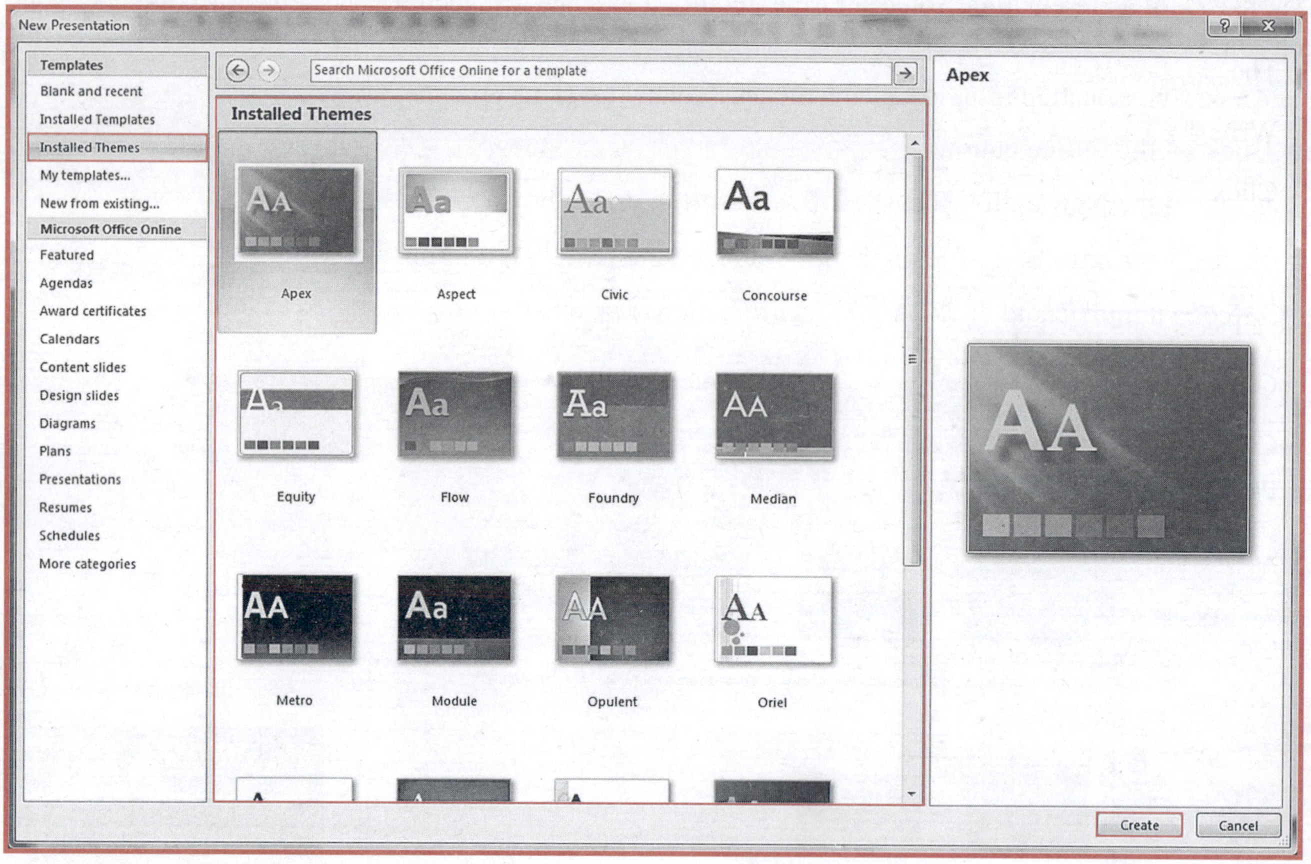

Fig. 6.6 *Creating a new presentation from an installed theme*

After you create a presentation, you can either work on it or save and close it for later use. To save a presentation, you can use the **Save** or the **Save As** option. To close a presentation you use the **Close** option.

Open a presentation file

To open an existing presentation file that is stored on the computer, follow the steps given below.

1. Click on the **Office** button.
2. Click on the **Open** option in the Offline button menu.
3. The **Open** dialog box appears. Select the file to be opened in the **File name:** box.
4. Click on the **Open** button.

Save a presentation file

Save option is used to save a presentation file along with the name given by the user. It takes the extension ***.pptx**.

Save As option is used to save the same file using different name or at a different location.

To save a file, follow the steps given below.

1. Click on the **Office** button.
2. Click on the **Save** option.
3. The **Save As** dialog box appears.
4. Write the name of the file in **File name:** box.
5. Click on the **Save** button.

Close a presentation file

To close a PowerPoint presentation, follow the steps given below.

1. Click on the **Office** button.
2. Click on the **Close** option in the **Office** button menu to close the active presentation (Fig. 6.7).

Fig. 6.7 *Office button menu*

FACT FILE

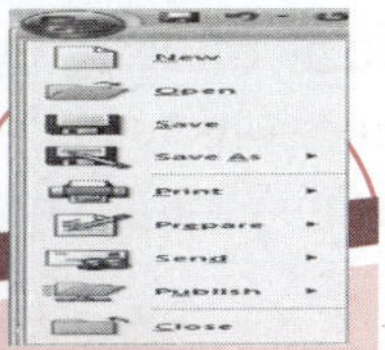

The **PowerPoint Options** dialog box, located in the Office menu button, enables you to customise the PowerPoint environment to fit to your specific requirements. The options available in this dialog box are: **Popular**, **Proofing**, **Save**, **Advanced**, **Customize**, **Add-Ins**, **Trust Centre** and **Resources**.

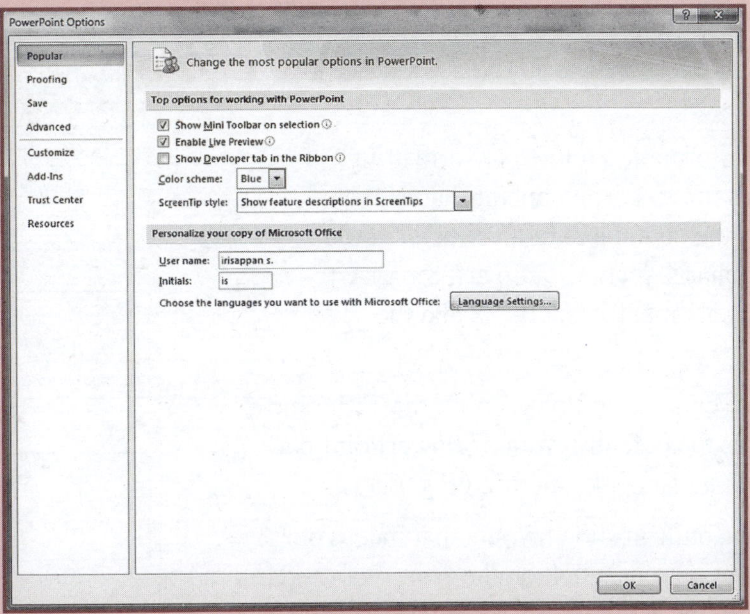

CHECK YOUR PROGRESS

A. How is Exit option in Office button different from Close option? **HOTS**

B. The Ribbon of Word 2007 is different from the Ribbon of PowerPoint 2007. Elucidate. (Hint: Number of tabs)

C. Explore different themes and templates available in PowerPoint 2007. Apply the Verve theme to one of your presentation.

D. Your computer teacher has assigned you the task of reviewing a PowerPoint presentation she created for a seminar on Importance of ICT. The presentation is in PowerPoint 2007 and you are new to PowerPoint 2007 interface. However, you are aware about the basic components. Therefore, before starting with the presentation, explore the PowerPoint 2007 interface.

1. List down all the tabs and groups in the Ribbon. Investigate what is their main functionality.
2. Explore the components of the status bar. Can you customise it?
3. Where is the Quick Access Toolbar? Can you change its position?

E. Differentiate between Installed themes and Installed templates.

Slide Group

The **Slides** group in the **Home** tab helps you to add and delete slides from your presentation. This group also has options to choose the slide layout and reset tool that resets all the layout setting to default. There are four tools in this group. They are: **New Slide**, **Layout**, **Reset** and **Delete** (Fig. 6.8).

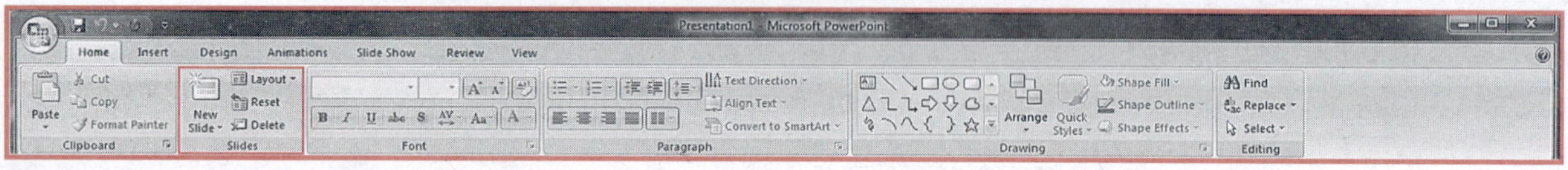

Fig. 6.8 *Slides group in the Home tab*

Layout

Slide layout contain all the information related to formatting, positioning and placeholders for all of the content that appears on a slide. Place holders are the containers in layouts that hold content such as text, tables, charts, pictures, clip art, SmartArt graphics, movies and sounds, theme, fonts, effects and the background of a slide.

When you create a blank presentation in PowerPoint, the **Title Slide** appears on the screen. This is the default layout of PowerPoint but there are other layouts that you can apply and use (Fig. 6.9).

In PowerPoint, you have nine built-in slide layouts that meet your specific needs. To open layout options, click on the **Home** tab and select the **Layout** button from the **Slide** group. A drop-down list appears. Select a layout and click on it to insert it.

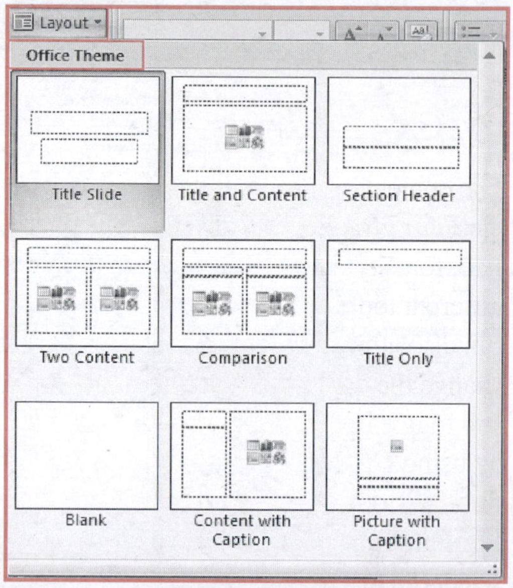

Fig. 6.9 *Layout tool*

New Slide

The New Slide tool is used to insert a new slide in a presentation (Fig. 6.10). It provides a list of option to select from. Click on black arrow next to new slide tool and a list of options appear. The options available in PowerPoint 2007 are:

- ***9 Slide Layouts:*** To select the layout for the new slide. The available layout options are **Title Slide**, **Title and Content**, **Section Header**, **Two Content**, **Comparison**, **Title Only**, **Blank**, **Content with Caption** and **Picture with Caption**.
- ***Duplicate Selected Slides:*** To create and insert a copy of the selected slide.
- ***Slides from Outline:*** To use slides from outlined document.
- ***Reuse Slides:*** To reuse slides from slide libraries or other PowerPoint files in your current presentation.

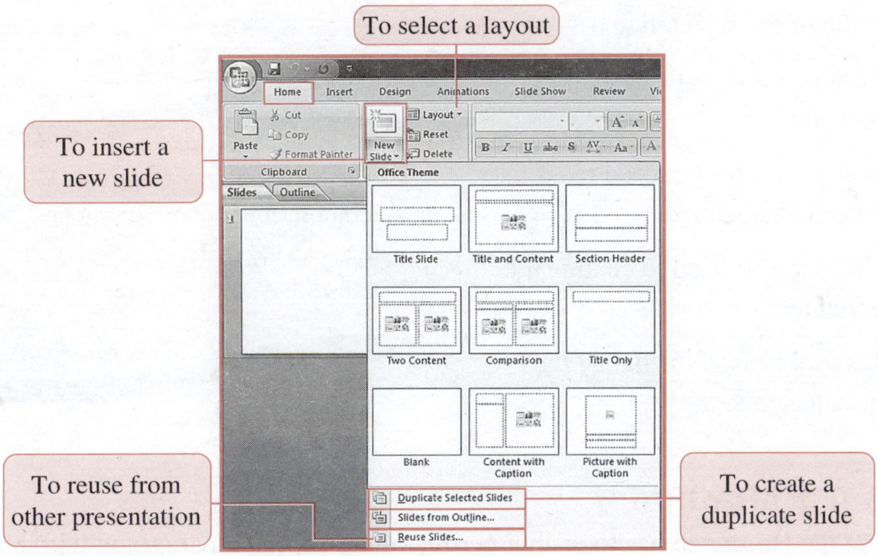

Fig. 6.10 *New Slide tool*

Reset and Delete

- ***Reset tool:*** This tool resets the position, size and formatting of the slide placeholders to their default settings.
- ***Delete tool:*** This tool removes the selected slide from the presentation.

Formatting a Slide

The content of the slides can be formatted using the **Font** group of the **Home** tab. Font face, font size, font style and font color can be changed using different tools available in the Font group. You can also adjust the spacing between characters; change the case of text to upper, lower, sentence and toggle case or give shadow effect to your text by using **Character Spacing**, **Change Case** and **Shadow** tools, respectively. Figure 6.11 shows the **Font** group and its tools. To use any of the tools, select the text you want to format and click on the tool. The various formatting options are:

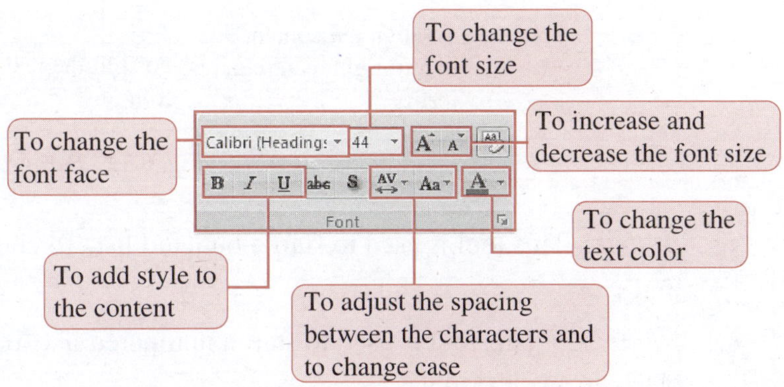

Fig. 6.11 *Font group*

- ***Font:*** This tool is used to change the font face of the selected text.
- ***Font Size:*** This tool is used to change the font size of the selected text.
- ***Grow Font:*** This tool is used to increase the font size of the selected text.
- ***Shrink Font:*** This tool is used to decrease the font size of the selected text.
- ***Clear All Formatting:*** This tool is used to clear all the formatting of the selected text and leaves just plain text.
- ***Bold, Italic and Underline:*** These tools are used to make the selected text bold, italic and underline it, respectively.
- ***Strikethrough:*** This tool is used to draw a line through the middle of the selected text.
- ***Shadow:*** This tool is used to give a shadow effect to the selected text.
- ***Character Spacing:*** This tool is used to adjust the spacing between characters.
- ***Change Case:*** This tool is used to change the case of the selected text.
- ***Font Color:*** This tool is used to change the font color of the selected text.

FACT FILE

The Live Preview feature in MS Office 2007 temporarily applies editing and formatting changes on the selected text and allows you to view the changes in real-time.

▶ FORMATTING A PARAGRAPH

The **Paragraph** group in the **Home** tab has tools that permit you to format a paragraph with bullets, numbering, indentation, line spacing, alignment and to convert text to SmartArt graphics. The options available in this group are (Fig. 6.12) listed below.

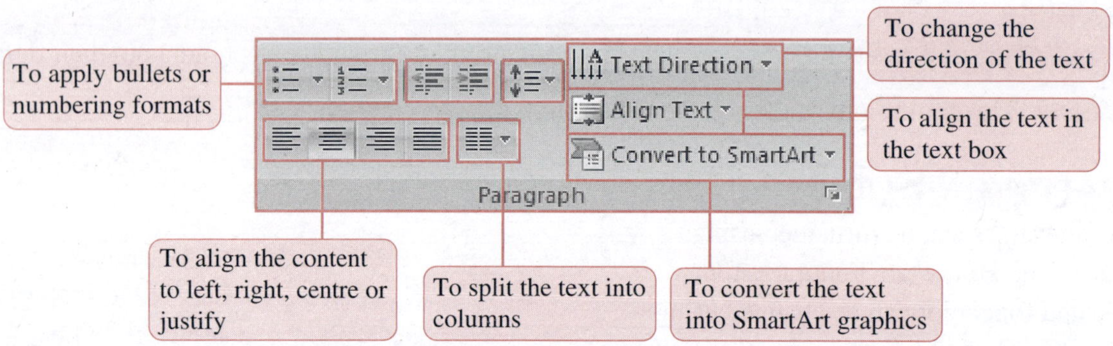

Fig. 6.12 *Paragraph group*

- ***Bullets:*** This tool is used to start a bulleted list. To choose different bullet style click on the black arrow next to it.
- ***Numbers:*** This tool is used to start a numbered list. To choose different numbering formats click on the black arrow next to it.

- ***Decrease List Level** and **Increase List Level:*** These tools are used to decrease and increase the indent levels, respectively.
- ***Line Spacing:*** This tool is used to specify the spacing between lines.
- ***Align Text Left:*** This tool is used to align the text to the left margin.
- ***Align Text Right:*** This tool is used to align the text to the right margin.
- ***Justify:*** This tool is used to align text to both the left and right margins.
- ***Columns:*** This tool is used to split the text into columns.
- ***Smart Art:*** This tool is used to convert the text into SmartArt graphic.
- ***Text Direction:*** This tool is used to change the orientation of text to vertical, stacked or rotate it to the desired direction.

Clipboard group

The **Clipboard** group of the **Home** tab have options to cut, copy and paste components (Fig. 6.13).

Copy and paste

To copy and paste data, follow the steps given below.

1. Select the item(s) that you wish to copy.
2. On the **Clipboard** group of the **Home** tab, click **Copy**.
3. Select the place(s) where you would like to copy the data.
4. On the **Clipboard** group of the **Home** tab, click **Paste**.

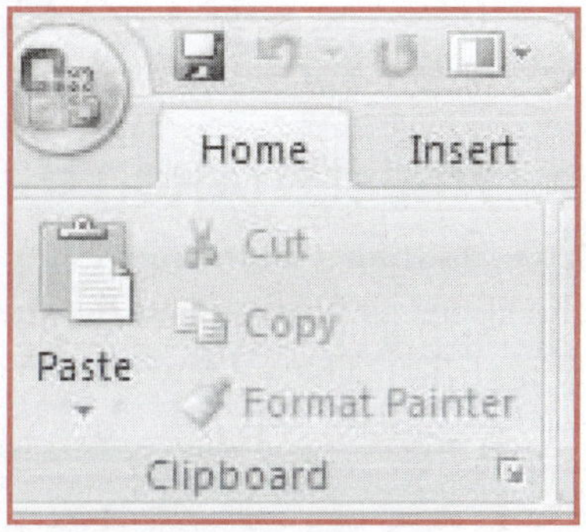

Fig. 6.13 *Clipboard group*

Cut and paste

To cut and paste data, follow the steps given below.

1. Select the item(s) that you wish to move (that is, cut and paste to another location).
2. On the **Clipboard** group of the **Home** tab, click **Cut**.
3. The data will be deleted from its original location.
4. Select the place(s) where you would like to copy the data.
5. On the **Clipboard** group of the **Home** tab, click **Paste**.

TRY THIS!

To undo or redo your most recent actions, click on the **Undo** and **Redo** buttons on the **Quick Access Toolbar**. You can also select text using **Select** and **Select All** buttons on the **Quick Access Toolbar**.

CHECK YOUR PROGRESS

A. Comparison and Two Content are two different slide layouts in PowerPoint 2007. They both are similar, but there is one elementary difference between them. Implement both the layouts in a presentation and with the help of an example, explain what sets them apart.

B. Complete the following activity.

1. Create a presentation on the topic 'My School' with minimum five slides.
2. Use Themes for slide background.
3. Display the activities of your school in each slide. (Such as, work experience, library, sports club and cultural activities).
4. Format the contents using Home tab tools you learnt so far.
5. Use Bullets and Numbering in atleast one of your slide.
6. Save the presentation as MySchool_nameofyourschool on your desktop.

C. Identify this tool 

. Is it present in Word 2007?

Presentation Views

Presentations can be viewed in a variety of ways. On the **View** tab, the **Presentation Views** group allows you to view the slides as **Normal**, **Slide Sorter**, **Notes Page**, **Slide Show**, **Slide Master**, **Handout Master**, and **Notes Master** (Fig. 6.14). These views are explained in Table 6.1.

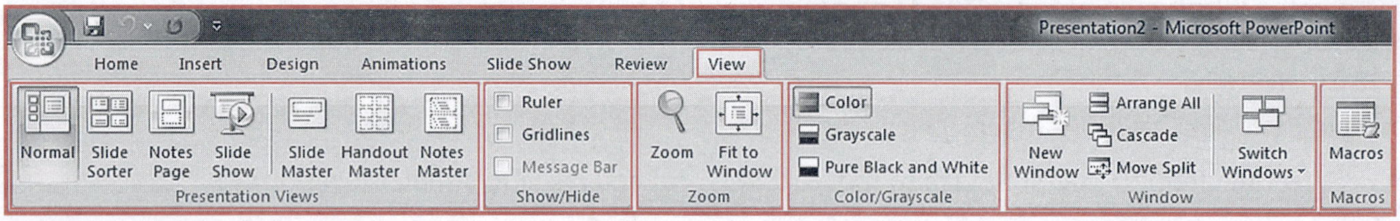

Fig. 6.14 *View group*

Table 6.1 *Presentation views*

Presentation Views	Description
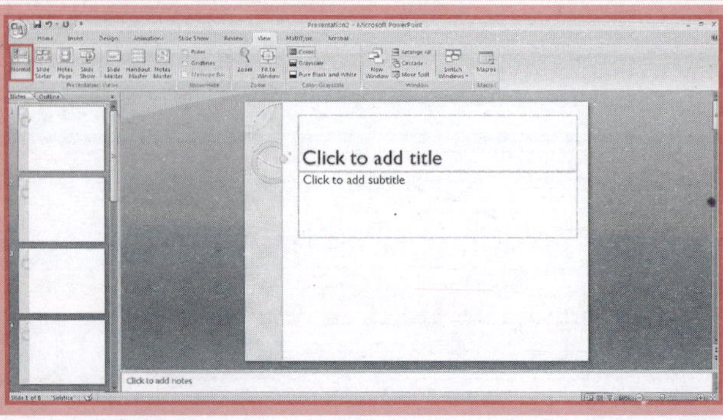	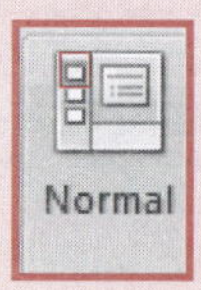 **Normal View:** It is the default view and it is known as the **main editing view**. It is used to write, edit and format the presentation. You can rearrange the slides using the **Outline** tab on left.

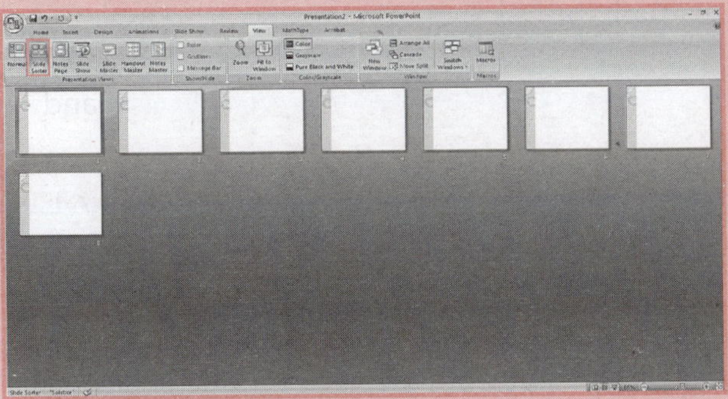

Slide Sorter View: You can view all the slides in a presentation on the screen. The slide number of each slide appears on the bottom right of each slide. You can rearrange the slides in this view.

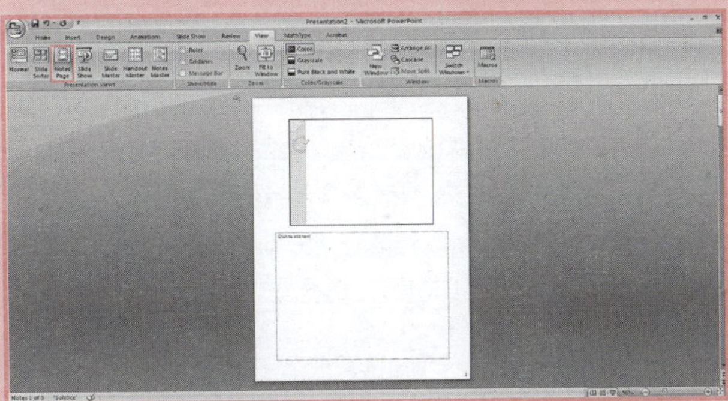

Notes Page View: Notes Page view is used to create speaker notes for the slides. It reminds the user about the topic of the slide that appears on the screen and provides the user with additional information that is not part of the slides.

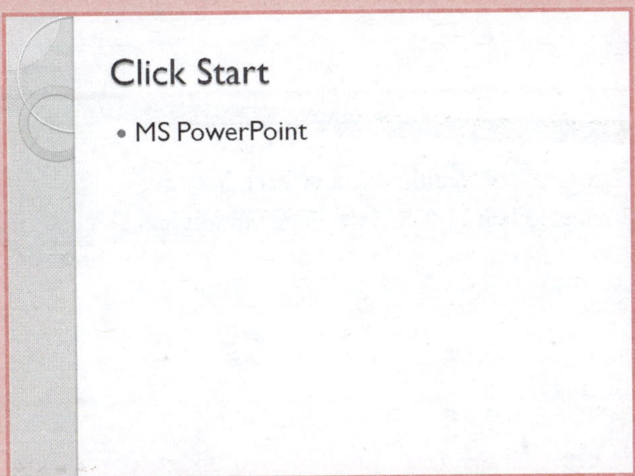

Slide Show View: The Slide Show view is used to display the presentation in full screen. You can use arrow keys, Home key End key and Enter key to move to first, next and last slide within a presentation.

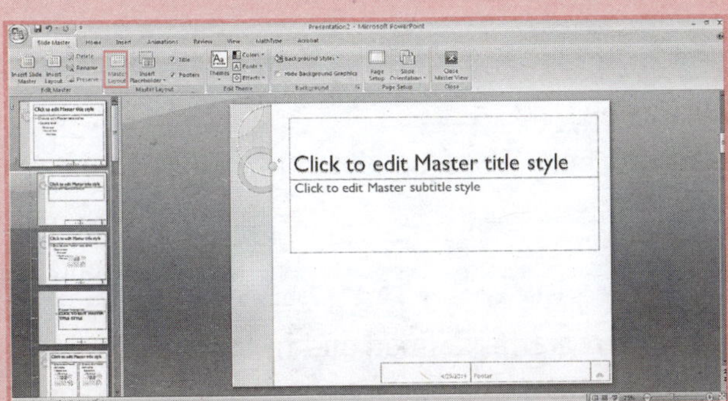

Slide Master View: A Slide Master is part of a template that stores information, including placements of text and objects on a slide, text and object placeholder sizes, text styles, backgrounds, color themes, effects, and animation.

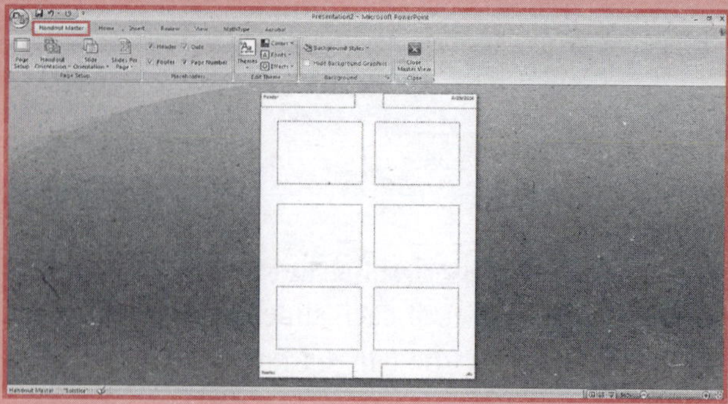

Handout Master View: This view is used to change the design and layout of the printed handouts. It displays the **Handout Master** tab with tools to change page size, orientation, slide orientation and number of slides to place in handouts.

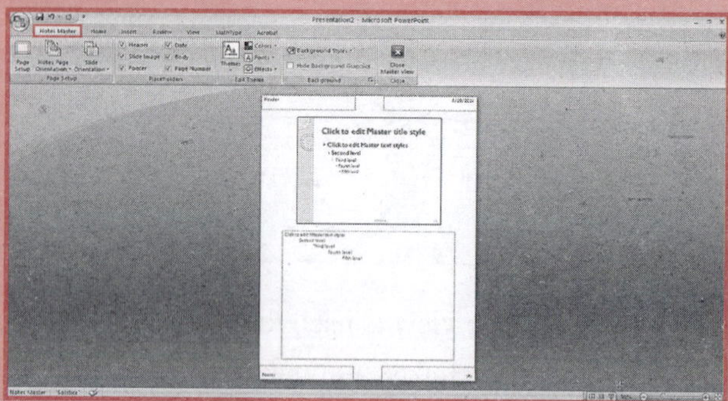

Notes Master View: This view determines the characteristics of printed speaker notes. It displays **Notes Master** tab with tools to edit the notes master. You can change the page setup, page orientation and insert headers, footers, themes, backgrounds, etc.

FACT FILE

In PowerPoint, a **Master** specifies the appearance of text, slide background color, animation effects, and any additional text or other objects that you want to add on each slide or page. Each PowerPoint presentation has at least three Masters. They are:

- **Slide Master:** It dictates the format of your slides
- **Handout Master:** It controls the look of printed handouts
- **Notes Master:** It determines the characteristics of printed speaker notes.

Inserting Text in Slides

The **Text** group of the **Insert** tab of PowerPoint 2007 helps you insert text box, WordArt, date, time, slide number, header and footers into a presentation.

Inserting WordArt

You can add WordArt in a presentation to enhance its appearance. Word Art are predefined and in-built styles that can be applied to text to create a visual effect (Fig. 6.15).

To apply WordArt, follow the steps given below.

1. Select the text you want to convert to WordArt.
2. Click on the **Insert** tab.
3. Click on the **WordArt** tool in the **Text** group. A drop-down list, with multiple choices, appears.
4. Choose the **WordArt** style you desire.
5. **Edit WordArt Text** box opens.
6. Choose the font type and font size you want in the **Font:** and **Size:** box. You can also make the text bold and italics. Make changes to the text in the **Text:** box.
7. Click on **OK**.

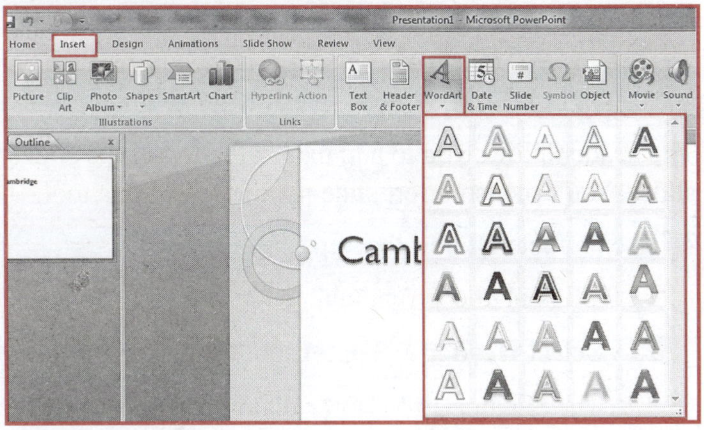

Fig. 6.15 *Inserting WordArt*

To modify the styles of WordArt: Even after inserting a WordArt in your presentation, you can modify it. To do so, follow the steps given below.

1. Select the **WordArt**.
2. Notice that **Drawing Tools Format** tab appears (Fig. 6.16).
3. In the **WordArt Styles** group you can change the text color, text outline color and text effect by clicking on the **Text Fill** tool, the **Text Outline** tool and the **Text Effects** tool, respectively.

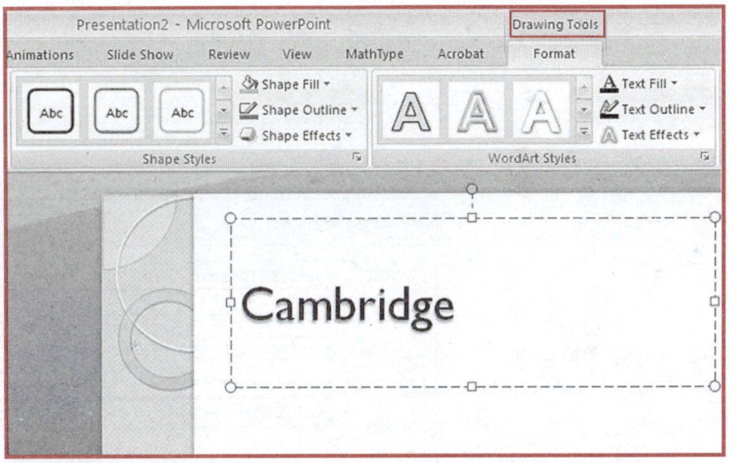

Fig. 6.16 *Modifying WordArt*

Inserting text box

The **Text Box** tool in the **Text** group of the **Insert** tab is used to insert a text box into a presentation. To add a text box, follow the steps given below.

1. Select the slide where you want to place the text box.
2. On the **Insert** tab, go to the **Text** group and click on the **Text Box** tool.
3. Click on the slide and drag the cursor to expand the text box.
4. Type the text in the text box.

NOTE: The moment you insert a text box, the **Drawing Tools Format** tab appears (Fig. 6.17). It has **Insert Shapes**, **Shape Styles**, **WordArt Styles**, **Arrange** and **Size** groups that help format both the text box and the text inside the text box.

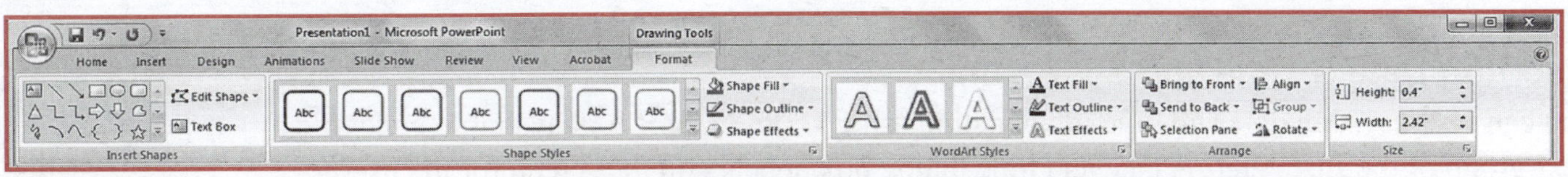

Fig. 6.17 *Drawing Tools Format tab*

Inserting Header and Footer

To repeat a text or logo on every page at the top or at the bottom of every slide, it is not necessary for you to type again and again. Instead, you can use the **Header & Footer** tool. It is used to create or edit the header or footer of the document.

The header allows you to add data at the top of the slides. The footer allows you to add data at the bottom of the slides. You can also insert slide number using this tool.

To insert a footer, follow the steps given below.

1. Click on the **Insert** tab.
2. Select **Header & Footer** tool from **Text** group.
3. The **Header and Footer** dialog box appears (Fig. 6.18).
4. Click the **Date and time**, **Slide number** and **Footer** checkbox to insert data and time, slide number and footer respectively, in your slides.
5. Select **Apply to All** button to apply it to all the slides or click on the **Apply** button to apply it to the current slide.

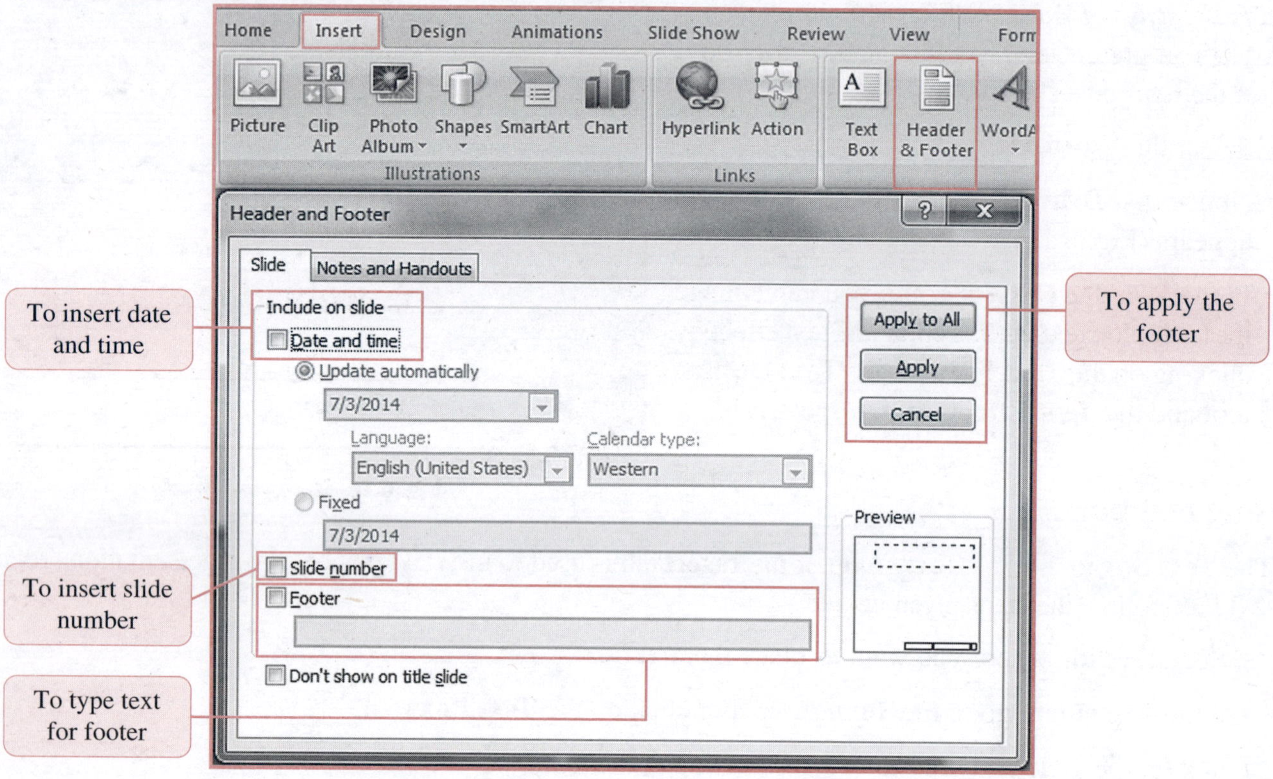

Fig. 6.18 *Header and Footer dialog box*

NOTE: You can add footer to both your slides as well as notes and handouts. In the **Header and Footer** dialog box, select the appropriate tab (**Slide** or **Notes and Handouts**) to insert them. However, a Header can only be added to notes and handouts.

Inserting Date & Time and Slide Number

You can insert system date and time in your slide using **Date & Time** tool available under the **Text** group of the **Insert** tab. A date and time dialog box appears on the screen for the user to select the date format to be inserted onto a slide. Slide number can also be inserted using **Slide Number** tool present in the same group.

▶ Slide Show

The **Slide Show** tab allows you to set up your presentation. This tab contains three groups: **Start Slide Show**, **Set Up** and **Monitors** (Fig. 6.19).

Fig. 6.19 *Slide Show tab*

Start Slide Show group

Under **Start Slide Show** group you have three tools: **From Beginning**, **From Current Slide, and Custom Slide Show**.

- ***From Beginning:*** This tool starts the slide show from the first slide of the presentation document.
- ***From Current Slide:*** This tool starts the slide show from the current slide.
- ***Custom Show:*** This tool is used to customise your slide show. It displays only the slides you select (Fig. 6.20).

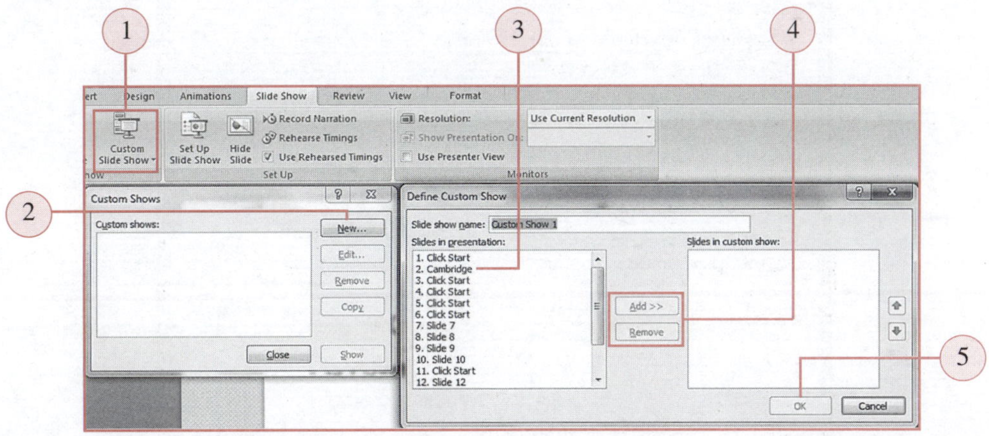

Fig. 6.20 *Setting up custom slide show*

Set Up group

Under **Set Up** group you have **Set Up Slide Show**, **Hide Slide**, **Record Narration**, **Rehearse Timings** and **Use Rehearsed Timings** tools (Fig. 6.21). This group allows you to set preferences for how the slide show will be presented. The options include:

- To run the show automatically or will be presented by a speaker
- To repeat the show continuously
- To show without Narration
- To show without Animation
- To show all slides or specific slides
- To advance slide automatically using timings or by clicking the mouse.

NOTE: The **Monitors** group is used to choose the screen resolution to use for the full-screen slide show. It is also used to set **Presenter View**. In this view, one monitor displays full screen slide show while another monitor displays special speaker view that includes timings and speaker notes.

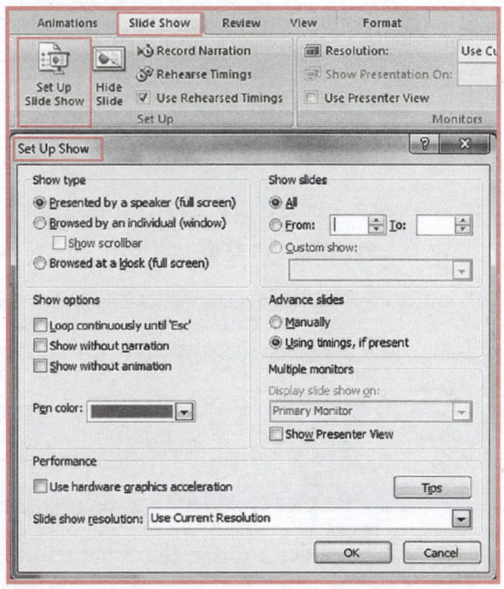

Fig. 6.21 *Set Up Slide Show*

ACTIVITY

To set up a slide show and rehearse and record slide timings.

1. Go to the **Slide Show** tab.
2. Click on the **Set Up Show** tool.
3. The **Set Up Show** dialog box appears.
4. In the **Show Type** section, select who will present the presentation; in the **Show slides** section, mention which all slides to include in your slide show; in the **Advanced slides** section, specify whether to use timings or manually move the slide show.

   NOTE: You can set other settings according to your requirement.

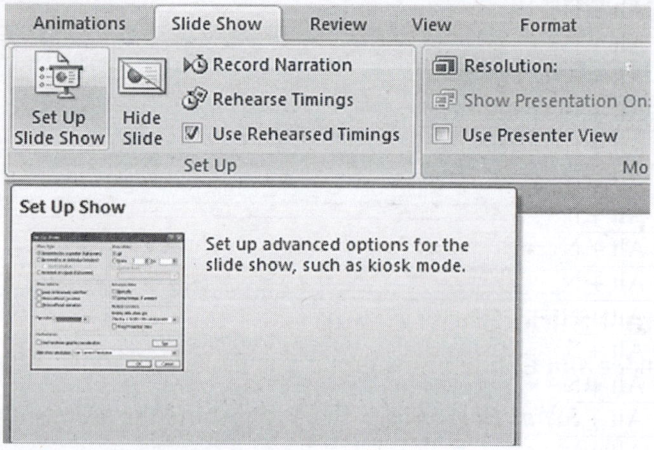

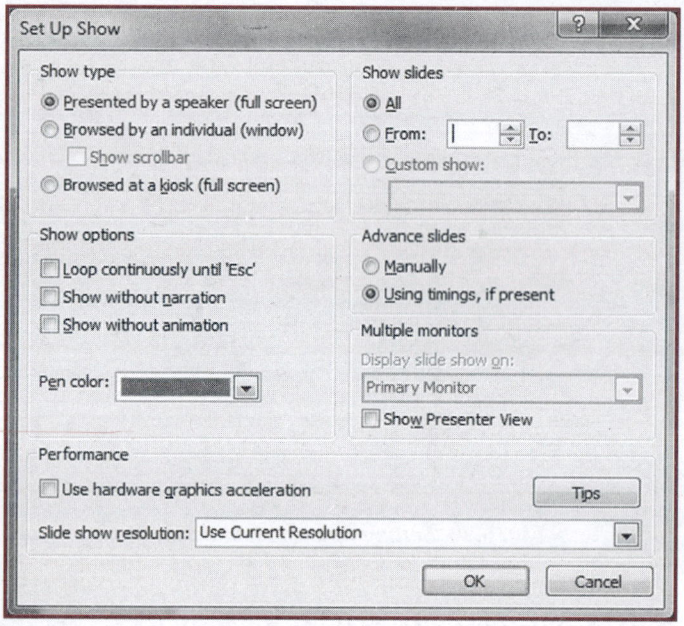

5. Click on **OK**.
6. In the **Set Up** group, click on **Rehearse Timings**.
7. The Rehearsal toolbar appears and the **Slide Time** box begins timing your presentation. The options available in the Rehearsal toolbar are:
   - **Next:** To move to the next slide
   - **Pause:** To temporarily stop recording the time
   - **Pause:** To restart recording the time after pausing
   - **Slide Time:** To set an exact time for a slide to appear, type the length of time in this box
   - **Repeat:** To restart recording the time from the current slide.
8. After you set the time for the last slide, a message box asks to keep the recorded slide timings or not. Click **Yes**.
9. Slide Sorter view appears and displays the time of each slide in your presentation.

Alt + H + L	To view slide layout options
Alt + H + K	To line spacing options
Alt + H + J	To split into columns
Alt + H + U	To start a bulleted list
Alt + H + N	To start a numbered list
Alt + H + 6	To set character spacing
Alt + N + X	To insert text box
Alt + N + H	To insert header and footer
Alt + N + W	To insert WordArt
Alt + N + D	To insert date and time
Alt + N + SN	To insert slide number
Alt + S + B	To start slide show from the beginning
Alt + S + C	To start slide show from the current slide
Alt + S + S	To setup Slide Show
Alt + W + L	Normal View
Alt + W + I	Slide Sorter View
Alt + W + T	Notes Page View
Alt + W + S	Slide Show View
Alt + W + M	Slide Master View
Alt + W + H	Handout Master View
Alt + W + K	Notes Master View
Ctrl + O	To open a presentation
Ctrl + B	To make the text bold
Ctrl + C	To copy
Ctrl + F10	To maximize presentation window
Ctrl + F9	To minimize presentation window
Ctrl + H	To replace
Ctrl + Home	To go to the first slide
Ctrl + I	To make the text italics
Ctrl + J	To Justify
Ctrl + L	To left align
Ctrl + Left Arrow	To move one word to the left
Ctrl + M	To insert new slide
Ctrl + Q	To exit from PowerPoint
Ctrl + R	To right align
Ctrl + Right Arrow	To move one word to right
Ctrl + Shift + >	To increase font size
Ctrl + T	To format the font
Ctrl + U	To underline
Ctrl + Up arrow	To move up one paragraph
Ctrl + W	To close the presentation
Ctrl + X	To cut
Ctrl + Y	To redo the last action
Ctrl + Z	To undo the last action
F1	To go to help
F5	To run presentation

CHECK YOUR PROGRESS

A. Create a presentation on the topic 'Save your Environment'. The topic should include one slide each on:

- Save water
- Keep your surroundings clean
- Go green
- Avoid plastic bags
- Don't pollute water and air

Use all the possible features of PowerPoint 2007 you have learnt so far.

B. Set up a custom slide show for the show presentation. Include only five slides in the slide show. HOTS

GLOSSARY

- **Installed Themes:** They are the set of predesigned formats that include text, layouts, background and color schemes which can be applied to any presentation.
- **Installed Templates:** It is a quick and easy way to create a Presentation using built-in templates.
- **Presentation:** It is a collection of multiple slides arranged in a systematic order with several components to present a slide show.
- **Slide:** It is a collection of text, images, pictures, graphs, charts, sound and animation.
- **Slide Layouts:** It contains formatting, positioning and placeholders for all of the content that appears on a slide.
- **Slide Show:** It is the presentation of series of slides created using a presentation tool.

NOW YOU KNOW

1. Microsoft Office button, Quick Access Toolbar, and Ribbon are the main components of PowerPoint 2007.
2. Office Button contains the functions of File Menu options of previous versions of PowerPoint.
3. The groups are logical collections of features designed to perform function that you will utilise in developing or editing your PowerPoint slides.
4. PowerPoint has in-built designs, pictures, clipart, graphics and templates which help the user to design the presentation in a professional manner.
5. Slide Pane is used to add contents on slides.
6. Installed Templates is equal to the AutoContent Wizard of previous versions of PowerPoint.
7. Normal View is the default view and it is called as main editing view.
8. Notes Page View is used to create speaker notes for the slides.
9. In PowerPoint, a Master specifies the appearance of text, slide background color, animation effects, and any additional text or objects that you want to display on each slide or page.
10. Slide Master dictates the format of your slides; Handout Master controls the look of printed handouts; and Notes Master determines the characteristics of printed speaker notes.

EXERCISE

FA

A Fill up the blanks.

1. A .... is a collection of text, images, pictures, graphs, charts, sound and animation.
2. The .... button contains the functions of File Menu options of previous versions of PowerPoint.
3. The .... toolbar contains tools that you use very often.
4. The Ribbon in PowerPoint 2007 has .... tabs.
5. The Installed Templates option is equal to the .... of previous versions of PowerPoint.
6. The default layout of the PowerPoint is .... slide.
7. The content of the slides can be formatted using .... group of Home Tab.
8. The .... view is used to display the presentation in full screen.
9. The .... Master dictates the format of the slides.
10. .... + ... keys are used to open an existing presentation.
11. The .... dialog box enables you to customise the PowerPoint environment to fit to your specific requirements.
12. The .... view includes the slide and the speaker notes.
13. .... master, ... master and .... master are the three masters of every PowerPoint presentation.
14. The .... group is used to choose the screen resolution to use for the full-screen slide show.
15. A .... can only be added to Notes and Handouts and not slides.

B Multiple choice questions.

1. Which keyboard shortcut key is used to bring you to the first slide of the presentation?

   a. Ctrl + F b. Ctrl + Home c. Home d. Ctrl + 1

2. There are .... layouts in Power Point 2007.

   a. 9 b. 24 c. 12 d. None of these

3. To create a copy of a slide you can simply click .... button.

a. Copy Slide   b. Blank Slide   c. Duplicate Slide   d. New Slide

4. To insert a new slide .... key is used.

a. Ctrl + N   b. Ctrl + S   c. Alt + N   d. Ctrl + M

5. In PowerPoint 2007, the saved presentation takes the extension ....

a. .ppt7   b. .ppt   c. .pptx   d. .ppts

6. .... function key is used to run a slide show.

a. F2   b. F1   c. F7   d. F5

7. To insert a text at the top of every page .... can be used.

a. Top notes   b. Heading   c. Header   d. Footer

8. The .... tool is used to reuse slides from Slide Libraries or other PowerPoint files in your current presentation.

a. Duplicate Slide   b. New Slide   c. Copy Slide   d. Reuse Slides

9. The .... tool is used to customise the slide show and display only the selected slides.

a. Live   b. Custom Show   c. Slide Show   d. Custom Slide Show

10. .... allows you to view your presentation with your speaker notes on one computer and on a different monitor you can view notes-free presentation for the audience.

a. Presenter View   b. Normal View   c. Notes View   d. Handout View

C Answer the following questions briefly.

1. Name any two software used to create presentation.
2. Name any two installed templates.
3. Name the view in which you can view all slides.
4. What is the extension of PowerPoint 2007 files?
5. Which key is used to decrease the font size of the selected text?

SA

D Answer the following questions.

1. What is the use of the slide sorter view?
2. Write a short note on three masters in PowerPoint 2007.
3. What are the groups present in the Home tab of PowerPoint 2007 Ribbon?

4. Can you rearrange the order of slides in Notes page view?
5. How can you insert date and time into your slide?

E Answer the following questions in detail.

1. How to set up a slide show?
2. Write a note on header and footer in PowerPoint 2007.
3. What are slide layouts? Which is the default layout?
4. How many types of slide views are present there in PowerPoint 2007?
5. What are the options present in slide show tab of PowerPoint 2007 Ribbon. Briefly explain the three groups present.

Application Based Questions

A. Shama divided her class into four equal groups. Each group represented a deliberation team. Team 1 and 2 were given the topic 'Documentation vs Presentation'. Team 3 and 4 were given the topic 'PowerPoint 2007 vs PowerPoint 2003'. Each group had to discuss and come up with ten points on the given topic. Suggest to the teams the specific points they can focus on and how to deal with them.

NOTE: Give atleast five suggestions to each team.

B. Kriti was exploring the PowerPoint 2007 interface and came across Installed Templates option. She asked her teacher about it. Her teacher explained the concept to her. Afterwards, she gave the following activity to Kriti. Help Kriti complete the activity.

Using templates create a presentation on the topic MS Office 2007. Follow the guidelines given below to complete this task.

- From the Installed Templates section select Widescreen Presentation template. Find pictures of Word, Excel, PowerPoint and Access window.
- Insert them in different slides.
- Write few lines about each program and format the content.
- Insert Slide Number.
- Create Header as 'MS Office 2007' and it should appear on all slides.
- Create footer as 'Activity 2'.

C. Ishan created a presentation for his sister's 16th birthday. The presentation has 16 slides; each slide corresponds to a year in her life. He now wants to add a common background to all the slides. Also, at the bottom of the page he wants to write Year1, Year2, Year3 and so on. Suggest how he can make these changes.

D. Raman was working on a presentation for his bank and at the same time creating speaker notes for himself. His son informed him that he can add notes into his PowerPoint presentation. However, Raman is worried that it will clutter his presentation and his personal notes will be visible to everyone in the audience. Help Raman understand how useful adding notes are for him. Also, explain which feature he can use to have a separate view for himself and the audience.

LAB WORK

A. Create a new presentation. Apply Title and Content slide layout to the first slide. Insert two blank slides and choose different layout for each. Apply Verve theme to the presentation. Add text box to each slide. In the text box, using WordArt, give headings. Save this file and exit PowerPoint.

B. Open the file you created earlier and add content to it. Make use of bullet and numbering on each slide. Set up the slide show and view the presentation in full screen mode.

C. Create a presentation to conduct a quiz on 'IT Icons'. Set up the Slide Show for this presentation. Follow the guidelines given below to complete this task.

- Create minimum five slides for Round 1 to Round 5 with at least five questions each.
- Round 1 – Name the IT Personalities (text only)
- Round 2 – Identify the icons (use pictures)
- Round 3 – Multiple Choice Questions
- Round 4 – Puzzle
- Round 5 – Rapid Fire Round (set timings for this slide)

D. Make a presentation for your school science project on 'Parts of the Atom'. Use WordArt on the title slide only. Use header and footer, to insert slide number on each slide. Add notes to each slide.

E. Explore the options present in the Office button. How do they help you publish and send your presentation to others? HOTS

MS Office 2010

Updates

In PowerPoint 2010:

- You can turn your mouse into a laser pointer during presentations. To use this feature, follow the steps given below.
  1. Start your PowerPoint presentation.
  2. Hold down the Ctrl key and click the left mouse button anywhere on the slide.
  3. The pointed arrow will automatically turn into a laser pointer on the slide.
- You can save your presentation as a video. PowerPoint 2010 allows you to make a video of your presentation that has perfectly synchronised audio and complex animations along with their timings. To use this feature, follow the steps given below.
  1. Click on the **File** menu.
  2. Select **Save & Send** option ⟶ **File Types** ⟶ **Create a Video**.
  3. In **Create a Video** pane, choose the appropriate options and click on the **Create Video** button.

TEACHER'S NOTES

1. Explore the PowerPoint 2007 backstage views with the students.
2. If possible, using multiple monitors and demonstrate how the Presenter View works.

7 Presentation Tools – II

SNAP RECAP

1. Microsoft Office button, Quick Access Toolbar and Ribbon are the main components of PowerPoint 2007 window.
2. The Slide Pane is used to add content on slides.
3. A PowerPoint 2007 presentation has minimum three masters: Slide Master, Handout Master and Notes Master.
4. Presentations can be viewed in different views: Normal, Slide Sorter, Notes Page, Slide Show, Slide Master, Handout Master, and Notes Master.

LEARNING OBJECTIVES

You will learn about:

1. Inserting Tables
2. Inserting Pictures
3. Inserting SmartArt
4. Inserting Charts
5. Inserting Sounds and Movies
6. Record Narration
7. Custom Animation
8. Slide Transition
9. Rehearse Timings

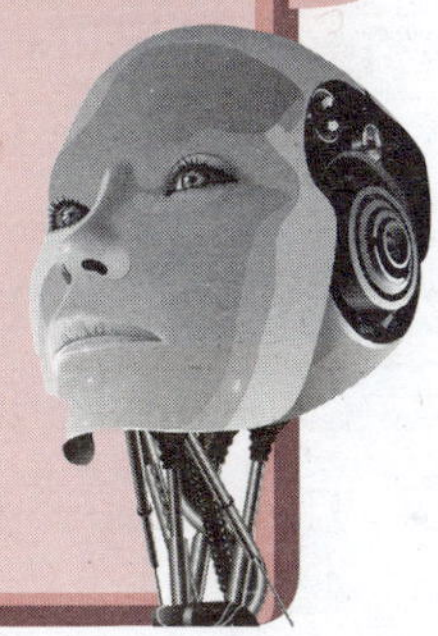

▶ INTRODUCTION

A presentation tool helps you to present a show effectively using pictures, diagrams, charts, video clips and sounds. The **Insert** tab in PowerPoint 2007 provides different tools to insert various components into a presentation. The **Insert** tab has five groups (Fig. 7.1). They are:

- Tables
- Illustrations
- Links
- Text
- Media Clips

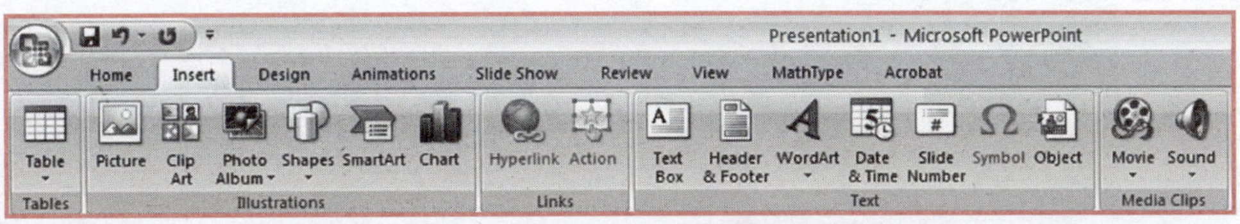

Fig. 7.1 *Insert tab*

▶ INSERTING TABLES

The **Table** tool in **Tables** group is used to organise the information in a tabular format. Tables are used to display data in a tabular format. To create a table, follow the steps given below (Fig. 7.2).

1. Place the cursor on the slide where you want to add the new table.
2. Click on the **Insert** tab.
3. Click the **Table** button on the **Tables** group. You can create a table in one of the four ways:
    a. Highlight the number of rows and columns.
    b. Click the **Insert Table...** option and enter the number of rows and columns.
    c. Click the **Draw Table** option and create your table by clicking and entering the rows and columns.
    d. Click the **Excel Spreadsheet** and enter data into the Excel spreadsheet that appears.

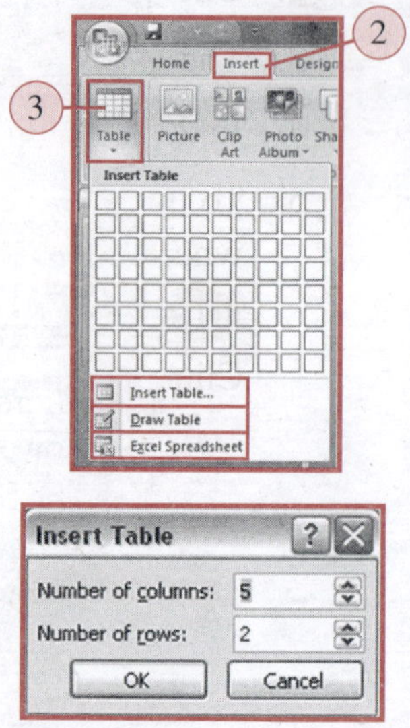

Fig. 7.2 *Inserting tables*

The options available in the **Table** tool are discussed below.

- ***Insert Table...:*** This tool is also used to insert a table in a slide. To insert a table, click on the **Insert Table...** option. A **Insert Table** dialog box appears. In the dialog box, type the number of columns and rows you want to create and click on **OK**. A table will be displayed on the slide.
- ***Draw Table:*** This tool is used to draw the borders of a table.
- ***Excel Spreadsheet:*** This tool is used to insert a spreadsheet on the current slide. Just click on the tool and a spreadsheet will appear on the slide.

▶ INSERT PICTURES

This option allows you to insert pictures from a file that is stored in the computer system. To insert a picture, follow the steps given below.

1. Click on the **Insert** tab.
2. Click the **Insert Picture** button in the **Illustrations** group.
3. In the **Insert Picture** dialog box that appears (Fig. 7.3), select the picture file and enter it in **File name:** box.
4. Click on the **Insert** button.
5. The selected picture will be inserted into the placeholder.

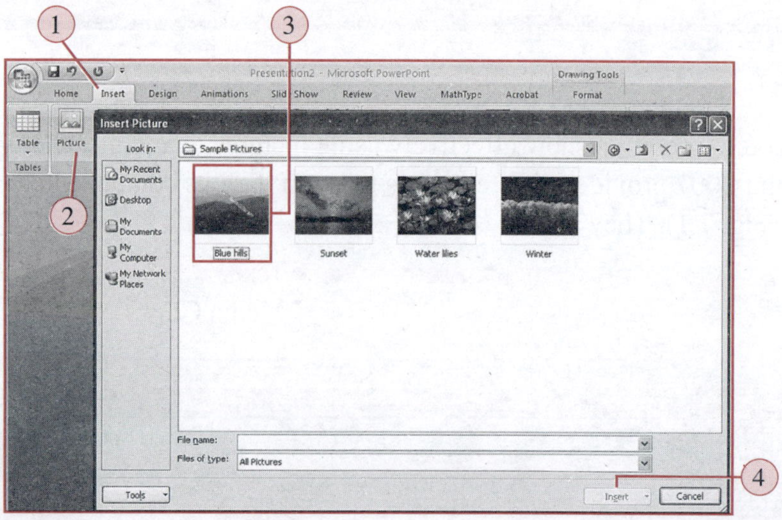

Fig. 7.3 *Insert Picture dialog box*

▶ Inserting Clip Art

PowerPoint 2007 has a collection of in-built pictures and art.
To insert them into your slide, follow the steps given below (Fig. 7.4).

1. Click on the **Insert** tab.
2. Click the **Clip Art** button in the **Illustrations** group.
3. The Clip Art task pane appears on the right side of the screen.
4. In the **Search for:** box, type the keywords and click on **Go**.
5. To insert the clip art on the slide, click on it and drag it to where you want.

   OR

   Click the black arrow next to the picture and choose the **Insert** option from the drop-down list that appears.

> **FACT FILE**
>
> To remove unwanted text from a picture or change it to a shape, **Crop** and **Crop to shape** tool respectively are used.

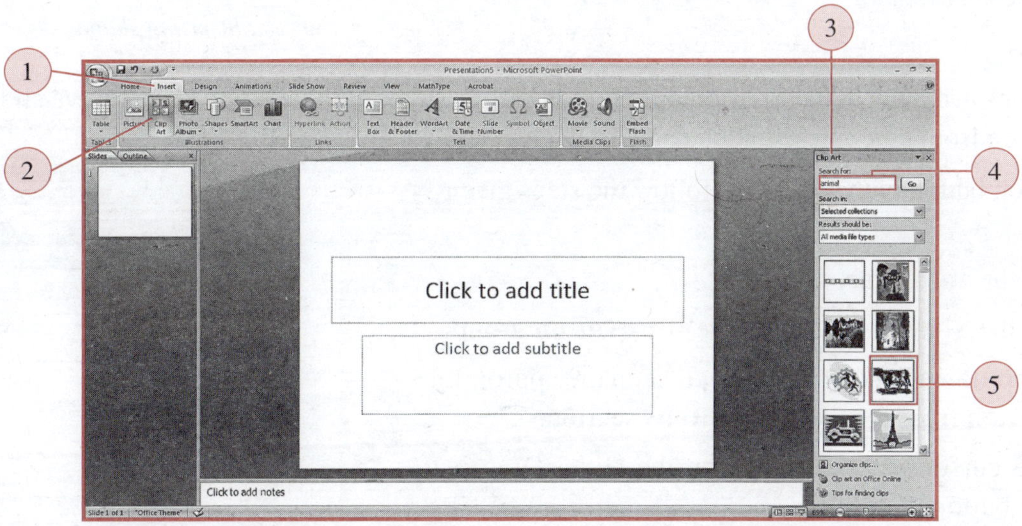

Fig. 7.4 *Inserting clip art*

Picture Tools Format tab

When you add a graphic to the presentation, an additional tab named **Picture Tools Format** appears on the Ribbon. This tab allows you to format pictures and graphics. It has four groups (Fig. 7.5). They are:

- ***Adjust group:*** The tools in this group help you control the brightness, contrast and color of the picture. You can also compress, change and reset the picture using tools in this group.
- ***Picture Styles group:*** The tools in this group help you to apply styles like a frame or a border around the picture and add effects to the picture.

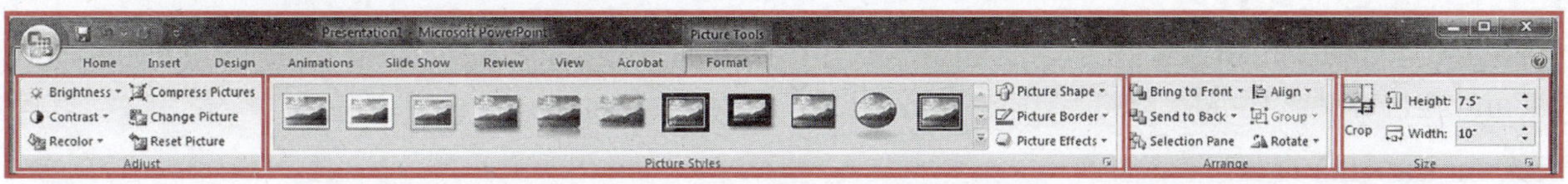

Fig. 7.5 *Picture Tools Format tab*

- ***Arrange group:*** The tools in this group help you to control the alignment and rotation of the picture.
- ***Size group:*** The tools in this group are used to crop and adjust the size of the picture.

▶ Inserting Shapes

The Shapes tool helps you insert different shapes in a slide. These shapes can be formatted and their color, size and direction can be changed. To add shapes to your presentation, follow the steps given below.

1. Click on the **Insert** tab.
2. Click on the **Shapes** button in the **Illustrations** group.
3. From the drop-down list select the shape you need (Fig. 7.6).

NOTE: The **Drawing Tools Format** tab is also used to format the shapes.

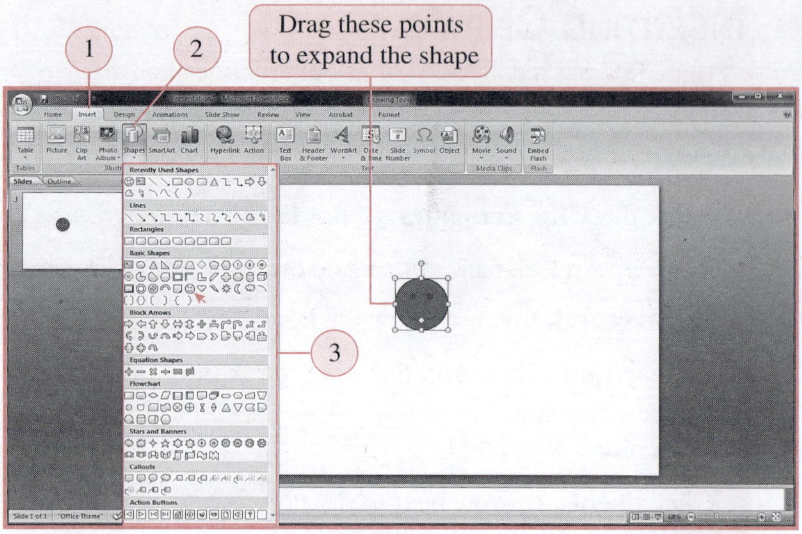

Fig. 7.6 *Inserting shapes*

Action Buttons

The Action Buttons available in the **Shapes** tool provide the facility to link to a web page/a file/a slide in the same presentation/a slide from other presentation using **hyperlinks**.

To create an action button with hyperlink, follow the steps given below.

1. Click on the **Insert** tab.
2. Click on the **Shapes** tool under the **Illustration** group.
3. In the drop-down list that appears, click on the appropriate action button from the **Action Buttons** section.
4. Place the cursor with plus sign on the slide. Drag it to place the button.
5. The action button appears on the screen along with the **Action Settings** dialog box (Fig. 7.7).

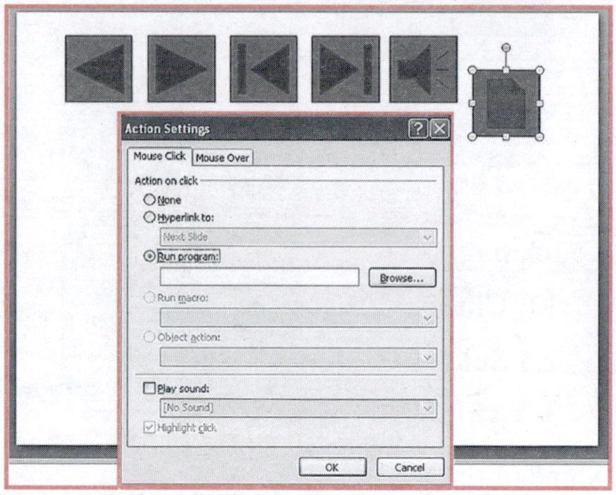

Fig. 7.7 *Action Settings dialog box*

6. Choose the action of the action button. You can choose between two options: **Mouse Click** or **Mouse Over**
7. Select the corresponding tab. Choose the action you desire from the **Action on click** section. The options available are: **None, Hyperlink to:** and **Run program:**. Select **Play sound:** checkbox to play sound on mouse-click and select **Highlight Click** Checkbox to highlight the mouse-click.
8. Click on **OK**.
9. Click on the action button, at the time of slide show, to trigger the action.

▶ Inserting SmartArt

SmartArt is a new feature in Office 2007 that allows you to choose from a variety of graphics, including flowcharts, lists, cycles and processes. To add SmartArt to your slides, follow the steps given below.

1. Click on the **Insert** tab.
2. Click the **SmartArt** button in the **Illustrations** group.
3. Click on the **SmartArt** of your choice from **Choose a SmartArt Graphic** dialog box (Fig. 7.8).
4. Click **OK**.

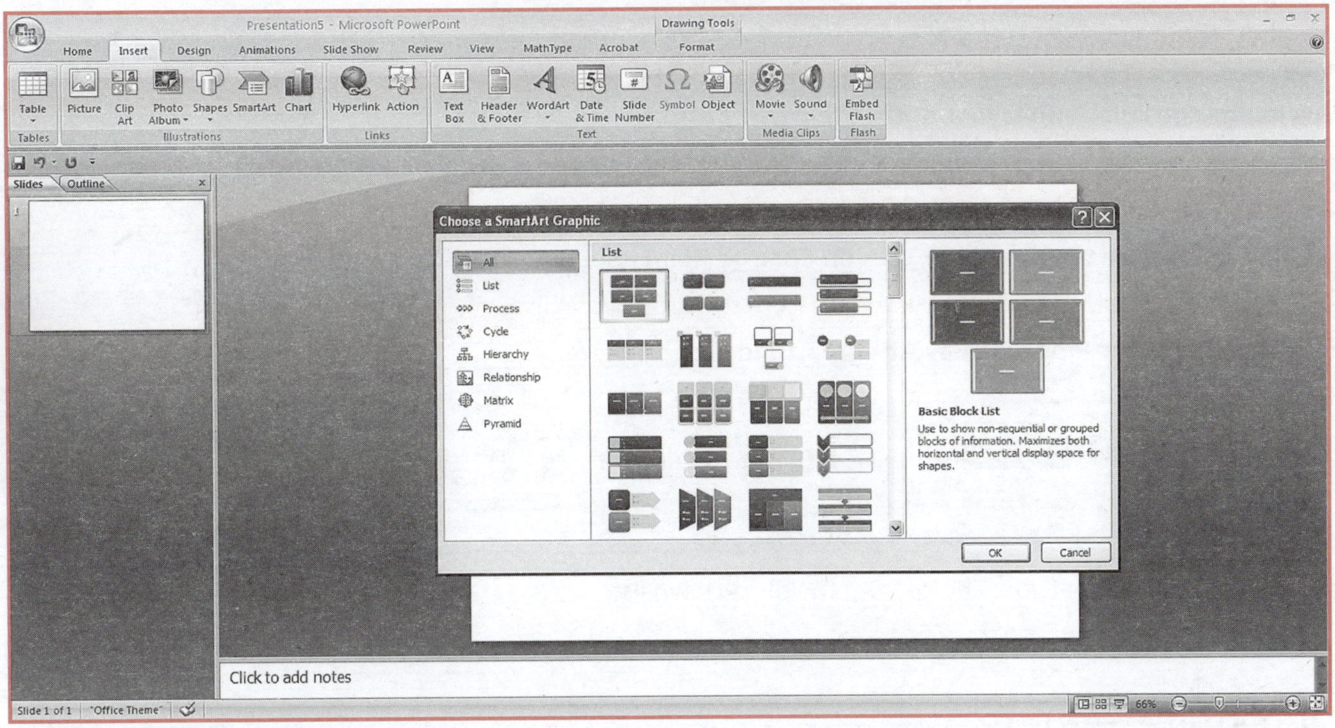

Fig. 7.8 *Choose a SmartArt Graphic dialog box*

5. The selected SmartArt graphic is added to your slide. Drag it to the desired location in the slide.

To format the SmartArt, follow the steps given below.

1. Click on the **SmartArt**. Two new tabs appear.
2. Select either the **SmartArt Tools Design** or the **SmartArt Tools Format** tab (Fig. 7.9).
3. Modify the SmartArt using the options available in the **Design** and **Format** tab.

Some of the tools available in the **SmartArt Tools Design** tab are: **Add Shape** to add another shape to the graphic; **Right to Left** to change the direction of the chosen element such as an arrow from right to left; **Promote** and **Demote** to promote and demote the level of the selected SmartArt graphic component; **Layouts** show more layouts in the same SmartArt graphic type; **Change Colors** to change the color combination of the elements in the SmartArt; **SmartArt Styles** to change the style of the selected SmartArt graphic.

Some of the tools available in the **SmartArt Tools Format tab** are: **Change Shape** to change the shape of the selected SmartArt graphic element; **Larger** and **Smaller** to make the selected SmartArt graphic element larger or smaller; **Shape Fill** and **Shape Outline** to change, add, or remove the shape fill and shape outline of the selected SmartArt graphic element; **WordArt Styles** to apply a WordArt style to the text contained in the selected SmartArt graphic element; **Arrange** allows you to reorder, align, group, and rotate the selected SmartArt graphic elements.

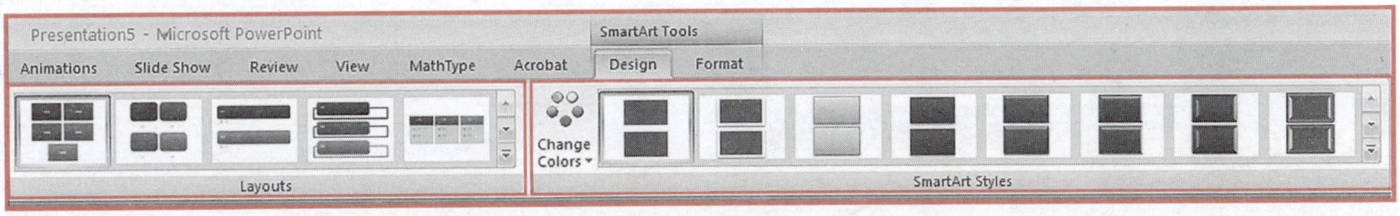

Fig. 7.9 *SmartArt Tools Design and Format tab*

ACTIVITY

To change the color and layout of the SmartArt graphic.

1. Click on the **SmartArt** graphic.
2. Go to the **SmartArt Tools Design** tab.
3. In the **SmartArt Styles** group, click on **Change Colors** option.
4. Select the color variation that you want from the drop-down list.
5. In the same tab, go to the **Layouts** group and click on **More**.

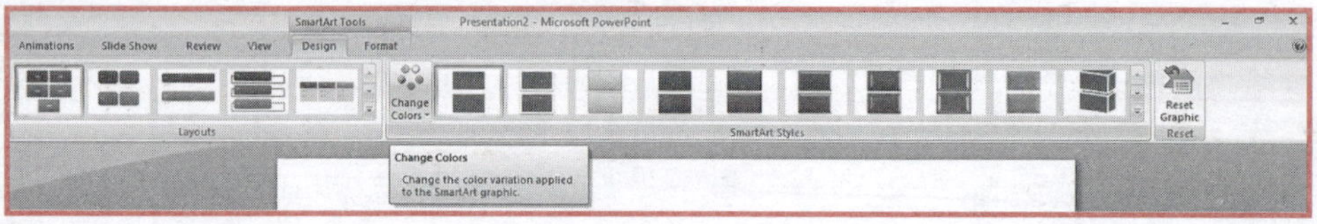

6. Select the layout of your choice from the drop-down list.

INSERTING CHARTS

Charts are used to display data in a pictorial form. It is easy to represent the comparison and growth values in the form of charts. To insert a chart, follow the steps given below.

1. Click on the **Insert** tab on the Ribbon.
2. In the **Illustrations** group, go to the **Charts** tool.
3. Click on the type of **Chart** you want to create.
4. Insert the data and label for the chart using **Data** and **Data Labels** options respectively.
   NOTE: When you insert a chart, the data is displayed in a separate spreadsheet window. It allows you to select, change and edit the data. The chart gets automatically updated with any change of data.
5. The chart is inserted into your presentation (Fig. 7.10).

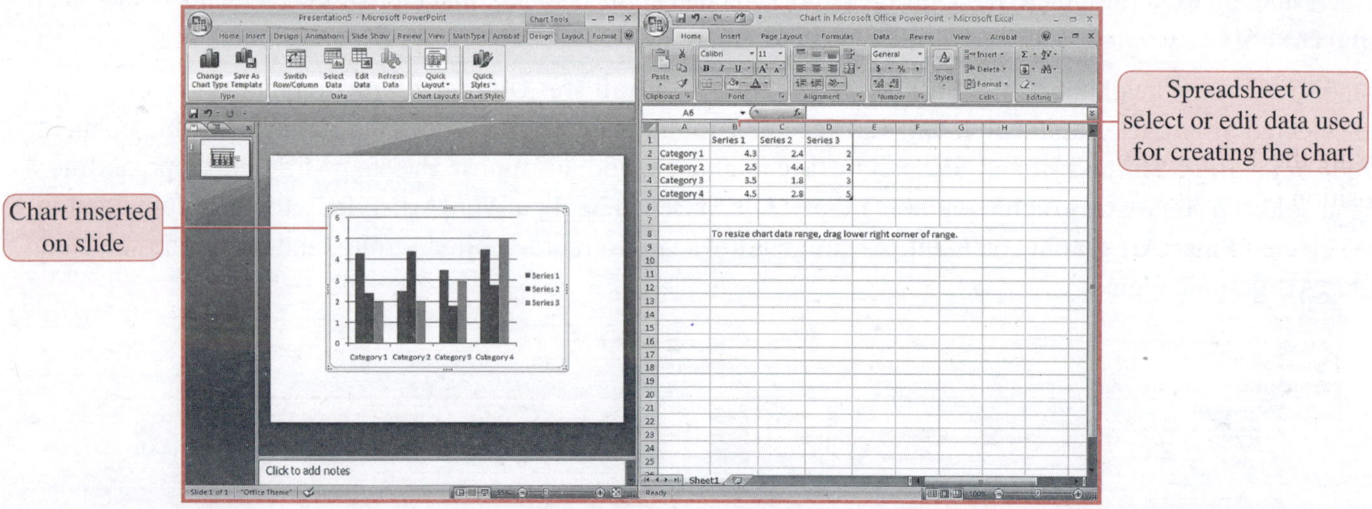

Fig. 7.10 *Inserting charts*

Components of a chart

The components of a chart are:

- *Chart area:* This includes the complete area of the entire chart.
- *X-axis:* This is the horizontal axis used to compare the data. It is also called **category axis**.
- *Y-axis:* This is the vertical axis used to plot the values. It is also known as **value axis**.
- *Data series:* They are the bars or other elements that show the data.
- *Category name:* These are the labels that are displayed on the X- and Y- axis.
- *Plot area:* It is the plotted chart area which includes plotted data, data series, X- and Y- axis.
- *Legend:* It represents the data series with different colors, patterns or symbols.

Chart Tools tab

The **Chart Tools tab** appear on the Ribbon when you click on the chart. There are three tabs: **Design**, **Layout**, and **Format**.

Using the **Design** tab, you can control the chart type, chart layout, chart styles and location of a chart (Fig. 7.11).

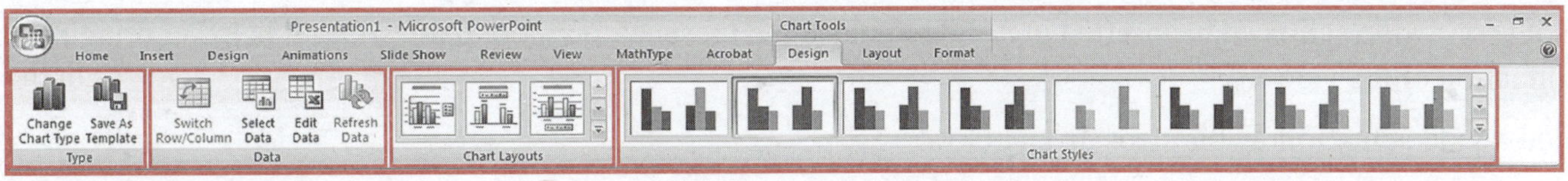

Fig. 7.11 *Chart Tools Design tab*

Using the **Layout** tab, you can control the insertion of pictures, text boxes, shapes, labels, backgrounds and data analysis in a chart (Fig. 7.12).

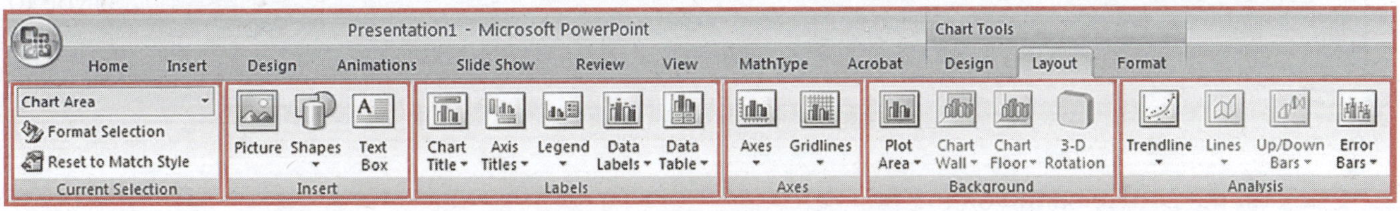

Fig. 7.12 *Chart Tools Layout tab*

Using the **Format** tab, you can format the chart area, shape styles, text styles and size. You can also arrange the position of objects in a chart (Fig. 7.13).

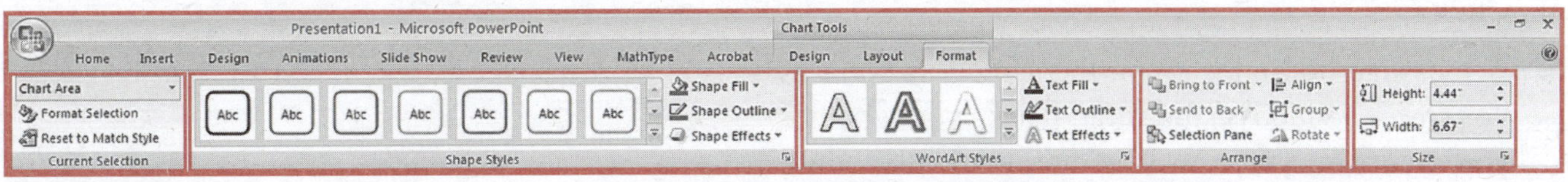

Fig. 7.13 *Chart Tools Format tab*

Editing chart data

To edit chart data, follow the steps given below.

1. Click on the chart. Notice three new additional tabs appear.
2. Click **Edit Data** on the **Data** group of the **Chart Tools Design** tab.
3. A spreadsheet appears. Edit data in the spreadsheet. The chart will be automatically updated.

Modifying chart labels and title

To modify the labels and titles, follow the steps given below.

1. Click on the chart. Notice three new additional tabs appear.
2. Click the **Chart Tools Layout** tab and select the **Labels** group.
3. Choose the appropriate title and label to change using the **Chart Title** and **Data Labels** tools.

▶ Inserting Media Clips

You can insert audio and video files into your presentation with the help of **Media** group in the **Insert** tab.

Inserting movies

A movie or a video clip can be inserted in a slide to make the presentation more interesting. It helps in bringing the attention of the viewers.

To add a video clip, follow the steps given below.

1. Click on the **Insert** tab (Fig. 7.14).

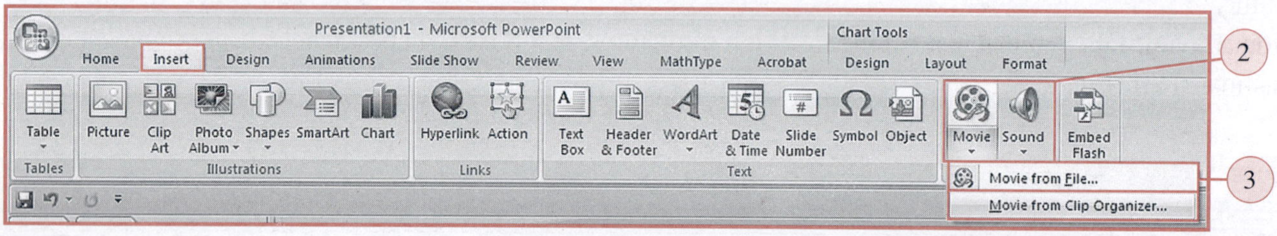

Fig. 7.14 *Inserting a video file*

2. Click on the **Movie** button on the **Insert** tab.
3. Choose either **Movie from File...** or **Movie from Clip Organizer...** option.
4. **Insert Movie** dialog box appears (Fig. 7.15). Select the movie to be inserted.
5. Click **OK**.
6. A message box appears on the screen as soon as you insert a video on the slide. It asks you whether you want the video to start automatically while presenting or you want to start playing it only when you click. Select the option as per your requirement (Fig. 7.16).

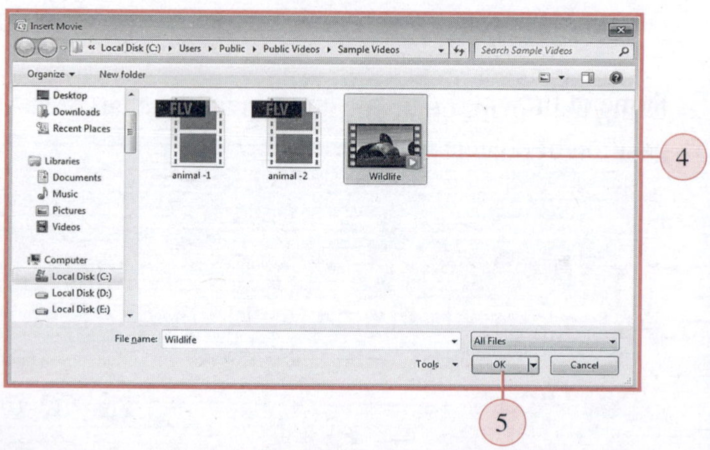

Fig. 7.15 *Insert Movie dialog box*

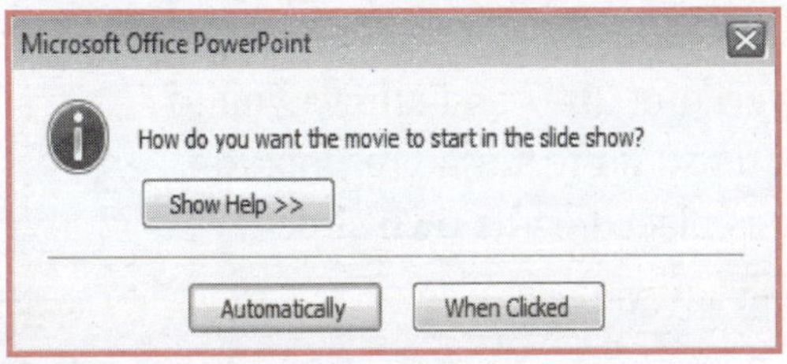

Fig. 7.16 *Microsoft Office Powerpoint message box*

NOTE: You can edit the movie using **Video Tools Format** tab that appears when you click on movie icon on the slide. You can also insert a movie from clip art gallery.

Insert sound

A presentation can be made more interesting and interactive by inserting sounds to its slide. The audio/sound can be user narration or an audio clip.

To add sound, follow the steps given below.

1. Click the **Sound** tool on the **Insert** tab.
2. Choose either **Sound from File…**, **Sound from Clip Organizer…**, **Play CD Audio Track…** or **Record Sound…** (Fig. 7.17).
3. The **Insert Audio** dialog box appears.
4. Select the audio you want and click on the **Insert** button.

To edit the audio, you use the **Sound Tools Options** tab that appears only after you add an audio file (Fig. 7.18).

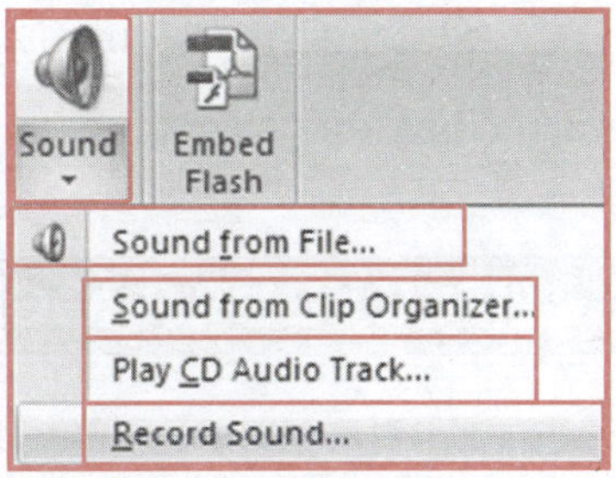

Fig. 7.17 *Sound tool in the Insert tab*

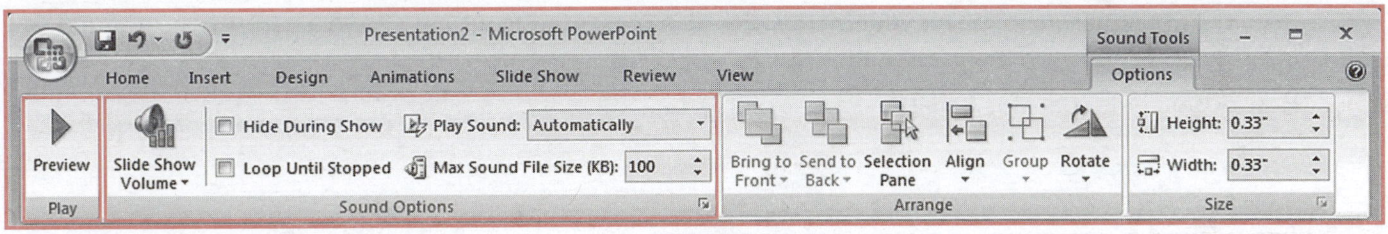

Fig. 7.18 *Sound Tools Options tab*

Some of the tools available in **Sound Tool Options** tab are:

- ***Preview:*** This is used to preview the video or audio before presenting the slide.
- ***Slide Show Volume:*** This is used to adjust the volume of the video or audio inserted.
- ***Hide During Show:*** This tool is used to hide the sound icon  that represents the video or audio.
- ***Loop Until Stopped:*** This tool is used to repeat the sound until it is stopped.
- ***Play Sound:*** It has three options viz. to play automatically, to play when clicked, and to play across slides.
- ***Max Sound File Size:*** It is used to specify the maximum size for embedding the sound in the presentation.

Inserting a photo album

The photo album feature is new in PowerPoint 2007 and allows you to easily create a photo album to share pictures. It creates a presentation based on a set of pictures. Each picture is placed on its own slide.

Fig. 7.19 *Inserting Photo album*

To create a photo album, follow the steps given below.

1. Go to the **Insert** tab.
2. Click **Photo Album** option in the **Illustrations** group (Fig. 7.19).
3. Select **New Photo Album...** option to create a new photo album or choose **Edit Photo Album** option to edit an existing album.
4. The **Insert Photo Album** dialog box appears. In **Insert picture from:** Section, click on **File/Disk...** to add pictures to the photo album.
5. Arrange the pictures in the order of the album by clicking the up/down arrows.
6. Add captions to the pictures, if necessary.
7. Click on **Create**.

CHECK YOUR PROGRESS

A. List the name and basic functions of the groups present in the Insert tab.

B. How can you insert an Excel worksheet on a slide?

C. Draw a circle and format it using the Drawing Tools Format tab.

D. Insert a SmartArt graphic in your presentation to depict a cyclic process.

E. Record a Christmas message for your friends. Create a presentation wishing them a happy new year and insert your recording in the presentation.

F. How do you enter data for a chart in PowerPoint?

▶ Animation Effects

Making an object like a text, a graphic, a chart or a picture move on a slide is called ***animation***. Animation makes the presentation more enhanced, impressive and interesting. Through animation you can highlight some important points of your presentation. You can animate an object in a presentation by applying movements, sound effects and visual effects. Animations also control the flow of information. You can insert animation in the slides by using the **Custom Animation** tool of the **Animations** group in the **Animations** tab (Fig. 7.20).

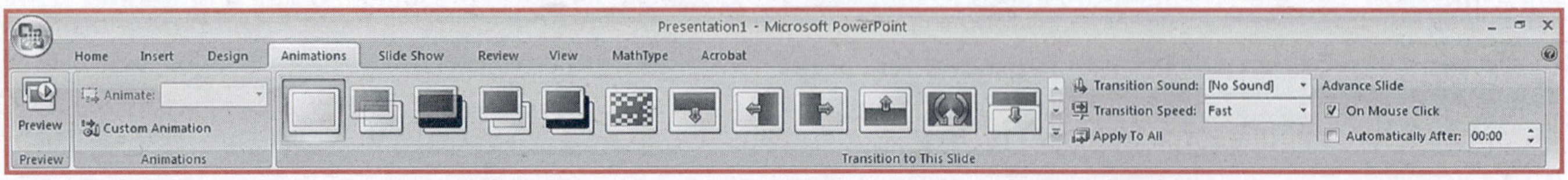

Fig. 7.20 *Animations tab*

Custom Animation

The Custom Animation effects are predefined special effects that you can add to objects on a slide.

To apply an animation effect, follow the steps as given below (Fig. 7.21).

1. Select the object.
2. Click the **Animations** tab on the Ribbon.
3. Click the **Custom Animation** tool in the **Animations** group.
4. In the **Custom Animation** task pane that appears on the right, click **Add Effect**.
5. Choose the appropriate effect from the drop-down list.
6. Click the **Preview** tab to visualise the effect of animation.
7. Click the **OK** button.

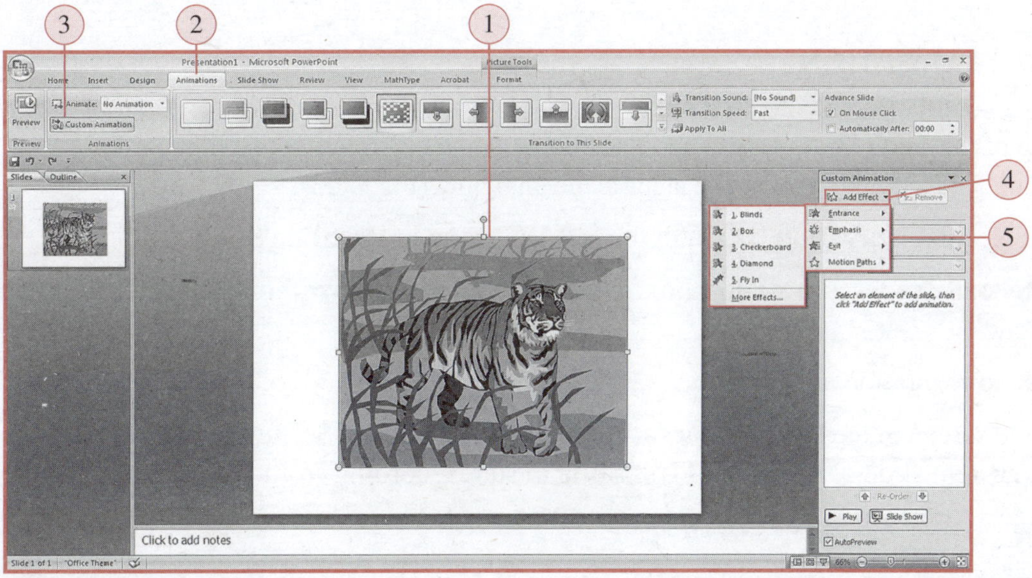

Fig. 7.21 *Applying Custom Animation*

Slide Transition

Slide Transition is used to add visual effects to the slide when a slide changes from one to another in a slide show view. You can apply these transition effects to a single slide or to all slides of a presentation.

To add slide transitions, follow the steps given below (Fig. 7.22).

1. Select the slide in which you want to apply transition.
2. Click the **Animations** tab.
3. Choose the appropriate animation from **Transition to This Slide** group.
4. A preview will be displayed for the current slide with the selected effect.
5. Select the desired speed from the **Transition Speed:** drop-down list.
6. Select the desired sound from the **Transition Sound:** drop-down list.
7. To advance the slide manually by clicking mouse, select **On Mouse Click** checkbox.
8. To advance the slide automatically to the next slide, select **Automatically After:** checkbox and enter the time in the adjoining box.

9. Use **Apply to all** tool to apply the selected transition effect to all slides.

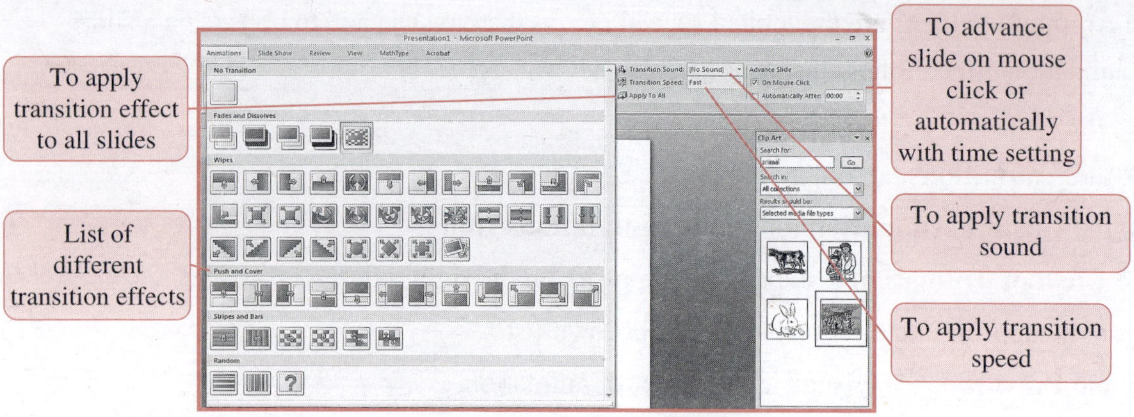

Fig. 7.22 *Applying Slide Transition*

Record Narration

If you want to add your narration with each slide, you can do so using **Record Narration** tool. It is available under the **Set Up** group of the **Slide Show** tab. To add narration, you need a microphone to record it.

To record narration for the slides, follow the steps as given below (Fig. 7.23).

1. Click the **Record Narration** button in the **Set Up** group of the **Slide Show** tab.
2. In the **Record Narration** dialog box, click on the **Set Microphone Level...** to check the levels of audio input.
3. Click **OK** to record the narration.
4. The second screen of the **Record Narration** dialog box appears. Select the **Current Slide** to start recording from the current slide or select the **First Slide** to start recording from the beginning of the presentation.

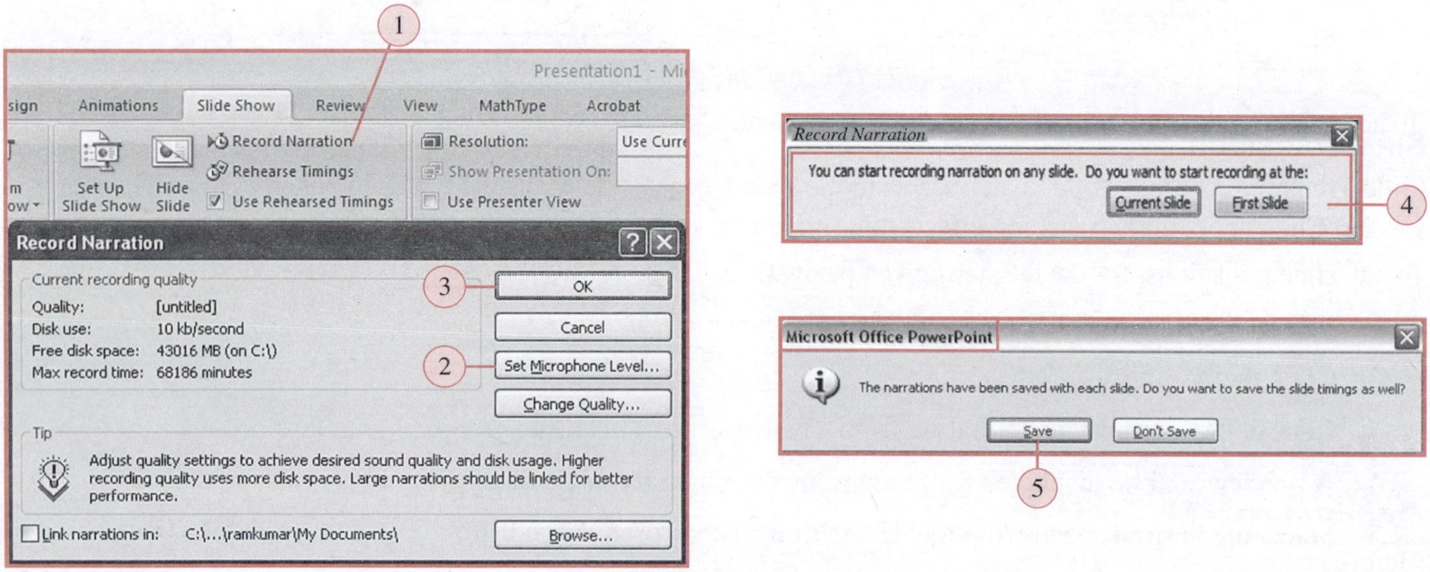

Fig. 7.23 *Recording narration*

NOTE: You can move through the slides and keep on adding narration from the first slide or the current slide.

5. To save the timings along with narration, click the **Save** button in the dialog box which is shown at the end.

6. When you run the slide show the narration will automatically play. While playing, PowerPoint does not allow any other sound on the slide to be played.

Rehearse Timings

The Rehearse Timings tool show a full screen slide show in which you can rehearse your presentation (Fig. 7.24). The amount of time you spend on each slide is recorded and you can save it to run the show automatically.

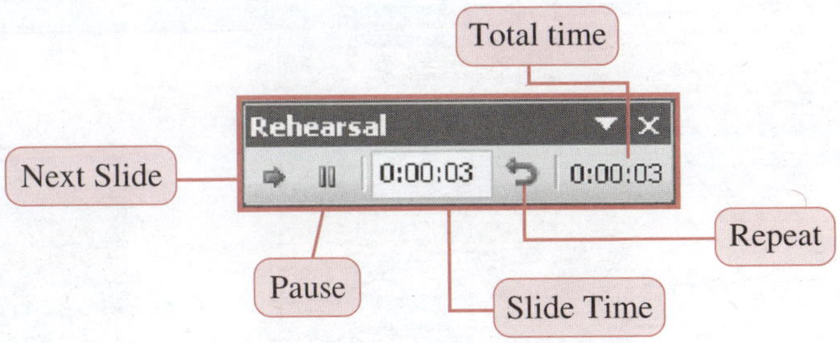

Fig. 7.24 *Rehearse Timings*

To rehearse the slide show, follow the steps given below.

1. Click the **Slide Show** tab.
2. Click the **Rehearse Timings** tool from the **Set Up** group.
3. Note down the timing for each slide which is displayed in the **Rehearsal** dialog box.

Printing Presentation Slides

There are many options for printing a presentation. They are (Fig. 7.25):

- ***Slides:*** This option prints the slides as you see them in presentation, that is, one slide per page.
- ***Handouts:*** This option allows you to specify the number of slides per page. For example, 1, 2, 3, 4, 6 or 9 per page.
- ***Notes Page:*** This option prints the slides along with the speaker notes.
- ***Outline View:*** This option will print only the outline of the presentation.

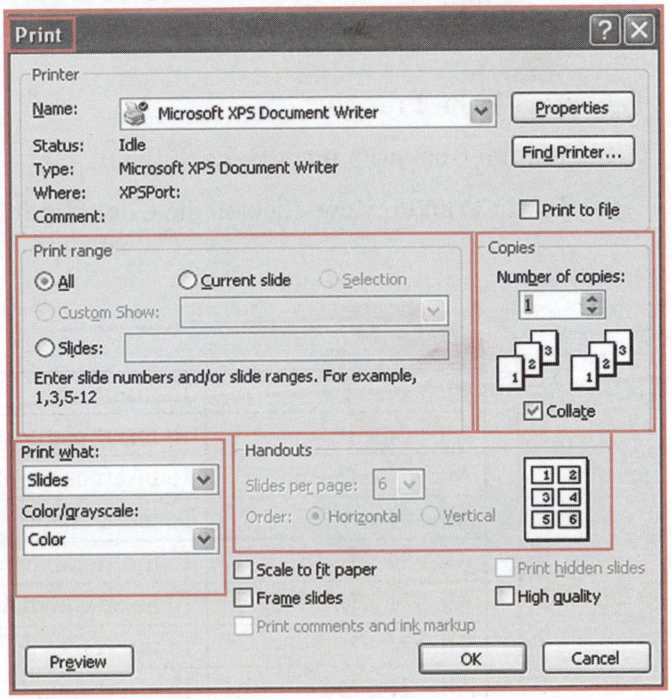

Fig. 7.25 *Printing a presentation*

To access the printing options, follow the steps given below.

1. Click on the **Office button**.
2. Click **Print**.
3. In the **Print** dialog box, go to the **Print range** section to select what you want to print; go to the **Number of copies:** section to specify the number of copies you need to print; go to the **Print what:** section to select the layout and color of the print; and go to the **Handouts** section to specify how many slides you want printed on one page.
4. Choose the format and click **OK** to print.

Print Preview

Before printing a file, you can check its preview (Fig. 7.26). To do so, follow the steps given below.

1. Click on the **Office** button.
2. Go to the **Print** option.

Fig. 7.26 *Print Preview tab*

3. Click **Print Preview**.
4. To print from print preview, click **Print**.
5. To exit Print Preview, click on the **Close Print Preview** button.

Quick Key

Alt + N + T	To insert table
Alt + N + P	To insert picture
Alt + N + C	To insert chart
Alt + N + S	To insert shape
Alt + N + F	To insert clip art
Alt + N + M	To insert SmartArt
Alt + N + V	To insert movies
Alt + N + O	To insert sounds
Alt + N + A	To insert photo album
Alt + A + P	To preview animation
Alt + A + C	To apply custom animation
Alt + A + T	To apply slide transition
Alt + A + U	To apply transition sound
Alt + A + E	To apply transition speed
Alt + A + L	To apply animation to all slides
Alt + A + M	To advance slide on mouse click

Alt + A + F	To advance slide automatically
Alt + A + I	To set timings to advance slide automatically after the timings
Alt + S + B	To start slide show from the beginning
Alt + S + C	To start slide show from the current slide
Alt + S + M	To customise slide show
Alt + S + S	To setup slide show
Alt + S + H	To hide slide
Alt + S + N	To record narration
Alt + S + T	To rehearse timings
Ctrl + K	To insert hyperlink
F1	To go to help
F5	To run presentation
F7	To check spelling

CHECK YOUR PROGRESS

A. Create a sample presentation with the steps outlining different weathers. Insert an image on each slide. Format the theme and background for this presentation. Replace the default font with Comic Sans. Spell Check the presentation. Save the presentation with the name it 'Different weathers'.

B. Create a presentation on cropping season and insert slides related to spring season from another presentation. Practice your timing. Edit them if the presentation is long.

C. Create a presentation to explain the workflow in an office, such as, a bank. Use SmartArt graphic, video clip and narration in the presentation.

D. What printing options are available in PowerPoint 2007?

GLOSSARY

- **Animation:** It refers to making an object like a text, a graphic, a chart or a picture move on a slide.
- **Charts:** This tool is used to display data in a pictorial form. It is easy to represent the comparison and growth values in the form of charts.
- **Custom Animation:** These effects are predefined special effects that you can add to objects on a slide.
- **Slide Transition:** They are used to add visual effects to the slide when a slide changes from one to another in a slide show view.
- **Table:** This tool in Tables group is used to organise the information in a tabular format.

NOW YOU KNOW

1. Action Buttons under Shapes tool provide the facility to link to a web page or a slide in the same presentation or a slide from other presentation using hyperlinks.
2. A movie or a video clips can be inserted in a slide to make the presentation more interesting and helps in bringing the attention of viewers.
3. The photo album feature is new in PowerPoint 2007 and allows you to easily create a photo album to share pictures.
4. Custom Animation effects are predefined special effects that you can add to objects on a slide.
5. Slide Transition is used to add visual effects to the slide when a slide changes from one to another in the slide show view.
6. Rehearse Timings show a full screen slide show in which you can rehearse your presentation.

EXERCISE

FA

A Fill in the blanks.

1. Action Buttons under Shapes tool provide the facility to link to a web page or a slide in the same presentation or a slide from other presentation using ....
2. The labels that are displayed on the X- and Y-axis are called ....
3. .... represents the data series with different colors, patterns or symbols.
4. Making an object move on a slide is called ....
5. Slide Transition tool is available under .... tab.

B Multiple choice questions.

1. To insert a picture in a slide, ... key is used.

   a. Alt + I + P b. Alt + Shift + P c. Alt + N + P d. Alt + P

2. The Rehearse Timings tool is present in .... tab.

   a. Insert b. Design c. Animations d. Slide Show

3. The .... tool shows a full screen slide show in which you can rehearse the presentation.

   a. Preview b. Rehearse Timings c. Slide Show d. Slide Sorter

4. The .... option allows you to specify the number of slides per page.

a. Print b. Print Preview c. Handouts d. File

5. .... when clicked, perform some action.

a. Action button b. Text box c. Sound d. None of these

6. Which of the following file format cannot be inserted as a picture to a presentation?

a. gif b. avi c. bmp d. All of these

7. The .... key will not be used to advance the slide during the slide show.

a. Esc b. Enter c. Page down d. Down arrow

8. The .... Tools tab appear on the Ribbon when you click on the chart.

a. Drawing b. Format c. Chart d. Data Sheet

9. Y- axis is also called as .... axis.

a. category b. data c. chart d. value

10. The .... show is used to customise the slide show.

a. Animate b. Custom Animation c. Transitions d. Preview

SA

C Answer the following questions.

1. What are the different speeds in slide transition speed mode? HOTS
2. Do you think that it is enough to place the action button on the slide to link a slide or web page? Why? HOTS
3. Name the tab in which Custom Animation tool is available. Give a situation where it is useful to use this tool.
4. How to add text in a built-in shape? HOTS
5. Name the tool that is used to remove the unwanted portion from the inserted picture.
6. What are two options available under Advance Slide? HOTS
7. What is the difference between these two tools:  HOTS
8. Name the tool that is used to add narration to your slides.
9. Name the tab in which photo album tool is available.
10. What are the various shapes available under Shapes tool?

D Answer the following questions in detail.

1. How to hide the sound icon from the slide? HOTS
2.  - Identify and explain these two icons.
3. What are the different tabs that you see when you click on the chart? Discuss.
4. Explore and explain any two transition effects.
5. How many types of slide views are there in PowerPoint 2007? HOTS
6. What is Custom Animation? Name any two custom animation effects.
7. What is the use of custom show?
8. What are the components of a chart?
9. Write a note on different options for printing a presentation?
10. Explain the tools available under Transition to This Slide group of animation tab.

Application Based Questions

A. Cathy is working on a presentation for her school's history project. In the conclusion, she wants to give a link to a slide from her economics presentation. Her mother suggests that she uses the Shapes tool to create a hyperlink. However, Cathy can not find the option. Help her.

B. Uday needs a countdown timer for a quiz contest he is organising. He asked one of his team members to help him create a countdown timer in PowerPoint 2007. The team member gave him the figure given below as a guide for creating the timer. Help Uday create the timer using tools such as Slide Reuse, Slide Transition and Custom Animation.

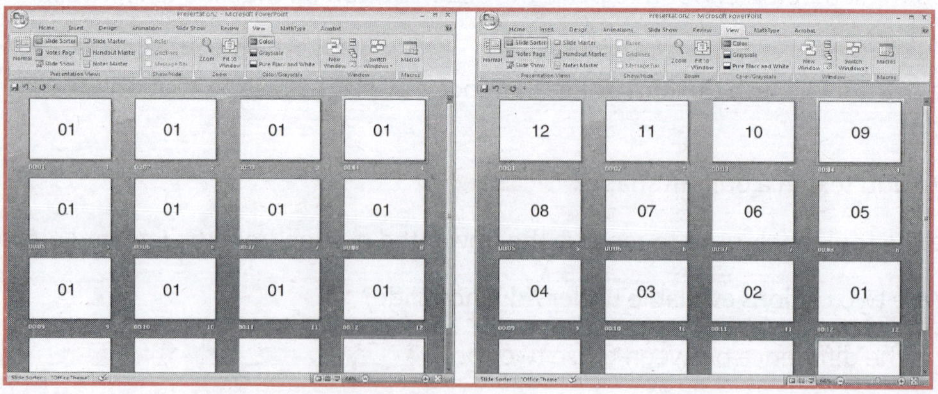

C. Raman created a presentation for his company's annual sales conference. While reviewing it, his manager suggested few improvements. Explain (give steps) how Raman will make the following changes.

1. Add a cover slide that specifies the location, date and timing of the conference.
2. Add a photo of the senior management along with all their names.

3. Insert a chart that depicts the forecast for the coming season.
4. Add the company header to the Handouts.
5. Record the total time of the presentation.

D. Saloni is working on a HR presentation for her company's new managing director. The finance team provided her the breakdown of total expense incurred by the HR department in the last fiscal year. She wants to add this data to her presentation in form of an Excel table and create a corresponding chart. What steps should she take to incorporate the Excel table and chart to her presentation?

E. Sharan is making a presentation, illustrating the growth of his NGO, for their annual fundraiser. Instead of using numbers and tables to depict the growth, he is thinking of using charts. Is it a more viable and effective option? If yes, then why? Justify your answer with an example.

F. Priya is creating a PowerPoint presentation for new recruits in her office. She doesn't want to overload the presentation with lot of animations. However, she wants to give special effects on transition from one slide to another. Can she do this? If yes, is it possible to set different transition speed or include sounds?

LAB WORK

A. Create a presentation on the topic 'Comparison of Symbian OS and Android OS in Smart Phones'. Add the following slides to complete the task.

- Slide 1: Features of Symbian OS
- Slide 2: Smart phones having Symbian OS (Insert suitable pictures)
- Slide 3: Features of Android OS
- Slide 4: Smart phones having Android OS (Insert suitable pictures)
- Slide 5: Create a table to compare the market sale of two OS based smartphones
- Slide 6: Insert a chart to show comparison
- Slide 7: Use SmartArt graphics to specify the data in an organised manner.

B. Create a small presentation, of not more than five slides, for your nephews 1st birthday. The presentation should run automatically and should not be more than two minutes long. It should have minimum text and the focus should be on graphics, audio and video clips of your nephew. Insert an action button that performs the actions automatically.

C. Create a sample presentation and take a printout of it to distribute it to the audience. It should include:

- The orientation of the handout should be Landscape.
- It should have the date at top and page number at the bottom.
- There should be four slides per page.
- The theme color scheme should be Apex.
- It should have a common background style.

D. Create a presentation for your English teacher's farewell party. The presentation should have minimum 10 slides and should include messages from the Principal, the management and the head of English department. Two to three slides should exclusively be devoted to images and video and audio clips. After creating the presentation, set up a slide show that run manually and can run at a kiosk. Record the messages from the Principal, the management and the head of English department.

MS Office 2010
Updates

In PowerPoint 2010:

- You can insert and play video from online sites, such as YouTube, during a slide show. Go to the **Insert** tab (⟶) **Video** (⟶) **Video from Web Site....** In the **Insert Video from WebSite** dialog box that appears, copy and paste the embed code and click on **Insert**.

  NOTE: You will need an active Internet connection during the presentation to stream live videos.

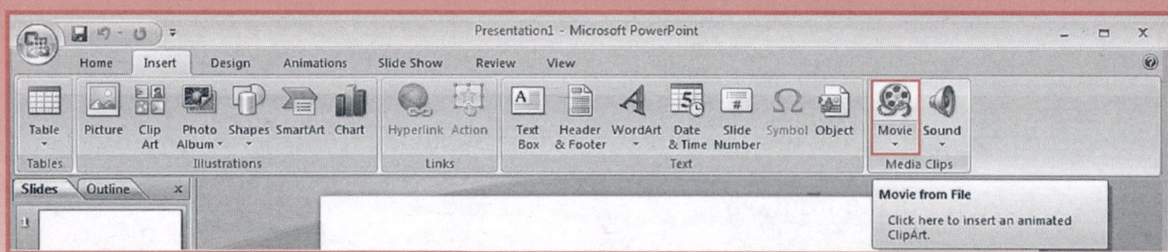

- You can remove background from a picture using the **Remove Background** feature. To remove the background, select the picture. In the **Picture Tools Format** tab that appears, click on the **Remove Background** button. A new **Background Removal** tab appears. Select the background you want to remove and keep using the **Mark Areas to Keep** and **Mark Areas to Remove** option. Click **Keep Changes**. The background is removed.

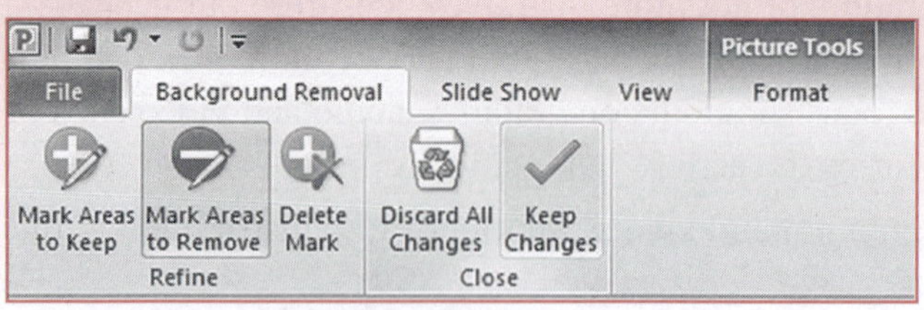

TEACHER'S NOTES

1. Explore different animation and transition with the students. Tell them the importance of animation timing and speed. Explain to them how presentations overloaded with animation, that are ill-timed, are not good.
2. If possible, help students create and then insert audio and videos into their presentations.

Worksheet 2

SECTION A

Fill in the blanks.

1. The ____________________ is present above the Ribbon and cannot be displayed on multiple lines.
2. The document views available in Word 2007 are ____________________, ____________________, ____________________ and ____________________.
3 The ____________________ option is used to highlight the text.
4. The ____________________ tool is used to insert page break into a document.
5. The ____________________ option in Word enables you to send the same letter to multiple recipients.
6. The Ribbon in PowerPoint 2007 has ____________________ tabs.
7. The ____________________ view is used to display the presentation in full screen.
8. The ____________________ includes the slide and the speaker notes.
9. Action Buttons under Shapes tool enables you to link an object to a web page or a slide using ____________________.
10. Making an object moving on a slide is called ____________________.

SECTION B

Answer the questions briefly.

1. Discuss different themes available in Word 2007.
2. What is a multilevel list? Explain with an example.
3. What is the use of the Symbol tool available under the Insert tab?
4. Differentiate between citation and footnote.
5. Define SmartArt.
6. What do you understand by the term slide transition?
7. How can you record a slide show? Name the tool that is used to add narration to the slides.
8. What is animation pane?
9. Where is the PowerPoint Options button present in PowerPoint 2007? What is its function?
10. What is the use of reading view in PowerPoint 2007?

Comprehensive Worksheet 1

SECTION A

Multiple choice questions.

1. Which one of the following is an open source operating system?

   a. Windows b. Linux c. Unix d. MS-DOS

2. Which of the following is an application software?

   a. MS-DOS b. MS Word c. Windows d. Unix

3. ____________________ is used to read the magnetic code written on the cheques or on credit cards.

   a. Magnetic Ink Character Reader b. Optical Character Recognition

   c. Optical Mark Reader d. Bar Code Reader

4. Winzip is a ____________________ program.

   a. backup b. file compression c. billing d. antivirus

5. Some specialised programs that come with Windows are grouped under the ____________________ heading.

   a. shareware b. desktop c. accessories d. control panel

6. Disk defragmenter is a ____________________.

   a. database program b. presentation program

   c. operating system d. utility software

7. One nibble is equal to ____________________ bit(s).

   a. 4 b. 8 c. 1 d. 1024

8. Which of the following is not a function of an operating system?

   a. File Management b. Process Management

   c. Memory Management d. Database Management

9. A laser printer is a/an ____________________.

   a. impact printer b. non-impact printer

   c. large printer d. slow printer

10. To align the text to centre ____________________ shortcut key is used.

    a. Ctrl + E b. Ctrl + C c. Ctrl + L d. Ctrl + R

SECTION B

Answer the questions.

1. Differentiate between bullets and numbering.
2. How DVD is different from CD?
3. What is the use of ecommerce?
4. What are the functions of the Review tab?
5. What is Custom Animation?
6. A garment factory maintains the details of arrival and departure of employees through system. Which type of software it is?
7. What are the three calculator modes available in Windows 7?
8. What is mail merge?
9. What is the purpose of F3 and F5 key in Notepad?
10. How do you use the Rehearse Timings tool?

SECTION C

Application based questions.

1. Investigate how computers are used in surgical operations. Also, list the advantages and limitations for both the patient and the hospital.
2. Investigate the different types of animations available in PowerPoint 2007.
3. Make a presentation on different key layouts on keyboards, especially with keyboards designed for use with languages other than English.
4. What are advantages of using touch screen devices as input devices? List the places around where you live that use touch screen devices.
5. List out the input and output devices designed for use by the blind people. Also, find out how computers help people with disability.
6. Find out the connection between Harald Gormsson, King of Denmark and Norway and Bluetooth.
7. With the help of real life examples, differentiate between data security and data confidentiality.
8. A company enters data for big commercial firms. Which spreadsheet package(s) will be most appropriate for them and why. Justify your answer with reasons.
9. Find out which type of network does a school, a hospital, a telephone exchange and a big MNC use. Is this choice of network suitable? If no, then why?
10. What do you understand by the term guided media? Explain with examples.

8 Spreadsheet Tools – I

SNAP RECAP

1. A spreadsheet tool is used to organise data in rows and columns.
2. A cell in a spreadsheet is an intersection of a row and a column.
3. Microsoft Excel is a spreadsheet program developed by Microsoft and is part of Microsoft Office package.
4. MS Excel allows you to create mathematical formulas and execute functions.

LEARNING OBJECTIVES

You will learn about:

1. Spreadsheets
2. MS Excel
3. Spreadsheet Terms
4. Components of MS Excel 2007
5. Creating and Saving a Worksheet
6. Modifying a Worksheet
7. Editing and Formatting a Worksheet

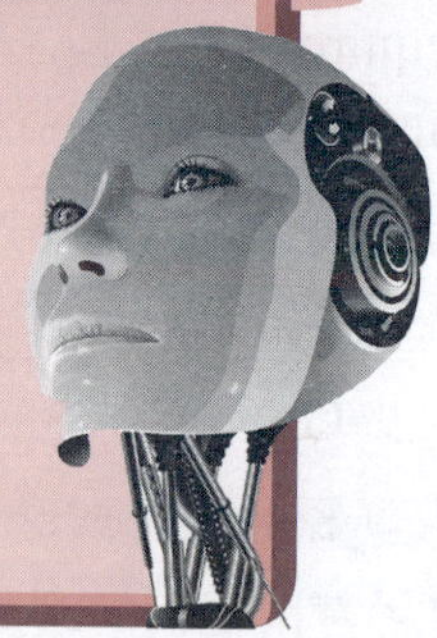

Introduction

A **spreadsheet software** is an application software that organises the information in rows and columns. Spreadsheet program helps you to create and manipulate the data stored electronically in rows and columns. Spreadsheet is like a big table or chart with data spread all over the page.

Spreadsheet software allows you:

- To easily enter and manipulate the data
- To calculate and analyse the data
- To use their built-in functions to make fast and accurate calculations
- To apply arithmetic, mathematical or statistical functions to numerical data
- To visualise and understand the data patterns
- To record data for financial analysis
- To represent the data in the form of charts and graphs.

There are various types of spreadsheet packages used for preparing worksheet and workbook. Some of them are Lotus 123, VisiCalc, Super Calc, Office Calc and MS Excel. MS Excel is the most powerful spreadsheet program.

▶ MS EXCEL

MS Excel is a spreadsheet program that runs on Microsoft Windows. It consists of rows, columns, mathematical functions, formatting tools, charts, graphs and other features. It is a very useful package for general calculations and business applications.

Some of the main features of MS Excel are listed below.

- Huge data can be organised without much effort.
- Built-in functions are used for both simple and complex calculations.
- The data can be represented pictorially in the form of charts and graphs.
- Any changes in data will automatically update the result of functions.
- It provides the facility to copy data, functions and formulas from one cell to another and from one worksheet to another so that you need not type the data or formula again.
- AutoFill feature in MS Excel is used to fill up the column and row instantly.
- Processing of data is very fast and accurate.

Starting MS Excel

A MS Excel file is referred as a **workbook**. Each workbook consists of several **worksheets**. Worksheets are like pages and workbook is like a notebook made of pages. By default, a MS Excel workbook displays three worksheets at the bottom with the names **Sheet1**, **Sheet2**, **Sheet3**. You can insert as many worksheets in a workbook as you want or require.

To invoke MS Excel 2007, follow the steps given below (Fig. 8.1).

1. Click on the **Start** button.
2. Click on **All Programs**.
3. Go to **Microsoft Office**.
4. Select **Microsoft Office Excel 2007**.
5. The first screen of **Microsoft Office Excel 2007** appears. By default a workbook is named Book1 (Fig. 8.2).

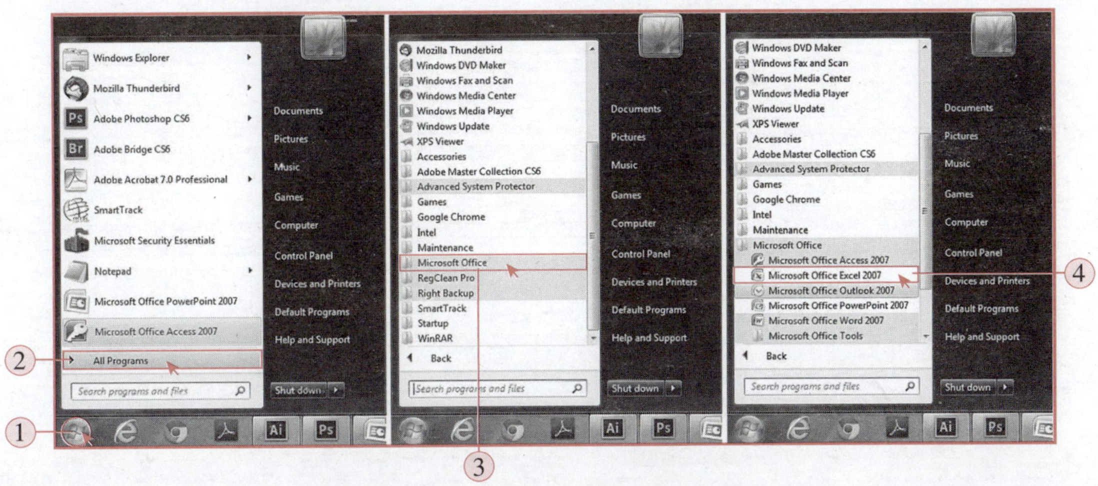

Fig. 8.1 *Starting MS Office Excel 2007*

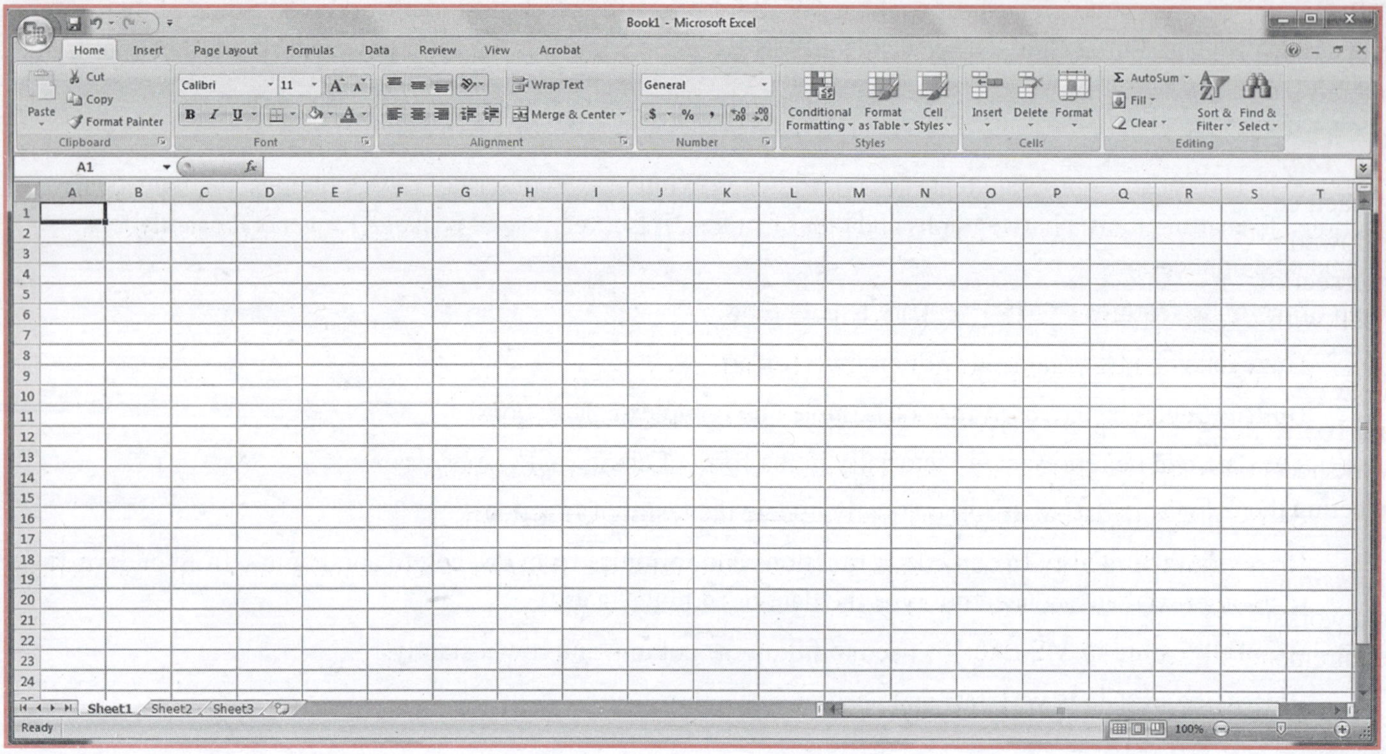

Fig. 8.2 *MS Office Excel 2007*

Spreadsheet terms

Before learning more about spreadsheets and MS Excel, it is important to learn some important and commonly used spreadsheet terms: **workbook**, **worksheet**, **cell**, **cell address**, **cell pointer** and **formula bar** (Fig. 8.3).

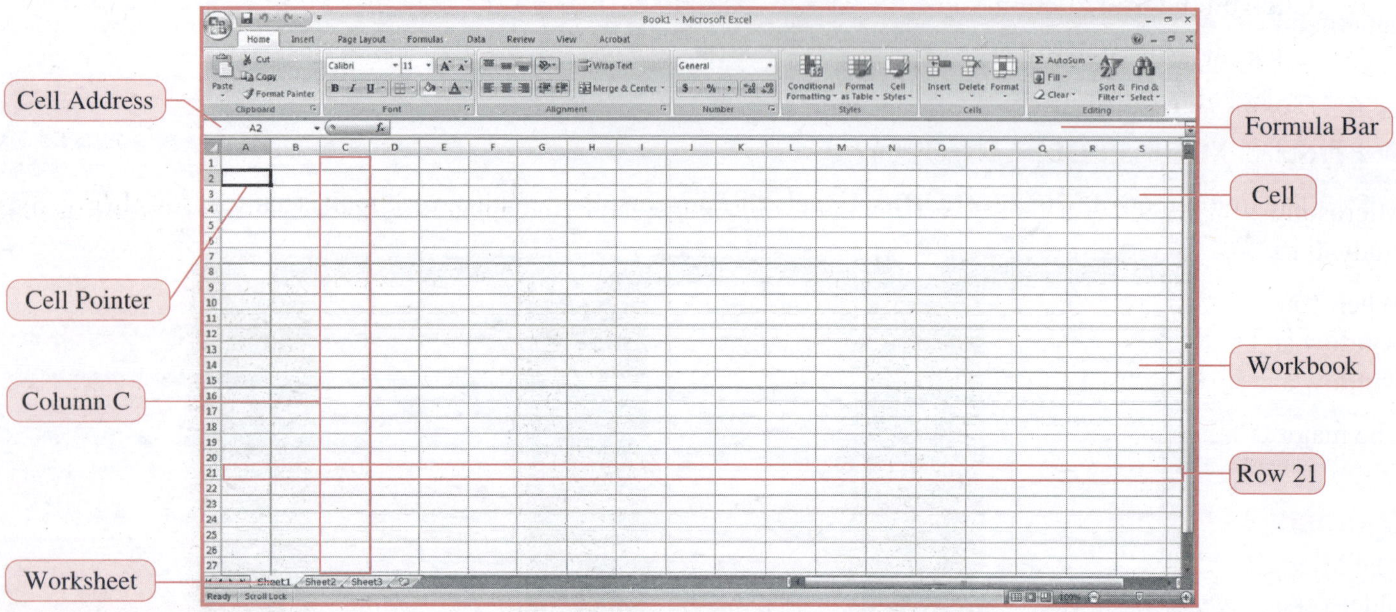

Fig. 8.3 *Some important spreadsheet terms*

Cell: A cell is a small rectangular box which is an intersection of a row and a column. It stores the data entered into a worksheet.

Cell Address: The cell address identifies the location of each cell. A cell address starts with column name followed by row number. For example, F5 cell is the intersection of F column and 5th row. You can refer to a cell with its address.

FACT FILE

The selected cell in any worksheet is called the **active cell.** In Figure 8.3, A2 is the active cell.

Rows and columns of a worksheet: The size of a worksheet is huge. In Excel 2007, there are **1048576 rows** and **16384 columns** (A to XFD). In total there are **17179869184 cells** (1048576 x 16384) in a worksheet. The entire worksheet can neither be viewed on screen at a time nor printed on a single page. It can only be printed on paper by selecting the data in small parts.

Worksheet: A worksheet is a rectangular sheet in which small boxes called cells are available. Data can be stored in a worksheet in form of rows and columns. A worksheet can be copied, renamed or moved according to user requirement. A spreadsheet is also known as worksheet.

Workbook: A workbook is a file in which worksheet(s) and charts are stored. You can store multiple worksheets, of similar type which are related to each other, in a single workbook.

Cell Pointer: In the spreadsheet, a cell remains highlighted with a black color border. This highlighted cell box is called cell pointer. It represents the active cell which is ready to accept the data or commands that you enter using a keyboard.

Formula Bar: The Formula bar is located below the Ribbon and next to the cell address box. This bar shows the data (numbers, names, formulas or functions) that you enter in an active cell.

MS Excel 2007

Microsoft Excel 2007 has many built-in functions to perform calculation, data analysis, statistical and financial study. It can display data as graphs, histograms and charts.

When you start MS Excel, two windows appear, one within the other. The outer window is called **application window** and it provides the user interface to interact with MS Excel. The inner window is known as **workbook window** and it is used for entering data.

The major components of MS Excel application windows are discussed here.

Microsoft Office Button

The Microsoft Office Button performs many of the functions that were previously located in the File menu of older versions of Excel. The options available in this button allows you to create a new workbook, open an existing workbook, save a workbook, print a workbook, send or share a work, or close a workbook (Fig. 8.4).

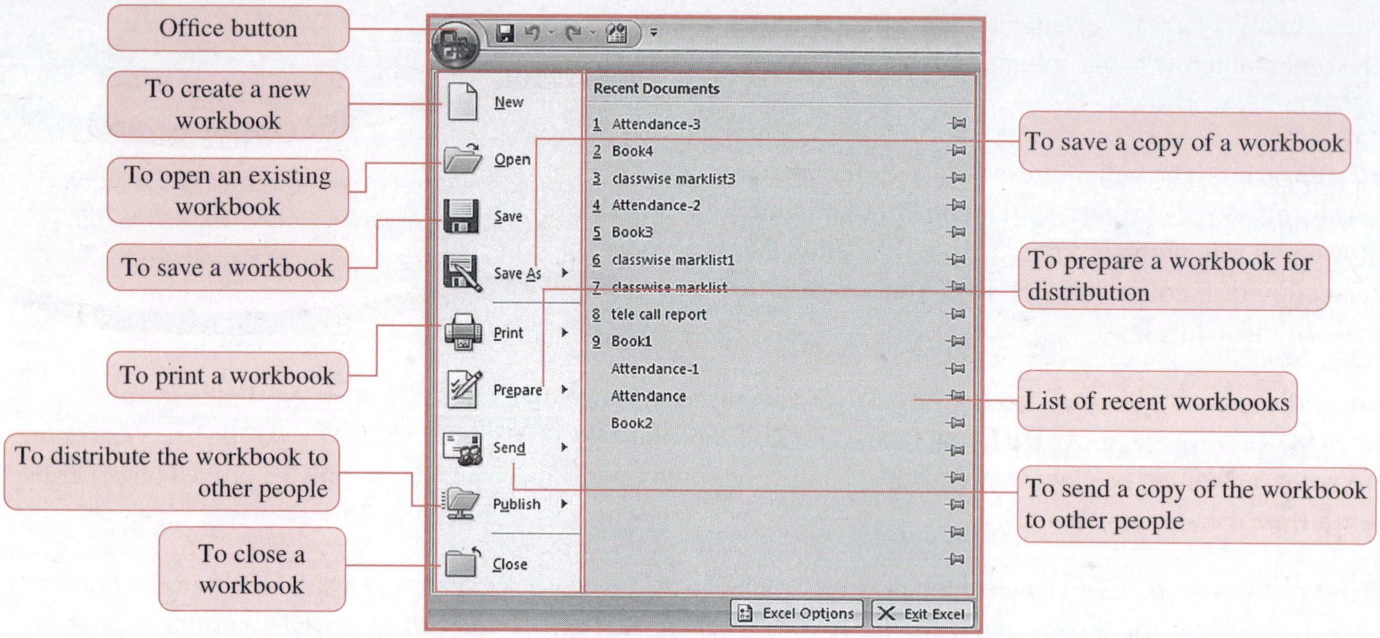

Fig. 8.4 *Office button menu*

NOTE: The **Close** option is used to close the current workbook while the **Exit Excel** option is used to close Excel 2007.

Ribbon

The Ribbon is a set of tabs available at the top portion of the MS Excel 2007 workbook. It has seven tabs: **Home**, **Insert**, **Page Layouts**, **Formulas**, **Data**, **Review**, and **View** (Fig. 8.5). Each tab is divided into **groups**. Each tab and its groups have a unique feature designed to perform functions that you may require to develop, format or edit your Excel 2007 spreadsheets. To view additional features within each group, click on the arrow at the bottom right corner of each group. It is known as **dialog box launcher**.

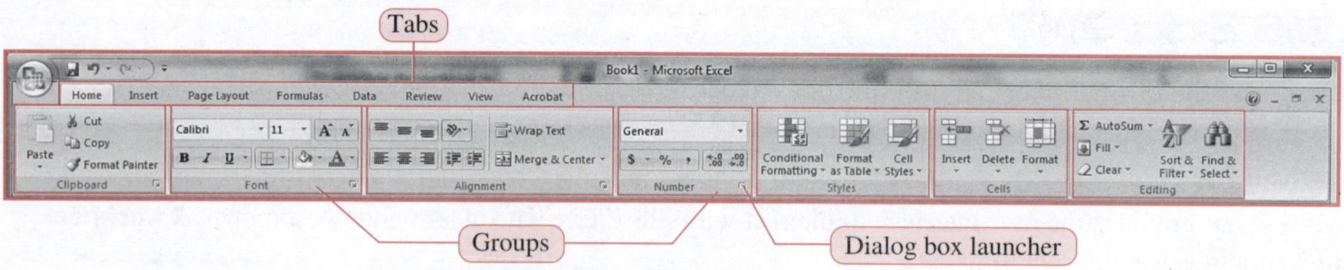

Fig. 8.5 *Ribbon*

Quick Access Toolbar

It provides easy access to commands that are frequently used. By default Save, Undo and Redo options are available in Quick Access Toolbar. However, you can customise the toolbar by adding shortcut options of your choice.

Fig. 8.6 *Quick Access Toolbar*

ACTIVITY

To customise the Quick Access Toolbar in MS Excel 2007.

1. Click on the downward arrow on the right of the **Quick Access Toolbar**.
2. The **Customize Quick Access Toolbar** drop-down list appears.
3. Select **More Commands. . .** option.
4. The **Excel Options** dialog box appears.

   NOTE: You can also open this dialog box by clicking on **Excel Option** button in the Office button menu.
5. Select the shortcut options you want to add to the toolbar and click on the **ADD>>** button. The options will be added to the Quick Access Toolbar.
6. Click on OK.

   NOTE: You can also change the position of the Quick Access Toolbar. To do so, select the **Show Below the Ribbon** option in the **Customize Quick Access Toolbar** drop-down list. The toolbar will move below the Ribbon.

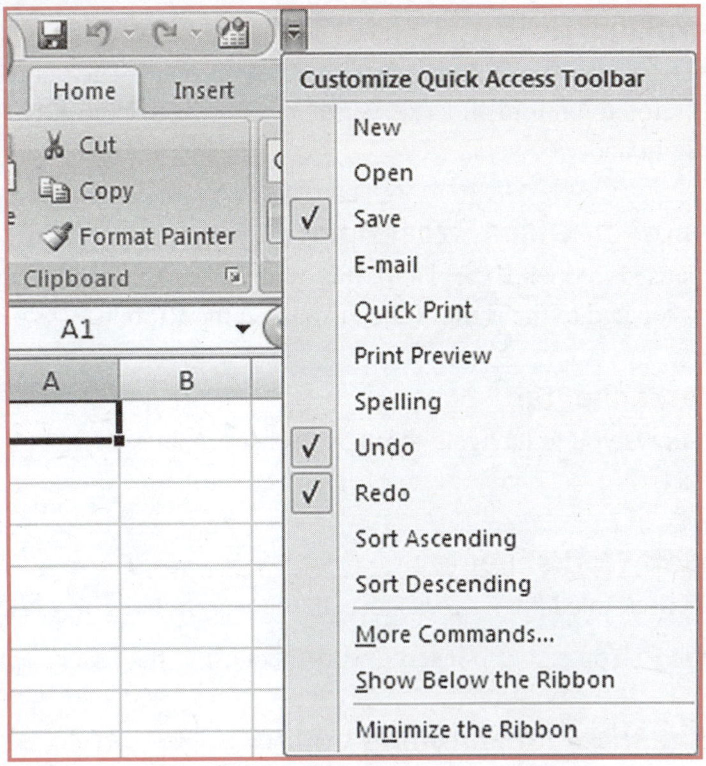

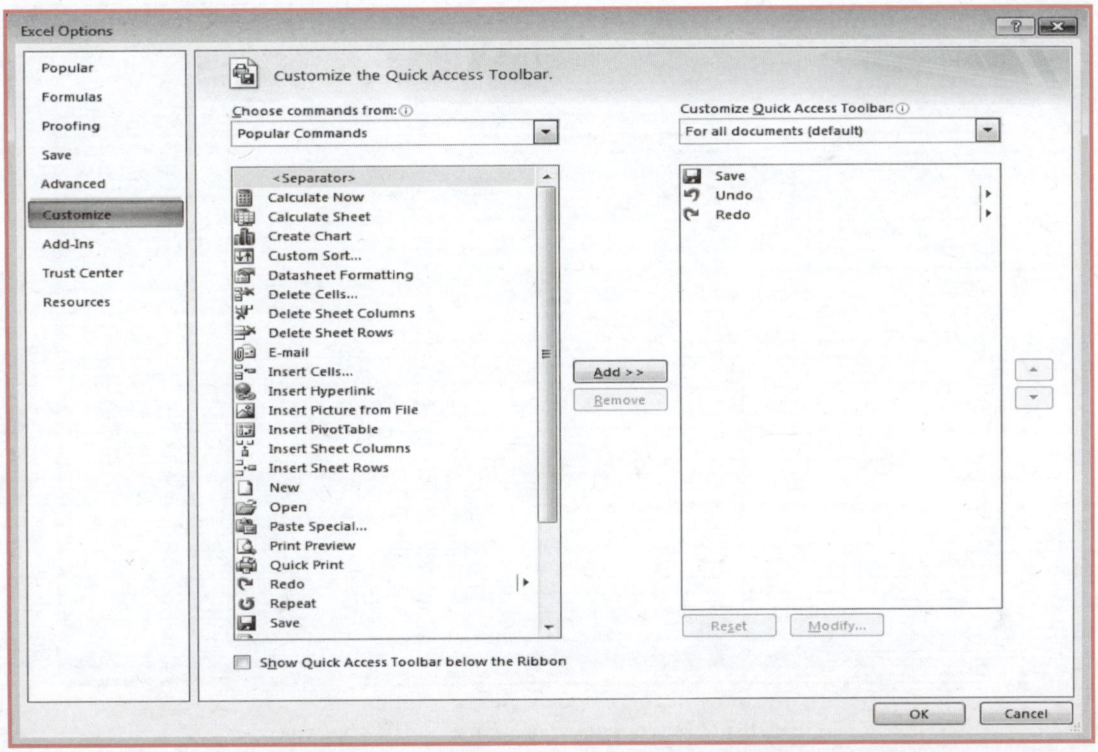

Title bar

It is present above the Ribbon and contains the name of the workbook. It is centrally aligned. On the right side of the title bar, you have the **Minimize**, **Restore Down** and **Close Down** options (Fig. 8.7).

Scroll bar

There are two scroll bars: vertical and horizontal. The vertical scroll bar is present at the right and is used to scroll from top to bottom and vice versa. The horizontal scroll bar is present at the bottom and it is used to scroll from left to right and vice versa.

Microsoft Office Excel Help

It is used to open Excel Help. It provides easy Excel tutorials on every topic from Excel formulas to Excel templates. It is located to the right of the last tab on the Ribbon.

Worksheet tab

It allows you to navigate through worksheets in a workbook. By default it shows three tabs: Sheet1, Sheet2 and Sheet3.

Insert Worksheet tab

It is used to add new worksheets in the workbook. The worksheet is inserted on the right (Fig. 8.7).

NOTE: You can also insert a worksheet using the **Insert** option in the **Cells** group of the **Home** tab.

Worksheet tab scrolling button

It allows you to scroll through the worksheets in your workbook, or take you to your first or last worksheet.

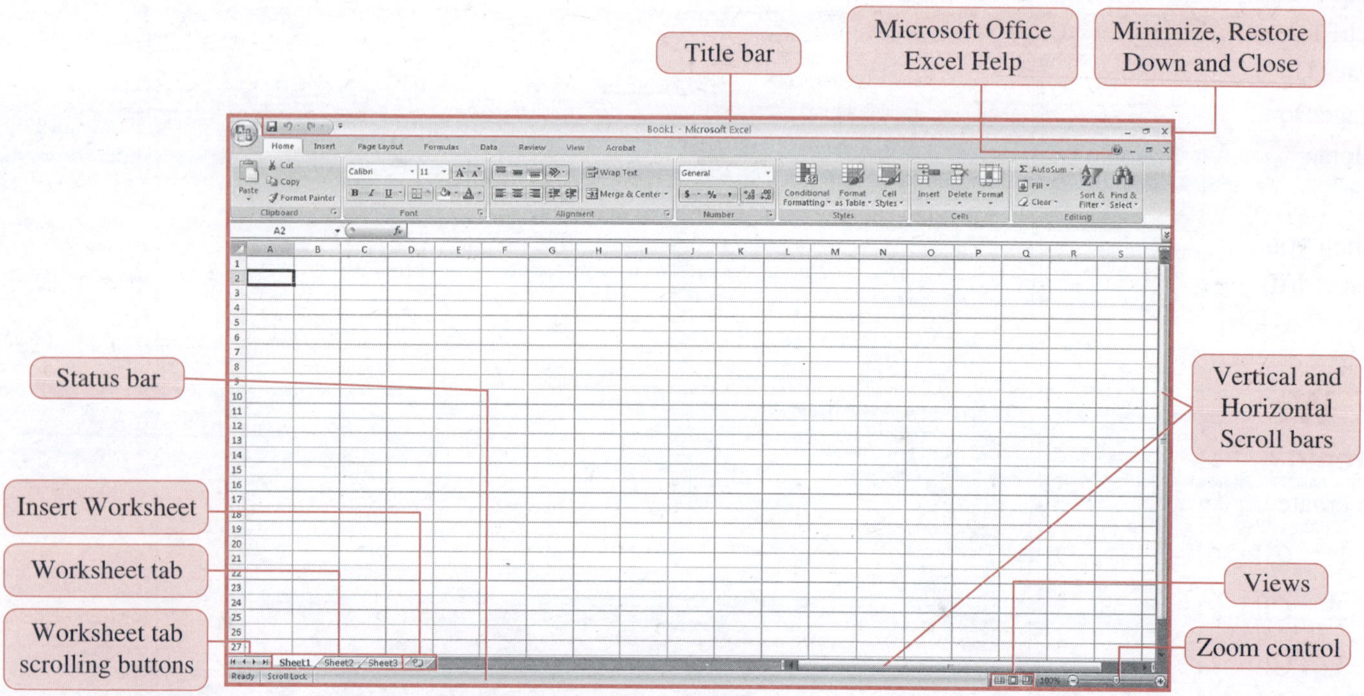

Fig. 8.7 *Components of MS Excel 2007 window*

View buttons

It provides different options to view your worksheet. The three options available in Excel 2007 are: **Normal**, **Page Layout** and **Page Break**.

Zoom control

It contains options to magnify or minimize the worksheet. The **Zoom Out** button allows you to view the content of your worksheet in smaller size while the **Zoom In** button provides an enlarged view. The **Zoom** button allows you to view and set the zoom percentage. You can also instantaneously zoom in and zoom out with the help of the **Zoom Slider**.

Data Input in a Workbook

You can enter a data in a cell by placing the mouse pointer in the cell. Once you left click on the cell you will notice that the boundary of the cell becomes bold and thick, demonstrating that it is an active cell. Type the data in the cell. To move the cell pointer from one cell to another, you can use arrow keys or tab key. With the help of the commands given in Table 8.1, you can easily go to any desired cell.

Table 8.1 *Commands to navigate between cells*

Command	Function
Right arrow key or Tab key	To move one column right
Left arrow key or Shift + Tab key	To move one column left
Up arrow Key or Shift + Enter key	To move one row up
Down arrow key or Enter key	To move one row down
Ctrl + left arrow key	To move to the first column of the selected row (Column A)
Ctrl + Right arrow key	To move to the last column of the selected row (Column XFD)
Ctrl + Up arrow key	To move to the first row of the worksheet (1st row)
Ctrl + down arrow key	To move to the last row of the worksheet (1048576th row)
Page Up key	To move one screen up
Page Down key	To move one screen down
Home	To move to the first column of the selected row

When you input data into a cell, it is simultanously filled in the formula bar. The three buttons, **Cancel**, **Enter** and **Insert Function**, appear to the left of the formula bar. Cancel button is used to delete the data entered; Enter button is used to enter the data; and Insert Function button is used to enter functions.

▶ Working with a Workbook

Create a workbook

To create a new workbook in Excel 2007, follow the steps given below.

1. Click on the **Office button**.
2. Click on the **New** option.
3. Choose **Blank Workbook**.
4. Click on the **Create** button.

NOTE: If you want to create a new document from a template, explore the templates and choose one that fits your needs.

ACTIVITY

To use an installed template to create a new workbook in Excel 2007.

1. Click on the **Office** button.
2. Click on the **New** option.
3. The **New Workbook** dialog box appears.
4. Click on **Installed Templates** option under **Templates** in the left pane.
5. In the middle pane, installed templates are displayed.
6. Select the desired template and click on **Create**.

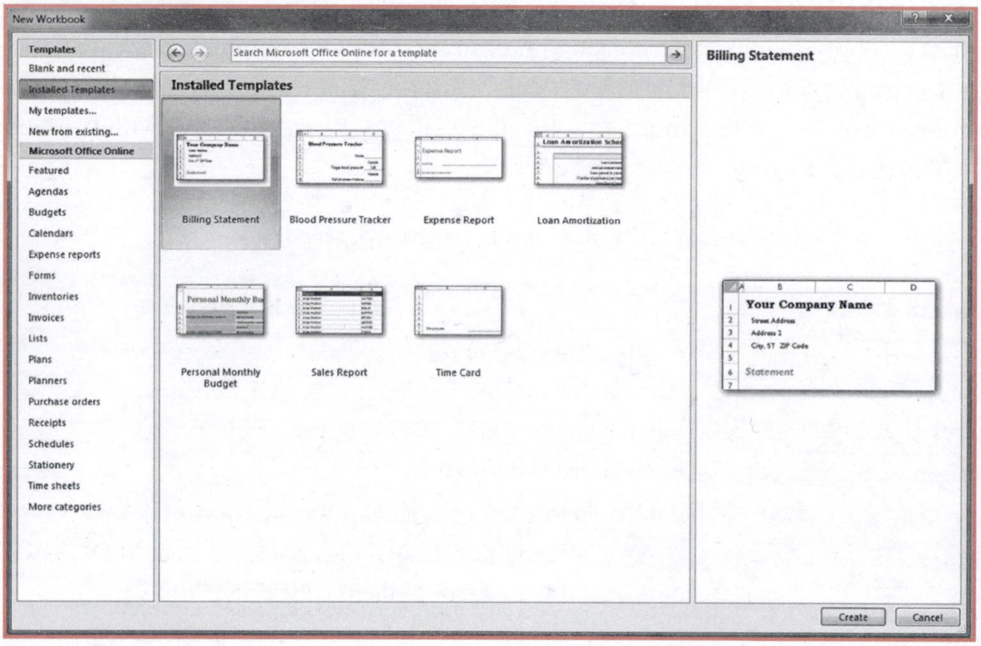

7. Customise the template as desired.
8. Save the file with a new name.

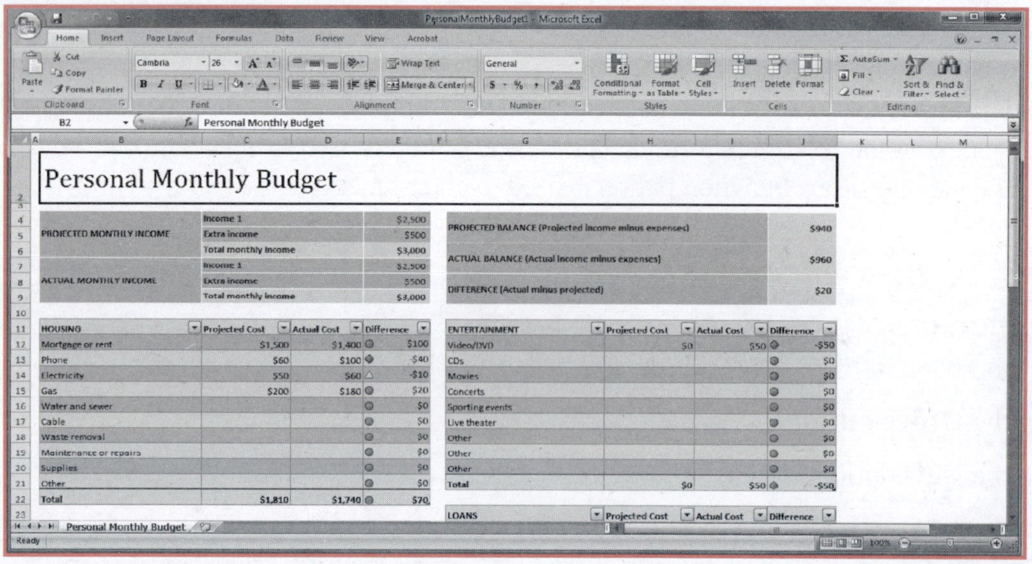

NOTE: You can also download templates offered by Microsoft directly from the New Workbook dialog box.

Save a workbook

To save a workbook in Excel 2007, follow the steps given below.

1. Click on the **Office button**.
2. Click on the **Save** option.
3. Enter the name of the workbook in **File name:** box and click on the **Save** button.
4. The saved file in MS Excel 2007 takes the extension **.xlsx**.

NOTE: To save a workbook with a different name or in a different versions of Excel (earlier version), or at a different location, use the **Save As** option.

Open a workbook

To open an existing workbook stored in your system, follow the steps given below.

1. Click on the **Office button**.
2. Click on the **Open** option.
3. Select the file you need to open, edit or modify.
4. Click on the **Open** button.

Print a worksheet

To print a selected portion of a worksheet, follow the steps given below.

1. Click on the **Office button**.
2. Click on the **Print** option.
3. Select the **Print Range** option (**All** / **Pages From…To**) or **Print What option** (**Selection/Active worksheet / Entire workbook**).
4. In the **Copies** section, type the number of copies you need in the **Number of copies box**.
5. Click on the **OK** button.

NOTE: Before printing, click on the **Print Preview** button, to preview the selected data for printing and if necessary, make changes before printing.

TRY THIS!

You can change the color of worksheet tabs. Right-click on the sheet and select the **Tab Color** option. From the **Theme Colors** dialog box, choose the color of your choice and just click on it.

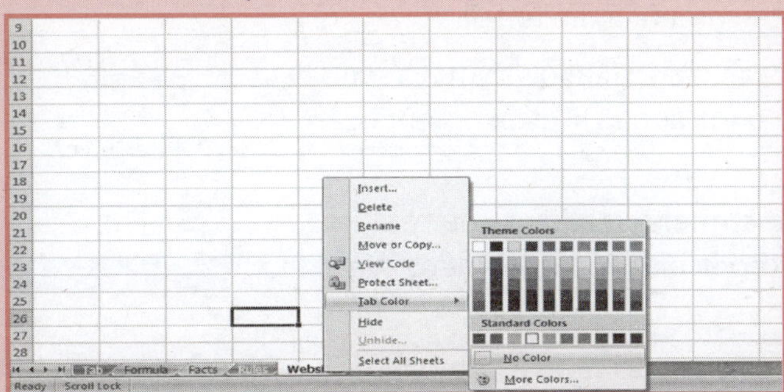

ACTIVITY

To explore and investigate the options available in the Prepare and Send options in the Office button menu.

1. Click on the **Office** button.
2. Click on the **Prepare** option.
3. **Prepare the document for distribution** menu list appears on the right.

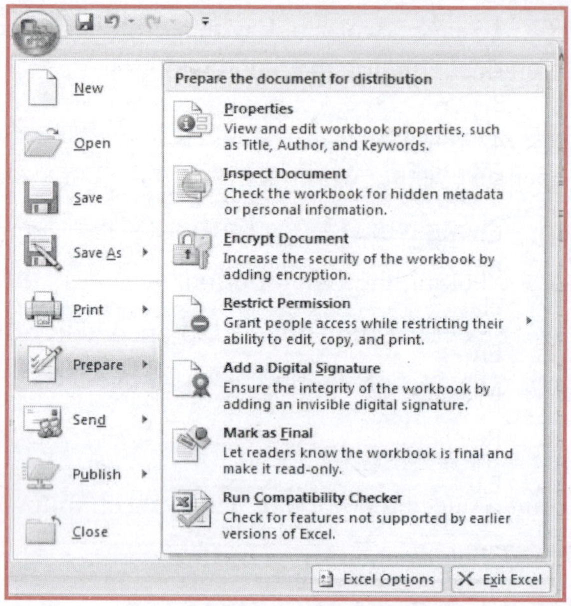

4. Using the menu list you can select the following options:
   a. **Properties:** This option allows you to view and edit properties of a workbook.
   b. **Inspect Document:** This option helps you to check a workbook for hidden personal data. Before sending any workbook, ensure that it is metadata free.
   c. **Encrypt Document:** It allows you to encrypt a workbook by setting up a password. Now the workbook can only be accessed by those who know the password.
   d. **Restrict Permission:** This option allows you to specify who can and who cannot modify the work.
   e. **Add a Digital Signature:** It allows you to add invisible digital signature to a workbook.
   f. **Mark as Final:** This option marks a workbook as final and locks it. It makes the workbook read-only and prevents further editing.
   g. **Run Compatibility Checker:** It is used to run compatibility check for features not supported by the previous versions of MS Excel.

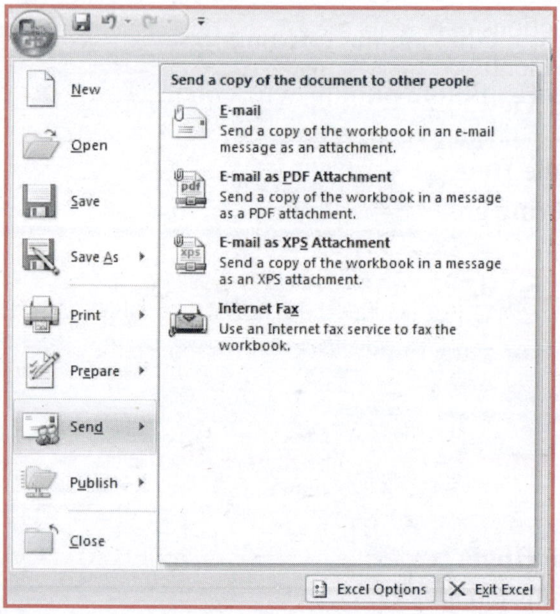

5. Now, click on the **Send** option.
6. **Send a copy of the document to other people** menu list appears on the right.
7. Using the menu list you can choose the following options:
   a. **E-mail:** It allows you to send a copy of the workbook as an attachment in an email.
   b. **E-mail as PDF Attachment:** It allows you to send a copy of the workbook as a PDF attachment in an email.
   c. **E-mail as XPS Attachment:** It allows you to send a copy of the workbook an XPS attachment in an email.
   d. **Internet Fax:** It allows you to send a copy of the workbook through Internet fax service.

CHECK YOUR PROGRESS

A. With the help of the Internet and your school library, find out the difference between Office Calc and MS Excel. HOTS

B. Explore different templates available in MS Excel 2007. Create two sample spreadbooks with the help of in-built MS Excel templates.

C. Write short notes on the following.

1. Lotus 123
2. Ribbon
3. Rows and Columns
4. Print Preview
5. Zoom controls

D. Create a workbook titled FriendsAddress. In the workbook, enter the Name, Phone Number, Address, Date of Birth and Emergency Contact details of five of your friends. Save the file as a PDF and email it to your class teacher.

E. Enumerate all the categories for which online templates are available. Download a template from Microsoft Online and use it to create a workbook.

F. Research and then write a short note on XPS.

G. Explore the options available in the Publish option in the Office button menu.

Modifying a Worksheet

MS Excel 2007 is used to perform arithmetic, logical and scientific calculations. Hence, after entering data in a worksheet, it is necessary to format, edit and manipulate the data based on your requirements. To add or delete, to format, to insert rows and columns, to insert picture and charts, to cut, copy and paste, to apply formulas and functions or to manipulate the data, you need to learn about the tabs, groups and tools available in Excel Ribbon. As mentioned earlier, there are seven tabs. They are: **Home**, **Insert**, **Page Layout**, **Formulas**, **Data**, **Review** and **View**.

In the **Home** tab you have seven groups. They are: **Clipboard**, **Font**, **Alignment**, **Number, Styles**, **Cells** and **Editing** groups (Fig. 8.8).

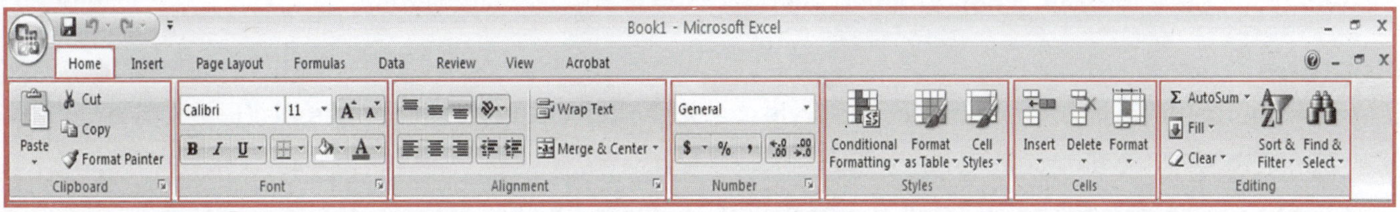

Fig. 8.8 *Home tab*

The **Home** tab is used to perform clipboard operations and basic text and cell formatting. Some common functions of this tab are listed below.

- It is used to copy or move the content from one place to another.
- It is used to apply formatting effects.

- It is used to format numbers with or without decimals and other specifications.
- It is used to apply style effects to cell with or without condition.
- It is used to insert and delete rows, columns and worksheets.
- It is used for sorting and filtering.

Clipboard group

Excel allows you to move, copy and paste cell and its content. The Cut, Copy and Paste options are available in the Clipboard group on the Home tab (Fig. 8.9).

- *Cut:* To cut the selection from the workbook and store it temporarily on the clipboard.
- *Copy:* To copy the selection from the workbook and store it temporarily on the clipboard.
- *Paste:* To paste the contents stored on the clipboard. For more options, such as, pasting the values, formatting, click the down arrow below the paste button and select the option according to requirement (Fig. 8.10).

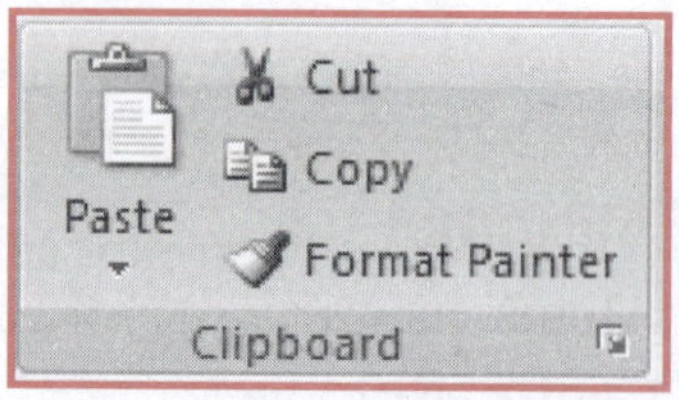

Fig. 8.9 *Clipboard group*

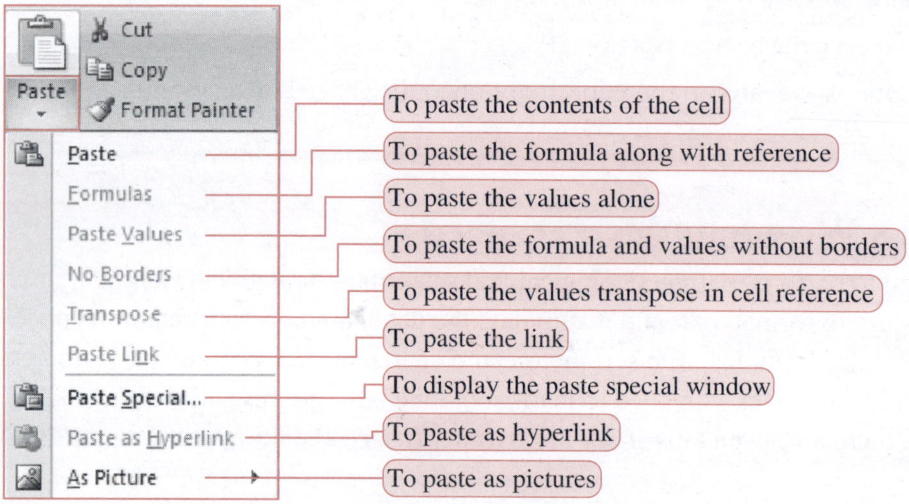

Fig. 8.10 *Paste options*

- *Format Painter:* Format Painter tool is used to copy the formatting from one place and apply it to another. To apply the same formatting effect to multiple places, double-click on the tool.

Font group

In a worksheet, font face, size, color, border and style can be modified using Font group tools (Fig. 8.11).

- *Font:* To state the desired font type of the selected text.
- *Font Size:* To state the desired font size of the selected text.
- *Grow Font and Shrink Font:* To increase and decrease font size of the selected text by one point.
- *Bold, Italic and Underline:* To make the selected text bold, italics or underline it, respectively.
- *Border:* To apply borders to the selected cell.
- *Fill Color:* To fill color in the selected cell(s).
- *Font Color:* To state the desired color of the selected text.

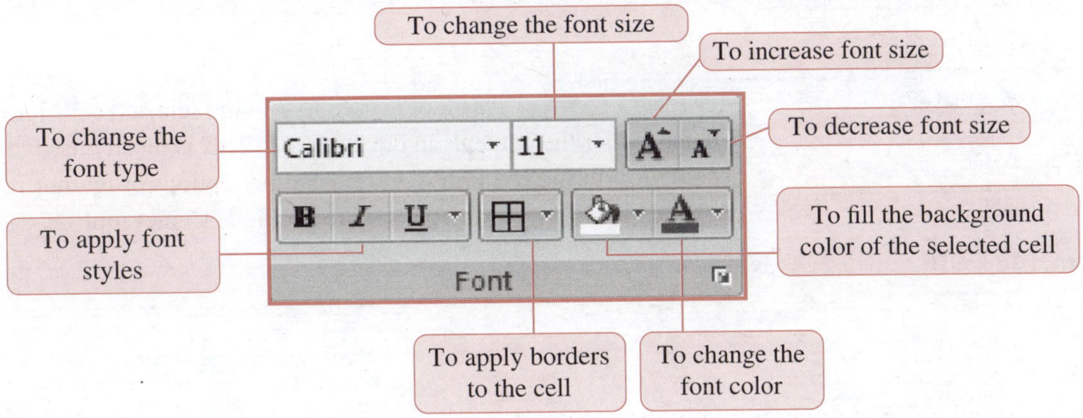

Fig. 8.11 *Font group*

Alignment group

Alignment group (Fig. 8.12) provides **Top**, **Bottom**, **Middle**, **Left**, **Centre**, **Right**, **Wrap Text** and **Merge & Centre** tools to align and organise the data in a cell of worksheet. The options in Alignment group are discussed in Table 8.2.

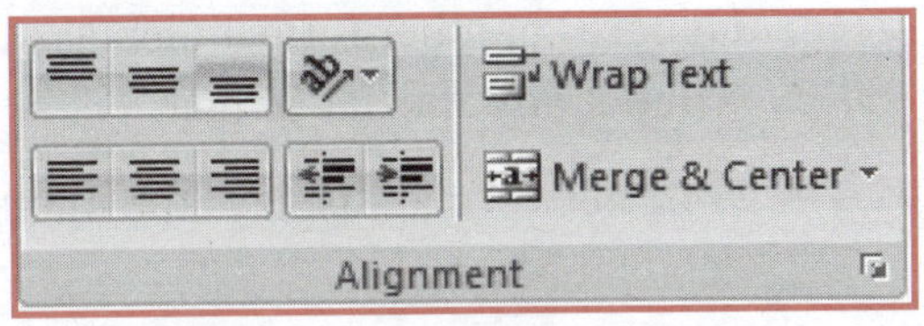

Fig. 8.12 *Alignment group*

Table 8.2 *Options in Alignment group*

Option	Description
	• **Top Align:** To align text to the top of the cell. • **Middle Align:** To align text between the top and bottom of the cell. • **Bottom Align:** To align text to the bottom of the cell.
	• **Left Align:** To align text to the left of the cell. • **Right Align:** To align text the right of the cell. • **Centre:** To align text to centre of the cell.
	• **Decrease:** To decrease the margin between the border and the text of the cell. • **Increase:** To increase the margin between the border and the text of the cell.
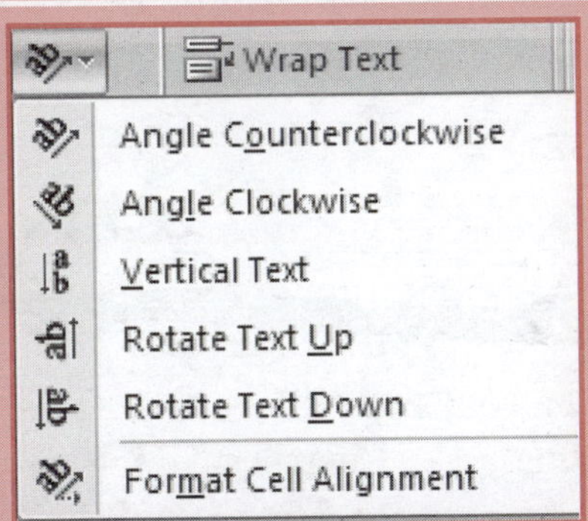	**Orientation:** To rotate text to a diagonal angle or vertical orientation. This is used for labeling narrow columns. To select the orientation, click the down arrow next to the tool to view and select all the available options.
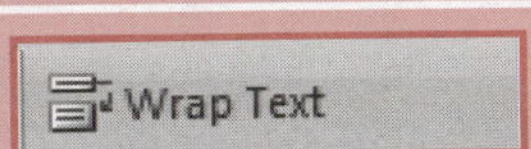	**Wrap Text:** To make all the content of the cell visible by displaying it on multiple lines.

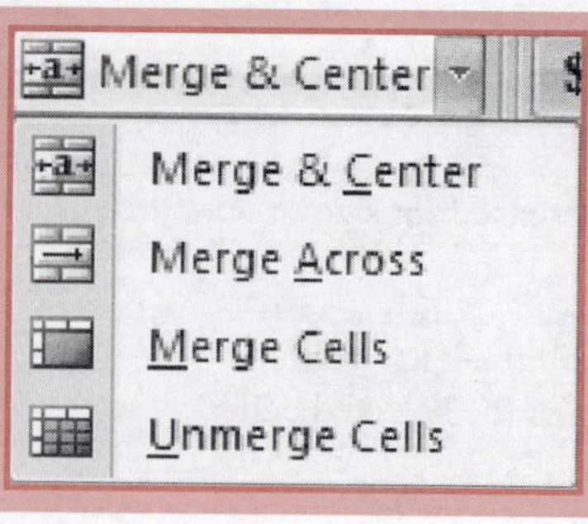

Merge and Center: This tool is used to join the selected cells into one larger cell and center the contents in the large cell. This is mostly used to create the heading for multiple columns. To select other options or to unmerge the cells, click the black arrow available next to Merge & Center tool.

Number group

Number Format tool allows you to choose how the values in a cell are displayed. To select the desired format for the content in the cell, click the black arrow next to general tool. The following options are available (Fig. 8.13):

- **General** number format displays the number without any special format.
- **Number** format displays the number with 2 decimal points.
- **Currency** format displays the number with decimal points along with a $ symbol.
- **Accounting** displays the number with decimal and $ symbol showing the value and $ symbol with spaces.
- **Short Date** format displays the data in mm/dd/yyyy (short date) format.
- **Long Date** format displays the data in day mm/dd/yyyy format.
- **Time** format displays the data in hrs:mm:sec a.m./p.m. format.
- **Percentage** format displays the data along with the % symbol.

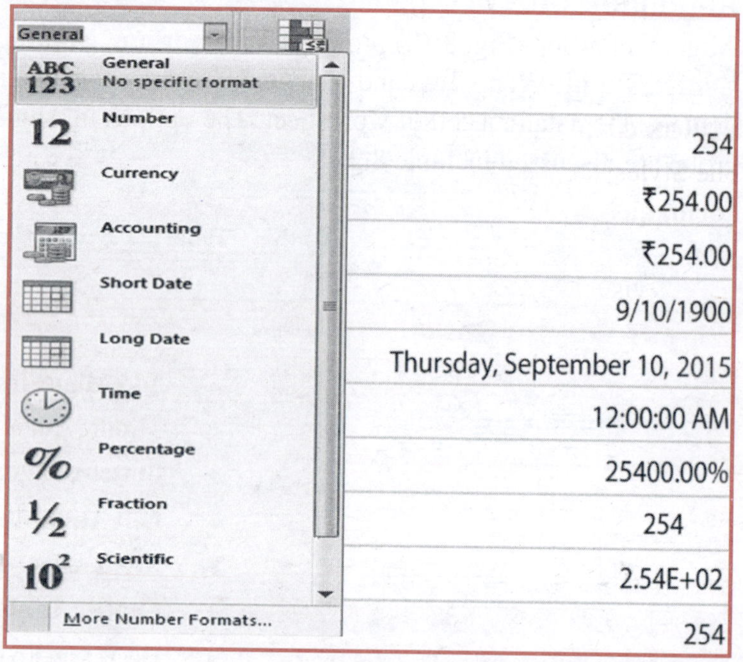

Fig. 8.13 *Numbers group*

- **Fraction** format displays the numbers as actual fraction, rather than decimal.
- **Scientific** format displays the number in exponential form.

FACT FILE

You can change the default currency symbol $ to € or other currency symbol using **Control Panel**. To do so, go to the **Control Panel** ⟶ **Region and Language** ⟶ **Additional Settings** ⟶ **Currency** ⟶ **Currency Symbol.**

CHECK YOUR PROGRESS

A. What are the elementary purpose of the following:

1. Alignment group
2. Number group

B. How is Wrap Text in Excel different from Word Wrap in Notepad? HOTS

C. How is Short Date function different from Long Date function? Explain with an example. HOTS

D. List down the names and functions of options available in the following drop-down list in the Alignment group:

1. Orientation 
2. Merge and Centre 

Styles group

The Styles group has three tools to apply quick styles to the cells in a worksheet. They are **Conditional Formatting**, **Format as Table** and **Cell Style**.

- ***Conditional Formatting:*** This tool is used to highlight interesting cells, emphasise unusual values and visualise data using data bars, color scales and icon sets based on the given criteria (Fig. 8.14).

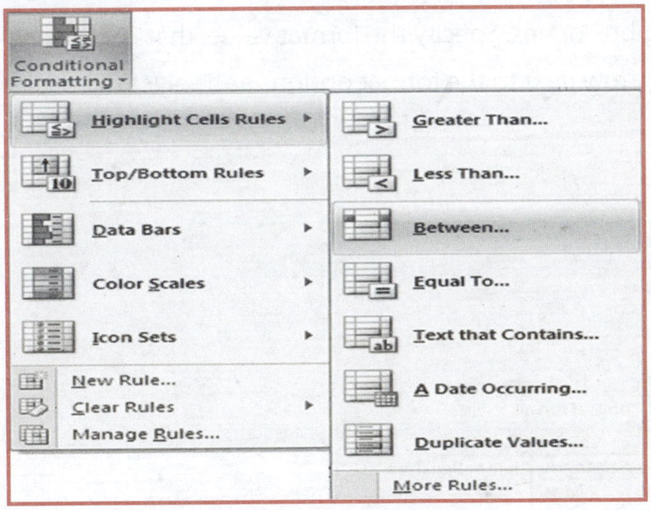

Fig. 8.14 *Conditional formatting*

ACTIVITY

To use conditional formatting to highlight students who are late to class.

1. Create a table with the following columns: Name of the Student, Class, Time of Arrival and Time of Departure. Enter atleast 10 entries.
2. Select the Time of Arrival column and click on the **Conditional Formatting** button in the **Styles** group on the **Home** tab.

3. A menu appears with different options for setting the criteria.
4. Go to the **Highlight Cells Rules** and then select **Greater Than. . .** option.

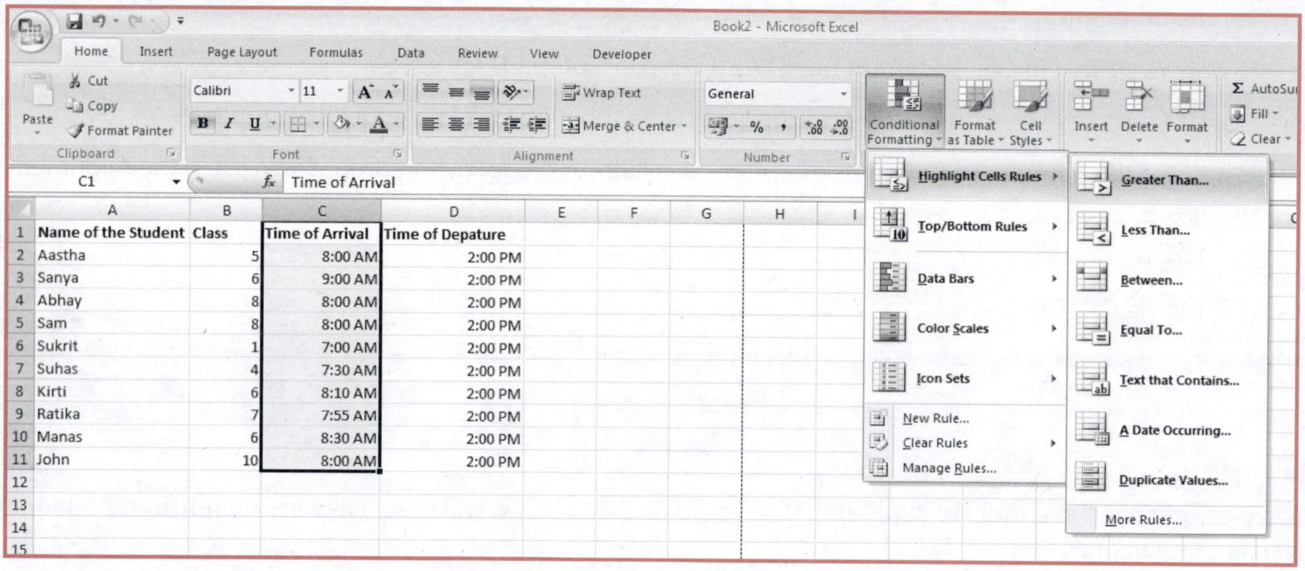

NOTE: Different criteria options are **Greater Than. . .**, **Less Than . . .**, **Between. . .**, **Equal To. . .**, **Text That Contains. . .**, **A Date Occurring. . .**, and **Duplicate Values. . ..**

5. The **Greater Than** dialog box opens. Specify the format value, that is, on or before 8 a.m.
6. Click on the drop-down arrow next to the format options and select the desired formatting.
7. Click on **OK**.

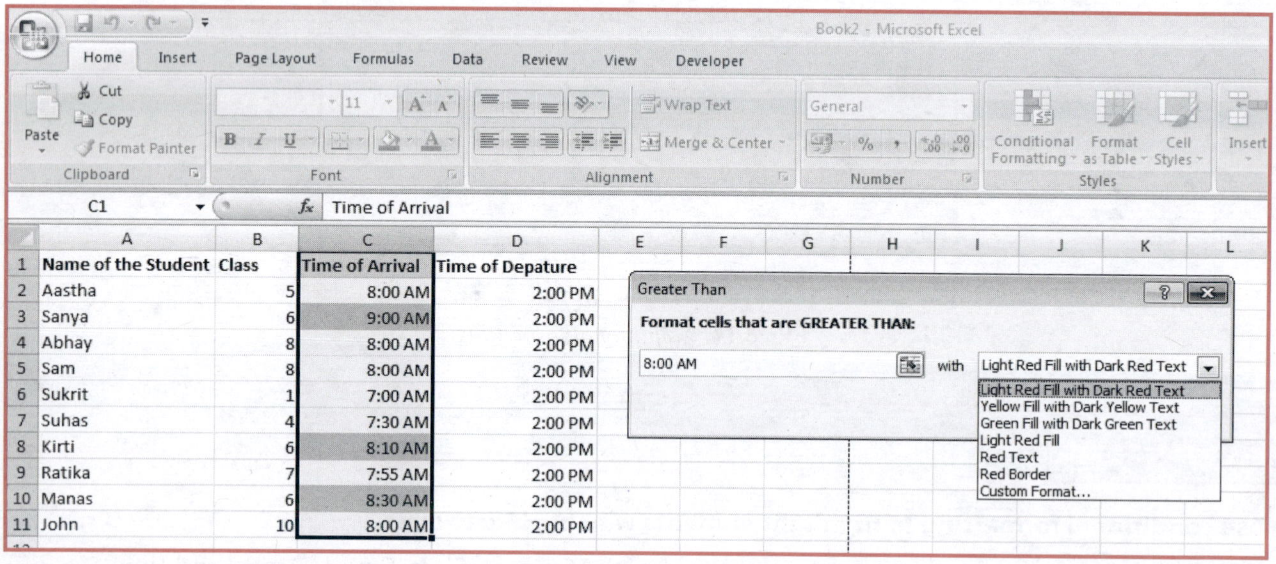

- ***Format as Table:*** This tool is used to quickly format a range of cells and convert it to a table by choosing a predefined table style (Fig. 8.15).

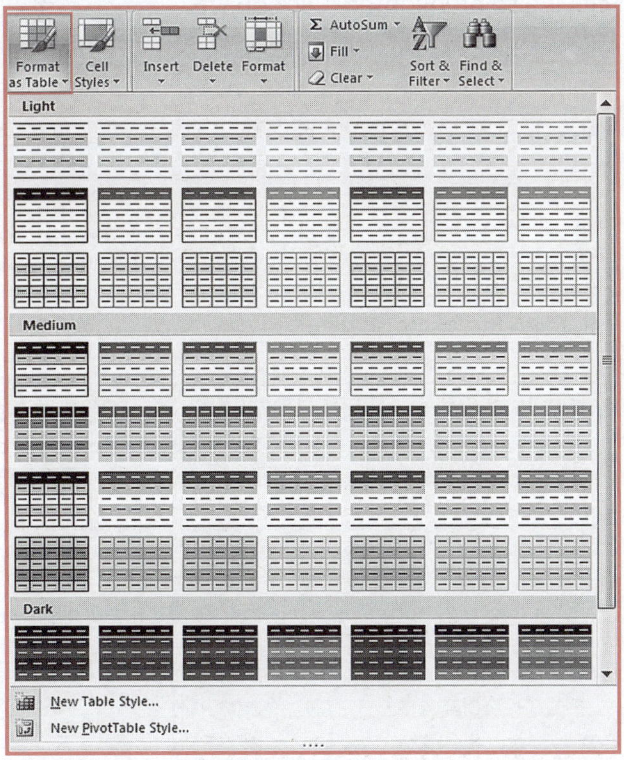

Fig. 8.15 *Format as Table*

ACTIVITY

To use the Format as Table option to apply predefined table styles.

1. Select the range of cells you want to convert to table.
2. Click on the **Format as Table** option in the **Styles** group on the **Home** tab.
3. A drop-down list of predefined styles appear. Click on the style of your choice.

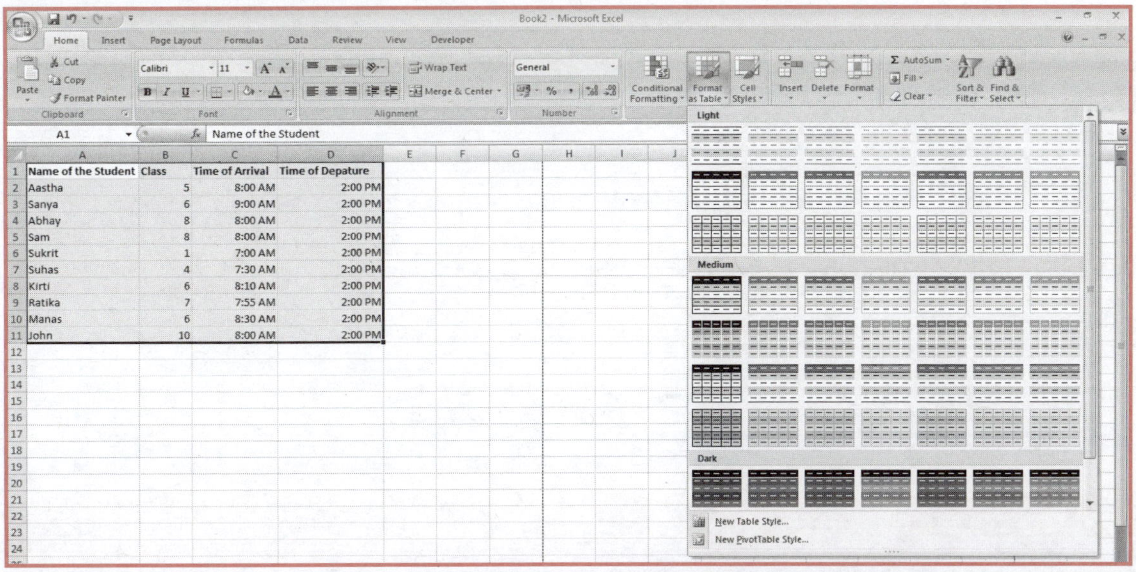

4. The **Format as Table** dialog box appears. It specifies the range of cells that has to be converted. Please note that the selected range of cell is also highlighted. Click on **OK**.

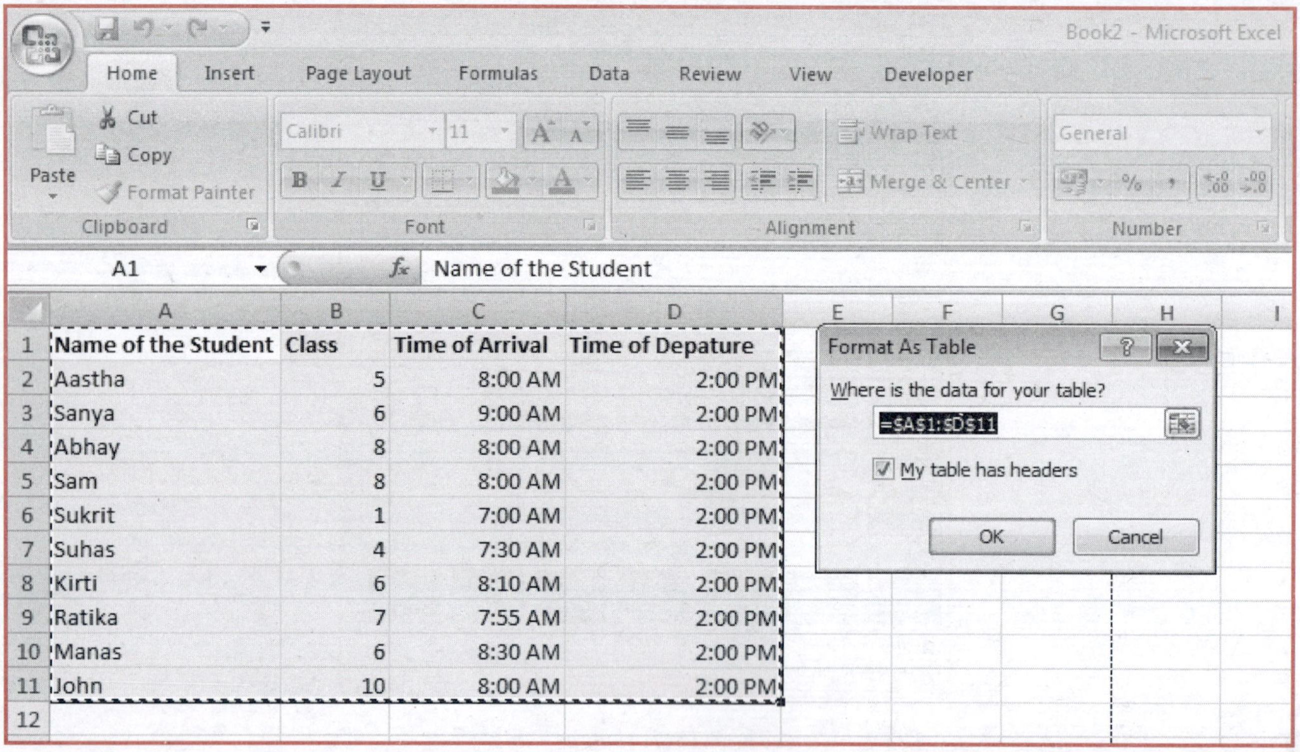

5. The predefined theme is applied. Also, a new **Table Tools Design** tab appears on the Ribbon. This tab is used to modify and format the table.

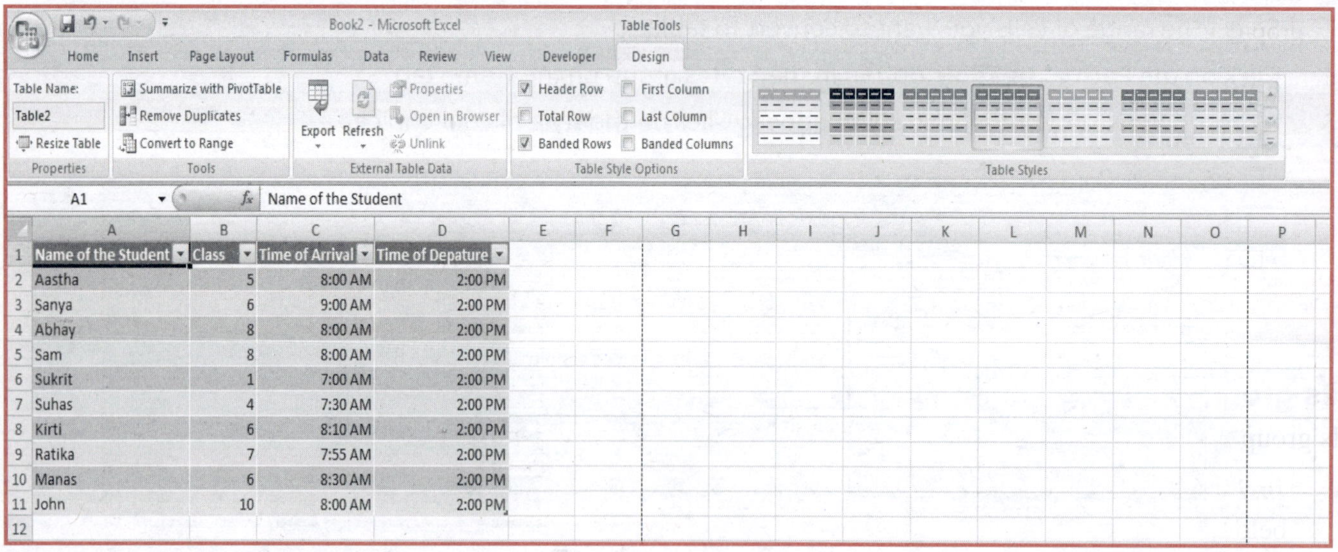

- ***Cell Style:*** This tool is used to quickly format a cell by choosing from pool of predefined styles. You can also define your own style for a cell (Fig. 8.16).

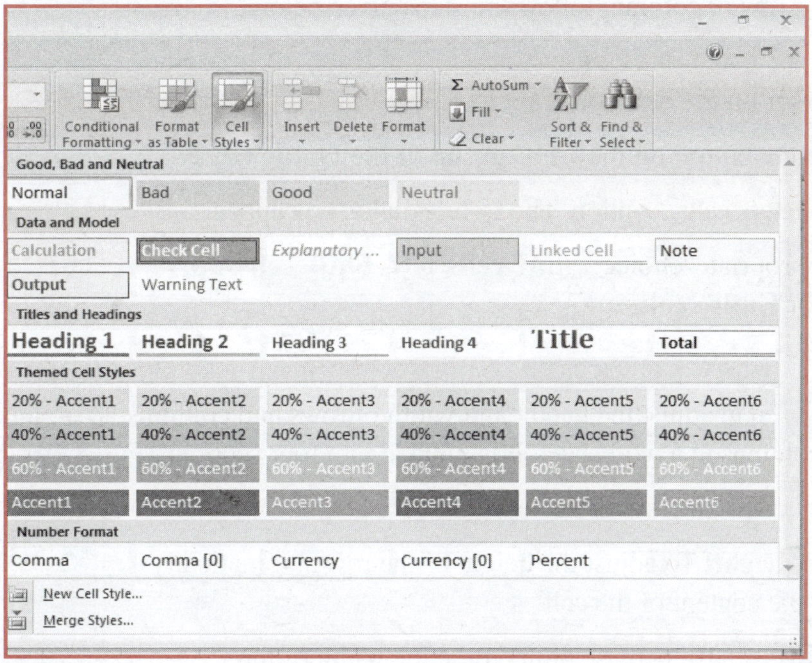

Fig. 8.16 *Cell style*

TRY THIS!

You can delete all the formatting with just one click. To do so, select the cell(s) and go to **Editing** group in the **Home** tab. Select **Clear** function to clear all formatting. You can also delete Comments and Content using options in Clear drop-down list.

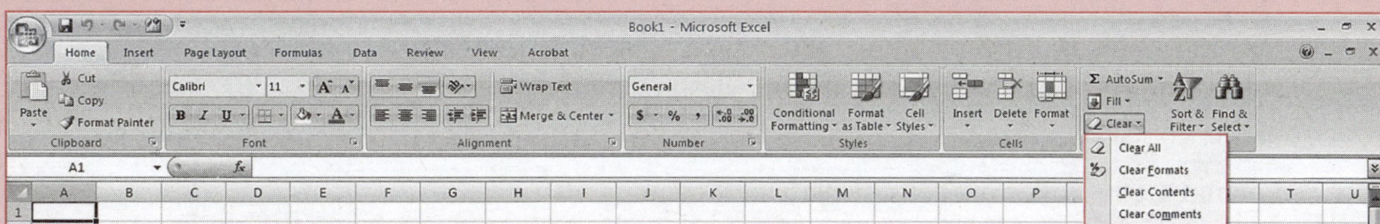

Cells group

Cells group provides you options to insert, delete and format cells.

- ***Insert:*** To insert a cell, row, column or a sheet, follow the steps given below (Fig. 8.17).
    1. Place the cursor in the row below where you want the new row, or in the column to the left of where you want the new column.
    2. Click on the **Insert** button on the **Cells** group of the **Home** tab.
    3. The **Insert** drop-down list appears. Select the desired option.

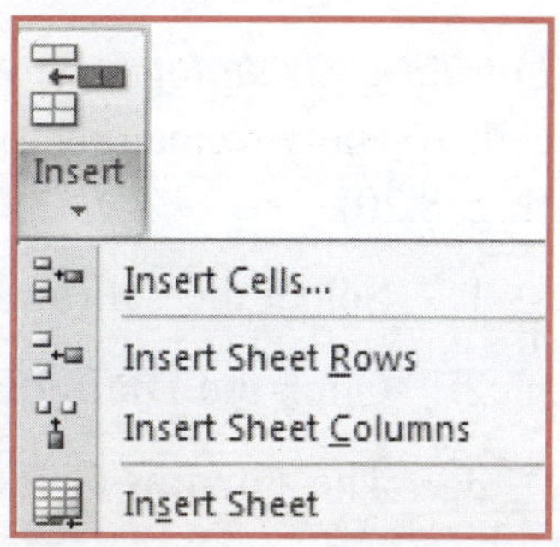

Fig. 8.17 *Insert option*

NOTE: The options available in **Insert** drop-down list are: **Insert cells...**, **Insert Sheet Rows**, **Insert sheet column** and **Insert sheet**.

- *Delete:* To delete a row or column, follow the steps given below (Fig. 8.18).
    1. Place the cursor on the cell you want to delete.
    2. Click the **Delete** button on the **Cells** group of the **Home** tab.
    3. Click on the **Delete cells...** option. The **Delete** dialog box appears.
    4. Click the appropriate choice: **Shift cells left**, **Shift cells up**, **Entire row** or **Entire column**.
    5. Press **OK**.

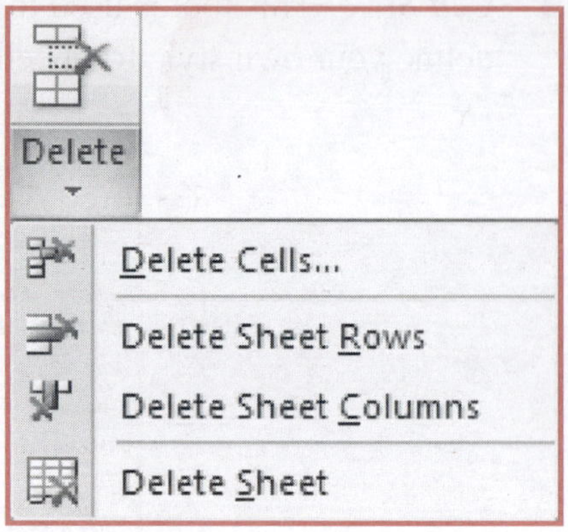

Fig. 8.18 *Delete option*

- *Format tool:* It is used to adjust the height and width of rows and columns; to organise sheets and to protect, hide and unhide columns in a worksheet. It is divided into four sections (Fig. 8.19). The options available are:
    - **Row Height…:** To increase or decrease the row height.
    - **Autofit Row Height:** To adjust the height of the row automatically according to the content of the cell.
    - **Column Width…:** To increase or decrease the width of the column.
    - **Autofit Column Width:** To adjust the width of the column automatically according to the content of the cell.
    - **Default Width…:** To set the default width of the column in the worksheet. The default width of a column is 8.43.
    - **Hide & Unhide:** To hide or unhide a row, column or a sheet.
    - **Protect Sheet…:** To protect your sheet with a password.
    - **Organize Sheets:** To copy, move, and rename a sheet. Using Tab color option, you can apply color to your sheet tab at the bottom of the worksheet.
    - **Format Cells…:** Format cells display the **Format Cell** dialog box. Number, Alignment, Font, Border, Fill and Protection are the different options available in this dialog box to format the cells.

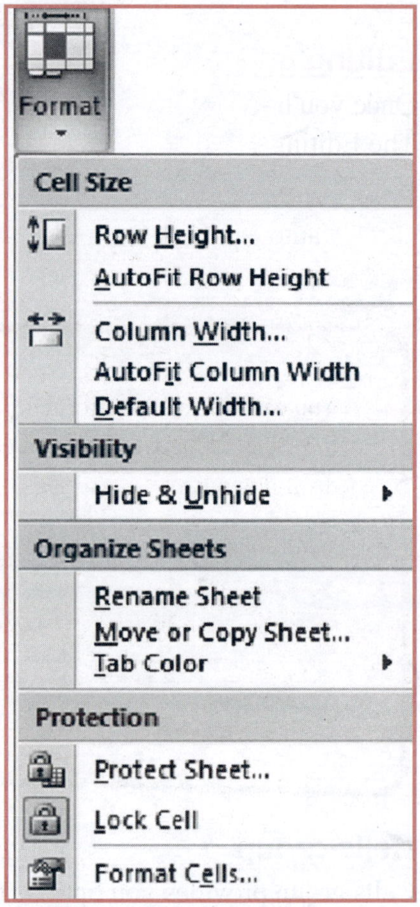

Fig. 8.19 *Format option*

Format Cells dialog box: In Excel, you can also apply specific formatting to a cell. To apply formatting to a cell or group of cells, follow the steps given below (Fig. 8.20).

1. Select the cell(s) that you want to format.
2. Click the **Dialog Box Launcher** on the **Font/Numbers/Alignment** group of the **Home** tab.
3. The **Format Cell** dialog box opens. Change formatting cell options as per your requirement.

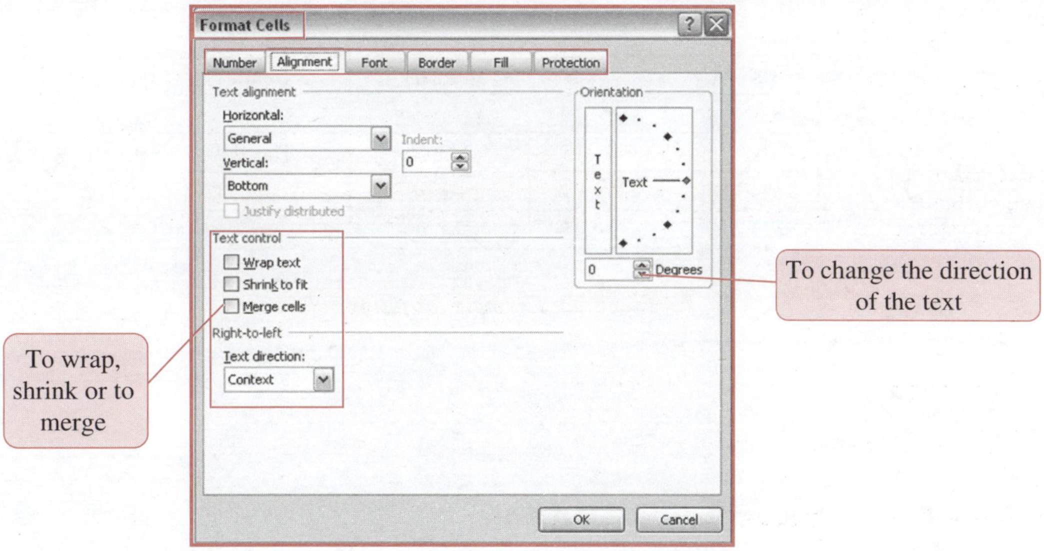

Fig. 8.20 *Format Cells dialog box*

Editing group

Once you have entered and saved data in a workbook, you need tools to alter, modify and manipulate the data. The Editing group provides such options.

- ***AutoSum:*** This tool is used to find the sum of values in a given range of cells automatically. To use AutoSum, follow the steps given below (Fig. 8.21).

  1. Type the values in horizontal or in vertical order.
  2. Select the range and click on the **AutoSum** tool available in the **Editing** group of **Home** tab.
     - **Sum:** The Sum function is used to find the sum of values in a given range of cells.
     - **Average:** The Average function is used to find out the average of the values in a given range of cells.
     - **Count:** The Count Function is used to count the number of entries in a given range of cells.
     - **Max:** The Maximum function returns the maximum of the given values in a range of cells.
     - **Min:** The Minimum function returns the minimum of the given values in a range of cells.
     - **More Functions:** This tool displays the Insert Function window for you to select the function you need.
  3. Click on the option you desire.

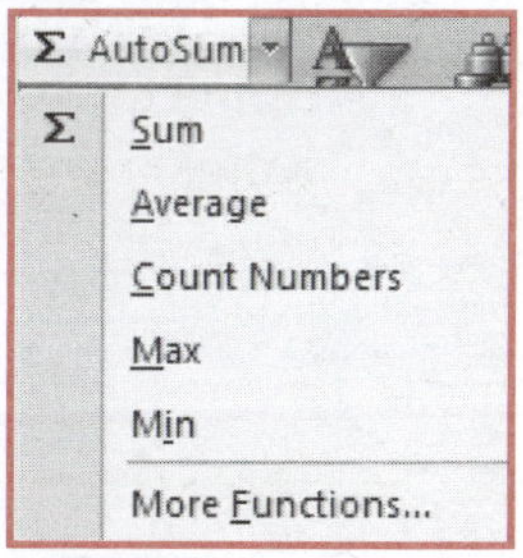

Fig. 8.21 *Autosum option*

- ***Auto Fill:*** The Auto Fill allows us to fill a range of cells in a row or column with a series of values (Fig. 8.22). To copy the same data to fill a range, type once. Select it and drag the small cross symbol at the bottom of right corner of the cell downwards till the last cell of the range. If you want to have a series of data (for example, days of the week (Fig. 8.23)) fill in the first two cells in the series and then use the Auto Fill feature.

  To use the Auto Fill function, follow the steps given below.

  1. Click on the **Fill Handle**.
  2. Drag the **Fill Handle** to fill the cells.

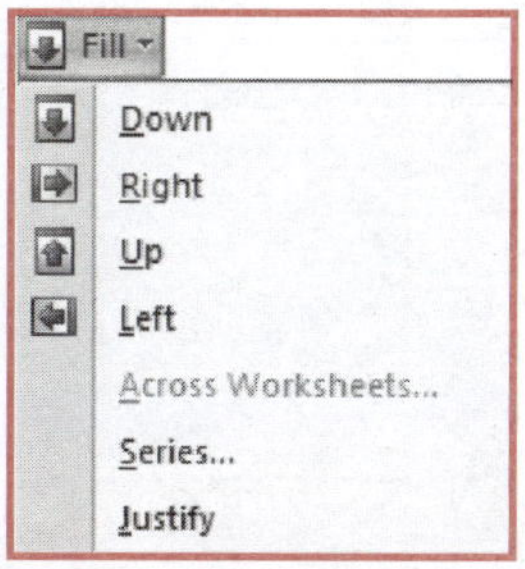

Fig. 8.22 *Fill option*

For example:

xls	5	5	January	Sunday
xls	5	10	February	Monday
xls	5	15	March	Tuesday
xls	5	20	April	Wednesday
xls	5	25	May	Thursday

Range filled with same value

Range filled with series

Fig. 8.23 *Example for filling cells*

ACTIVITY

To use the Auto Fill and AutoSum functions in a table.

1. Create a sample table consisting of names and roll number of students and marks of five subjects. The table should have ten records.
2. The first column is Roll Number. Fill the first two values and then drag the **Fill Handle** to automatically fill the values.
3. Use **Conditional Formatting** option in the **Styles** group of the **Home** tab to highlight student who scored less than 33 (passing score) in any subject.

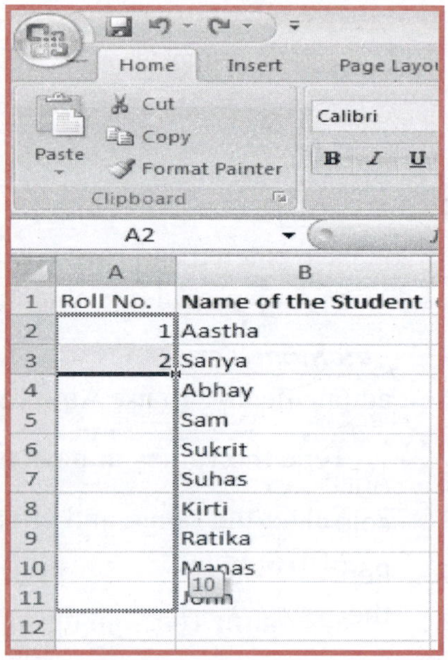

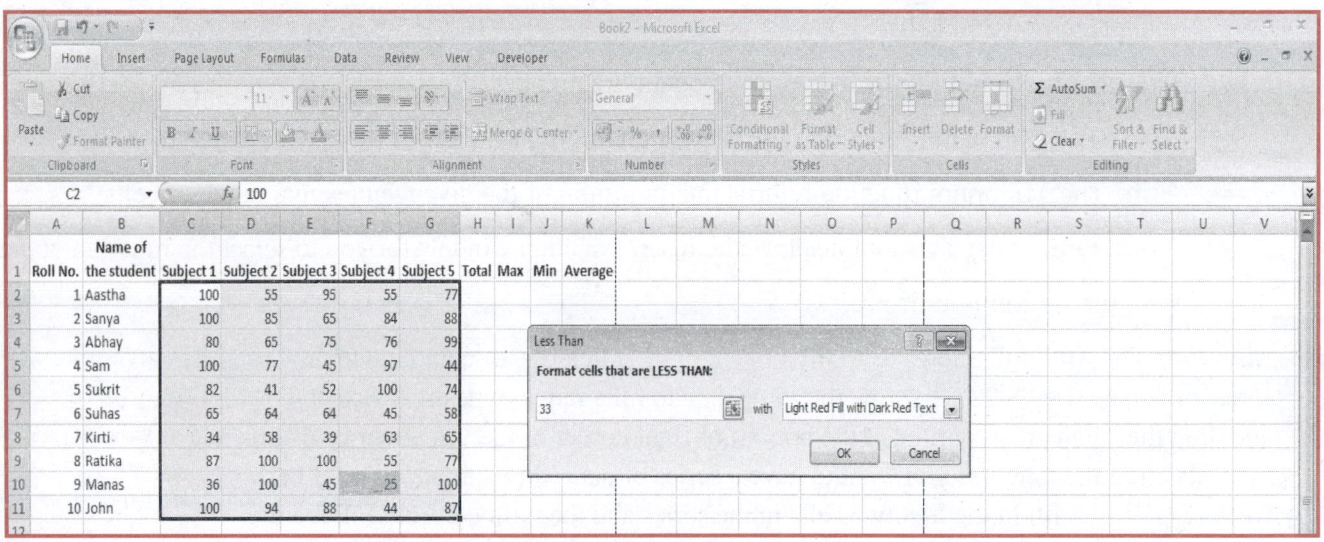

4. Go to the H2 cell, click on the **AutoSum function** button in the **Editing** group of the **Home** tab. Select the range of cell whose total you want and the Sum function is automatically applied.
5. Press **Enter**.

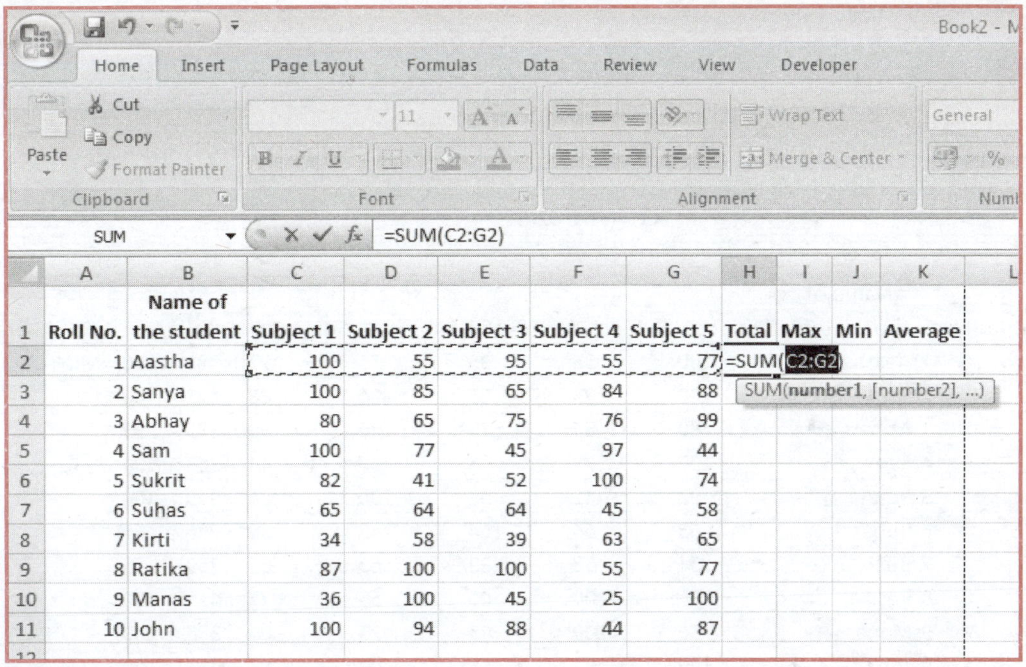

6. Again drag the **Fill Handle** downwards to copy the Sum formulae and automatically fill the values in the column.
7. Repeat the steps to find the maximum marks a student scored. Use **Max** in **AutoSum** function and then use the **Auto Fill** option to copy the formulae to the entire column.

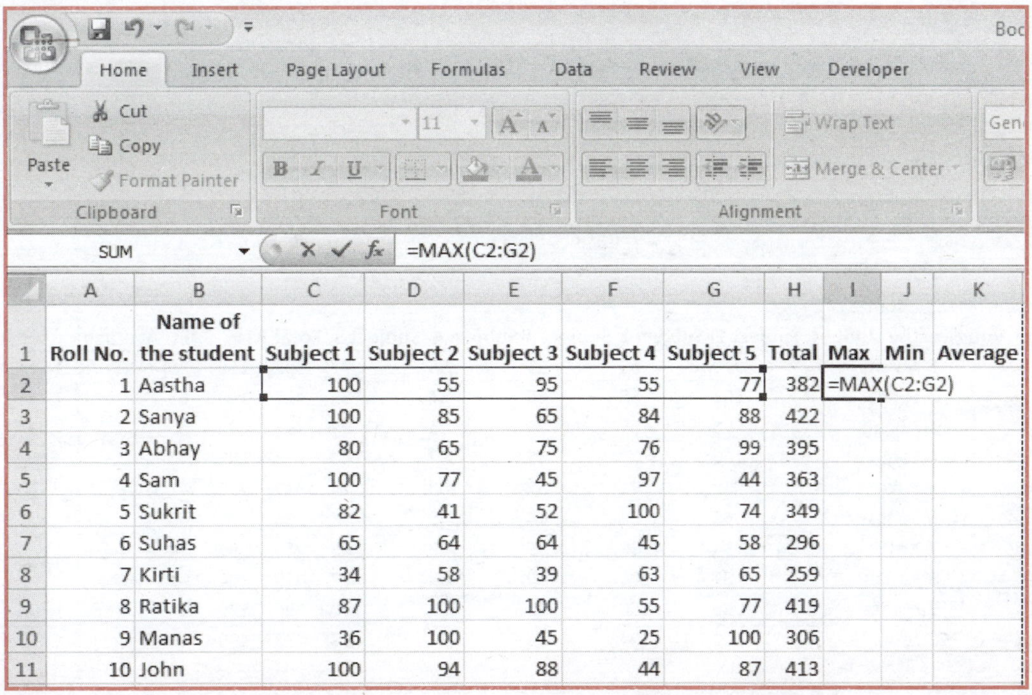

8. Repeat the steps to find the minimum marks a student scored. Use **Min** in **AutoSum** function and then use the **Auto Fill** option to copy the formulae to the entire column.

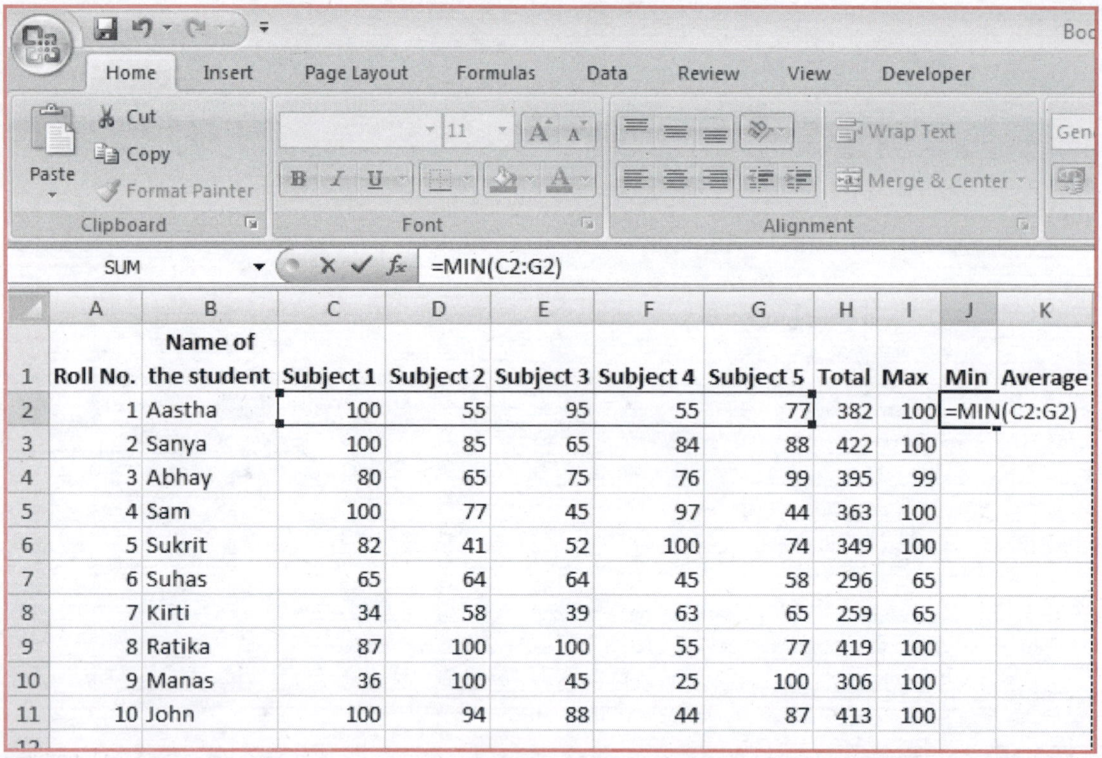

	A	B	C	D	E	F	G	H	I	J	K
1	Roll No.	Name of the student	Subject 1	Subject 2	Subject 3	Subject 4	Subject 5	Total	Max	Min	Average
2	1	Aastha	100	55	95	55	77	382	100	=MIN(C2:G2)	
3	2	Sanya	100	85	65	84	88	422	100		
4	3	Abhay	80	65	75	76	99	395	99		
5	4	Sam	100	77	45	97	44	363	100		
6	5	Sukrit	82	41	52	100	74	349	100		
7	6	Suhas	65	64	64	45	58	296	65		
8	7	Kirti	34	58	39	63	65	259	65		
9	8	Ratika	87	100	100	55	77	419	100		
10	9	Manas	36	100	45	25	100	306	100		
11	10	John	100	94	88	44	87	413	100		

9. Again repeat the steps to find the average marks a student scored. Use **AVERAGE** in **AutoSum** function and then use the **Auto Fill** option to copy the formulae to the entire column.

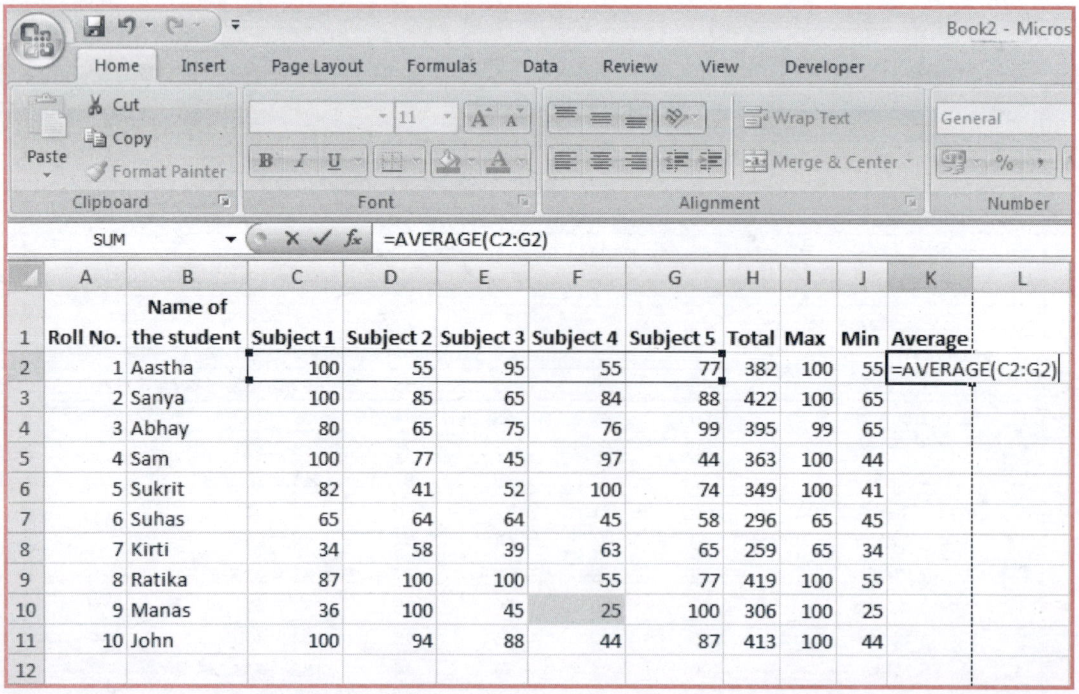

	A	B	C	D	E	F	G	H	I	J	K	L
1	Roll No.	Name of the student	Subject 1	Subject 2	Subject 3	Subject 4	Subject 5	Total	Max	Min	Average	
2	1	Aastha	100	55	95	55	77	382	100	55	=AVERAGE(C2:G2)	
3	2	Sanya	100	85	65	84	88	422	100	65		
4	3	Abhay	80	65	75	76	99	395	99	65		
5	4	Sam	100	77	45	97	44	363	100	44		
6	5	Sukrit	82	41	52	100	74	349	100	41		
7	6	Suhas	65	64	64	45	58	296	65	45		
8	7	Kirti	34	58	39	63	65	259	65	34		
9	8	Ratika	87	100	100	55	77	419	100	55		
10	9	Manas	36	100	45	25	100	306	100	25		
11	10	John	100	94	88	44	87	413	100	44		
12												

Sort & Filter: **Sorting** is the process of arranging data in ascending or descending order to analyse the data easily. The most common type of sorting is alphabetical ordering, which can be done in ascending or descending order (Fig. 8.24). The **Custom Sort** option is used to define the sort column, values and order of sorting. You can add levels to sort more than one column. The header row can be avoided while sorting by clicking **My data has headers** button. You can also filter out the data temporarily according to the criteria (Fig. 8.25).

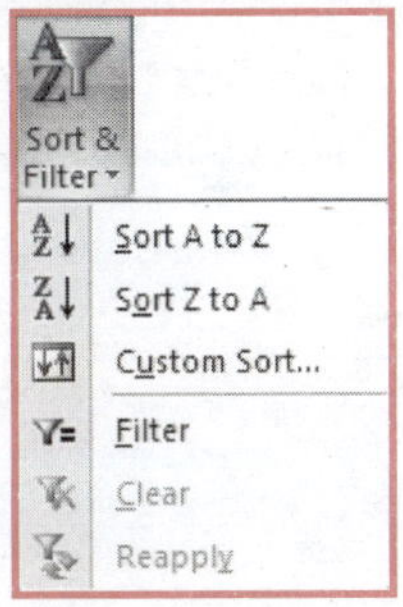

Fig. 8.24 *Sort & Filter option*

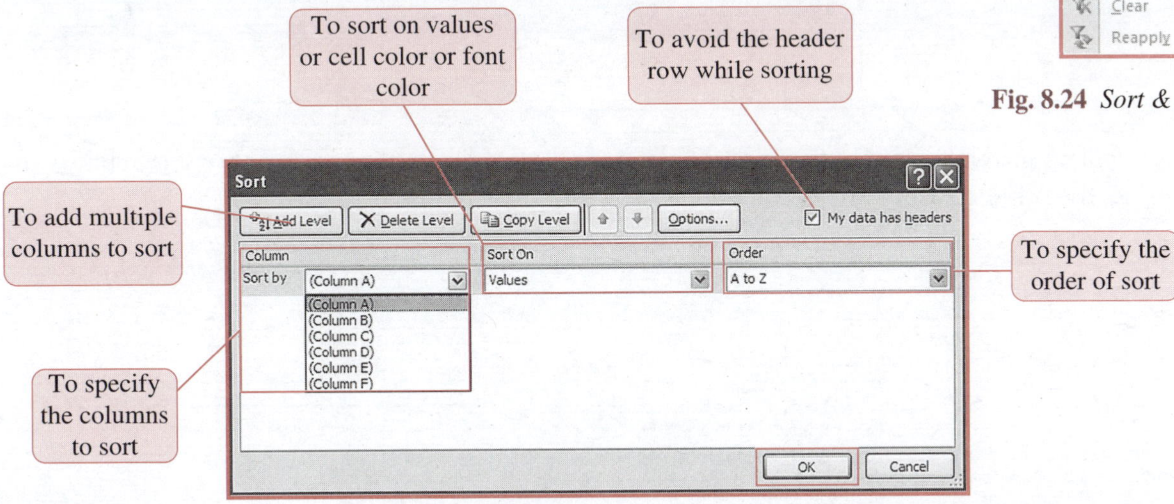

Fig. 8.25 *Sorting data*

You can sort in alphabetical order; from largest to smallest or from smallest to largest; on multiple levels.

Filtering allows you to display only data that meets certain criteria. You can filter data using the AutoFilter feature to display only the data that meets specified criteria. Filtered data can be copied, manipulated, and printed without having to move it to a new spreadsheet. Using AutoFilter, you can filter data by selecting criteria from a list, by numerical conditions, or by color.

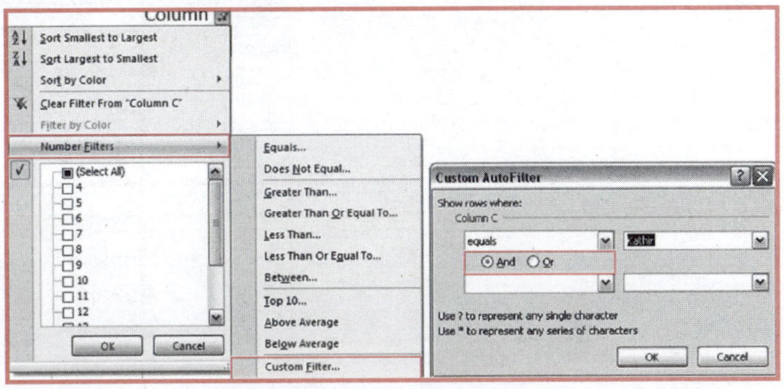

Fig. 8.26 *Applying filters*

Filtering can be done using direct values (Smallest to Largest, Largest to Smallest, color) or based on conditions given in **Number filters** option (Fig. 8.26).

You can also customise your filter using the **Custom Filter** option which takes you to **Custom AutoFilter** option that provides you a dailog box to accept one or more criteria.

ACTIVITY

To use the sorting and filtering options on the table created in the previous activity.

1. Click on column header B to select the entire column B.
2. In the **Editing** group of the **Home** tab, click on the **Sort & Filter** option.
3. A drop-down list appears. From the list, select **Sort A to Z** option.

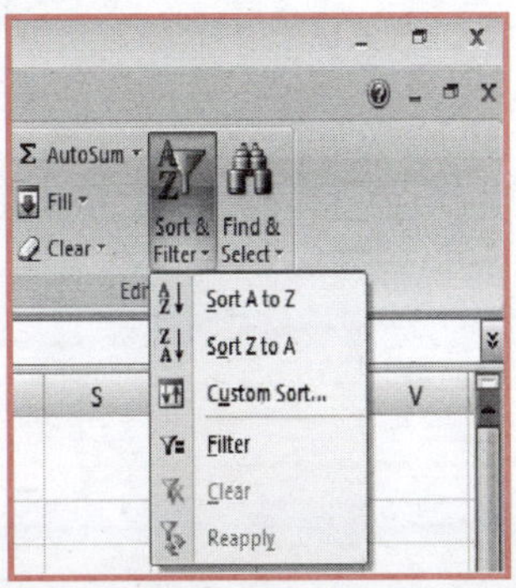

4. The **Sort Warning** dialog box appears. It reminds you that the adjacent cells are not included in the sort selection. Click on the **Sort** button to proceed.

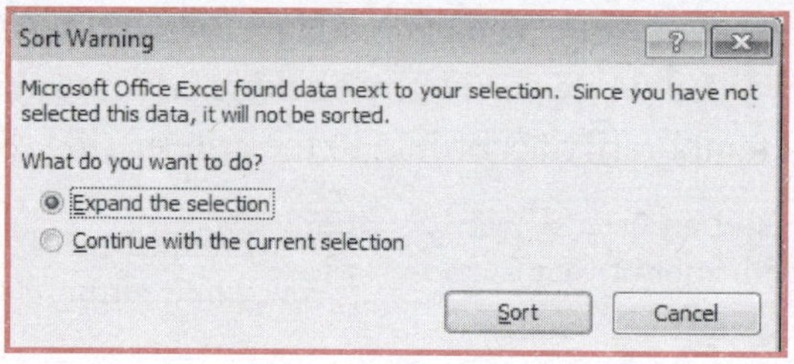

5. The data will be sorted in alphabetical order, from A to Z. Please note that since only column B was selected for sorting, the other columns are rearranged as per sorting in column B.

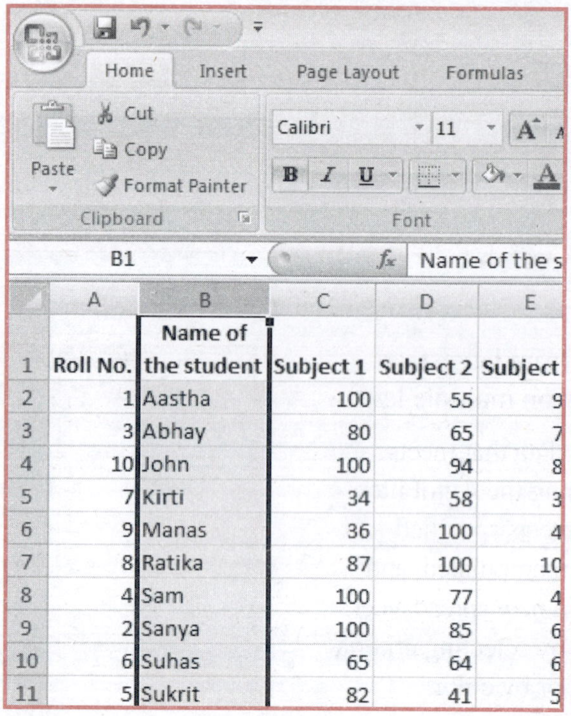

	A	B	C	D	E
1	Roll No.	Name of the student	Subject 1	Subject 2	Subject
2	1	Aastha	100	55	9
3	3	Abhay	80	65	7
4	10	John	100	94	8
5	7	Kirti	34	58	3
6	9	Manas	36	100	4
7	8	Ratika	87	100	10
8	4	Sam	100	77	4
9	2	Sanya	100	85	6
10	6	Suhas	65	64	6
11	5	Sukrit	82	41	5

6. To sort on multiple levels, click on the **Custom Sort...** option in the **Sort & Filter** option drop-down list.
7. The **Sort** dialog box appears.

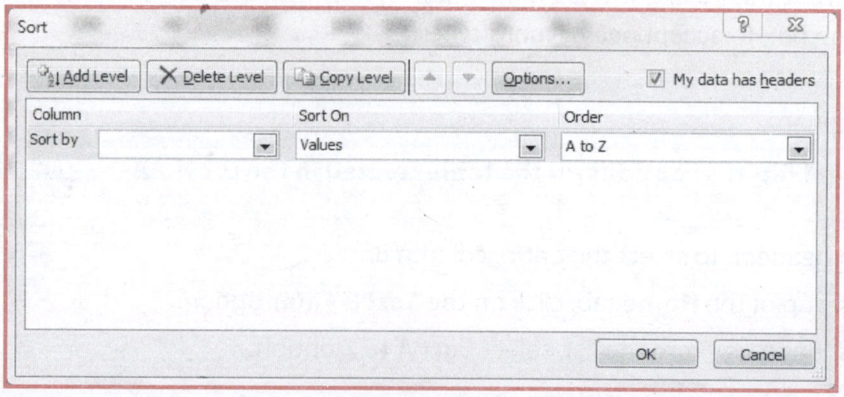

8. In the **Sort by** box, mention the name of the column you want to sort. In the **Sort on** box select what to sort on. In the **Order** box, choose the order of the results. To add another level, click on the **Add Level** button.

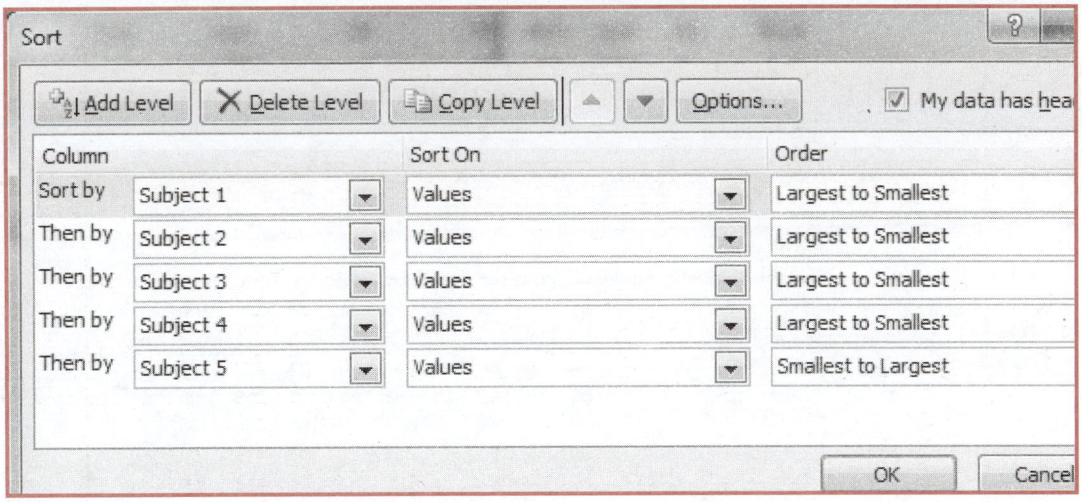

9. Click on **OK**.
10. Now, select column C. From the **Sort & Filter** drop-down list, select **Filter** option.
11. A downward arrow head appears in C1 cell. Click on the arrow to open the **Filter** drop-down list.

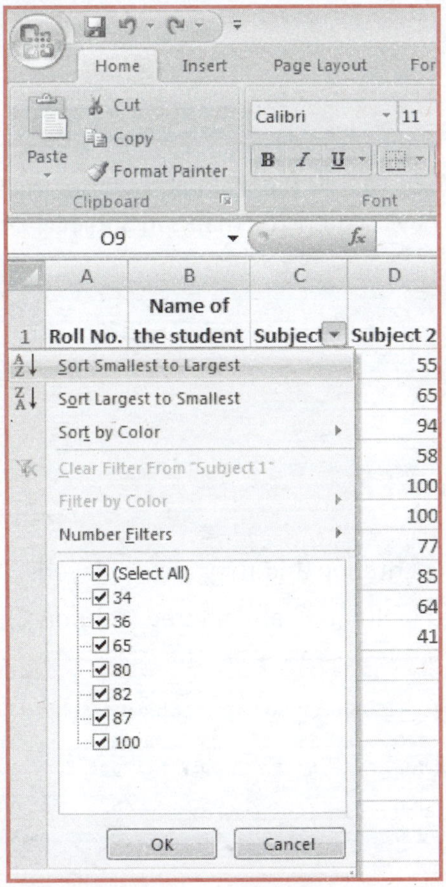

12. Go to the **Numbers Filters** option in the **Filter** drop-down list and select **Equals…** .

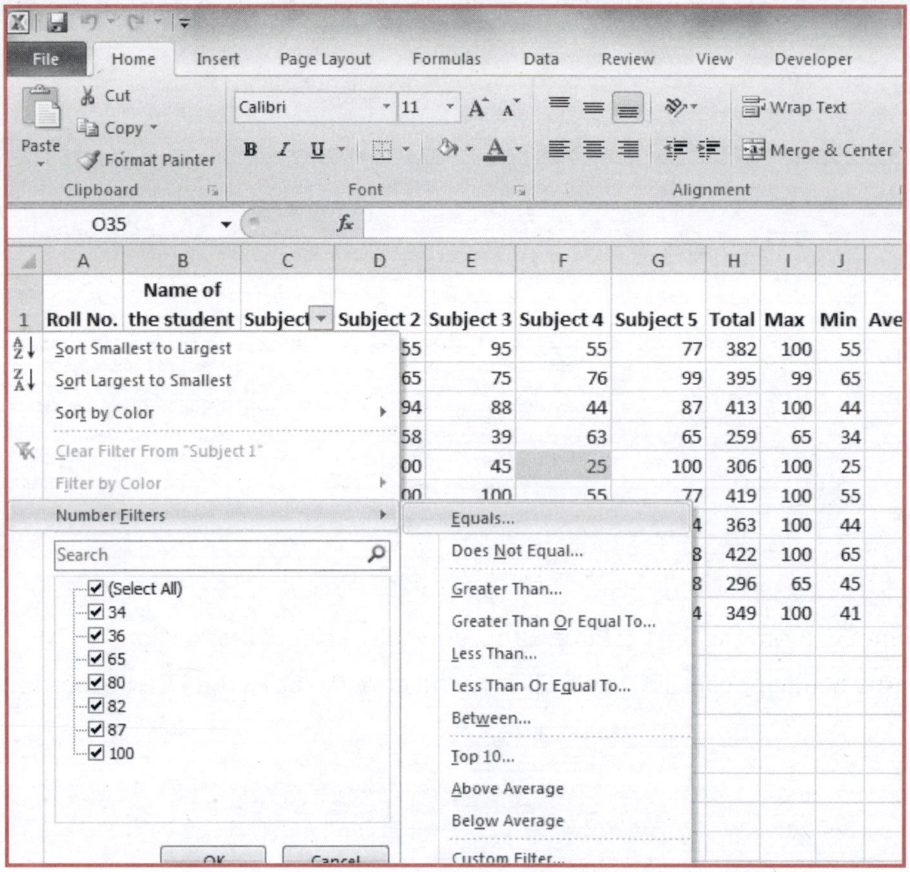

13. The **Custom AutoFilter** dialog box appears. In the dialog box, enter the filtering criteria. In this case, the criterion is to show records of students who have scored 100 marks in Subject1 or scored more than 90 marks in Subject1.

14. There are four records that fulfill the criterion and they are displayed.

NOTE: Here, the records are both sorted (column B) and filtered (column C).

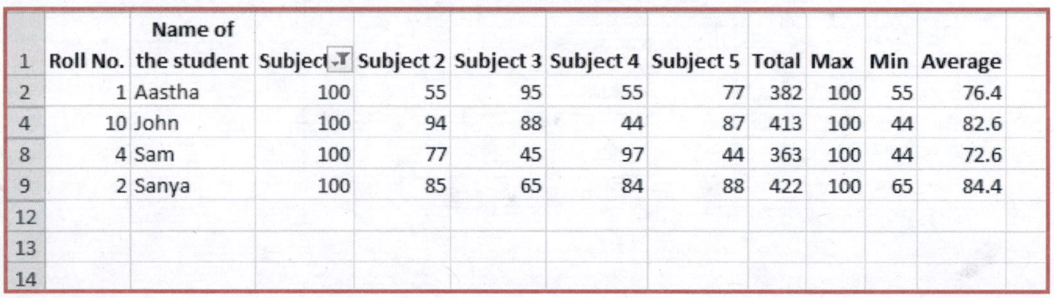

	Roll No.	Name of the student	Subject1	Subject 2	Subject 3	Subject 4	Subject 5	Total	Max	Min	Average
2	1	Aastha	100	55	95	55	77	382	100	55	76.4
4	10	John	100	94	88	44	87	413	100	44	82.6
8	4	Sam	100	77	45	97	44	363	100	44	72.6
9	2	Sanya	100	85	65	84	88	422	100	65	84.4
12											
13											
14											

TRY THIS!

You can also filter unique items from a list. To do so, go to **Data** tab → **Sort & Filter** group → **Filter** tool. In filter group, choose **Advanced Filter** option and check the **Unique records only** option. Click **OK**.

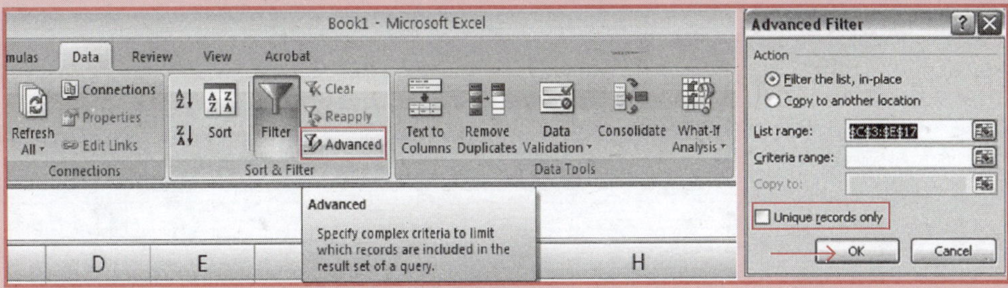

- ***Find & Select:*** This group helps you to find a value, formulae and comment. If necessary, you can also replace and make changes.

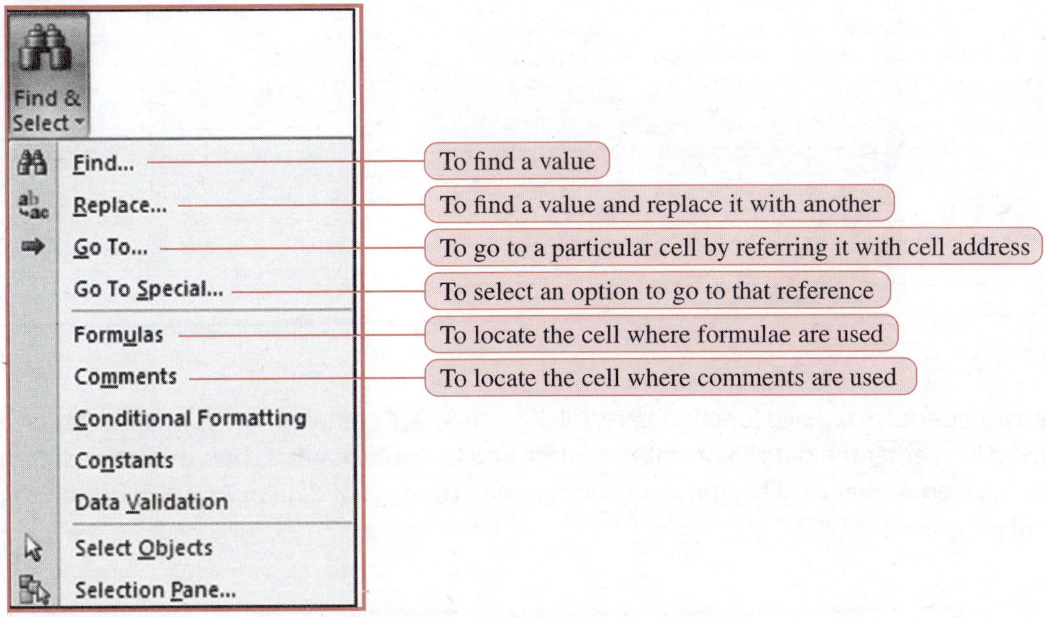

Fig. 8.27 *Find & select option*

ACTIVITY

To find text in a workbook.

1. Select **Find & Select** option in the **Editing** group of the **Home** tab.
2. A drop-down list appears. Select the **Find** option.

   NOTE: You can also go to **Find** option by pressing **Ctrl+F**.
3. The **Find and Replace** dialog box appears.

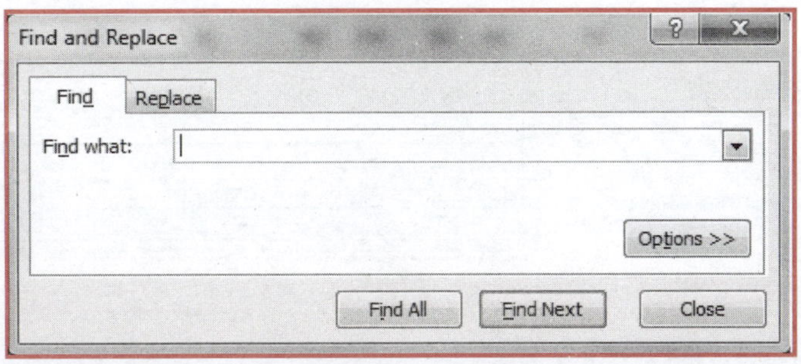

4. In the **Find what:** box, enter the data you want to search.
5. Click on the **Find All** to find all the instance of the data entered.
6. The **Find and Replace** dialog box expands and contains a list of all the instance of the data.
7. Click **Close**.

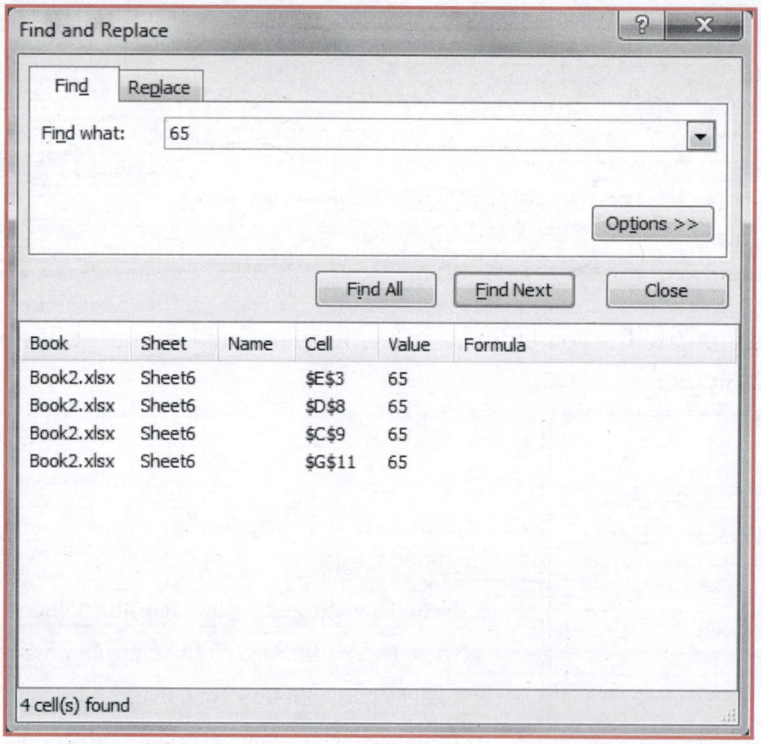

NOTE: You can also perform replace function here. Click on the **Replace** tab in the **Find and Replace** dialog box. In the **Find what:** box, enter the data you want to replace and in **Replace what:** box, enter the data you want to replace it with. Click on **Replace All** button to replace all the instances of data or **Replace** button to preview and replace particular instances of data.

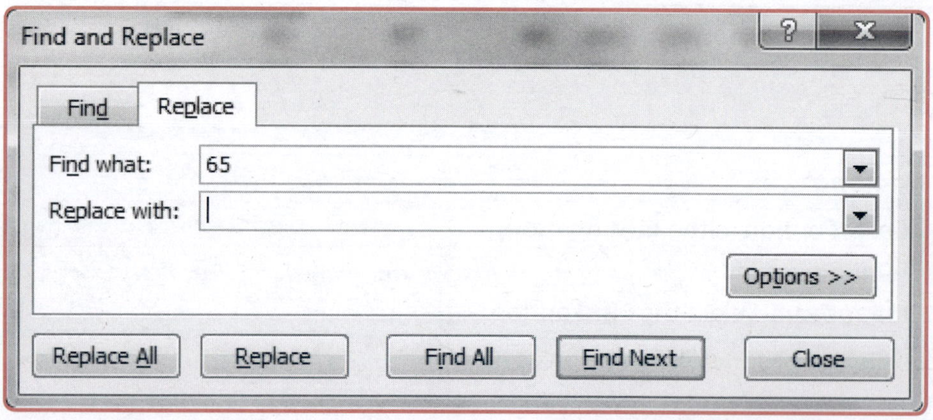

Quick Key

Ctrl + 1	To display Format Cells dialog box
Ctrl + 2	To apply/remove bold format from the selected text
Ctrl + 3	To apply/remove italic format
Ctrl + 4	To apply/remove underlining format
Ctrl + D	To use the fill down command to copy the contents and format of the topmost cell
Ctrl + R	To use the fill right command to copy the contents and format of the leftmost cell
Ctrl + F	To find a text
Ctrl + A	To select all in a worksheet
Ctrl + N	To create a new workbook
Ctrl + O	To open an existing workbook
Ctrl + Shift + &	To apply outline border to the selected cell(s)
Ctrl + Shift + –	To remove outline border to the selected cell(s)
Ctrl + Shift + $	To apply currency number format for the selected cell
Ctrl + '+'	To display Insert dialog box (to insert column or row)
Ctrl + '–'	To display Delete dialog box (to delete column or row)
Ctrl + Shift + F	To display Format Cells dialog box highlighting the font menu
Shift + F11	To insert new worksheet
F2	To edit the content of an active cell

CHECK YOUR PROGRESS

A. Create a sample table consisting of names, age, address, phone number and email address of five friends and apply the following:

1. Conditional formatting
2. Format the table using either Light or Dark table style.

B. Explore and give a reasoned answer:

1. Difference between Protect Sheet and Lock Cell **HOTS**
2. Difference between Conditional Formatting and Sorting.

C. In a spreadsheet, fill dates for one month using autofill feature.

D. In the table created above, sort the name of friends in ascending order.

E. Investigate and give steps to:

1. Clear all conditional formatting
2. Create new table styles
3. Apply cell styles to heading in a table.

F. Explain different options available in the Editing group of the Home tab. Write short notes on all the options.

GLOSSARY

- **Auto Fill:** It allows you to fill a range of cells in a row or column with a series of values.
- **Cell:** It is a small rectangular box which is an intersection of a row and a column.
- **Cell address:** It identifies the location of each cell.
- **Cell Pointer:** It is the highlighted cell box that represents the active cell.
- **Ribbon:** It is a set of tabs available at the top portion of the Excel workbook.
- **Spreadsheet software:** It is an application software that organises the information in rows and columns.
- **Sorting:** It is the process of arranging data in ascending or descending order in order to analyse the data easily.
- **Workbook:** It is a file in which worksheet and charts are stored.
- **Worksheet:** It is a rectangular sheet in which small box called cells are available.

NOW YOU KNOW

1. MS Excel is an application software which is used to perform arithmetic, logical and scientific calculations.
2. There are 1048576 rows and 16384 columns (A to XFD). There are 17179869184 cells (1048576 × 16384) in a worksheet.
3. Excel file is referred as a workbook which consists of several worksheets.
4. An entire worksheet can neither be viewed on one screen nor printed in one go.
5. You can format your cells, tables and worksheets with the help of options given in various groups of Home tab.

EXERCISE

FA

A Fill in the blanks.

1. In MS Excel 2007, a worksheet has .... columns and .... rows.
2. By default, a workbook contains .... worksheets.
3. To fill the range of cells with 5,10,15, ..., ... option is used.

4. The content of the selected cell is displayed on the .... bar.

5. In Excel 2007, number is .... aligned and text is .... aligned.

6.  tool is available in .... tab.

7. A .... is a file in which, worksheets and charts are stored.

8. The highlighted cell box that represents the active cell is called ....

9. .... + ... keys are used to display the Format Cells dialog box.

10. The intersection of column F and 5th row is referred as ....

11. You can also customise your filter using .... option.

12. The saved file in Excel 2007, takes the extension ....

B Multiple choice questions.

1. The currency symbol can be changed using the .... utility of Control Panel.

   a. Device Manager b. Recovery c. Region and Language d. System

2. In a worksheet, the active cell is highlighted by .... border.

   a. dashed line b. dotted line c. dark black d. No

3. The default column width in Excel 2007 is .... points. HOTS

   a. 8.33 b. 8.43 c. 8.12 d. 8.24

4. The name of last column in Excel 2007 is ....

   a. XV b. AV c. XVD d. XFD

5. If you are in 4th row and 5th column, then that cell is referred as ....

   a. E4 b. 5D c. E5 d. D4

6. A collection of worksheet is called ....

   a. workgroup b. workbook c. spreadsheet d. None of these

7. Excel 2007 contains .... rows and .... columns.

   a. 65536 rows and 256 columns b. 1048576 rows and 16384 columns

   c. 63536 rows 280 columns d. 1022345 rows and 65536 columns

8. The Merge & Center option is present in .... group.

   a. Clipboard b. Alignment c. Styles d. Cells

9. The formatting tools are available in .... tab.

   a. Home b. Insert c. Review d. Data

10. The display on the name box shows C4. This means that ....

a. That you are in 3rd column, 4th row

b. That you are in 4th column and 3rd row

c. That you are 4th row, 4th column

d. That you are in C row, 2nd column

C Answer the following questions briefly.

1. Define worksheet.
2. Write the steps to invoke Excel 2007.
3.  Identify this tool.
4. My data has headers This option is available in Custom Sort Window. What is the purpose of this? HOTS
5. Write a short note on Clear option.

SA

D Answer the following questions.

1. Write a short note on Find & Replace option.
2. Explain Custom Sort.
3. What are the options available in the Numbers group?
4. Define AutoSum function.
5. What are Cell Styles?

E Answer the following questions in detail.

1. What are the two different keyboard shortcut keys to apply or remove bold style to the content of a cell?
2. Explain AutoFill option.
3. Write down the features of MS Excel 2007.
4. Differentiate between Sorting and Filtering.
5. Write down different alignment options available in MS Excel 2007. How are they different from options available in MS Word 2007?

Application Based Questions

A. Ravi has a monthly income of Rs. 11000. His fixed monthly outgoings are: Rs. 4000 for rent, Rs. 2000 for food, Rs. 1000 for electricity, Rs. 1500 for conveyance, Rs. 500 for phone and Rs. 250 for cable television. He wants to make a worksheet with his monthly income, monthly expenses and the amount left over per day. Which MS Office 2007 application can he use? Help him create the aforementioned.

B. Lima was asked to create a schedule for specialised computer classes in her institute. Her manager gave her a paper based schedule (as given here) and asked her to recreate it using Excel 2007.

1	NAME OF THE COURSE	TIMINGS		NUMBER OF STUDENTS	COURSE FEES
2		SHIFT 1	SHIFT 2		
3	C++	08:00 – 09:30 AM	1:00 – 2:30 PM	23	RS. 6000/-
4	.NET	09:30 – 11:00 AM	2:30 – 4:00 PM	22	RS. 7000/-
5	PHOTOSHOP	11:00 – 12:30 PM	4:00 – 5:30 PM	18	RS. 5000/-

However, while working, Lima faced difficulties listed below. Help her.

1. How are the cells merged in Line 1?
2. How is Column 2 split in to 2 columns (from line 3 to line 5)?
3. How are the numbers inserted to the left of each row?
4. Is it possible to add another column next to last column? If yes, then how?

C. Nina wants to create an electronic attendance sheet for the month of October for her class. She found a sample online but she does not know Excel 2007. Give steps, along with appropriate screenshots, to help her create the attendance sheet. In the screenshots mark the tabs, groups and tools being used.

NAME OF CLASS - TEACHER'S NAME

Attendance Sheet - October 2014

Date	Ben	Rashmi	Suman	Jim	Shivangi	Terry	Manav	Malvika
1/10								
2/10								
3/10								
6/10								
7/10								
8/10								
9/10								
10/10								
13/10								
14/10								
15/10								
16/10								
17/10								

D. Sameer is creating an online directory for his office. His company has over 1000 employees and all their information is on paper. Enumerate the steps involved in converting a paper directory into an Excel 2007 workbook. Also, list all the columns he should insert in his workbook. Explain the utility of Sort and Filter option in a huge database like this.

LAB WORK

A. Teresa is the class teacher of class IX. She has to store the following details in a worksheet. Help her to complete the task.

KK PUBLIC SCHOOL								
Roll No.	Name	Lang I	Lang II	Math	Science	Social	Total	Average

B. Look at the table given below and follow the instructions to complete the activity.

THE APPROXIMATE DISTANCE OF CITIES FROM DELHI STATION		
CITY	DISTANCE	NO. OF STATION
Dilshad Garden	25.1	21
Jahangirpuri	17.36	15
Noida	47.3	42
Yamuna Bank	6.25	21

1. Change the column width to 20
2. Change the row width to 30
3. Merge and centre the heading
4. Apply bold style to heading
5. Apply format and layouts for the given data

C. Smita created a table of her monthly expenses. The table is given below.

Date	Description	Category	Amount
1/11/14	Shopping	Food	INR 19,955.00
1/11/14	Rug	Home	INR 700.00
2/11/14	Flight	Travel	INR 35,550.00
2/11/14	Petrol	Car	INR 9,000.00
2/11/14	Cinema Tickets	Entertainment	INR 3,200.00
2/11/14	Dinner Out	Food	INR 5,075.00
18/11/14	Medicine	Medical	INR 350.00
21/11/14	Shoes	Personal Items	INR 80.00
22/11/14	Gift	Other	INR 800.00
23/11/14	Telephone	Utilities	INR 1,000.00

Based on this table, answer these questions.

1. For which month and year is the table?
2. What is the total amount of money Smita spent in the given month? Which formula will you use to find the total?
3. How much money did she spend on different modes of transportation?
4. Create a similar monthly budget for yourself.

D. Ask your parents for last six months electricity and water bills. Create a table to display your monthly consumption of both water and electricity; the total expenditure on both the utilities; average consumption of water per month; and during which month you used the least electricity.

MS Office 2010 Updates

In Excel 2010:

- You have the new **Backstage View**, which basically provides the same commands found under the File menu in previous version of Excel. In backstage view, options come with a preview screen and information tabs. For example, when you select the print option, a preview of the print job is automatically displayed.

  Backstage View also provides access to various Page and Print settings, such as Duplexing, Orientation, Margins and Scaling. The Save and Send option provides buttons for emailing, publishing, and saving files, as well as options to create PDF or XPS documents are also present.

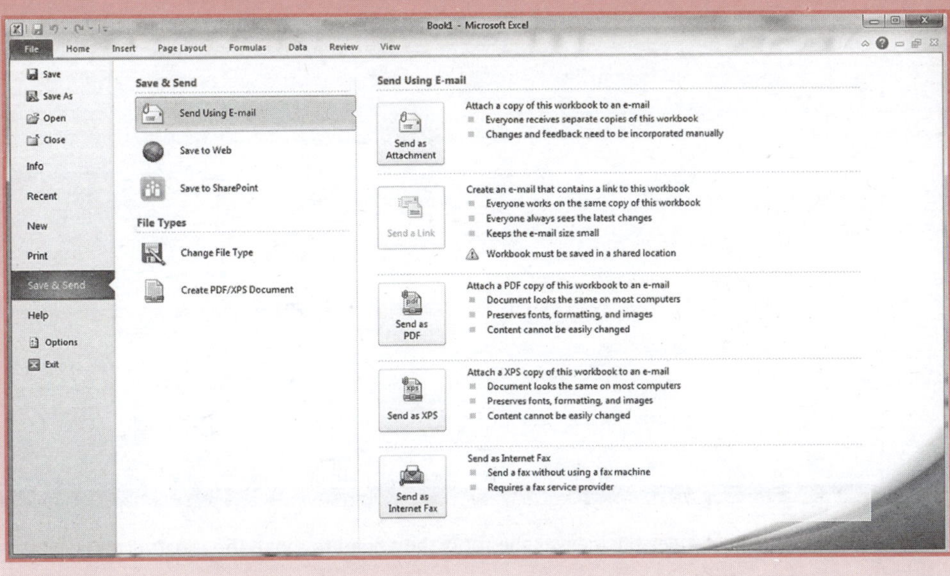

- You can add your own tabs and groups to the Ribbon. To do so, click on **File** → **Options** → **Customize Ribbon** → **New Tab/New Group.**

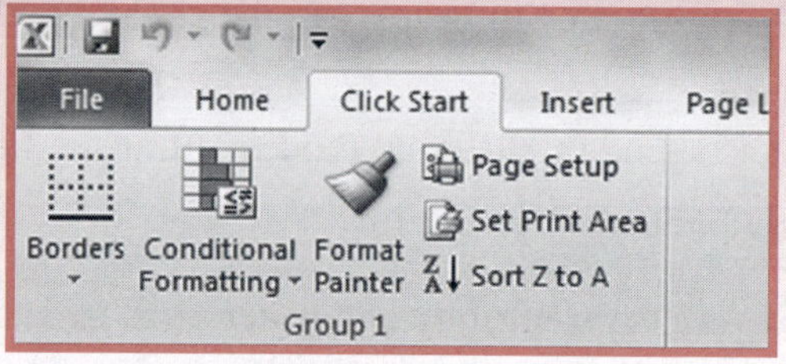

TEACHER'S NOTES

1. Explain to the students how Microsoft Excel gives businesses the tools they need to make the most of their data.
2. Features like Find & Replace, Sorting and Filtering are very useful while dealing with huge database. Using a sample database, talk to the students about their usefulness.

9 Spreadsheet Tools - II

SNAP RECAP

1. MS Excel is used to perform arithmetic, logical and scientific calculations.
2. A workbook consists of several worksheets.
3. Conditional Formatting, Format as Table and Cell Style are three quick styles that can be applied to cells in a worksheet.
4. AutoSum tool is used to find the sum of values in a given range of cells automatically.
5. Auto Fill tool is used to fill a range of cells in a row or column with a series of values.

LEARNING OBJECTIVES

You will learn about:

1. Insert Shapes and Pictures
2. Charts
3. Formulae
4. Cell Reference
5. Functions
6. Formulae Tab

INTRODUCTION

You can add pictures, clip art, shapes and charts to make your MS Excel workbook more attractive and understandable. Excel 2007 offers variety of chart types to choose from. You can format them and change their design and layout as per your requirements.

Excel also has a range of formulae and functions which help you to perform different types of calculation.
In this chapter, you will learn more about Charts, Formulae and Functions. You will also learn how to add shapes, pictures and clip art; cell referencing; freezing cells; and printing titles.

▶ Adding Pictures and Shapes

The **Insert** tab is used to insert tables, charts, text and links. It has **Tables**, **Illustrations**, **Charts**, **Links** and **Text** groups in it. Each group has tools that help add different components to a worksheet (Fig. 9.1).

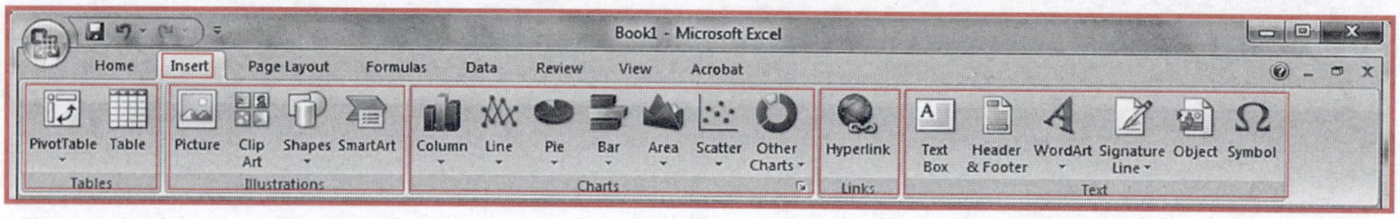

Fig. 9.1 *Insert tab*

To insert a picture

You can easily add a picture stored in your computer to your workbook (Fig. 9.2) by following the steps given below.

1. Go to the **Insert** tab.
2. Click on the **Picture** button.
3. The **Insert Picture** dialog box appears. Browse for the picture in your files.
4. Select the picture.
5. Click on the **Insert** button.

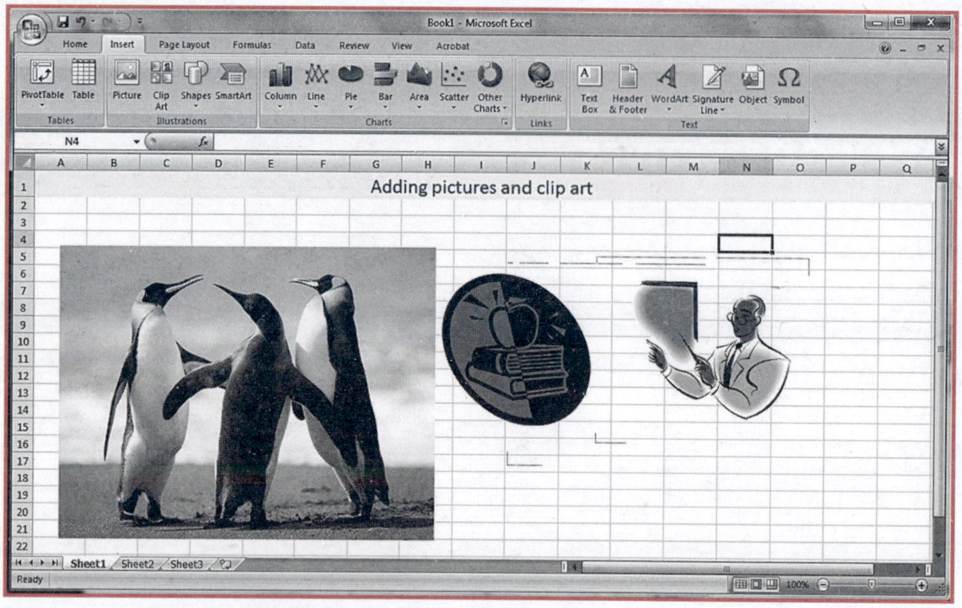

Fig. 9.2 *Adding pictures and clip art in Excel 2007 worksheet*

To insert a picture from clip art

Excel has a repository of built-in images on almost every topic. These images are known as clip arts and can be added to your worksheet. Follow the steps given below to insert a clipart.

1. Go to the **Insert** tab.
2. Click on the **Clip Art** button.
3. The **Clip Art** task pane opens on the right side of the workbook.

4. Search your picture by writing the keyword(s) in the **Search for:** box.
5. Select the clip art picture from the list of options that appears.
6. Click on the image to insert it in workbook and drag it to where you want it.

OR

Double-click on the image to insert it in worksheet. The image will be copied where the cursor is currently placed.

NOTE: You can edit your pictures and clip art using the additional **Picture Tools Format** tab which appears on the Ribbon only after you add an image or a clip art.

FACT FILE

You can also add a **SmartArt** graphic. A SmartArt is a visual representation of your data and information. It can be created quickly and easily with the help of different in-built layouts. They help you to effectively communicate your message or and ideas with the help of graphics and not just text. To insert a SmartArt graphic, go to **Insert** tab → **Illustrations** group → **SmartArt**. **Choose a SmartArt Graphic** dialog box appears. Select a graphic and click on **OK**. Edit the graphic as per your need. Some examples of SmartArt graphic are shown here.

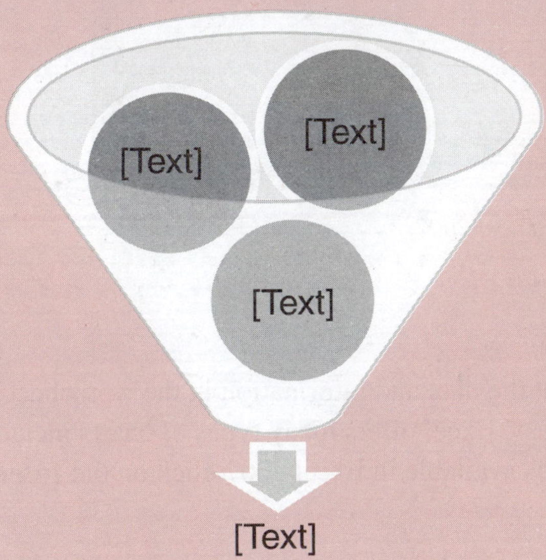

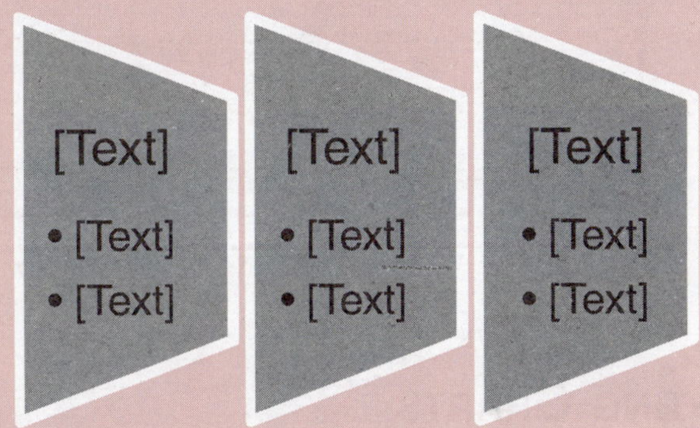

To Insert a shape

You can add shapes to your file. The available shapes include lines, basic geometric block arrows, equation shapes, flowcharts, callouts, stars and banners. You can also combine multiple shapes to make a drawing or a more complex shape.

To insert a shape into a worksheet, follow the steps given below (Fig. 9.3).

1. Click on the **Insert** tab.
2. Go to the **Shapes** button. A drop-down list appears.
3. Click on the shape you want to draw. A drawing canvas appears.
4. Drag the cursor to increase or decrease the size of the selected shape.

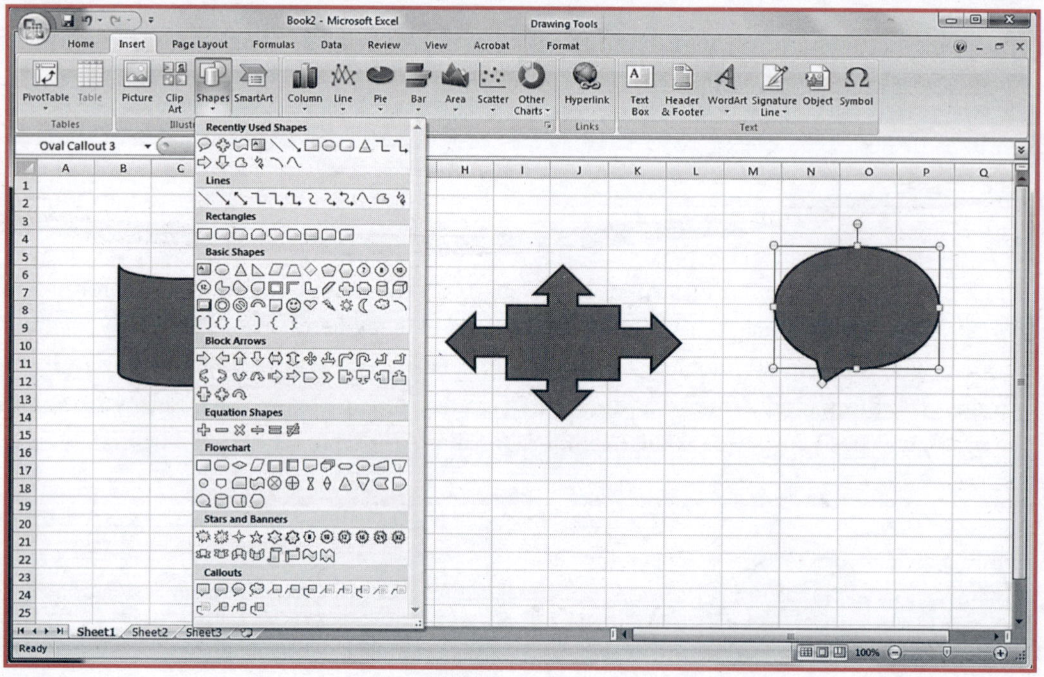

Fig. 9.3 *Adding shapes in Excel 2007*

▶ INSERTING CHARTS

A chart is an important feature of Excel that allows you to present the data and information in the worksheet in a pictorial form. This makes the comparison and analysis of data easy. Excel offers many types of charts including, Column, Line, Pie, Bar, Area, Scatter and more. To view the charts available in Excel 2007 click on the **Insert** tab on the Ribbon.

Create a chart

To create a chart, follow the steps given below.

1. Select the **cells** that contain the data you want to use in the chart.
2. Click on the **Insert** tab on the Ribbon and go to the **Charts** group (Fig. 9.4).
3. In the **Charts** group, click on the type of **Chart** type you want to create.
4. A drop-down list consisting of number of chart types appears.
5. Click on the desirable chart type to insert it into the workbook.

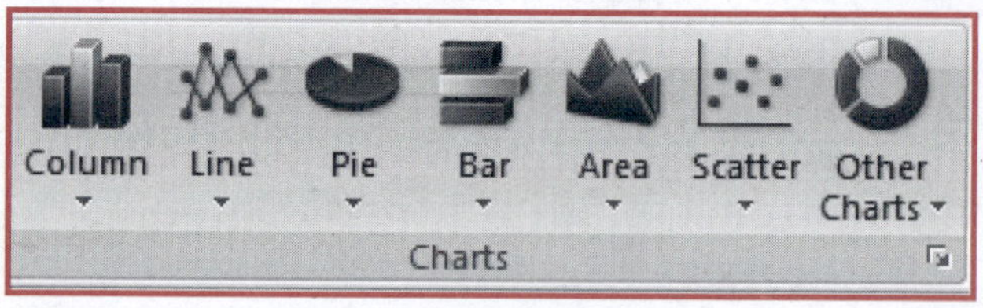

Fig. 9.4 *Charts group*

FACT FILE

You can change the chart type after you create your chart. To do so, click inside the chart. Go to the **Chart Tools Design** tab ⟶ **Type** group ⟶ **Change Chart Type**. The **Change Chart Type** dialog box appears. Select a new chart type and click on **OK**.

Charts in MS Excel

The different types of charts available in Excel 2007 are discussed below.

XY or Scatter chart: It compares pairs of values. It shows relationship among numeric values, such as scientific, statistical and engineering data. One set of values is shown vertically and the other horizontally. It combines these values into single data points and show them in irregular clusters (Fig. 9.5).

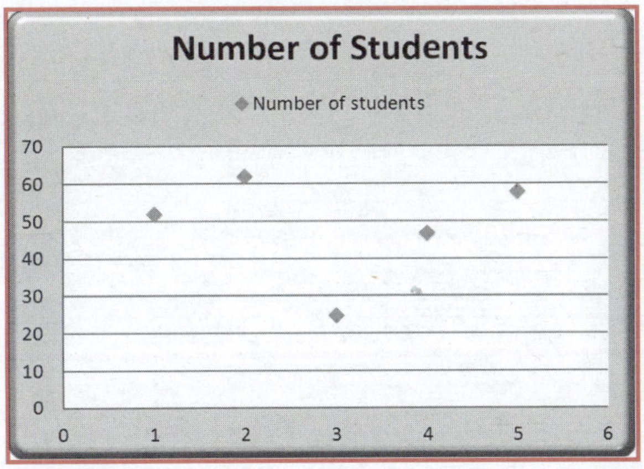

Fig. 9.5 *Scatter chart*

Column chart: It compares values across categories. The categories are shown horizontally and values are shown vertically. They are useful for showing data changes over a period of time (Fig. 9.6).

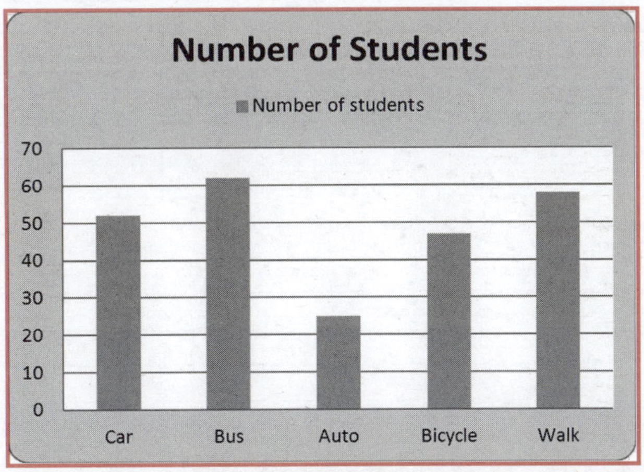

Fig. 9.6 *Column chart*

Pie chart: It takes a circular shape. It displays the contribution of each value to the total. The data points are displayed as a percentage of the whole pie (Fig. 9.7).

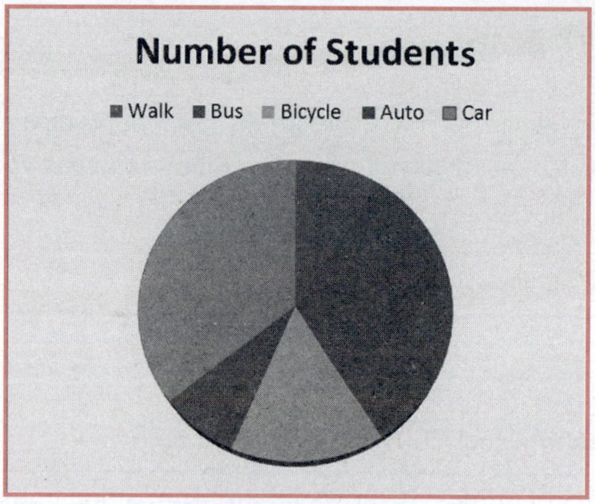

Fig. 9.7 *Pie chart*

Bar chart: It shows comparison among individual items. The categories are shown vertically and values are shown horizontally (Fig. 9.8).

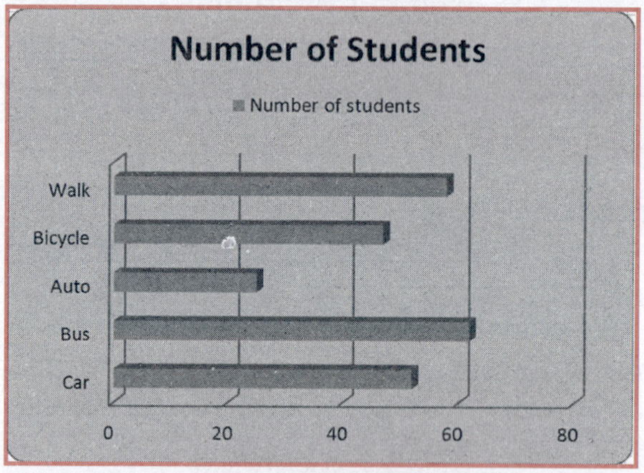

Fig. 9.8 *Bar chart*

Line chart: It shows the movement in data at equal intervals. The categories are shown horizontally and the values are displayed vertically. They are useful for showing data trends at equal intervals (Fig. 9.9).

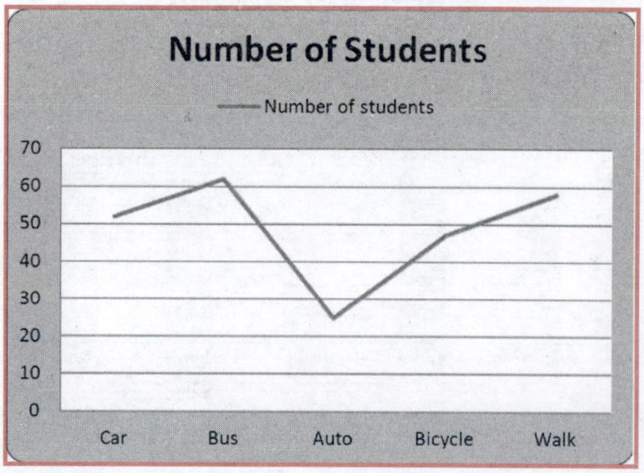

Fig. 9.9 *Line chart*

Area chart: It emphasises on the differences between several sets of data over a period of time. The area between axis and line is emphasised with color and texture. Data point markers are not displayed. They are useful for showing magnitude of change in data over a period of time (Fig. 9.10).

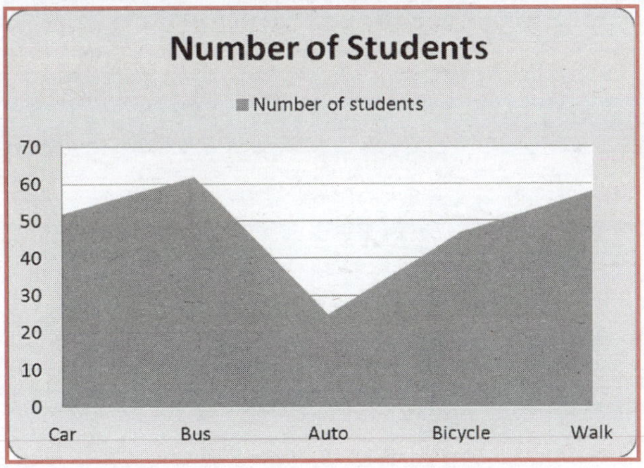

Fig. 9.10 *Area chart*

Doughnut chart: It displays the contribution of each value, like a pie chart, however, it can contain more than one series. Each ring of the doughnut represents a data series (Fig. 9.11).

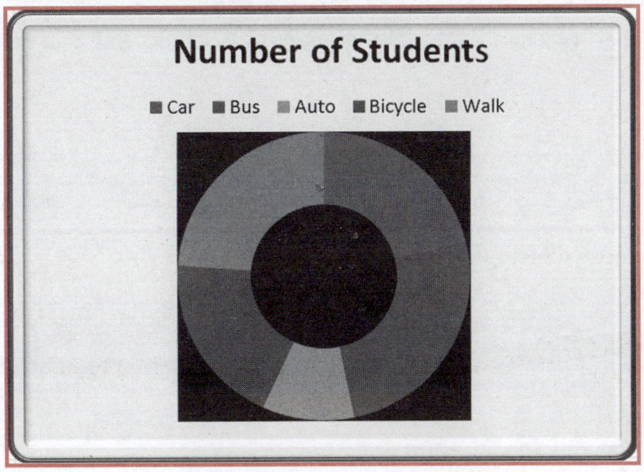

Fig. 9.11 *Doughnut chart*

Bubble chart: It is almost similar to scatter chart. But it can compare three values (Fig. 9.12).

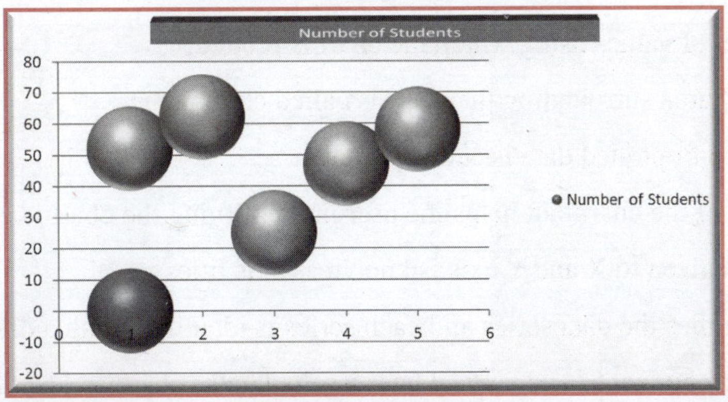

Fig. 9.12 *Bubble chart*

Radar chart: It is used when the categories are not compared directly. It displays values relative to a centre point. A line connects all the values in the series (Fig. 9.13).

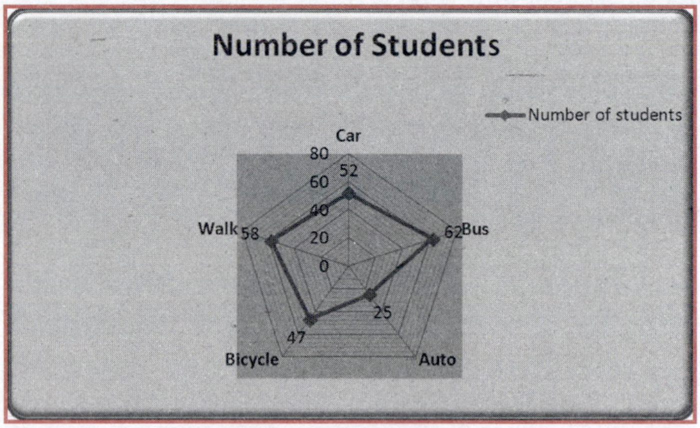

Fig. 9.13 *Radar chart*

FACT FILE

You can also create your own chart types in Excel 2007. Some of the charts that can be created are:

- Gantt charts
- Combination charts
- Organisation charts
- Histogram and pareto (sorted histogram) charts.

Components of a chart

The main components of a chart are listed below.

- ***X-Axis:*** This is the horizontal axis. It is also referred to as **category axis**.
- ***Y-Axis:*** This is the vertical axis. It is also referred to as **value axis**.
- ***Data Series:*** It is a set of values using which the chart is plotted.
- ***Chart Area:*** The total area surrounding the chart is called chart area.
- ***Plot Area:*** The portion of plotted data is called plot area.
- ***Chart Title:*** The title of the chart that helps the user in identifying the chart is called chart title.
- ***Axis Titles:*** The titles given to X and Y axis is known as axis titles.
- ***Legend:*** Legend identifies the data series and each series is identified with a different color.
- ***Gridlines:*** These are the horizontal and vertical lines inserted in the charts to identify the value of each data point.
- ***Data Label:*** This label provides the additional information about data.

Chart Tools tab

When you click on the chart that is inserted in a worksheet, you will note that three new tabs: **Design**, **Layout** and **Format** appear on the Ribbon (Fig. 9.14). These tabs are used to change the design, labels, axes, background and the layout of the chart.

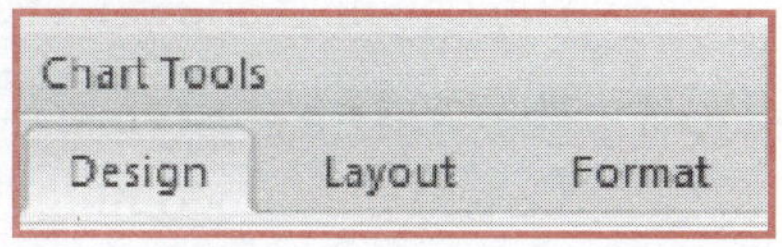

Fig. 9.14 *Chart Tools tabs*

- Under **Design** tab you have **Type** group, **Data** group, **Chart Layouts** group, **Chart Styles** group and **Location** group. Some of the tools available in this tab are discussed below (Fig. 9.15).
  - The **Chart Type** tool is used to change the type of the chart. You can save the chart as templates using the **Save As Template** tool.
  - The **Switch Row/Column** under the **Data** group is used to swap the data of X-axis over to Y-axis.
  - The **Select data** tool is used to change the data range included in the chart.
  - The **Move Chart** is used to move the chart to another sheet or tab in a workbook.
  - Styles can be applied to the charts using the **Chart Styles** tool.

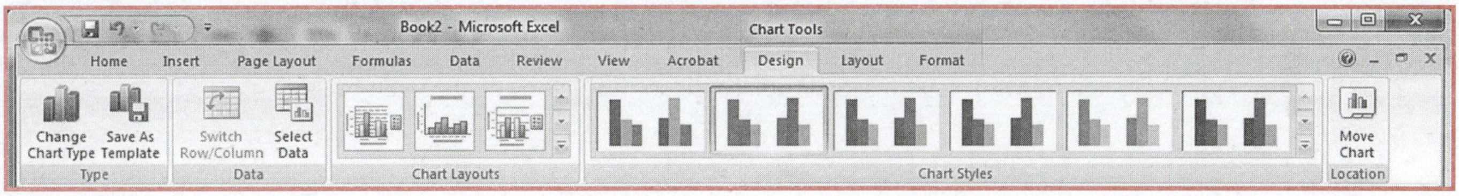

Fig. 9.15 *Chart Tools Design tab*

- Under **Layout tab** you have **Current Selection**, **Insert**, **Labels**, **Axes**, **Background**, **Analysis** and **Properties** group. The components of charts can be modified using tools in this tab. Some of the tools available in this tab are discussed below (Fig. 9.16).
  - The **Chart Title** tool is used to format the title of the chart.
  - You can insert picture, clip art and SmartArt into your chart using the **Insert** group.
  - The **Labels** group helps modify the chart titles, legends and axis titles.
  - You can also fill color in the chart background with the **Background** group.

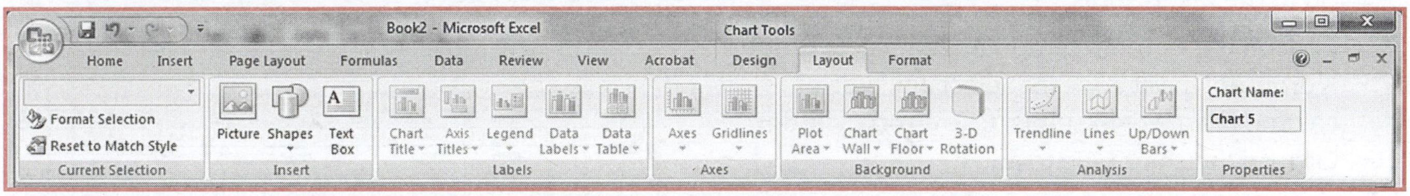

Fig. 9.16 *Chart Tools Layout tab*

- Under **Format tab** you have **Current Selection**, **Shape Styles**, **Word Art Styles**, **Arrange** and **Size** group to apply styles to the chart inserted in a worksheet. Some of the tools available in this tab are discussed below (Fig. 9.17).

- The **Shape Styles** group has **Shape Fill** and **Shape Outline** tools to modify the color and outline of a chart. You can also add effects like Glow, Shadow and 3-D rotation using the **Shape Effects** tool.
- The **WordArt Styles** group helps in modifying the font size, font type, font design, font color, font effects of the text contained in the chart.
- The **Arrange** group sets the position of the chart, viz. the text in the worksheet and the **Size** group adjusts the size of the chart.

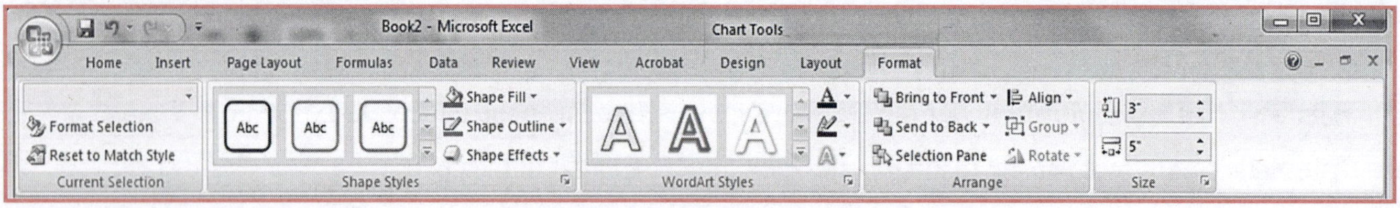

Fig. 9.17 *Chart Tools Format tab*

TRY THIS!

You can copy a chart created in MS Excel to MS Word. To do so, follow the steps given below.

1. Select the chart.
2. Click on the **Copy** option on the **Clipboard** group of the **Home** tab.
3. Go to the **Word** document where you want the chart to be located.
4. Click on the **Paste** option on the **Clipboard** group of the **Home** tab.

ACTIVITY

To create a column chart and customise it using Chart Tools tab.

1. Select the cells containing the data you want in your chart.
2. Go to the **Insert** tab.
3. Click on the **Column** button in the **Charts** group. A drop-down list appears. Select any type of column chart. For example, **Clustered Cylinder**. Click on the chart type to add it.

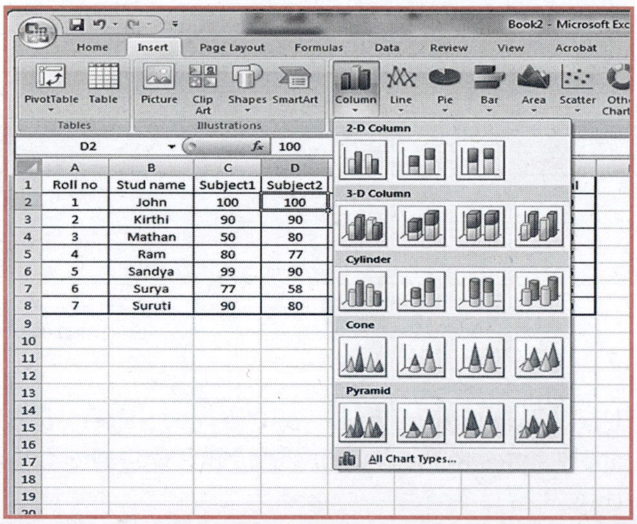

4. The moment you insert a chart, **Chart Tools** tab (**Design**, **Layout** and **Format**) appear.

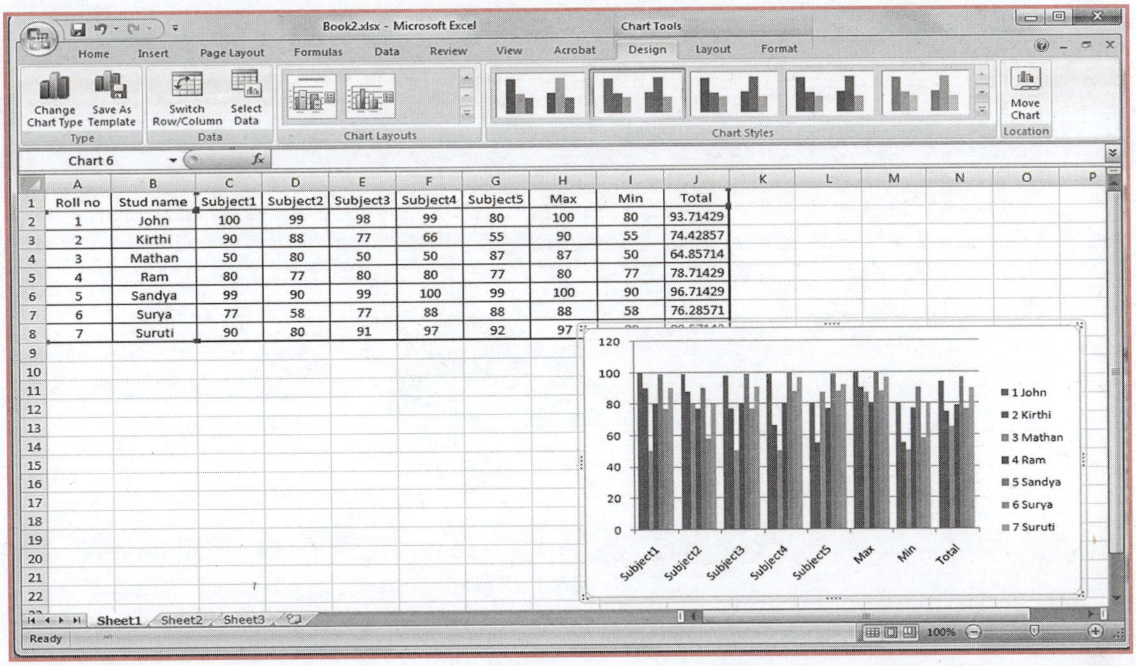

5. Go to **Chart Styles** tool in the **Chart Tools Design** tab. Click on the chart style that you want to use.

6. To change the layout of the chart, click on the **Quick Layout** tool. A drop-down list consisting of different layout appears. Select a layout of your choice.

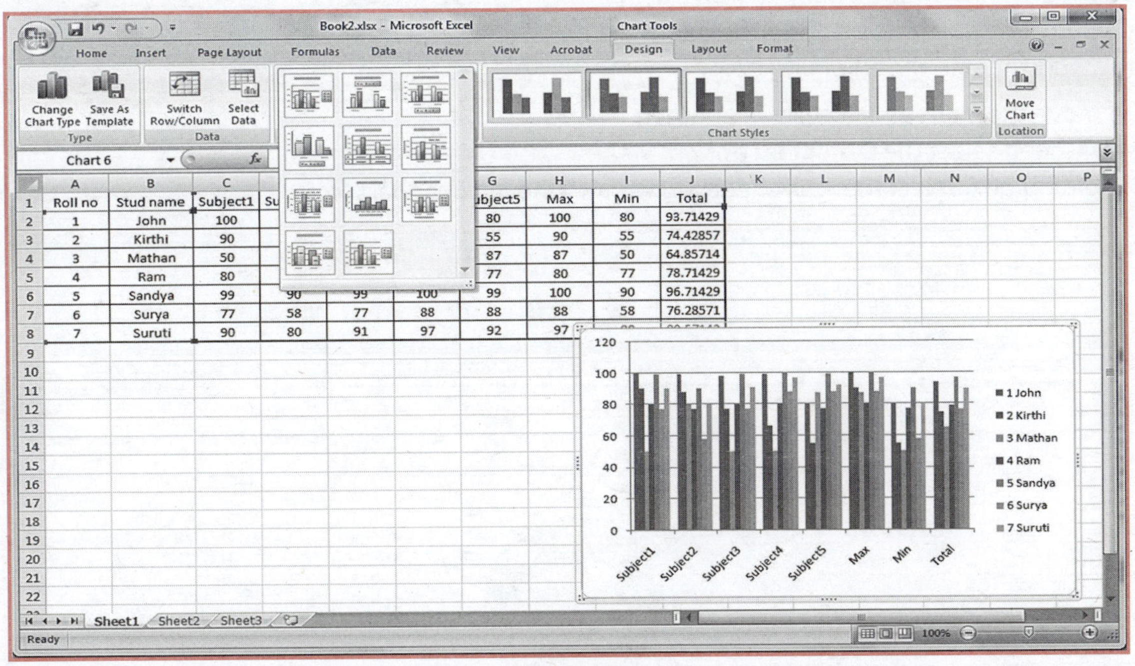

7. Click on the **Change Chart Type** option in the **Type** group of the **Chart Tools Design** tab to change the chart type. In the **Change Chart Type** dialog box, select the new chart type and click on **OK**.

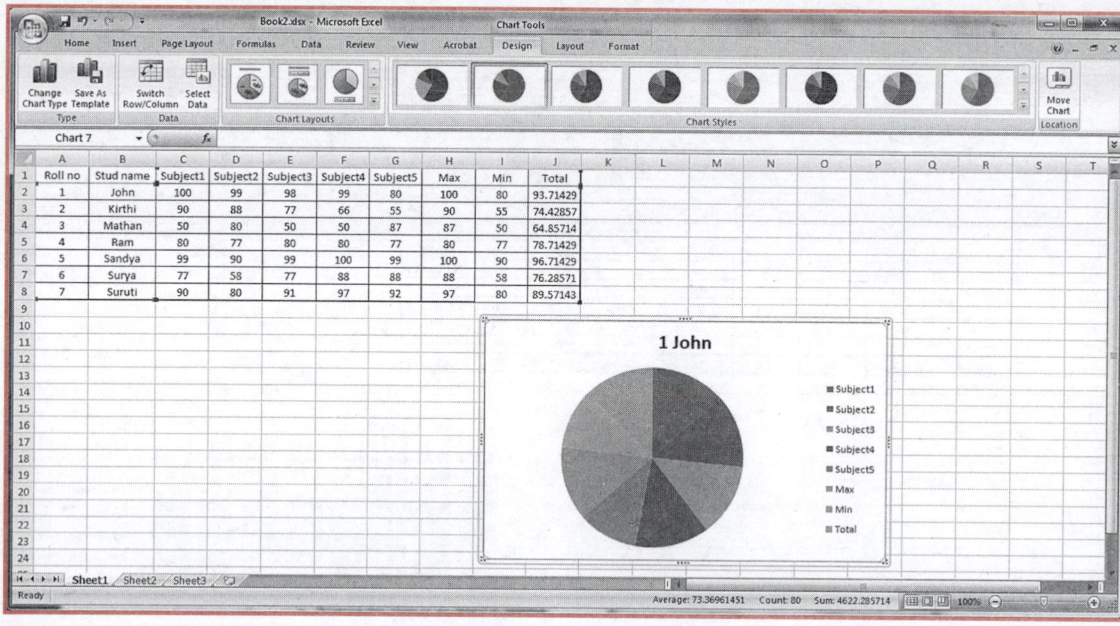

8. In case you need to move your chart to another location, select the **Move Chart** option in the **Location** group of the **Chart Tools Design** tab. The **Move Chart** dialog box appears.

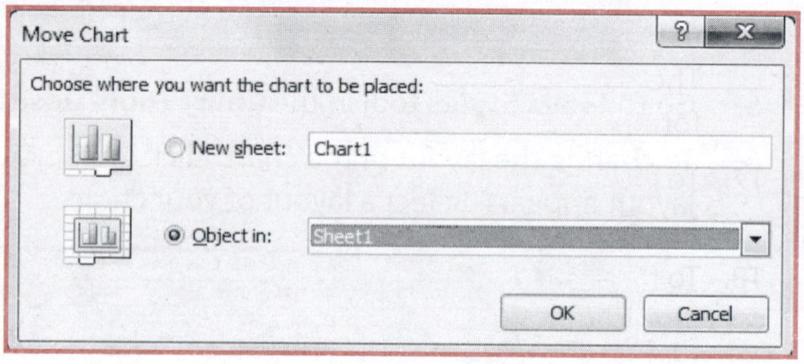

9. In the dialog box, you have two options.
   - Select the **New Sheet:** option to move the chart to a new worksheet. Type the name of the worksheet in the adjoining box.
   - To move the chart as an object in another worksheet, select the **Object in:** option. In the adjoining box, select the worksheet you want to move your chart to.

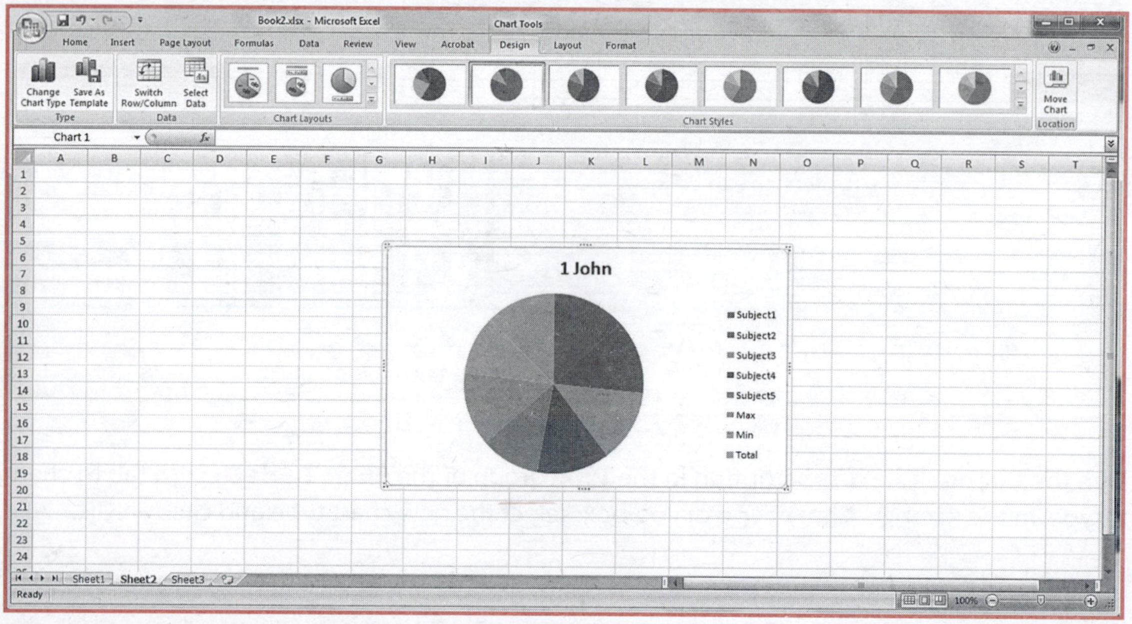

10. To save your chart as a template, go to the **Save As Template** option in the **Type** group of the **Chart Tools Design** tab. In the **Save Chart Template** dialog box, type the name of the template in the **File name:** box and in the **Save as type:** select **Chart Template Type**. Click on **Save**.
11. To add a title to a chart, go to the **Labels** group of the **Chart Tools Layout** tab. Select **Chart Title** tool.
12. The Chart Title drop-down list appears. It has the following options:
    - **None:** It means that you don't want to display a title. It is the default choice. This option is also used for removing a chart title.
    - **Centered Overlay Title:** It displays the title over the chart and the title is centrally aligned. However, it does not change the existing size of the chart.
    - **Above Chart:** It displays the title over the chart and the title is centrally aligned but it adds room at the top so that the title does not obstruct with the chart.
13. Select an option. A box appears on the chart. Double-click on the box and type the desired title.
14. Similarly, you can also modify the axis titles, legends, data labels and data table by using **Axis Titles**, **Legend**, **Data Labels** and **Data Table** tools, respectively, from the **Labels** group of the **Chart Tools Layout** tab.
15. To change the format of a selected chart element, click on the arrow next to the **Chart Elements box** in the **Current Selection** group of the **Chart Tools Layout** tab. Select the chart element that you want to format.
16. In the **Current Selection** group, click on **Format Selection** tool. The **Format Chart Area** dialog box. Click on a category and select the formatting options that you want.

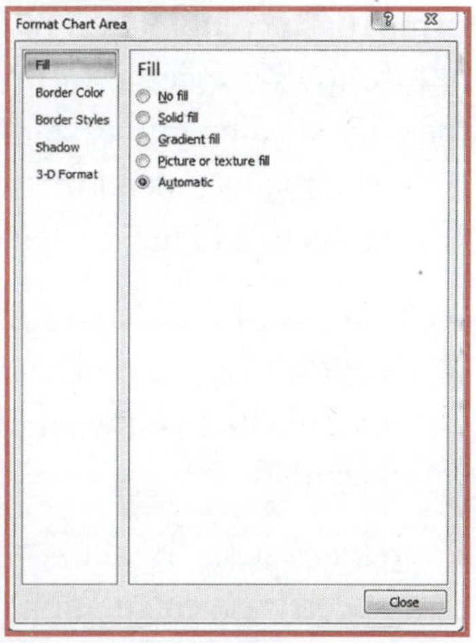

17. To insert a picture, shape or a text box, go to the **Insert** group of the **Chart Tools Layout** tab.
18. To fill background color in the chart floor and chart wall, select **Chart Floor** and **Chart Wall** tool in the **Background** group of the **Chart Tools Layout** tab.
19. To change the name of the chart, go to **Properties** group of the **Chart Tools Layout** tab. In the **Chart name:** box type the name of the chart.
20. To format the shape of the chart elements, go to the **Shape Styles** group in **Chart Tools Format** tab. Use the **Shape Style**, **Shape Fill**, **Shape Outline** and **Shape Effects** tools to modify the shapes.
21. To format the text in the chart, go to the **WordArt Style group** in **Chart Tools Format** tab. Use the **Text Fill**, **Text Outline** and **Text Effects** tools to select the formatting options that you want.

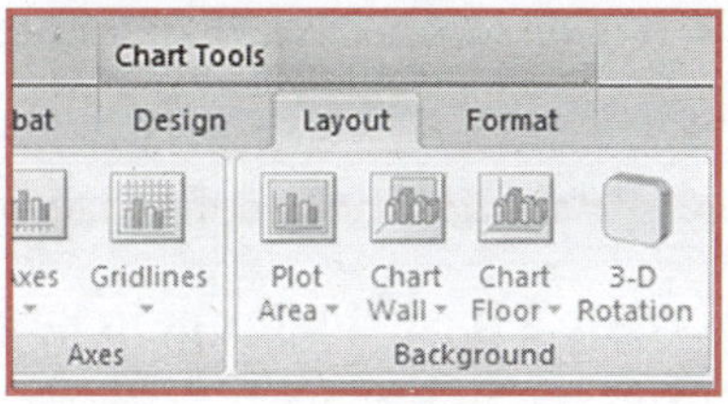

CHECK YOUR PROGRESS

A. Using the Insert tab in MS Excel, you can add more components like Headers and Footers, Signature Line. Word Art and Hyperlinks. You have already learnt how to add them in a Word document. Using the same steps, add them to your workbook. HOTS

B. In the month of April 2014, Rohan spent his monthly salary amounting to INR 25,500 on different items as given below. Represent the data in the form of a bar chart.

Items	Clothing	Education	Food	Bills	Miscellaneous	Saving
Amount Spent	2000	6000	5000	5000	2000	5500

C. Note down the number of hours you spend on the following activities in a day after school hours. Tabulate the information as per the following table and represent it in a pie chart.

S.No	Activity	Time (in minutes)
1.	Homework	
2.	Playing outdoor games	
3.	Playing games with computer	
4.	Reading books	
5.	Watching TV	
6.	Helping your mother	

Formulae

A formula is a combination of operators, operands and an equal to sign. It follows a specific format in Excel. All the formulae created for mathematical calculations starts with an equal to (=) sign. The operands can be a constant value, a cell reference or a function.

3500	5500	9000
4500	6500	=C19+D19

For example, to add the contents of two cells A1 and A2, the formula would be written as: **= A1 + A2**

The elements of an Excel formula are listed below.

- ***Cell References:*** The cell or range of cells that you want to use in your calculation.
- ***Operators:*** Symbols (+, –, *, /) that specify the calculation to be performed.
- ***Constants:*** Numbers or text values that do not change.
- ***Functions:*** Predefined formulas in Excel.

To create a basic formula in Excel, follow the steps given below.

- Select the cell where you want to apply the formula.
- Type = (the equal sign) followed by the formula and press **Enter** key.

FACT FILE

The order in which mathematical operators and syntax are applied in Excel is as follows:

1. Parentheses
2. Exponents
3. Multiplication and Division
4. Addition and Subtraction

You can remember this order by its mnemonic phrase, *Please Excuse My Dear Aunt Sally.*

In Microsoft Excel 2007, mathematical computations are typically done by built-in functions. Excel has a library of several hundred functions on the **Formulas** Tab. They let you perform a number of mathematical and statistical calculations. For example, you can use the sum function to add numbers, average function to compute averages on a list of numbers, the PMT function to figure out payment on a loan, so on and so forth.

ACTIVITY

To apply basic formula in Excel.

1. To find the total of five subjects in the following table, go to H2 cell.
2. Type =C2+D2+E2+F2+G2.
3. Press Enter.

	A	B	C	D	E	F	G	H	I
1	Roll No.	Name of the student	Subject 1	Subject 2	Subject 3	Subject 4	Subject 5	Total	Percentage
2	1	Aastha	100	55	95	55	77	=C2+D2+E2+F2+G2	
3	3	Abhay	80	65	75	76	99		
4	10	John	100	94	88	44	87		
5	7	Kirti	34	58	39	63	65		
6	9	Manas	36	100	45	25	100		
7	8	Ratika	87	100	100	55	77		
8	4	Sam	100	77	45	97	44		
9	2	Sanya	100	85	65	84	88		
10	6	Suhas	65	64	64	45	58		
11	5	Sukrit	82	41	52	100	74		

4. Drag the fill handle downwards to automatically fill the values in column H.
5. To find the percentage, divide the total marks achieved by the maximum marks (500) and divide it by 100.
6. Type =(H2/500)*100 in cell I2.
7. Press Enter.

	A	B	C	D	E	F	G	H	I
1	Roll No.	Name of the student	Subject 1	Subject 2	Subject 3	Subject 4	Subject 5	Total	Percentage
2	1	Aastha	100	55	95	55	77	382	=(H2/500)*100
3	3	Abhay	80	65	75	76	99	395	
4	10	John	100	94	88	44	87	413	
5	7	Kirti	34	58	39	63	65	259	
6	9	Manas	36	100	45	25	100	306	
7	8	Ratika	87	100	100	55	77	419	
8	4	Sam	100	77	45	97	44	363	
9	2	Sanya	100	85	65	84	88	422	
10	6	Suhas	65	64	64	45	58	296	
11	5	Sukrit	82	41	52	100	74	349	
12									

8. Drag the fill handle downwards to automatically fill the values in column I.

▶ Cell Reference

The cell in a worksheet is a location where rows and columns intersect. A particular cell is identified in a formula using its cell reference.

In Excel, cell reference is of three types. They are:

- Relative reference
- Absolute reference
- Mixed reference

Relative reference

A relative reference refers to the cells that are relative to the position of the formula. When you write a formula in one cell and copy it to another cell, the contents of the cell will not be copied. The formula used in the cell will be copied, in terms of the position of cell relative to the cell containing the formula. This is called relative reference. It is used in formulae that use relative values and values that are not fixed.

=B2+C2

B	C	D	E
Practicals	Theory	Total	
48	40	=B2+C2	
50	85	135	
62	48	110	

=B3+C3

B	C	D
Practicals	Theory	Total
48	40	88
50	85	135
62	48	110

Fig. 9.18 *Relative reference*

In Excel, relative reference is a cell reference in a formula that changes when a formula is copied from one cell to another, to reflect the new position. When the formula of D2 is copied to D3, it will be copied as = **B3 + C3**. A formula copied from one cell to another adjusts itself according to the position of the cell.

Absolute reference

For absolute reference contains a formula which does not change when the formula from one cell is copied to another cell. Cells are referred by their fixed position in the worksheet. This is done by using $ symbol before both the row number and the column name.

=B2-C2

B	C	D	E
Cost	Discount	Price after discount	
20000	1000	19000	
22000		21000	

=B3-C2

B	C	D	E
Cost	Discount	Price after discount	
20000	1000	19000	
22000		21000	

Fig. 9.19 *Absolute reference*

In the above example, cell D2 holds the formula = **B2 – C2**. The C2 reference is absolute here. The content remains same when it is copied to next cell, that is, 20000 –1000 = 19000 in D2. While copying the formula with absolute reference, B2 changes to B3 whereas the absolute reference C2 remains the same. Thereby, D3 holds the value 22000 – 1000 = 21000.

Mixed reference

A mixed reference is a combination of both relative and absolute reference. In absolute reference the $ sign is used before both the row number and the column name. In mixed reference, the $ sign is used either before the row number or before the column name. If there is no $ sign, then it is relative reference.

In Figure 9.20(a), \$c\$2 (discount) is an absolute reference. However, the discount is variable in this case and this gives the wrong output. Here, you can use mixed reference. The formula will be = **B2 – \$C2** (Fig. 9.20(b)).

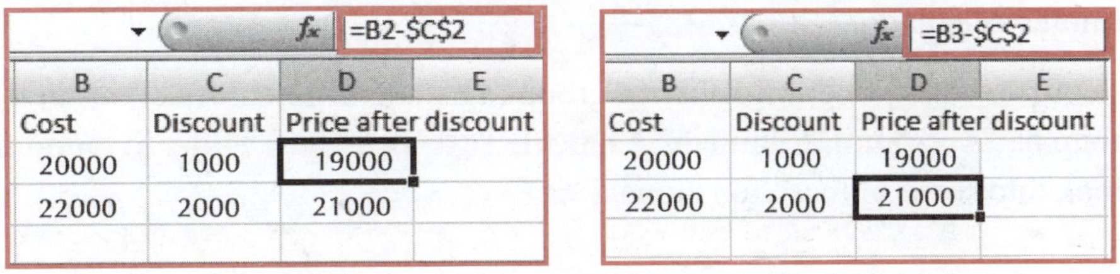

(a)

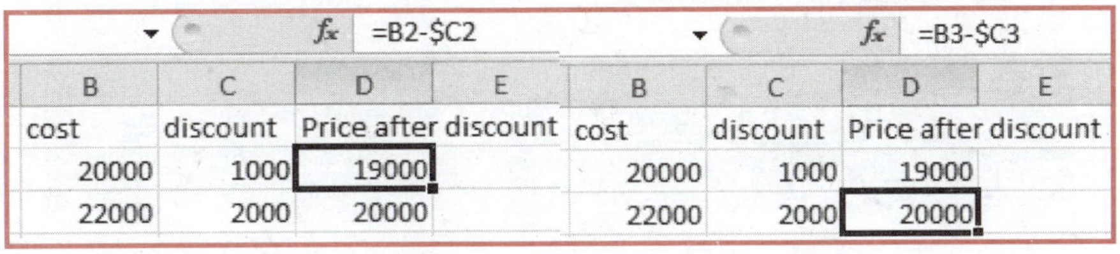

(b)

Fig 9.20 *Mixed Reference*

Some common errors while applying the formula in a worksheet are given in Table 9.1.

Table 9.1 *Some common formula errors*

Error	Description
#REF!	The cell referred is not valid or deleted
#value!	The formula has an invalid operator
####	The width of the column is not enough to accommodate the result of the formula
#NUM	The number used in formula is not acceptable
#Name	The cell referred is not known to Excel

CHECK YOUR PROGRESS

A. Try the following formula and match them to the answers given in the right column. **HOTS**

S.no	Formula	Answer
1.	= 2 + 3^2 * 5 / 3	550
2.	= 20 * 4 /5 + 10	17
3.	= (2 + (3^3)*4)/2	26
4.	= (45+33+99-32)*4	580
5.	= 125/5*20+50	55

B. Open a new worksheet. Create a row header as given below. Add atleast five entries. Calculate Gross Salary and Net Pay using the formula given in the table.

Employee Name	Basic	DA	HRA	CCA	Gross Salary	PF	Net Pay
					= Basic + DA + HRA + CCA		= Gross Salary – PF

▶ FORMULAS TAB

Functions are predefined formulae that perform calculations by using the contents of the cell. Functions are used to perform simple and complex calculations.

The Formulas tab in Excel 2007 has **Function Library** group to handle different functions in a worksheet (Fig. 9.21). The function library group has **AutoSum**, **Financial**, **Logical**, **Text**, **Date and Time**, **Trigonometry** and **Scientific** functions in it. Let us look into some of these functions.

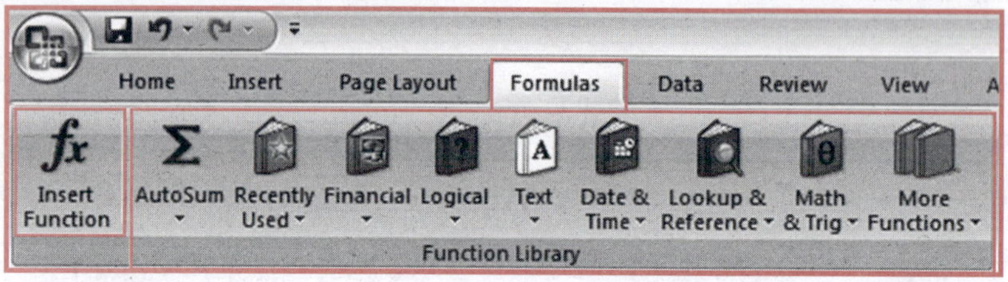

Fig. 9.21 *Functions Library group*

Insert Function

The **Insert Function** tool in the **Function Library** allows the user to edit the formula in the current cell by choosing functions and editing the arguments. To do so, follow the steps given below.

1. Type the values in the cell range.
2. Click on the **Insert Function** tool from the **Formulas** tab.
3. Search the function in **Search for a function:** box and select a function to insert it into your worksheet.

Function Library

The following options are available in the **Function Library** group of the Formula tab.

- ***AutoSum:*** This tool is used to display the result of a simple calculation such as Sum, Average, Count, Min, Max and other functions of the selected cells (Fig. 9.22).
- ***Recently used Functions:*** This tool is used to browse and select a function from a list of recently used functions.
- ***Financial Functions:*** This tool is used to browse and select a function from a list of financial function such as ACCRINT (accrued interest) and CUMPRINC (Cumulative principal).
- ***Logical Functions:*** This tool provides a list of logical functions such as AND, IF and FALSE.
- ***Text Function:*** This tool provides a list of functions such as CHAR and BAHTEXT that converts numbers to text and returns the ASCII code.

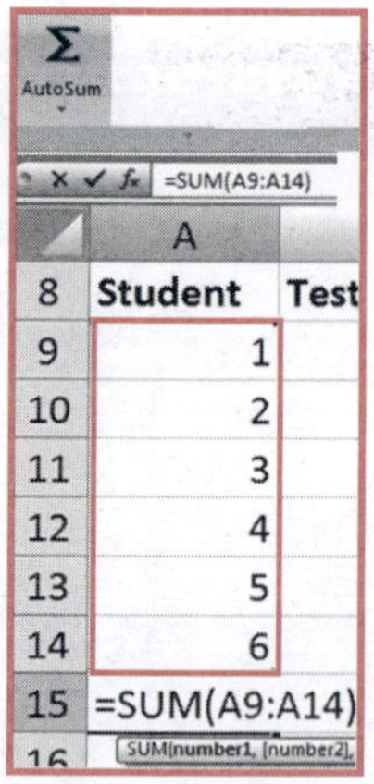

Fig. 9.22 *Autosum tool*

- ***Date & Time:*** This provides a list of date and time related functions such as EDATE, and EOMONTH.
- ***Math & Trig:*** This provides a list of trigonometry functions such as ACOS and ASIN.
- ***More Functions:*** This provides a list of statistical and engineering functions.

Syntax of some common functions

1. ***Sum() function:*** To add all the numbers given in the arguments.
   Syntax: SUM(number1, number2, number3,...) or SUM(Starting Cell reference : Ending Cell reference)
   NOTE: You can use the same syntax for Average, Min, Max functions except for the name of function.

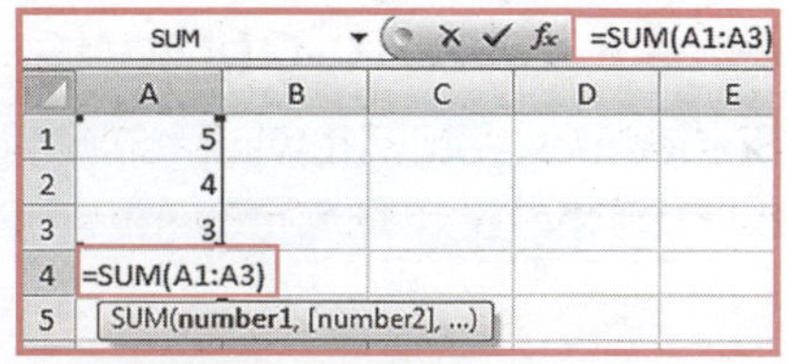

Fig 9.23 *Sum() function*

2. ***IF function:*** It is used to check whether the given condition is true and returns the value accordingly.
   Syntax: = IF(Condition, True Value, False Value)
   For example: = IF(A4 > 50,"SATISFACTORY","UNSATISFACTORY")

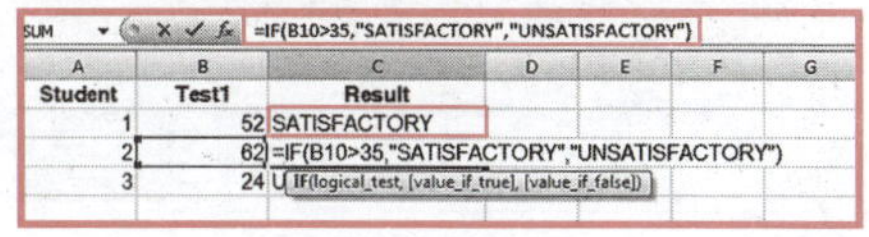

Fig 9.24 *IF function*

CHECK YOUR PROGRESS

A. Open a new worksheet to create a table to show the sales figure achieved by the employees during the month of April 2015. Find out the average sales figure, maximum and minimum sales figure. Calculate incentive of 5% of sales for the employees who achieved the target (greater than 2,00,000) using if function.

- Insert a column chart to compare the sales of all employees.
- Merge and centre the company name.
- Insert a suitable logo.
- Format the data by applying font color and style.
- Align it to centre.
- Adjust the row height and column width.

MEDI PHARMA LIMITED			
S.No	**Name of the Employee**	**Sales Amount**	**Incentive (if any)**
1.	Sunil Agarwal	2,30,000	
2.	Anil Kulkarni	4,50,000	
3.	Mini Menon	3,45,000	
4.	Vishal Jhamb	1,50,000	
5.	Camilla Thomas	2,00,000	
	Total Sales		
	Average		
	Maximum		
	Minimum		

B. Use a sample table to apply any five formulae using Insert Function tool in the Function Library. Give syntax of each formula separately too.

▶ Text to Columns

Sometimes you will want to split data of one cell into two or more cells. You can do this easily by utilising the convert the **Text to Columns** tool in the **Data Tools** group of the **Data** tab (Fig. 9.25).

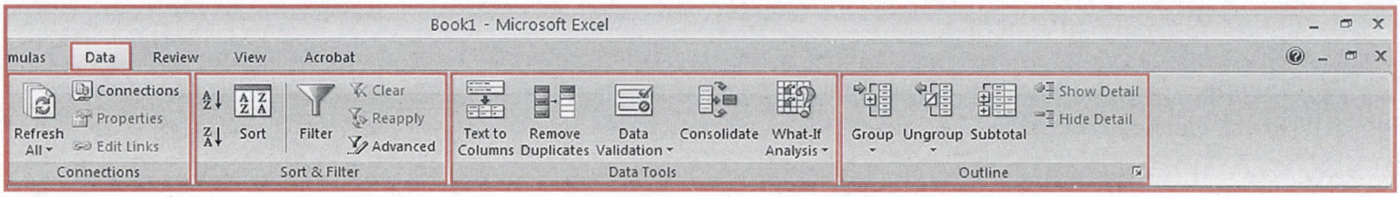

Fig. 9.25 *Text to Columns is present in Data Tools group*

To convert text to columns, follow the steps given below.

1. Highlight the column in which you wish to split the data.
2. Click the **Text to Columns** button present in the **Data Tools** group of **Data** tab.
3. Click **Delimited** if you have a comma or tab separating the data, or click **Fixed width** to set the data separation at a specific size (Fig. 9.26).
4. Click on the **Finish** button.

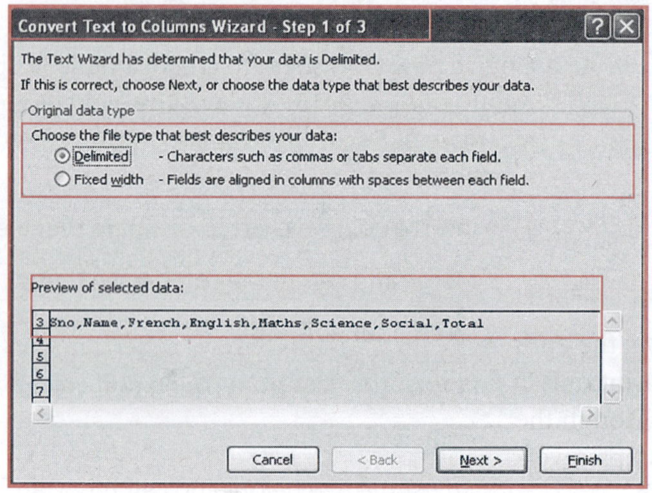

Fig. 9.26 *Convert Text to Columns Wizard*

▶ Print Titles

The print titles function allows you to repeat the column and row headings at the beginning of each new page to make the reading of multiple page sheet easier when printed. To print titles, the steps are as follows.

1. Go to the **Page Layout** tab on the Ribbon (Fig. 9.27).
2. Click the **Print Titles** button in the **Page Setup** group.
3. The **Page Setup** dialog box appears. Go to the **Sheet** tab.
4. In the **Print Titles** section, click the **Rows to repeat at top:/Column to repeat at top:** box to select the rows/columns to be repeated (Fig. 9.28).
5. Select the **Page order**.
6. Check the **Print Preview**.
7. Click on **OK**.

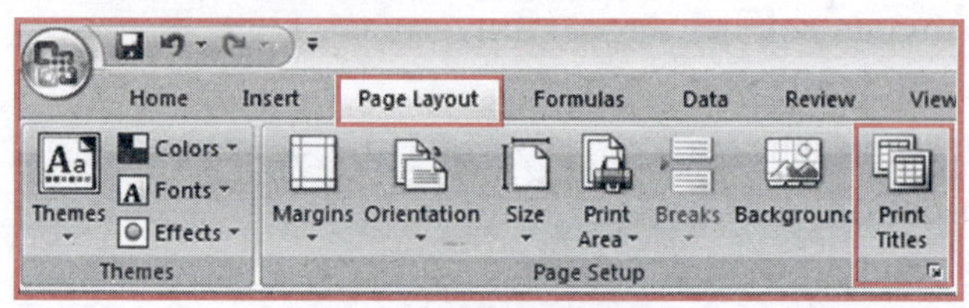

Fig. 9.27 *Page Layout tab*

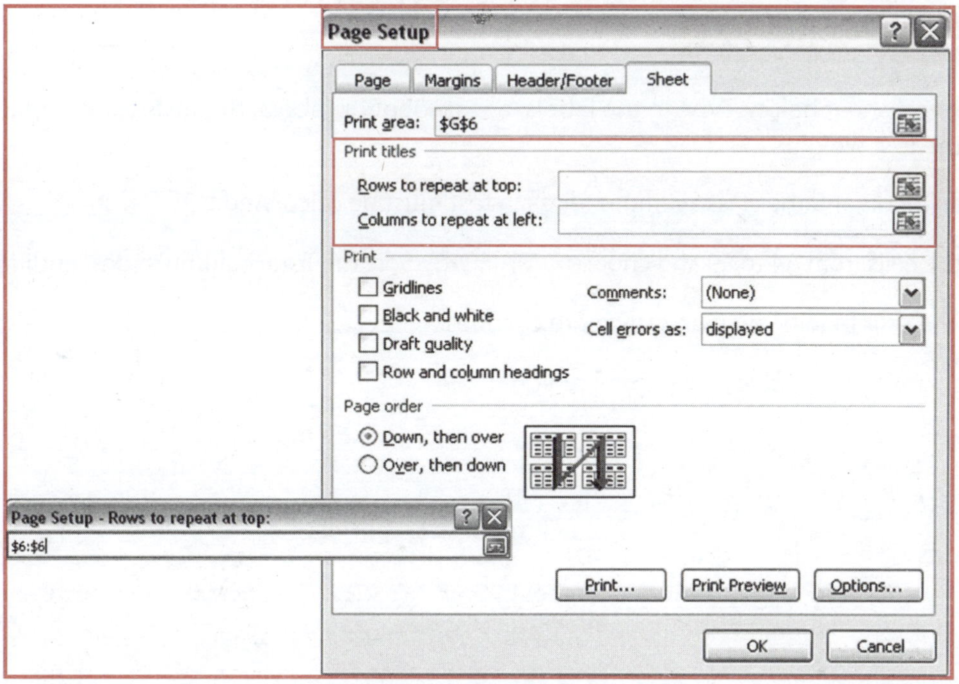

Fig. 9.28 *Page Setup dialog box*

PRINT A SELECTED RANGE

As the entire worksheet is too long to fit in a page, you can also print only a portion of a worksheet. This can be easily done through the **Print Area** function. To print a range follow the steps given below.

1. Select the area to be printed.
2. Click the **Print Area** button on the **Page Setup** group of the **Page Layout** tab.
3. Click on **Set Print Area** option (Fig. 9.29).

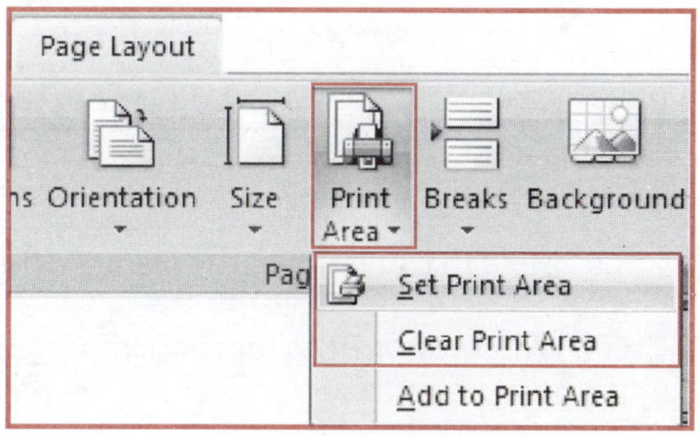

Fig. 9.29 *Print Area tool*

FREEZE ROWS AND COLUMNS

You can select a particular portion of a worksheet to stay static while you work on other parts of the sheet. This is accomplished through the **Freeze Rows and Columns** function. To freeze a row or column, follow the steps given below.

1. Click the **Freeze Panes** button in **Window** group of the **View** tab (Fig. 9.30).
2. Either select a section to be frozen or click the defaults of top row or left column.
3. To unfreeze, click the **Freeze Panes** button.
4. Click **Unfreeze** Panes.

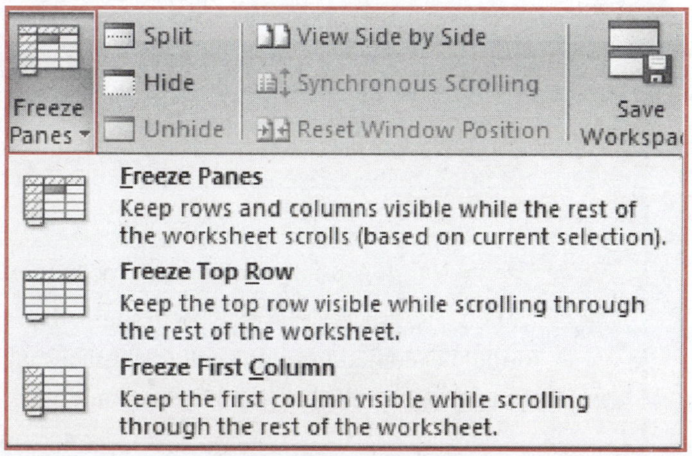

Fig. 9.30 *Freeze Panes tool*

CHECK YOUR PROGRESS

A. Create the worksheet below. Type in the labels, the student numbers, the test results (which are out of 100), and the test weights.

- The total marks and the class averages for each test must be calculated.
- Select the cells from A4 to E9 and choose DATA|SORT. Sort the Total column in descending order.
- Freeze the cells before you make any more changes.
- Add a chart of your choice to supplement your table.

S.NO	A	B	C	D	E
1.	**First Semester Result**				
2.					
3.	**Student**	**Test1**	**Test2**	**Test3**	**Total**
4.	1	45	50	45	46.25
5.	2	60	65	55	58.75
6.	3	35	45	30	35
7.	4	70	65	75	71.25
8.	5	50	50	60	55
9.	6	56	60	55	56.25
10.					
11.	**Class Average**	52.5	55.83333	53.33333	
12.					

B. How to convert text to column? What is the purpose of Delimited and Fixed width options in this process?

C. Why is Print Titles function important in multipage?

GLOSSARY

- **Chart:** It is a graphical representation of the information contained in the worksheet.
- **Freeze Row/Column:** It is used to lock the selected cells from any more change.
- **Functions:** They are predefined formulae that perform calculations by using the contents of the cell.
- **Mixed Reference:** It is a combination of both relative and absolute reference.
- **Print Area:** It is used to print only a portion of a worksheet.
- **Relative Reference:** It refers to the cells that are relative to the position of the formula, that is, when a formula is copied from one cell to another, only the formula is copied in terms of the position of the cell relative to the cell containing the formula.
- **Absolute Reference:** It contains a formula which does not change when it is copied from one cell to another cell, that is, cells are referred by their fixed position in the worksheet.

- **Formula:** It is a combination of operators, operands and an equal to sign that follows a specific format and are used for mathematical calculations.
- **Functions:** They are predefined formulas that perform simple and complex calculations by using the contents of the cell.
- **Cell Reference:** It refers to a cell or a range of cells on a worksheet.

NOW YOU KNOW

1. AutoSum tool is used to display the result of a simple calculation.
2. Chart Type tool is used to change the type of the chart.
3. Chart Title tool is used to format the title of the chart.
4. Legend identifies the data series and each series is identified with a different color.
5. The print titles function allows you to repeat the column and row headings at the beginning of each new page to make reading a multiple page sheet easier to read when printed.
6. You can select a particular portion of a worksheet to stay static while you work on other parts of the sheet through the Freeze Rows and Columns Function.

EXERCISE

FA

A Fill in the blanks.

1. .... error message is shown when the cell referred is not known to Excel.
2. Copying the formula $C3 refers to .... reference.
3. .... are predefined formulae that perform calculations by using the contents of the cell.
4. The .... function is used to print a portion of a worksheet.
5. The .... tool provides a list of logical functions such as AND, IF and FALSE.
6. The Date & Time tool is available under .... tab.
7. The intersection of column F and 5th row is referred as ....
8. The Chart Title tool is available under Chart Tools........................... tab.
9. To add the contents of two cells A1 and A2, the formula would be written as ....
10. .... reference has no $ symbol in it.

B Multiple choice questions.

1. A formula in MS Excel always begins with a .... sign.

   a. = b. @ c. ! d. $

2.

	A	B	C
1	COST	DISCOUNT	
2	2000	=IF(A2>2000,200,0)	

If you press enter key after typing this formula, the value of B2 will be ....

   a. 200 b. 0 c. 20 d. None of these

3. To add all the numbers in the range A1 to A10, you use .... function.

   a. =ADD(A1:A10) b. =SUM(A1:A10) c. =SUMTOT(A1:A10) d. =TOT(A1:A10)

4. A value in a formula that does not change is called a ....

   a. constant b. variable c. cell reference d. cell address

5. .... reference changes automatically when it is copied to another cell.

   a. Absolute b. Relative c. Mixed d. Cell

6. Reference in Excel is of .... types.

   a. 3 b. 4 c. 2 d. 5

7. The .... function allows you to repeat the column and row headings at the beginning of each new page.

   a. Print Header b. Print Titles c. Chart Title d. None of these

8. CUMPRINC is a .... function.

   a. logical b. general c. financial d. statistical

9. The #NUM error message is displayed when ....

   a. The number used in the formula is not acceptable

   b. The cell reference is incorrect

   c. The formula entered is invalid

   d. The width of the column cannot accommodate the result

10. Identify this tool 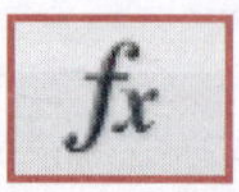

.

   a. Insert Function b. AutoSum c. Equation d. Insert Formula

SA

C Answer the following questions.

1. What is the other name for XY chart?
2.  Identify this tool.
3. How is doughnut chart different from pie chart? Explain with the help of an example.
4. What are the three new tabs that appear on the Ribbon under Chart Tools tab when a chart inserted in a worksheet is clicked?
5. What is a category axis?

D Answer the following questions in detail.

1. Differentiate between column chart and bar chart.
2. Identify and label the components of the chart given below.

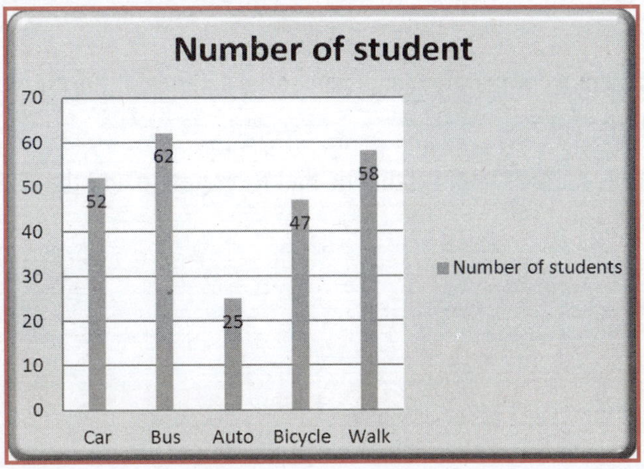

3. Write a short notes on any four common errors that you get when you apply a formula in a worksheet. HOTS
4. What is the use of IF function? Explain with an example.
5. What are the three types of references?
6. How is absolute reference different from relative reference?
7. Explain different types of charts.
8. How to convert text to columns? Give steps.
9. What are functions?
10. How do you print titles at the beginning of every new page? Give steps.

Application Based Questions

A. Payal was asked to calculate the sum of the contents in the range of cell A1 to A5 without using any function. Help her to complete this task.

B. Kavita is the class teacher of class X. She has to store the student name, roll number and marks of five different subjects in a worksheet. Help her to complete the task.

- Write the formula to calculate total marks.
- Write the formula to calculate average marks.
- Fill the roll number in 1,2,3... series.
- Find the minimum, maximum marks.
- Also, write the name of the school on the top of the worksheet and center align it to all the selected columns.

C. Salman is a data entry operator in the human resource department of an IT firm. He has to store data of employees of different department. His manager asked him to create a worksheet for every department, rename all the tabs according to the department and color them so that they can be distinguished easily. Help him.

D. Sana owns a chain of departmental stores. She stores the weekly sales figure of every store separately. However, she wants to combine all the data in one sheet and insert a chart to show the overall growth of all her stores. Investigate whether she can do this or not.

E. Ashish wants to graphically represent a comparative analysis of the salaries of his employees. Suggest the most suitable chart type for achieving the same.

F. After completing his class database, Gaurav realised that he had forgotten to add the date of birth column in the spreadsheet. Can he add the same now?

LAB WORK

A. Draw and complete the sample table given. Follow the instructions given below to complete the activity.

- Change the column width to 20 and the row width to 30.
- Apply a border to all the cell that has data in it.
- Apply bold style to heading.
- Insert a pie chart.
- Apply format and layouts for the given data.

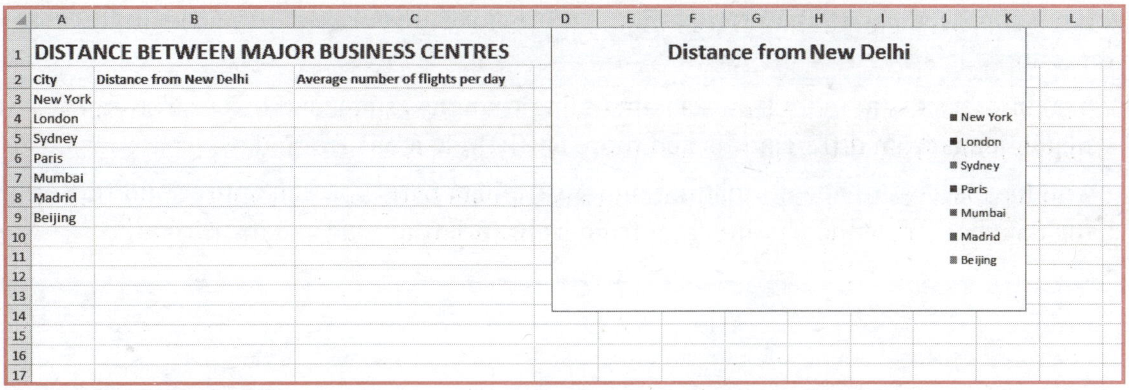

	A	B	C
1	DISTANCE BETWEEN MAJOR BUSINESS CENTRES		
2	City	Distance from New Delhi	Average number of flights per day
3	New York		
4	London		
5	Sydney		
6	Paris		
7	Mumbai		
8	Madrid		
9	Beijing		

B. Your school is planning to buy new equipments for the school girl's cricket team. List down all the equipment's required. Create a table in Excel with the following headers: Product, Price, Quantity, and Total Cost. Fill in the products you are planning to buy, their quantity, price and the total cost per product. At the bottom of the table, give the grand total. Use functions and formulae to perform all the calculations.

C. Create a table that list the weather report of last 20 days. Select 10 records from the table and insert a pie chart. Select the other 10 records and insert a column chart. Use both the charts to analyse the weather. State which is easier to understand?

D. In the above table, freeze the rows that contain weather report for the second week of the month.

MS Office 2010
Updates

In MS Excel 2010:

- You can create tiny charts that fit in a cell called **sparklines**. They are used to visually summarise trends alongside data. They are generally used to show data trends. To add sparklines, go to the **Insert** tab. In the **Sparklines** group, click the type of sparkline that you want to create: **Line**, **Column**, or **Win/Loss**.

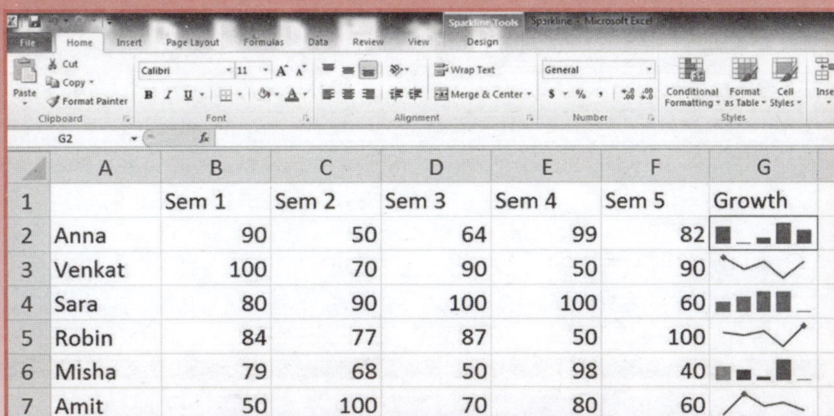

	A	B	C	D	E	F	G
1		Sem 1	Sem 2	Sem 3	Sem 4	Sem 5	Growth
2	Anna	90	50	64	99	82	
3	Venkat	100	70	90	50	90	
4	Sara	80	90	100	100	60	
5	Robin	84	77	87	50	100	
6	Misha	79	68	50	98	40	
7	Amit	50	100	70	80	60	

- You have improved conditional formatting that provides greater formatting flexibility. Some new features are:
  - You have access to more icon sets, including triangles, stars, and boxes. You can also mix and match icons from different sets and more easily hide icons from view.
  - You have access to new formatting options for data bars. You can apply solid fills or borders to the data bar, or set the bar direction from right-to-left instead of left-to-right.

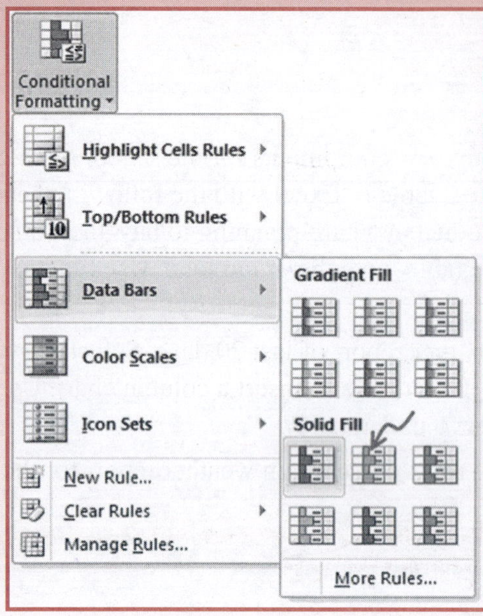

TEACHER'S NOTES

1. Talk to the students about how Excel helps in mathematics and formulae.
2. In Excel huge databases can be created, however printing them is problematic. Help them print huge databases.

10 Communication Technology

SNAP RECAP

1. A network consists of two or more computers linked together for sharing resources.
2. A type of network that can be used only by the users of an organisation is called Intranet.
3. Network technology includes the transfer of Video, Audio and data.

LEARNING OBJECTIVES

You will learn about:

1. What is a Network?
2. Advantages of a Network
3. Network Topologies
4. Types of Network
5. Home Networking
6. Network Devices
7. Wired Technology
8. Wireless Technology
9. Internet and its Applications
10. World Wide Web

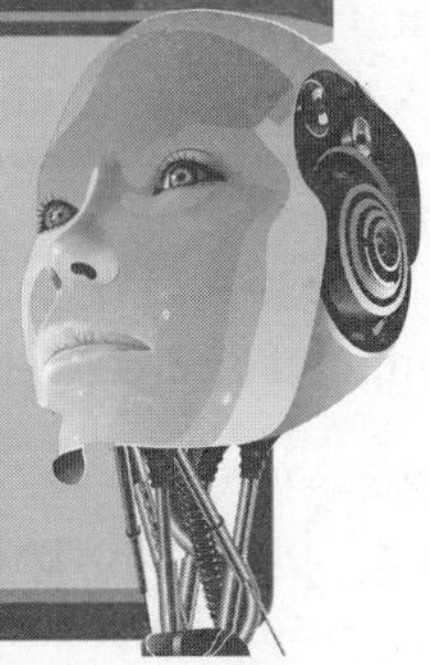

INTRODUCTION

The process of connecting two or more computers or devices, using hardware and software components, thus enabling them to communicate with each other as well as transfer and share data and information between them is called **computer networking**. A **computer network** may exist between computer systems housed within a building or between computer systems placed around the world (Fig. 10.1).

A system consisting of connected nodes made to share data, hardware and software is called a computer network.

Fig. 10.1 *Computer networking*

A computer network usually consist of two or more computers, computer servers, cables, network hubs, switches, routers, bridges, modem and network interface card (Fig. 10.2).

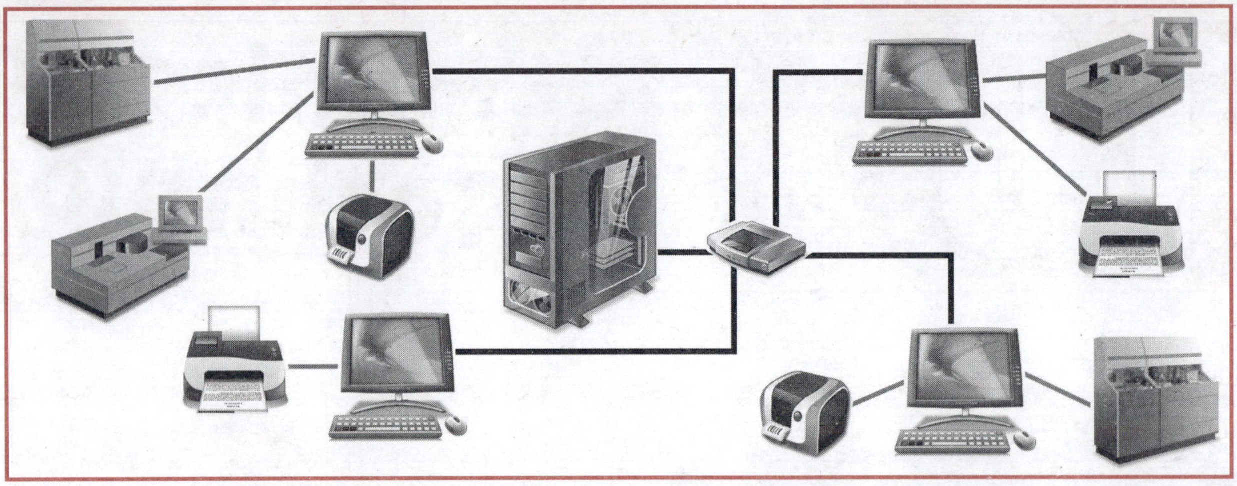

Fig. 10.2 *Components of a network*

Server(s) is a powerful computer/group of computers that controls the entire network. The computers at workstations that are connected to the main server are called **clients**. A client is also called a **node**.

To facilitate communication over the network, you require a **network interface card**. It is a hardware component that identifies every node in a network. You can also communicate through a **wireless network adaptor** that can be easily plugged into a USB port. The various hardware components are connected to each other by cables.

Another important component of a computer network is a **MODEM**. It stands for **MO**dulator and **DEM**odulator. It is a hardware device that enables a computer to transmit data over telephone and cable lines by converting the digital data used by a computer into an analog signal used on phone lines; and then converting the analog signal back to digital signal at the receiving end. There are two different types of modem: Wireless and Wired.

Advantages of a Network

Computer network have many advantages. Some of them are listed below.

- ***Sharing Resources:*** Networking allows you to share devices. For example, several computers can be connected to a single expensive printer; you can play a CD from one computer while sitting on another computer. Storage devices, printers, scanners and computer programs are examples of shareable resources.
- ***Sharing Information:*** The information present on a single computer is made available to other computers connected to a network. Networking helps exchange data and information among computers in a network.
- ***Sharing Software:*** Software programs can be installed once on the main server and accessed by all the computers on the network. This saves time and cost.
- ***Simultaneous Access:*** In a stand-alone computer, the information or the resources connected to it cannot be accessed by any other computer. Networking allows several users to access all applications and resources simultaneously.
- ***Easier Backups:*** In a network, if a particular computer does not have a CD/DVD drive to copy, burn or take backup of the CD/DVD, then you can use another computer which has a CD/DVD drive for the aforementioned tasks.
- ***Communication:*** As several computers are connected in a network, one can send and receive messages easily. Voice mails and video calls can also be done easily.

Topology

In computer networking, **topology** refers to the layout of connected devices. Topology denotes the shape of a network or the network's layout. A **network topology** determines how different nodes in a network are connected to each other and how they communicate.

Main types of topologies

Different types of network topologies are listed below.

- Linear Bus topology
- Star topology
- Ring topology
- Tree topology

FACT FILE

Network services are applications hosted by computer servers on a network. They provide certain functionality to the members or users of the network.

Linear Bus Topology

In linear bus topology, all the devices/nodes are connected to a central cable which has exactly two end points (Fig. 10.3). Ethernet and Local Talk networks use a linear bus topology.

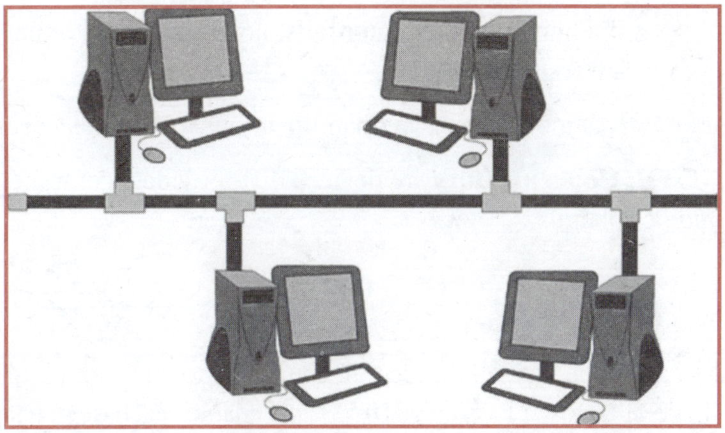

Fig. 10.3 *Linear Bus topology*

Advantages of linear bus topology

Some of the advantages of a linear bus topology are listed below.

- It is easy to connect a computer or a peripheral device to a linear bus topology.
- It requires less cable length than other topologies and hence is cheapest in terms of cabling cost.
- Central back up permits to store all the work/information at one place.

Disadvantages of linear bus topology

Some of the disadvantages of a linear bus topology are listed below.

- The entire network shuts down if there is a break in the main cable.
- Terminators are required at both the ends of backbone cable.
- It is difficult to identify the problem in linear bus topology because the entire network shuts down.
- It can not to be used as a stand-alone solution in a large building.

Star Topology

In a star topology, all the devices are connected to a central hub file server. Nodes or workstations and peripherals devices communicate across the network by passing data through the hub (Fig. 10.4). Compared to linear bus topology, it is more difficult to install star topology because there is more cabling involved. The protocols used with star configurations are usually Ethernet or Local Talk.

Advantages of star topology

Some of the advantages of a star topology are listed below.

- In star topology, data packets do not pass through excessive number of nodes. In any communication, almost three devices and two links are involved.
- Even if one cable fails, network will continue to operate. There will be no disruptions to the network when connecting or removing devices.
- It is easy to detect faults in the network and to remove parts.

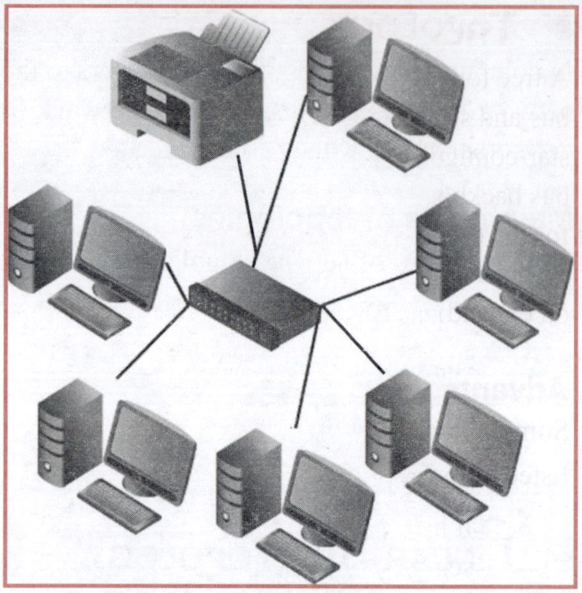

Fig. 10.4 *Star topology*

Disadvantages of star topology

Some of the disadvantages of a star topology are listed below.

- It requires more cable length than linear bus topology.
- If a hub or concentrator fails, nodes attached to that hub are disabled.
- It is more expensive than linear bus topologies because of the cost of the concentrators.

NOTE: Concentrators are devices that provide a central connection point for cables from workstations, servers and peripherals.

Ring Topology

In a ring topology, all devices are connected to one another in shape of a closed loop (Fig. 10.5). This enables each device to be connected directly to two other devices, one on either side of it.

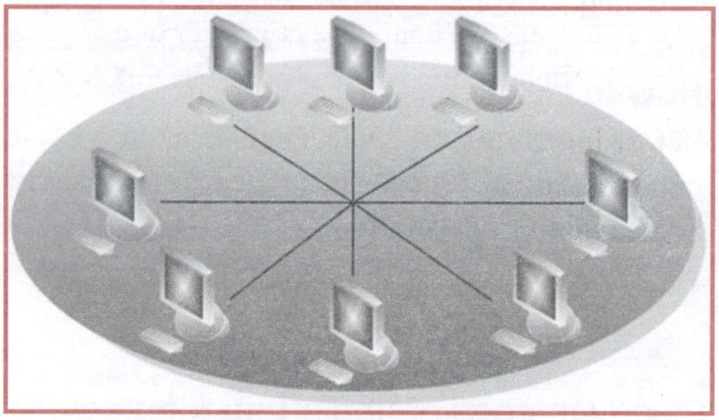

Fig. 10.5 *Ring topology*

Advantages of ring topology

Some of the advantages of a ring topology are listed below.

- In ring topology, all the traffic flows only in one direction at very high speed. This helps reduce chances of collision.
- Even when the load on the network increases, its performance is better than other topologies.
- Additional components do not affect the performance of a network.

Disadvantages of ring topology

Some of the disadvantages of a ring topology are listed below.

- Each data must pass through all the computers between source and destination. This makes it slower than other topologies.
- If one workstation or port goes down the entire network gets affected.
- Network cards, used in this topology, are expensive as compared to Ethernet cards and hubs.

▶ Tree Topology

A tree topology combines characteristics of linear bus and star topologies. It consists of groups of star-configured workstations connected to a linear bus backbone cable (Fig. 10.6). Tree topologies allow for the expansion of an existing network and enable organisations, such as schools, to configure (and later on expand) a network to meet their growing needs.

Fig. 10.6 *Tree topology*

Advantages of tree topology

Some of the advantages of a tree topology are listed below.

- It has point-to-point wiring for individual segments.
- It is supported by several hardware and software vendors.

Disadvantages of tree topology

Some of the disadvantages of a tree topology are listed below.

- In tree topology, the overall length of each segment is limited by the type of cabling used.
- If the backbone line breaks, the entire segment goes down.
- It is more difficult to configure and wire than other topologies.

How to choose a topology?

Before installing a network, it is important to choose a suitable topology for your deployment environment. The important parameters to consider while choosing a topology are requirement, cost, future expansion needs, etc. Some other important parameters are:

- Money
- Length of cable needed
- Cable type
- Infrastructure and hardware available
- Maintenance and troubleshooting
- Future growth

FACT FILE

Network resilience is the ability of a computer network to provide and maintain an acceptable level of service in the face of faults and challenges.

A linear bus network is the least expensive way to install a network; you do not have to purchase concentrators. It also uses comparatively shorter lengths of cable and thus reduces the cost. But its maintenance and troubleshooting is complicated because the entire network shuts down when there is a break anywhere in the system. With a star topology, expanding a network is easily done by adding another concentrator. However, it is costlier than linear bus topology. The most common cable used in schools is unshielded twisted pair, which is most often used with star topologies. Later in the chapter you will learn more about different types of cables used in a network.

CHECK YOUR PROGRESS

A. What is computer networking?

B. Differentiate between star and linear bus topology.

C. List out advantages of a computer network.

D. Give two limitations each of any three topologies.

E. With the help of the Internet find out more about two different types of modem. HOTS

Types of Network

One way to categorise the different types of computer network designs is by their scope or scale. For historical reasons, the networking industry refers to nearly every type of design as some kind of ***area network***. Some common examples of an area network types are listed and discussed below.

- **LAN:** Local Area Network
- **WAN:** Wide Area Network
- **MAN:** Metropolitan Area Network

Local Area Network (LAN)

A Local Area Network (LAN) is a network that connects network devices over a relatively short distance (Fig. 10.7). It interconnects computers in a limited area such as home, school, computer laboratory or office building. LAN is advantageous as it allows sharing of expensive resources such as printers; it has central back-up; it allows exchange of data across network and much more.

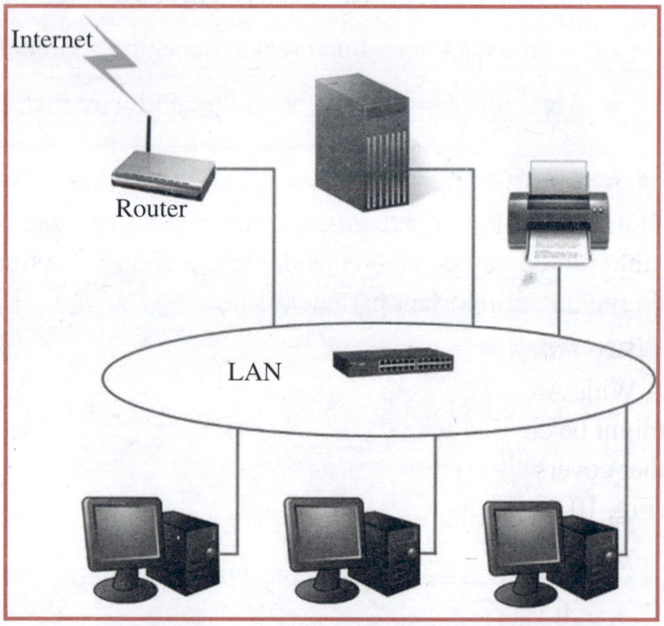

Fig. 10.7 *LAN*

Some important features of LAN are listed below.

- It has limited geographical range, usually a few kilometres.
- It has high speed data transfer rates that vary from 10 to 100 mbps.
- Bus and Ring topology are the most commonly used topologies.
- It provides full time connectivity to local services.
- It supports a variety of transmission medium, such as cable and wireless transmission.
- Cabling is the primary transmission medium. Coaxial or CAT 5 cables are usually used for connections.
- Due to short distances, errors and noise is minimum.
- It is low cost. The installation, expansion and maintenance of LAN is simple and scalable.

For example, a computer lab in a school will have LAN.

Metropolitan Area Network (MAN)

A Metropolitan Area Network (MAN) as the name indicates, is a network that links locations together from across different locations in a general geographical area (Fig. 10.8). A newspaper/media company employ a MAN. Branch offices in different cities could coordinate stories that appear in localised publications with the help of MAN. One of the biggest advantage of MAN is bandwidth of the connecting links which makes it very fast.

Some important features of MAN are listed below.

- The network size falls intermediate between LANs and WANs. It covers between 5 km to 50 kms area.
- The data transfer rate is low compared to LAN.
- It connects number of LAN's to form larger network, so that resources can be shared.

For example, organisations with different branches located in the city.

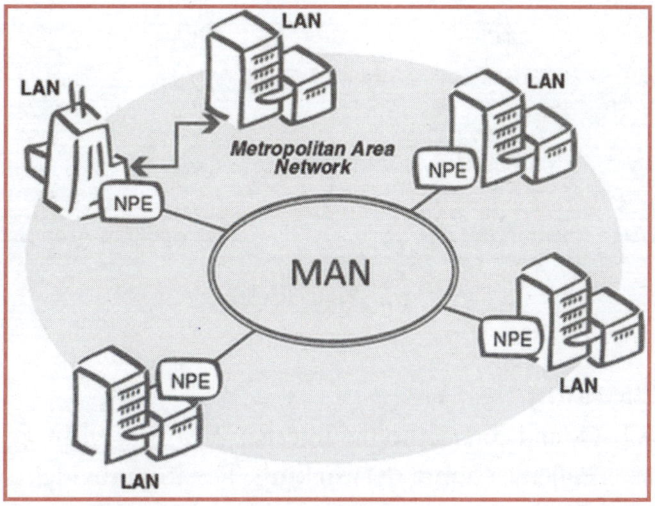

Fig. 10.8 *MAN*

Wide Area Network (WAN)

A Wide Area Network (WAN), in comparison to a MAN, is not restricted to a geographical location, although it might be confined within the bounds of a state or a country. A wide area network is a telecommunication network that covers a broad area, that is, any network that links across metropolitan, regional, or national boundaries (Fig. 10.9). The Internet is an example of a worldwide public WAN.

Some important features of WAN are listed below.

- It is distinguished in terms of geographical range. It is a country and worldwide network.
- It contains multiple LAN's and MAN's.
- It uses satellites and microwave relays.
- It mainly uses fibre optic cable.
- It has high speed data transfer rates that support advanced features, such as voice communication.
- It may be used in guided (wired) or unguided (wireless) medium of transmission.
- Leased lines, fibre optic, microwave and satellite channels can be used as the transmission medium.

For example, the Internet.

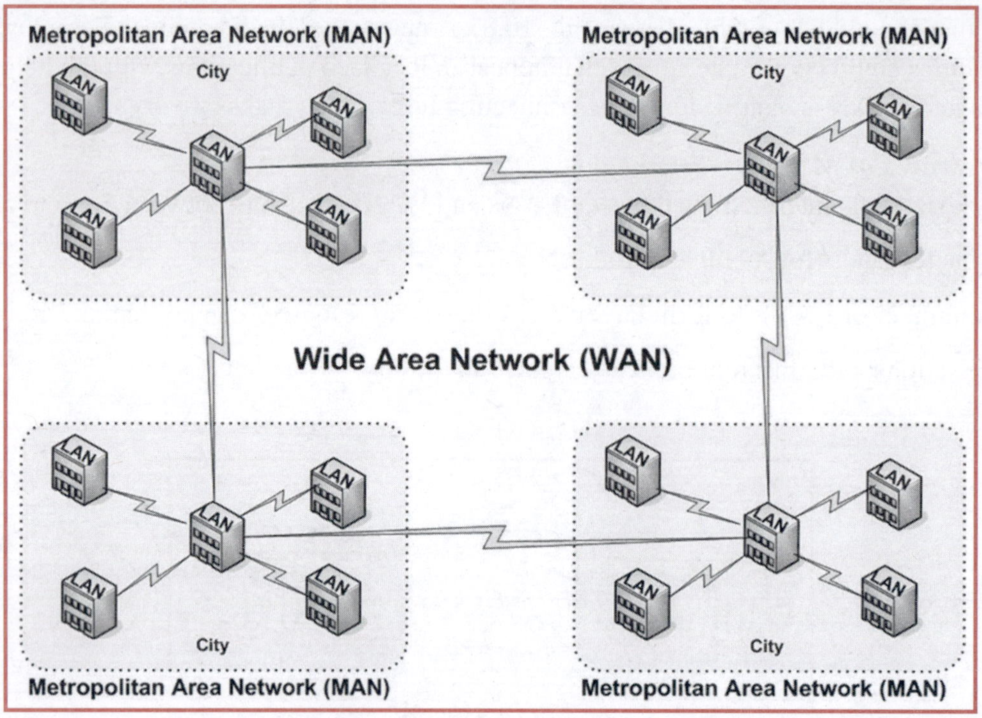

Fig. 10.9 *WAN*

LAN, WAN and Home Networking

Residences typically employ one LAN and connect to the Internet WAN via an **Internet Service Provider (ISP)** using a **broadband modem**. This is called as **home networking**. The ISP provides a WAN IP address to the modem, and all of the computers on the home network use LAN (so-called *private*) IP addresses.

Other Types of Area Networks

While LAN and WAN are the most popular network types mentioned, there were also other area networks available for communication. They are listed below.

- *SAN:* Storage Area Network, System Area Network, Server Area Network, or sometimes called Small Area Network
- *CAN:* Campus Area Network, Controller Area Network, or sometimes called Cluster Area Network
- *PAN:* Personal Area Network
- *DAN:* Desk Area Network
- *WLAN:* Wireless Local Area Network

FACT FILE

In 1965, Thomas Merrill and Lawrence G Roberts created the first Wide Area Network (WAN).

Today, computer networks are the core of modern communication. All modern aspects of the **Public Switched Telephone Network** (PSTN) are computer-controlled, and telephony increasingly runs over the Internet Protocol, although not necessarily the public Internet.

CHECK YOUR PROGRESS

A. With the help of the Internet and library, answer the following questions. HOTS

1. Give three disadvantages of LAN, WAN and MAN.
2. Write a short note on PAN, CAN and SAN.
3. What is PSTN?

B. Differentiate between WLAN and WAN.

NETWORKING TECHNOLOGY

For transmitting data between two systems, a communication medium is required. Various types of mediums are available and the choice depends upon the type, cost, transfer rate and overall data transmission efficiency of it. Basically, a computer networking can be established in two ways. They are:

- Wired technology
- Wireless technology

WIRED TECHNOLOGY

When a wire is used to connect two computers it is called wired technology. It is a method where the data is transmitted from one place to another through a physical medium. In **cable networks** and **telephone networks** the data transmission is through wired technology. There are various kinds of wires or cables that are used for the transmission of data. They are co-axial cable, ethernet cable and optical fibre cable.

Co-axial cable

In this cable, there are two conductors. An inner conductor is surrounded by an insulating medium which is again surrounded by an outer conductor (Fig. 10.10). It is mainly used by cable TV operators and high speed broadband networks.

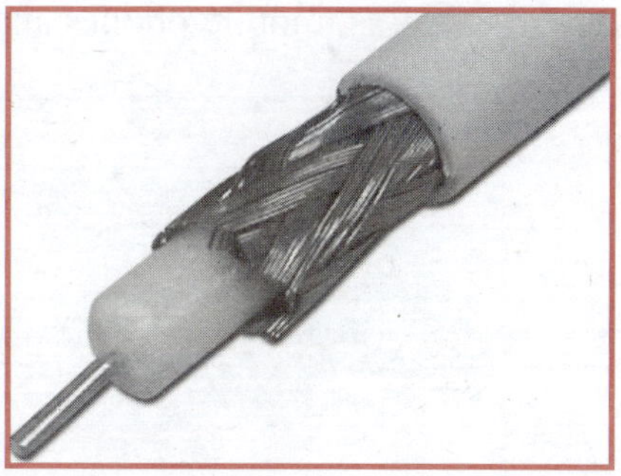

Fig. 10.10 *Co-axial cable*

Some of the features of coaxial cable are listed below.

- It has high data transmission rate.
- It is cheaper than any other medium.
- It covers long distances.
- Its outer plastic jacket protects you from shocks and jerks.

Ethernet cable

Ethernet cables are used to connect together the network devices such as hubs, switches and computers. It consists of devices attached to a common medium (co-axial cable or twisted pair) that provides a path for the signals to travel (Fig. 10.11). Each end of its cable has a jack with eight pins to plug into the ethernet port of different devices. It is the most widely used technology for LAN.

Some ot the features of ethernet cable are listed below.

- It is widely available.
- It is less expensive.
- It provides stable connectivity.

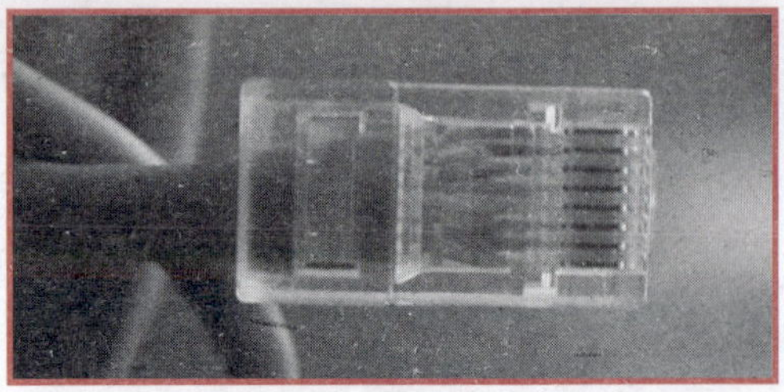

Fig. 10.11 *Ethernet cable*

Optical fibre cable

Optical fiber cables are made of glass or plastic fibres (Fig. 10.12). The glass core transmits light when the refractive index changes. Hence, these are used to transfer data in the form of light beams. They have higher data transfer rates and can carry signals over large distances.

Some of the features of optical fibre cable are listed below.

- It has fast data transmission rates.
- Data can be carried over long distances without loss.
- It has higher data security.

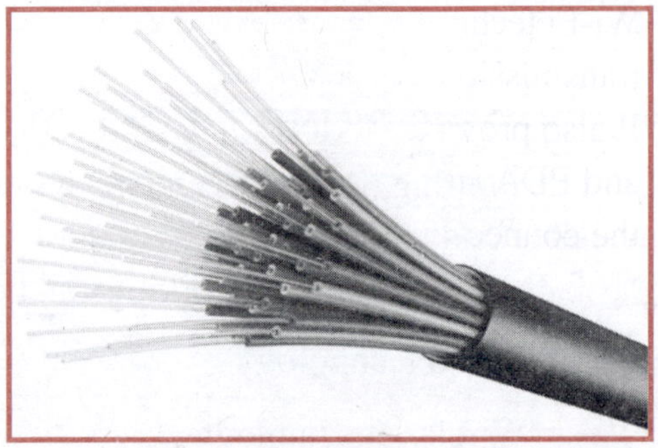

Fig. 10.12 *Optical fibre cable*

Wireless Technology

Wireless technology is a method of communication that uses radio frequencies or infrared waves to transmit data between devices on a LAN. As it does not use cables or wires, it is known as wireless technology.

Bluetooth

Bluetooth is a wireless technology used to transmit data from one device to another. It relies on low frequency radio waves and the protocol software enables it to transmit data to other devices over short distances. It can automatically detect and communicate with other bluetooth devices without any user input. It is used to connect devices, such as, digital cameras, mobile phones and personal computers (Fig. 10.13).

Fig. 10.13 *Bluetooth transmissions*

Infrared Radiation

Infrared technology offers low power requirements and low circuitry costs. These are portable and highly secure. No wires are required but the transmitter and receiver must be in line of sight (Fig. 10.14). Its performance drops off with longer distances. These radiations can also be blocked by walls, people, table, chair, etc. Infrared waves are used in TV remote control.

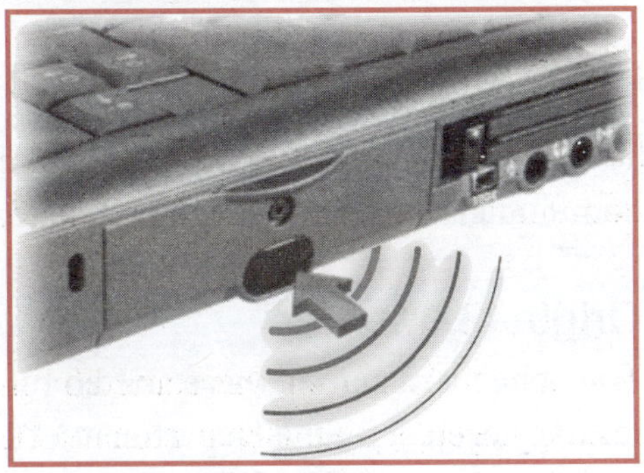

Fig. 10.14 *Infrared radiations*

Wireless Fidelity

Wi-Fi technology is more powerful and gives a high speed of data transmission as compared to Bluetooth. It uses high frequency radio waves. It also provides wireless Internet connections for computers, mobile phones and PDA (Personal Digital Assistants) (Fig. 10.15). Though, Wi-Fi is flexible, the connection gets affected due to weather conditions, such as rains and thunderstorms.

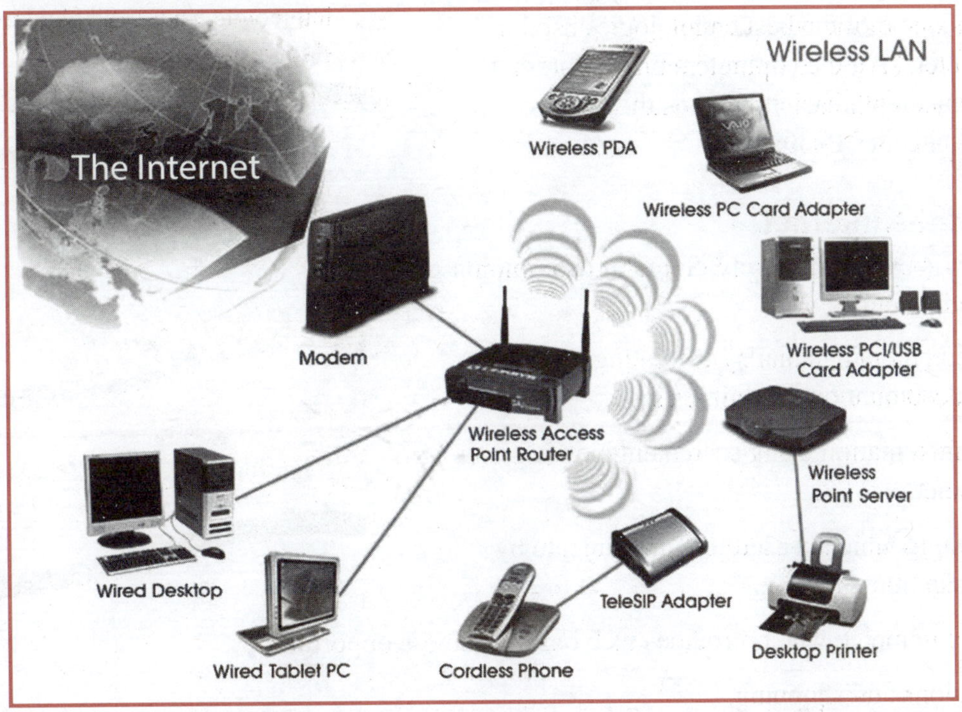

Fig. 10.15 *Wi-Fi*

FACT FILE

Public places such as airports, hotels, bookstores and shops which offers Wi-Fi access are called **hotspots**.

▶ INTERNET

The Internet is a network of millions of computers linked to each other by wired and wireless technologies. It enables communication between computers across the world.

Origin of Internet

The concept of Internet was started by the US Government in the year 1969. It was originally developed for a military project by the Department of Defense of the US under the name **ARPANET (Advanced Research Project Agency Network)**. The basic aim of ARPANET was to create a network that allows the users of a research computer at one university to access and exchange information with the users of research computers at other universities.

Today, the Internet is one of the best technologies used in the world of computers. All the computers on the Internet are able to communicate with each other as they follow same set of rules, known as **Protocol**.

FACT FILE

Interspace is a multi-user virtual environment that automatically interconnect related logical spaces within shared virtual world.

Applications of the Internet

Nowadays, Internet is used extensively. Some of its common applications are listed below.

- Sending and receiving emails by creating a web based email account on the email sites.
- Searching information using search engine programs on the Internet.
- Online chatting which is used to communicate by means of instant messaging.
- Electronic commerce which provides web based business opportunities.
- Online auctions and shopping.
- Reservations and cancellations of tickets (Railways, Airways, etc.).
- Uploading and downloading files through File Transfer Protocol (FTP).
- Online teaching and learning.
- Video Conference, that is, telecommunication technology to interact via two-way video and audio transmissions.

FACT FILE

Exploring the web or net is called **surfing**.

Requirements to connect to the Internet

For connecting to the Internet, you require the following:

- **Computer with high RAM**, minimum 1GB RAM
- **Modem**, with 56 kbps speed
- **Telephone line**, that carries the transmitted information from one point to another.

- **Speakers**, **Microphone**, **Webcam** (optional) and **CD/DVD** drive
- **Web browser**, a software that is used to connect and work with the Internet
- **Internet account** from an Internet Service Provider (ISP); some popular ISPs are VSNL, BSNL and Airtel.

World Wide Web

The World Wide Web is a collection of information that contains various documents, pictures and sound effects that are stored on the computer around the world. It enables the user to view a wide variety of information, including news, business and activities across the world. In general, WWW refers to the online information available on net or pages on different websites. It is the leading information retrieval service of the Internet.

Some common web terms

Web: It is the collection of information on the network.

Web Page: Each and every page of a website is called a web page.

Website: The large collection of related web pages on the net is known as a website.

Uniform Resource Locator (URL): It refers to the address of any resource on the Internet. Every resource has its own unique address. The user can go to a particular website using this URL.

The method of identifying computers by name is called **letter addressing system**. It is also known as **domain naming system** (DNS). The last three letters of the web address are important. These letters provide information about the kind of organisation the web address belongs to. For example,

.com	Commercial organisation
.net	Networking organisation
.edu	Educational institution
.org	Non-profit organisation
.gov	Government organisation

Web Browser: It is the software program that is used to access web pages. Some popular web browsers are Microsoft Internet Explorer, Mozilla Firefox, Google Chrome and Netscape Navigator. The browser allows the user to send and receive information through web server on the monitor.

Web Server: It is a computer that stores web pages. It accepts request and sends response to the user on the Internet.

FACT FILE

- **Intranet** is a network that is under the control of a single administrative entity. It refers to a network within an organisation. Usually, an intranet is the internal LAN of an organisation. Intranet can be understood as a private extension of the Internet confined to an organisation.
- **Extranet** is a network that is also under the administrative control of a single organisation, however it supports limited connection to a specific external network. For example, an organisation may provide access to portions of its intranet to share data with its business partners or customers. While intranets are generally restricted to employees of the organisation, extranets may also be accessed by customers, suppliers, or other approved parties.

CHECK YOUR PROGRESS

A. With the help of the Internet, do the following:

1. Collect more information regarding MAN. Also, list out the places where MAN is used and for what purpose it is used.
2. Prepare a project about the origin of network. Describe the hardware and software that makes up a network.

B. Present a comparison chart for network topologies.

C. Create a PowerPoint presentation on the following:

1. Comparison between wired and wireless technology
2. Applications of Internet.

D. Write a short note on customer services typically provided by an Internet Service Provider.

GLOSSARY

- **Chatting:** It is an online communication by means of instant messaging.
- **Computer Network:** It is a system consisting of connected nodes made to share data, hardware and software.
- **Letter Addressing System:** It referes to web addresses using .com, .net, .in and .edu.
- **Surfing:** It refers to exploring the Internet for topics of your interest.
- **Topology:** It refers to the shape of a network or the network's layout.
- **URL:** It is the unique address of a website.
- **Web Browser:** It is the software used to access web pages.
- **Web Page:** Each and every page of a website is known as a web page.
- **Web Server:** It is a computer that stores web pages.
- **World Wide Web:** It is a collection of information that contains various documents, pictures and sound effects that was stored on computers around the world.

NOW YOU KNOW

1. A system consisting of connected nodes made to share data, hardware and software is called a computer network.
2. Sharing resources, sharing information, easier backups, communication and multiple access are the advantages of networking.
3. In computer networking, topology refers to the layout of connected devices.
4. In a linear bus topology, all devices are connected to a central cable.
5. In a star topology, all devices are connected to a central hub.

6. In a ring topology, all devices are connected to one another in the shape of a closed loop.
7. A tree topology combines characteristics of linear bus and star topologies.
8. LAN, MAN and WAN are the common examples of area network.
9. A LAN connects network devices over a relatively short distance.
10. A MAN is a network that links locations together from across different locations in a general geographical area.
11. A WAN is a telecommunication network that covers a broad area, that is, any network that links across metropolitan, regional or national boundaries.
12. When a wire is used to connect two or more computers it is termed as wired technology.

EXERCISE

FA

A Fill in the blanks.

1. The process of connecting two or more computers is called ....
2. .... refers to the shape of a network or the network's layout.
3. .... is a computer network that interconnects computers in a limited area.
4. A network that links locations together from across different locations in a general geographical area is called ....
5. A telecommunication network that covers a broad area is called ....
6. The first graphical browser was ....
7. .... is used to connect your computer to the telephone line.
8. .... provides an Internet account to its user.
9. The software that is used to connect and work with the Internet is ....
10. .... provides wireless Internet connections for computers, mobile phones and PDA.

B Multiple choice questions.

1. The communication between two or more computers is set up by a ....

   a. network b. WAN c. LAN d. MAN

2. Which of the following is not a web browser?

   a. Gmail b. Firefox c. Internet Explorer d. Google Chrome

3. .... is the process of getting a file from any location on your computer with the help of the Internet.

   a. Uploading b. Copying c. Downloading d. None of these

4. The large collection of related web pages on the net is called as a ....

   a. web document b. website c. web browser d. webpages

5. Communicating by means of instant messaging is called ....

   a. chatting b. teleconference c. video conference d. email

6. .... cables are made of glass or plastic fibre.

   a. Coaxial b. Twisted c. Ethernet d. Optical fibre

7. .... waves are used in TV remote control.

   a. Wi-Fi b. Bluetooth c. Infrared d. All of these

8. The type of networking used by a cable TV operator is ....

   a. WAN b. LAN c. MAN d. CAN

9. Data within the building can be sent through ....

   a. Bluetooth b. Wi–Fi c. Infrared d. None of these

10. Data from one mobile phone to another can be transferred using ....

    a. wired technology b. infrared c. wi-fi d. bluetooth

C Give expansions for the following. HOTS

1. SAN ....
2. CAN ....
3. WLAN ....
4. PAN ....
5. DAN ....
6. URL ....
7. ARPANET ....
8. MODEM ....
9. ISP ....
10. BPS ....

SA

D Identify the topology and name what all components will be required in each topology.

1. 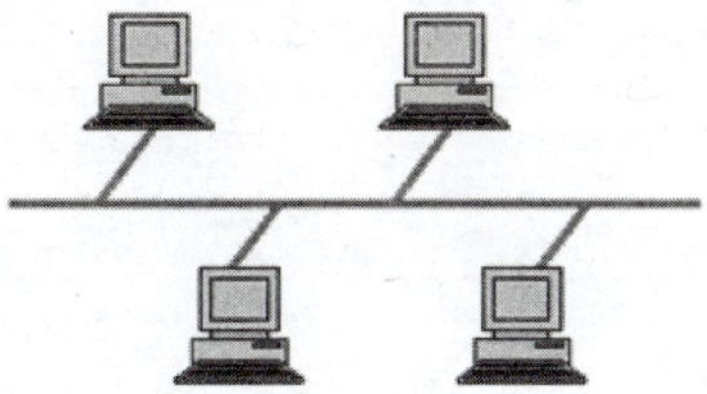

2. 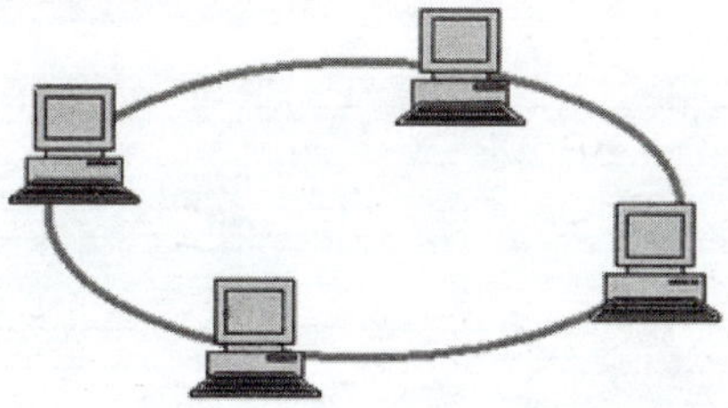

3. 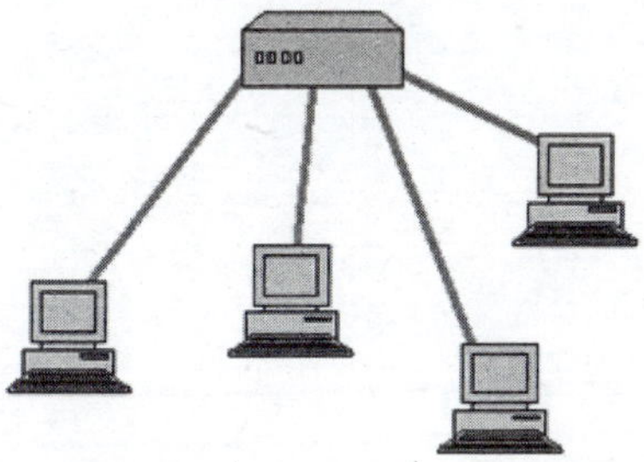

4. 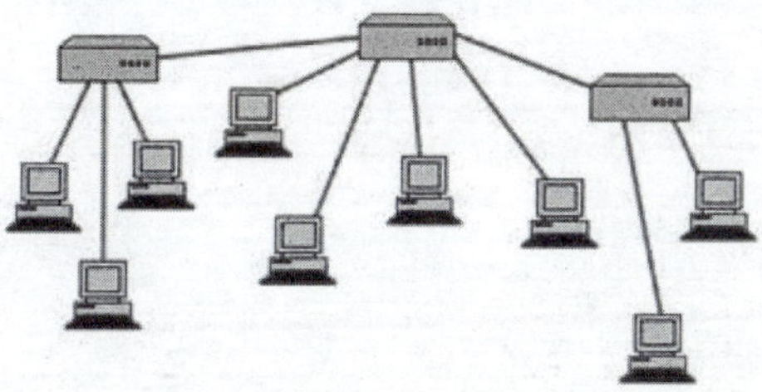

E Answer the following questions in detail.

1. What is network? What are the advantages of a network?
2. Draw and explain any two network topologies.
3. Explain LAN, WAN and MAN. Give examples.
4. What are the factors that needs to be considered while choosing a topology?
5. Discuss and list out the disadvantages of the Internet.
6. What are the hardware and software requirements for connecting a computer system with Internet?
7. Write a brief note on bluetooth.
8. What are the features of optical fibre cable?
9. List out the applications of the Internet.
10. Explain any five web terms.

Application Based Questions

A. Rohit's father identified five sites that Rohit frequently visits. He took screenshots of their home pages and created the table given below. He asked Rohit to recall their URL and asked him to explain why he visits these websites frequently.

S.NO.	WEB PAGE	URL	Purpose
1.	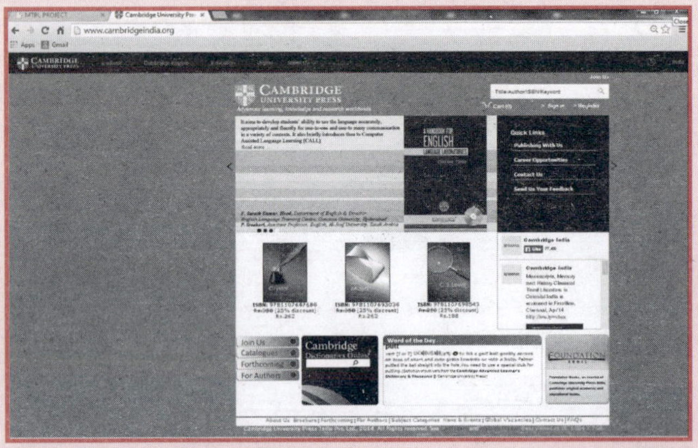		
2.	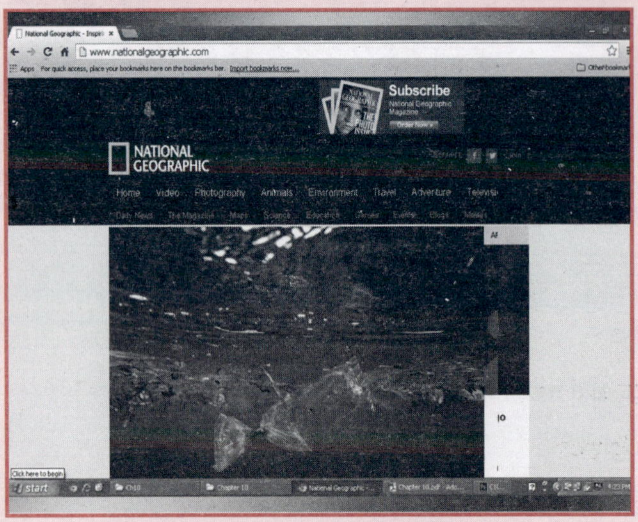		
3.	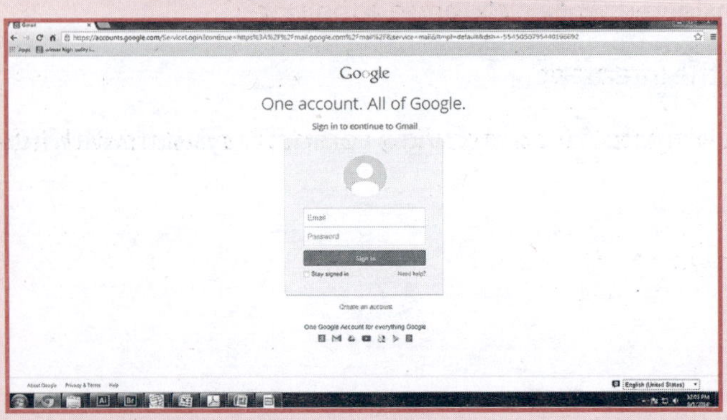		

4.

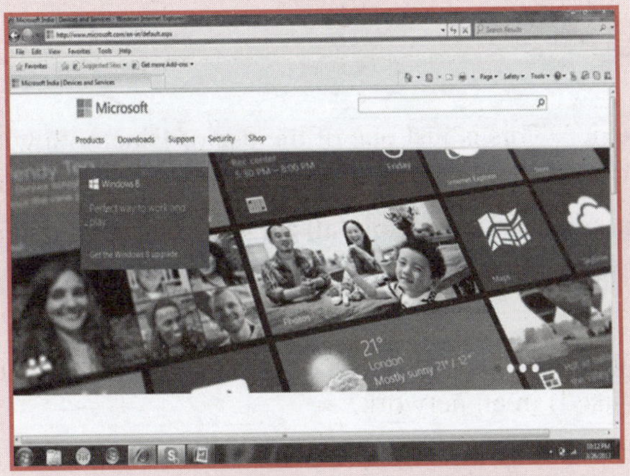

5.

B. How has networking changed communication between offices that are located in different continent?

C. Raman recently acquired a shop in an upcoming business district. However, his manufacturing unit is 70 kms away. For smooth and easy communication he wants to set up a network between his two units. Which network is most suitable for him and why?

D. What type of network is used by online shopping websites like Amazon and Flipkart?

E. As a brand consultant, Surbhi regularly travels for work. How can she access the Internet and her email id while travelling?

F. An accounting firm recently hired 40 more people and to accommodate them they rented the floor above them. An IT consultant advised them to install a network. However, the firm is not too keen. List both advantages and disadvantages of implementing the network. What is your recommendation?

G. What type of network would the following use?

1. A training centre that occupies two adjoining buildings.
2. A university whose campus is spread all across a state.
3. A company that has offices in different states in a country.
4. A bank that has offices in different countries across the globe.

H. Atul is planning to install either Wi-Fi or broadband connection at home. Which is a better option for him and why? Justify.

I. Advancement in computer technology has enabled employees to work from home. List some of the advantages.

J. Ratika's school has installed multimedia tablets at various spots in her school. What kind of Internet connection and network do you think they use?

LAB WORK

A. Bluetooth makes the mobile phone a hands free device. This is just one of the use of Bluetooth with mobile phones. Investigate other uses of Bluetooth in devices such as mobile phones, tablets and laptops.

B. Envision a computer network for you and your parents. Firstly, list out all the resources and devices you have. Then, draw a simple diagram to show how computers and other devices may be connected in your home network.

C. Make a PowerPoint presentation on different form of cabling that can be used in a network. If possible, show the class different cables that are (or can be used) in an network.

D. Harjeet went to Srinagar with her family. She clicked many photographs with her mobile phone. Now she wants to transfer the photos onto her laptop and email them to her aunt. However, her laptop's Bluetooth is not working. Suggest an alternative way.

E. Visit a library in your city that uses the Internet. Observe how the Internet changed the library experience for both the staff members and the patrons?

TEACHER'S NOTES

1. Discuss with class how the Internet enables us to access heavy multimedia content from across the globe.
2. With lots of real-life examples, differentiate between the Internet and the Intranet.

11 Content Technology

SNAP RECAP

1. Binary is the primary language used by computers to communicate.
2. The hardware components of a computer are the electronic and mechanical parts, such as, monitor, printer, keyboard and mouse.
3. The software components of a computer are the computer programs, such as, Microsoft Office and antivirus utility.
4. Data abstraction refers to handling the data in a meaningful way.

LEARNING OBJECTIVES

You will learn about:

1. Data
2. Information
3. Multimedia
4. Hardware and Software requirements for Multimedia
5. Components of Multimedia
6. Uses of Multimedia
7. Animation
8. File Types

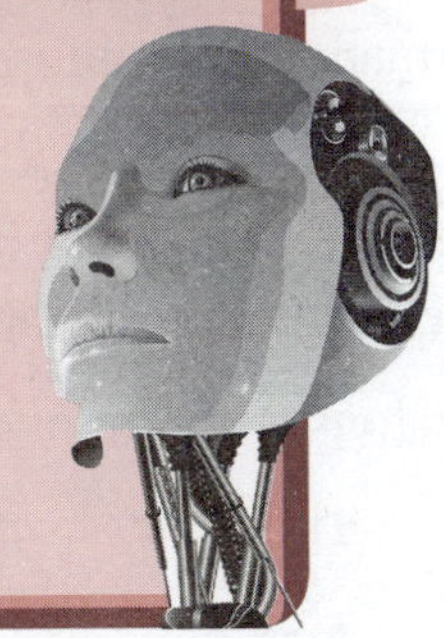

INTRODUCTION

A computer needs some data or information from the user to process and present the desired output. A number, a text, or an image, whatever you input, for a computer it is just a data. In its raw form data has no meaning. It needs to be processed and interpreted to get meaningful and useful information. For example, 'The human skeleton is made of bones' can be considered data while a book on different types of bones and their characteristics can be considered information. In this chapter, you will learn about data and how it is different from information. Also, concept of multimedia and animation will be introduced in this chapter.

FACT FILE

In a computer system, data is stored in binary form, '0' and '1', that is, whenever you input data into a computer system, it is first converted to digital form. Each character on the keyboard has its own code that consists of eight binary digits. For example,

A 01000001

a 01100001

▶ DATA

Data refers to any number, alphabet, special character or the combination of all, that a user inputs into a computer. The computer operates on this unstructured data to provide useful and meaningful results. In a computer system, numbers, alphabets, sound and picture, all are referred to as data (Fig. 11.1). However, data has no meaning at the time of input as it consists of just fact based on records and observations. For example, a Student's Name, Admission Number, Address and Contact Details are the data for the student personal detail file.

Fig. 11.1 *Data*

▶ INFORMATION

The main function of a computer is to convert the meaningless data into useful information. *The processed data is called information*. For example, the input numbers 76, 99, 88, 67 and 78 in Figure 11.2, are some numbers which have no meaning of their own. However, the total and average of these five numbers can be obtained by processing the given data numbers. The resultant total and the resultant average is called information. This information is derived from the data you input.

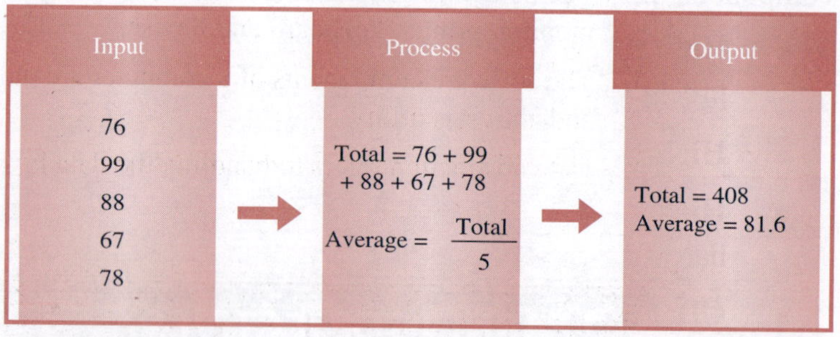

Fig. 11.2 *Input–Process–Output*

When you feed input (data) into a computer, it processes the data and produce the output (information). This output is then sent either to an output device or stored in the computer memory for further processing (Fig. 11.3).

Decisions and actions are taken based on this information. For decision to be meaningful, information should be:

- Timely
- Accurate
- Complete

The integration of this information and human understanding of the subject is referred to as ***knowledge***. Knowledge is derived from information just as information is derived from data. The difference between data, information and knowledge is the level of abstraction. Data has the lowest level of abstraction and knowledge has the highest level of abstraction.

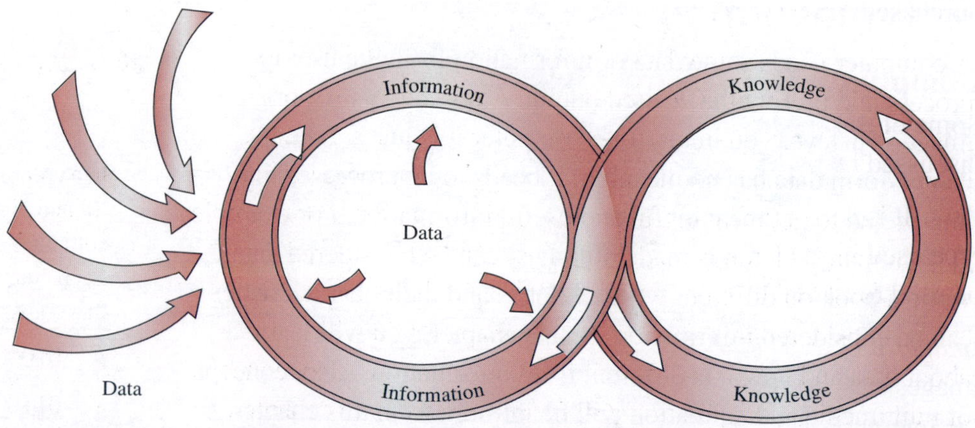

Fig. 11.3 *Data–Information–Knowledge*

▶ Multimedia

The word *multi* means *many* and the word *multimedia* means *many media*. In simple words, *multimedia is the combination of various types of medias, such as text, pictures, graphics, audio, video and animation.* (Fig. 11.4). Due to the integration of all these different mediums, multimedia content occupies more memory space. Multimedia is used in various fields like education, entertainment, business, art and science.

Fig. 11.4 *Multimedia*

Hardware requirements for multimedia

For effectively producing and running multimedia application, your computer require certain hardware components. Some of them are listed below.

- **High speed processor**, preferably a Pentium processor
- **High RAM**, minimum 2GB
- **High storage capacity**, at least 250GB hard disk
- **CD/DVD drive**
- **Color monitor**
- **Microphone/Speakers**
- **Digital camera**

FACT FILE

Singer Bob Goldstein coined the term multimedia in July 1966 to promote the opening of his show, LightWorks at L'Oursin. It was only by 1990s that the term multimedia took on its current meaning.

Software requirements for multimedia

For running and authoring multimedia applications, you need certain software programs that allow you to manipulate images, delete or cut undesirable noises from an audio file, delete scenes from a video file, provide animation, etc. Some software programs commonly used for creating multimedia content are Microsoft PowerPoint, Microsoft Expression Web, Adobe Dreamweaver, Adobe Photoshop and Adobe Premiere. While some programs have to be purchased, others are available free of charge.

Components of multimedia

Some of the components of a multimedia project are discussed below (Fig. 11.5).

Fig. 11.5 *Components of multimedia*

Text: It is the most common and fundamental media type used in a multimedia document. Hypertext can also be used to link text to another page or another link.

Image: It enhances the look of a multimedia document. Images can be imported from various places, such as, the Internet or a digital camera.

Audio: It provides narration or background music for a multimedia document. You can add audio files from the Internet or from a resource CD/DVD. You can also create your own audio file using a microphone.

Animation: It refers to the manipulation of still images so that they give an illusion of visual motion. Visual effects such as wipes, fades and swirls are simple forms of animation.

Video: It can be created with images and animations. Video data is the most complex form of data. You can either create your own video files or import video files from different sources.

FACT FILE

Audacity is an audio editor used for recording, editing and mixing sounds.

Uses of multimedia

Multimedia is one of the most powerful medium of communication and is used extensively in various fields like art, education, entertainment, engineering, medicine, business and science (Fig. 11.6). Some of the uses of multimedia are listed below.

- ***Multimedia in education:*** Nowadays, classroom learning is not limited to conventional methods and make use of interactive audio-visual means. **Edutainment**, that is, Educational Entertainment, a term used by The Walt Disney Company in early as 1948, is on the rise. Classrooms are becoming more and more interactive and both educators and learners are making extensive use of ICT tools.
- ***Multimedia in games:*** The gaming industry heavily uses multimedia elements to give varied audio, video and special effects to their games that makes them more entertaining.
- ***Multimedia in business:*** The business application of multimedia includes business to business and interoffice communications, presentations, demos, conferencing, training and company websites.

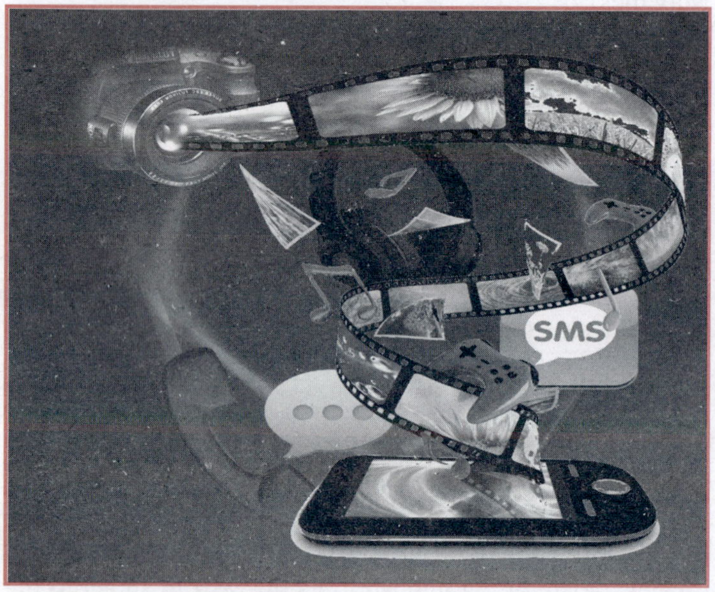

Fig. 11.6 *Uses of multimedia*

- ***Multimedia in entertainment:*** The entertainment industry uses multimedia to develop special effects and animations for movies, television and video games.

CHECK YOUR PROGRESS

A. Name any two:

1. essential hardware components required for running multimedia applications
2. components of multimedia.

B. Define information. Explain the relationship between information and knowledge.

C. Make a list of various multimedia software that you use.

D. Apart from the uses of multimedia given above, multimedia is used extensively in other fields too. List 10 other uses of multimedia from your everyday life. HOTS

▶ Animation

Fig. 11.7 *Animation*

Animation is created from drawn pictures using real time visuals. It is merely the quick display of a sequence of images to create an illusion of movement (Fig. 11.7). Most of the cartoon movies are created on the basis of animation. Animations make static presentations come alive.

Multimedia files have their own formats with extensions like, ***.fla**, ***.swf** (Flash files); ***.dir**, ***.dcr** (Director files); ***.max** (3-D Studio Max files). Some of the software programs used for animation are:

- Animate
- Animator-DV
- Jumpwel
- Toon Boom Animation

FACT FILE

Adobe Flash is the most common software program used for adding animations and interactivity to web pages. Adobe Flash consists of a player, a file format and an authoring tool.

▶ File Types

A file format determines the application to be used for opening a file. The following are the different types of files used in multimedia (Fig. 11.8).

Fig. 11.8 *Different multimedia file formats*

Image file type

Pictures give an enhanced look to a multimedia file. They can be downloaded, copied or drawn. Some of the drawing software available are Paint and CorelDraw. The different file formats to store bitmaps and vector graphics are:

Windows meta file	*.wmf
Autocad format	*.dxf
JPEG	*.jpg
GIF files	*.gif

Audio file type

Some of the commonly used file formats for storing audio files in a computer system are:

MIDI	*.midi, *.mid, *.smf
MP3	*.mp3, *.mp4
MPEG	*.mpg, *.mpv
WAV	*.wav

Video file type

Video files have various different formats and extensions based on the technology used. Some commonly used video file formats are:

MPEG	*.mpg, *.mpeg
QuickTime	*.mov
Flash	*.swf, *.flv
MP4	*.mp4

FACT FILE

A picture or an image stored in an electronic format is called **graphic**.

FACT FILE

Musical Instrument Digital Interface (MIDI) is a communication standard developed for electronic musical instruments and computers. MIDI is the quickest, easiest and most flexible tool to create your own original audio for a multimedia project.

Conclusion

Today, there are plenty of media technologies being used to create a complete multimedia project. A virtual reality application presents 3-D effects and multi-sensory information. This provides the virtual reality of audio and video with the sense of touch. In gaming software, biofeedback is introduced and the player gets vibration when he/she is affected in the game. Business and companies have realised the power of multimedia. Video conferencing, business presentations, Smart Card/Magnetic Swipe card for employees and digital attendance are all so common in the corporate world today. Classroom across schools and colleges are getting more and more tech-savvy. Multimedia, undoubtedly, is enjoying widespread use in all aspects of our life.

This merging of many different technologies to create one wholesome entity is known as **convergence of technology**. *Convergence of technology can be defined as interlinking of different computing technologies, information technologies and communication networks that has arisen as the result of the evolution and popularisation of the Internet and the activities, products and services that have emerged in the digital media space*. Take for example, the mobile phones today. There use is not limited to mobile telephony only. They are used for calling, messaging, emailing, browsing the web, audio and video conferencing, photography, videography, sound recording, GPS and gaming. This is a classic example of convergence of varied different technologies to create a separate entity.

ACTIVITY

To create a small movie clip using still images.

1. Click on the **Start** button ⟶ **All Programs** ⟶ **Windows Live Movie Maker**.
2. In the **Add** group in the **Home** tab, click on the **Add videos and photos** option.

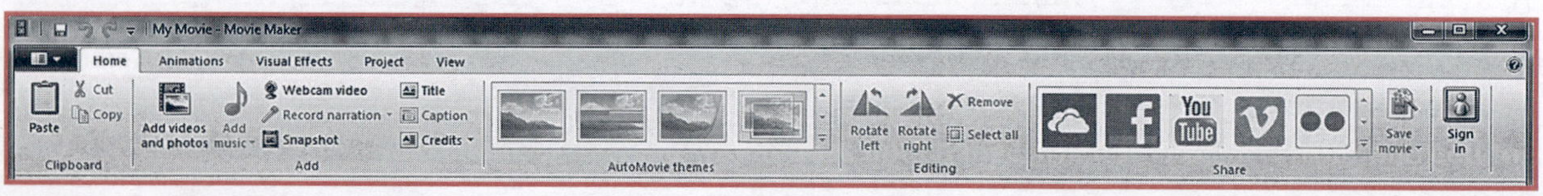

3. The **Add Videos and Photos** dailog box appears. Click on the photo to add it. To select multiple images, press the **Ctrl** button and click on multiple images to add them to the storyboard area on the left.

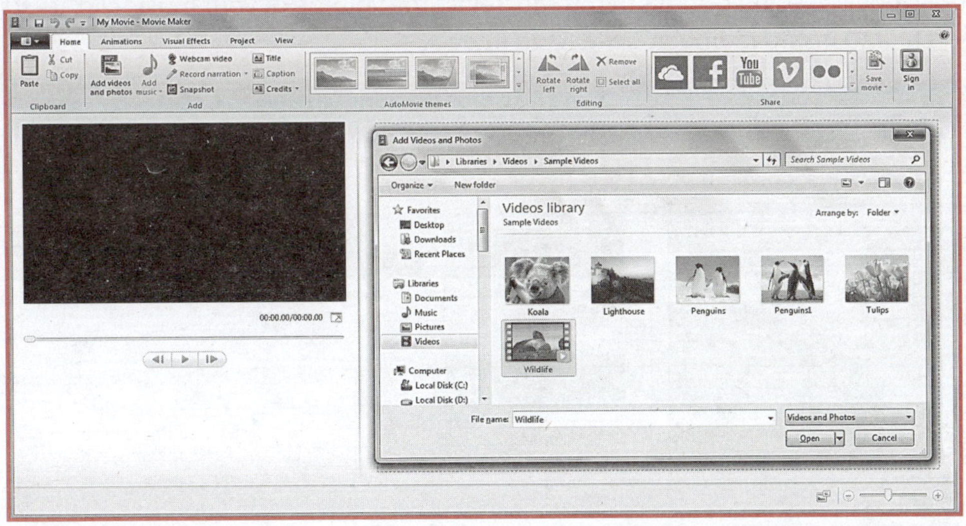

4. A new tab **Video Tools Edit** appears. In this tab, go to the **Duration** option in the **Adjust** group. Here, set how long a picture should display.

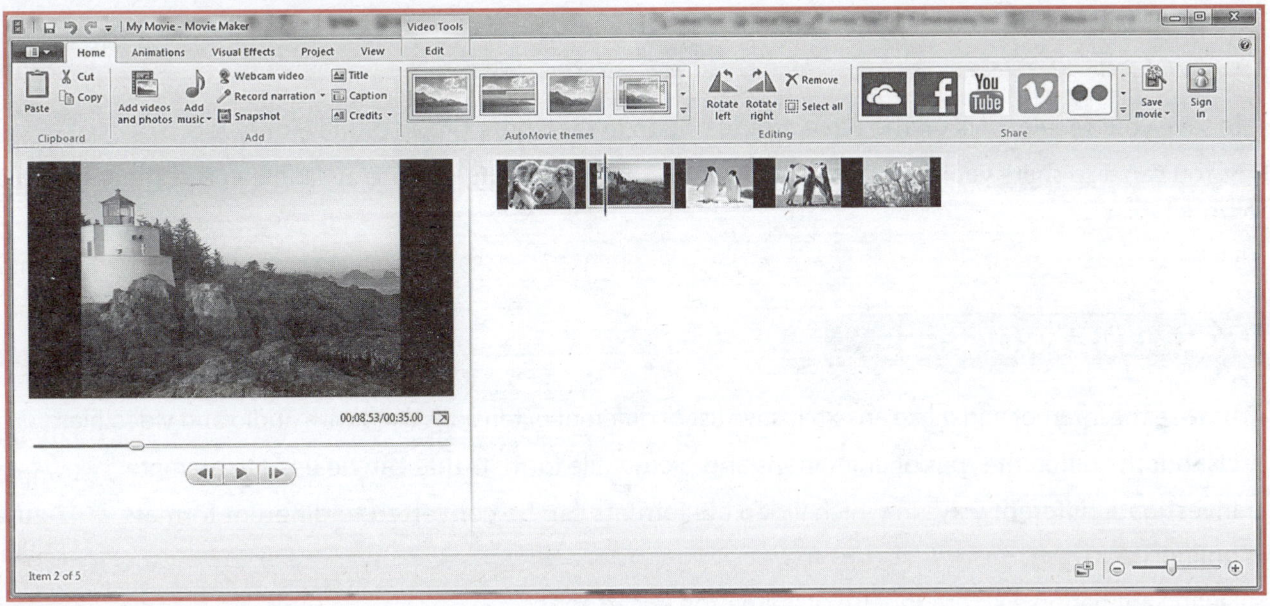

NOTE: After adding the images to the storyboard area, you can change their sequence by just dragging them around.

5. Go to the **Animations** tab. There are two groups in this tab: **Transitions** and **Pan and zoom**. Click on the thumbnail of an image to select it.

   a. To add movement, click the **More** button in the **Pan and zoom** group and select an option in the gallery.

   b. To add transitions, click the **More** button in the **Transitions** group and select an option in the gallery.

NOTE: While applying Transitions and Pan and zoom options, you can see live preview of every option.

6. To give effects to your images, go to the **Effects** group in **Visual Effects** tab and select an option in the gallery.

7. To add music to your movie, click on **Add music** option in the **Add** group of the **Home** tab. The **Add music** dailog box appears. Browse and add the clip of your choice. You will notice an additional tab, **Music Tools Options** appears. Using options in this tab, select the volume of your music clip, its starting and end point and add fading in and fading out effects to it.

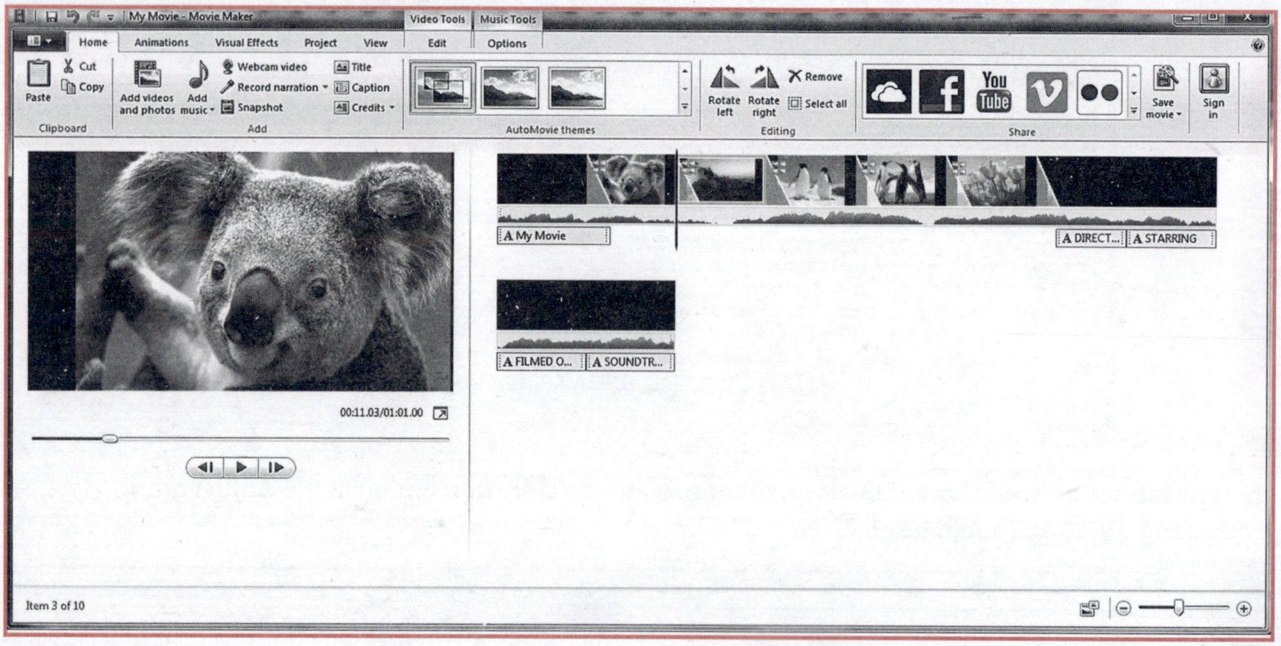

8. To save your movie, click on the **Save movie** option in the **Share** group of the **Home** tab.

NOTE: You can also share your movie on YouTube and Facebook using options available in the **Share** group of the **Home** tab.

CHECK YOUR PROGRESS

A. Browse the Internet and make an exhaustive list of different extensions used with audio and video files.

B. List out the different types of animations and picture file formats that can be used to animate.

C. Investigate different ways in which video file formats can be converted to different formats online. HOTS

D. Define animation. Explore the use of animation in cartoons.

GLOSSARY

- **Animation:** It is the quick display of a sequence of images to create an illusion of movement.
- **Data:** It refers to some number, alphabet, special character or the combination of all.
- **Information:** It is the data that is proccessed and has meaning now.

- **MIDI (Musical Instrument Digital Interface):** It is a communication standard developed for electronic musical instruments and computers.
- **Multimedia:** It is a combination of various types of media such as text, pictures, graphics, audio, video and animation.

NOW YOU KNOW

1. A computer needs a data or information to process and present the output.
2. A data has no meaning at the time of input.
3. The main function of a computer is to convert the meaningless data into useful information.
4. You can create video games, animation movies, add special effects to audio and video in movies using different multimedia tools.
5. Animation makes static presentations come alive.

EXERCISE

FA

A Fill in the blanks.

1. .... is a combination of various types of medias such as text, pictures, graphics, audio, video and animation.
2. Paint and CorelDraw are .... software.
3. The main function of a computer is to convert the meaningless data into useful ....
4. A picture or an image stored in an electronic format is called ....
5. The .... movies are created on the basis of animation.

B Multiple choice questions.

1. A data is a/an ....

   a. text b. number c. image d. All of these

2. An image stored in an electronic format is a ....

a. picture b. presentation c. animation d. graphic

3. MIDI stands for ....

a. Musical Instrument Digital Interface
b. Musical Instrumental Device Interface
c. Musical Instrumental Digital Integrated
d. Musical Instrumental Digital Image

4. Which of the following is the most complex form of data?

a. Video b. Audio c. Text d. None of these

5. .... makes static presentation alive by providing the movements.

a. Audio b. Animation c. Editing d. All of these

C Browse the Internet and find the full form of following type of files. HOTS

1.*.mpg ....
2. *.gif ....
3. *.avi ....
4. *.bmp ....
5. *.swf ....
6. *.wmf ....
7. *.mpf ....
8. *.smf ....
9. *.dxf ....
10. *.mov ....

SA

D Answer the following questions.

1. Define data.
2. What is multimedia? Name any two audio file formats used in multimedia.
3. What is MIDI?
4. What is the file format of an audio file that is recorded using Sound Recorder in Windows 7? HOTS
5. Elucidate animation with examples.

E Answer the following questions in detail.

1. What are the components of multimedia? Enumerate different uses of multimedia?
2. With the help of an example, differentiate between data and information.
3. List out different file formats used in multimedia. Also, explain how various browsers support different file formats. HOTS
4. List out the hardware and software requirements for a multimedia project.
5. Why do we need a computer system with high processor to load a multimedia project? HOTS

Application Based Questions

A. Rashmi and Anubhuti were asked by their school, St. Mary's High School, to create a video for the school's century celebration. However, when they visited the school multimedia lab they found it severely lacking in resources. So, they decided to write to the school administration asking them to buy unavailable and outdated resources. They created a table that had pictures and names of all the necessary resources; but the school asked them to provide more information. Help them fill the table below to submit to the administration.

Component	Name	Function	Multimedia Element	File Format

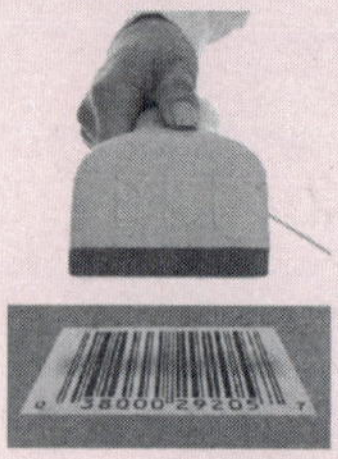				

B. Sanya has five still images of a horse. She wants to create an illusion of a running horse with these images. Can she achieve this? If yes, then suggest a way she can do so. Give steps. **HOTS**

LAB WORK

A. Complete the following activity.

1. Create a movie on the topic 'Application of Multimedia' (in education, entertainment, web designing or business).
2. Draw and apply animations and video effects.
3. Add sound files by recording your narration using microphone.
4. Add an appropriate video clip.
5. Add text wherever necessary (not more than two lines).

B. Using PowerPoint 2007 create a sample presentation and apply different animation and transition effects to it.

TEACHER'S NOTES

1. Conduct a class discussion on different software programs used in different operating system. If possible, show the students some popular multimedia software packages.
2. Ask the students to collect information on history of Walt Disney Animation Studios and make a five minute presentation on Walt Disney Animation Studios' use of animation in movies.

Worksheet 3

SECTION A

Fill in the blanks.

1. By default, a MS Excel 2007 worksheet contains ____________________ sheets.
2. In Excel, number is ____________________ aligned and text is ____________________ aligned.
3. ____________________ are predefined formulas that perform calculations by using the contents of the cell.
4. The ____________________ function is used to print titles on each printed page.
5. The Currency tool is available under ____________________ tab.
6. In MS Excel, there are three types of cell referencing. They are ____________________, ____________________ and ____________________ reference.
7. ____________________ refers to the shape of a network or the network's layout.
8. ____________________ is a graphical browser.
9. ____________________ provides wireless Internet connections for computers, mobile phones and PDA.
10. ____________________ is a combination of various types of medias like, text, picture, graphic, audio video and animation.

SECTION B

Answer the questions briefly.

1. Enumerate different types of charts available in MS Excel 2007.
2. Differentiate between category axis and value axis?
3. Name and draw four network topologies.
4. What factor needs to be considered while choosing a topology?
5. What are the hardware and software requirements to connect a computer system with the Internet?
6. What is the difference between the Internet and the World Wide Web?
7. What are the features of optical fibre cable?
8. List out the applications of the Internet.
9. What is multimedia?
10. Differentiate between data and information using a mathematical example.

12 Programming in C

SNAP RECAP

1. A program is a set of instructions written in a specific language that a computer can understand.
2. An assembler, an interpreter and a compiler are the language translators.
3. Programming languages, such as BASIC, C and C++ are used to develop software programs.
4. A language translator helps in converting a source code to a machine code.

LEARNING OBJECTIVES

You will learn about:

1. Algorithm
2. Flowchart
3. Introduction to C
4. Constant, Variable, Identifier and Keyword
5. Data Types
6. Declaration of a Variable
7. Input–Output functions in C
8. Operators in C
9. Control structures in C
10. Arrays in C
11. Functions in C

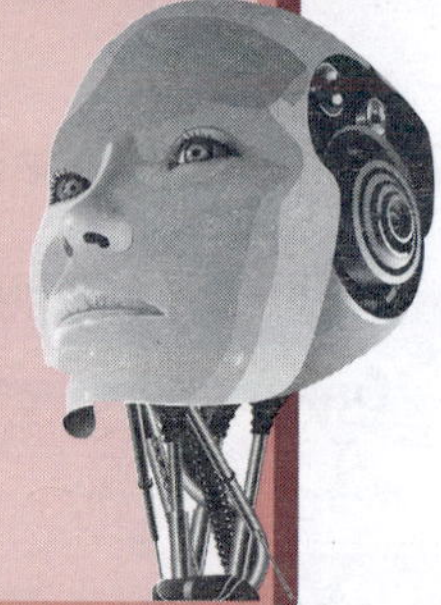

INTRODUCTION

Any work given to a computer requires systematic planning and thinking. As the computer cannot think on its own, the person who is instructing the computer needs to estimate, plan, analyse and give specific and appropriate instructions to the computer so that it can complete the work or solve the problem. The steps involved in this are given below.

1. Analyse the problem.
2. Write down the requirements of solving the problem (the variables, constants and formulae to be used).
3. Write the **algorithm** to solve the problem.
4. Draw a **flowchart** to understand the flow of the program.
5. Convert the algorithm and flowchart to **program statements**.

6. Eliminate the bugs, if any.
7. Test the program by giving suitable values for the correct execution and output.
8. For the record, maintain a document about the complete flow of program to reuse and modify.

Before you get into the structure of a C program, you need to learn about writing algorithms and drawing flowcharts as they both play an important role in designing a program.

ALGORITHM

The step-by-step instruction for solving a problem is called an ***algorithm***. It is written in simple English. Every algorithm begins with the **Start** command and ends with the **Stop** command. *If the programmer uses the programming language commands to write an algorithm, then it is called a* ***pseudocode***.

Rules for writing an algorithm

While writing an algorithm, some rules need to be followed. They are listed here.

- An algorithm should have 'Start' at the beginning and 'Stop' at the end.
- Each instruction has to be written as a separate statement; one below the other.
- An algorithm should have proper input to accept or assign values to process.
- The processing statement should be clear enough to execute without an error.
- An algorithm should produce an output to display the result.

For example: An algorithm to add two numbers:

1. Start
2. Accept two numbers (Number1, Number2)
3. Add the two numbers and store their total in Sum (Sum = Number1 + Number2)
4. Print the numbers and their sum
5. Stop.

CHECK YOUR PROGRESS

A. Write an algorithm to find the simple interest by accepting principal amount, rate of interest and number of years.
(**Hint:** SI = (P x N x R) / 100)

B. Write an algorithm to find the area of a square, if the length of a side is 26.5 cm.

FLOWCHART

The pictorial representation of the steps involved in solving a problem is called a **flowchart**. It depicts the flow of the computational paths as a picture. Each symbol in a flowchart represents a particular operation. Some of the symbols used in flowcharts and their purpose are given in Table 12.1.

Table 12.1 *Symbols used in flowcharts*

Symbol	Name	Purpose
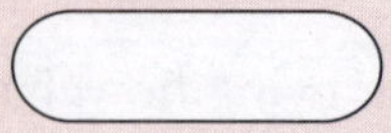	Oval shape (Start/Termination)	It shows the starting and terminating point of a process.
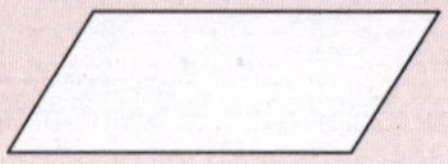	Parallelogram shape (Data)	It shows the input and the output step.
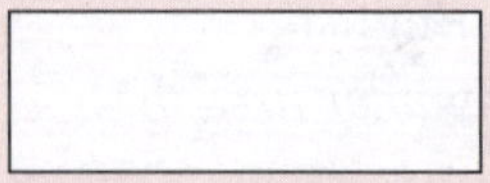	Rectangle shape (Process)	It shows a process or an action step to be carried out.
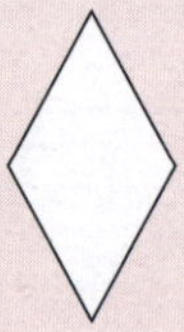	Rhombus shape (Decision)	It is used to check the validity of the data. It indicates that a decision has to be made.
	Circle shape (Connector)	It is used to show the connectivity from one point to another in a process. It is usually labelled with a capital letter A, B, C, and so on, to show the matching jump points.
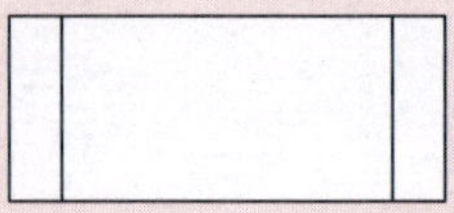	Predefined process (Subroutine)	It is a marker for another process step or some of the process flow steps. It depicts a subprocess.
	Rounded rectangle shape (Alternate process)	It depicts an alternate to the normal process step.
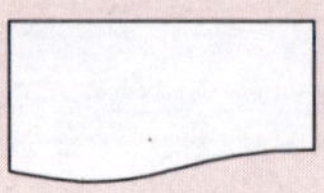	Document	It is used to produce a document.
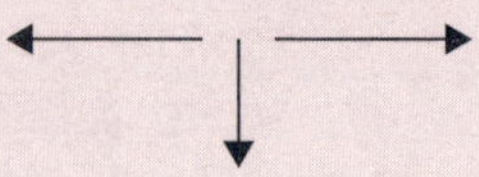	Flow lines with arrow head	It indicates the flow of a program.

Rules for creating a flowchart

Some rules that need to be followed while creating a well-drawn flowchart are listed below.

- Every flowchart must begin with a Start symbol.
- The flow of sequence is generally from the top of the page to the bottom of the page. (This may vary with loop step).
- Arrow-heads must be used on flow lines to specify the flow of direction.
- The connectors should be labelled with same letter to match the previous step with jump points.

For example:

1. To calculate simple interest

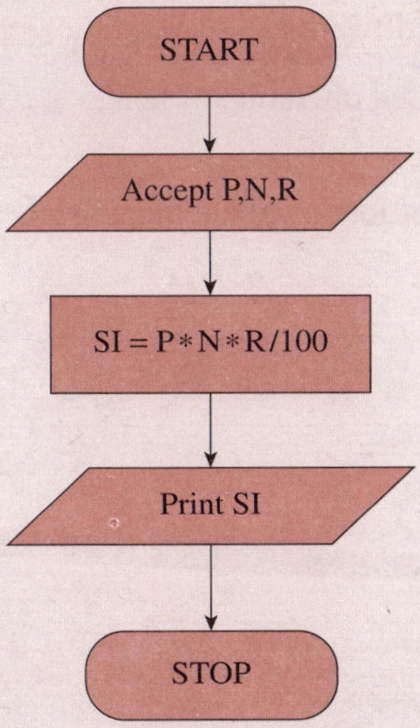

2. To calculate area of a square

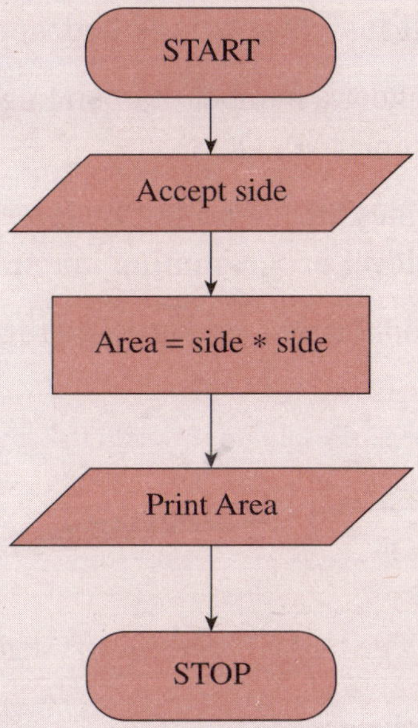

CHECK YOUR PROGRESS

Write the algorithm and draw a flowchart for the following.

A. Accept basic pay, DA, HRA, CCA and calculate gross pay of an employee.
(**Hint:** Gross pay = Basic pay + DA + HRA+ CCA)

B. Accept marks of any five subjects. Calculate and print their total and average.

▶ INTRODUCTION TO C

A **program** is a set of statements which are executed to achieve a specific task. These statements are written using a programming language. The correct syntax or grammar of the language is followed for proper execution. Programming languages are broadly classified into two categories: **low-level programming language** and **high-level programming language**. Machine and symbolic languages are considered as low-level programming languages and the statements written using language similar to English are termed as high-level programming languages.

C is a high-level programming language developed by Dennis Ritchie at Bell Laboratories in 1972. Most of its principles and ideas were taken from the earlier languages like B, BCPL and CPL.

FACT FILE

BCPL stands for Basic Combined Programming Language. B language was a scaled down version of BCPL.

Features of C language

Some of the main features of C programming language are listed below.

- C programs are efficient, fast and highly portable.
- C is well suited for writing both application software and system software.
- C runs under a number of operating systems including the CUI based operating system. For example, MS DOS.
- C combines the features of high-level language and functionality of low-level language. Hence, it is called **middle level programming language**.
- C is a popular general purpose programming language.

FACT FILE

The source code for Unix operating system is coded in C.

STRUCTURE OF A C PROGRAM

A C program comprises different sections. They are:

- Header file section
- Main function
- Declaration section
- Executable part
- Comments (optional)

Header file

A C program depends upon the header files for the definition of functions that are used in a program. The extension of a header file is ***.h**. It has to be declared along with `#include` statement.

Main function

The execution of every C program begins with the `main()` function. Every C program must contain the `main()` function. The program execution starts with the **curly opening brace** ({) and ends with the **curly closing brace** (}). The declaration and executable parts have to be declared between these two braces.

Declaration section

This block declares all the variables that are used in the executable part. The initialisation of variables is also done in this part.

Syntax:

```
<data type> <var> = Value;
```

For example: `int a = 5;`

Executable part

This part of the program contains a single statement or a set of statements depending on the task to be achieved.

Comments

To understand the flow of a program, the programmer can include comments in the program. They are useful for documentation. *Comments are the statements that are placed between the* ***delimiters*** */* and */.* Comment statements are non-executable statements.

For example: </*The following statement is used to find the sum of two numbers */>

Once you write a C program, you must run it through a **C compiler**. The complier will convert the program into an executable code that the computer can execute. There are number of compilers like **Microsoft's Visual C++ environment** and **Borland Turbo C++**. In this book **Turbo C++ compiler** is used (Fig. 12.1).

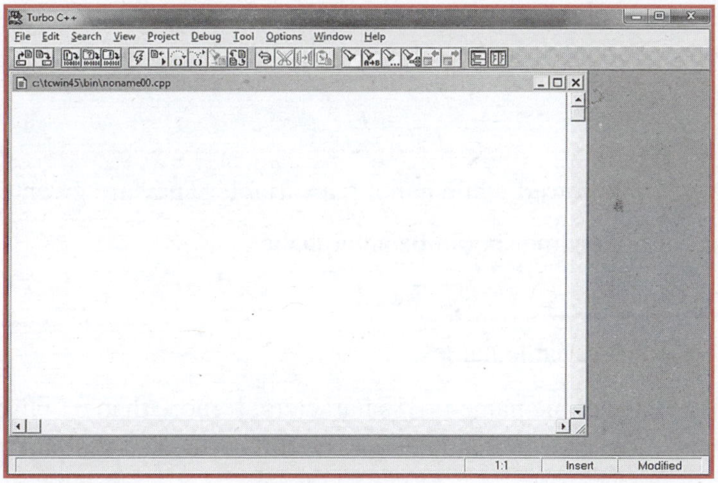

Fig. 12.1 *Turbo C++*

To compile a program in Turbo C++, press **Alt + F9**. If there is any error in the program, it will be listed as a message in the message window. Debug the error and execute the program by pressing **Ctrl + F9**.

NOTE: A C program is saved with ***.C** file extension.

A simple C program

Let us write a simple C program (Fig. 12.2).

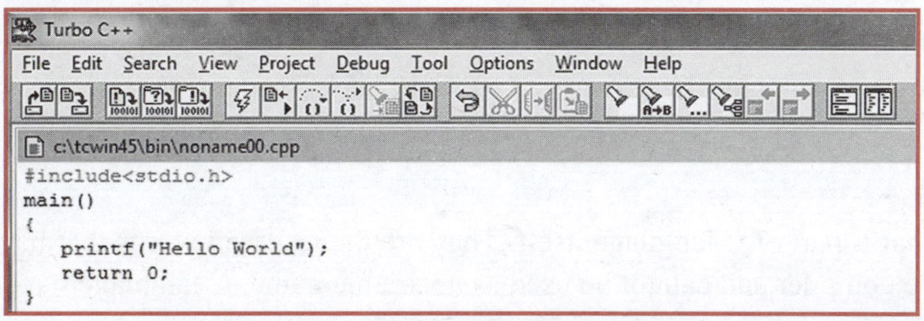

INPUT

Fig. 12.2 *Input*

The output of the code given in Figure 12.2 is shown in Figure 12.3.

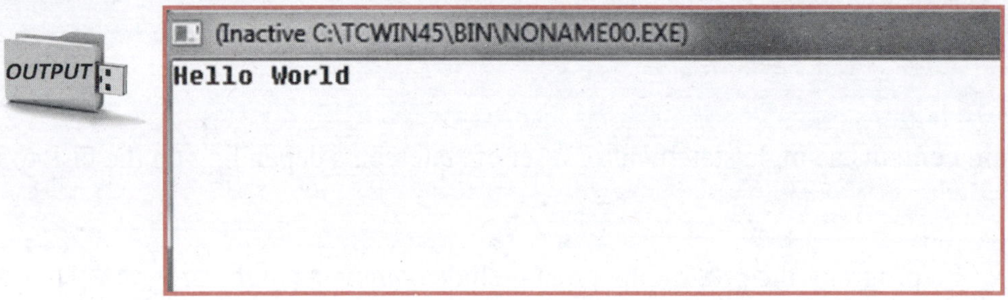

Fig. 12.3 *Output*

NOTE: C language is a case sensitive language.

▶ C VARIABLE

A variable is an entity that may change its value. In a program, the results of the processing statements are stored in the computer's memory. To make use of these values or to retrieve them we give names to these memory locations. These names are called **variables**. Variables are used for storing data. For example, `a = 5`.

Rules for naming a variable

There are some rules that need to be followed while naming a variable. They are given below.

- The first character of a variable name should be an alphabet.
- No special character, except underscore, is allowed.
- C keywords cannot be used as variable names.
- The maximum length of the variable name is 31 characters. If more than 31 characters are used to define a variable, the character (s) after the 31st character will be truncated. You will not get an error message.

NOTE: Identifier is a symbolic and unique name given to C entities to identify them during the execution of a program. Identifiers are user-defined names, consisting of a sequence of letters and digits but name of an identifier should begin with a letter. Like a variable name, only underscore can be used in an identifier.

▶ C CONSTANT

A number or a string is called C constant. *Constants are the values assigned to a variable used in a program.* C constants are classified into two types. They are:

- **Numeric constants,** for example, 4, 80, –30, 0.45, etc.
- **String constants,** for example, "F", "Venue", "10/12/12", 54, 7th street, etc.

▶ C KEYWORD

A keyword is a word that is part of C language itself. They are the reserved words that have predefined meaning assigned to them by the compiler and cannot be used as a variable name. C language have 32 keywords. They are given in Table 12.2.

Table 12.2 *C keywords*

Char	Signed	Break	For
Auto	Const	Sizeof	Case
If	Extern	Double	Struct
Continue	Goto	Register	Enum
Typedef	Default	Return	Static
Float	Union	Do	Switch
Volatile	Int	Unsigned	Else
While	Long	Void	Short

CHECK YOUR PROGRESS

A. Identify whether the following variable names are valid or not.

1. Hello 2. 1stname 3. Name.surname
4. Int 5. Sal90

B. How are constants different from variables? Explain.

C. Find out what is the meaning of the following keywords. HOTS

1. Typedef 2. Union 3. Register
4. Static 5. Void

D. With the help of your school library and the Internet, write a short note on identifiers.

DATA TYPES

It is necessary to declare a variable in C language because you need to explain to the computer about the type of data you store in the variable. Data type help the computer to find out the type of value that will be stored in the variable, operations that can be done on values of that type, and the way values of that type can be stored. The fundamental data types in C language are given in Table 12.3.

Table 12.3 *Data types in C*

Name	Description	Size	Range
Char	Character or small integer	1 byte	Signed: –128 to 127 Unsigned: 0 to 255
Short or Int	Short integer	2 bytes	Signed: –32768 to 32767 Unsigned: 0 to 65535
Long	Long integer	4 bytes	Signed: –2147483648 to 2147483647 Unsigned: 0 to 4294967295
Boolean	Boolean value	1 byte	True or False
Float	Floating point number	4 bytes	+/– 3.4e +/– 38 (~7 digits)
Double	Double precision floating point number	8 bytes	+/– 1.7e +/– 308 (~15 digits)
Long Double	Long double precision floating point number	8 bytes	+/– 1.7e +/– 308 (~15 digits)

Format descriptor

Format descriptors define how the input or output data is to be represented and interpreted internally. These are the conversion specifications that are also called **control variables**. These control variables are enclosed within double quotes. Some of them are given in Table 12.4.

Table 12.4 *Format descriptors in C*

Format Descriptor	Meaning
%d	Print and scan as signed decimal integer
%u	Print and scan as unsigned decimal integer
%s	Print and scan as a string
%f	Print and scan as a float pointing number
%e	Print and scan as scientific notation
%c	Print and scan as a character
%lf	Print and scan as double (long float)

Escape sequence

Escape sequences are special strings used to control the output generated from a C program on the monitor or on any other output device. When a **backslash (\)** is used in front of a selected group of characters, the compiler tells the computer to escape from the way these characters would normally be interpreted. Some of the common escape sequences are given in Table 12.5.

Table 12.5 *Escape sequences in C*

Escape Sequence	Meaning
\n	To start a newline
\t	To start in next horizontal tab
\v	To start in next vertical tab
\a	To produce beep sound
\f	To start on next page (formfeed)
\r	Carriage return
\\	To print backslash
\’	To print single quote
\”	To print double quote

▶ DECLARING A VARIABLE

Declaration explains to the computer the type of data to be used in a program. To declare a variable is to specify the data type followed by a valid variable name.

Syntax:

```
Data type variablename;
```

For example:

- `int a;` *where,* `a` *is an integer variable*
- `char c;` *where,* `c` *is of character data type*

- `char snam[20];` *where,* `snam` *is a character string of length 20*
- `float esal;` *where,* `esal` *is a floating point variable*
- `double exp;` *where,* `exp` *is a double variable*

INPUT AND OUTPUT FUNCTIONS

There is no keyword for the purpose of input and output in C language. Only **library functions** are used for input and output. There are plenty of library functions available in C. These files are classified into various groups and each group is kept in the header file.

The input/output functions are kept in the header file called **stdio.h (standard input output header file). scanf**, **printf**, **getchar**, **putchar** and **puts** functions are available in stdio.h. Similarly, the mathematical functions are in **math.h** and string functions are in **string.h**. Hence, whenever you want to use these library functions it is necessary to include the corresponding header file at the beginning of the C program.

Scanf( ) function

The **scanf**( ) function is an important input function that reads input from stdio.h file and stores the data in the other arguments. It can be used to accept a set of values through a keyboard.

Syntax:

```
scanf("Format Descriptors", address of the variables);
```

For example:

```
scanf("%d", &a);

scanf("%s","%d", "%c", a, &b, &c);
```

NOTE: %d indicates that the variable `<a>` is an integer variable. The numeric variable is preceded by an ampersand symbol (`&`), which refers to the address of the variable.

printf( ) function

The **printf**( ) function is one of the most important and frequently used function in C. It is used to print any combination of string, number and character on the screen or on a paper. It prints the output according to the format and other arguments passed to printf( ). The syntax for printf( ) function is:

Syntax:

```
printf("escape sequences format descriptors", variable name);
```

For example:

```
printf("\n %d %c", a, c);

printf("a=%d, b=%d", a, b);
```

where, `a` is a numeric variable and `c` is a character variable.

Let us write a simple program using scanf() and printf() function. The following program (Fig. 12.4) accepts the student name, student number and class from the user and displays it (Fig. 12.5).

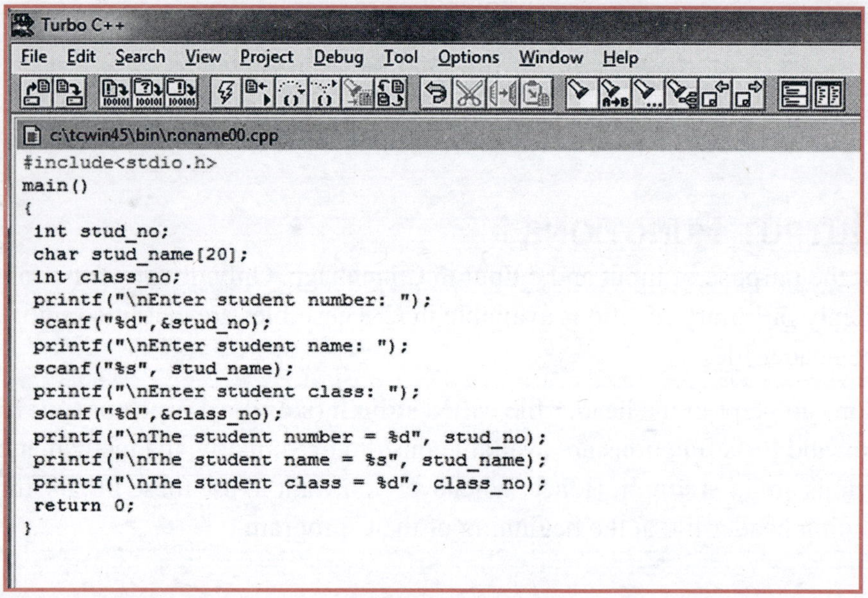

Fig. 12.4 *Input*

Fig. 12.5 *Output*

CHECK YOUR PROGRESS

A. Write a program in C to print any five idioms.

B. Write a program in C to print any five keywords and their purpose.

C. Find the errors in the following C program. Explain the errors and rewrite the code.

```
#include <stdio.h>
main()
{
  int a
  printf("Enter an integer\n");
  scanf("d%", &a);
  printf("Integer that you have entered is %d\n", a);
  return;
}
```

D. Make a list of commonly used library functions in C.

▶ OPERATORS

An operator is a symbol that tells the compiler to perform specific operations required for processing. It indicates an operation to be performed on data to yield a new value. C provides operators such as:

- Arithmetic operator
- Assignment operator
- Relational operator
- Logical operator
- Ternary/Conditional operator
- Increment and Decrement operator
- Sizeof operator

Arithmetic operator

An arithmetic operator is used for numerical calculations between two constant values or variables in which the values are stored. Different arithmetic operators that are used in C language are given in Table 12.6.

Table 12.6 *Arithmetic operators in C*

Operator	Name and Purpose
+	Addition operator to add
–	Subtraction operator to subtract
*	Multiplication operator to multiply
/	Division operator to get the quotient
%	Modulus operator to get the remainder

For example: To accept two numbers from the user and display their sum, write the code as shown in Figure 12.6. The output is given in Figure 12.7.

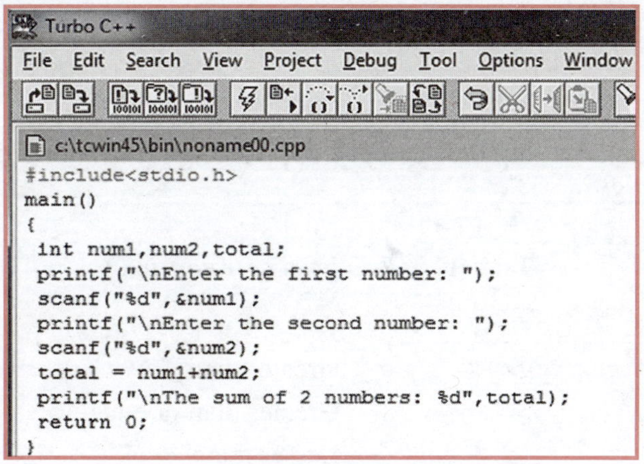


```
#include<stdio.h>
main()
{
 int num1,num2,total;
 printf("\nEnter the first number: ");
 scanf("%d",&num1);
 printf("\nEnter the second number: ");
 scanf("%d",&num2);
 total = num1+num2;
 printf("\nThe sum of 2 numbers: %d",total);
 return 0;
}
```

INPUT

Fig. 12.6 *Input*

OUTPUT

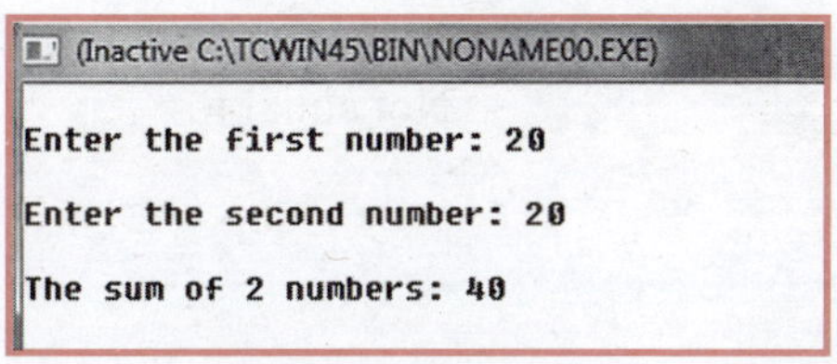

Fig. 12.7 *Output*

CHECK YOUR PROGRESS

Write the following C programs using arithmetic operators.

A. To print the difference and product of two numbers.

B. To print the area of a circle by accepting radius using scanf( ) function.

C. To print the quotient and remainder of a number.

D. To print the perimeter of a rectangle by accepting the length and breadth from the user.

Assignment operator

An assignment operator (=) is used to assign a value, a variable or an expression to a variable in a program. The assignment operators used in C are given in Table 12.7.

Table 12.7 *Assignment operators in C*

Operator	Name	Purpose
=	Assignment	To assign a value from right side to left
+=	Add AND assignment	To add right operand to left and assign the result to left operand
−=	Subtract AND assignment	To subtract right operand from left and assign the result to left operand
*=	Multiply AND assignment	To multiply right operand to the left and assign the result to left operand
/=	Divide AND assignment	To multiply right operand from the left and assign the result to left operand
%=	Modulus AND assignment	To find the modulus using two operands and assign the result to left operand

For example:

```
a = 5;          b = a;
a = a+5;   or      a+ = 5;
a = a-5;   or      a- = 5;
```

Relational operator

A relational operator provides the relationship between two expressions. If the condition is True, it returns the value 1, else it will return value 0 (Table 12.8).

Table 12.8 *Relational operators in C*

Operator	Purpose
>	Greater than
>=	Greater than or equal to
<	Lesser than
<=	Lesser than or equal to
==	Equal to
!=	Not equal to

For example:

```
printf(a>b);
```

Logical operator

A logical operator is used to combine two expressions containing relational operators. The logical operators used in C are given in Table 12.9.

Table 12.9 *Logical operators in C*

Operator	Name	Purpose
&&	AND	Returns true if both operands have non-zero value.
||	OR	Returns true if any of the two operands have non-zero value.
!	NOT	Negates the state of its operand.

For example:

```
printf("\n" a>b && a>c);
```

Ternary operator

It is an operator operating on three operands. It is a shortcut to an `if else` statement that you will learn later in the chapter. It is also called **conditional operator**. The `?:` operator returns one of two values depending on the result of an expression.

Syntax:

```
Expression 1 (condition) ? Expression 2 : Expression 3
```

In above statement, if expression 1 evaluates to true, then expression 2 is evaluated and if expression 1 evaluates to false, then expression 3 is evaluated.

For example:

```
res=(a>b ? a : b);
```

where, if the condition `a>b` *is true, then the* `res` *variable stores the value* `a` *and if the condition is false, it stores the value* `b`.

Sizeof operator

The sizeof operator is used to calculate the size of any data type. It is measured in the number of bytes required to represent the type.

For example:

`printf("\n%d",, sizeof(a));` *where,* `a` *is an integer variable*

`printf("\n %d", sizeof(2015);` *where,* `2015` *is a numeric constant*

`printf("\n%d", sizeof("welcome");` *where,* `welcome` *is a string constant*

`printf("\n%d",sizeof(float));` *where,* `float` *is a data type used in C*

Increment / Decrement operator

The increment operator ++ adds 1 to its operand. The decrement operator -- subtracts 1 from its operand. `a = a + 1;` is the same as `a++;` and `a=a-1;` is the same as `a--`.

Both the increment and decrement operator can either precede or follow the operand.

For example:

```
a = a+1;
```

can be written as

`++a; (prefix)` *or as*

`a++; (postfix)`

NOTE: If you are using prefix form then increment or decrement will be done before rest of the expression is evaluated and if you are using postfix form then increment or decrement will be done after the complete expression is evaluated.

For example: To increment a number in prefix and postfix form, the input (Fig. 12.8) and the corresponding output (Fig. 12.9) are given here.

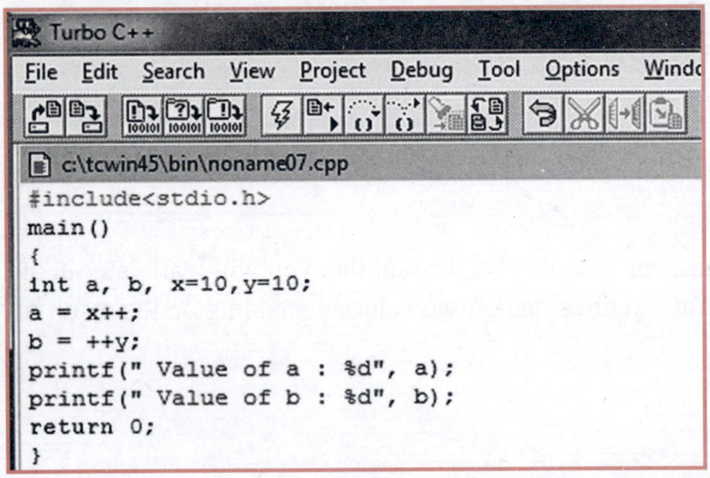

Fig. 12.8 *Input*

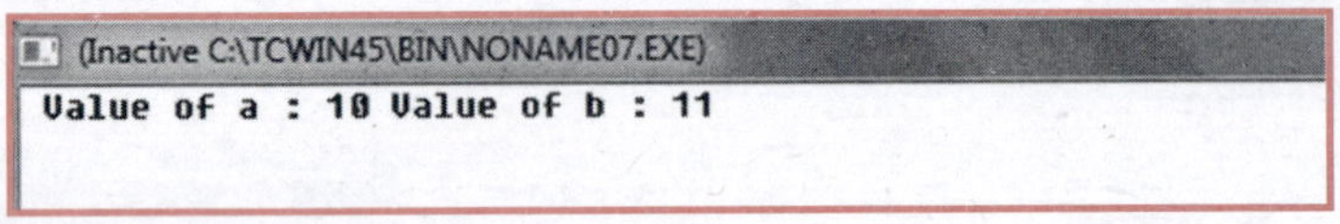

Fig. 12.9 *Output*

ACTIVITY

A. To use different assignment operators in a C program. Find out the output.

```
#include <stdio.h>
main()
{
   int a = 21;
   int c;
   c =  a;
   printf("Line 1 - =  Operator Example, Value of c = %d\n", c );
   c +=  a;
   printf("Line 2 - += Operator Example, Value of c = %d\n", c );
   c -=  a;
   printf("Line 3 - -= Operator Example, Value of c = %d\n", c );
   c *=  a;
   printf("Line 4 - *= Operator Example, Value of c = %d\n", c );
   c /=  a;
   printf("Line 5 - /= Operator Example, Value of c = %d\n", c );
   c  = 200;
   c %=  a;
```

```
    printf("Line 6 - %= Operator Example, Value of c = %d\n", c );
    c <<=  2;
    printf("Line 7 - <<= Operator Example, Value of c = %d\n", c );
    c >>=  2;
    printf("Line 8 - >>= Operator Example, Value of c = %d\n", c );
    c &=  2;
    printf("Line 9 - &= Operator Example, Value of c = %d\n", c );
    c ^=  2;
    printf("Line 10 - ^= Operator Example, Value of c = %d\n", c );
    c |=  2;
    printf("Line 11 - |= Operator Example, Value of c = %d\n", c );
    return 0;
}
```

B. To use sizeof and ternary operator in a C program. Find out the output.

```
#include <stdio.h>
main()
{
    int a = 4;
    short b;
    double c;
 /* example of sizeof operator */
    printf("Line 1 - Size of variable a = %d\n", sizeof(a) );
    printf("Line 2 - Size of variable b = %d\n", sizeof(b) );
    printf("Line 3 - Size of variable c = %d\n", sizeof(c) );
 /* example of ternary operator */
    a = 10;
    b = (a == 1) ? 20: 30;
    printf( "Value of b is %d\n", b );
    b = (a == 10) ? 20: 30;
    printf( "Value of b is %d\n", b );
    return 0;
}
```

CHECK YOUR PROGRESS

A. Write the equivalent C statement using increment/decrement/assignment operator for the following.

1. m1 = m1+1;
2. age = age –1;
3. a = a – b;
4. n = n*5;

B. Write a C program for the following.

1. To add three numbers.
2. Using the ternary operator print the greater of two numbers.
3. Find the sum, difference and product of two numbers.
4. Accept radius of a circle and calculate its area.
5. Accept a number. Calculate and print its square and cube.

▶ CONTROL STRUCTURES

In general, computer carry out the instruction in sequential order starting from first statement to last statement. This is the normal flow of control, from top to bottom. C language possesses decision making capabilities and supports statements known as **control statements** or **decision making statements**. It uses the logical expression. It controls the order of execution and changes the control flow in a program.

C supports the following control structure:

- if statement
- switch statement
- goto statement.

If statement

The `if statement` is a decision making statement used to control the flow of execution. It is a two-way decision statement and is used with an expression.

Syntax:

```
if(condition)
{
    Statement/s to be executed if the condition is true
}
```

This control structure checks for a condition. If the condition is true, then the statement or a set of statements is/are executed and move to the next statement. If the condition is false then it skips the statement.

For example: To accept a number from the user and check whether it is 1 or not, write the code as shown in Figure 12.10. The output is given in Figure 12.11.

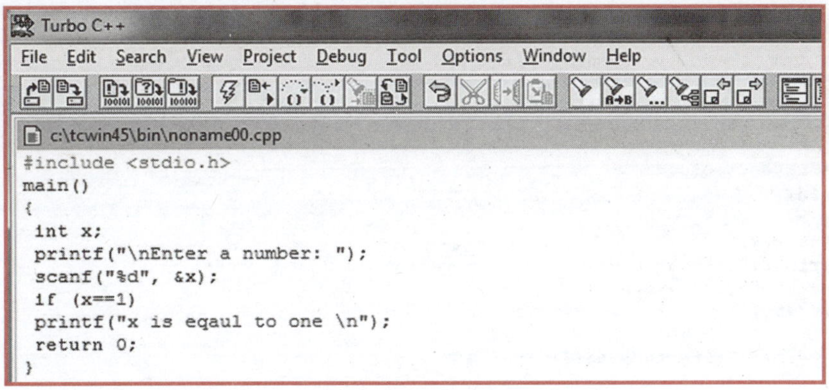

Fig. 12.10 *Input*

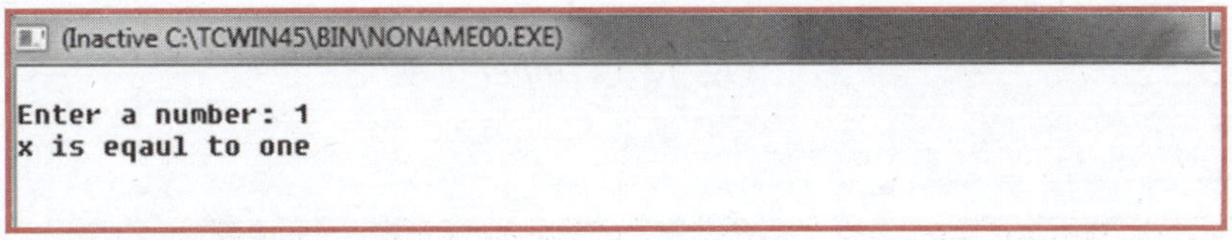

Fig. 12.11 *Output*

If else statement

The `if else` statement is an extension of the simple `if` statement. When the condition in `if` statement evaluates to false, it would be necessary to execute some code instead of leaving it to the next statement. In such a case, `else` statement is used to execute another statement or a set of statements.

Syntax:

```
if(condition)
{
true - block statement/s
}
else
{
false - block statement/s
}
```

If the condition is true then the true–block statements are executed otherwise the false–block statements are executed.

For example: To accept two numbers from the user and check which is the greater number, write the code as shown in Figure 12.12. The output is given in Figure 12.13.

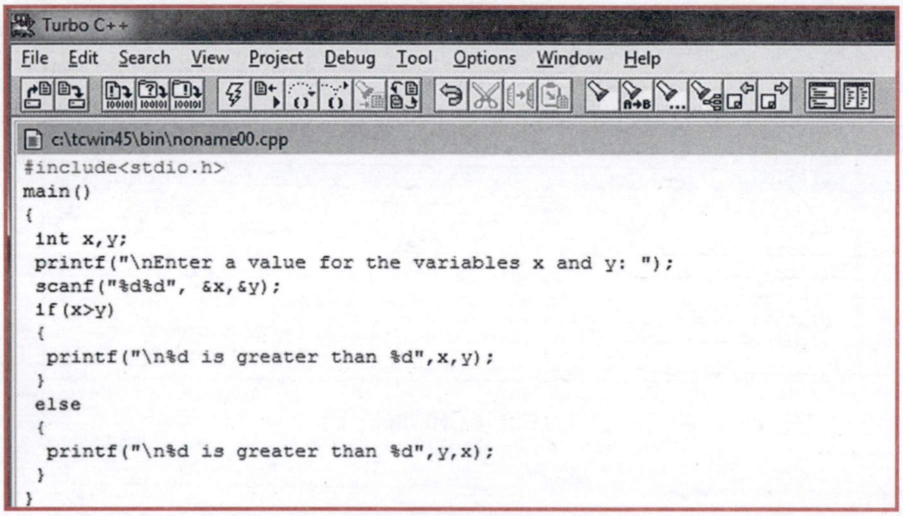


```
#include<stdio.h>
main()
{
 int x,y;
 printf("\nEnter a value for the variables x and y: ");
 scanf("%d%d", &x,&y);
 if(x>y)
 {
  printf("\n%d is greater than %d",x,y);
 }
 else
 {
  printf("\n%d is greater than %d",y,x);
 }
}
```

Fig. 12.12 *Input*

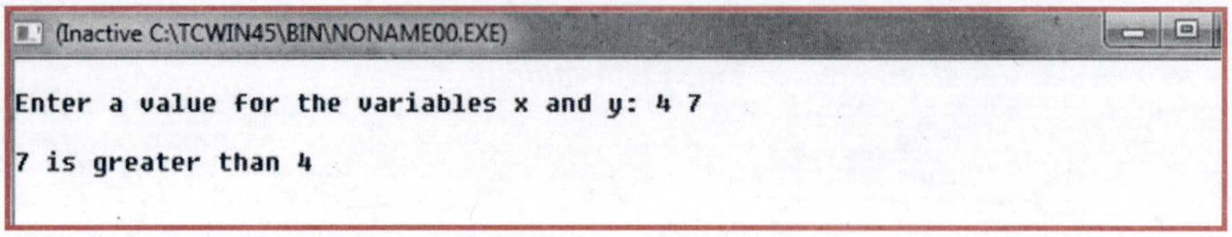


```
Enter a value for the variables x and y: 4 7

7 is greater than 4
```

Fig. 12.13 *Output*

If else if statement

This statement is used to check for the multiple conditions.

Syntax:

```
if(condition)
{
Statement/s;
}
elseif(condition)
{
Statement(s);
}
else
{
Statement(s);
}
```

For example: To accept a number from the user and check whether it is a positive or a negative number, write the code as shown in Figure 12.14. The output is given in Figure 12.15.

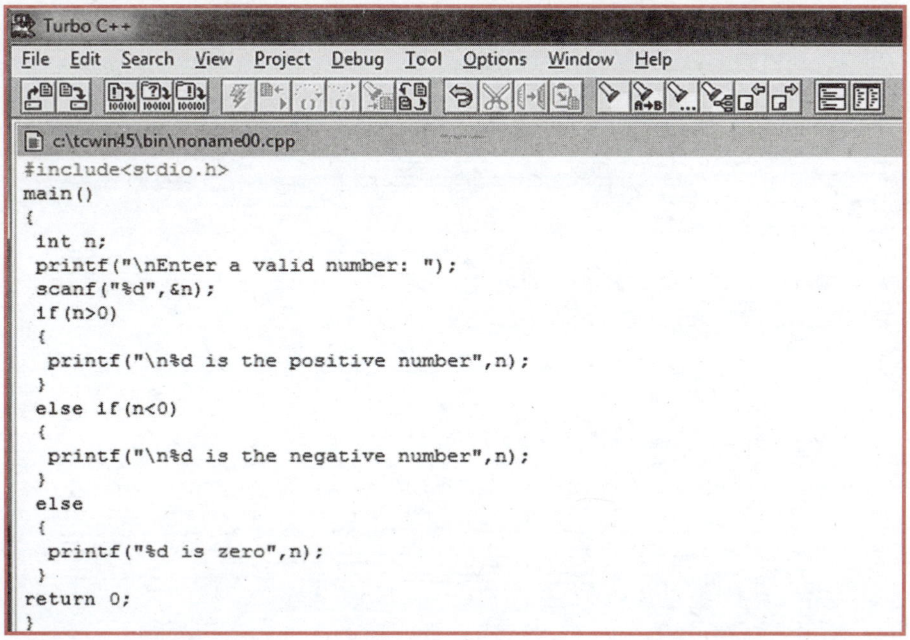

Fig. 12.14 *Input*

Fig. 12.15 *Output*

Nested if statements

An `if` statement within another `if` statement is called `nested if` statement.

Syntax:

```
if(condition 1)
 {
      /* Executes when condition 1 is true */
      if(condition 2)
      {
           /* Executes when condition 2 is true */
      }
 }
```

ACTIVITY

To write a nested C source code program. Find out the output.

```
#include <stdio.h>
main ()
{
    int a = 10;
    int b = 20;
    if( a == 10 )
    {
        if( b == 20 )
        {
            printf("Value of a is 10 and b is 20\n" );
        }
    }
    printf("Exact value of a is : %d\n", a );
    printf("Exact value of b is : %d\n", b );
    return 0;
}
```

Switch statement

The `switch` and `case` statements help control complex conditional and branching operations. It is used to make a decision between many alternatives.

The switch variable can either be an integer or a character data type. The value in the case label can either be a numeric or a character constant. The switch variable is evaluated and checks whether the case label constant is equal to that of the switch variable or expression. If any of the case label matches, the statement within the case is executed and control is transferred to the statements after the switch body using break statement. If no such case value matches, the control transfers to the default statement if any.

NOTE: Default is optional.

Syntax:

```
switch(expression/variable)
 {
 case value1:
     Statement/s;
     break;
```

```
case value 2:
    Statement/s;
    break;
default:
    Statement/s;
break;
}
```

For example: To accept a grade from the user and display an appropriate response, write the code as shown in Figure 12.16. The output is given in Figure 12.17.

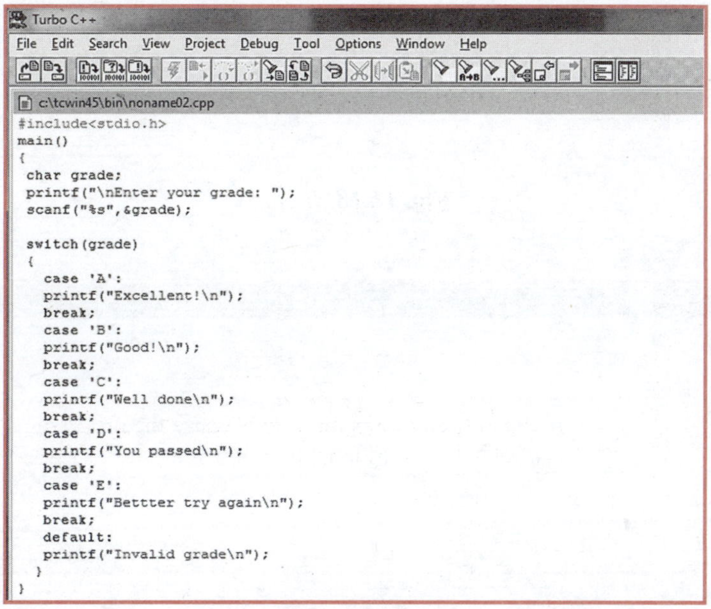

Fig. 12.16 *Input*

Fig. 12.17 *Output*

GOTO statement

A goto statement in C provides an unconditional jump from the goto line to a labelled statement in the same function block.

Syntax:

```
goto label;
.
.
.
label: statement;
```

For example: Write the code as given in Figure 12.18. The output is shown in Figure 12.19.

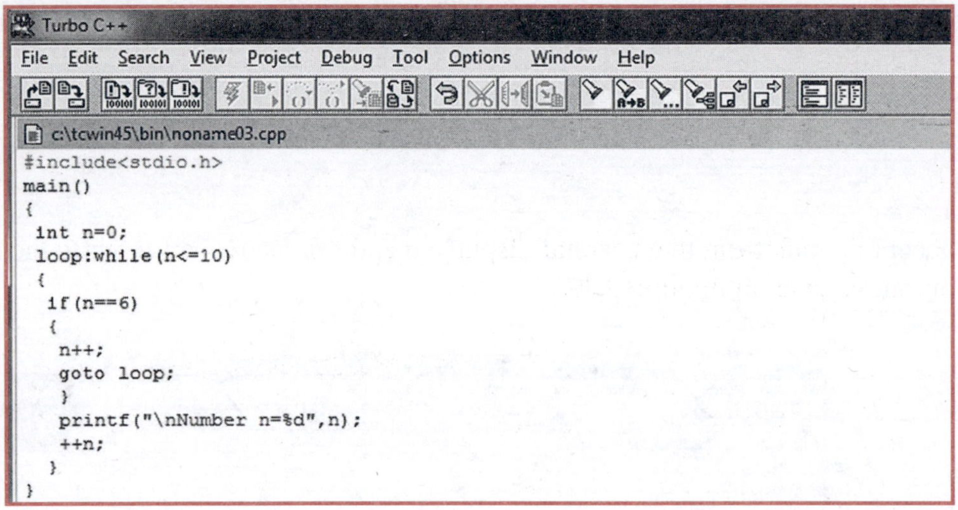

Fig. 12.18 *Input*

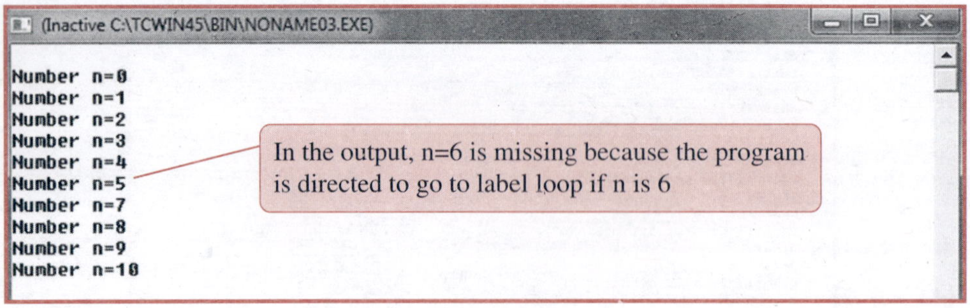

Fig. 12.19 *Output*

CHECK YOUR PROGRESS

A. Write a program in C programming language to:

1. Find the greatest of three numbers.
2. Accept a number and find whether it is divisible by 5.
3. Accept class and print the message according to the category given in the right side using `if else if` statement if the class is between:
   a. 1–5: Primary School
   b. 6–8: Middle School
   c. 9–10: High School
   d. 11–12: Senior Secondary School

B. Using `switch` case, find the square and cube of a number. Accept a number to find the square and cube. Accept a character. If the character variable is 's', then find the square of the number and if it is 'c', then find the cube of the number. If it is other than 's' and 'c' print a message that character entered is invalid.

▶ Loop Structures

In general, we may have to repeat certain small tasks. In programming, repeating some tasks until a condition is satisfied is called **looping**. In C there are three loop structures available. They are:

- while loop
- do while loop
- for next loop

while loop

The `while` loop repeats a statement(s) until the given condition proves false.

Syntax:

```
while(condition)
{
     Statement/s;
}
```

The `while` loop checks the condition and if the condition is false at the beginning, the loop will not execute even once.

FACT FILE

In `while` and `do while` loop, it is necessary to include the increment or decrement step along with the other processing statements. Otherwise, it the loop will become an indefinite loop.

For example: To print numbers from 10 to 1 using while loop, write the code as shown in Figure 12.20. The output is given in Figure 12.21.

INPUT

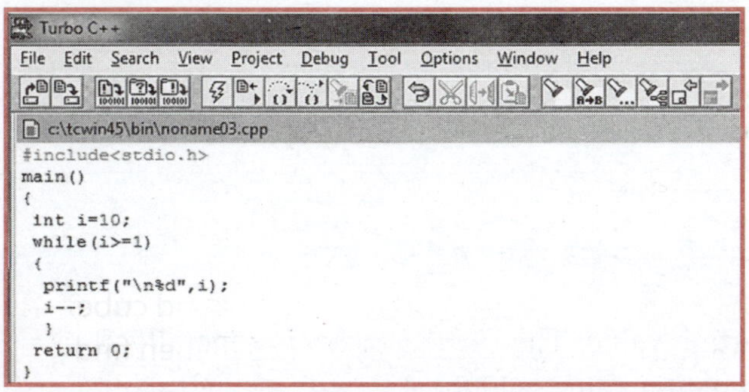

Fig. 12.20 *Input*

OUTPUT

Fig. 12.21 *Output*

do while Loop

This is similar to the `while` loop except for the fact that the condition occurs at the end of the loop body, unlike in `while` loop where the condition is given at the beginning. As the loop checks the condition only at the end of the loop, the statements are executed at least once. The condition then checks the data and loops back to read again.

Syntax:

```
do
{
    Statement/s;
} while(condition);
```

For example: To print the numbers from 1 to 10 using do while loop, write the code as shown in Figure 12.22. The output is given in Figure 12.23.

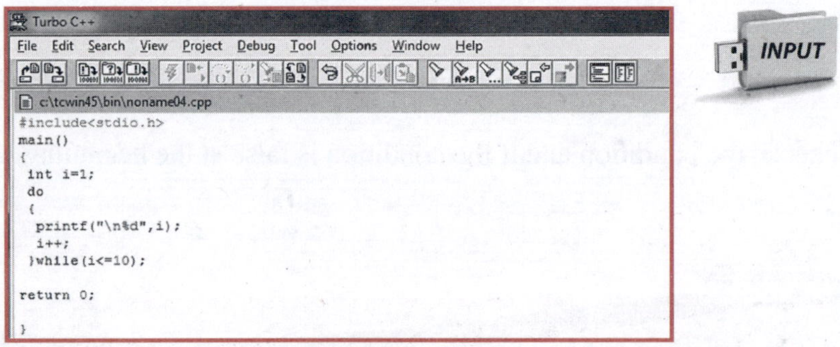

Fig. 12.22 *Input*

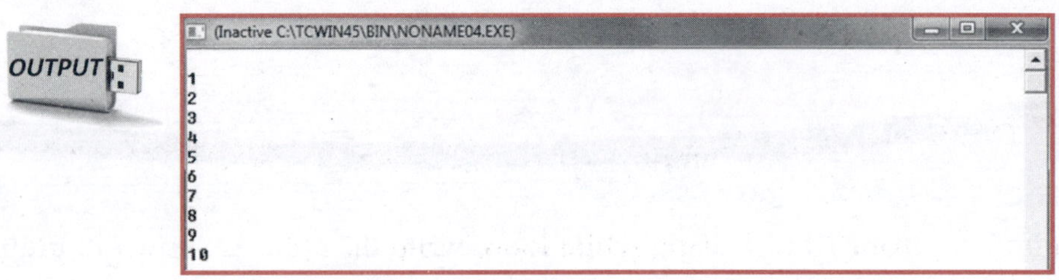

Fig. 12.23 *Output*

for Loop

It is a counter loop. `for` loop allows automatic initialisation to a counter variable.

Syntax:

```
For(initialization, condition, increment/decrement)
{
    Statement/s;
}
```

The `initialization` is used to set a counter variable to its starting value. The `condition` is generally a relational statement that checks the counter variable against a termination value, and the `increment/decrement` increments/decrements the counter value. The loop repeats until the condition becomes false.

For example: To print the numbers from 10 to 20 using `for` loop, write the code as shown in Figure 12.24. The output is given in Figure 12.25.

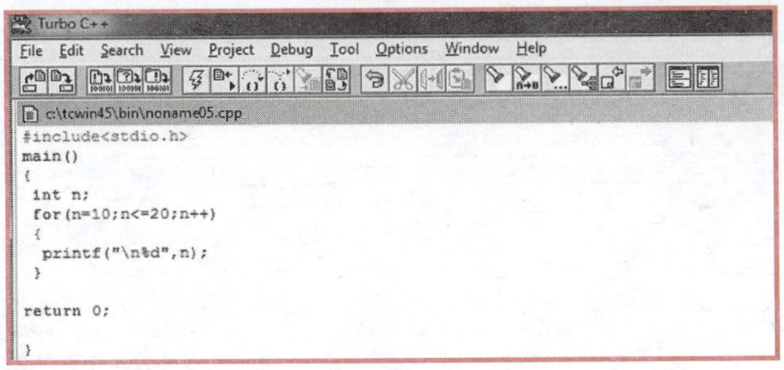

Fig. 12.24 *Input*

Fig. 12.25 *Ouput*

Break and Continue statements in a loop

- ***Break:*** To exit a loop before the condition is satisfied, you can use the `break` statement. This is useful as it stops running the loop because a condition, other than the loop end condition, has been met.
- ***Continue:*** It is possible to skip the rest of the commands in an active loop and start from the first line by giving `continue` statement in the middle. This instructs the program to ignore the commands given after `continue` and take the control back to the beginning of the loop.

For example: Write the code as given in Figure 12.26. The output (Fig. 12.27) is also given.

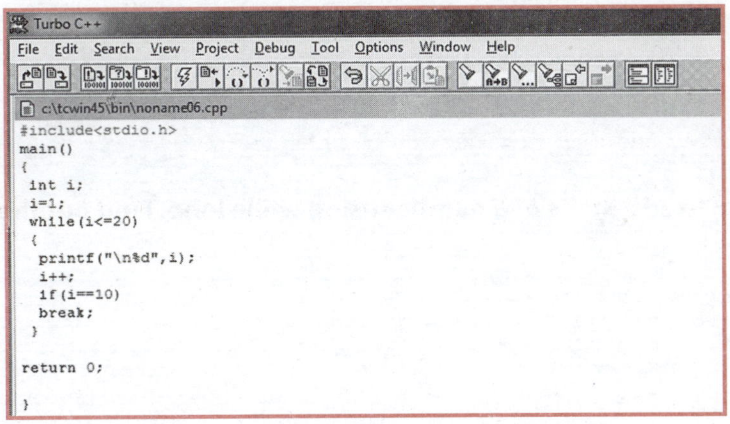

Fig. 12.26 *Input*

Fig. 12.27 *Output*

ACTIVITY

A. To write a C program to find HCF or GCD using while loop. Find out the output.

```
#include<stdio.h>
main()
{
    int num1,num2;

    printf("Enter two integers: ");
    scanf("%d %d",&num1,&num2);
    printf("HCF of %d and %d is ",num1 , num2);

    while(num1!=num2)
    {
        if(num1>num2)
            num1-=num2;
        else
            num2-=num1;
    }

    printf("%d",num1);

    return 0;
}
```

B. To write a C program to add digits of a number using while loop. Find out the output.

```
#include <stdio.h>
main()
{
    int n, sum = 0, remainder;
    printf("Enter an integer\n");
    scanf("%d",&n);

    while(n != 0)
    {
        remainder = n % 10;
        sum = sum + remainder;
```

```
    n = n / 10;
  }
  printf("Sum of digits of entered number = %d\n",sum);
  return 0;
}
```

C. To write a C program to find factorial using for loop. Find out the output.

```
#include <stdio.h>
main()
{
  int c, n, fact = 1;
  printf("Enter a number to calculate it's factorial\n");
  scanf("%d", &n);
  for (c = 1; c <= n; c++)
    fact = fact * c;
  printf("Factorial of %d = %d\n", n, fact);
  return 0;
}
```

D. To write a C program to reverse numbers. Find out the output.

```
#include <stdio.h>
main()
{
   int n, reverse = 0;

   printf("Enter a number to reverse\n");
   scanf("%d",&n);

   while (n != 0)
   {
      reverse = reverse * 10;
      reverse = reverse + n%10;
      n = n/10;
   }
   printf("Reverse of entered number is = %d\n", reverse);

   return 0;
}
```

▶ ARRAYS

C language provides a data structure called the **array**, which can store a fixed-size sequential collection of elements of the same type. Instead of declaring individual variables you can declare one array variable if they all belong to same data type. Each element in the array variable can be indicated by an **index**. The lowest address corresponds to the first element and the highest address corresponds to the last element.

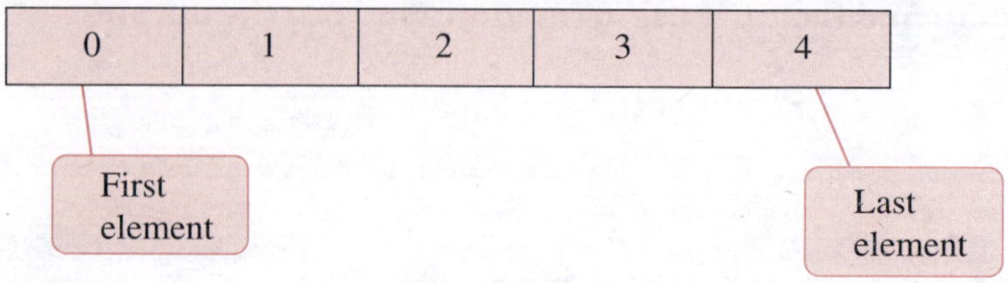

Arrays are of three types. They are:

- Single dimensional array
- Two dimensional array
- Multi-dimensional array

Single dimensional array

Arrays that are specified by a single subscript are called single dimensional array. To declare an array in C, specify the type of the element and number of elements required by an array.

Syntax:

```
Data type array variablename[number of elements];
```

The number of elements in an array is the **array size**. Array size must be an integer constant greater than zero.

For example: To declare an array named bonus with 10 elements, you write:

```
float bonus[10];
```

This will allocate 10 consecutive locations for the float variable bonus.

NOTE: You can initialise array in C either one by one.
For example:

```
Bonus[0]=2000;

Bonus[1]=1500;

Bonus[2]=2000;

Bonus[3]=1500;

Bonus[4]=2000;
```

Or, by using a single statement. For example,

```
Bonus[5] = {2000,1500,2000,1500,2000};
```

FACT FILE

To write a separate statement to accept values for each and every element in an array is time consuming. As it is repetition, it is better to use *for* loop to accept the values for the elements in an array.

For example: To input marks of n number of subjects and print their total. The input (Fig. 12.28) and output (Fig. 12.29) are given.

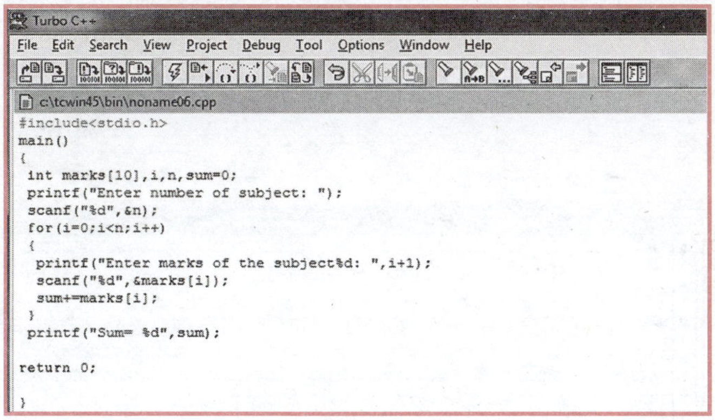


```
#include<stdio.h>
main()
{
 int marks[10],i,n,sum=0;
 printf("Enter number of subject: ");
 scanf("%d",&n);
 for(i=0;i<n;i++)
 {
  printf("Enter marks of the subject%d: ",i+1);
  scanf("%d",&marks[i]);
  sum+=marks[i];
 }
 printf("Sum= %d",sum);

return 0;

}
```

Fig.12.28 *Input*

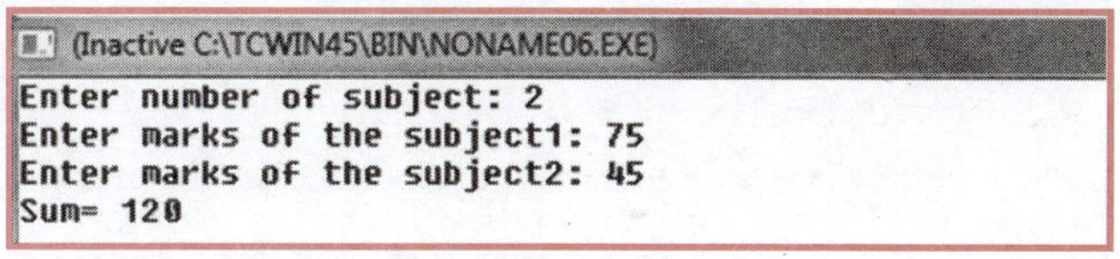


```
Enter number of subject: 2
Enter marks of the subject1: 75
Enter marks of the subject2: 45
Sum= 120
```

Fig.12.29 *Ouput*

Like an integer array, a group of characters can also be stored in a character array called **string**. To store a string "COMPUTER" in an array called fnam, write declaration statement as:

```
Char fnam[8];
```

For example: To accept your name and print using character array, write the code given in Figure 12.30. The corresponding output (Fig. 12.31) is also shown.

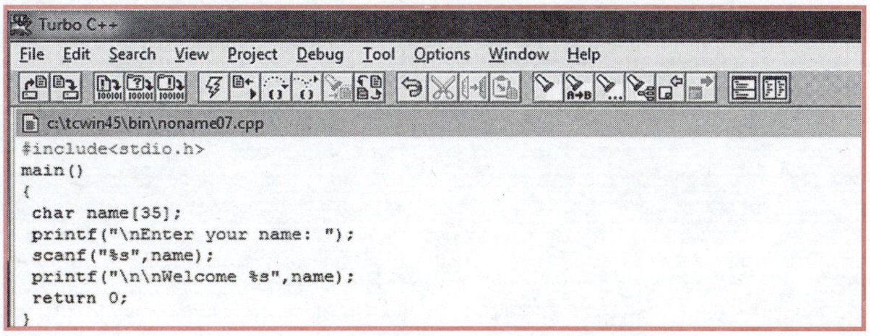


```
#include<stdio.h>
main()
{
 char name[35];
 printf("\nEnter your name: ");
 scanf("%s",name);
 printf("\n\nWelcome %s",name);
 return 0;
}
```

Fig.12.30 *Input*

```
Enter your name: Irish

Welcome Irish
```

Fig.12.31 *Output*

Two dimensional array

An array that has two indices is known as a two dimensional array. Tables and Matrices are executed on computers using two dimensional arrays in which the first index signifies row and the second index signifies column.

NOTE: An array with more than one index is called a **multi-dimensional array**.

Syntax:

```
Datatype arrayname [][];
```

For example: Write the code as given in Figure 12.32. The corresponding output is given in Figure 12.33.

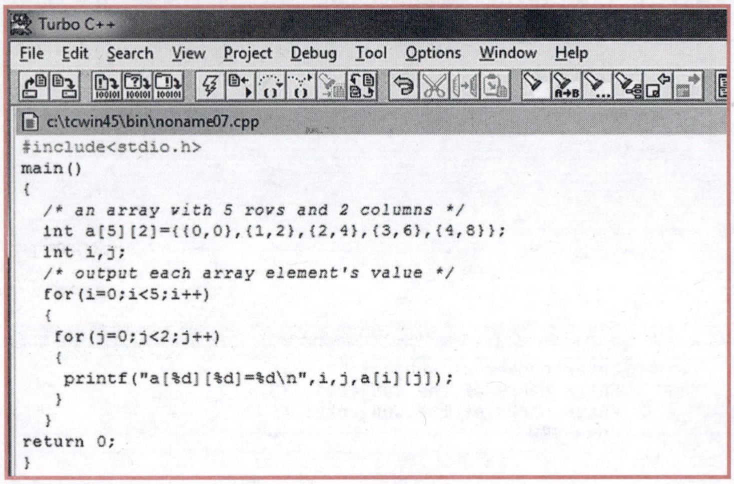

Fig.12.32 *Input*

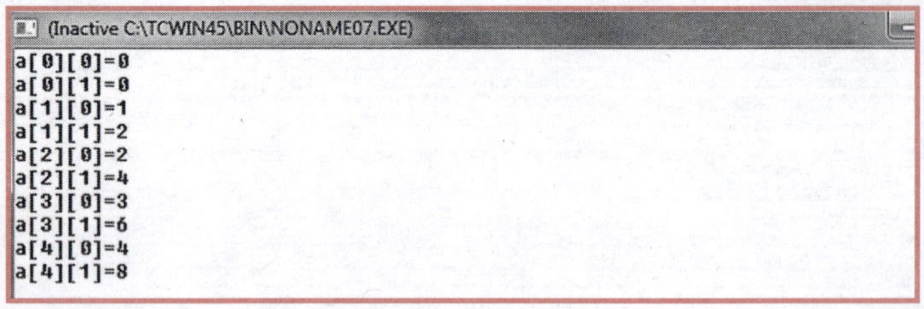

Fig.12.33 *Output*

ACTIVITY

A. To write a C program to calculate average using arrays. Find out the output.

```
#include <stdio.h>
main(){
    int n, i;
    float num[100], sum=0.0, average;
    printf("Enter the numbers of data: ");
    scanf("%d",&n);
    while (n>100 || n<=0)
    {
        printf("Error! number should be in range of (1 to 100).\n");
        printf("Enter the number again: ");
        scanf("%d",&n);
    }
  for(i=0; i<n; ++i)
   {
      printf("%d. Enter number: ",i+1);
      scanf("%f",&num[i]);
      sum+=num[i];
   }
   average=sum/n;
   printf("Average = %f",average);
   return 0;
}
```

B. To write a C program to display largest element of an array. Find out the output.

```
#include <stdio.h>
main(){
    int i,n;
    float arr[100];
    printf("Enter total number of elements(1 to 100): ");
    scanf("%d",&n);
    printf("\n");
    for(i=0;i<n;++i)  /* Stores number entered by user. */
    {
       printf("Enter Number %d: ",i+1);
       scanf("%f",&arr[i]);
    }
    for(i=1;i<n;++i)  /* Loop to store largest number to arr[0] */
    {
       if(arr[0]<arr[i]) /* Change < to > if you want to find smallest element*/
           arr[0]=arr[i];
    }
    printf("Largest element = %f",arr[0]);
    return 0;
}
```

CHECK YOUR PROGRESS

A. Accept your five main subject marks using array. Calculate and print the total and average.

B. Accept a string using character array and print it in reverse order.

C. Create a program to read matrix elements and display them using two dimensional array.

Functions

Function is a block of statements which perform some specific task and return a single value to the calling function. There are two types of functions in C language. They are:

- ***Library functions:*** Predefined functions in C language
- ***User-defined functions:*** Functions written by a programmer

Library functions in C

C language supports a big collection of library functions. To include these functions in any of the C program, you have to include the respective header file. Some of the functions are discussed below.

Functions under stdio.h

Some important functions under stdio.h header files are given in Table 12.10.

Table 12.10 *Functions under stdio.h*

Name of the Function	Purpose	Syntax	Example
printf( )	To display the output as per the format given	printf("format descriptor", &varname); or printf("\n<message>");	printf("%d",a);
getchar( )	To accept a single character from the user	variable name = getchar();	a=getchar();
putchar( )	To display the output (single character only)	putchar(variable name);	putchar(a);
gets( )	To read a string including blank spaces	gets(variable name);	gets(snam);
puts()	To display the output string	puts("message"); or puts(variable name);	puts("welcome"); or puts(snam);

FACT FILE

Getchar(), putchar(), gets() and puts() do not support the format descriptors and hence you cannot accept numeric values using these functions.

Functions under stdlib.h

Some important conversion functions come under stdlib header files. They are given in Table 12.11.

Table 12.11 *Functions under stdlib.h*

Name of the Function	Purpose	Syntax	Example
atof()	To convert a string to a floating point	atof(string);	C=atof("3443.45");
atoi()	To convert a string into an integer value	atoi(string);	C=atoi("3233");

Functions under string.h

String functions are used for string manipulations. Some are given in Table 12.12.

Table 12.12 *Functions under string.h*

Name of the Function	Purpose	Syntax	Example
strcat()	To join two strings and store the result in the first string	strcat(string1, string2);	strcat("click", "start");
strncat()	To join only n character of string2 to string1	strncat(string1, string2, n);	strncat("click", "start", 4);
strlwr()	To convert a string from uppercase to lowercase	strlwr(string);	strlwr("bytes");
strupr()	To convert a string from lowercase to uppercase	strupr(string);	strupr("bits");
strrev()	To reverse the given string	strrev(string);	strrev("yahoo");
strcmp()	To compare the given 2 strings. It is case-sensitive	strcmp(string1, string2);	strcmp("cam", "cam");
stricmp()	It is similar to strcmp but it ignores the case difference	stricmp(string1, string2)	stricmp("cam", "Cam");
strncmp()	To compare n characters of string2 with string1	strncmp(string1, string2, n);	strncmp("hello", "welcome", 2);
strchr()	To find the first occurrence of the given character in a given string and prints the string from that position	strchr(string1, search character);	strchr("cambridge", "m");
strlen()	To find the length of the given string	strlen(string);	strlen("technology");
strcpy()	To copy string2 to string1. The string1 will be replaced with string2	strcpy(string1, string 2);	strcpy("c.sc", "ict");
strncpy()	To copy only n characters of string2 to string1	strncpy(string1, string 2, n);	strncpy("click", "start", 4); only star will be copied to string 1.

Functions under math.h

Math functions are used for mathematical manipulations. Some of them are given in Table 12.13.

Table 12.13 *Functions under math.h*

Name of the Function	Purpose	Syntax	Example
abs()	To return the positive number (ignores the sign)	abs(variable);	abs(–45);
pow()	To find the power of a given number	pow(variable, power value);	pow(2,3);
sqrt()	To return the positive square root of a given number	sqrt(number/variable);	sqrt(64);
exp()	To find the exponential value	exp(double value);	exp(3444.44);
Floor	To return the smallest integer for a floating number	floor(float number);	float(35.55);

Functions under time.h

Some important functions under time.h header files are given in Table 12.14.

Table 12.14 *Functions under time.h*

Name of the Function	Purpose	Syntax	Example
time()	To return the time of the day	time();	time();
ctime()	To convert date and time to a string	ctime();	ctime();

NOTE: To use all functions given above, you should include the appropriate header files at the beginning of the program.

ACTIVITY

A. To write a C program to find out the square root using library function. Find out the output.

```
#include <stdio.h>
#include <math.h>
main()
{
    float num,root;
    printf("Enter a number to find square root.");
    scanf("%f",&num);
    root=sqrt(num);             /* Computes the square root of num and stores in
    root. */
    printf("Square root of %.2f=%.2f",num,root);
    return 0;
}
```

B. To write a C program to find absolute value of a number. Find out the output.

```
#include <stdio.h>
#include <math.h>

main()
{
  int n, result;

  printf("Enter an integer to calculate it's absolute value\n");
  scanf("%d", &n);

  result = abs(n);
```

```
  printf("Absolute value of %d = %d\n", n, result);

  return 0;
}
```

C. To write a C program to clear the screen and move the cursor to upper left hand corner of screen. Find out the output.

```
#include<stdio.h>
#include<conio.h>

main()
{
   printf("Press any key to clear the screen.\n");

   getch();

   clrscr();

   printf("This appears after clearing the screen.\n");
   printf("Press any key to exit...\n");

   getch();
   return 0;
}
```

D. To write a C program to get current date and time. Find out the output.

```
#include <stdio.h>
#include <time.h>

main ()
{
   time_t curtime;

   time(&curtime);

   printf("Current time = %s", ctime(&curtime));

   return 0;
}
```

CHECK YOUR PROGRESS

A. Calculate and print the sum of numbers from 1 to 1000 using while loop.

B. Accept any 10 numbers (only positive numbers). If the number is <=0, print a message that you cannot enter zero or negative numbers and break the loop. Find the sum of 10 numbers.

C. Using do while loop print the multiples of 17.

D. Print the numbers from 1 to 500 in a horizontal row (using escape sequence). Calculate and print the sum of the numbers using for loop.

E. Accept a string using gets function.

1. Find the length of the string.
2. Convert it to uppercase and print the same.
3. Convert it to lowercase and print the same.
4. Print the reverse of the string.
5. Accept another string and copy the new string to the first string.
6. Print the length of the new string.
7. Compare both the strings.

F. Accept a number and find its square root.

G. Accept a negative number and print it as a positive number.

H. Complete the following crossword.

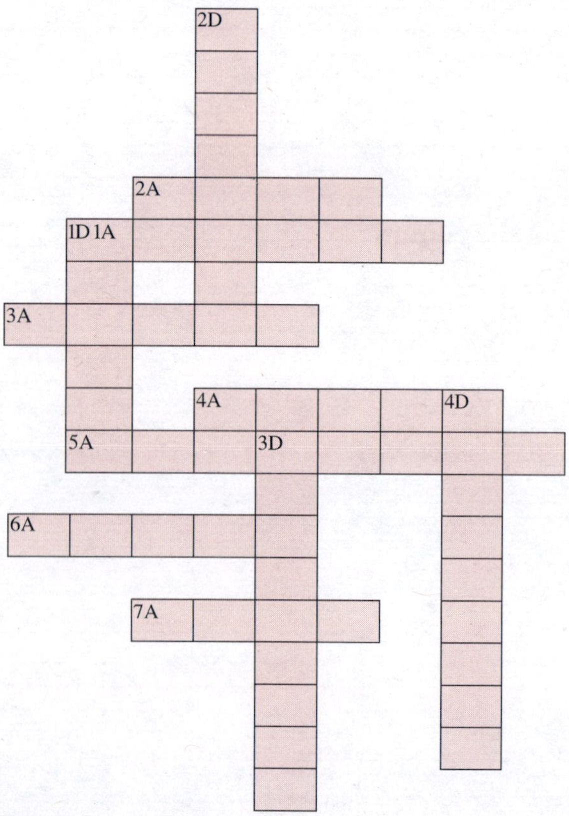

Across:

1. to be declared as a character array
2. header file that hold mathematical functions
3. collection of elements in a single variable
4. a function used to read data in a formatted form
5. memory location to store values
6. loop statement that checks the condition first
7. displays string output without using %s

Down:

1. function that is used to reverse a string
2. conditional operator
3. name used to refer a variable
4. pictorial representation of a program

GLOSSARY

- **Algorithm:** It refers to step-by-step instruction written in simple English to solve a problem.
- **Array:** It can store a fixed size sequential collection of elements of the same type.
- **Array Size:** It refers to the number of elements in an array.
- **Control Structure:** It controls the order of execution and changes the control flow in a program.
- **Escape Sequences:** They are special strings used to control output from the C program on the monitor or on any output device.
- **Flow Chart:** It is the pictorial representation of the steps involved in solving a problem.
- **Format Descriptors:** It define how the input or output data is to be represented and interpreted internally.
- **Function:** It is a block of statements which perform some specific task and return a single value to the calling function.
- **Identifier:** It is a unique name used to refer to a variable.
- **Library Functions:** They are the predefined functions in C language.
- **Nested if statement:** It refers to if statement within another if statement.
- **Operator:** It is a symbol that tells the compiler to perform specific operations required for processing.
- **Program:** It is a set of statements which will be executed to achieve a specific task.
- **Pseudo Code:** It is an algorithm written using programming language.
- **Single Dimensional Array:** They are arrays that are specified by a single subscript.
- **User-Defined Functions:** These functions are written by a programmer.

NOW YOU KNOW

1. C language combines the features of high-level language and functionality of low-level language and hence it is called as middle level language.
2. C language uses 32 keywords.
3. C is developed by Dennis Ritchie and most of its principles and ideas were taken from the earlier languages like B, BCPL and CPL.
4. The person who is instructing the computer need to estimate, plan, analyse and give instructions to solve the problem.
5. There is no keyword for the purpose of Input and Output in C language.
6. The strings and arrays variable need not be preceded with an ampersand symbol.
7. In prefix form, the increment or decrement will be done before rest of the expression and in postfix form the increment or decrement will be done after the complete expression is evaluated.
8. The switch variable can either be an integer or character data type.
9. It is possible to skip the rest of the commands in the active loop and starts from the first line by giving continue statement in the middle.
10. Before using a function, you should include the appropriate header files at the beginning of the program.

EXERCISE

FA

A Fill in the blanks.

1. To write an algorithm using a programming language keywords is called ....
2. The printf function is used to .... results on the screen.
3. A .... statement in C language provides an unconditional jump.
4. The step-by-step instruction in solving a problem is called ....
5. The pictorial representation of the steps involved in solving a problem is called ....
6. A .... is a set of statements which will be executed to achieve a specific task.
7. C is a high-level language developed by ....
8. Machine and symbolic languages were considered as .... level languages.
9. The source code for .... operating system is coded in C.
10. .... files has to be declared along with # include statement.
11. .... statements are non-executable statements.
12. To compile your C program, press .... + ... keys.
13. .... are the values assigned to a variable used in a program.
14. The maximum length of the variable name is .... characters.
15. Like a variable name, only an .... can be used in an identifier.
16. C language uses 32 ....
17. The format descriptor .... is used to print and scan as a string.
18. There is no keyword for the purpose of .... and .... in C language.
19. The .... and .... variable need not be preceded with an ampersand symbol.
20. .... are used to combine two expressions containing relational operators.
21. A ternary operator is also known as a .... operator.
22. The .... operator is used to calculate the size of any data type.
23. .... is used to make a decision between many alternatives.
24. In switch case, if no case value matches, the control transfers to the .... statement.
25. Predefined functions in C language are called ....

B Multiple choice questions.

1. To show the input and output step in a flowchart .... symbol is used.

   a. 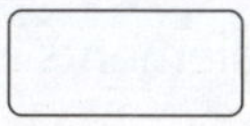 b.  c.  d. 

2. The extension of a header files is ....

   a. *.c b. *.hdr c. *.h d. *.hdf

3. The program execution starts from the ....

   a. (b. { c. [d. }

4. The delimiters/* and */refers to ....

   a. multiplication b. multiply and divide

   c. divide and multiply d. None of these

5. To compile your program, press .... key.

   a. Alt + F9 b. F9 c. F10 d. F5

6. The maximum length of the variable name is .... characters.

   a. 32 b. 31 c. 30 d. 24

7. Control variables are enclosed within ....

   a. {} b. < > c. ( ) d. " "

8. The scanf, printf, getchar, putchar and puts functions are available in .... header files.

   a. stdlib.h b. string.h c. stdio.h d. All of these

9. %d indicates that the variable is a/an .... variable.

   a. character b. float c. integer d. double

10. .... is referred as divide AND assignment operator.

    a. /& b. /= c. %= d. /*

11. The two special characters used in ternary operator are .... and ....

    a. ?; b. }; c. ?: d. {;

12. Adding 1 to the variable "a" can be expressed as ....

    a. a=a+1; b. a++; c. a+=1; d. All of these

13. .... statement is used to check for the multiple conditions.

    a. if else if b. if else c. if endif d. if

14. The .... statement is optional in switch case.

    a. break b. default c. continue d. case

15. In for loop syntax, the third expression is ....

a. Increment/decrement
b. ?:
c. printf()
d. scanf()

16. It is better to use .... statement to accept the values for the elements in an array.

a. for loop
b. while loop
c. do while
d. None of these

17. To read input from the user as per the format given .... function is used.

a. getchar
b. gets
c. printf
d. scanf

18. To read a string along with blank spaces .... function is used.

a. gets
b. getchar
c. scanf
d. putchar

19. To join n characters of string2 to string1 .... function is used.

a. strjoin
b. strncat
c. stradd
d. strcat

20. .... is the function similar to strcmp but ignores the case difference.

a. strcmp
b. stricmp
c. strncmp
d. strrcmp

C Differentiate the following.

1. Variable and Constant
2. Strcpy and Strncpy
3. Scanf and Printf
4. Scanf and Gets
5. = and ==
6. & and &&
7. while loop and do while loop
8. / and %
9. %d and %u
10. Postfix increment operator and Prefix increment operator

D Answer the following questions briefly.

1. What is an algorithm?
2. What is flowchart?
3. What is pseudocode?
4. What is a program?
5. Write a short note on BCPL.
6. How are the programming languages classified?

7. Give an example of a low-level programming language.
8. Name the operating systems in which the source code is written in C.
9. What is the extension of a header file used in C?
10. How to declare header files in C?
11. What are non-executable statements?
12. What is the extension of saved C program files?
13. What is a variable?
14. Define identifier.
15. How many keywords are there in C?
16. What value a boolean data type can hold?
17. What are format descriptors?
18. What does %e format descriptor stands for?
19. What are control variables?
20. Write the syntax to declare a variable in C.
21. Name the header file in which input and output functions are kept in.
22. In scanf("%d", &a); what does the & stands for?
23. Name the data type need not be preceded with an ampersand symbol while using scanf() function.
24. What is an operator?
25. What is the purpose of % operator?
26. What is the use of Add AND operator?
27. What is the other name for ternary operator?
28. What are the two special characters used in ternary operator?
29. Name the loop which executes the block of statements at least once irrespective of the condition given.
30. Define array.

SA

E Answer the following questions.

1. Draw any four symbols used in flowchart and write their meaning.
2. How to instruct a computer to solve a problem?
3. Name the different sections of a structure of C program.
4. List the different operators used in C language.

5. What are the functions kept under stdlib.h?
6. Explain any two math functions.
7. Name and explain any three types of arrays used in C.
8. Write the features of C language.
9. What are the rules for assigning a variable name in C?
10. Write the syntax of for loop.

F Answer the following questions in detail.

1. Explain the structure of C program in detail.
2. Explain any five string functions with syntax.
3. With an example give a note on different if statements used in C.
4. Write a note on different operators used in C with an example.
5. Draw the different symbols of flowchart and write their name and purpose.
6. Write a brief note on ternary operator.
7. How to declare a string in C?
8. What is the purpose of break and continue function in a while loop?
9. Explain any four format descriptors and escape sequences.
10. Draw a flowchart to find the greatest of two numbers.

Application Based Questions

A. Lima heads the student welfare committee and maintains records of all her students. The records include Attendance Details, Unit Test Marks, Examination Marks and Extra Curricular Activities. All her records exist in Excel 2007. In an IT Training Seminar for Teachers in her school, she asked the trainer if there is an alternate way. He suggested that the school should hire someone to create software for maintaining these records. The school put out an advertisement for the same and asked the interested programmers to write an algorithm and draw the flowchart (for the following four groups) to understand the flow of their design and present it to the school.

Group 1: List out the steps to maintain records for Class Attendance Register.

Group 2: List out the steps to maintain records for Unit Test Records.

Group 3: List out the steps to maintain records for Examination Records.

Group 4: List out the steps to consolidate both the assessments (reducing to 10%, 30%, etc).

B. Priya found the following program in a Cyber Olympiad paper. The question asked the students to identify the error in the program. She debugged the program but is apprehensive to run it, as she fears that it may be a virus. Investigate what the following program does and is it harmful?

```
#include<stdlib.h>
int main()
```

```
{
system("C:\\Windows\\System32\\ipconfig");
return 0;
}
```

C. Mallika works for a local planning and zoning commission. Part of her job entails her to maintain and preserve parks in residential area. She regularly has to calculate and compare areas of parks in different area. Help her design a program to calculate the area of a rectangle park plot. Use conio.h library class.

D. Sachin wrote a C program to find greatest in 3 numbers. He used different operators to design his program. However, his teacher asked him to use a control structure because it would simplify the code. Help him.

LAB WORK

A. Find error in the following program and rewrite the correct code.

1.
```
#include <stdio.h>
main()
{
int n, first = 0, second = 1, next, c;
printf("Enter the number of terms\n");
scanf("%d", n);
print("First %d terms of Fibonacci series are :-\n", n);
for ( c = 0 c < n ; c+ )
{
if ( c <= 1 )
next = c;
else
{
next = first + second;
first = second;
second = next;
}
printf("%d\n",next);
}
return 0;
}
```

2.
```
#include <stdio.h>
main()
{
 int n, c;
 printf("Enter a number\n");
 scanf("%d", &n);     if ( n == 2 )
 printf("Prime number.\n");
 else
 {
 for ( c = 2 ; c <= n - 1 ; c++ )
 {
 if ( n c == 0 )
 break;
 }
 if ( c != n )
 printof("Not prime.\n");
 else
printf("Prime number.\n");
return 0;
}
```

B. Create a flowchart and then write C program code to check whether the number is a palindrome number or not.

1. Get the number from user.
2. Reverse it.
3. Compare it with the number entered by the user.
4. If both are same then print palindrome number.
5. Else print not a palindrome number.

C. Write a C program to find the quotient and remainder of two integers entered by the user.

D. Write a C program to check whether a number is positive or negative or zero.

E. Examine the code given below and determine its purpose. Justify your answer with an output.

```
#include <stdio.h>

int main()
```

```
{
    int n,i;
printf("Enter a positive integer: ");
    scanf("%d",&n);
    printf("Factors of %d are: ", n);
    for(i=1;i<=n;++i)
    {
        if(n%i==0)
            printf("%d ",i);
    }
    return 0;
}
```

TEACHER'S NOTES

1. Explain to the students what all qualities a good program should have.
2. Discuss different errors/bugs that can arise in a program code.

13 Societal Impacts of IT – I

SNAP RECAP

1. The World Wide Web was developed in 1989 by Tim Berners Lee.
2. The World Wide Web is a system of interconnected servers that contains interlinked hypertext documents.
3. The web is made up of web client, web server and Internet Service Provider.
4. Some of the basic uses of the web are email solutions, e-commerce, education and entertainment.

LEARNING OBJECTIVES

You will learn about:

1. Information Technology
2. Plagiarism
3. Intellectual Property Rights
4. Copyright ©
5. Piracy
6. Internet Hacking
7. Privacy and Security
8. Careers in IT

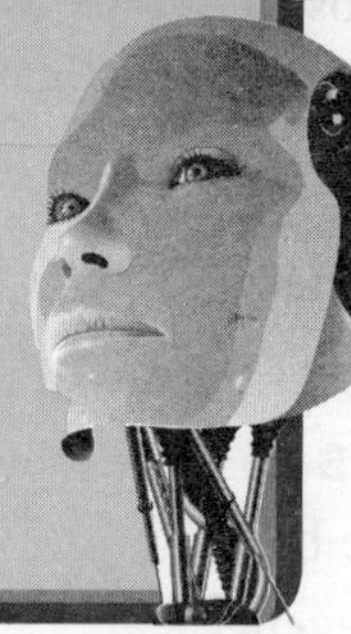

Introduction

Information Technology (**IT**) is used to store, process, retrieve, distribute and secure information. It involves the use of computer hardware, software, database management, communication and network technologies. Nowadays, information technology is used in all walks of life, such as, education, business, manufacturing, designing, entertainment, research and development. This is becauses IT helps in effective and smooth functioning of the day-to-day life. However, at the same time it can also be used to cause harm. Threats to a computer system can be both internal and external. There are people who violate the system by trying to gain unauthorised access to system for monetary gains. The advancement in technology makes it possible for unethical and criminal activities to be carried out in a

Fig. 13.1 *Global IT*

more sophisticated way. Considering the increase in negative impacts of information technology, it is necessary that, as a citizen, each one of us should be aware of moral and ethical issues and develop a good sense of responsibility towards it. Some of the major issues discussed in this chapter are plagiarism, intellectual property rights, copyright ©, piracy, internet hacking, privacy and security.

Plagiarism

The act of copying the contents of somebody else's work and reusing it as your own, especially from one website to another, is called **plagiarism** (Fig. 13.2). The Internet has made it easy to access, download and copy information. This has led to an increase in cases of plagiarism. However, using quotation marks or acknowledging the source of information does not constitute plagiarism. Paraphrasing also constitutes plagiarism if the source is not quoted. The example given below constitutes plagiarism.

Fig. 13.2 *Plagiarism*

For example:

Original	Paraphrase
The US has only lost approximately 30 percent of its forest area, most of this in the nineteenth century.	Only 30 percent of the original forest area has been lost.
The loss has not been higher mainly because population pressure has never been as great there as in Europe.	Europe has fared slightly worse due to greater population pressure.
The doubling of US farmland from 1880 to 1920 happened almost without affecting the total forest area as most was converted from grasslands.	Even though US farmland doubled from 1880 to 1920, little forest area was affected since the farms appeared on grasslands.

Types of plagiarism

On the basis of type of copying done, plagiarism can be classified as:

- ***Ghost Writer:*** The writer copies another person's work and presents it as his/her own.
- ***Photocopy:*** The writer copies a certain portion of text from one source, without making any changes.
- ***Self Stealer:*** The writer copies from his/her own work.
- ***Potluck Paper:*** The writer copies from different sources making some simple changes.

To avoid plagiarism, a few simple steps can be taken. Some of them are:

- Plan the work
- Take permission from the authors
- Acknowledge the sources
- Use quotations
- Develop the content in its original form
- Avoid paraphrasing.

FACT FILE

Stealing of another person's ideas, thoughts and expression also amounts to plagiarism.

▶ Intellectual Property Rights

The rights related to literary works, inventions and discovery is called **Intellectual Property Rights (IPR)**. Even though you can easily download information from the Internet, you cannot use this information for commercial purpose without the original author's permission. For example, many pirated software are commonly used today. This is violation of the intellectual property rights law.

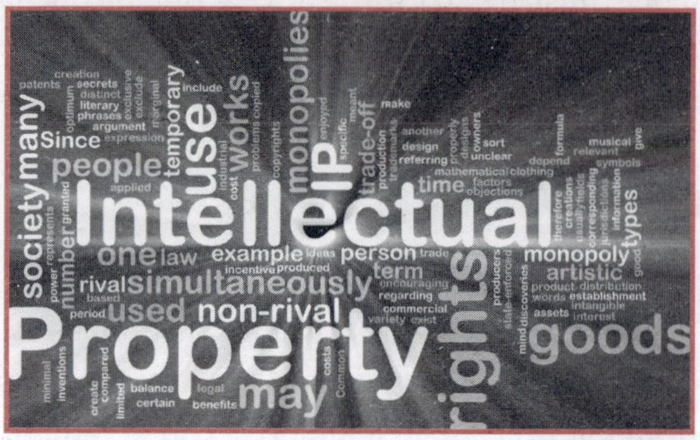

Fig. 13.3 *IPR*

In computer industry, Intellectual Property Rights (Fig. 13.3) are affected by:

- Copyright
- Patents
- Undisclosed information
- Contract

It is necessary to protect these rights as it may affect an individual or an organisation in many ways, such as:

- The owner may lose his/her share from the profit of selling their intellectual product.
- It may affect the economic growth of an organisation as the growth of the company depends on the profit of selling the products.
- Some pirated software may affect the computer system with virus or other threats.

Copyright ©

Copyright, denoted by the symbol ©, is a legal right granted to the creator of an original work. Only the creator of the copyrighted work has the rights to use and distribute it. It is unlawful to use the copyrighted material without the prior permission of the original owner (Fig. 13.4).

Fig. 13.4 *Copyright*

The illegitimate use of materials held by copyright is known as **piracy**. Piracy mostly targets software, film and music.

NOTE: Copyright is subject to a statutorily determined term. Once the copyright term expires, the copyrighted work enters the public domain and can be freely used by anyone.

Piracy

There are different types of piracy such as Software Piracy, Internet Piracy, Pre-Installed Software Piracy and On-line Auction Piracy.

Fig. 13.5 *Piracy*

- The illegal reproduction or the distribution of software applications is called **software piracy**.
- Downloading software through the Internet without authorisation is called **internet piracy**.

- Installing a copy of a particular software to more than one computer is called **pre-installed software piracy**.
- Selling an unauthorised software online, using legal terms, is called **online auction piracy.**

FACT FILE

The process of creating and distributing illegal copies of software and selling them at low price is called **counterfeiting**.

Encryption and decryption

Encryption is the process of encoding the content from plain text into ciphertext (unknown form) that cannot be easily understood by all the users. A key is used to encrypt text. The encryption key is programmed by a programmer and only an authorised person, who knows the key, can use and read it. Encryption is used to ensure the security while carrying out sensitive transaction.

Decryption is the process of converting the ciphertext into plain text using the key which is used to encrypt data. If the cipher is stronger, it is hard for an unauthorised person to decipher it. Simple ciphers include the substitution of letters for numbers and the rotation of letters in the alphabet.

Internet hacking

Internet hacking (Fig. 13.6) is a kind of crime in which a hacker breaks into your computer/website to access or to modify your programs or information when you are connected to the Internet.

Fig. 13.6 *Internet hacking*

FACT FILE

Counter hacking is the process of identifying who hacked your system to gain access to your information.

FACT FILE

NAT stands for Network Address Translation. It is a technology that allows a home network to share Internet access. A single cable modem or DSL modem could connect all the computers in a house to the Internet simultaneously. Additionally, NAT keeps the home network secure from hackers. By not forwarding requests that originate from the Internet to the computer, a NAT device blocks mischief.

Privacy

Privacy (Fig. 13.7) refers to one's personal (or professional) information. It refers to identification of an individual. For example, personal information like name, address, date of birth, contact information and ID issue. In today's scenario millions of individuals are exposed to privacy threats. Many Internet sites provide counter measures to their users for protection of their personal information and against attack from unauthorised personal.

Fig. 13.7 *Privacy*

In order to protect the privacy of an Internet user, **authentication cookies** are usually used by the Internet sites. They help the website identify whether the correct user is logged in or not and from which account they are logged in.

A **cookie** is used to track your preferences and hence to show you similar websites that might interest you. However, sometimes these benefits can also have negative impacts. For example, one of the most common ways of theft of information by the hackers is by gaining access to your user name and password that are saved by a cookie. **Third-party cookies** are extremely dangerous because they save the same information that a regular cookie does, and then they give out this information to unauthorised people.

FACT FILE

The process of stealing information like password and credit card details is called **phishing**. It is an attempt to scam the user into surrendering their private information that is used for identity theft. Communications from social web sites, auction sites, banks and online payment processors are normally used to lure the innocent.

Computer Security and Integrity of Information

Computer security and integrity of information refers to techniques designed to protect your system from unauthorised access, intentional theft or manipulation which can cause serious damage to an individuals and organisations. Computer security breaches are divided into different categories. They are listed below.

- ***Hardware:*** Hardware like phone lines, cables and modems are vulnerable to security breaches.
- ***Software:*** This includes password cracking and infecting the files through virus files.
- ***Network:*** Networks are generally used to transmit data and information that can be hacked/stolen and reveals private, sensitive and confidential information about an organisation.

Integrity refers to the authenticity of the information. Your computer system is at risk when someone tries to modify your data. By implementing an Information Integrity, you can manage the risk to your computer system by preventing and monitoring information errors, enhancing security and providing protection.

How to secure your system?

There are various measures that can be taken for data security and integrity. Some of them are:

- Install firewall, antivirus, anti-spyware programs on your system
- Give password protection to your files and folders
- Use data encryption technology to encode your information
- Allot the access of information to an authorised person who will have access control
- Voice recognition, fingerprint recognition can also be applied to restrict usage
- An organisation can also assign an individual or a team to monitor the misuse of information, if any.

Conclusion

There are numerous laws to control computer crimes and numerous measures to control security breaches. Laws are revised and many websites are dedicated to educate people about the causes, prevention and ethical issues. It is important to be aware and vigilant.

CHECK YOUR PROGRESS

A. Create a poster on different threats to create awareness among society.

B. Investigate and make a presentation on Secure Sockets Layer. HOTS

C. Divide the class into two groups. Ask one group to be the attacker and the other to be the defender. Act out what all threat a computer faces and how they can be resolved.

Careers in IT

There are wide varieties of career opportunities available for capable and experienced IT professionals (Fig. 13.8). IT professionals are responsible for designing, developing, supporting and managing computer hardware, software and networks. Today, IT professionals are working in major areas of business including banking, finance, health care, retail and manufacturing sectors. Some of the career opportunities available to IT professionals are discussed below.

Fig. 13.8 *Careers in IT*

Computer operator

Computer operators are needed to operate the vast computer system and various devices attached to it; which include loading the system, input output devices, software and recording the performance.

Computer faculty

A computer faculty is needed to teach IT in a school, college and various other institutes.

Computer programmer

A computer programmer writes software code for different types of applications using computer languages, such as, Java, C++ and VB.

Web designer

A web designer designs web pages and websites for the world wide web.

System analyst

A system analyst is responsible for analysing and designing a particular application based on the technical and behavioral aspects.

Graphic animator

An animator creates animations using animation software like Flash, Photoshop and Maya. They can work in a variety of fields including films, video games and the Internet.

Database administrator

A database administrator is responsible for storage and management of electronic data. They are responsible for the design, implementation, maintenance and repair of an organisation's database using various DBMS software, such as, Access and Oracle.

Software tester

Software testing involves operation of application, evaluating the output, identifying and eliminating the bugs and to check the functionality of the software.

There are more careers in IT field apart from what was mentioned above that you can make of. They are: Server Administrator, E-Commerce Consultant, IT Consultant, Mobile Application Developer, Multimedia Developer, Sound Editor, Network Security Manager and so on.

CHECK YOUR PROGRESS

A. Find out the hidden terms related to Societal Impacts of IT in the word grid.

A	F	E	W	Q	S	C	N	Q	L	D	M
G	D	P	G	W	A	D	H	W	K	Y	N
N	S	S	L	E	C	F	J	E	C	R	H
I	J	C	D	A	X	R	U	A	H	E	A
H	L	V	J	T	G	T	R	R	G	W	C
S	C	O	P	Y	R	I	G	H	T	Z	K
I	F	R	K	U	P	U	A	Y	B	J	E
H	H	J	I	I	F	J	A	R	V	H	R
P	J	J	O	K	C	N	V	X	I	F	S
L	K	L	P	L	I	M	C	Z	D	S	U
C	D	S	E	C	U	R	I	T	Y	G	M

B. With the help of the Internet find out what is the job profile of the following people.

1. Server administrator
2. Mobile application developer
3. Multimedia developer
4. Network security manager

GLOSSARY

- **Counterfeiting:** It is the process of creating and distributing illegal copies of software and selling them at low price.
- **Ghost writer:** They are a type of plagiarists who copy another person's work, word for word and passes it as their own.
- **Intellectual Property Rights:** They are the rights related to literary works, inventions and discoveries.
- **Internet hacking:** It is the act of breaking into your computer/website to access or modify your programs or information when you are connected to the Internet.
- **Internet Piracy:** It is downloading a software through the Internet without authorisation.
- **Online Auction Piracy:** It refers to selling of unauthorised software through the Internet using legal terms.
- **Phishing:** It is the process of stealing information like password and credit card details.
- **Plagiarism:** It is the act of copying the content of someone else's work and reusing it as your own especially, from one website to another.
- **Pre-installed software Piracy:** It refers to installing a copy of particular software to more than one computer.
- **Software Piracy:** It is the illegal reproduction or the distribution of software applications.

NOW YOU KNOW

1. The symbol © refers to a copyrighted content. It means that all the material and information related to the content is copyrighted and the creator is the sole owner.
2. Data encryption, controlling the access of information and physical checks are some of the methods used to ensure computer security.
3. Privacy refers to one's information or to the identity of an individual.
4. Integrity refers to the authenticity of the information. Integrity is at risk when someone tries to modify the data.
5. A database administrator is responsible for storage and management of electronic data.
6. There are wide varieties of career opportunities available for capable and experienced IT professionals.

EXERCISE

FA

A Fill in the blanks.

1. .... is a type of plagiarism where the writer copies another person's work, word for word and passes it as his own.
2. .... refers to the authenticity of the information.
3. The symbol .... denotes that it is copyrighted.
4. Downloading a software through the Internet without authorisation is called ....
5. A .... is responsible for storage and management of electronic data.
6. You should provide .... to your important files and folders.
7. A .... designs web pages and websites.
8. .... technology is used to encode your information.
9. .... involves operation of application, evaluating the output, identifying and eliminating the bugs and to check the functionality of a software.
10. ....is responsible for analysing and designing a particular application based on the technical and behavioural aspects.

B Multiple choice questions.

1. Copying the contents of someone else's work is called ....

   a. copyright b. plagiarism c. backup d. None of these

2. A person who designs web pages and websites for the World Wide Web is called a ....

   a. web designer b. developer c. designer d. programmer

3. This process involves the evaluation of operation and output.

   a. Editing b. Evaluating c. Testing d. Checking

4. If you are an IT professional, you can be a/an ....

   a. System Engineer b. Programmer c. Animator d. All of these

5. The process of creating and distributing illegal copies of software and selling them at low price is called ....

   a. selling b. auctioning c. distribution d. counterfeiting

6. To secure your computer you can ....

   a. install an antivirus program
   b. use pen drives
   c. connect to the Internet
   d. update your operating system

7. Intellectual property rights are applicable to ....

   a. literary works b. discoveries c. inventions d. All of these

8. Encryption is ....

   a. stealing of one's data
   b. coding the data
   c. copying the data
   d. authorised copy of data

9. NAT stands for ....

   a. Network Address Translate
   b. Network Add Translation
   c. Network Address Translation
   d. Net Address Translation

10. What is not plagiarism?

    a. Ghost Writer
    b. Self Stealer
    c. Potluck Paper
    d. Theft

C State whether the following statements are True or False.

1. It is unlawful to use someone else's materials and information without their prior permission.
2. The legal reproduction or the distribution of software applications is called software piracy.
3. To take the necessary permission from the original author of the work and acknowledge the source of information for using it is called plagiarism.
4. An animator creates web pages and websites.
5. The process of stealing information like password and credit card details is called phishing.
6. It is necessary to give password protection to your important files and folders.
7. Ghost writer is not a type of plagiarist.
8. Software piracy refers to the unauthorised copying of software.
9. The illegitimate use of materials held by copyright is known as piracy.
10. Encryption is the process of decoding the content from plain text into ciphertext .

D Match the careers with the task given.

1.	Creating animations for video games and movies	a.	Computer Programmer
2.	Developing web pages	b.	Database Administrator
3.	Eliminating bugs from programs	c.	Animator
4.	Developing software using computer languages	d.	Web Designer
5.	Responsible for storing and managing data	e.	Software Tester

E Answer the following questions briefly.

1. What is the full form of IPR?
2. Name any two types of plagiarism.
3. What does this © symbol refers to?
4. Name any one career opportunity in IT which does not require an engineering degree.
5. Who is responsible for maintaining and storing data in an organised database?

SA

F Answer the following questions.

1. Define Information Technology.
2. What is internet hacking?
3. What do you mean by Intellectual Property Rights?
4. Vinay is a businessman. He travels constantly. While on tours, he has to pay his bills through Internet using credit card so that he meets all the deadlines. Suggest to him a security method to protect his credit card details while using Internet.

G Answer the following questions in detail.

1. Explain any two career opportunities in IT.
2. What are the different types of software piracies?
3. What is plagiarism? Give methods to avoid it.
4. Explain privacy with an example.

Application Based Questions

A. Human behaviour is one of the biggest threat to the security of a computer system. A majority of the viruses, bugs, spywares and spams can be evaded by adapting our behaviour while using the Internet. Make a list of ten such suggestions/measures. Some of them are given below.

1. Do not click on links in pop-up windows.
2. Do not click on links in emails.
3. Do not respond to spam/junk email.
4. Do not respond to or click on links in emails that look exactly like email from your bank, credit card company or retail stores.

B. What online resources do you use to keep abreast of web security issues? Can you give an example of a recent web security vulnerability or threat?

C. Plagiarism is widespread. Explain, using examples, how following type of plagiarism are practiced. HOTS

1. Copy and paste plagiarism
2. Word switch plagiarism
3. Style plagiarism
4. Metaphor plagiarism
5. Idea plagiarism

D. Rohan deleted Roshini's science assignment stored on one of the computers at school computer lab because of low disk space. Was it the right thing to do? Justify.

LAB WORK

A. Create a presentation to show the societal impacts of IT. Suggest some ways of securing your computer from threats.

B. Follow the steps given below to secure your system.

1. Install a good antivirus software program.
2. Run manual weekly spyware scans using programs like Spybot.
3. Set Windows Updates to install automatically.
4. Create software firewall by updating Windows Firewall setting.

TEACHER'S NOTES

1. Tell the students about Microsoft Security Essentials and Hardware Firewalls (Routers).
2. If possible, review different antivirus and anti-spyware programs available in the market today.

Worksheet 4

SECTION A

Fill in the blanks.

1. The step-by-step instruction used in solving a problem is called ____________________.
2. The source code for ____________________ operating system is coded in C.
3. To compile a C program, press ____________________ keys.
4. The format descriptor are also called ____________________.
5. The ____________________ and ____________________ variable need not be preceded with an ampersand symbol.
6. Predefined functions in C language are called ____________________.
7. ____________________ is responsible for planning, designing, implementing and maintaining a network.
8. © symbol denotes that it is ____________________.
9. Downloading a software through the Internet without any authorisation is known as ____________________.
10. A ____________________ is responsible for storage and management of electronic data.

SECTION B

Answer the questions briefly.

1. What is the extension of a header file used in C? How to declare header files in C?
2. What value can double and long data type can hold?
3. What is the purpose of the sizeof operator?
4. What does %f stand for?
5. Define array.
6. Name and explain control structures supported in C.
7. Explain plagiarism.
8. Enumerate different types of careers in IT.
9. What is Internet hacking?
10. What do you understand by Security and Integrity of Information? Write a brief note.

Comprehensive Worksheet 2

SECTION A

Multiple choice questions.

1. Which one of the following is spreadsheet software?

   a. MS Excel　　b. Office Calc　　c. Lotus 123　　d. Notepad

2. Which one of the following is not a Chart Tools tab?

   a. Design　　b. Layout　　c. Location　　d. Format

3. ____________________ reference does not change when copied to another cell.

   a. Absolute　　b. Variable　　c. Relative　　d. Mixed

4. ____________________ network connects computers that are geographically separated but in the same metropolitan city.

   a. MAN　　b. CAN　　c. WAN　　d. LAN

5. A non-profit organisations are identified by ____________________.

   a. com　　b. net　　c. edu　　d. org

6. The step-by-step instruction used for solving a problem is called____________________.

   a. algorithm　　b. flowchart　　c. BPCL　　d. None of these

7. The processed data is called ____________________.

   a. information　　b. knowledge　　c. Both a and b　　d. None of these

8. ____________________ define how the input or output data is to be represented and interpreted internally.

   a. Format Descriptors　　b. Control Variables

   c. Both a and b　　d. None of these

9. It is a valid variable name.

   a. int a　　b. char c　　c. char snam[20];　　d. floa esal

10. ____________________ is a decision making statement used to control the flow of execution.

    a. If statement　　b. Switch statement　　c. goto statement　　d. ifso statement

SECTION B

Answer the questions.

1. What is the difference between chart area and chart wall?
2. Explain the different formats present in Numbers group of MS Excel 2007?
3. What is the use of formulas in MS Excel 2007?
4. What is cell referencing? Explain different types of cell references in MS Excel 2007.
5. What is computer networking?
6. Differentiate between wireless and wired technology.
7. Differentiate between data and information.
8. Enumerate and explain the components of multimedia.
9. What are the different operators used in C programming language?
10. Discuss, with example, different control structures supported by C programming language.

SECTION C

Application based questions.

1. What do you understand by the term spreadsheet? Give five general features of different types of spreadsheet tool.
2. Rama wants to calculate the difference between column B and C, and store it in column D. She types the formula, B-C but the result is inaccurate. Why? How can she rectify her mistake?
3. What type of network is used by Indian Railways? Briefly discuss its advantages and disadvantages.
4. Sam is sitting in his hotel lobby where a band is playing for a school group. The lobby is also a wi-fi hotspot. However, Sam is unable to access the Internet. Why?
5. Differentiate between Intellectual Property Rights and Copyright.
6. How is piracy different from privacy? Explain with example.
7. Sweta wants to be a software tester. What will be her job description?
8. Your grandfather recently bought a new laptop. To ensure its safety and integrity, what all steps should he take before using it.
9. Rohit is working on a sales presentation for the annual sales meet. He is making the presentation in PowerPoint 2007 but all his data is in Excel 2007. How can he integrate both the application to produce an impactful presentation?
10. C has directly or indirectly influenced many languages, like, C#, Java, JavaScript and Python. Justify the statement with examples.

IT Applications - I

PROJECT 1

Using MS Word 2007, create a greeting card to wish your friends a Happy New Year.

- Use **Word Art** option in the **Text** group of **Insert** tab to highlight your wishes.
- Add photos using the **Pictures** option in the **Illustrations** group of the **Insert** tab to enhance the look of your card.
- Give border and background color using **Page Borders** and **Page Colors** options in the **Page Background** group of the **Insert** tab.
- Use minimum text.

Here is a sample greeting card.

PROJECT 2

Using MS Word 2007, create a poster for a Swimming Course.

- Insert the information given below and format the same with **Font Color** and **Styles** options present in the **Font** group of the **Home** tab.
  - For Women and Children
  - Rate: INR 100/- per hour
  - Weekend classes also available
- Insert a related picture and clip art using the **Illustrations** group of the **Insert** tab.
- Use the **Page Border** and **Page Color** options in the **Page Background** group of the **Page Layout** tab to format the page.
- Use the **Word Art** option in the **Text** group of the **Insert** tab to give the heading (that is, Summer Coaching Camp).
- Make all the text (except the heading) italics using the **Italic** option in the **Font** group of the **Home** tab.
- Insert a picture watermark using the **Custom Watermark...** in the **Watermark** option present in the **Page Background** group of the **Page Layout** tab.

Here is a sample poster.

PROJECT 3

Using MS Word 2007, design an invitation card for your parent's 25th wedding anniversary.

- Use the **Page Borders** and **Page Color** options in the **Page Background** group of the **Page Layout** tab.
- Type the content to invite and format the same using **Home** tab tools.
- Align the content to centre using the **Centre** option in the **Paragraph** group of the **Home** tab.
- Insert an image as page background. To do so, go to **Page Layout** tab ⟹ **Page Color** option ⟹ **Fill Effects....** In the **Fill Effects** dialog box, select the **Picture** tab. Click on the **Select Picture...** button to insert an image as page background.

Here is a sample invitation.

PROJECT 4

Write a letter to a computer dealer asking him to send quotation for new computers for your office. Specify the configuration of the machine you intend to buy. Send the letter to atleast five companies using Mail Merge feature of MS Word 2007.

- Apply the formatting effects using **Font**, **Paragraph** and **Style** group, wherever needed.
- Apply **Bold** style to subject and sender's name.
- Use **Word Art** option in the **Text** group of the **Insert** tab to insert the company's name and make it look like company's letter head.
- Use **Bold** options in the **Font** group of the **Home** tab.
- Use the **Spelling and Grammar** option in the **Proofing** group of the **Review** tab to carry out a spell check on your document.
- Use **Start Mail Merge** and **Select Recipients** option in the **Start Mail Merge** group of the **Mailing** tab to send the letter to five different companies.

Here is a sample letter.

TECH BYTES Pvt Ltd

26, MODEL COLONY, SHAHDARA, NEW DELHI - 14

Date: 5.5.15

From
Vinod Mehra
Tech Bytes Pvt Ltd
New Delhi

To
<<As per mailing list>>

Sir / Madam
Sub: Procurement of Computers

It is proposed that we procure 50 desktop systems of the following configurations for our organisation. You are requested to send your quotations in a sealed envelope on or before 31.5.2014. The sealed quotations will be opened on 2.6.2014 afternoon.

Configuration:

Processor	*Intel I3 – 1.3 GHz*
RAM	*4 GB*
Hard Disk Capacity	*500 GB – SATA*
Monitor	*14" LED monitor*
Keyboard	*104 keys*
Mouse	*Optical USB mouse*
Storage drive	*DVD Drive R/W*
USB Ports	*Front 2, back 4*
Multimedia Kit	*Headphone with mike*

The lowest quotations will be given work order for supply of desktop systems. The desktop systems should be supplied within 15 working days from the date of the receipt of the work order.

Yours faithfully,

Vinod Mehra
(System – Admin)

PROJECT 5

Create a spreadsheet to tabulate the class marks student wise.

- Insert 10 student records with name, number and marks of five main subjects.
- Calculate total and average using **Sum** and **Average** functions. You can insert these functions by using the **Insert function** or **AutoSum** option in the **Function Library** group of the **Formulas** tab.
- Find the maximum marks and minimum marks using **Max** and **Min** function in the **AutoSum** option in the **Functions Library** group of the **Formulas** tab.
- Insert a chart to compare the data. Go to the **Insert** tab ⟹ **Charts** group.

Here is a sample table and a sample chart.

NATIONAL PUBLIC SCHOOL								
S.No.	**Student Name**	**Lang I**	**Lang II**	**Maths**	**Science**	**Social Science**	**Total**	**Average**
1	Atul	89	89	90	95	90	453	90.6
2	Faraz	88	97	96	93	95	469	93.8
3	Vijay	66	57	69	73	69	334	66.8
4	Chris	77	87	78	82	79	403	80.6
5	Kiron	88	89	87	84	89	437	87.4
6	Varun	85	90	89	87	90	441	88.2
7	Shivani	44	67	70	74	72	327	65.4
8	Remy	66	67	74	78	72	357	71.4
9	Aastha	88	88	90	96	92	454	90.8
10	Akshay	99	97	98	95	93	482	96.4

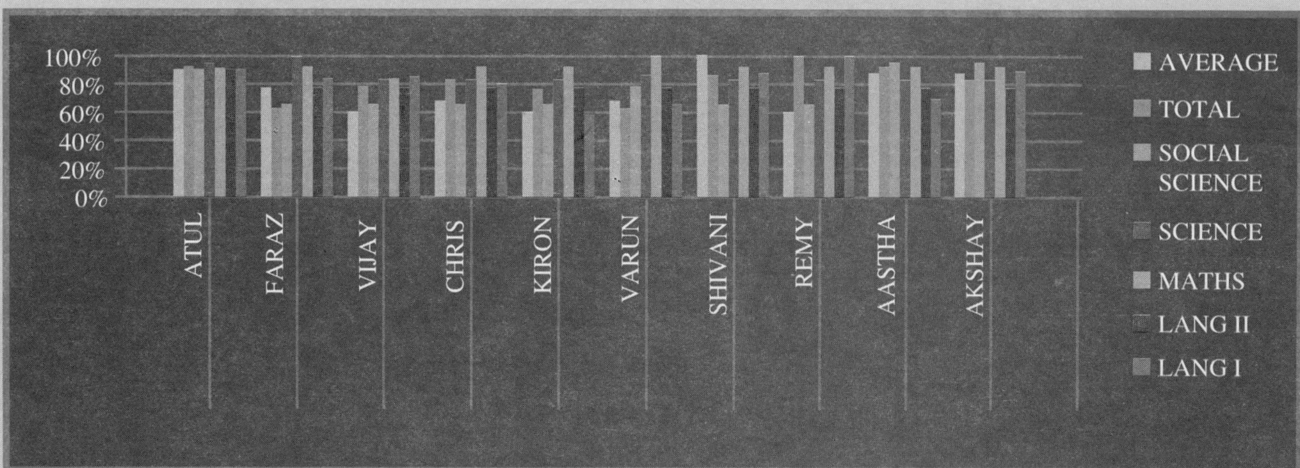

PROJECT 6

Create a spreadsheet to display the cricket score record.

- Insert minimum five records with column name Team, Total Matches, Won, Lost, Net Run Rate and Points.
- Using **Conditional Formatting** option in the **Styles** group of the **Home** tab, apply different shading to each row.
- Find the maximum run rate holder using **Max** function in the **AutoSum** option in the **Function Library** group of the **Formulas** tab.
- Insert a chart to compare the performance of all the teams. Using **Chart Tools** tab, format the chart.

  NOTE: The **Chart Tools** tab has three tabs: **Design**, **Layout** and **Format**. Use atleast one group in each of the **Chart Tools** tab to format the chart.
- Set print area using the **Print Area** option in the **Page Setup** group of the **Page Layout** tab.
- Sort the team names alphabetically using the **Sort** option in the **Sort and Filter** group of the **Data** tab.
- Save the spreadsheet as a PDF file.

Here is a sample table and a sample chart.

INDIAN PREMIER LEAGUE 2015					
Team	**Total Matches**	**Won**	**Lost**	**Net Run Rate**	**Points**
Chennai Super Kings	14	10	4	0.636	20
Delhi Daredevils	13	3	10	– 0.737	6
Kings XI Punjab	13	5	8	– 0.018	10
Kolkota Knight Riders	14	6	8	– 0.044	12
Mumbai Indians	14	10	4	0.551	20
Pune Warriors	14	2	12	– 1.314	4
Rajasthan Royals	14	10	4	0.506	20
Royal Challengers	14	8	6	0.475	16
Sunrisers Hyderabad	14	8	6	– 0.117	16

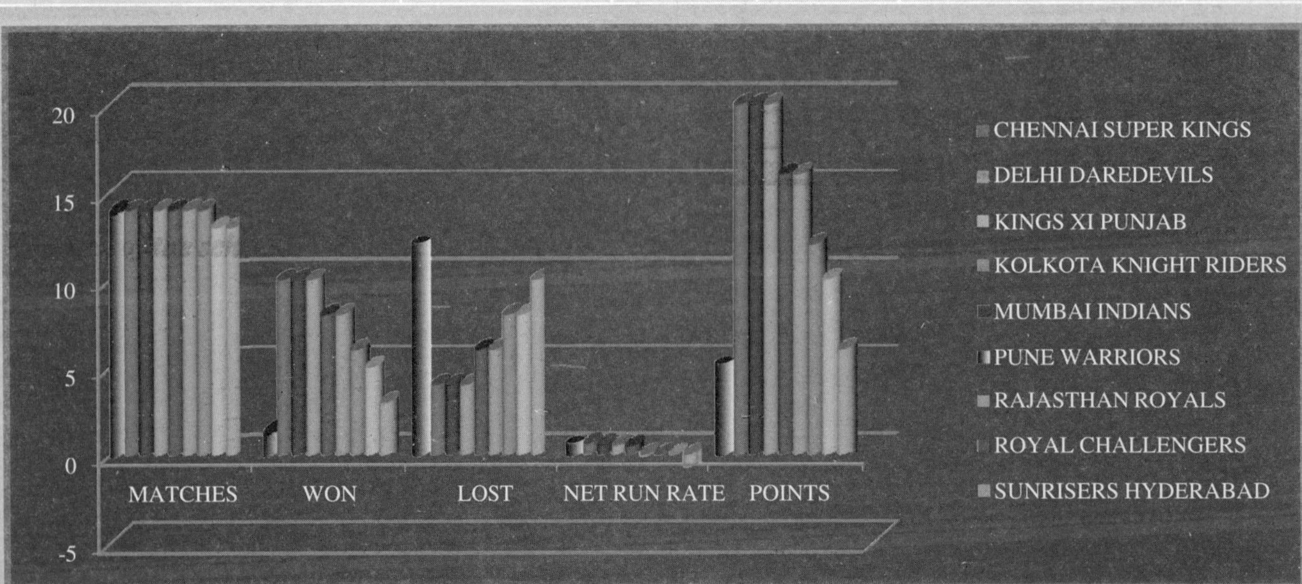

PROJECT 7

Create a spreadsheet to tabulate the weather forecasting report of four major cities according to months.

- Collect and insert records. Give appropriate title to the report.
- Format the content using the **Font Color**, **Shades** and **Styles** options in the **Home** tab.
- Insert chart to compare the data among all cities.
- Insert another chart to compare data for a particular city. Use different chart type for each city.
- Insert a theme using **Themes** option in the **Themes** group of the **Page Layout** tab.

Here is a sample table and sample charts.

COMPARISON OF WEATHER REPORT – CITY WISE				
Month	**Chennai**	**Mumbai**	**Kolkata**	**Delhi**
APR	38	36	37	37
MAY	39	38	38	40
JUN	35	37	38	37
JUL	34	34	36	36
AUG	32	30	35	35
SEP	32	28	32	30
OCT	32	26	32	26

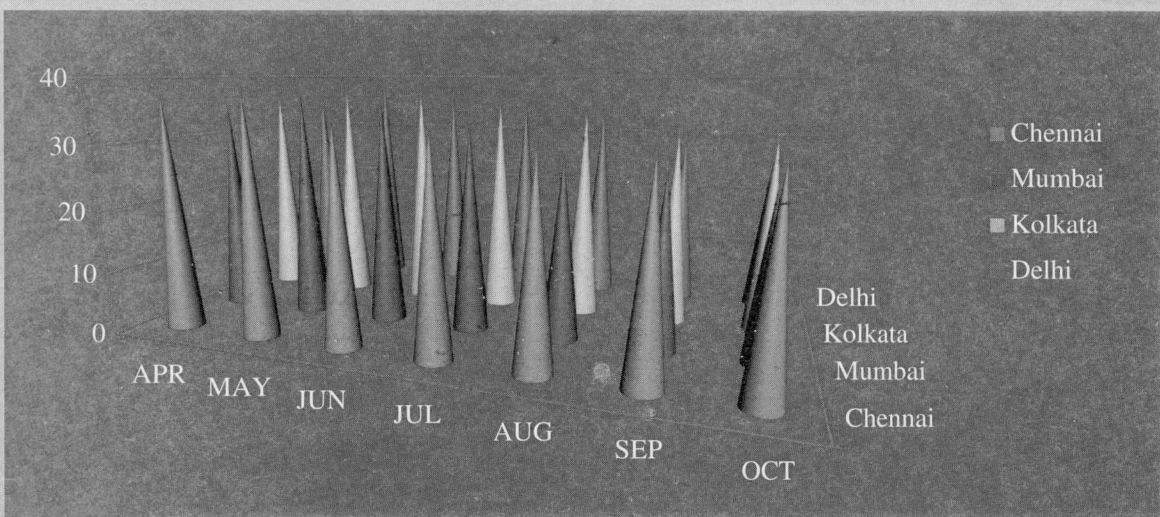

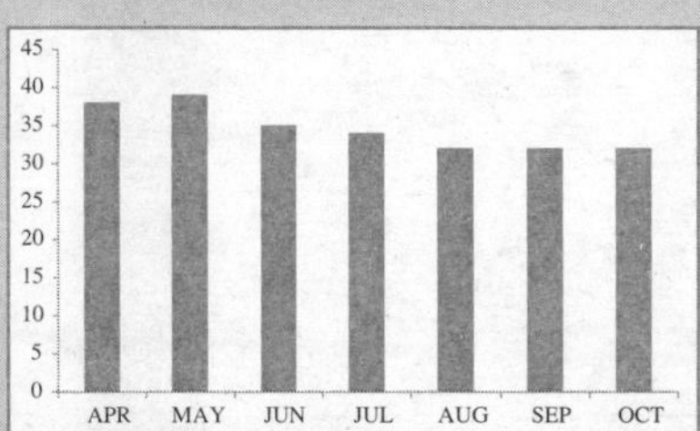

Chennai

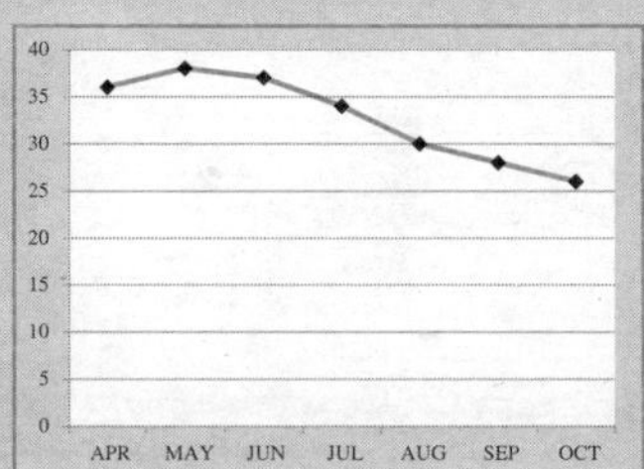

Mumbai

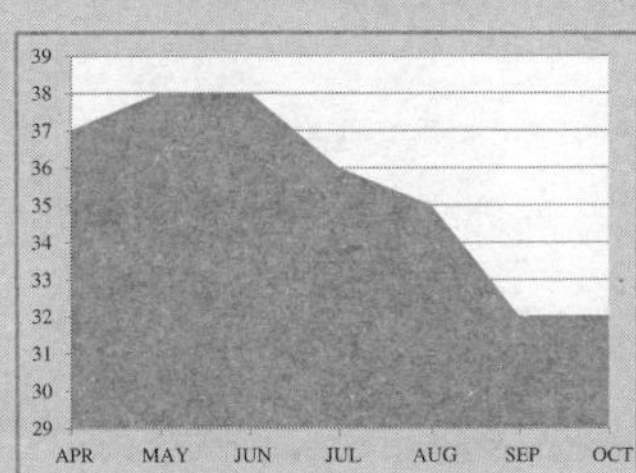

Kolkata

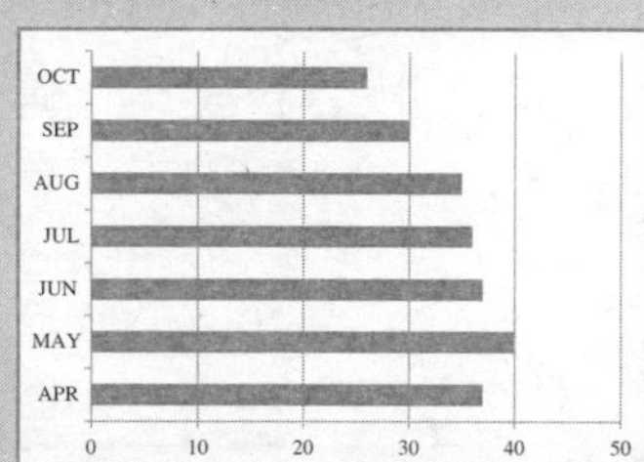

Delhi

PROJECT 8

Create a promotional presentation for a playschool. Use an installed PowerPoint 2007 template.

- Add minimum five slides.
- Use an installed PowerPoint 2007 template. Go to **File** menu ⟹ **New**. In **New** option you have templates and themes that can be used.
- Add pictures to show different activities of the school using the **Images** group of the **Insert** tab.
- Format the text using **Font** group in the **Home** tab and **Text** group in **Insert** tab.

Here is a sample presentation.

PROJECT 9

Create a presentation on any topic from your school science/social studies book.

- Insert minimum five slides.
- Use the **Themes** group in the **Design** tab to apply background to the slides.
- Browse the Internet to collect related pictures and insert them in your slides using the **Picture** option in the **Illustrations** group of the **Insert** tab.
- Apply **Custom Animation** and **Slide Transition** to all slides. Both the options are present in the **Animations** tab.

Here is a sample presentation on the topic Harmful Effects Associated with Plastic Dispersal.

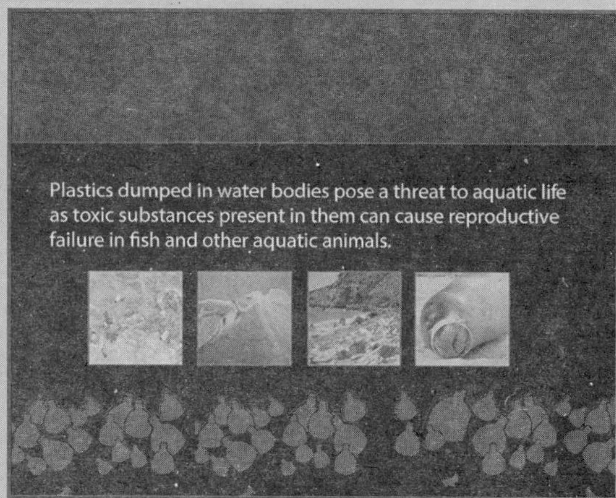

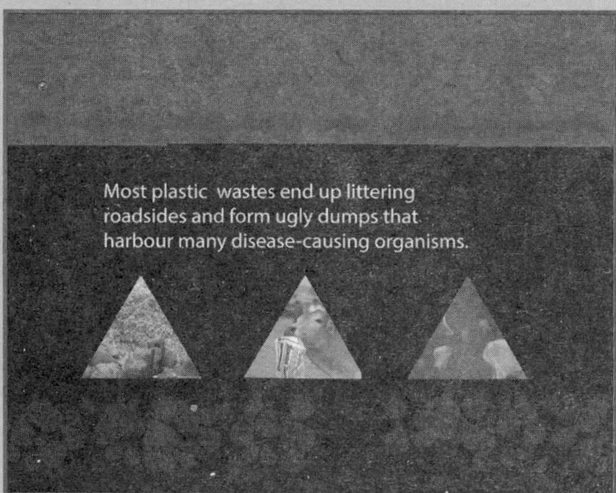

PROJECT 10

Create a presentation on any science topic from your textbook.

- Using the **Background Style** option in the **Background** group of the **Design** tab apply background to all the slides.
- Insert SmartArt (**Insert** tab ⟹ **Illustration** group ⟹ **SmartArt option**) and pictures (**Insert** tab ⟹ **Images** group ⟹ **Picture option**)
- Add **Custom Animation** and **Slide Transition** to all slides.
- Set up a slides show using the **Set up slide show** option in the **Set up** group of **slide show** tab.
- Use minimun text.

Here is the sample presentation on the topic Agricultural Practices.

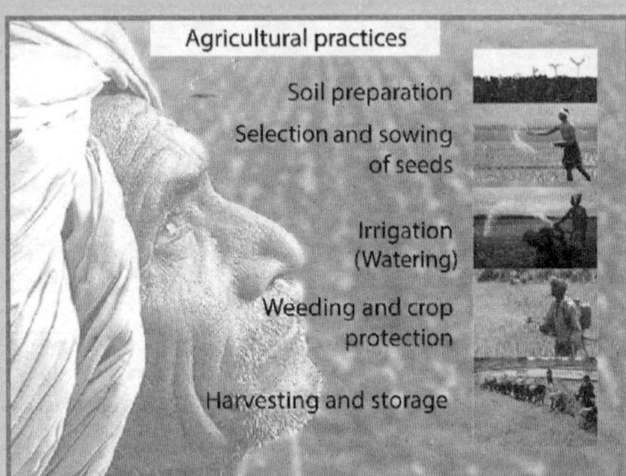

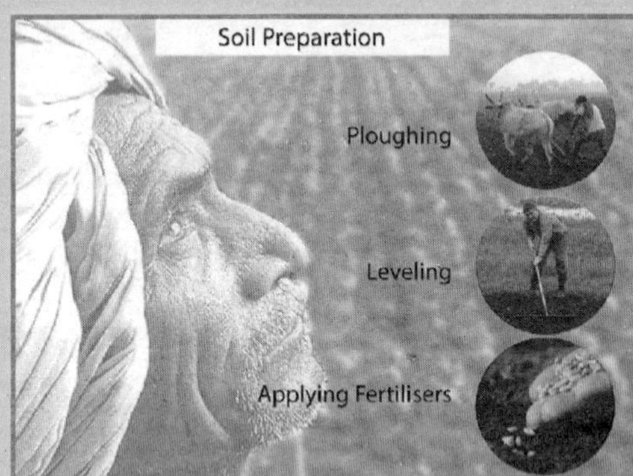

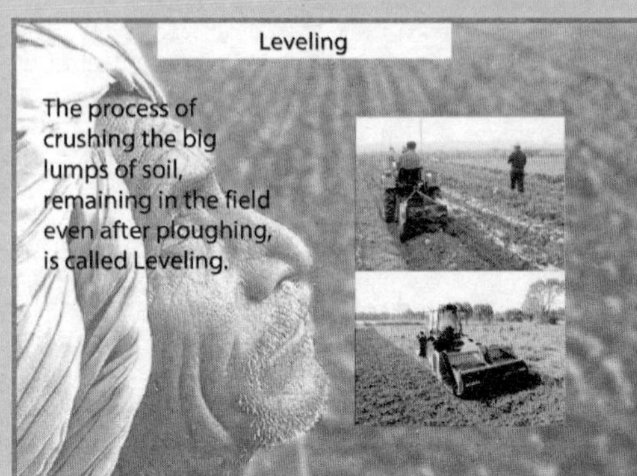

PROJECT 11

Create a presentation to promote a product.

- Insert the picture of the product using **Picture** option in the **Images** group of the **Insert** tab.
- Highlight the features of the product using formatting options present in **Font** and **Paragraph** group of the **Home** tab.
- Mention the discounts, if any.
- Use as many features of PowerPoint 2007 as you can to give animation effects.

Here is the sample presentation to advertise cricket bats.

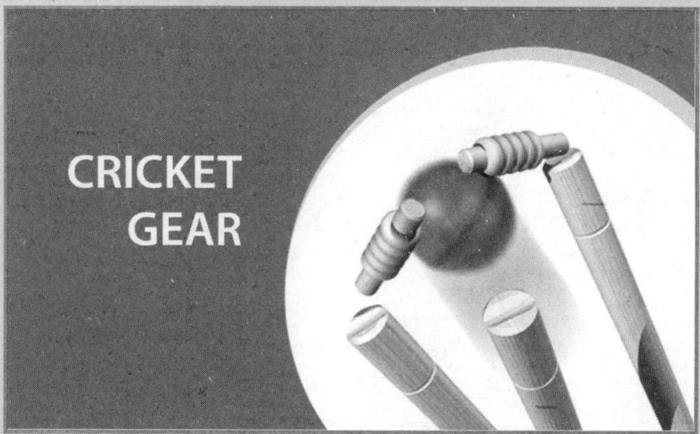

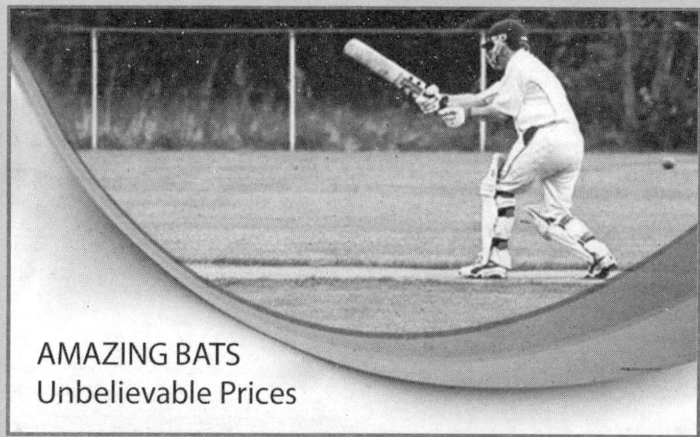

PROJECT 12

Write a C source code to check whether the entered year is leap year using `if else` statement.

```
#include <stdio.h>
main()
{
      int year;
      printf("Enter a year: ");
      scanf("%d",&year);
      if(year%4 == 0)
      {
          if( year%100 == 0) /* Checking for a century year */
          {
              if ( year%400 == 0)
                 printf("%d is a leap year.", year);
              else
                 printf("%d is not a leap year.", year);
          }
          else
             printf("%d is a leap year.", year );
      }
      else
         printf("%d is not a leap year.", year);
      return 0;
}
```

PROJECT 13

Write a C source code to generate multiplication table.

NOTE: In this code you can mention the range of the multiplication table.

```
#include <stdio.h>
main()
{
    int n, range, i;
    printf("Enter an integer to find multiplication table: ");
    scanf("%d",&n);
    printf("Enter range of multiplication table: ");
    scanf("%d",&range);
    for(i=1;i<=range;++i)
```

```
    {
        printf("%d * %d = %d\n", n, i, n*i);
    }
    return 0;
}
```

PROJECT 14

Write a C source code to create a simple calculator for addition, subtraction, multiplication and division using `switch case` statement.

```
# include <stdio.h>
main()
{
    char o;
    float num1,num2;
    printf("Enter operator either + or - or * or divide : ");
    scanf("%c",&o);
    printf("Enter two operands: ");
    scanf("%f%f",&num1,&num2);
    switch(o) {
        case '+':
            printf("%.1f + %.1f = %.1f",num1, num2, num1+num2);
            break;
        case '-':
            printf("%.1f - %.1f = %.1f",num1, num2, num1-num2);
            break;
        case '*':
            printf("%.1f * %.1f = %.1f",num1, num2, num1*num2);
            break;
        case '/':
            printf("%.1f / %.1f = %.1f",num1, num2, num1/num2);
            break;
        default:
            /* If operator is other than +, -, * or /, error message is shown */
            printf("Error! operator is not correct");
            break;
    }
    return 0;
}
```

PROJECT WORK

Complete the following case studies.

1. Create a multi-lingual greeting card. (Use regional language fonts)
2. Create a report about a recent educational trip you went on.
3. Send a birthday party invitation to your friends using mail merge feature of Word 2007.
4. Create a spreadsheet to list out the groceries and their prices at different shops. Insert a chart to represent the comparison of prices in different shops.
5. Create a spreadsheet to compare the number of hours you spend on academics, hours you spend with your homework activities, hours you spend with your computer system, hours you spend for your extra coaching for academic excellence, hours you spend on outdoor games and cultural activities. Insert a chart and format the same using Chart Tools.
6. Being a student, you may have a personal collection of books at home. Categorise them as academic-based, value-based, novels, comics and horror type books. Using spreadsheet, tabulate the category of books and the number of books you have in each category. Find out the category for which you have the maximum and minimum number of books. Insert a chart to analyse the data in a better way.
7. Create a presentation on Trends in Wi-Fi Technology. Add the following topics.
   - About Internet
   - How to connect internet
   - Wired and Wireless Technology used
   - Advantages of Wi-Fi
   - Wi-Fi devices
8. Create a presentation on Rain Water Harvesting. Add the following topics.
   - Water – Introduction
   - Need of Water
   - Why do you need to save water?
   - Rain – Main source of water
   - How to save rain water?
   - Features of Rain Water Harvesting
9. Write a C program code to add and display the sum of two integers entered by the user.
10. Write a C program code to check whether the character entered by the user is a vowel or not. Use the `if else` statement.

Sample Test Paper 1 – Solved

1. Rimi wants to make sure that there is consistency in design and color in the English presentation that she is making. How can she achieve this?
2. Rohit wants to apply to an institution for scholarship. For the scholarship, he has to email the institution his application along with the copies of his certificates. Which of the following device should he use to capture the digital copy of his certificates?

   a) Joystick b) Scanner c) Printer d) Light Pen
3. Kanan wants to see all the slides in her presentation simultaneously. Suggest which view she should use to see all the slides simultaneously.
4. Give an example of mixed referencing with respect to Excel.
5. A bank cheque normally has some special numbers printed on it. Which device is used to read these special characters?
6. Given below are two newspaper articles from different newspapers. What has the writer of the second article done? Can such a situation be avoided?

   Daily News, August 26, 1997: Sheep rearing (original)
   "The sheep was put on its back and pinned it between the workers legs. Then, reaching for his clippers, he went to work."

   Network News, December 16, 2010: Ladakh Sheep rearing
   "With a little persuasion, the worker pulled the sheep onto its back and pinned it between his legs. Then, reaching for his clippers, he went to work."
7. Paul wants to insert graphics objects in his PowerPoint presentation. Name any two graphics objects which he can insert in his presentation.
8. Anmol is interested in developing content for World Wide Web using programming and development tools. Suggest an appropriate career for him.
9. Shalini wants to book a train ticket. Can she book the ticket using the Internet? If yes, then state one advantage of using the Internet.
10. Ivan cannot move from one slide to the next in a slide show. Name two methods do to so?
11. Arjun was asked by his manager to print handouts of his presentation but he does not know what they are. Explain the meaning of handouts to him.
12. Name the input device used to sense and read thick and thin black stripes present on the items usually sold at supermarkets.

13. How would you refer to the range starting from 1st column, 1st row and spread till 4th column and 5th row?
14. In which view can you apply animation on the text or objects?

15. Anna has written a letter which she wants to send to 4 banks.

11/22, Green Park,
New Delhi,
India
2-March-2015

Dear <title> <surname><Address line>
I am Anna Jose, the general manager of the 'InstaDigital Solutions Ltd.' and the holder of the current account number <account_no>.
I would like you to send me the statement of the account for the last 3 months. I need to present this statement to the tax authorities next week. I request you to kindly send the statement at the earliest.

In reference to the above, I would like to point out that I need the statement from 01.05.14 until 01.08.14.
A prompt reply will be highly appreciated.

Thanking in advance,

Anna Jose
(General Manager)
InstaDigital Solutions Ltd.

Now answer the questions.

i. Anna wants to send the letter with same content to 4 banks with similar request. The addresses of all such banks along with corresponding account numbers are stored in a separate document. Name the feature which will help Anna achieve the same.
ii. Name the two files that Anna has to use to be able to send letters to all the banks.
iii. Identify the merge fields in the given document.
iv. Anna wants to keep a record of all the changes/ corrections that she makes in this document. Name the feature used to achieve the same.

16. The Spell Check tool will find errors in which of the following?

a) It in a beautiful, sunny day.
b) It is a beautiful sunny.
c) It isa beautiful, sunny day.
d) Is a beautiful sunny day.

17. Fill in the blanks by choosing one of the types of software listed in the box given below.

database	**desktop publisher (DTP)**	**spreadsheet**	**word processor**

a) A___________is most suitable for producing a school magazine.
b) A___________is most suitable for producing school accounts.

18. Why is secondary storage needed in a computer? Explain briefly.

19. Identify the device. List its features.

20. Name three functions that can be performed in Slide Sorter view of a presentation.

21. What is the function of Preview/Play button in Custom Animation? Explain briefly.

22. What is an action button? Write 'True' for correct and 'False' for incorrect statements pertaining to 'Action Buttons'.

a) You can create our own action buttons on a slide.

b) An action button can link a document to a website on the Internet.

23. Suppose you have bought all hardware components required for assembling a computer. After assembling the computer system, which will be the very first software to be installed?

a) Hardware driver

b) Operating system

c) Antivirus software

d) Word processing software

24. Which of the following is not a function of an operating system?

a) File Management

b) Memory Management

c) Resource Management

d) Database Management

25. Suppose you have to type a particular text many times in a Word document. Write one way by which you do not have to retype it again and again.

26. Arrange the following memory units in ascending order of their storage capacities.

Kilobyte, Byte, Terabyte, Megabyte

27. Text 1 shows part of an article handwritten by an author on 'Eating Breakfast'. Text 2 shows the same text after Ms. Jacob has typed it in Word.

Text 1

For those who always skip breakfast, you should stop that habit now! You've heard many times that "Breakfast is the most important meal of the day." Now, recent research confirms that one of the worst practices you can develop may be avoiding breakfast.

Text 2

For those who always skip breakfast, you should stop that habit now! You've heard many times that "Breakfast is the most important meal of the day." Now, recsent resaerch confirms that one of the worst practices you can develop may be avoiding breakfast.

What should Ms. Jacob have done before printing out the work to make sure that the two underlined words were correct?

28. A few output devices and tasks are given. Select the output device most appropriate for the task given below.

Output devices
Dot Matrix Printer, Laser Printer, Plotter, Inkjet Printer, Speakers

Tasks
a) Producing 1000 letters quickly, to be sent to members of a club

b) Producing a graph of a patient's heart beat in a hospital

c) Producing an audible warning signal

29. How can you insert a sound file in a PowerPoint presentation?

30. Which option would you use to display the digit 2 in the formula H_20?

31. Which one of the following is not a Custom Animation effect?

a) Fly in
b) Appear
c) Jump
d) Checkerboard

32. Differentiate between RAM and ROM.

33. Name one specific software/tool for each of the following category.

a) Antivirus software
b) Encryption Tool
c) Operating System
d) Disk Utility Software
e) Browser

34. Sugandh has used a word processor to write her history homework. Here is some of her homework.

Quit India Speech by Mahatma Gandhi on August 8th 1942. "Everybody will be his own master. It is to join a struggle for such democracy that I invite you today. Once you realise this you will forget all the differences, and think of yourselves as Indians only, engaged in the common struggle for independence."

a) Choose two tools that Sugandh can use to make the title stand out.

Spelling Checker, Print Preview, Cut Paste, Bold, Underline, StrikeOut

b) How can she find the synonym of the term 'struggle'?

35. Absolute cell Referencing occurs when ____________ .

a) Formula is dragged and the cell reference adjusts automatically.

b) Formula is dragged but the cell references do not adjust.

c) $ symbol is automatically added with each cell value.

d) Spreadsheet is saved with 'absolute' as file name.

36. A domain name ending with org belongs to ____________ .

a) An educational institution

b) An organization

c) A site that is highly organised

d) A commercial website

37. What is the difference between PROM, EPROM and EEPROM?

38. Name the different operators used in C programming langauge.

39. Are multi-dimensional arrays different from two dimensional arrays?

40. What can you do with the Internet?

a) Exchange information with friends and colleagues

b) Access pictures, sounds, video clips and other media elements

c) Find diverse perspective on issues from a global audience

d) All of the above

41. Which of the following actions can be performed using the tools present in Page Setup group of Word?

a) Margins

b) Paper Size

c) Page Orientation (Landscape or Portrait)

d) All of the above

42. What is the difference between a file and a folder?

43. What are data types? Explain in respect to C programming lanaguge.

44. Yashima has made a Help Document for her new 3-D game. The content is ready but she wants to add attractive borders on each page. Name a Word 2007 feature she can use to do the same?

45. What are library functions? Name any two library functions available in C programming language.

46. What do you understand by the term convergence of technology? Explain with the help of an example.

47. How can you secure your computer system?

48. The maximum length of a variable name in C programming language is ____________ characters.

a) 32 b) 31 c) 30 d) 24

49. Jolly is typing a letter for her boss and wants to use a pound sign £ in the letter. Which feature of Word can she use to insert the sign?

50. Prabhat has a setup a new typesetting business. He wants to try out few software and see their strengths and weakness before purchashing them. Which category of software/shareware will serve his purpose?

Answer Key – Sample Test Paper 1

1. She should create her presentation using some suitable template.

   OR

   She should use master slides.
2. b) Scanner
3. Slide sorter view
4. A$1
5. Magnetic Ink Character Recognition
6. Writer of the second article has done plagiarism. To avoid such a situation, the writer of the second article must take permission from the author of the first article, acknowledge his sources, use quotations, develop the content in its original form and avoid paraphrasing in the article.
7. Pictures and SmartArt
8. Web Developer
9. Yes. It will save her time. (Or any other relevant advantage)
10. Using cursor control keys
    Using mouse click
11. Handouts are printouts of slides of a presentation. Usually these slides are small sized versions of the slides printed multiple slides per page.
12. Bar Code Reader
13. A1:D5
14. Normal View
15. i. Main Document and Data Source

    ii. <title>, <surname>, <Address line>, <account_no>

    iii. Review
16. c) It isa beautiful, sunny day.
17. a) desktop publisher

    b) spreadsheet
18. Secondary memory is stored in secondary storage devices like hard disk, CD-ROM, DVD and floppy disk. It is permanent in nature. It is non-volatile and helps prevent loss of data. Also, a computer's working memory is finite and limited in size so it cannot always hold the data we need. So, secondary memory is used.
19. Pen Drive. It is a flash memory storage device. It is easy to carry and copy. It is portable and writable. The capacity of a pen drive ranges from 256 MB to 32 GB.
20. The three functions of Slide Sorter View are:
    - Rearranging slides
    - Hiding slides
    - Adjusting the view
21. It is used to play or preview animation.
22. Action Buttons under Shapes tool provide the facility to link to a web page or a slide in the same presentation or a slide from other presentation using hyperlinks.

    a) True

    b) True
23. b) Operating system
24. d) Database Management
25. Copy and Paste
26. Byte, Kilobyte, Megabyte, Terabyte
27. Spell and Grammar check

28. a) Dot Matrix printers
 b) Laser printers
 c) Speakers
29. Using the Sound tool in the Insert tab.
30. Subscript
31. c) Jump
32. RAM stands for Random Access Memory. It is known as temporary memory as its contents are erased as soon as the computer is turned off. Static RAM (SRAM) and Dynamic RAM (DRAM) are the two types of RAM. ROM stands for Read Only Memory. The data is not erased or lost even if the computer is turned off. It is known as read only memory because its contents cannot be modified.
33. a) Vipre
 b) WinZip
 c) Linux
 d) Disk Defragmentor
 e) Mozilla Firefox
34. a) Bold, Underline
 b) Thesaurus tool
35. b) Formula is dragged but the cell references do not adjust.
36. b) An organisation
37.

PROM	EPROM	EEPROM
It can only be programmed once and cannot be erased.	It can be erased by exposing it to ultraviolet light.	It can be erased using electric signals.
Its contents cannot be altered.	Its content can be written again but the entire content has to be rewritten, even if there is a small change.	There is no need to delete the whole content for a small change. The part that needs modification can be altered in isolation but the process is expensive.

38. C provides operators such as:
 - Arithmetic operator
 - Assignment operator
 - Relational operator
 - Logical operator
 - Ternary /Conditional operator
 - Increment and Decrement operator
 - Size of operator
39. An array that has two indices is known as a two dimensional array. An array with more than one index is called a multi-dimensional array.
40. d) All of the above
41. d) All of the above
42. The difference between the two is that files store data, while folders store files and other folders.
43. Data type help the computer to find out the type of value that will be stored in the variable, operations that can be done on values of that type, and the way values of that type can be stored. The fundamental data types in C language are int, char, short, long, float, double, etc.
44. Borders tool
45. Library functions are the predefined functions in C programming language. stdio.h and stdlib.h are two library functions available in C.
46. Convergence of technology can be defined as interlinking of different computing technologies, information technologies and communication networks that has arisen as the result of the evolution and popularisation of the Internet and the activities, products and services that have emerged in the digital media space. For example, the mobile phones today. There use is not limited to mobile telephony only. They are used for calling, messaging, emailing, browsing the web, audio and video conferencing, photography, videography, sound recording, GPS and gaming. This is a classic example of convergence of varied different technologies to create a separate entity.

47. Some ways to secure your system are:
- Install firewall, antivirus, anti-spyware programs on your system
- Give password protection to your files and folders
- Use data encryption technology to encode your information
- Allot the access of information to an authorised person who will have access control
- Voice recognition, fingerprint recognition can also be applied to restrict usage
- An organisation can also assign an individual or a team to monitor the misuse of information, if any.

48. b) 31

49. Symbols tool

50. DeskTop Publishing software

Sample Test Paper 2 – Unsolved

1. Mini has made a presentation for her new advertisement campaign. The content is ready but she does not have time to design the background. However, she has chosen a color scheme for the presentation. Name the feature which will help her create a professional looking presentation without devoting much time.
2. Girish wants to store data of his monthly expenditure for a period of one year. He also wants to perform some calculations and analysis. Suggest one Microsoft Office application that Girish can use for this.
3. Daniel is not able to understand the difference between Normal view and Outline view in PowerPoint 2007. Write a note explaining the difference between both. Give an example for better understanding.
4. Slide Transition and Custom Animations are two options available in PowerPoint 2007. Which option helps you to add special effects on text boxes and images in the presentation? At what stage can you add these effects: designing phase or slide show? Also, give steps to add these special effects to an image of the Sun. Show the Sun rising from the west.
5. Fareeda is trying to put many pictures and text on a particular slide. Whenever she is re-positioning the text box, all the picture objects shift to different positions. Which option should she use to fix positions of all the picture objects in one go in a particular manner?
6. Out of the following external files, which one(s) help you include sound in a presentation?

   JPEG, WAV, GIF, BMP, MP3
7. The formula in cell A2 is = B2+C3. If we copy this formula to cell F2, what will the formula be?
8. What will be the cell address of the cell formed by the intersection of the fifth column and the eighth row?
9. Differentiate between relative referencing and mixed referencing with respect to Excel 2007.
10. Name the toolbar/tab in Excel 2007 which has all the options of changing the font properties. Make a list of all the options present and give one use of each.
11. What extra hardware is required for adding and testing narration in PowerPoint 2007?
12. Out of the following list pick out the option(s) that is not a type of plagiarism. Justify.

    a) Adding new content b) Potluck paper c) Ghost writer d) Photocopy
13. Amit has learnt photo editing and now he is planning to make a career in web designing. Out of the following, which option(s) are essential for him to learn and why?

    a) C++ b) HTML c) Spreadsheet Packaged d) Presentation Package
14. Define the terms plagiarism and intellectual property rights. Use the definition and examples to clearly bring out the difference between the two.
15. Name the cells included in the range reference A1:B2.
16. In Excel 2007, what is the column immediately next to column Z?
17. Allena is interested in transferring few songs from her mobile phone to Sanya's mobile phone. Suggest to her a suitable wireless option she may opt for doing the same.
18. Suggest any two ways through which plagiarism can be checked and reduced.
19. Define the following terms.

    i) Firewall ii) Cyber crime
20. From the following list identify the features which are available in both PowerPoint 2007 and Excel 2007. Also, name the tool used.

    a) Spell check facility b) Headers and footers c) Adding water marks/backgrounds d) Macros
21. A garment shop is planning to connect all computers in their office building that is spread over an area of 50 meters. Suggest the most economical cable type, which has high data transfer speed, that can be used to connect these computers. Which type of network will be formed by connecting these computers?
22. Explain the usage of the Rehearse Timings tool present in PowerPoint 2007.
23. From the following techniques which one is suitable for maintaining data integrity and which one is suitable for ensuring security of information? Give reasons.
    - Data encryption and password protection
    - Backing up data regularly

24. Alex has created a bar chart in Excel 2007. Now he is making a presentation on a related topic and wants the same bar chart to be included in one of the slide of the presentation. Suggest two ways he can copy the chart. Give steps describing both the ways.

25. Briefly explain how the groups present in the Reference tab of Word 2007 can help you prepare the school annual report.

26. Mani recently joined a construction company as a marketing executive. During her orientation she was shown a presentation about the company. She however is not satisfied with it and wants to make it better. Using her presentation skills, she intends to make the following changes. Suggest the features she can use to accomplish the following changes.

    i. Add the company's logo

    ii. Add audio to each slide to explain the content of the slide

    iii. Add an effect to mark shifting from one slide to another during a slide show

    iv. Connect slide 4 to slide 9 directly

    v. Add slide numbers automatically at the bottom of each page

27. Give the following answers with respect to a spreadsheet.

    i. Cell A1 contains the number 20 and B1 contains 3. What will be the contents of cell C1, if the formula = A1+B1*2^3 is entered in cell C1?

    ii. The contents of cell A1, B1, C1, and D1 are 10, -20, 30 & -40 respectively. What will be the value displayed in cell E1 which contains the formula = MIN (A1:D1)?

    iii. Cell D3 contains the formula =B3+C3 and this formula is copied to cell E3. What will be the copied formula in cell E3?

28. Cambridge India maintain their employee salary details in a spreadsheet. A sample data of 7 employees is shown below. Complete the steps given below.

    i. Write formulae for the operations (a) to (e).

    ii. Answer the questions (f) to (h) based on the spreadsheet given below along with the relevant cell address.

	A	B	C	D	E	F
1	NAME	BASIC	HRA	DA	PF	NET SALARY
2	Surinder	50000	20000	-	600	-
3	Kanika	56000	20000	-	600	-
4	Aashish	35000	15000	-	400	-
5	Harjit	45000	15000	-	500	-
6	Abhijit	60000	25000	-	700	-
7	Jyoti	75000	30000	-	700	-
8	Amita	25000	10000	-	300	-
9	Maximum					-
10	No.of Emp					=

    a. To calculate DA as 25% of BASIC+HRA for each employee and display the same in column D.

    b. To calculate the NET SALARY as BASIC+HRA+DA-PF for each employee and display in column F.

    c. To find the maximum NET SALARY and display in cell F9.

    d. To count the number of Employees and display in cell B10.

    e. The manager wants to know how many employees from the above data are eligible for the bonus. The criteria being that the employees having a salary greater than 45000 are not eligible for the bonus. Write the formula the manager should use for achieving the same and display the number of employees in cell F10.

    f. The manager realises that he has forgotten to add the S.No. column in the above spreadsheet. Which feature will help him automate the typing of sequential numbers?

    g. The manager wants to graphically represent a comparative analysis of the salaries of employees. Suggest the most suitable chart type for achieving the same.

    h. If the salary of an employee changes, will the manager have to redo all the calculations for that particular employee? Explain.

29. In the letter given on the next page, the line numbers are given on the right hand side of the lines of the document. Observe the letter document and answer the questions given below.

    i. In the document, identify the lines and write the line numbers for line(s) that contains superscript text.

    ii. Which feature has been used to give numbering in lines 28–30?

    iii. The manager wants to send the letter with same content to all customers with similar complaints. The addresses of all such customers are stored in a separate document. Name the feature which will help the manager achieve the same.

iv. The manager wants to keep a record of all the changes/corrections that he makes in this document. Name the feature used to achieve the same.

From:

Customer Help Manager,
Fountain Spray Corporation,
New City 4

To,

Yanran Philip
R-900, JalyaanVihar
King Nagar

Subject: Reply to Complaint no. A-349562

Dear Madam

This is the reference to your complaint no A-349562 with regard to our Automatic Spray System Model 978. We would like to inform you the following:

1. The defect informed by you is not covered in our Warranty Terms.
2. The defective part is required to be imported from Japan.
3. As a privileged customer of ours, company will be able to give 50% discount on the part along with free installation at your premises.

Kindly let us know your decision in this regard.

In your best service!

Sincerely yours

Anika Palan
Custcare@Autospray.com
www.AutoSpray978.com

30. The principal of AksharVidya Primary School has employed Vijay Kumar to enter marks of all the students in each examination in result processing software. What would be the designation of Vijay?

a) Data entry operator b) Digital content manager c) Web designer d) Programmer

31. Ratika is logging into her Gmail account and one of her friends is trying to peep in so that she can figure out her password. Which of the following issue(s) is being infringed?

a) Plagiarism b) Privacy c) Intellectual Rights d) None of these

32. In a presentation document, in order to type '2' in the mathematical expression A.X2+B.X+C=0, which one of the following options you would use?

a) Insert Clipart b) Subscript c) Italics style d) Superscript

33. In a presentation, Sachin has to change all occurrences of the word 'Calcutta' with 'Kolkata'. Which one of the following options is most appropriate to do the task

a) Copy and Paste b) Find and Replace c) Cut and Paste d) All of these

34. Members of 'Nibbles & Bytes', the computer club of a school wants to prepare and print participation certificate for all the participants in their annual interschool symposium. They want to use a spreadsheet, where the detail of the participating students along with the events and schools are entered. Which of the following office techniques is most appropriate to get the desired result?

a) Copy and Paste b) Find and Replace c) Mail Merge d) Cut and Paste

35. Reshma is making a science project presentation on Sustainable Development using PowerPoint 2007. She wants to add the phrase 'Sustainable Development' at the top of each page. Which option she should use?

a) Footer b) Header c) Watermark d) Bullets

36. A student wants to create a digital story teller on the famous story 'Rabbit and Tortoise'. He has downloaded some images of rabbit, tortoise and forest. He wants to add background music, voice over and animation. Which one of the Office tool should he use?

a) Word processing software b) Presentation software c) Spreadsheet software d) Database Management System Software

37. Which of the following can be performed in Slide Sorter view of PowerPoint 2007?

a) Rearranging slides b) Deleting slides

c) Make global changes to several slides at one time d) All of these

38. In PowerPoint 2007, the entry effect as one slide replaces another slide in a slide show is called ....

a) Animation b) Slide Transition c) Custom Animation d) Rehearse Timing

39. Vanya has made a presentation on Global Warming. She wants to run her slide show automatically while she speaks on the topic in the class. Which option should she use?

a) Custom Animation b) Rehearse Timing c) Slide Transition d) None of these

40. Computer teacher of Shanti Education School wants to graphically analyse the performance of her students in the last three computer tests. Which one of the following Office tools she should use to get graphical report in most effective manner?

a) Word processing software b) Presentation software c) Spreadsheet software d) Database Management System Software

41. The total marks scored by students are entered in a spreadsheet as shown below.

Name	Marks
Aman	445
Rahman	432
Anita	456
Amisha	421
George	442
Fatima	487

If we want to have merit list of these students (student marks appearing in descending order with corresponding name) which one of the following options will accomplish the task in one go.

a) Copy and Paste b) Reverse c) Search d) Sort

42. In a spreadsheet, which one of the following reference changes rows and columns automatically when it is copied to a new cell?

a) Relative reference b) Absolute reference c) Mixed reference d) All of these

43. The Auto Fill feature in Excel ....

a) extends a sequential series of data

b) automatically adds a range of cells values

c) applies a border around the selected cells

d) fills the selected cells with a background color

44. It is an offence as per cyber laws to use a software without paying the license fee to the copyright owner company if that software belongs to the class of:

a) shareware b) freeware c) open source d) proprietary software.

45. Sameera, who was born in 1995, is thinking of a password for her online bank account. Which one of the following you would suggest for strengthening the security of her account?

a) Sam95 b) a99p54c66 c) samniza1995 d) sam1995

46. Divya is writing a letter to her brother and wants to add her recent photographs in the letter. Which Word 2007 option should she use to insert the images? But before, how can she transfer the pictures from her mobile phone and camera to her computer.

47. Aastha inserted a text box in her document and she wants to give shadow and 3-D effect to it. How can she achieve this? Give steps.

48. Sameer wants the logo of his company to appear as ghost text on every letter his company sends. How can he do this?

49. How can you customise the Quick Access Toolbar in Microsoft Office 2007?

50. Give 10 important features of Windows 7.

Answer Key

CHAPTER 1

A. Fill in the blanks.

1. wired
2. pointing device
3. trackball
4. flat, stylus
5. Magnetic Ink Character Recognition
6. Arithmetic and Logic, Control, Memory
7. impact
8. Plotters
9. mid-range
10. ecommerce

B. Multiple choice questions.

1. b	2. a	3. b	4. d	5. a
6. a	7. d	8. b	9. b	10. d
11. d	12. b	13. a	14. a	15. d
16. c	17. c	18. d	19. a	20. c

C. State whether the following statements are True or False.

1. True	2. False	3. False	4. False	5. True
6. True	7. False	8. True	9. True	10. False
11. True	12. False	13. True	14. False	15. True

CHAPTER 2

A. Fill in the blanks.

1. software
2. Operating system
3. Multitasking
4. specific purpose application software
5. CUI, GUI
6. MS-DOS
7. assembly, machine
8. antivirus
9. DeskTop Publishing
10. defragmentation

B. Multiple choice questions.

1. a	2. d	3. b	4. c	5. b
6. a	7. b	8. c	9. d	10. c

CHAPTER 3

A. Fill in the blanks.

1. Recycle Bin
2. maximized or restored
3. Programmer
4. Word wrap
5. peek
6. shortcut
7. sub folders
8. Desktop gadgets
9. Quick Launch bar
10. Notepad

B. Multiple choice questions.

1. d	2. a	3. b	4. b	5. c
6. a	7. c	8. c	9. d	10. c
11. b	12. c	13. a	14. a	15. c
16. d	17. c	18. a	19. b	20. a

C. Identify the tools and write the name of the accessories in which they are available.

Date and Time tool in WordPad

Line spacing tool in WordPad

Freeform selection tool in Paint

Zoom in tool in Paint and WordPad

Grow font tool in WordPad

Text highlight color in WordPad

Superscript tool in WordPad

Fill with color tool in Paint

Magnifier tool in Paint

Text tool in Notepad, WordPad and Paint

CHAPTER 4

A. Fill in the blanks.

1. Word processing
2. Quick Access toolbar
3. Jump page
4. Print Layout, Full screen reading, Web Layout, Outline, Draft
5. docx, pdf
6. Find, Replace, Select
7. Strikethrough
8. D, Shift + D
9. Styles
10. Zoom 100%, One Page, Two Pages, Page Width

B. Multiple choice questions.

1. b	2. c	3. c	4. a	5. b
6. c	7. b	8. d	9. a	10. a

CHAPTER 5

A. Fill in the blanks.

1. Pages, Tables, Illustrations, Links, Header & Footer, Text, Symbols
2. Blank Page
3. Tables Tool Design
4. SmartArt
5. Links
6. Signature Line
7. Office
8. Remove watermark
9. Main document, data source file
10. Review

B. Multiple choice questions.

1. d	2. c	3. b	4. a	5. c
6. c	7. c	8. c	9. d	10. a

C. Match the following options with the appropriate tabs.

1. d	2. f	3. e	4. g	5. c
6. a	7. b			

CHAPTER 6

A. Fill in the blanks.

1. Slide
2. Office
3. Quick Access Toolbar
4. Seven
5. Auto content wizard
6. Title
7. Font
8. Slide Show
9. Slide
10. Ctrl + O
11. PowerPoint Options
12. Notes Page
13. Slide, Handout, Notes
14. Monitors
15. Header

B. Multiple choice questions.

1. b	2. a	3. c	4. d	5. c
6. d	7. c	8. d	9. b	10. a

CHAPTER 7

A. Fill in the blanks.

1. hyperlinks
2. category name
3. legend
4. animation
5. Animations

B. Multiple choice questions.

1. c	2. d	3. b	4. c	5. a
6. b	7. a	8. c	9. d	10. a

CHAPTER 8

A. Fill in the blanks.

1. 16384, 1048576
2. 3
3. Auto Fill
4. Address
5. right, left
6. Home
7. workbook
8. cell pointer
9. Ctrl + 1
10. F5
11. custom filter
12. xlsx

B. Multiple choice questions.

1. c	2. c	3. b	4. d	5. a
6. b	7. b	8. b	9. a	10. a

CHAPTER 9

A. Fill in the blanks.

1. #Name
2. mixed
3. Functions
4. Print Area
5. Logical function
6. Formulas
7. F5
8. Layout
9. =A1+A2
10. Relative

B. Multiple choice questions.

1. a	2. b	3. b	4. a	5. b
6. a	7. b	8. c	9. a	10. a

CHAPTER 10

A. Fill in the blanks.

1. computer networking
2. Topology
3. LAN
4. MAN
5. WAN
6. mosaic
7. Modem
8. Internet Service Provider
9. web browser
10. Wi-fi technology

B. Multiple choice questions.

1. a	2. a	3. c	4. b	5. a
6. d	7. c	8. c	9. b	10. d

C. Give expansions for the following.

1. SAN: Storage Area Network
2. CAN: Campus Area Network
3. WLAN: Wireless Local Area Network
4. PAN: Personal Area Network
5. DAN: Desk Area Network
6. URL: Uniform Resource Locator
7. ARPANET: Advanced Research Project Agency
8. MODEM: Modulator Demodulator
9. ISP: Internet Service Provider
10. BPS: Bits Per Second

CHAPTER 11

A. Fill in the blanks.

1. Multimedia
2. drawing
3. information
4. graphic
5. cartoon

B. Multiple choice questions.

1. d 2. d 3. a 4. a 5. b

C. Browse the Internet and find the full form of following type of the files.

1. mpg: Moving Pictures expert group
2. gif: Graphics interchange format files
3. avi: Audio Video interleaved file
4. bmp: Bitmap file
5. swf: Shock wave flash file
6. wmf: Windows meta format file
7. mpf: Media Package file
8. smf: Standard Mamogram Form
9. dxf: Data exchange Format file
10. mov: quick time content files (short form)

CHAPTER 12

A. Fill in the blanks.

1. pseudo code
2. print
3. goto
4. algorithm
5. flowchart
6. program
7. Dennis Ritchie
8. low
9. Unix
10. Header
11. Comment
12. Alt, F9
13. Constant
14. 31
15. underscore
16. keywords
17. %S
18. input and output
19. strings and arrays
20. Logical operators
21. conditional
22. sizeof
23. Switch case
24. default
25. library functions

B. Multiple choice questions.

1. c	2. c	3. b	4. d	5. a
6. b	7. d	8. c	9. c	10. b
11. c	12. d	13. a	14. b	15. a
16. a	17. d	18. a	19. b	20. b

CHAPTER 13

A. Fill in the blanks.

1. Ghost writer
2. Integrity
3. ©
4. internet piracy
5. database administrator
6. password protection
7. web designer
8. Data encryption
9. Software testing
10. System analyst

B. Multiple choice questions.

1. b	2. a	3. c	4. d	5. d
6. a	7. d	8. b	9. c	10. d

C. State whether the following statements are True or False.

1. True	2. False	3. False	4. False
5. True	6. True	7. False	8. True
9. True	10. False		

D. Match the careers with the task given.

1. c 2. d 3. e 4. a 5. b

Cheat Sheet

Chapter 1

• The characteristics of a computer are speed, accuracy, diligence, versatility, reliability and storage. The three main units of a computer are: input unit, processing unit and output unit.

• **Input Unit:** It controls the functions of input devices like keyboard and mouse.

• **Control Unit:** It controls and directs the functions of all components of a computer.

• **Memory Unit:** It stores programs and data received through the input unit.

• **Arithmetic and Logic Unit:** It is used to perform arithmetic and logical operations on data received from the memory unit; and transfer the same to the main memory.

• **Output Unit:** It is used to display the result of processing, in form of either a hard copy or a softcopy.

• The memory capacity of a computer system can be defined in terms of the following units.

4 bits = 1 nibble	1024 KB = 1 Megabyte (MB)
8 bits = 2 nibbles, 1 byte	1024 MB = 1 Gigabyte (GB)
1024 bytes = 1 Kilobyte (KB)	1024 GB = 1 Terabyte (TB)

• **Primary Memory:** It is the main memory of the computer. It is directly accessible to the CPU. It is of two types: Random Access Memory (RAM) and Read Only Memory (ROM); where RAM is temporary and ROM is permanent.

• **Secondary Memory:** It is the cheapest form of memory. It is slow as compared to the main memory. It refers to the secondary storage devices like hard disk, CD-ROM, DVD, floppy disk, etc. It is permanent in nature.

• **RAM:** It stands for Random Access Memory. It is known as temporary memory as its contents are erased as soon as the computer is turned off. Static RAM (SRAM) and Dynamic RAM (DRAM) are the two types of RAM.

• **ROM:** It stands for Read Only Memory. The data is not erased or lost even if the computer is turned off. It is known as read only memory because its contents cannot be modified.

• **Dynamic RAM:** It deletes the data when the power is on and hence it requires refresh command to restore. It is very slow. Most of the computers contain DRAM chips.

• **Static RAM:** It retains the data as long as the power is on. It gives fast access to data. It is expensive.

• **Super Computer:** They are the fastest computers. The memory capacity of a super computer is in gigabytes or in terabytes and its storage capacity is in pixabytes. Its processing speed lies in the range of 400–10000 MFLOPS.

• **CD-ROM:** It stands for Compact Disc Read Only Memory. It is used to store data up to 700 MB. It is an optical storage device. The data once stored in a CD-ROM cannot be modified.

• **CD-RW:** The capacity of CD-RW is as same as CD-ROM. It is an optical storage device. The data once written can be modified, deleted and rewritten.

• **DVD:** It stands for Digital Versatile Disk. It is like a CD but its storage capacity is more than that of a CD (from 4 GB to 47 GB). It is an optical storage device.

• **Blue Ray:** It can store large amount of data as compared to a DVD. It can store data up to 25 GB of data. It gives HD (High density) data video experience to the viewer.

• **Printer:** It is used to print the output generated by the processing unit (CPU) on a paper. This output is known as hard copy.

• **Plotter:** It is an output device used to print graphics, diagrams and maps.

• **Laser printer:** It is used to print high quality text and images. It can print about 100 pages in a minute. Laser printers are used in DeskTop Publishing (DTP).

• **Inkjet printer:** The speed of this printer is less as compared to laser printer; but at the same time it is less expensive. It is used in small offices, in schools and at home.

• **Impact printer:** In this printer the paper comes in direct contact with the printer head. For example: Daisy Wheel printers and Dot Matrix printers.

• **Non-Impact printer:** In this printer the paper does not come in the direct contact with the printer head. For example: Laser printers and Inkjet printers.

• **Webcam:** It is a camera that is usually placed on the top of the monitor. It is used to take pictures and record movies. It is used primarily for video conferencing over the Internet.

• **Touch screen:** It is a special monitor that allows the user to input information by touching the screen that can detect touch. Many mobile phones today have touch screens.

• **MICR:** Its stands for Magnetic Ink Character Recognition. It is used to read the magnetic code written on the cheques or on credit cards. It provides a secure and high speed method of scanning and processing information.

• **BCR:** It stands for Bar Code reader. It is used to read the pattern of bars on the items you buy from the market. The stripes of the bar code are sensed and read by BCR. BCR can be hand-held optical readers or fixed readers.

• **Storage devices:** They are the secondary memory devices that are used to store data and programs.

Chapter 2

• **Software:** It is the set of programs and procedures that helps in performing various operations on a computer.

• **System Software:** It manages, controls and coordinates the hardware component of a computer. It also performs the task of storage management. It includes: Operating system, Language translators and Utility software.

• **Application software:** It is used for a specific purpose of work that benefits the user. It is designed to handle specialised tasks like documentation, creating spreadsheets, drawing, creating graphics, employee payroll and school results. It can be categorised into: General purpose application software and Specific purpose application software

- **Presentation software:** It is used to display information in the form of slide show on screen by developing slides.
- **Spreadsheet software:** It is used to create spreadsheets, do various calculations, handling data, inserting charts, analysing data and display the data in an organised manner.
- **Word processing software:** It is used to create, edit and format a document quickly and efficiently.
- **Utility software:** It is a program that supports the computer hardware and software by performing a small range of tasks. Utilities protect the computer from virus attacks, loss of data, security and storage, cleaning, repairing, compressing and creating backup of data.
- **Antivirus utility:** It scans the system, recognises a virus, alerts the user and cleans the system.
- **Backup utility:** It is used to take a backup of file on a backup storage device so that the files can be retrieved when the data is lost or damaged.
- **Translator:** It is used to convert instructions to machine code and vice versa.
- **Assembler:** It converts assembly language programs (low-level language) to machine level language programs and vice versa.
- **Compiler:** It converts the high-level language programs into machine level language programs and vice versa. It converts the entire program at one time and displays all the errors of the program with line numbers.
- **Interpreter:** It converts high-level language programs (BASIC, VISUAL BASIC) into machine level language programs and vice versa. It converts and executes the program line by line. It cannot resume the next line unless the error is rectified.
- **Character User Interface:** A CUI operating system requires you to type commands (using a keyboard) to interact with a computer. It is sequence oriented in nature, that is, each command is executed in an order.
- **Graphical User Interface:** A GUI operating system requires you to make use of graphics and images to interact with a computer. GUI makes interactions with computers really easy; a user just has to click the mouse.
- Input and Output Management, Processor Management, Memory Management, Resource Management, Information Management, Utility Management are some of the important functions of an operating system.
- **Single user operating system:** The processor has to execute only one program at a time, and hence the memory management is not difficult for this type of operating system.
- **Multi-user operating system:** It allows more than one user to access the operating system at the same time. Network techniques are adapted to establish this.
- **Multitasking operating system:** It allows you to execute more than one program at a given time. It allows different devices to perform their own processing independently, without the involvement of CPU.
- **Real-time operating system:** It provides random enquiries from remote locations. They are dedicated systems and their tasks are processed immediately.
- **Batch processing operating system:** It accepts tasks and places them sequentially to execute. The tasks can be stored and executed whenever the computer is idle.
- **Time sharing operating system:** It allows access to CPU and other files through many remotely placed systems called remote terminals. This allows users to run several different programs concurrently on one or more than one.
- **Encryption:** It is the process of converting data into an unknown form.
- **Decryption:** It is the process of converting the encrypted code back to its original form.

Chapter 3

- **Operating System:** It is the system software that acts as an interface between the user and the computer hardware.
- The main functions of an operating system are: Process management, Main memory management, Input output system management, File management and Security management.
- Some common operating systems used in personal computers are: Windows, Linux and Mac OS.
- MS-DOS can be accessed from the Windows operating system. Click on Start ⟹ Run. In the Run dialog box, type command or cmd.
- **Linux:** It is a non-proprietary software. Linux is known as Open Source because it allows individuals and companies to sell, distribute and copy or download its code.
- **Microsoft Windows:** It is a GUI based operating system. It is user-friendly and allows the user to interact with the computer by clicking the buttons of a mouse.
- Some of the common tasks of mouse:
  - **Click:** It is used to select a file or an object on the screen (by pressing mostly the left button of the mouse).
  - **Double-click:** It is used to execute an application (by pressing the mouse buttons twice quickly).
  - **Drag:** It is used to move the object from one place to another.
  - **Scroll:** It is used to scroll the screen or a document up and down.
- The main components of Windows 7 desktop are: Icons, Start button, Quick Launch bar, Task bar, Notification Area and Show Desktop.
- In Windows 2007, you can display two application windows side-by-side.
- **Task bar:** It is the long horizontal bar at the bottom of the desktop. It shows the applications or programs that are currently opened.
- **Quick Launch bar:** It is used to open programs quickly with a single-click. It is just to the right of the Start button.
- **Jump List:** It is a new feature in Windows 7. It shows the recent documents, websites or playlists.
- **Peek feature:** It is a new feature in Windows 7 that allows you to peer past all your opened windows and show the desktop.
- **Notification Area:** It is at the right end of the taskbar. It has volume control, system clock and other associated programs.
- **Gadgets:** They are the mini programs that offer information and easy access to the tools that are frequently used.
- **Recycle Bin:** It holds the deleted files and folders until they are completely deleted from the hard disk.
- **Subfolder:** It refers to a folder inside another folder.
- **On-screen keyboard:** To activate on-screen keyboard: Start ⟹ All Programs ⟹ Accessories ⟹ Ease of Access ⟹ On-Screen keyboard.
- **Calculator:** It helps you to perform arithmetic and scientific calculations. Windows 7 calculator provides the advanced capabilities of a programming, scientific and statistical calculator.
- **Paint:** It is a program of Windows 7 that is used to create drawings on a blank drawing area or in existing pictures.

• **Word wrap:** This feature of Notepad automatically adjusts the width of each line of text in a document according to the width of the screen. It is available under Font menu of the Notepad.

• **Print Preview:** This option is used to preview and make changes, if any, before printing the document.

• **Smartphone:** It is a hybrid of a cell phone and a personal computer.

• **Android:** It is a Linux-derived mobile OS backed by Google, along with major hardware and software developers (such as Intel, HTC, ARM, Samsung, Motorola and eBay, to name a few), that forms the Open Handset Alliance.

Chapter 4

• **Microsoft Office Word 2007:** It is a word processing tool which has a range of editing, formatting and layout options. It is part of the Microsoft Office 2007 suite.

• **Ribbon:** It is a panel located on top of MS Office Word 2007 interface. It consists of seven default tabs which are further divided into groups. Each group has buttons to give commands to perform a specific function.

• Print Layout, Full screen reading, Web Layout, Outline and Draft are the different views available under Document Views group of the View tab.

• **Save:** This option is used to save a new document so that it can be used or modified in future.

• **Save As:** This option is used to save a document in another name or type or location.

• New, Open, Save, Print Preview, Undo, Redo, Quick Print are the different tools available under Quick Access Toolbar. The toolbar can be customised.

• **Editing:** It is the process of modifying an existing document by inserting or deleting some content, or embedding pictures, charts and tables.

• **Formatting:** It is the process of changing the appearance of text in a document and making it attractive.

• Office, Civic, Clarity, Essential are some of the themes that can be applied to a document. The Office theme is the default theme of Word 2007.

• **Templates:** They are the preselected styles and settings that are available to create a new document.

• **Multilevel list:** This tool is used to list items at different levels rather than at one level. A list can be picked from the gallery or can be created.

• **Format Painter:** This tool is used to copy the formatting from one place and apply it to another selection.

Chapter 5

• Proofing, Language, Comments, Tracking, Changes, Compare and Protect groups are available in the Review tab of Word 2007.

• Word 2007 provides a facility of creating and inserting tables in a document. You can insert or draw a table in a document using Table tools which are available under the Insert tab.

• **Table Tools Design** and **Table Tools Layout** are the two contextual tabs that appear on inserting a table. They are used to change the design and layout of the table.

• **Data group:** This group is present in Table Tools Layout tab and has Sort, Repeat Header Rows, Convert to Text and Formula tools.

• **Merge Cells tool:** It is used to merge two or more selected cells into one cell.

• **AutoFit tool:** It is used to resize the column width automatically based on the size of the text in the cell.

• **Links group:** This group is present in the Insert tab and has three tools: Hyperlink, Bookmark and Cross-reference.

• **Text group:** This group is present in Insert tab and has Text Box, Quick Parts, WordArt, Drop Cap, Signature Line, Date & Time and Object tools.

• **Page Setup group:** This group is present in Page Layout tab and has Margins, Page Orientation and Size tools.

• **Header tool:** It is used to create or edit the header content of a document. The content of the header will appear at the top of each page in a document.

• **Footer tool:** It is used to create or edit the footer content of the document. The content of the footer will appear at the bottom of each page in a document.

• **Mail Merge:** It provides a way to create custom documents for bulk mailings. It combines the main document with a data source file.

• **Track Changes tool:** It allows you to see what changes have been made to a document including insertion, deletion and formatting changes. This tool is found on the Review tab.

• **Smart Art tool:** It is a collection of graphics you can use to organise and visually communicate information within a document. It includes timelines, processes and workflow.

• **Shapes tool:** Lines, Basic shapes, Block Arrows, Rectangles, Equation shapes, Flowchart, Stars and Banners, Callout are the different categories of shapes available under Shapes tool of Insert tab.

• **Equation tool:** It is used to insert common mathematical equations or to build up your own equations using a library of math symbols.

• **Watermark tool:** It is used to insert a watermark. A watermark is often used to indicate that a document is to be treated as confidential, urgent, etc.

• **Thesaurus tool:** It suggests other words with a similar meaning to the word you have selected. This allows you to view the synonyms of the selected text.

• **Word Count tool:** It is used to find out the number of words, characters, paragraphs and lines in the document. It is available under the Proofing group of the Review tab.

• **Themes tool:** It is used to change the overall design of the entire document including colors, fonts and effects.

• **Alignment tool:** It is used to align the text to left, right, top, bottom, center or middle of a document.

• **Hyperlink tool:** It is used to create a link to a web page, a picture, a program or an email address.

• **Bookmark tool:** It is used to assign a name to a specific point in a document. You can make a hyperlink to jump directly to a bookmarked location.

• **Citation tool:** It is used to add a quotation or a reference from a book. You can select from the list of sources or you can create a new one.

Chapter 6

• Clipboard, Slides, Font, Paragraph, Drawing and Editing are the different groups available under the Home tab of PowerPoint 2007.

• **Slide Layouts tool:** It contains formatting, positioning and placeholders for all of the content that appears on a slide. Place holders are the containers in layouts that hold content such as text, tables, charts, pictures, clip art, SmartArt, movies and sounds. It also contains the theme, fonts, effects and the background of a slide. Title Slide is the default layout of PowerPoint 2007.

- **Slide Master:** It is a part of a template that stores information, including placements of text and objects on a slide, text and object placeholder sizes, text styles, backgrounds, color themes, effects, and animation.
- **Presentations Views:** A presentation can be viewed in a variety of manners. On the View tab, the Presentation Views group allows you to view the slides as Normal, Slide Sorter, Notes Page, Slide Show, Slide Master, Handout Master, and Notes Master.
- **Normal view:** It is the default view and it is called the main editing view. It is used to write, edit and format the presentation. You can rearrange the slides using the Outline tab.
- **Slide Sorter view:** It allows you to view all the slides in a presentation on the screen. The slide number of each slide appears at the right bottom of it. You can also rearrange the slides in this view.
- **Handout Master view:** It is used to change the design and layout of the printed slide handouts. It displays the Handout Master tab with tools to change page size, orientation, slide orientation and number of slides to place in a handout.
- **Notes Master view:** It displays the slide notes in a page view. It determines the characteristics of printed speaker notes and allows editing the notes master.
- **Notes Page view:** It is used to create speaker notes for the slides. The notes are only visible to the speaker and are not visible to the audience.
- You cannot rearrange the slides in Notes Page view. However, slides can be rearranged using Slide Sorter view.
- **Date & Time tool:** It is used to insert system date and time into a slide. It is available in the Text group of the Insert tab.
- **Header & Footer tool:** It is used to repeat a text or logo on every slide at the top or at the bottom. Headers allow adding data at the top of the slides. Footer allows adding data at the bottom of the slides. You can also insert slide number using this tool.
- **Setup Slide Show:** It option allows you to set preferences for how the slide show will be presented.

Chapter 7

- **Shapes tool:** Recently used shapes, lines, rectangles, basic shapes, block arrows, equation shapes, flowcharts, stars and banners, callouts and action buttons are the different shapes available under the Shapes tool.
- **Action Button tool:** In a slide, when an Action Button is placed, the Action Settings dialog box appears immediately. This box helps hyperlink the slide to another slide or web page.
- **Photo album tool:** It is available under Images group of Insert tab and is used to insert a photo album into a presentation.
- **Crop tool:** It is used to remove the unwanted portion from an inserted picture.
- **Media group:** It has tools to insert audio and video files into a presentation.
- **Sound Tools tab:** This tab appears only after you add an audio file. Play, Sound Options, Arrange and Size are the different groups available under this tab. These groups have tools to play a sound automatically, to playback upon clicking an object, to preview sound, to loop sound, to set volume, etc.
- **Animation:** It refers to making an object like a text, a graphic, a chart or a picture move on a slide.
- **Custom Animation tool:** This tool is used to apply predefined special effects to the objects on a slide.
- **Slide Transition tool:** This tool is used to add visual effects to the slide when a slide changes from one slide to another in a slide show. The transition effects can be applied to a single slide or to all the slides of a presentation.
- Fast, Medium and Slow are the different speed options available under the Slide Transition Speed tool.
- **Custom Show:** This tool is used to customise your slide show. It displays only the slides you select. This tool is available under the Slide Show tab.
- To advance the slide manually by clicking mouse during a slide show, select **On Mouse Click** checkbox.
- To advance the slide automatically to the next slide during a slide show, select **Automatically After** checkbox.
- **Record Narration tool:** It is used to narration with each slide. It is available under Set up group of Slide Show tab. A microphone is required to record narration.
- **Rehearse Timings tool:** It is used to show a full screen slide show in which you can rehearse your presentation. The amount of time you spend on each slide is recorded and you can save it to run the show automatically.

Chapter 8

- MS Excel is a spreadsheet program that runs on Microsoft Windows. It consists of rows, columns, mathematical functions, formatting tools, charts, graphs and other features.
- To start Excel 2007: Click Start ⟹ All Programs ⟹ Microsoft Office 2007 ⟹ Microsoft Office Excel 2007.
- Some of the main features of MS Excel are:
  - A huge data can be organized without taking much effort.
  - Built-in functions are used for calculating both simple and complex calculations.
  - The data can be represented pictorially in the form of charts and graphs.
  - Any changes in data will be automatically updated in the result of functions.
  - Excel provides the facility to copy data, functions and formulas from one cell to another and from one worksheet to another so that you need not type the data or formula again.
  - AutoFill feature in Excel is used to fill up the column or row instantly.
  - Processing of data is very fast and accurate.
- **Worksheet:** It is a rectangular sheet in which small boxes called cells are available. Data can be stored in a worksheet in form of rows and columns. A spreadsheet is also known as worksheet.
- **Workbook:** It is a file in which worksheet(s) and charts are stored. You can store multiple worksheets, of similar type which are related to each other, in a single workbook.
- There are seven tabs in Excel 2007: Home, Insert, Page Layout, Formulas, Data, Review and View.

• **Styles group:** It has three tools to apply quick styles to the cells in a worksheet. They are Conditional Formatting, Format as Table and Cell Style.

• **Number group:** General, Accounting, Currency, Percentage Style, Comma Style, Short Date, Long Date, time are the various options available under Number group.

• **Alignment group:** This group provides Top, Bottom, Middle, Left, Center, Right, Wrap Text and Merge & Center tools to align and organise the data in a cell of a worksheet.

• **AutoFill:** This tool is used to fill up the column or row instantly. To copy the same data to fill a range, type once. Select it and drag the small cross symbol at the bottom of right corner of the cell downwards till the last cell of the range.

• **Conditional Formatting:** This tool is used to highlight interesting cells, emphasise unusual values and visualise data using data bars, color scales and icon sets based on the given criteria.

• **Find tool:** It is used to find a specific text within a document.

• **Replace tool:** It is used to replace the selected text with the new text.

• **Filtering:** It refers to the process of narrowing down the data in the worksheet, allowing you to view only the information you need.

• **Sorting:** It refers to the process of arranging data in ascending or descending order to analyse the data easily.

• **Custom Sort:** It is used to define the sort column, values and order of sorting. You can add levels to sort more than one column.

• **Clear option:** It clears the filtering and sorting options applied to a range of data.

• **AutoSum tool:** It is used to find the sum of values in a given range of cells automatically.

• **Cell Style tool:** It is used to quickly format a cell by choosing from the gallery of predefined styles.

Chapter 9

• **Insert Tab:** It is used to insert tables, charts, text and links in a worksheet.

• **Clip Art:** They are the built-in images in Excel that can be added to your worksheet.

• **SmartArt:** It is a visual representation of your data and information. It can be created quickly and easily with the help of different in-built layouts.

• **Chart:** It is a graphical representation of the information contained in the worksheet.

• **Pie Chart:** It takes a circular shape. It displays the contribution of each value to the total. The data points are displayed as a percentage of the whole pie.

• **Doughnut Chart:** It displays the contribution of each value, like a pie chart, however, it can contain more than one series.

• **Column Chart:** It compares values across categories. The categories are shown horizontally and values are shown vertically.

• **XY or Scatter Chart:** It compares pairs of values. It shows relationship among numeric values, such as scientific, statistical and engineering data. One set of values is shown vertically and the other horizontally.

• **Bar Chart:** It shows comparison among individual items. The categories are shown vertically and values are shown horizontally.

• **Line Chart:** It shows the movement in data at equal intervals. The categories are shown horizontally and the values are displayed vertically.

• **Area Chart:** It emphasises on the differences between several sets of data over a period of time. The area between axis and line is emphasised with color and texture.

• **Bubble Chart:** It is almost similar to scatter chart. But it can compare three values.

• **Radar Chart:** It is used when the categories are not compared directly. It displays values relative to a centre point.

• When you click on the chart that is inserted in a worksheet, you will note that three new tabs: **Design**, **Layout** and **Format** appear on the Ribbon.

• **Formula:** It is a combination of operators, operands and an equal to sign.

• **Cell Reference:** It refers to a cell or a range of cells on a worksheet.

• **Relative Reference:** It refers to the cells that are relative to the position of the formula, that is, when a formula is copied from one cell to another, only the formula is copied in terms of the position of the cell relative to the cell containing the formula.

• **Absolute Reference:** It contains a formula which does not change when it is copied from one cell to another cell, that is, cells are referred by their fixed position in the worksheet.

• **Mixed Reference:** It is a combination of both relative and absolute reference.

• **Functions:** They are predefined formulae that perform calculations by using the contents of the cell.

• **Insert Function Tool:** It is present in the Function Library and allows the user to edit the formula in the current cell by choosing functions and editing the arguments.

• **Text to Columns Tool:** It is used to split data of one cell into two or more cells.

• **Print Titles Tool:** It allows you to repeat the column and row headings at the beginning of each new page to make the reading of multiple page sheet easier when printed.

• **Freeze Rows and Columns Tool:** It is used to make a particular portion of a worksheet static while you work on other parts of the sheet.

Chapter 10

• **Computer Networking:** It is the process of connecting two or more computers or devices, using hardware and software components, thus enabling them to communicate with each other as well as transfer and share data and information between them.

• **Server:** It is a powerful computer/group of computers that controls the entire network.

• **Clients:** They are the computers at workstations that are connected to the main server are called. A client is also called a node.

• **Modem:** It is a hardware device that enables a computer to transmit data over telephone and cable lines by converting the digital data used by a computer into an analog signal used on phone lines; and then converting the analog signal back to digital signal at the receiving end.

- **Some of the advantages of a computer network are:**
  - Sharing Resources
  - Sharing Information
  - Sharing Software
  - Simultaneous Access
  - Easier Backups
  - Communication
- **Network Topology:** It determines how different nodes in a network are connected to each other and how they communicate.
- **Linear Bus Topology:** In this all the devices/nodes are connected to a central cable which has exactly two end points.
- **Star Topology:** In this all the devices are connected to a central hub file server. Nodes or workstations and peripherals devices communicate across the network by passing data through the hub.
- **Ring Topology:** In this all devices are connected to one another in shape of a closed loop. This enables each device to be connected directly to two other devices, one on either side of it.
- **Tree Topology:** It combines characteristics of linear bus and star topologies. It consists of groups of star-configured workstations connected to a linear bus backbone cable.
- The important parameters to consider while choosing a topology are requirement, cost, future expansion needs, cable type, length of cable needed, infrastructure and hardware available, maintenance and troubleshooting, etc.
- **LAN:** It is a network that connects network devices over a relatively short distance. It interconnects computers in a limited area such as home, school, computer laboratory or office building.
- **MAN:** It is a network that links locations together from across different locations in a general geographical area.
- **WAN:** It is a telecommunication network that covers a broad area, that is, any network that links across metropolitan, regional, or national boundaries.
- **Wired Technology:** It is a method of communication in which a wire is used to connect two computers.
- **Wireless Technology:** It is a method of communication that uses radio frequencies or infrared waves to transmit data between devices on a LAN.
- **Internet:** It is a network of millions of computers linked to each other by wired and wireless technologies. It enables communication between computers across the world.
- **World Wide Web:** It is a collection of information that contains various documents, pictures and sound effects that are stored on the computer around the world. It enables the user to view a wide variety of information, including news, business and activities across the world.
- **Letter Addressing System:** It is the method of identifying computers by name. It is also known as domain naming system (DNS). The last three letters of the web address are important. These letters provide information about the kind of organisation the web address belongs to.

Chapter 11

- **Data:** It refers to any number, alphabet, special character or the combination of all that a user inputs into a computer.
- **Information:** It is the processed data.
- **Knowledge:** It is the integration of information and human understanding of the subject.
- **Multimedia:** It is the combination of various types of medias, such as text, pictures, graphics, audio, video and animation.
- **Some of the hardware requirements for multimedia are:**
  - High speed processor, preferably a Pentium processor
  - High RAM, minimum 2GB
  - High storage capacity, at least 250 GB hard disk
  - CD/DVD drive
  - Color monitor
  - Microphone/Speakers
  - Digital camera
- **Some of the components of a multimedia project are:**
  - Text
  - Audio
  - Animation
  - Video
- **Some of the uses of multimedia are:**
  - You can create video games, animation movies; give special effects to audio and video in movies.
  - You can create 3-D effects in images.
  - You can create interesting presentations which provides the interactive learning for students in classroom.
  - You can create well designed and attractive web pages.
- **Animation:** It is created from drawn pictures using real time visuals. It is merely the quick display of a sequence of images to create an illusion of movement.
- **File Type:** A file format determines the application to be used for opening a file.
- **Some file formats used in multimedia:**
  - **MPG:** Moving Pictures Expert Group
  - **GIF:** Graphics Interchange Format file
  - **AVI:** Audio Video Interleaved file
  - **BMP:** Bitmap file
  - **SWF:** Shock Wave Flash file
  - **WMF:** Windows Meta Format file
  - **MPF:** Media Package file
  - **SMF:** Standard Mamogram Form
  - **DXF:** Data eXchange Format file
  - **MOV:** Quick Time Content files
- **Convergence of Technology:** It can be defined as interlinking of different computing technologies, information technologies and communication networks that has arisen as the result of the evolution and popularisation of the Internet and the activities, products and services that have emerged in the digital media space.

Chapter 12

- **Algorithm:** It refers to step-by-step instruction for solving a problem.
- Some rules need to be followed while writing an algorithm:
  - It should have 'Start' at the beginning and 'Stop' at the end
  - Each instruction has to be written as a separate statement; one below the other

* It should have proper input to accept or assign values to process
* The processing statement should be clear enough to execute without an error
* It should produce an output to display the result.

• **Flowchart:** It refers to pictorial representation of the steps involved in solving a problem. It depicts the flow of the computational paths as a picture.

• Some rules that need to be followed while creating a well-drawn flowchart:

* Every flowchart must begin with a Start symbol and end with a Stop symbol
* The flow of sequence is from the top to bottom
* Arrow-heads must be used to specify the flow of direction.
* The connectors should be labelled with same letter to match the previous step with jump points.

• **Program:** It is a set of statements which are executed to achieve a specific task. These statements are written using a programming language.

• Programming languages are broadly classified into two categories: **low-level programming language** and **high-level programming language**.

• **Some of the main features of C programming language are:**

* It is efficient, fast and highly portable
* It is well suited for writing both application software and system software
* It runs under a number of operating system including the CUI based operating system
* It combines the features of high-level language and functionality of low-level language.

• A C program comprises of Header file section, Main function, Declaration section, Executable part and Comments (optional).

• **Variable:** It is a name given to the temporary memory location where data can be stored temporarily.

• **Constant:** It is a value assigned to a variable used in C programs.

• **Some rules that need to be followed while naming a variable:**

* The first character of a variable name should be an alphabet
* No special character, except underscore, is allowed
* C keywords cannot be used as variable names
* The maximum length of the variable name is 31 characters.

• **Data Type:** It helps the computer to find out the type of value that will be stored in the variable, operations that can be done on values of that type, and the way values of that type can be stored.

• **Format Descriptors:** They define how the input or output data is to be represented and interpreted internally. These are the conversion specifications.

• **Escape Sequences:** They are special strings used to control the output generated from a C program on the monitor or on any output device. When a backslash (\) is used in front of a selected group of characters, the compiler tells the computer to escape from the way these characters would normally be interpreted.

• **scanf( ) Function:** It reads input from stdio.h file and stores the data in the other arguments. It can be used to accept a set of values through keyboard.

• **printf( ) Function:** It is used to print any combination of string, number and character on the screen or on a paper.

• **Operator:** It is a symbol that tells the compiler to perform specific operations required for processing. C provides operators such as Arithmetic operator, Assignment operator, Relational operator, Logical operator, Ternary / Conditional operator, Increment and Decrement operator and Sizeof operator.

• **if Statement:** It is a decision making statement used to control the flow of execution. It is a two-way decision statement and is used with an expression.

• **switch...case Statement:** It helps control complex conditional and branching operations. It is used to make a decision between many alternatives.

• **goto Statement:** It provides an unconditional jump from the goto line to a labelled statement in the same function block.

• **Looping:** It refers to repeating some tasks until a condition is satisfied. In C there are three loop structures available: while loop, do while loop and for next loop.

• **while Loop:** It repeats a statement/s until the given condition proves false.

• **do while Loop:** This is similar to the while loop except for the fact that the condition occurs at the end of the loop body, unlike in while loop where the condition is given at the beginning. As the loop checks the condition only at the end of the loop, the statements are executed at least once.

• **for Loop:** It is a counter loop. For loop allows automatic initialization to a counter variable.

• **Break Statement:** It is used to exit a loop before the condition is satisfied.

• **Continue Statement:** It is used to skip the rest of the commands in the active loop and take the control back to the beginning of the loop.

• **Array:** It refers to a data structure, which can store a fixed-size sequential collection of elements of the same type.

• Arrays are of three types: Single Dimensional array, Two Dimensional array and Multi-Dimensional array.

• **Function:** It is a block of statement which performs some specific task and return a single value to the calling function. There are two types of functions in C: Library function and User-defined function.

Chapter 13

• **Plagiarism:** It is the act of copying the contents of somebody else's work and reusing it as your own, especially from one website to another.

• **To avoid plagiarism:**

* Plan the work
* Take permission from the authors
* Acknowledge the sources
* Use quotations
* Develop the content in its original form
* Avoid paraphrasing

• **Intellectual Property Rights:** They are the rights related to literary works, inventions and discoveries.

- **Copyright:** It is denoted by the symbol ©. It is a legal right granted to the creator of an original work. Only the creator of the copyrighted work has the rights to use and distribute it.
- **Encryption:** It is the process of encoding the content from plain text into ciphertext (unknown form) that can only be decoded with the help of a key.
- **Decryption:** It is the process of converting the ciphertext into plain text using the key which is used to encrypt data.
- **Internet Hacking:** It is a kind of crime in which a hacker breaks into your computer/website to access or to modify your programs or information when you are connected to the Internet.
- **Privacy:** It refers to identification of an individual. For example, personal information like name, address, date of birth, contact information and ID issue.
- **Cookie:** It is used to track your preferences and hence to show you similar websites that might interest you.
- **Authentication Cookies:** They are used by the Internet sites to identify whether the correct user is logged in or not and from which account they are logged in.
- **Integrity:** It refers to the authenticity of the information.